Managing change

W9-BUX-689

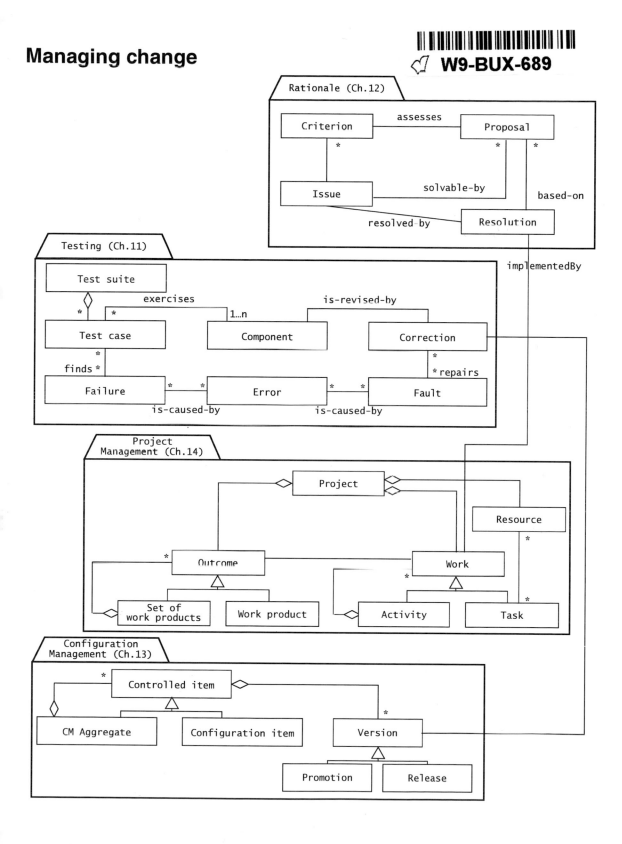

Object-Oriented Software Engineering

Using UML, Patterns, and Java™

Third Edition

Bernd Bruegge & Allen H. Dutoit

Technical University of Munich
Department of Computer Science
Munich, Germany

Carnegie Mellon University
School of Computer Science
Pittsburgh, PA, United States

Prentice Hall

Boston   Columbus   Indianapolis   New York   San Francisco   Upper Saddle River
Amsterdam   Cape Town   Dubai   London   Madrid   Milan   Munich   Paris   Montreal   Toronto
Delhi   Mexico City   Sao Paulo   Sydney   Hong Kong   Seoul   Singapore   Taipei   Tokyo

Vice President and Editorial Director, ECS: *Marcia J. Horton*
Editor in Chief: *Michael Hirsch*
Executive Editor: *Tracy Dunkelberger*
Assistant Editor: *Melinda Haggerty*
Editorial Assistant: *Allison Michael*
Director of Marketing: *Margaret Waples*
Marketing Manager: *Erin Davis*

Marketing Coordinator: *Kathryn Ferranti*
Senior Managing Editor: *Scott Disanno*
Senior Operations Supervisor: *Alan Fischer*
Operations Specialist: *Lisa McDowell*
Art Director: *Kenny Beck*
Cover Designer: *Bruce Kenselaar*
Media Editor: *Dan Sandin*

Copyright © 2010, 2004, 2000 Pearson Education, Inc., publishing as Prentice Hall. All rights reserved. Manufactured in the United States of America. This publication is protected by Copyright, and permission should be obtained from the publisher prior to any prohibited reproduction, storage in a retrieval system, or transmission in any form or by any means, electronic, mechanical, photocopying, recording, or likewise. To obtain permission(s) to use material from this work, please submit a written request to Pearson Education, Inc., Permissions Department, One Lake Street, Upper Saddle River, NJ, 07458.

Many of the designations by manufacturers and seller to distinguish their products are claimed as trademarks. Where those designations appear in this book, and the publisher was aware of a trademark claim, the designations have been printed in initial caps or all caps.

Quote of Chapter 1 from *Object-Oriented Analysis and Design with Applications* by Booch, © 1994 Benjamin Cummings Publishing Company Inc. Reprinted by permission of Pearson Education, Inc.
Quotes of Chapters 2 & 12 from *Zen and the Art of Motorcycle Maintenance* by Robert Pirsig, © 1974 by Robert Pirsig. Reprinted by permission of HarperCollins Publishers Inc. William Morrow. For British Commonwealth excluding Canada, *Zen and the Art of Motorcycle Maintenance* by Robert M. Pirsig published by Bodley Head. Used by persmission of The Random House Group Limited.
Quote of Chapter 6 from *The Emperor's Old Clothes* by C. A. R. Hoare, © 1981 Association for Computing Machinery, Inc. Reprinted by permission.
Quote of Chapter 13 from *Chapterhouse: Dune* by Frank Herbert, © 1985 by Frank Herbert. Used by permission of Berkeley Publishing Group, a division of Penguin Group (USA) Inc.
All other chapter quotes are in the public domain or fall within the realm of fair use.
Book photos: *Bernd Bruegge, Rich Korf, and Blake Ward*

Library of Congress Cataloging-in-Publication Data on File

10 9 8 7 6

Prentice Hall
is an imprint of

www.pearsonhighered.com

ISBN 10: 0-13-606125-7
ISBN 13: 978-0-13-606125-0

To Goeg, Toby, and Clara.
—B.B.

To my family:
Vicky, Eleni, Anna-Maria, Michelle, and Chris
with love.
—A.H.D.

Foreword

Over ten years ago, I read about a software engineering course taught by Bernd Bruegge at Carnegie-Mellon University. In software engineering courses at many other universities, small groups of 3 or 4 students were assigned several toy problems during a semester with deadlines of less than a month. On such small projects, one strong programmer can carry the whole team by brute force. It isn't necessary to learn communication skills, use modeling tools, or deal with the ambiguities of actual problems. Students come away unprepared for the complexities of real-world development. In Bruegge's course, the entire class worked on a single, semester-long project to produce a query-oriented navigation system for the city of Pittsburgh. They had to build on the interactive mapping system produced by the previous semester's class. The clients were managers for the county planning department and port authority. The geographic and bus schedule data had misspellings, inaccuracies, and incompatible formats. The students produced an accepted system of over 27,000 lines of code. What a difference from the toy projects taught at many other places! Students came away from the course with an appreciation of the need for strategy, organization, and tools to deal with the complexity and messiness of the real world. They learned software engineering the only way one learns any craft—by practicing it on realistic cases.

This book is a reflection of that pragmatic philosophy of software development as an engineering discipline. The authors adopt a point of view—an object-oriented approach using UML—that makes the many facets of software engineering approachable to students. They cover both the modeling techniques and the human communications skills needed to achieve success. They also include several chapters on managing change, a topic that appears in every real project but which is often neglected in texts. Readers of this book will gain a solid appreciation of the rich scope and complexity of software engineering.

I particularly enjoyed the many illuminating anecdotes selected from a wide range of fields. These provide lively examples of problems large and small that illustrate the subtleties and traps that engineers must confront. Any book that makes relevant examples of Polynesian navigation, the tangled history of the text of Tolkien's *Lord of the Rings*, and grandmother's recipe for trimming hams is not only useful but also fun to read.

Jim Rumbaugh

Preface

The K2 towers at 8,611 meters in the Karakorum range of the western Himalayas. It is the second highest peak of the world and is considered the most difficult 8000er to climb. An expedition to the K2 typically lasts several months in the summer, when the weather is most favorable. Even in summer, snowstorms are frequent. An expedition requires thousands of pounds of equipment, including climbing gear, severe weather protection gear, tents, food, communication equipment, and pay and shoes for hundreds of porters. Planning such an expedition takes a significant amount of time in the life of a climber and requires dozens of participants in supporting roles. Once on site, many unexpected events, such as avalanches, porter strikes, or equipment failures, will force the climbers to adapt, find new solutions, or retreat. The success rate for expeditions to the K2 is currently less than 40%.

The United States National Airspace System (NAS) monitors and controls air traffic in the United States. The NAS includes more than 18,300 airports, 21 air route traffic control centers, and over 460 control towers. These add up to more than 34,000 pieces of equipment, including radar systems, communication switches, radios, computer systems, and displays. The current infrastructure is aging rapidly. The computers supporting the 21 air route traffic control centers, for example, are IBM 3083 mainframes that date back to the early 1980s. In 1996, the United States government initiated a program to modernize the NAS infrastructure, including improvements such as satellite navigation, digital controller/pilot communications, and a higher degree of automation in controlling the air routes, deciding the order in which aircraft land, and controlling ground traffic as aircraft move from and to the runways. Such a complex infrastructure, however, can only be modernized incrementally. Consequently, while new components offering new functionality are introduced, older components still need to be supported. For example, during the transition period, a controller will have to be able to use both analog and digital voice channels to communicate with pilots. Finally, the modernization of the

NAS coincides with a dramatic increase in global air traffic, predicted to double within the next 10–15 years. The previous modernizing effort of the NAS, called the Advanced Automation System (AAS), was suspended in 1994 because of software-related problems, after missing its initial deadline by several years and exceeding its budget by several billions of dollars.

Both of the above examples discuss complex systems in which external conditions can trigger unexpected changes. Complexity puts the problem beyond the control of any single individual. Change forces participants to move away from well-known solutions and to invent new ones. In both examples, several participants need to cooperate and develop new techniques to address these challenges. Failure to do so results in failure to reach the goal.

This book is about conquering complex and changing software systems.

The theme

The application domain (mountain expedition planning, air traffic control, financial systems, word processing) usually includes many concepts that software developers are not familiar with. The solution domain (user interface toolkits, wireless communication, middleware, database management systems, transaction processing systems, wearable computers) is often immature and provides developers with many competing implementation technologies. Consequently, the system and the development project are complex, involving many different components, tools, methods, and people.

As developers learn more about the application domain from their users, they update the requirements of the system. As developers learn more about emerging technologies or about the limitations of current technologies, they adapt the system design and implementation. As quality control finds defects in the system and users request new features, developers modify the system and its associated work products. The result is continuous change.

Complexity and change represent challenges that make it impossible for any single person to control the system and its evolution. If controlled improperly, complexity and change defeat the solution before its release, even if the goal is in sight. Too many mistakes in the interpretation of the application domain make the solution useless for the users, forcing a retreat from the route or the market. Immature or incompatible implementation technologies result in poor reliability and delays. Failure to handle change introduces new defects in the system and degrades performance beyond usability.

This book reflects more than 10 years of building systems and of teaching software engineering project courses. We have observed that students are taught programming and software engineering techniques in isolation, often using small problems as examples. As a result, they are able to solve well-defined problems efficiently, but are overwhelmed by the complexity of their first real development experience, when many different techniques and tools need to be used and different people need to collaborate. Reacting to this state of affairs, the typical undergraduate curriculum now often includes a software engineering project course, organized as a single development project.

The tools: UML, Java, and Design Patterns

We wrote this book with a project course in mind. The book can be used, however, in other situations as well, such as short and intensive workshops or short-term R&D projects. We use examples from real systems and examine the interaction among state-of-the art techniques, such as UML (Unified Modeling Language), Java-based technologies, design patterns, design rationale, configuration management, and quality control. Moreover, we discuss project management related issues that are related to these techniques and their impact on complexity and change.

The principles

We teach software engineering following five principles:

Practical experience. We believe that software engineering education must be linked with practical experience. Students can understand complexity only by working with a complex system—that is, a system that no single student can completely understand.

Problem solving. We believe that software engineering education must be based on problem solving. Consequently, there are no right or wrong solutions, only solutions that are better or worse relative to stated criteria. Although we survey existing solutions to real problems and encourage their reuse, we also encourage criticism and the improvement of standard solutions.

Limited resources. If we have sufficient time and resources, we could perhaps build the ideal system. There are several problems with such a situation. First, it is not realistic. Second, even if we had sufficient resources, if the original problem rapidly changes during the development, we would eventually deliver a system solving the wrong problem. As a result, we assume that our problem-solving process is limited in terms of resources. Moreover, the acute awareness of scarce resources encourages a component-based approach and reuse of knowledge, design, and code. In other words, we support an engineering approach to software development.

Interdisciplinarity. Software engineering is an interdisciplinary field. It requires contributions from areas spanning electrical and computer engineering, computer science, business administration, graphic design, industrial design, architecture, theater, and writing. Software engineering is an applied field. When trying to understand and model the application domain, developers interact regularly with others, including users and clients, some of whom know little about software development. This requires viewing and approaching the system from multiple perspectives and terminologies.

Communication. Even if developers built software for developers only, they would still need to communicate among themselves. As developers, we cannot afford the luxury of being able to communicate only with our peers. We need to communicate alternatives, articulate solutions, negotiate trade-offs, and review and criticize others' work. A large number of failures in software engineering projects can be traced to the communication of inaccurate information or to missing information. We must learn to communicate with all project participants, including, most importantly, the client and the end users.

These five principles are the basis for this book. They encourage and enable the reader to address complex and changing problems with practical and state-of-the-art solutions.

The book

This book is based on object-oriented techniques applied to software engineering. It is neither a general software engineering book that surveys all available methods nor a programming book about algorithms and data structures. Instead, we focus on a limited set of techniques and explain their application in a reasonably complex environment, such as a multi-team development project that includes 20 to 60 participants. Consequently, the book also reflects our biases, our strengths, and our weaknesses. We hope, nevertheless, that all readers will find something they can use. The book is structured into 16 chapters organized into three parts, which can be taught as a semester-long course.

Part I, *Getting Started*, includes three chapters. In this part, we focus on the basic skills necessary for a developer to function in a software engineering context.

- In Chapter 1, *Introduction to Software Engineering*, we describe the difference between programming and software engineering, the current challenges in our discipline, and basic definitions of concepts we use throughout the book.
- In Chapter 2, *Modeling with UML*, we describe the basic elements of a modeling language, UML, used in object-oriented techniques. We present modeling as a technique for dealing with complexity. This chapter teaches the reader how to read and understand UML diagrams. Subsequent chapters teach the reader how to build UML diagrams to model various aspects of the system. We use UML throughout the book to model a variety of artifacts, from software systems to processes and work products.
- In Chapter 3, *Project Organization and Communication*, we introduce basic concepts of project organization and communication. Developers and managers spend more than half of their time communicating with others, either face-to-face or via E-mail, groupware, video conference, or written documents. Whereas modeling deals with complexity, communication deals with change. We describe project organizations and discuss what constitutes effective communication.

In Part II, *Dealing with Complexity*, we focus on methods and technologies that enable developers to specify, design, and implement complex systems.

- In Chapter 4, *Requirements Elicitation*, and Chapter 5, *Analysis*, we describe the definition of the system from the users' point of view. During requirements elicitation, developers determine the functionality users need and a usable way of delivering it. During analysis, developers formalize this knowledge and ensure its completeness and consistency. We focus on how UML is used to deal with application domain complexity.

- In Chapter 6, *System Design: Decomposing the System*, and Chapter 7, *System Design: Addressing Design Goals*, we describe the definition of the system from the developers' point of view. During this phase, developers define the architecture of the system in terms of design goals and a subsystem decomposition. They address global issues, such as the mapping of the system onto hardware, the storage of persistent data, and global control flow. We focus on how developers can use architectural styles, components, and UML to deal with solution domain complexity.

- In Chapter 9, *Object Design: Specifying Interfaces*, Chapter 9, *Object Design: Specifying Interfaces*, and Chapter 10, *Mapping Models to Code*, we describe the detailed modeling and construction activities related to the solution domain. During this phase, developers identify and adapt design patterns and frameworks to realize specific subsystems. They refine and specify precisely the interfaces of classes using constraint languages such as UML's Object Constraint Language. Finally, they map the detailed object design model to source code and database schema.

- In Chapter 11, *Testing*, we describe the validation of system behavior against the system models. Testing detects faults in the system, including those introduced during changes to the system or its requirements. Testing activities include unit testing, integration testing, and system testing. We describe several testing techniques, such as whitebox, blackbox, path testing, state-based testing, and inspections, and discuss their application to object-oriented systems.

In Part III, *Managing Change*, we focus on methods and technologies that support the control, assessment, and implementation of changes throughout the development of a system.

- In Chapter 12, *Rationale Management*, we describe the capture of design decisions and their justifications. The models developed during requirements elicitation, analysis, and system design help us deal with complexity by providing different perspectives on *what* the system should be doing and *how* it should do it. To be able to deal with change, we need also to know *why* the system is the way it is. Capturing design decisions, considered alternatives, and their argumentation enables us to access the rationale of the system.

- In Chapter 13, *Configuration Management*, we describe techniques for modeling the project history. Configuration management complements rationale in helping us deal with change. Version management records the evolution of the system. Release management ensures consistency and quality across the components of a release. Change management ensures that modifications to the system are consistent with project goals.

- In Chapter 14, *Project Management*, we describe techniques for initiating a software development project, tracking its progress, and dealing with risks and unplanned events. We focus on organizations, roles, and management activities that allow a large number of participants to collaborate and deliver a high-quality system within planned constraints.

- In Chapter 15, *Software Life Cycle*, we describe software life cycles, such as Boehm's Spiral Model and the Unified Software Development Process, that provide an abstract model of development activities. In this chapter, we also describe the Capability Maturity Model, which is used for assessing the maturity of organizations.

- In Chapter 16, *Methodologies: Putting It All Together*, we describe methodologies and heuristics for applying the material covered in the other chapters to concrete situations. No matter how thorough the requirements elicitation or detailed the planning, projects of any realistic size encounter unexpected events and changes. Dealing with uncertainty makes real projects and systems look very different from projects and systems examined in textbooks. In this chapter, we describe several different methodologies, discuss issues that need to be addressed in every project, and present three case studies of actual projects.

The topics above are strongly interrelated. To emphasize their relationships, we selected an iterative approach. Each chapter consists of five sections. In the first section, we introduce the issues relevant to the topic with an illustrative example. In the second section, we describe briefly the activities of the topic. In the third section, we explain the basic concepts of the topic with simple examples. In the fourth section, we detail the technical activities with examples from real systems. Finally, we describe management activities and discuss typical trade-offs. In Chapters 4–10, we present a running case study of a complex multi-user game management system called ARENA. By repeating and elaborating on the same concepts in increasingly complex examples, we hope to provide the reader with an operational knowledge of object-oriented software engineering.

The courses

Building a large, complex system can be compared with climbing a big mountain. It is good to have a route description, but the route can never be completely mapped out, as new crevasses may open anytime. Even though we map out our software engineering knowledge in this book, changes will occur and methods that we believe in now may be out of date soon.

How can we teach students to cope with such rapidly changing conditions? For us, the most important thing to pass on to a student is not only knowledge of the map, but also the ability to negotiate the terrain. Although it is wise to study the description of a route, there is no substitute for the experience of actually traveling the route.

We wrote this book for a semester-long software engineering project course for senior or graduate students. We assume that students have experience with a programming language such as C, C++, C#, or Java. We expect that students have the necessary problem-solving skills to attack technical problems, but we do not expect that they have been exposed to the complex or changing situations typical of system development. This book can also be used for other types of courses, such as short, intensive professional courses.

Project and senior-level courses.   A project course should include all the chapters of the book, roughly in the order presented. An instructor may consider teaching more advanced project management concepts from Chapter 14, *Project Management*, early in the course so that students become familiar with planning and controlling.

Introductory-level course.   An introductory course with homework should focus on the first three sections of each chapter. The fourth section and the case study can be used as material for homework and can simulate the building of a minisystem using paper for UML diagrams, documents, and code.

Short technical course.   The book can also be used for a short, intensive course geared toward professionals. A technical course focusing on UML and object-oriented methods could use the chapter sequence 1, 2, 4, 5, 6, 7, 8, 9, 10, 11, covering all development phases from requirements elicitation to testing. An advanced course would also include Chapter 12, *Rationale Management*, and Chapter 13, *Configuration Management*.

Short management course.   The book can also be used for a short, intensive course geared toward managers. A management course focusing on managerial aspects such as communication, risk management, rationale, maturity models, and UML could use the chapter sequence 1, 2, 3, 14, 15, 16, 12, 13.

Changes since the second edition

This edition started as an upgrade of our book to UML 2 and to the latest advances in agile methods. In the process, we also added new material about system design and testing. We thank Tracy Dunkelberger, our publisher, for her patience. We made the following changes:

- *Comprehensive upgrade to the latest UML and OCL standards.* We revised most diagrams in the book to take advantage of the latest advances of UML and OCL. In particular, we use component diagrams with ball-and-socket notation during system and object design.
- *Expanded material on agile methods.* In the second edition, we introduced coverage of the XP methodology in Chapter 16. In this edition, we extended the material on agile methods to Scrum and Rugby and consequently adapted the material on testing, configuration management, and project management in Chapters 11, 13, and 14.
- *New material on continuous integration.* A practice of agile methods, used in other contexts as well, is the continuous integration of software changes into main production trunk. While this practice allows integration problems to be identified, and thus resolved, much earlier, its realization presents initially many challenges. We present this new material in Chapter 13, *Software Configuration Management*.

- *New material on U2TP and automated testing.* In our teaching, we found the extensions of the UML 2 Testing Profile facilitate the discussion of testing concepts, in particular, the distinction between the testing system and the system under test. This also allowed us to extend the material on testing to automated testing and automatic test generation.
- *Improvements of the case study and examples throughout.* Since the last edition, we received a lot of feedback about the case study and the examples in this book. We are grateful of this feedback and consequently implemented many suggestions, too numerous to enumerate here in detail.

Typographical conventions

We use the following conventions throughout the book:

- A new term appears in **bold** when defined the first time.
- Book titles, chapter titles, and emphasized terms appear in *italics*.
- The names of systems and of modeling elements (e.g., class, attribute, operation, state, variable) appear in `monospaced font`.
- The names of abstract classes appear in *`italics monospaced font`*.
- Object names appear <u>underlined</u> in figures.
- URLs appear in <u>underlined roman</u>.
- Source code appears in `monospaced font`, with reserved keywords in **bold** and comments in *`italics`*.

Production notes

This book was written and composed using Adobe Framemaker. The final print images were generated as PDF files using Adobe Acrobat Distiller.

About the authors

Dr. Bernd Bruegge has been studying and teaching Software Engineering at Carnegie Mellon University for 20 years, where he received his masters and doctorate degrees. He received his Diplom from the University of Hamburg. He is now a university professor of Computer Science with a chair for Applied Software Engineering at the Technische Universität München and an adjunct faculty member of Carnegie Mellon University. He has taught object-oriented software engineering project courses on the text materials and website described in this book for 15 years. He won the Herbert A. Simon Excellence in Teaching Award at Carnegie Mellon University in 1995. Bruegge is also an international consultant and has used the techniques in this book to design and implement many real systems, including an engineering feedback system for DaimlerChrysler, an environmental modeling system for the U.S. Environmental Protection Agency, and an accident management system for a municipal police department, to name just a few.

Dr. Allen Dutoit works in the aerospace industry in the area of avionics software development. He received his M.S. and Ph.D. from Carnegie Mellon University and his Diplôme d'Ingénieur from the Swiss Federal Institute of Technology in Lausanne. He has taught software engineering project courses with Professor Bruegge since 1993, both at Carnegie Mellon University and the Technische Universität München, where they used and refined the methods described in this book. Dutoit's research covered several areas of software engineering and object-oriented systems, including requirements engineering, rationale management, distributed development, and prototype-based systems. He was previously affiliated with the Software Engineering Institute and the Institute for Complex Engineered Systems at Carnegie Mellon University.

Opener Pictures

The pictures at the beginning of each chapter are from an Alpine-style ascent of the West Rib of Denali (6,193 m) made by one of the authors before starting to work on this book. During this trip, the analogy between software development and mountaineering became more than obvious. The pictures chronicle the climb, showing our expedition car on the Alaskan Canadian Highway, a view of Mt. Robson with the Kain Face (Chapter 1), a view of Denali from the plane (Chapters 2 and 4), the beginning of the West Rib (Chapter 3), a look 1000 meters down from the top of the West Rib showing our foot tracks on the East Kahiltna Glacier (Chapter 5), Mt. Foraker from Camp 5 (Chapter 6), a beautiful but difficult edge around 5,000m (Chapter 7), the Base Camp of the normal route where we reused the remains of an igloo (Chapter 8), the landing area for Doug Geeting's plane (Chapter 9), a bivouac place at the top of the West Rib named "Hotel Crux," because one cannot dig an area big enough for a tent (Chapter 10), crossing the Bergschrund (Chapter 11), a fresh avalanche area (Chapter 12), Denali with the Cassin Ridge (Chapter 13), plans for different routes to the summit (Chapter 14), a "horizontal" sunrise at the start of the Cassin Ridge (Chapter 15), and the summit of Denali (Chapter 16).

The cover picture shows the summit of K2.

Acknowledgments

This book has witnessed much complexity and change during its development. In 1989, the first author (B.B.) originally set out to teach software engineering in a single-project course format. The goal was to expose students to the important issues in software engineering by solving real problems described by real clients with real tools under real constraints. The first course, listed as 15-413 in the Carnegie Mellon catalog of courses, had 19 students, used SA/SD, and produced 4,000 lines of code. Heavily influenced by the book by James Rumbaugh and his colleagues on object-oriented modeling and design, we have used object-oriented methods since then. We taught several distributed versions of the course involving up to 100 students from Carnegie Mellon and Technische Universität München, resulting in systems with up to 500 pages of documentation and 50,000 lines of code. We currently are teaching a distributed course involving students from University of Otago in New Zealand and Technische Universität München.

The drawback of project courses is that instructors do not escape the complexity and change that their students experience. Instructors quickly become participants in the development themselves, often acting as project managers. We hope that this book will help both instructors and students conquer this level of complexity and change.

Somehow, in spite of much energy spent on the course, we found time to write and complete this textbook and its subsequent revision, thanks to the help and patience of numerous students, clients, teaching assistants, support staff, coinstructors, reviewers, Prentice Hall staff, and most of all, our families. Some have contributed to improving the course, others have provided constructive feedback on successive drafts, and yet others were simply there when the going got tough. Over the past 20 years, we have indebted ourselves to many people whom we acknowledge here.

The participants of the project courses. Workstation Fax (1989), Interactive Maps (1991), Interactive Pittsburgh (1991), FRIEND (1992, 1993, 1994), JEWEL, GEMS (1991, 1994, 1995), DIAMOND (1995, 1996), OWL (1996, 1997), JAMES (1997, 1998), PAID (1998, 1999), STARS (1999, 2000, 2001), TRAMP (2001, 2002), ARENA (2002, 2003), CampusTV (2004, 2005), Virtual Symphony Orchester (2005), WALOS (2006), and DOLLI (2007, 2008).

The people who supported the projects. For their commitment, for their kindness, and for getting us out of trouble when we needed it: Martin Bauer, Ulrich Bauer, Catherine Copetas, Oliver Creighton, Ava Cruse, Barry Eisel, Luca Girardo, Dieter Hege, Mariss Jansons, Joyce Johnstone, SiegfriedKiese, Siegfried Klinkhammer, Rafael Kobylinski, Marc Lindike, Asa MacWilliams, Monika Markl, Key Maerkl and his Aritus Quartet, Pat Miller, Martin Ott, Ralf Pfleghar, Martin Pittenauer, Harald Ranner, Joachim Reichel, Max Reiss, Barbara Sandling, Christian Sandor, Ralph Schiessl, Arno Schmackpfeffer, Helma Schneider, Stephan Schoenig, Steffen Schwarz, Martin Wagner, Uta Weber, Timo Wolf, and Michael Zaddach.

The colleges, coinstructors, and friends who influenced us. Mario Barbacci, Len Bass, Ben Bennington, Elizabeth Bigelow, Roberto Bisiani, Naoufel Boulila, Harry Q Bovik, Andreas Braun, Manfred Broy, Sharon Burks, Marvin Carr, Mike Collins, Robert Coyne, Douglas Cunningham, Michael Ehrenberger, Kim Faught, Peter Feiler, Allen Fisher, Laura Forsyth, Eric Gardner, Helen Granger, Thomas Gross, Volker Hartkopf, Bruce Horn, David Kauffer, Gudrun Klinker, Kalyka Konda, Suresh Konda, Rich Korf, Birgitte Krogh, Sean Levy, Frank Mang, K. C. Marshall, Dick Martin ("Tang Soo"), Horst Mauersberg, Roy Maxion, Russ Milliken, Ira Monarch, Rhonda Moyer, Robert Patrick, Brigitte Pihulak, Mark Pollard, Martin Purvis, Raj Reddy, Yoram Reich, James Rumbaugh, Johann Schlichter, Mary Shaw, Jane Siegel, Daniel Siewiorek, Asim Smailagic, Mark Stehlik, Eswaran Subrahmanian, Stephanie Szakal, Tara Taylor, Michael Terk, Günter Teubner, Marc Thomas, Walter Tichy, Jim Tomayko, Blake Ward, Alex Waibel, Art Westerberg, Jeannette Wing, and Tao Zhang.

Reviewers who gave us constructive feedback and who helped us get many details right: Martin Barrett, Brian Berenbach, Alex Borgida, Ramsey Bualuan, Dave Chesney, Andrea De Lucia, Debora East, Thomas Eichhorn, Henry Etlinger, Ray Ford, Jim Helm, Jonas Helming, Korbinian Herrmann, Allen Holliday, John Keklak, Robert Lechner, Max Koegel, Jonathan Maletic, Jeff McKinstry, Bruce Maxim, Gerhard Mueller, Michael Nagel, Helmut Naughton, Barbara Paech, Dennis Pagano, Daniel Paulish, Joan Peckham, Gary Pollice, David Rine, Florian Schneider, Ingo Schneider, Anthony Sullivan, Damla Turgut, and the many anonymous reviewers for their constructive and detailed comments. All remaining errors are ours.

Everybody at Prentice Hall who helped us making this book a reality, in particular Alan Apt, our first publisher, for never losing faith; Lakshmi Balasubramanian, Toni Holm, Patrick Lindner, Camille Trentacoste, Jake Warde, and, for this edition, Tracy Dunkelberger, Scott Disanno, and many others who worked hard toward the completion of this book, but whom we did not have the opportunity and pleasure to meet personally.

And finally, our families, to whom we dedicate this book and without whose infinite love and patience this enterprise would never have been possible.

Contents at a Glance

Table of Contents

PART I
Getting Started

1

Introduction to Software Engineering

The amateur software engineer is always in search of magic, some sensational method or tool whose application promises to render software development trivial. It is the mark of the professional software engineer to know that no such panacea exists.

—Grady Booch, in *Object-Oriented Analysis and Design*

The term software engineering was coined in 1968 as a response to the desolate state of the art of developing quality software on time and within budget. Software developers were not able to set concrete objectives, predict the resources necessary to attain those objectives, and manage the customers' expectations. More often than not, the moon was promised, a lunar rover built, and a pair of square wheels delivered.

The emphasis in software engineering is on both words, *software* and *engineering*. An engineer is able to build a high-quality product using off-the-shelf components and integrating them under time and budget constraints. The engineer is often faced with ill-defined problems and partial solutions, and has to rely on empirical methods to evaluate solutions. Engineers working in such application domains as passenger aircraft design and bridge construction have successfully met similar challenges. Software engineers have not been as successful.

The problem of building and delivering complex software systems on time has been actively investigated and researched. Everything has been blamed, from the customer ("What do you mean I can't get the moon for $50?") to the "soft" in software ("If I could add that one last feature ...") to the youth of this discipline. What is the problem?

Complexity and change

Useful software systems are complex. To remain useful they need to evolve with the end users' need and the target environment. In this book, we describe object-oriented techniques for conquering complex and changing software systems. In this chapter, we provide a motivation for object-oriented techniques and define the basic concepts used throughout this book.

1.1 Introduction: Software Engineering Failures

Consider the following examples [Neumann, 1995]:

Year 1900 bug

In 1992, Mary from Winona, Minnesota, received an invitation to attend a kindergarten. Mary was 104 at the time.

Leap-year bug

A supermarket was fined $1000 for having meat around 1 day too long, on February 29, 1988. The computer program printing the expiration date on the meat labels did not take into account that 1988 was a leap year.

Interface misuse

On April 10, 1990, in London, an underground train left the station without its driver. The driver had taped the button that started the train, relying on the system that prevented the train from moving when doors were open. The train operator had left his train to close a door which was stuck. When the door was finally shut, the train simply left.

Security

CERT (Computer Emergency Response Team) at the Software Engineering Institute is a government-funded organization for assisting the community in dealing with security incidents, vulnerabilities, and security know-how. The number of security incidents reported to CERT from the United States increased from 252 incidents in 1990 to 21,756 in 2000, and more than 40,000 incidents were reported in 2001.

Late and over budget

In 1995, bugs in the automated luggage system of the new Denver International Airport caused suitcases to be chewed up. The airport opened 16 months late, $3.2 billion over budget, with a mostly manual luggage system.

Late and over budget (2)

In 2002, the Swanick Air Traffic Control system covers all the enroute air traffic over England and Wales. The system was delivered substantially over budget (cost £623 million, originally planned at £350 million) and 6 years late. Two major upgrades of the system were delivered after training of the traffic controllers had started.

On-time delivery

After 18 months of development, a $200-million system was delivered to a health insurance company in Wisconsin in 1984. However, the system did not work correctly: $60 million in overpayments were issued. The system took 3 years to fix.

Unnecessary complexity

The C-17 cargo plane by McDonnell Douglas ran $500 million over budget because of problems with its avionics software. The C-17 included 19 onboard computers, 80 microprocessors, and 6 different programming languages.

Each of the failures described above resulted from a software-related problem. In some cases, developers did not anticipate seldom-occurring situations (a person living more than 100 years, leap years impacting expiration dates). In other cases, developers did not anticipate the user actively misusing the system (taping down a button, exploiting security holes in network software). In yet other cases, system failures resulted from management failures (late and over-budget delivery, on-time delivery of an incorrect system, unnecessary complexity).

Software systems are complex creations. They perform many functions; they are built to achieve many different, and often conflicting, objectives. They comprise many components; many of their components are custom made and complex themselves. Many participants from different disciplines take part in the development of these components. The development process and the software life cycle often spans many years. Finally, complex systems are difficult to understand completely by any single person. Many systems are so hard to understand, even during their development phase, that they are never finished: these are called *vaporware*.

Software development projects are subject to constant change. Because requirements are complex, they need to be updated when errors are discovered and when the developers have a better understanding of the application. If the project lasts many years, the staff turn-around is high, requiring constant training. The time between technological changes is often shorter than the duration of the project. The widespread assumptions of a software project manager that all changes have been dealt with and that the requirements can be frozen will lead to the deployment of an irrelevant system.

In the next section, we present a high-level view of software engineering. We describe software engineering from the perspective of science, engineering, and knowledge acquisition and formalization. In Section 1.3, we describe in more detail the main terms and concepts we use in this book. In Section 1.4, we provide an overview of the development activities of software engineering. In Section 1.5, we provide an overview of the managerial activities of software engineering.

1.2 What Is Software Engineering?

Software engineering is a **modeling** activity. Software engineers deal with complexity through modeling, by focusing at any one time on only the relevant details and ignoring everything else. In the course of development, software engineers build many different models of the system and of the application domain.

Software engineering is a **problem-solving** activity. Models are used to search for an acceptable solution. This search is driven by experimentation. Software engineers do not have infinite resources and are constrained by budget and deadlines. Given the lack of a fundamental theory, they often have to rely on empirical methods to evaluate the benefits of different alternatives.

Software engineering is a **knowledge acquisition** activity. In modeling the application and solution domain, software engineers collect data, organize it into information, and formalize it into knowledge. Knowledge acquisition is not sequential, as a single piece of additional data can invalidate complete models.

Software engineering is a **rationale-driven** activity. When acquiring knowledge and making decisions about the system or its application domain, software engineers also need to capture the context in which decisions were made and the rationale behind these decisions. Rationale information, represented as a set of issue models, enables software engineers to understand the implication of a proposed change when revisiting a decision.

In this section, we describe in more detail software engineering from the perspectives of modeling, problem solving, knowledge acquisition, and rationale. For each of these activities, software engineers have to work under people, time, and budget constraints. In addition, we assume that change can occur at any time.

1.2.1 Modeling

The purpose of science is to describe and understand complex systems, such as a system of atoms, a society of human beings, or a solar system. Traditionally, a distinction is made between *natural sciences* and *social sciences* to distinguish between two major types of systems. The purpose of natural sciences is to understand nature and its subsystems. Natural sciences include, for example, biology, chemistry, physics, and paleontology. The purpose of the social sciences is to understand human beings. Social sciences include psychology and sociology.

There is another type of system that we call an artificial system. Examples of artificial systems include the space shuttle, airline reservation systems, and stock trading systems. Herbert Simon coined the term *sciences of the artificial* to describe the sciences that deal with artificial systems [Simon, 1970]. Whereas natural and social sciences have been around for centuries, the sciences of the artificial are recent. Computer science, for example, the science of understanding computer systems, is a child of the twentieth century.

Many methods that have been successfully applied in the natural sciences and humanities can be applied to the sciences of the artificial as well. By looking at the other sciences, we can learn quite a bit. One of the basic methods of science is **modeling**. A model is an abstract representation of a system that enables us to answer questions about the system. Models are useful when dealing with systems that are too large, too small, too complicated, or too expensive to experience firsthand. Models also allow us to visualize and understand systems that either no longer exist or that are only claimed to exist.

Fossil biologists unearth a few bones and teeth preserved from some dinosaur that no one has ever seen. From the bone fragments, they reconstruct a model of the animal, following rules of anatomy. The more bones they find, the clearer their idea of how the pieces fit together and the higher the confidence that their model matches the original dinosaur. If they find a sufficient number of bones, teeth, and claws, they can almost be sure that their model reflects reality accurately, and they can guess the missing parts. Legs, for example, usually come in pairs. If the left leg is found, but the right leg is missing, the fossil biologists have a fairly good idea what the missing leg should look like and where it fits in the model. This is an example of a model of a system that no longer exists.

Today's high-energy physicists are in a position similar to that of a fossil biologist who has found most of the bones. Physicists are building a model of matter and energy and how they fit together at the most basic, subatomic level. Many years of experiments with particle accelerators have given high-energy physicists enough confidence that their models reflect reality and that the remaining pieces that are not yet found will fit into the so-called standard model. This is an example of a model for a system that is claimed to exist.

Both system modelers, fossil biologists and high-energy physicists, deal with two types of entities: the real-world system, observed in terms of a set of phenomena, and the application domain model, represented as a set of interdependent concepts. The system in the real world is a dinosaur or subatomic particles. The application domain model is a description of those aspects of the real-world system that are relevant to the problem under consideration.

Software engineers face similar challenges as fossil biologists and high-energy physicists. First, software engineers need to understand the environment in which the system has to operate. For a train traffic control system, software engineers need to know train signaling procedures. For a stock trading system, software engineers need to know trading rules. The software engineer does not need to become a fully certified train dispatcher or a stock broker; they only need to learn the application domain concepts that are *relevant* to the system. In other terms, they need to build a model of the application domain.

Second, software engineers need to understand the systems they could build, to evaluate different solutions and trade-offs. Most systems are too complex to be understood by any one person, and most systems are expensive to build. To address these challenges, software engineers describe important aspects of the alternative systems they investigate. In other terms, they need to build a model of the solution domain.

Object-oriented methods combine the application domain and solution domain modeling activities into one. The application domain is first modeled as a set of objects and relationships. This model is then used by the system to represent the real-world concepts it manipulates. A train traffic control system includes train objects representing the trains it monitors. A stock trading system includes transaction objects representing the buying and selling of commodities. Then, solution domain concepts are also modeled as objects. The set of lines used to depict a train or a financial transaction are objects that are part of the solution domain. The idea of object-oriented methods is that the solution domain model is a transformation of the application domain model. Developing software translates into the activities necessary to identify and describe a system as a set of models that addresses the end user's problem. We describe in more detail modeling and the concepts of objects in Chapter 2, *Modeling with UML*.

1.2.2   Problem Solving

Engineering is a **problem-solving** activity. Engineers search for an appropriate solution, often by trial and error, evaluating alternatives empirically, with limited resources and incomplete knowledge. In its simplest form, the engineering method includes five steps:

1. Formulate the problem.
2. Analyze the problem.
3. Search for solutions.
4. Decide on the appropriate solution.
5. Specify the solution.

Software engineering is an engineering activity. It is not algorithmic. It requires experimentation, the reuse of pattern solutions, and the incremental evolution of the system toward a solution that is acceptable to the client.

Object-oriented software development typically includes six development activities: requirements elicitation, analysis, system design, object design, implementation, and testing. During requirements elicitation and analysis, software engineers formulate the problem with the client and build the application domain model. Requirements elicitation and analysis correspond to steps 1 and 2 of the engineering method. During system design, software engineers analyze the problem, break it down into smaller pieces, and select general strategies for designing the system. During object design, they select detail solutions for each piece and decide on the most appropriate solution. System design and object design result in the solution domain model. System and object design correspond to steps 3 and 4 of the engineering method. During implementation, software engineers realize the system by translating the solution domain model into an executable representation. Implementation corresponds to step 5 of the engineering method. What makes software engineering different from problem solving in other sciences is that change occurs in the application and the solution domain while the problem is being solved.

Software development also includes activities whose purpose is to evaluate the appropriateness of the respective models. During the analysis review, the application domain model is compared with the client's reality, which in turn might change as a result of modeling. During the design review, the solution domain model is evaluated against project goals. During testing, the system is validated against the solution domain model, which might be changed by the introduction of new technologies. During project management, managers compare their model of the development process (i.e., the project schedule and budget) against reality (i.e., the delivered work products and expended resources).

1.2.3   Knowledge Acquisition

A common mistake that software engineers and managers make is to assume that the acquisition of knowledge needed to develop a system is linear. This mistake is not made by software managers alone; it can be found in other areas as well. In the 17th century, a book was published that offered to teach all the German poems by pouring them into the student's head in 6 hours with a funnel.[1] The idea of using a funnel for learning is based on the widespread assumption that our mind is a bucket that is initially empty and can be filled in a linear fashion. Material enters through our senses, accumulates, and is digested. Popper calls this linear acquisition model for knowledge "the bucket theory of the mind." Among the many other things that are wrong with this theory (described in [Popper, 1992]) is the assumption that knowledge is conceived as consisting of things that can fill a bucket; that is, the fuller the bucket, the more we know.

Knowledge acquisition is a nonlinear process. The addition of a new piece of information may invalidate all the knowledge we have acquired for the understanding of a system. Even if we had already documented this understanding in documents and code ("The system is 90% coded, we will be done next week"), we must be mentally prepared to start from scratch. This has important implications on the set of activities and their interactions we define to develop the software system. The equivalent of the bucket theory of the mind is the sequential waterfall model for software development, in which all steps of the engineering method are accomplished sequentially.

There are several software processes that deal with this problem by avoiding the sequential dependencies inherent in the waterfall model. **Risk-based development** attempts to anticipate surprises late in a project by identifying the high-risk components. **Issue-based development** attempts to remove the linearity altogether. Any development activity—analysis, system design, object design, implementation, testing, or delivery—can influence any other activity. In issue-based development, all these activities are executed in parallel. The difficulty with nonsequential development models, however, is that they are difficult to manage.

1.2.4 Rationale

When describing the acquisition or evolution of knowledge, we are even less well equipped than when describing the knowledge of an existing system. How does a mathematician derive a proof? Mathematical textbooks are full of proofs, but rarely provide hints about the proof derivation. This is because mathematicians do not think this background is important. Once the axioms and the rules of deduction have been stated, the proof is timeless.

For software engineers, the situation is different. Assumptions that developers make about a system change constantly. Even though the application domain models eventually stabilize once developers acquire an adequate understanding of the problem, the solution domain models are in constant flux. Design and implementation faults discovered during testing and usability problems discovered during user evaluation trigger changes to the solution models. Changes can also be caused by new technology. The availability of a long-life battery and of high-bandwidth wireless communication, for example, can trigger revisions to the concept of a portable terminal.

---

1. G. P. Harsdoerfer (1607–1658), "Poetischer Trichter, die teutsche Dicht- und Reimkunst, ohn Behuf der lateinischen Sprache, in 6 Stunden einzugießen," Nuernberg, 1630.

Change introduced by new technology often allows the formulation of new functional or nonfunctional requirements. A typical task of software engineers is to change a currently operational software system to incorporate this new enabling technology. To change the system, it is not enough to understand its current components and behavior. It is also necessary to capture and understand the context in which each design decision was made. This additional knowledge is called the **rationale** of the system.

Capturing and accessing the rationale of a system is not trivial. First, for every decision made, several alternatives may have been considered, evaluated, and argued. Consequently, rationale represents a much larger amount of information than do the solution models. Second, rationale information is often not explicit. Developers make many decisions based on their experience and their intuition, without explicitly evaluating different alternatives. When asked to explain a decision, developers may have to spend a substantial amount of time recovering its rationale. In order to deal with changing systems, however, software engineers must address the challenges of capturing and accessing rationale.

1.3 Software Engineering Concepts

So far, we have presented a high-level view of software engineering from the perspectives of modeling, problem solving, knowledge acquisition, and rationale. In this section, we describe the main terms and concepts we use throughout the book.[2] A Project, whose purpose is to develop a software system, is composed of a number of Activities. Each Activity is in turn composed of a number of Tasks. A Task consumes Resources and produces a WorkProduct. A WorkProduct can be either a System, a Model, or a Document. Resources are either Participants, Time, or Equipment. A graphical representation of these concepts is shown in Figure 1-1. Each rectangle represents a concept. The lines among the rectangles represent different relationships between the concepts. For example, the diamond shape indicates aggregation: a Project includes a number of Activities, which includes a number of Tasks. The triangle shape indicates a generalization relationship; Participants, Time, and Equipment are specific kinds of Resources. Figure 1-1 is represented in the Unified Modeling Language (UML) notation. We use UML throughout the book to represent models of software and other systems. Intuitively, you should be able to understand this diagram without full knowledge of the UML semantics. Similarly, you can also use UML diagrams when interacting with a client or a user, even though they may not have any knowledge of UML. We describe the semantics of these diagrams in detail in Chapter 2, *Modeling with UML*.

---

2. As much as possible, we follow the definitions of the IEEE standards on Software Engineering [IEEE Std. 610.12-1990].

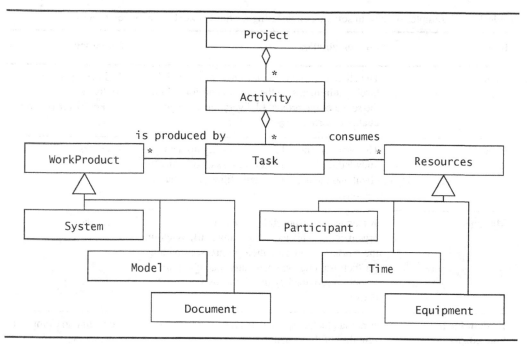

Figure 1-1 Software engineering concepts depicted as a UML class diagram [OMG, 2009].

1.3.1 Participants and Roles

Developing a software system requires the collaboration of many people with different backgrounds and interests. The client orders and pays for the system. The developers construct the system. The project manager plans and budgets the project and coordinates the developers and the client. The end users are supported by the system. We refer to all the persons involved in the project as **participants**. We refer to a set of responsibilities in the project or the system as a **role**. A role is associated with a set of **tasks** and is assigned to a participant. The same participant can fill multiple roles.

Consider a TicketDistributor system:

TicketDistributor is a machine that distributes tickets for trains. Travelers have the option of selecting a ticket for a single trip or for multiple trips, or selecting a time card for a day or a week. The TicketDistributor computes the price of the requested ticket based on the area in which the trip will take place and whether the traveler is a child or an adult. The TicketDistributor must be able to handle several exceptions, such as travelers who do not complete the transaction, travelers who attempt to pay with large bills, and resource outages, such as running out of tickets, change, or power.

Treating the development of this TicketDistributor as a software engineering project, Table 1-1 provides examples of roles for this example.

Table 1-1   Examples of roles in software engineering for the `TicketDistributor` project.

Role	Responsibilities	Examples
Client	The client is responsible for providing the high-level requirements on the system and for defining the scope of the project (delivery date, budget, quality criteria).	Train company that contracts the `TicketDistributor`.
User	The user is responsible for providing domain knowledge about current user tasks. Note that the client and the user are usually filled by different persons.	Travelers
Manager	A manager is responsible for the work organization. This includes hiring staff, assigning them tasks, monitoring their progress, providing for their training, and generally managing the resources provided by the client for a successful delivery.	Alice (boss)
Human Factors Specialist	A human factors specialist is responsible for the usability of the system.	Zoe (Human Computer Interaction specialist)
Developer	A developer is responsible for the construction of the system, including specification, design, implementation, and testing. In large projects, the developer role is further specialized.	John (analyst), Marc (programmer), & Zoe (tester)[a]
Technical Writer	The technical writer is responsible for the documentation delivered to the client. A technical writer interviews developers, managers, and users to understand the system.	John

a.   As `TicketDistributor` is a small project, Zoe fills both the human factor specialist and the tester roles, and John fills the analyst and the technical writer roles.

1.3.2   Systems and Models

We use the term **system** as a collection of interconnected parts. Modeling is a way to deal with complexity by ignoring irrelevant details. We use the term **model** to refer to any abstraction of the system. A `TicketDistributor` for an underground train is a system. Blueprints for the `TicketDistributor`, schematics of its electrical wiring, and object models of its software are models of the `TicketDistributor`. Note that a development project is itself a system that can be modeled. The project schedule, its budget, and its planned deadlines are models of the development project.

1.3.3 Work Products

A **work product** is an artifact that is produced during the development, such as a document or a piece of software for other developers or for the client. We refer to a work product for the project's internal consumption as an **internal work product**. We refer to a work product that must be delivered to a client as a **deliverable**. Deliverables are generally defined prior to the start of the project and specified by a contract binding the developers with the client. Table 1-2 describes examples of work products for the TicketDistributor example.

Table 1-2 Examples of work products for the TicketDistributor project.

Work product	Type	Description
Specification	Deliverable	The specification describes the system from the user's point of view. It is used as a contractual document between the project and the client. The TicketDistributor specification describes in detail how the system should appear to the traveler.
Operation manual	Deliverable	The operation manual for the TicketDistributor is used by the staff of the train company responsible for installing and configuring the TicketDistributor. Such a manual describes, for example, how to change the price of tickets and the structure of the network into zones.
Status report	Internal work product	A status report describes at a given time the tasks that have been completed and the tasks that are still in progress. The status report is produced for the manager, Alice, and is usually not seen by the train company.
Test manual	Internal work product	The test plans and results are produced by the tester, Zoe. These documents track the known defects in the prototype TicketDistributor and their state of repair. These documents are usually not shared with the client.

1.3.4 Activities, Tasks, and Resources

An **activity** is a set of tasks that is performed toward a specific purpose. For example, requirements elicitation is an activity whose purpose is to define with the client what the system will do. Delivery is an activity whose purpose is to install the system at an operational location. Management is an activity whose purpose is to monitor and control the project such that it meets its goals (e.g., deadline, quality, budget). Activities can be composed of other activities. The delivery activity includes a software installation activity and an operator training activity. Activities are also sometimes called **phases**.

A **task** represents an atomic unit of work that can be managed: A manager assigns it to a developer, the developer carries it out, and the manager monitors the progress and completion of the task. Tasks consume resources, result in work products, and depend on work products produced by other tasks.

Resources are assets that are used to accomplish work. Resources include time, equipment, and labor. When planning a project, a manager breaks down the work into tasks and assigns them to resources.

Table 1-3 describes examples of activities, tasks, and resources in software engineering.

Table 1-3   Examples of activities, tasks, and resources for the TicketDistributor project.

Example	Type	Description
Requirements elicitation	**Activity**	The requirements elicitation activity includes obtaining and validating requirements and domain knowledge from the client and the users. The requirements elicitation activity produces the specification work product (Table 1-2).
Develop "Out of Change" test case for TicketDistributor	**Task**	This task, assigned to Zoe (the tester) focuses on verifying the behavior of the ticket distributor when it runs out of money and cannot give the correct change back to the user. This activity includes specifying the environment of the test, the sequence of inputs to be entered, and the expected outputs.
Review "Access Online Help" use case for usability	**Task**	This task, assigned to John (the human factors specialist) focuses on detecting usability issues in accessing the online help features of the system.
Tariff Database	**Resource**	The tariff database includes an example of tariff structure with a train network plan. This example is a resource provided by the client for requirements and testing.

1.3.5   Functional and Nonfunctional Requirements

Requirements specify a set of features that the system must have. A **functional requirement** is a specification of a function that the system must support, whereas a **nonfunctional requirement** is a constraint on the operation of the system that is not related directly to a function of the system.

For example, *The user must be able to purchase tickets* and *The user must be able to access tariff information* are functional requirements. *The user must be provided feedback in less than one second* and *The colors used in the interface should be consistent with the company colors* are nonfunctional requirements. Other nonfunctional requirements may include using specific hardware platform for the system, security requirements, how the system should deal with failures and faults, and how to provide backward compatibility with an old system that the client is unwilling to retire.

1.3.6   Notations, Methods, and Methodologies

A **notation** is a graphical or textual set of rules for representing a model. The Roman alphabet is a notation for representing words. UML (Unified Modeling Language [OMG, 2009]), the notation we use throughout this book, is a notation for representing object-oriented models. The use of notations in software engineering is common and predates object-oriented concepts. Data flow diagrams [De Marco, 1978] is a notation for representing systems in terms of data sources, data sinks, and data transformations. Z [Spivey, 1989] is a notation for representing systems based on set theory.

A **method** is a repeatable technique that specifies the steps involved in solving a specific problem. A recipe is a method for cooking a specific dish. A sorting algorithm is a method for ordering elements of a list. Rationale management is a method for justifying change. Configuration management is a method for tracking change.

A **methodology** is a collection of methods for solving a class of problems and specifies how and when each method should be used. A seafood cookbook with a collection of recipes is a methodology for preparing seafood if it also contains advice on how ingredients should be used and what to do if not all ingredients are available. Royce's methodology [Royce, 1998], the Object Modeling Technique (OMT [Rumbaugh et al., 1991]), the Booch methodology [Booch, 1994], and Catalysis [D'Souza & Wills, 1999] are object-oriented methodologies for developing software.

Software development methodologies decompose the process into activities. OMT provides methods for three activities: *Analysis*, which focuses on formalizing the system requirements into an object model, *System Design*, which focuses on strategic decisions, and *Object Design*, which transforms the analysis model into an object model that can be implemented. The OMT methodology assumes that requirements have already been defined and does not provide methods for eliciting requirements. The Unified Software Development Process also includes an *Analysis* activity and treats *System Design* and *Object Design* as a single activity called *Design*. The Unified Process, unlike OMT, includes a *Requirements Capture* activity for eliciting and modeling requirements. Catalysis, while using the same notations as the Unified Process, focuses more on reuse of design and code using patterns and frameworks. All of these methodologies focus on dealing with complex systems.

In this book, we present a methodology for developing complex and changing systems. During the course of our teaching and research ([Bruegge, 1992], [Bruegge & Coyne, 1993], [Bruegge & Coyne, 1994], [Coyne et al., 1995]), we have adapted and refined methods from a variety of sources. For activities modeling the application domain, such as requirements elicitation and analysis, we describe methods similar to those of OOSE [Jacobson et al., 1992].

For solution domain modeling activities, such as system design and object design, we describe object-oriented activities similar to those of OMT. For change-related activities, we focus on rationale management, which originated from design rationale research [Moran & Carroll, 1996], and configuration management, which originated from the maintenance of large systems [Babich, 1986].

1.4 Software Engineering Development Activities

In this section, we give an overview of the technical activities associated with object-oriented software engineering. Development activities deal with the complexity by constructing and validating models of the application domain or the system. Development activities include

- Requirements Elicitation (Section 1.4.1)
- Analysis (Section 1.4.2)
- System Design (Section 1.4.3)
- Object Design (Section 1.4.4)
- Implementation (Section 1.4.5)
- Testing (Section 1.4.6).

Figure 1-2 depicts an overview of the relationship among these activities and their products. In Section 1.5, we give an overview of the managerial activities associated with software engineering. In Chapter 14, *Project Management*, and in Chapter 15, *Software Life Cycle*, we discuss in more detail the modeling, planning, and software engineering activities.

1.4.1 Requirements Elicitation

During **requirements elicitation**, the client and developers define the purpose of the system. The result of this activity is a description of the system in terms of actors and use cases. Actors represent the external entities that interact with the system. Actors include roles such as end users, other computers the system needs to deal with (e.g., a central bank computer, a network), and the environment (e.g., a chemical process). Use cases are general sequences of events that describe all the possible actions between an actor and the system for a given piece of functionality. Figure 1-3 depicts a use case for the TicketDistributor example we discussed previously. We describe requirements elicitation, including use cases and nonfunctional requirements, in detail in Chapter 4, *Requirements Elicitation*.

1.4.2 Analysis

During **analysis**, developers aim to produce a model of the system that is correct, complete, consistent, and unambiguous. Developers transform the use cases produced during requirements elicitation into an object model that completely describes the system. During this activity, developers discover ambiguities and inconsistencies in the use case model that they resolve with the client. The result of analysis is a system model annotated with attributes, operations, and

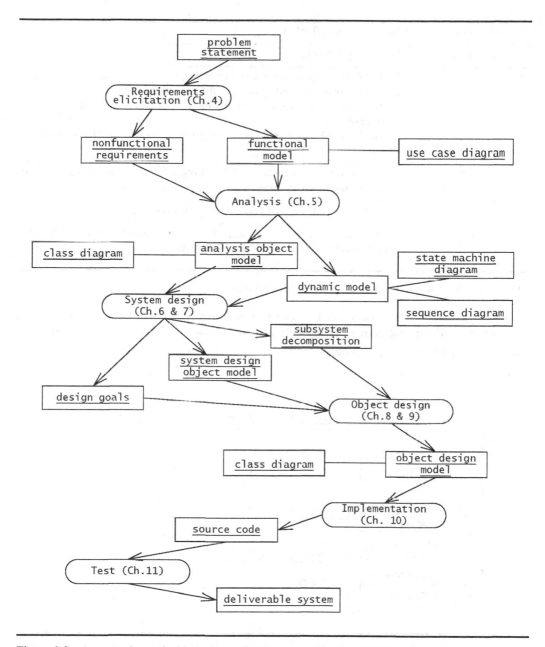

Figure 1-2 An overview of object-oriented software engineering development activities and their products. This diagram depicts only logical dependencies among work products. Object-oriented software engineering is iterative; that is, activities can occur in parallel and more than once.

Use case name	PurchaseOneWayTicket
Participating actor	Initiated by Traveler
Flow of events	1. The Traveler selects the zone in which the destination station is located. 2. The TicketDistributor displays the price of the ticket. 3. The Traveler inserts an amount of money that is at least as much as the price of the ticket. 4. The TicketDistributor issues the specified ticket to the Traveler and returns any change.
Entry condition	The Traveler stands in front of the TicketDistributor, which may be located at the station of origin or at another station.
Exit condition	The Traveler holds a valid ticket and any excess change.
Quality requirements	If the transaction is not completed after one minute of inactivity, the TicketDistributor returns all inserted change.

Figure 1-3 An example of use case, PurchaseOneWayTicket.

associations. The system model can be described in terms of its structure and its dynamic interoperation. Figure 1-4 depicts an example of dynamic model for the TicketDistributor. Figure 1-5 depicts an example of object model for the TicketDistributor.

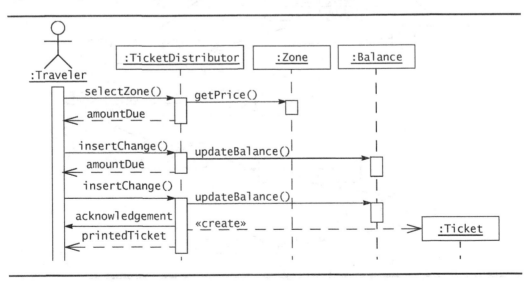

Figure 1-4 A dynamic model for the TicketDistributor (UML sequence diagram). This diagram depicts the interactions between the actor and the system during the PurchaseOneWayTicket use case and the objects that participate in the use case.

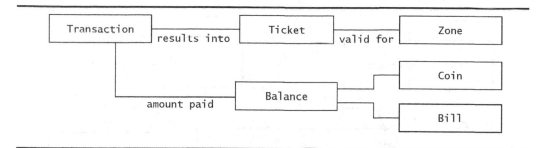

Figure 1-5 An object model for the `TicketDistributor` (UML class diagram). In the `PurchaseOneWayTicket` use case, a `Traveler` initiates a transaction that will result in a `Ticket`. A `Ticket` is valid only for a specified Zone. During the `Transaction`, the system tracks the `Balance` due by counting the `Coins` and `Bills` inserted.

We describe analysis, including object models, in detail in Chapter 5, *Analysis*. We describe in detail the UML notation for representing models in Chapter 2, *Modeling with UML*.

1.4.3   System Design

During **system design**, developers define the design goals of the project and decompose the system into smaller subsystems that can be realized by individual teams. Developers also select strategies for building the system, such as the hardware/software platform on which the system will run, the persistent data management strategy, the global control flow, the access control policy, and the handling of boundary conditions. The result of system design is a clear description of each of these strategies, a subsystem decomposition, and a deployment diagram representing the hardware/software mapping of the system. Whereas both analysis and system design produce models of the system under construction, only analysis deals with entities that the client can understand. System design deals with a much more refined model that includes many entities that are beyond the comprehension (and interest) of the client. Figure 1-6 depicts an example of system decomposition for the `TicketDistributor`. We describe system design and its related concepts in detail in Chapter 6, *System Design: Decomposing the System*, and in Chapter 7, *System Design: Addressing Design Goals*.

1.4.4   Object Design

During **object design**, developers define solution domain objects to bridge the gap between the analysis model and the hardware/software platform defined during system design. This includes precisely describing object and subsystem interfaces, selecting off-the-shelf components, restructuring the object model to attain design goals such as extensibility or understandability, and optimizing the object model for performance. The result of the object design activity is a detailed object model annotated with constraints and precise descriptions for each element. We describe object design and its related concepts in detail in Chapter 8, *Object Design: Reusing Pattern Solutions*, and Chapter 9, *Object Design: Specifying Interfaces*.

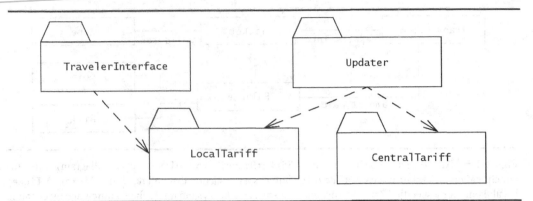

Figure 1-6 A subsystem decomposition for the `TicketDistributor` (UML class diagram, packages represent subsystems, dashed lines represent dependencies). The `TravelerInterface` subsystem is responsible for collecting input from the `Traveler` and providing feedback (e.g., display ticket price, returning change). The `LocalTariff` subsystem computes the price of different tickets based on a local database. The `CentralTariff` subsystem, located on a central computer, maintains a reference copy of the tariff database. An `Updater` subsystem is responsible for updating the local databases at each `TicketDistributor` through a network when ticket prices change.

1.4.5   Implementation

During **implementation**, developers translate the solution domain model into source code. This includes implementing the attributes and methods of each object and integrating all the objects such that they function as a single system. The implementation activity spans the gap between the detailed object design model and a complete set of source code files that can be compiled. We describe the mapping of UML models to code in Chapter 10, *Mapping Models to Code*. We assume the reader is already familiar with programming concepts and knows how to program data structures and algorithms using an object-oriented language such as Java or C++.

1.4.6   Testing

During **testing**, developers find differences between the system and its models by executing the system (or parts of it) with sample input data sets. During unit testing, developers compare the object design model with each object and subsystem. During integration testing, combinations of subsystems are integrated together and compared with the system design model. During system testing, typical and exception cases are run through the system and compared with the requirements model. The goal of testing is to discover as many faults as possible such that they can be repaired before the delivery of the system. The planning of test phases occurs in parallel to the other development activities: System tests are planned during requirements elicitation and analysis, integration tests are planned during system design, and unit tests are planned during object design. We describe these issues in more detail in Chapter 11, *Testing*.

1.5 Managing Software Development

In this section, we briefly describe the activities involved in managing a software engineering project. Management activities focus on planning the project, monitoring its status, tracking changes, and coordinating resources such that a high-quality product is delivered on time and within budget. Management activities not only involve managers, but also most of the other project participants as well. Management activities include

- Communication (Section 1.5.1)
- Rationale Management (Section 1.5.2)
- Software Configuration Management (Section 1.5.3)
- Project Management (Section 1.5.4)
- Software Life Cycle (Section 1.5.5).

Software maintenance, which we do not cover in this book, includes the development activities that occur after the delivery of the system to the client. Traditionally, software maintenance has been distinguished from the other development activities as it is highly change driven and is performed by a different team than the original development team. As modern software engineering projects become more change driven, the distinction between construction activities and maintenance activities is blurred. Many of the activities described in this book can carry on to maintenance, including object design, implementation, testing, rationale management, and software configuration management.

1.5.1 Communication

Communication is the most critical and time-consuming activity in software engineering. Misunderstandings and omissions often lead to faults and delays that are expensive to correct later in the development. Communication includes the exchange of models and documents about the system and its application domain, reporting the status of work products, providing feedback on the quality of work products, raising and negotiating issues, and communicating decisions. Communication is made difficult by the diversity of participants' backgrounds, by their geographic distribution, and by the volume, complexity, and evolution of the information exchanged.

To deal with communication issues, project participants have many tools available. The most effective one is conventions: When participants agree on notations for representing information, on tools for manipulating information, and on procedures for raising and resolving issues, they already have eliminated substantial sources of misunderstanding. Examples of notations include UML diagrams, templates for writing documents and meeting minutes, and identification schemes for naming software components. Examples of tools include Computer Aided Software Engineering (CASE) tools for maintaining models, word processors for generating documents, and interchange formats for publishing information. Examples of procedures include meeting procedures for organizing, conducting, and capturing a meeting, review procedures for reviewing documents and providing feedback, and inspection procedures for detecting defects in models or source code. The selected conventions do not need to be the best available; they only need to be shared and agreed on by everybody. We describe communication issues in detail in Chapter 3, *Project Organization and Communication*.

1.5.2   Rationale Management

Rationale is the justification of decisions. Given a decision, its rationale includes the problem that it addresses, the alternatives that developers considered, the criteria that developers used to evaluate the alternatives, the debate developers went through to achieve consensus, and the decision. Rationale is the most important information developers need when changing the system. If a criterion changes, developers can reevaluate all decisions that depend on this criterion. If a new alternative becomes available, it can be compared with all the other alternatives that were already evaluated. If a decision is questioned, they can recover its rationale to justify it.

Unfortunately, rationale is also the most complex information developers deal with during development, and thus, the most difficult to update and maintain. To deal with this challenge, developers capture rationale during meetings and on-line discussions, represent rationale with issue models, and access rationale during changes. We describe these issues in detail in Chapter 12, *Rationale Management*.

1.5.3   Software Configuration Management

Software configuration management is the process that monitors and controls changes in work products. Change pervades software development. Requirements change as the client requests new features and as developers improve their understanding of the application domain. The hardware/software platform on which the system is built changes as new technology becomes available. The system changes as faults are discovered during testing and are repaired. Software configuration management used to be in the realm of maintenance, when improvements are incrementally introduced in the system. In modern development processes, however, changes occur much earlier than maintenance does. Thus, changes during development can be dealt with using configuration management at all stages.

Configuration management enables developers to track changes. The system is represented as a number of configuration items that are independently revised. For each configuration item, its evolution is tracked as a series of versions. Selecting versions enables developers to roll back to a well-defined state of the system when a change fails.

Configuration management also enables developers to control change. After a baseline has been defined, any change needs to be assessed and approved before being implemented. This enables management to ensure that the system is evolving according to project goals and that the number of problems introduced into the system is limited. We describe these issues in detail in Chapter 13, *Configuration Management*.

1.5.4   Project Management

Project management does not produce any artifact of its own. Instead, project management includes the oversight activities that ensure the delivery of a high-quality system on time and within budget. This includes planning and budgeting the project during negotiations with the client, hiring developers and organizing them into teams, monitoring the status of the project, and intervening when deviations occur. Most project management activities are beyond the scope of this book. We describe, however, the project management activities that are visible to the developers and techniques that make the development–management communication more effective. We describe these issues in detail in Chapter 14, *Project Management*.

1.5.5   Software Life Cycle

In this chapter, we describe software engineering as a modeling activity. Developers build models of the application and solution domains to deal with their complexity. By ignoring irrelevant details and focusing only on what is relevant to a specific issue, developers can more effectively resolve issues and answer questions. The process of developing software can also be viewed as a complex system with inputs, outputs, activities, and resources. It is not surprising, then, that the same modeling techniques applied to software artifacts are used for modeling software processes. A general model of the software development process is called a *software life cycle*. We describe software life cycles in Chapter 15, *Software Life Cycle*.

1.5.6   Putting It All Together

After reading Chapters 1–15 in this book, you will have an overview of the current state-of-the-art methods in object-oriented software engineering, which you can view as a thick cookbook of recipes. In practice, however, a cookbook is rarely enough for the novice to cook a complete meal. Moreover, not all ingredients are always available, and the cook has to improvise to bridge the gaps.

Chapter 14, *Project Management*, focuses on planning and controlling projects. Chapter 15, *Software Life Cycle*, focuses on modeling, improving, and repeating software life cycle processes. Both chapters, because they focus on techniques and models, take an optimistic view of project execution. In Chapter 16, *Methodologies: Putting It All Together*, we examine what happens outside of textbook situations. We provide methodologies and heuristics for adapting the building blocks presented in the other chapter to specific situations. In particular, we describe several agile and heavier methodologies.

1.6 ARENA Case Study

In each chapter, we introduce concepts and activities using increasingly complex examples, starting with toy examples from the classroom and moving to actual examples from project courses or from real systems. Moreover, to put the activities of each chapter in the context of the overall software engineering project, we also use a single, comprehensive case study throughout the book, describing the development of a system called ARENA.

ARENA is a multi-user, Web-based system for organizing and conducting tournaments. ARENA is game independent in the sense that organizers can adapt a new game to the ARENA game interface, upload it to the ARENA server, and immediately announce and conduct tournaments with players and spectators located anywhere on the Internet. Organizers can also define new tournament styles, describing how players are mapped to a set of matches and how to compute an overall ranking of players by adding up their victories and losses (hence, figuring out who won the tournament). To recoup their operational costs, organizers can also invite potential sponsors to display advertisement banners during games.

In the section entitled "ARENA Case Study" located at the end of each chapter, we discuss issues, design decisions, and trade-offs specific to the chapter in the context of ARENA. We also relate these issues to the parts of the case study presented in previous chapters, thereby emphasizing inter-chapter dependencies. For example:

- In Chapter 4, *Requirements Elicitation*, we describe how developers write an initial set of use cases based on information provided by a client. We define in more detail how tournaments should be organized and announced, and how players apply for new tournaments. In the process, we generate more questions for the client and uncover ambiguities and missing information about the system.

- In Chapter 5, *Analysis*, we describe how an object model and a behavior model are constructed from the use case model. We also examine how the development of these models leads to more refinements in the use case model and in the discovery of additional requirements. For example, we define more formally the concept of exclusive sponsorship, describe the workflow associated with deciding on the sponsorship of a tournament, and consolidate the object model.

- In Chapter 7, *System Design: Addressing Design Goals*, we select a client server architecture and a framework for realizing the system, and address issues such as data storage and access control. We examine different mechanisms for authenticating users on the Web, identify the persistent objects we need to store (e.g., game state, tournament results, player profiles), and decompose ARENA into smaller subsystems that can be handled by single programmers.

- In Chapter 8, *Object Design: Reusing Pattern Solutions*, and in Chapter 9, *Object Design: Specifying Interfaces*, we identify additional solution domain objects to fill the gap between the system design and the implementation. We reuse template solutions by selecting design patterns for addressing specific issues. For example, a strategy pattern is used to encapsulate different tournament styles.

- In Chapter 10, *Mapping Models to Code*, we translate the UML models we built so far into Java code, and reexamine the object design as new optimization issues are discovered. In this chapter, we illustrate the tight iteration between object design and implementation.

The work products associated with the ARENA system, along with a demonstration, are available from http://wwwbruegge.in.tum.de/OOSE/WebHome.

1.7 Further Reading

The fundamental issues associated with software engineering are not new and have been written about for several decades.

In the *Mythical Man Month* [Brooks, 1995], first published in 1975, Frederick Brooks reflects on his experience with developing an operating system for the IBM 360 mainframe, a multi-million dollar, multi-year project that went over budget and schedule. Since then, different techniques, tools, and methods have enabled software engineers to tackle more complex and challenging problems, only to experience failures that are more expensive and more spectacular. Many basic lessons of this landmark book are still applicable today.

In *Computer-Related Risks* [Neumann, 1995], Peter Neumann relates a collection of computer-related failures, examine roots causes and effects of these failures, and discusses what might be done to avoid them. *Computer-Related Risks* is a sobering account that should be read by any software engineer who dreams of building and mastering complex systems.

Objective Knowledge: An Evolutionary Approach [Popper, 1992] is an essay about knowledge construction. Karl Popper breaks from traditional knowledge theories dating back to Aristotle and proposes that scientific knowledge, once stated in a human language, becomes a separate entity that grows through selection. As software engineering is a collaborative knowledge-gathering and construction activity, Popper's book can be useful to stimulate critical thinking and provide a different perspective on the field.

In this book, we focus on object-oriented software engineering and target senior-level software engineering project courses. Consequently, we leave out several historical and management topics that are traditionally included in software engineering books, such as software metrics, cost estimation, and formal methods. An overview of these topics can be found in more general software engineering textbooks, such as *Software Engineering* [Sommerville, 2006] and *Software Engineering: A Practitioner's Approach* [Pressman, 2009].

1.8 Exercises

1-1   What is the purpose of modeling?

1-2   A programming language is a notation for representing algorithms and data structures. List two advantages and two disadvantages of using a programming language as the sole notation throughout the development process.

1-3   Consider a task you are not familiar with, such as designing a zero-emissions car. How would you attack the problem?

1-4   What is meant by "knowledge acquisition is not sequential"? Provide a concrete example of knowledge acquisition that illustrates this.

1-5   Hypothesize a rationale for the following design decisions:

- "The TicketDistributor will be at most one and a half meters tall."

- "The TicketDistributor will include two redundant computer systems."

- "The TicketDistributor interface will consist of a touch screen for displaying instructions and accessing commands and a single button for aborting transactions."

1-6   Specify which of these statements are functional requirements and which are nonfunctional requirements:

- "The TicketDistributor must enable a traveler to buy weekly passes."

- "The TicketDistributor must be written in Java."

- "The TicketDistributor must be easy to use."

- "The TicketDistributor must always be available."

- "The TicketDistributor must provide a phone number to call when it fails."

1-7   Specify which of these decisions were made during requirements or system design:

- "The TicketDistributor is composed of a user interface subsystem, a subsystem for computing tariff, and a network subsystem for managing communication with the central computer."

- "The TicketDistributor hardware uses PowerPC processor chips."

- "The TicketDistributor provides the traveler with online help."

1-8   In the following description, explain when the term account is used as an application domain concept and when as a solution domain concept:

"Assume you are developing an online system for managing bank accounts for mobile customers. A major design issue is how to provide access to the accounts when the customer cannot establish an online connection. One proposal is that accounts are made available on the mobile computer, even if the server is not up. In this case, the accounts show the amounts from the last connected session."

1-9   What is the difference between a task and an activity?

1-10 A passenger aircraft is composed of several millions of parts and requires thousands of persons to assemble. A four-lane highway bridge is another example of complexity. The first version of Word for Windows, a word processor released by Microsoft in 1989, required 55 person-years, resulted into 249,000 lines of source code, and was delivered 4 years late. Aircraft and highway bridges are usually delivered on time and within budget, whereas software is often not. Discuss what are, in your opinion, the differences between developing an aircraft, a bridge, and a word processor that would cause this situation.

References

[Babich, 1986]   W. Babich, *Software Configuration Management*, Addison-Wesley, Reading, MA, 1986.

[Booch, 1994]   G. Booch, *Object-Oriented Analysis and Design with Applications,* 2nd ed. Benjamin/Cummings, Redwood City, CA, 1994.

[Brooks, 1995]   F. P. Brooks, *The Mythical Man Month: Anniversary Edition: Essays on Software Engineering*, Addison-Wesley, Reading, MA, 1995.

[Bruegge, 1992]   B. Bruegge, "Teaching an industry-oriented software engineering course," *Software Engineering Education,* SEI Conference, Lecture Notes in Computer Sciences, Vol. 640, pp. 65–87, Springer-Verlag, October 1992.

[Bruegge & Coyne, 1993]   B. Bruegge & R. Coyne, "Model-based software engineering in larger scale project courses," *IFIP Transactions on Computer Science and Technology,* Vol. A-40, pp. 273–287, Elsevier Science, Netherlands, 1993.

[Bruegge & Coyne, 1994]   B. Bruegge & R. Coyne, "Teaching iterative object-oriented development: Lessons and directions," in J. L. Diaz-Herrera (ed.), *7th Conference on Software Engineering Education,* Lecture Notes in Computer Science, Vol. 750, pp. 413–427, Springer-Verlag, 1994.

[Coyne et al., 1995]   R. Coyne, B. Bruegge, A. Dutoit, & D. Rothenberger, "Teaching more comprehensive model-based software engineering: Experience with Objectory's use case approach," in L. Ibraham (ed.), *8th Conference on Software Engineering Education,* Lecture Notes in Computer Science, pp. 339–374, Springer-Verlag, April 1995.

[De Marco, 1978]   T. De Marco, *Structured Analysis and System Specification.* Yourdon, New York, 1978.

[D'Souza & Wills, 1999]   D. F. D'Souza & A. C. Wills, *Objects, Components, and Frameworks with UML: The Catalysis Approach*, Addison-Wesley, Reading, MA, 1999.

[IEEE Std. 610.12-1990]   *IEEE Standard Computer Dictionary: A Compilation of IEEE Standard Computer Glossaries*, New York, NY, 1990.

[Jacobson et al., 1992]   I. Jacobson, M. Christerson, P. Jonsson, & G. Overgaard, *Object-Oriented Software Engineering—A Use Case Driven Approach*, Addison-Wesley, Reading, MA, 1992.

[Moran & Carroll, 1996]   T. P. Moran & J. M. Carroll (eds.), *Design Rationale: Concepts, Techniques, and Use*, Lawrence Erlbaum Associates, Mahwah, NJ, 1996.

[Neumann, 1995]   P. G. Neumann, *Computer-Related Risks*, Addison-Wesley, Reading, MA, 1995.

[OMG, 2009]   Object Management Group, *OMG Unified Modeling Language Specification. Version 2.2*, 2009. http://www.omg.org.

[Popper, 1992]   K. Popper, *Objective Knowledge: An Evolutionary Approach*, Clarendon, Oxford, 1992.

[Pressman, 2009]   R. S. Pressman, *Software Engineering: A Practitioner's Approach*, 7th ed., McGraw-Hill, 2009.

[Royce, 1998]   W. Royce, *Software Project Management: A Unified Framework*, Addison-Wesley, Reading, MA, 1998.

[Rumbaugh et al., 1991]   J. Rumbaugh, M. Blaha, W. Premerlani, F. Eddy, & W. Lorensen, *Object-Oriented Modeling and Design*, Prentice Hall, Englewood Cliffs, NJ, 1991.

[Simon, 1970]   H. A. Simon, *The Sciences of the Artificial*, MIT Press, Cambridge, MA, 1970.

[Sommerville, 2006]   I. Sommerville, *Software Engineering*, 8th ed., Addison-Wesley, Reading, MA, 2006.

[Spivey, 1989]   J. M. Spivey, *The Z Notation, A Reference Manual*, Prentice Hall, Hertfordshire, UK 1989.

Modeling with UML

Every mechanic is familiar with the problem of the part you can't buy because you can't find it because the manufacturer considers it a part of something else.

—Robert Pirsig, in *Zen and the Art of Motorcycle Maintenance*

Notations enable us to articulate complex ideas succinctly and precisely. In projects involving many participants, often of different technical and cultural backgrounds, accuracy and clarity are critical as the cost of miscommunication increases rapidly.

For a notation to enable accurate communication, it must come with a *well-defined* semantics, it must be *well suited* for representing a given aspect of a system, and it must be *well understood* among project participants. In the latter lies the strength of standards and conventions: when a notation is used by a large number of participants, there is little room for misinterpretation and ambiguity. Conversely, when many dialects of a notation exists, or when a very specialized notation is used, the notation users are prone to misunderstandings as each user imposes its own interpretation. We selected UML (Unified Modeling Language, [OMG, 2009]) as a primary notation for this book because it provides a spectrum of notations for representing different aspects of a system and has been accepted as a standard notation in the industry.

In this chapter, we first describe the concepts of modeling in general and object-oriented modeling in particular. We then describe five fundamental notations of UML that we use throughout the book: use case diagrams, class diagrams, interaction diagrams, state machine diagrams, and activity diagrams. For each of these notations, we describe its basic semantics and provide examples. We revisit these notations in detail in later chapters as we describe the activities that use them. Specialized notations that we use in only one chapter are introduced later, such as UML deployment diagrams in Chapter 6, *System Design: Decomposing the System*, and PERT charts in Chapter 14, *Project Management*.

2.1 Introduction

UML is a notation that resulted from the unification of OMT (Object Modeling Technique [Rumbaugh et al., 1991]), Booch [Booch, 1994], and OOSE (Object-Oriented Software Engineering [Jacobson et al., 1992]). UML has also been influenced by other object-oriented notations, such as those introduced by Mellor and Shlaer [Mellor & Shlaer, 1998], Coad and Yourdon [Coad et al., 1995], Wirfs-Brock [Wirfs-Brock et al., 1990], and Martin and Odell [Martin & Odell, 1992].

The goal of UML is to provide a standard notation that can be used by all object-oriented methods and to select and integrate the best elements of precursor notations. For example, UML includes the use case diagrams introduced by OOSE and uses many features of the OMT class diagrams. UML also includes new concepts that were not present in other major methods at the time, such as extension mechanisms and a constraint language. UML has been designed for a broad range of applications. Hence, it provides constructs for a broad range of systems and activities (e.g., distributed systems, analysis, system design, deployment). System development focuses on three different models of the system (see Figure 1-2):

- The **functional model**, represented in UML with use case diagrams, describes the functionality of the system from the user's point of view.
- The **object model**, represented in UML with class diagrams, describes the structure of the system in terms of objects, attributes, associations, and operations. During requirements and analysis, the object model starts as the *analysis object model* and describes the application concepts relevant to the system. During system design, the object model is refined into the *system design object model* and includes descriptions of the subsystem interfaces. During object design, the object model is refined into the *object design model* and includes detailed descriptions of solution objects.
- The **dynamic model**, represented in UML with interaction diagrams, state machine diagrams, and activity diagrams, describes the internal behavior of the system. Interaction diagrams describe behavior as a sequence of messages exchanged among a *set of objects*, whereas state machine diagrams describe behavior in terms of states of an *individual object* and the possible transitions between states. Activity diagrams describe behavior in terms control and data flows.

In this chapter, we describe UML diagrams for representing these models. Introducing these notations represents an interesting challenge: understanding the purpose of a notation requires some familiarity with the activities that use it. However, it is necessary to understand the notation before describing the activities. To address this issue, we introduce UML iteratively. In the next section, we first provide an overview of the five basic notations of UML. In Section 2.3, we introduce the fundamental ideas of modeling. In Section 2.4, we revisit the five basic notations of UML in light of modeling concepts. In subsequent chapters, we discuss these notations in even greater detail when we introduce the activities that use them.

2.2 An Overview of UML

In this section, we briefly introduce five UML notations:

- Use Case Diagrams (Section 2.2.1)
- Class Diagrams (Section 2.2.2)
- Interaction Diagrams (Section 2.2.3)
- State Machine Diagrams (Section 2.2.4)
- Activity Diagrams (Section 2.2.5).

2.2.1 Use Case Diagrams

Use cases are used during requirements elicitation and analysis to represent the functionality of the system. Use cases focus on the behavior of the system from an external point of view. A use case describes a function provided by the system that yields a visible result for an actor. An actor describes any entity that interacts with the system (e.g., a user, another system, the system's physical environment). The identification of actors and use cases results in the definition of the boundary of the system, that is, in differentiating the tasks accomplished by the system and the tasks accomplished by its environment. The actors are outside the boundary of the system, whereas the use cases are inside the boundary of the system.

For example, Figure 2-1 depicts a use case diagram for a simple watch. The WatchUser actor may either consult the time on their watch (with the ReadTime use case) or set the time (with the SetTime use case). However, only the WatchRepairPerson actor can change the battery of the watch (with the ChangeBattery use case).

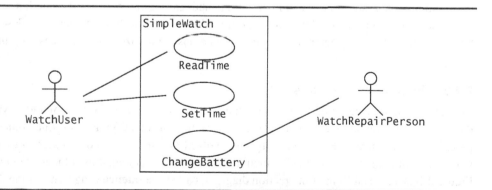

Figure 2-1   A UML use case diagram describing the functionality of a simple watch. The WatchUser actor may either consult the time on her watch (with the ReadTime use case) or set the time (with the SetTime use case). However, only the WatchRepairPerson actor can change the battery of the watch (with the ChangeBattery use case). Actors are represented with stick figures, use cases with ovals, and the boundary of the system with a box enclosing the use cases.

2.2.2   Class Diagrams

Class diagrams are used to describe the structure of the system. Classes are abstractions that specify the common structure and behavior of a set of objects. Objects are instances of classes that are created, modified, and destroyed during the execution of the system. An object has state that includes the values of its attributes and its links with other objects.

Class diagrams describe the system in terms of objects, classes, attributes, operations, and their associations. For example, Figure 2-2 is a class diagram describing the elements of all the watches of the SimpleWatch class. These watch objects all have an association to an object of the PushButton class, an object of the Display class, an object of the Time class, and an object of the Battery class. The numbers on the ends of associations denote the number of links each SimpleWatch object can have with an object of a given class. For example, a SimpleWatch has exactly two PushButtons, one Display, two Batteries, and one Time. Similarly, all PushButton, Display, Time, and Battery objects are associated with exactly one SimpleWatch object.

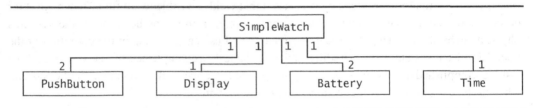

Figure 2-2   A UML class diagram describing the elements of a simple watch.

At the analysis level, associations represent existence relationships. For example, a SimpleWatch requires the correct number of PushButtons, Displays, Batteries, and Time. In this example, the association is symmetrical: PushButton cannot perform its function without a SimpleWatch. UML also allows for one-directional relationships, which we describe in Section 2.4.2. At the implementation level, associations are realized as references (i.e., pointers) to objects.

2.2.3   Interaction Diagrams

Interaction diagrams are used to formalize the dynamic behavior of the system and to visualize the communication among objects. They are useful for identifying additional objects that participate in the use cases. We call objects involved in a use case **participating objects**. An interaction diagram represents the interactions that take place among these objects. For example, Figure 2-3 is a special form of interaction diagram, called a **sequence diagram**, for the SetTime use case of our simple watch. The left-most column represents the WatchUser actor who initiates the use case. Labeled arrows represent stimuli that an actor or an object sends to other objects. In this case, the WatchUser presses button 1 twice and button 2 once to set her watch a minute ahead. The SetTime use case terminates when the WatchUser presses both buttons simultaneously.

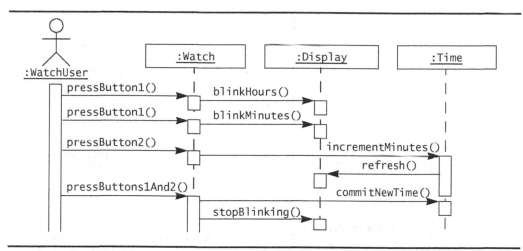

Figure 2-3 Λ UML sequence diagram for the Watch. The left-most column represents the timeline of the WatchUser actor who initiates the use case. The other columns represent the timeline of the objects that participate in this use case. Object names are <u>underlined</u> to denote that they are instances (as opposed to classes). Labeled arrows are stimuli that an actor or an object sends to other objects.

2.2.4   State Machine Diagrams

State machine diagrams describe the dynamic behavior of an individual object as a number of states and transitions between these states. A state represents a particular set of values for an object. Given a state, a transition represents a future state the object can move to and the conditions associated with the change of state. For example, Figure 2-4 is a state machine diagram for the Watch. A small black circle initiates that BlinkHours is the initial state. A circle surrounding a small black circle indicates that StopBlinking is a final state. Note that this diagram represents different information than the sequence diagram of Figure 2-3. The sequence diagram focuses on the messages exchanged between objects as a result of external events created by actors. The state machine diagram focuses on the transitions between states as a result of external events for an individual object.

2.2.5   Activity Diagrams

An activity diagram describes the behavior of a system in terms of activities. Activities are modeling elements that represent the execution of a set of operations. The execution of an activity can be triggered by the completion of other activities, by the availability of objects, or by external events. Activity diagrams are similar to flowchart diagrams in that they can be used to represent control flow (i.e., the order in which operations occur) and data flow (i.e., the objects that are exchanged among operations). For example, Figure 2-5 is an activity diagram representing activities related to managing an Incident. Rounded rectangles represent activities; arrows between activities represent control flow; thick bars represent the

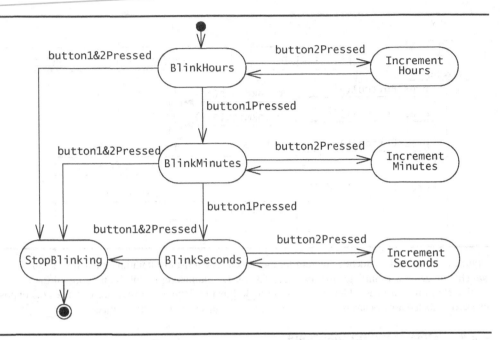

Figure 2-4   A UML state machine diagram for SetTime use case of the Watch.

synchronization of the control flow. The activity diagram of Figure 2-5 depicts that the AllocateResources, CoordinateResources, and DocumentIncident can be initiated only after the OpenIncident activity has been completed. Similarly, the ArchiveIncident activity can be initiated only after the completion of AllocateResources, Coordinate-Resources, and DocumentIncident. These latter three activities, however, can occur concurrently.

This concludes our first walkthrough of the five basic notations of UML. Now, we go into more detail: In Section 2.3, we introduce basic modeling concepts, including the definition of

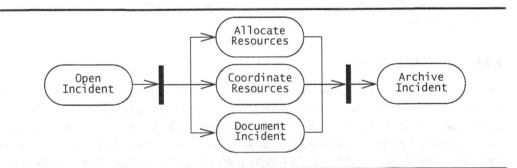

Figure 2-5   An example of a UML activity diagram. Activity diagrams represent behavior in terms of activities and their precedence constraints. The completion of an activity triggers an outgoing transition, which in turn may initiate another activity.

systems, models, types, and instances, abstraction, and falsification. In Sections 2.4.1–2.4.5, we describe in detail use case diagrams, class diagrams, sequence diagrams, state machine diagrams, and activity diagrams. We illustrate their use with a simple example. Section 2.4.6 describes miscellaneous constructs, such as packages and notes, that are used in all types of diagrams. We use these five notations throughout the book to describe software systems, work products, activities, and organizations. By the consistent and systematic use of a small set of notations, we hope to provide the reader with an operational knowledge of UML.

2.3 Modeling Concepts

In this section, we describe the basic concepts of modeling. We first define the terms **system**, **model**, and **view**, and discuss the purpose of **modeling**. We explain their relationship to programming languages and terms such as **data types**, **classes**, **instances**, and **objects**. Finally, we describe how object-oriented modeling focuses on building an abstraction of the system environment as a basis for the **system model**.

2.3.1 Systems, Models, and Views

A **system** is an organized set of communicating parts. We focus here on engineered systems, which are designed for a specific purpose, as opposed to natural systems, such as a planetary system, whose ultimate purpose we may not know. A car, composed of four wheels, a chassis, a body, and an engine, is designed to transport people. A watch, composed of a battery, a circuit, wheels, and hands, is designed to measure time. A payroll system, composed of a mainframe computer, printers, disks, software, and the payroll staff, is designed to issue salary checks for employees of a company. Parts of a system can in turn be considered as simpler systems called **subsystems**. The engine of a car, composed of cylinders, pistons, an injection module, and many other parts, is a subsystem of the car. Similarly, the integrated circuit of a watch and the mainframe computer of the payroll system are subsystems. This subsystem decomposition can be recursively applied to subsystems. Objects represent the end of this recursion, when each piece is simple enough that we can fully comprehend it without further decomposition.

Many systems are made of numerous subsystems interconnected in complicated ways, often so complex that no single developer can manage its entirety. **Modeling** is a means for dealing with this complexity. Complex systems are generally described by more than one model, each focusing on a different aspect or level of accuracy. Modeling means constructing an abstraction of a system that focuses on interesting aspects and ignores irrelevant details. What is interesting or irrelevant varies with the task at hand. For example, assume we want to build an airplane. Even with the help of field experts, we cannot build an airplane from scratch and hope that it will function correctly on its maiden flight. Instead, we first build a scale model of the air frame to test its aerodynamic properties. In this scale model, we only need to represent the exterior surface of the airplane. We can ignore details such as the instrument panel or the engine. In order to train pilots for this new airplane, we also build a flight simulator. The flight simulator needs to accurately represent the layout and behavior of flight instruments. In this case, however, details about the exterior of the plane can be ignored. Both the flight simulator and the scale model are much less complex than the airplane they represent. Modeling allows us to deal with complexity through a divide-and-conquer approach: For each type of problem we want to solve (e.g., testing aerodynamic properties, training pilots), we build a model that only focuses on the issues relevant to the problem. Generally, modeling focuses on building a model that is simple enough for a person to grasp completely. A rule of thumb is that each entity should contain at most 7 ± 2 parts [Miller, 1956].

Modeling also helps us deal with complexity by enabling us to incrementally refine simple models into more detailed ones that are closer to reality. In software engineering, as in all engineering disciplines, the model usually precedes the system. During analysis, we first build a model of the environment and of the common functionality that the system must provide, at a level that is understandable by the client. Then we refine this model, adding more details about the forms that the system should display, the layout of the user interface, and the response of the system to exceptional cases. The set of all models built during development is called the **system model**. If we did not use models, but instead started coding the system right away, we would have to specify all the details of the user interface before the client could provide us with feedback. Thus we would lose much time and resources when the client then introduces changes.

Unfortunately, even a model may become so complex that it is not easily understandable. We can continue to use the divide-and-conquer method to refine a complex model into simpler models. A **view** focuses on a subset of a model to make it understandable (Figure 2-6). For example, all the blueprints necessary to construct an airplane constitute a model. Excerpts necessary to explain the functioning of the fuel system constitute the fuel system view. Views may overlap: a view of the airplane representing the electrical wiring also includes the wiring for the fuel system.

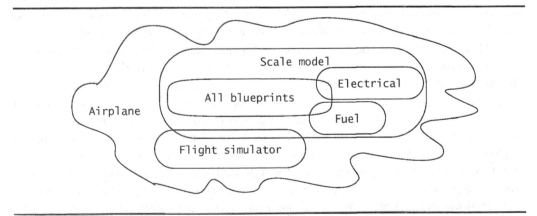

Figure 2-6   A model is an abstraction describing a subset of a system. A view depicts selected aspects of a model. Views and models of a single system may overlap each other.

Notations are graphical or textual rules for representing views. A UML class diagram is a graphical view of the object model. In wiring diagrams, each connected line represents a different wire or bundle of wires. In UML class diagrams, a rectangle with a title represents a class. A line between two rectangles represents a relationship between the two corresponding classes. Note that different notations can be used to represent the same view (Figure 2-7).

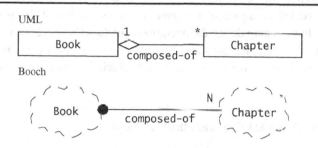

Figure 2-7 Example of describing a model with two different notations. The model includes two classes, Book and Chapter, with the relationship, Book is composed of Chapters. In UML, classes are depicted by rectangles and aggregation associations by a line terminated with a diamond. In the Booch notation, classes are depicted by clouds, and aggregation associations are depicted with a line terminated with a solid circle.

In software engineering, there are many other notations for modeling systems. UML describes a system in terms of classes, events, states, interactions, and activities. Data flow diagrams [De Marco, 1978] depict how data is retrieved, processed, and stored. Z Schemes [Spivey, 1992] represent the system in terms of invariants (conditions that never change) and in terms of what is true before and after the execution of an operation. Each notation is tailored for a different problem.

In the next sections, we focus in more detail on the process of modeling.

2.3.2   Data Types, Abstract Data Types, and Instances

A **data type** is an abstraction in the context of a programming language. A data type has a unique name that distinguishes it from other data types. It denotes a set of values that are members of the data type (i.e., the **instances** of the data type) and defines the structure and the operations valid in all instances of the data type. Data types are used in typed languages to ensure that only valid operations are applied to specific instances.

For example, the name int in Java corresponds to all the signed integers between -2^{32} and $2^{32} - 1$. The valid operations on this type are all the integer arithmetic operations (e.g., addition, subtraction, multiplication, division) and all the functions and methods that have parameters of type int (e.g., mod). The Java run-time environment throws an exception if a floating point operation is applied to an instance of the int data type (e.g., trunc or floor).

An **abstract data type** is a data type defined by an implementation-independent specification. Abstract data types enable developers to reason about a set of instances without looking at a specific implementation of the abstract data type. Examples of abstract data types are sets and sequences, which can be mathematically defined. A system may provide different implementations of the set abstract data type, each optimizing different criteria (e.g., memory consumption, insertion time). However, a developer using a set only needs to understand its semantics and need not be aware of the internal representation of the set. For example, the abstract data type `Person` may define the operations `getName()`,[1] `getSocialSecurityNumber()`, and `getAddress()`. The fact that the social security number of the person is stored as a number or as a string is not visible to the rest of the system. Such decisions are called **implementation decisions**.

2.3.3   Classes, Abstract Classes, and Objects

A **class** is an abstraction in object-oriented modeling and in object-oriented programming languages. Like abstract data types, a class encapsulates both structure and behavior. Unlike abstract data types, classes can be defined in terms of other classes by using inheritance. Assume we have a watch that also can function as a calculator. The class `CalculatorWatch` can then be seen as a refinement of the class `Watch`. This type of relationship between a base class and a refined class is called **inheritance**. The generalization class (e.g., `Watch`) is called the **superclass**, the specialized class (e.g., `CalculatorWatch`) is called the **subclass**. In an inheritance relationship, the subclass refines the superclass by defining new attributes and operations. In Figure 2-8, `CalculatorWatch` defines functionality for performing simple arithmetic that regular `Watch`es do not have. Superclass and subclass are relative terms. The same class can be a subclass with respect to one class and a superclass with respect to another class.

When an inheritance relationship serves only to model shared attributes and operations, that is, if the generalization is not meant to be instantiated, the resulting class is called an **abstract class**. Abstract classes often represent generalized concepts in the application domain, and their names are italicized. For example, in chemistry, `Benzene` can be considered a class of molecules that belongs to the abstract class *OrganicCompound* (Figure 2-9). *OrganicCompound* is a generalization and does not correspond to any one molecule; that is, it does not have any instances. In Java, `Collection` is an abstract class providing a generalization for all collection classes. However, there are no instances of the class `Collection`. Rather, all collection objects are instances of one of the subclasses of Collection, such as `LinkedList`, `ArrayList`, or `HashMap`. Note that not all generalizations are abstract classes. For example, in Figure 2-8 the `Watch` class is not an abstract class as it has instances. When modeling software systems,

---

1. We refer to an operation by its name followed by its arguments in parentheses. If the arguments are not specified, we suffix the name of the operation by a pair of empty parentheses. We describe operations in detail in the next section.

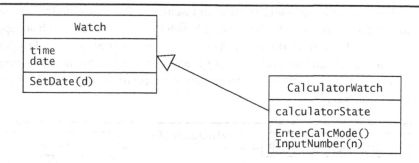

Figure 2-8 A UML class diagram depicting two classes, Watch and CalculatorWatch. CalculatorWatch is a refinement of Watch, providing calculator functionality not found in normal watches. In a UML class diagram, classes and objects are represented as boxes with three compartments: the first compartment depicts the name of the class, the second depicts its attributes, the third its operations. The second and third compartments can be omitted for brevity. An inheritance relationship is displayed by a line with a triangle. The triangle points to the superclass, and the other end is attached to the subclass.

abstract classes sometimes do not correspond to an existing application domain concept, but rather are introduced to reduce complexity in the model or to promote reuse.

A class defines the **operations** that can be applied to its instances. Operations of a superclass can be inherited and applied to the objects of the subclass as well. For example, in Figure 2-8, the operation SetDate(d), setting the current date of a Watch, is also applicable to CalculatorWatches. The operation EnterCalcMode(), however, defined in the CalculatorWatch class, is not applicable in the Watch class.

A class defines the **attributes** that apply to all its instances. An attribute is a named slot in the instance where a value is stored. Attributes have a unique name within the class and the type. Watches have a time and a date attribute. CalculatorWatches have a calculatorState attribute.

An **object** is an instance of a class. An object has an identity and stores attribute values. Each object belongs to exactly one class. In UML, an instance is depicted by a rectangle with its name underlined. This convention is used throughout UML to distinguish between instances and

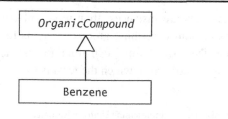

Figure 2-9 An example of abstract class (UML class diagram). *OrganicCompound* is never instantiated and only serves as a generalization class. The names of abstract classes are italicized.

classes.[2] In Figure 2-10, `simpleWatch1291` is an instance of `Watch`, and `calculatorWatch1515` is an instance of `CalculatorWatch`. Note that, although the operations of `Watch` are applicable to `calculatorWatch1515`, `calculatorWatch1515` is not an instance of the class `Watch`. The attributes of an object can be visible to other parts of the system in some programming languages. For example, Java allows the implementor to specify in great detail which attributes are visible and which are not.

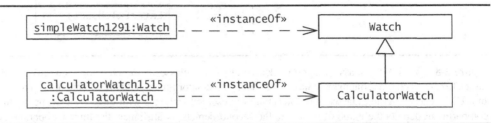

Figure 2-10   A UML class diagram depicting instances of two classes. `simpleWatch1291` is an instance of `Watch`. `calculatorWatch1515` is an instance of `CalculatorWatch`. Although the operations of `Watch` are also applicable to `calculatorWatch1515`, the latter is not an instance of the former.

2.3.4   Event Classes, Events, and Messages

Event classes are abstractions representing a kind of event for which the system has a common response. An **event**, an instance of an event class, is a relevant occurrence in the system. For example, an event can be a stimuli from an actor (e.g., "the `WatchUser` presses the left button"), a time-out (e.g., "after 2 minutes"), or the sending of a message between two objects. Sending a **message** is the mechanism by which the sending object requests the execution of an operation in the receiving object. The message is composed of a name and a number of arguments. The receiving object matches the name of the message to one of its operations and passes the arguments to the operation. Any results are returned to the sender.

For example, in Figure 2-11, the `:Watch` object computes the current time by getting the Greenwich time from the `:Time` object and the time difference from the `:TimeZone` object by sending the `getTime()` and the `getTimeDelta()` messages, respectively. Note that `:Watch` denotes an undesignated object of class `Watch`.

Events and messages are instances: they represent concrete occurrences in the system. Event classes are abstractions describing groups of events for which the system has a common response. In practice, the term "event" can refer to instances or classes. This ambiguity is resolved by examining the context in which the term is used.

---

2. Underlined strings are also used for representing Uniform Resource Locators (URLs). To improve readability, we do not use an underlined font in the text, but rather, we use the same font to denote instances and classes. In general, this ambiguity can be resolved by examining the context. In UML diagrams, however, we always use an underlined font to distinguish instances from classes.

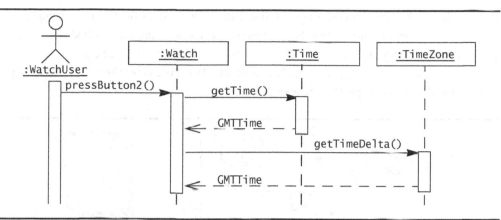

Figure 2-11 Examples of message sends (UML sequence diagram). The Watch object sends the getTime() message to a Time object to query the current Greenwich time. It then sends the getTimeDelta() message to a TimeZone object to query the difference to add to the Greenwich time. The dashed arrows represent the replies (i.e., message results that are sent back to the sender).

2.3.5 Object-Oriented Modeling

The **application domain** represents all aspects of the user's problem. This includes the physical environment, the users and other people, their work processes, and so on. It is critical for analysts and developers to understand the application domain for a system to accomplish its intended task effectively. Note that the application domain changes over time, as work processes and people change.[3]

The **solution domain** is the modeling space of all possible systems. Modeling in the solution domain represents the system design and object design activities of the development process. The solution domain model is much richer and more volatile than the application domain model. This is because the system is usually modeled in much more detail than the application domain. Emerging technologies (also called technology enablers), deeper understanding of implementation technology by the developers, and changes in requirements trigger changes to the solution domain models. Note that the deployment of the system can change the application domain as users develop new work processes to accommodate the system.

Object-oriented analysis is concerned with modeling the application domain. **Object-oriented design** is concerned with modeling the solution domain. Both modeling activities use the same representations (i.e., classes and objects). In object-oriented analysis and

---

3. The application domain is sometimes further divided into a user domain and a client domain. The client domain includes the issues relevant to the client, such as, operation cost of the system, impact of the system on the rest of the organization. The user domain includes the issues relevant to the end user, such as, functionality, ease of learning and of use.

design, the application domain model is also part of the system model. For example, an air traffic control system has a `TrafficController` class to represent individual users, their preferences, and log information. The system also has an `Aircraft` class to represent information associated with the tracked aircraft. `TrafficController` and `Aircraft` are application domain concepts that are encoded into the system (Figure 2-12).

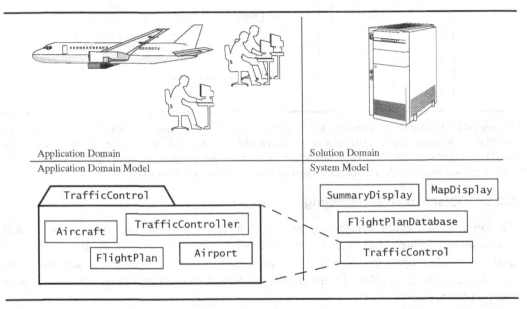

Figure 2-12   The application domain model represents entities of the environment that are relevant to an air traffic control system (e.g., aircraft, traffic controllers). The system model represents entities that are part of the system (e.g., map display, flight plan database). Note that in object-oriented analysis and design, the application domain model is part of the system model. The system model refines the application domain model to include solution domain concepts, such as `SummaryDisplay`, `MapDisplay`, and `FightPlan-Database`. (For more details, see Chapter 5, *Analysis*.)

Modeling the application domain and the solution domain with a single notation has advantages and disadvantages. On the one hand, it can be powerful: solution domain classes that represent application concepts can be traced back to the application domain. Moreover, these classes can be encapsulated into subsystems independent of other implementation concepts (e.g., user interface and database technology) and be packaged into a reusable toolkit of domain classes. On the other hand, using a single notation can introduce confusion because it removes the distinction between the real world and the model of it. The solution domain is bound to be simpler and biased toward the solution. To address this issue, we use a single notation and, in cases of ambiguity, we distinguish between the two domains. In most cases, we are referring to the model (e.g., "an `Aircraft` is associated with a `FlightPlan`" is a statement about the model).

2.3.6   Falsification and Prototyping

A model is a simplification of reality in the sense that irrelevant details are ignored. Relevant details, however, need to be represented. **Falsification** [Popper, 1992] is the process of demonstrating that relevant details have been incorrectly represented or not represented at all; that is, the model does not correspond to the reality it is supposed to represent.

The process of falsification is well known in other sciences: researchers propose different models of a reality, which are gradually accepted as an increasing amount of data supports the model, then rejected once a counterexample is found. Near the end of the 18th century, for example, it was discovered that the orbit of the planet Mercury did not exactly match the orbit predicted by Newton's theory of gravity. Later, Einstein's general theory of relativity predicted a slightly different orbit that better matched the results. In other words, Newton's theory was falsified in favor of Einstein's. Note, however, that we still use Newton's theory for practical applications on Earth, because the differences predicted by both theories are small in these situations and Newton's theory is much simpler. In other words, the details ignored by Newton's theory are not relevant for the scales we are accustomed to.

We can apply falsification to software system development as well. For example, a technique for developing a system is **prototyping**: when designing the user interface, developers construct a prototype that only simulates the user interface of a system. The prototype is then presented to potential users for evaluation—that is, falsification—and modified subsequently. In the first iterations of this process, developers are likely to throw away the initial prototype as a result of feedback from the users. In other terms, users falsify the initial prototype, a model of the future system, because it does not accurately represent relevant details.

Note that it is only possible to demonstrate that a model is incorrect. Although in some cases, it is possible to show mathematically that two models are equivalent, it is not possible to show that either of them correctly represents reality. For example, formal verification techniques can enable developers to show that a specific software implementation is consistent with a formal specification. However, only field testing and extended use can indicate that a system meets the needs of the client. At any time, system models can be falsified due to changes in the requirements, in the implementation technology, or in the environment.

2.4 A Deeper View into UML

We now describe in detail the five main UML diagrams we use in this book.

- **Use case diagrams** represent the functionality of the system from a user's point of view. They define the boundaries of the system (Section 2.4.1).
- **Class diagrams** represent the static structure of a system in terms of objects, their attributes, operations, and relationships (Section 2.4.2).
- **Interaction diagrams** represent the system's behavior in terms of interactions among a set of objects. They are used to identify objects in the application and implementation domains (Section 2.4.3).

- **State machine diagrams** represent the behavior of nontrivial objects (Section 2.4.4).
- **Activity diagrams** are flow diagrams used to represent the data flow or the control flow through a system (Section 2.4.5).

2.4.1 Use Case Diagrams

Use cases and actors

Actors are external entities that interact with the system. Examples of actors include a user role (e.g., a system administrator, a bank customer, a bank teller) or another system (e.g., a central database, a fabrication line). Actors have unique names and descriptions.

Use cases describe the behavior of the system as seen from an actor's point of view. Behavior described by use cases is also called **external behavior**. A use case describes a function provided by the system as a set of events that yields a visible result for the actors. Actors initiate a use case to access system functionality. The use case can then initiate other use cases and gather more information from the actors. When actors and use cases exchange information, they are said to **communicate**. We will see later that we represent these exchanges with communication relationships.

For example, in an accident management system, field officers (such as a police officer or a fire fighter) have access to a wireless computer that enables them to interact with a dispatcher. The dispatcher in turn can visualize the current status of all its resources, such as police cars or trucks, on a computer screen and dispatch a resource by issuing commands from a workstation. In this example, field officer and dispatcher can be modeled as actors.

Figure 2-13 depicts the actor FieldOfficer who invokes the use case ReportEmergency to notify the actor Dispatcher of a new emergency. As a response, the Dispatcher invokes the

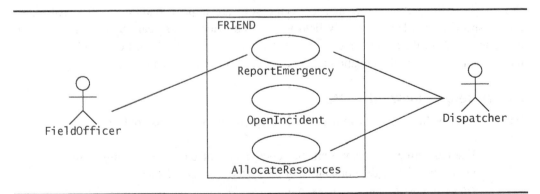

Figure 2-13 An example of a UML use case diagram for First Responder Interactive Emergency Navigational Database (FRIEND), an accident management system. Associations between actors and use cases denote information flows. These associations are bidirectional: they can represent the actor initiating a use case (FieldOfficer initiates ReportEmergency) or a use case providing information to an actor (ReportEmergency notifies Dispatcher). The box around the use cases represents the system boundary.

OpenIncident use case to create an incident report and initiate the incident handling. The Dispatcher enters preliminary information from the FieldOfficer in the incident database (FRIEND) and orders additional units to the scene with the AllocateResources use case.

For the textual description of a use case, we use a template composed of six fields (see Figure 2-14) adapted from [Constantine & Lockwood, 2001]:

- The **name** of the use case is unique across the system so that developers (and project participants) can unambiguously refer to the use case.

- **Participating actors** are actors interacting with the use case.

- **Entry conditions** describe the conditions that need to be satisfied before the use case is initiated.

Use case name	ReportEmergency
Participating actors	Initiated by FieldOfficer Communicates with Dispatcher
Flow of events	1. The FieldOfficer activates the "Report Emergency" function of her terminal.
	2. FRIEND responds by presenting a form to the FieldOfficer.
	3. The FieldOfficer fills out the form by selecting the emergency level, type, location, and brief description of the situation. The FieldOfficer also describes possible responses to the emergency situation. Once the form is completed, the FieldOfficer submits the form.
	4. FRIEND receives the form and notifies the Dispatcher.
	5. The Dispatcher reviews the submitted information and creates an Incident in the database by invoking the OpenIncident use case. The Dispatcher selects a response and acknowledges the report.
	6. FRIEND displays the acknowledgment and the selected response to the FieldOfficer.
Entry condition	• The FieldOfficer is logged into FRIEND.
Exit condition	• The FieldOfficer has received an acknowledgment and the selected response from the Dispatcher, OR • The FieldOfficer has received an explanation indicating why the transaction could not be processed.
Quality requirements	• The FieldOfficer's report is acknowledged within 30 seconds. • The selected response arrives no later than 30 seconds after it is sent by the Dispatcher.

Figure 2-14   An example of a use case, ReportEmergency.

- The **flow of events** describes the sequence of interactions of the use case, which are to be numbered for reference. The common case (i.e., cases that are expected by the user) and the exceptional cases (i.e., cases unexpected by the user, such as errors and unusual conditions) are described separately in different use cases for clarity. We organize the steps in the flow of events in two columns, the left column representing steps accomplished by the actor, the right column representing steps accomplished by the system. Each pair of actor–system steps represents an interaction.

- **Exit conditions** describe the conditions satisfied after the completion of the use case.

- **Quality requirements** are requirements that are not related to the functionality of the system. These include constraints on the performance of the system, its implementation, the hardware platforms it runs on, and so on. Quality requirements are described in detail in Chapter 4, *Requirements Elicitation*.

Use cases are written in natural language. This enables developers to use them for communicating with the client and the users, who generally do not have an extensive knowledge of software engineering notations. The use of natural language also enables participants from other disciplines to understand the requirements of the system. The use of the natural language allows developers to capture things, in particular special requirements, that cannot easily be captured in diagrams.

Use case diagrams can include four types of relationships: communication, inclusion, extension, and inheritance. We describe these relationships in detail next.

Communication relationships

Actors and use cases communicate when information is exchanged between them. **Communication relationships** are depicted by a solid line between the actor and use case symbol. In Figure 2-13, the actors FieldOfficer and Dispatcher communicate with the ReportEmergency use case. Only the actor Dispatcher communicates with the use cases OpenIncident and AllocateResources. Communication relationships between actors and use cases can be used to denote access to functionality. In the case of our example, a FieldOfficer and a Dispatcher are provided with different interfaces to the system and have access to different functionality.

Include relationships

When describing a complex system, its use case model can become quite complex and can contain redundancy. We reduce the complexity of the model by identifying commonalities in different use cases. For example, assume that the Dispatcher can press at any time a key to access a street map. This can be modeled by a use case ViewMap that is included by the use cases OpenIncident and AllocateResources (and any other use cases accessible by the Dispatcher). The resulting model only describes the ViewMap functionality once, thus reducing complexity of the overall use case model. Two use cases are related by an include relationship if one of them includes the second one in its flow of events. In use case diagrams, **include relationships** are depicted by a dashed open arrow originating from the including use case (see Figure 2-15). Include relationships are labeled with the string «include».

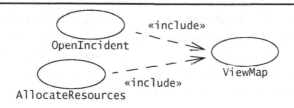

Figure 2-15   An example of an «include» relationship (UML use case diagram).

Use case name	AllocateResources
Participating actor	Initiated by Dispatcher
Flow of events	. . .
Entry condition	• The Dispatcher opens an Incident.
Exit condition	• Additional Resources are assigned to the Incident. • Resources receives notice about their new assignment. • FieldOfficer in charge of the Incident receives notice about the new Resources.
Quality requirements	At any point during the flow of events, this use case can **include** the ViewMap use case. The ViewMap use case is initiated when the Dispatcher invokes the map function. When invoked within this use case, the system scrolls the map so that location of the current Incident is visible to the Dispatcher.

Figure 2-16   Textual representation of include relationships of Figure 2-15. "Include" in **bold** for clarity.

We represent include relationships in the textual description of the use case with one of two ways. If the included use case can be included at any point in the flow of events (e.g., the ViewMap use case), we indicate the inclusion in the *Quality requirements* section of the use case (Figure 2-16). If the included use case is invoked during an event, we indicate the inclusion in the flow of events.

Extend relationships

Extend relationships are an alternate means for reducing complexity in the use case model. A use case can extend another use case by adding events. An extend relationship indicates that an instance of an extended use case may include (under certain conditions) the behavior specified by the extending use case. A typical application of extend relationships is the specification of exceptional behavior. For example (Figure 2-17), assume that the network connection between the Dispatcher and the FieldOfficer can be interrupted at any time. (e.g., if the FieldOfficer enters a tunnel). The use case ConnectionDown describes the set of events taken by the system and the actors while the connection is lost. ConnectionDown extends the use cases OpenIncident and AllocateResources. Separating exceptional behavior from common behavior enables us to write shorter and more focused use cases. In the textual representation of a use case, we represent extend relationships as entry conditions of the extending use case. For example, the extend relationships depicted in Figure 2-17 are represented as an entry condition of the ConnectionDown use case (Figure 2-18).

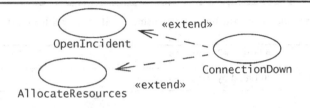

Figure 2-17   An example of an «extend» relationship (UML use case diagram).

Use case name	ConnectionDown
Participating actor	Communicates with FieldOfficer and Dispatcher.
Flow of events	...
Entry condition	This use case **extends** the OpenIncident and the AllocateResources use cases. It is initiated by the system whenever the network connection between the FieldOfficer and Dispatcher is lost.
Exit condition	...

Figure 2-18   Textual representation of extend relationships of Figure 2-17. "Extends" in **bold** for clarity.

The difference between the include and extend relationships is the location of the dependency. Assume that we add several new use cases for the actor Dispatcher, such as UpdateIncident and ReallocateResources. If we modeled the ConnectionDown use case with include relationships, the authors of UpdateIncident and ReallocateResources use cases need to know about and include the ConnectionDown use case. If we used extend relationships instead, only the ConnectionDown use case needs to be modified to extend the additional use cases. In general exception cases (such as help, errors, and other unexpected conditions) are modeled with extend relationships. Use cases that describe behavior commonly shared by a limited set of use cases are modeled with include relationships.

Inheritance relationships

An **inheritance relationship** is a third mechanism for reducing the complexity of a model. One use case can specialize another more general one by adding more detail. For example, FieldOfficers are required to authenticate before they can use FRIEND. During early stages of requirements elicitation, authentication is modeled as a high-level Authenticate use case. Later, developers describe the Authenticate use case in more detail and allow for several different hardware platforms. This refinement activity results in two more use cases: AuthenticateWithPassword which enables FieldOfficers to login without any specific hardware, and AuthenticateWithCard which enables FieldOfficers to login using a smart card. The two new use cases are represented as specializations of the Authenticate use case (Figure 2-19). In the textual representation, specialized use cases inherit the initiating actor and the entry and exit conditions from the general use case (Figure 2-20).

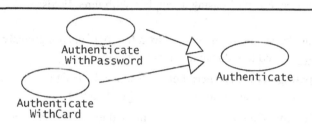

Figure 2-19 An example of an inheritance relationship (UML use case diagram). The Authenticate use case is a high-level use case describing, in general terms, the process of authentication. AuthenticateWithPassword and AuthenticateWithCard are two specializations of Authenticate.

Use case name	AuthenticateWithCard
Participating actor	**Inherited** from Authenticate use case.
Flow of events	1. The FieldOfficer inserts her card into the field terminal.
	2. The field terminal acknowledges the card and prompts the actor for her personal identification number (PIN).
	3. The FieldOfficer enters her PIN with the numeric keypad.
	4. The field terminal checks the entered PIN against the PIN stored on the card. If the PINs match, the FieldOfficer is authenticated. Otherwise, the field terminal rejects the authentication attempt.
Entry condition	**Inherited** from Authenticate use case.
Exit condition	**Inherited** from Authenticate use case.

Figure 2-20 Textual representation of inheritance relationships of Figure 2-19.

Note that extend relationships and inheritance relationships are different. In an extend relationship, each use case describes a different flow of events to accomplish a different task. In Figure 2-17, the OpenIncident use cases describes the actions that occur when the Dispatcher creates a new Incident, whereas the ConnectionDown use case describes the actions that occur during network outages. In Figure 2-19, AuthenticateWithPassword and Authenticate both describe the same task, each at different abstraction levels.

Scenarios

A use case is an abstraction that describes all possible scenarios involving the described functionality. A **scenario** is an instance of a use case describing a concrete set of actions. Scenarios are used as examples for illustrating common cases; their focus is on understandability. Use cases are used to describe all possible cases; their focus is on completeness. We describe a scenario using a template with three fields:

- The **name** of the scenario enables us to refer to it unambiguously. The name of a scenario is underlined to indicate that it is an instance.
- The **participating actor instances** field indicates which actor instances are involved in this scenario. Actor instances also have underlined names.
- The **flow of events** of a scenario describes the sequence of events step by step.

Note that there is no need for entry or exit conditions in scenarios. Entry and exit conditions are abstractions that enable developers to describe a range of conditions under which a use case is invoked. Given that a scenario only describes one specific situation, such conditions are unnecessary (Figure 2-21).

2.4.2   Class Diagrams

Classes and objects

Class diagrams describe the structure of the system in terms of classes and objects. **Classes** are abstractions that specify the attributes and behavior of a set of objects. A class is a collection of objects that share a set of attributes that distinguish the objects as members of the collection. **Objects** are entities that encapsulate state and behavior. Each object has an identity: it can be referred individually and is distinguishable from other objects.

In UML, classes and objects are depicted by boxes composed of three compartments. The top compartment displays the name of the class or object. The center compartment displays its attributes, and the bottom compartment displays its operations. The attribute and operation compartments can be omitted for clarity. Object names are underlined to indicate that they are instances. By convention, class names start with an uppercase letter. Objects in object diagrams may be given names (followed by their class) for ease of reference. In that case, their name starts

Scenario name	warehouseOnFire
Participating actor instances	bob, alice:FieldOfficer john:Dispatcher
Flow of events	1. Bob, driving down main street in his patrol car, notices smoke coming out of a warehouse. His partner, Alice, activates the "Report Emergency" function from her FRIEND laptop. 2. Alice enters the address of the building, a brief description of its location (i.e., northwest corner), and an emergency level. In addition to a fire unit, she requests several paramedic units on the scene given that area appears to be relatively busy. She confirms her input and waits for an acknowledgment. 3. John, the Dispatcher, is alerted to the emergency by a beep of his workstation. He reviews the information submitted by Alice and acknowledges the report. He allocates a fire unit and two paramedic units to the Incident site and sends their estimated arrival time (ETA) to Alice. 4. Alice receives the acknowledgment and the ETA.

Figure 2-21   The warehouseOnFire scenario for the ReportEmergency use case.

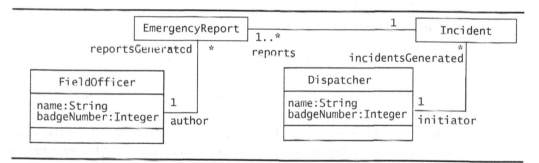

Figure 2-22   An example of a UML class diagram: classes that participate in the ReportEmergency use case. Detailed type information is usually omitted until object design (see Chapter 9, *Object Design: Specifying Interfaces*).

with a lowercase letter. In the FRIEND example (Figures 2-22 and 2-23), Bob and Alice are field officers, represented in the system as FieldOfficer objects called bob:FieldOfficer and alice:FieldOfficer. FieldOfficer is a class describing all FieldOfficer objects, whereas Bob and Alice are represented by two individual FieldOfficer objects.

In Figure 2-22, the FieldOfficer class has two attributes: a name and a badgeNumber. This indicates that all FieldOfficer objects have these two attributes. In Figure 2-23, the bob:FieldOfficer and alice:FieldOfficer objects have specific values for these attributes: "Bob. D." and "Alice W.", respectively. In Figure 2-22, the FieldOfficer.name attribute is of type String, which indicates that only instances of String can be assigned to the FieldOfficer.name attribute. The type of an attribute is used to specify the valid range of

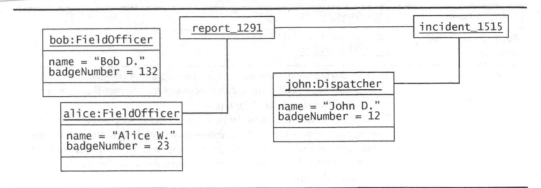

Figure 2-23   An example of a UML object diagram: objects that participate in warehouseOnFire.

values the attribute can take. Note that when attribute types are not essential to the definition of the system, attribute type decisions can be delayed until object design. This allows the developers to concentrate on the functionality of the system and to minimize the number of trivial changes when the functionality of the system is revised.

Associations and links

A **link** represents a connection between two objects. **Associations** are relationships between classes and represent groups of links. Each FieldOfficer object also has a list of EmergencyReports that has been written by the FieldOfficer. In Figure 2-22, the line between the FieldOfficer class and the EmergencyReport class is an association. In Figure 2-23, the line between the alice:FieldOfficer object and the report_1291:EmergencyReport object is a link. This link represents a state that is kept in the system to denote that alice:FieldOfficer generated report_1291:EmergencyReport.

In UML, associations can be symmetrical (bidirectional) or asymmetrical (unidirectional). All the associations in Figure 2-22 are symmetrical. Figure 2-24 depicts an example of one-directional association between Polygon and Point. The **navigation** arrow at the Point end of the association indicates that the system only supports navigation from the Polygon to the Point. In other words, given a specific Polygon, it is possible to query all Points that make up

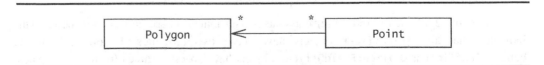

Figure 2-24   Example of a one-directional association. Developers usually omit navigation during analysis and add navigation information during object design, when they make such decisions (see Chapter 8, *Object Design: Reusing Pattern Solutions*, and Chapter 9, *Object Design: Specifying Interfaces*).

the `Polygon`. However, the navigation arrow indicates that given a specific `Point`, it is not possible to find which `Polygons` the `Point` is part of. UML allows navigation arrows to be displayed on both ends of an association. By convention, however, an association without arrows indicates that navigation is supported in both directions.

Association class

Associations are similar to classes, in that they can have attributes and operations attached to them. Such an association is called an **association class** and is depicted by a class symbol that contains the attributes and operations and is connected to the association symbol with a dashed line. For example, in Figure 2-25, the allocation of `FieldOfficers` to an `Incident` is modeled as an association class with attributes `role` and `notificationTime`.

Any association class can be transformed into a class and simple associations as shown in Figure 2-26. Although this representation is similar to Figure 2-25, the association class representation is clearer in Figure 2-25: an association cannot exist without the classes it links. Similarly, the `Allocation` object cannot exist without a `FieldOfficer` and an `Incident`. Although Figure 2-26 carries the same information, this diagram requires careful examination of the association multiplicity. We examine such modeling trade-offs in Chapter 5, *Analysis*.

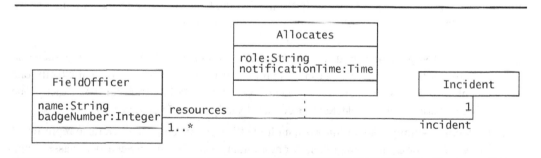

Figure 2-25   An example of an association class (UML class diagram).

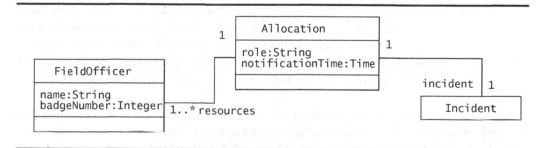

Figure 2-26   Alternative model for `Allocation` (UML class diagram).

Roles

Each end of an association can be labeled by a **role**. In Figure 2-22, the roles of the association between EmergencyReport and FieldOfficer are author and reportsGenerated. Labeling the end of associations with roles allows us to distinguish among the multiple associations originating from a class. Moreover, roles clarify the purpose of the association.

Multiplicity

Each end of an association can be labeled by a set of integers indicating the number of links that can legitimately originate from an instance of the class connected to the association end. This set of integers is called the **multiplicity** of the association end. In Figure 2-22, the association end author has a multiplicity of 1. This means that all EmergencyReports are written by exactly one FieldOfficer. In other terms, each EmergencyReport object has exactly one link to an object of class FieldOfficer. The multiplicity of the association end reportsGenerated role is "many," shown as a star. The "many" multiplicity is shorthand for 0..n. This means that any given FieldOfficer may be the author of zero or more EmergencyReports.

In UML, an association end can have an arbitrary set of integers as a multiplicity. For example, an association could allow only a prime number of links and thus, would have a multiplicity 1, 2, 3, 5, 7, 11, 13, and so forth. In practice, however, most of the associations we encounter belong to one of the following three types (see Figure 2-27):

- A **one-to-one association** has a multiplicity 1 on each end. A one-to-one association between two classes (e.g., PoliceOfficer and BadgeNumber) means that exactly one link exists between instances of each class (e.g., a PoliceOfficer has exactly one BadgeNumber, and a BadgeNumber denotes exactly one PoliceOfficer).

- A **one-to-many association** has a multiplicity 1 on one end and 0..n (also represented by a star) or 1..n on the other. A one-to-many association between two classes (e.g., FireUnit and FireTruck) denotes composition (e.g., a FireUnit owns one or more FireTrucks, a FireTruck is owned exactly by one FireUnit).

- A **many-to-many association** has a multiplicity 0..n or 1..n on both ends. A many-to-many association between two classes (e.g., FieldOfficer and IncidentReport) denotes that an arbitrary number of links can exist between instances of the two classes (e.g., a FieldOfficer can write many IncidentReports, an IncidentReport can be written by many FieldOfficers). This is the most complex type of association.

Adding multiplicity to associations increases the amount of information we capture from the application or the solution domain. Specifying the multiplicity of an association becomes critical when we determine which use cases are needed to manipulate the application domain objects. For example, consider a file system made of Directories and Files. A Directory can

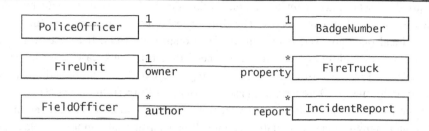

Figure 2-27 Examples of multiplicity (UML class diagram). The association between PoliceOfficer and BadgeNumber is one-to-one. The association between FireUnit and FireTruck is one-to-many. The association between FieldOfficer and IncidentReport is many-to-many.

contain any number of *FileSystemElements*. A *FileSystemElement* is a concept that denotes either a Directory or a File. In case of a strictly hierarchical system, a *FileSystemElement* is part of exactly one Directory, which we denote with a one-to-many multiplicity (Figure 2-28).

If, however, a File or a Directory can be simultaneously part of more than one Directory, we need to represent the aggregation of *FileSystemElement* into Directories as a many-to-many association (see Figure 2-29).

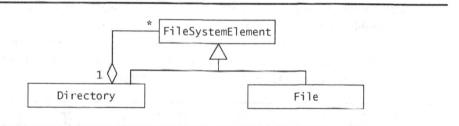

Figure 2-28 Example of a hierarchical file system. A Directory can contain any number of *FileSystemElements* (a *FileSystemElement* is either a File or a Directory). A given *FileSystemElement*, however, is part of exactly one Directory.

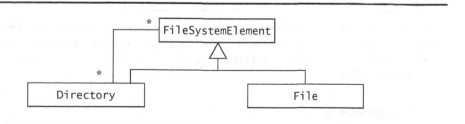

Figure 2-29 Example of a nonhierarchical file system. A Directory can contain any number of *FileSystemElements* (a *FileSystemElement* is either a File or a Directory). A given *FileSystemElement* can be part of many Directories.

This discussion may seem to be considering detailed issues that could be left for later activities in the development process. The difference between a hierarchical file system and a nonhierarchical one, however, is also in the functionality it offers. If a system allows a given File to be part of multiple Directories, we need to define a use case describing how a user adds an existing File to existing Directories (e.g., the Unix link command or the Macintosh MakeAlias menu item). Moreover, use cases removing a File from a Directory must specify whether the File is removed from one Directory only or from all Directories that reference it. Note that a many-to-many association can result in a substantially more complex system.

Aggregation

Associations are used to represent a wide range of connections among a set of objects. In practice, a special case of association occurs frequently: **aggregation**. For example, a State contains many Counties, which in turn contain many Townships. A PoliceStation is composed of PoliceOfficers. A Directory contains a number of Files. Such relationships could be modeled using a one-to-many association. Instead, UML provides the concept of an aggregation, denoted by a simple line with a diamond at the container end of the association (see Figures 2-28 and 2-30). One-to-many associations and aggregations, although similar, cannot be used interchangeably: aggregations denote hierarchical aspects of the relationship and can have either one-to-many or many-to-many multiplicity, whereas one-to-many associations imply a peer relationship. For example, in Figure 2-30, the PoliceOfficers are part of the PoliceStation. In Figure 2-22, a FieldOfficer writes zero or many EmergencyReports. However, the FieldOfficer is not *composed* EmergencyReports. Consequently, we use an association in the latter case and an aggregation in the former case.

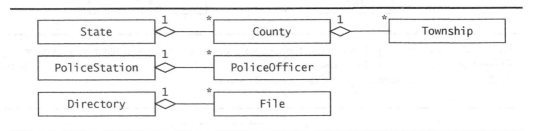

Figure 2-30 Examples of aggregations (UML class diagram). A State contains many Counties, which in turn contains many Townships. A PoliceStation has many PoliceOfficers. A file system Directory contains many Files.

Qualification

Qualification is a technique for reducing multiplicity by using keys. Associations with a 0..1 or 1 multiplicity are easier to understand than associations with a 0..n or 1..n multiplicity. Often in the case of a one-to-many association, objects on the "many" side can be distinguished from one another using a name. For example, in a hierarchical file system, each file belongs to exactly one directory. Each file is uniquely identified by a name in the context of a directory. Many files can have the same name in the context of the file system; however, two files cannot share the same name within the same directory. Without qualification (see top of Figure 2-31), the association between Directory and File has a one multiplicity on the Directory side and a zero-to-many multiplicity on the File side. We reduce the multiplicity on the File side by using the filename attribute as a key, also called a **qualifier** (see top of Figure 2-31). The relationship between Directory and File is called a **qualified association**.

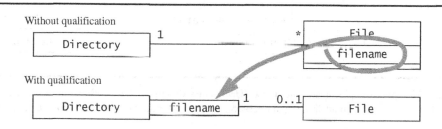

Figure 2-31   Example of how a qualified association reduces multiplicity (UML class diagram). Adding a qualifier clarifies the class diagram and increases the conveyed information. In this case, the model including the qualification denotes that the name of a file is unique within a directory.

Reducing multiplicity is always preferable, as the model becomes clearer and fewer cases have to be taken into account. Developers should examine each association that has a one-to-many or many-to-many multiplicity to see if a qualifier can be added. Often, these associations can be qualified with an attribute of the target class (e.g., filename in Figure 2-31).

Inheritance

Inheritance is the relationship between a general class and one or more specialized classes. Inheritance enables us to describe all the attributes and operations that are common to a set of classes. For example, FieldOfficer and Dispatcher both have name and badgeNumber attributes. However, FieldOfficer has an association with EmergencyReport, whereas Dispatcher has an association with Incident. The common attributes of FieldOfficer and Dispatcher can be modeled by introducing a *PoliceOfficer* class that is specialized by the FieldOfficer and the Dispatcher classes (see Figure 2-32). *PoliceOfficer*, the generalization, is called a **superclass**. FieldOfficer and Dispatcher, the specializations, are called the **subclasses**. The subclasses **inherit** the attributes and operations from their parent class. Abstract classes (defined in Section 2.3.3) are distinguished from concrete classes by *italicizing* the name of abstract classes. In Figure 2-32, *PoliceOfficer* is an abstract class. Abstract classes are used in object-oriented modeling to classify related concepts, thus reducing the overall complexity of the model.

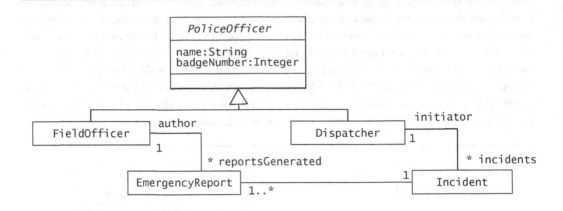

Figure 2-32 An example of an inheritance (UML class diagram). *PoliceOfficer* is an abstract class which defines the common attributes and operations of the FieldOfficer and Dispatcher classes.

Object behavior is specified by **operations**. An object requests the execution of an operation from another object by sending it a **message**. The message is matched up with a **method** defined by the class to which the receiving object belongs or by any of its superclasses. The methods of a class in an object-oriented programming language are the implementations of these operations.

The distinction between operations and methods allows us to distinguish between the specification of behavior (i.e., an operation) and its implementation (i.e., a set of methods that are possibly defined in different classes in the inheritance hierarchy). For example, the class Incident in Figure 2-33 defines an operation, called assignResource(), which, given a FieldOfficer, creates an association between the receiving Incident and the specified Resource. The assignResource() operation may also have a side effect such as sending a notification to the newly assigned Resource. The close() operation of Incident is responsible for closing the Incident. This includes going over all the resources that have been assigned to the incident over time and collecting their reports. Although UML distinguishes operations from methods, in practice, developers usually do not and simply refer to methods.

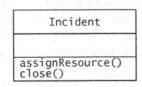

Figure 2-33 Examples of operations provided by the Incident class (UML class diagram).

Applying class diagrams

Class diagrams are used for describing the structure of a system. During analysis, software engineers build class diagrams to formalize application domain knowledge. Classes represent participating objects found in use cases and interaction diagrams, and describe their attributes and operations. The purpose of analysis models is to describe the scope of the system and discover its boundaries. For example, using the class diagram pictured in Figure 2-22, an analyst could examine the multiplicity of the association between `FieldOfficer` and `EmergencyReport` (i.e., one `FieldOfficer` can write zero or more `EmergencyReports`, but each `EmergencyReport` is written by exactly one `FieldOfficer`) and ask the user whether this is correct. Can there be more than one author of an `EmergencyReport`? Can there be anonymous reports? Depending on the answer from the user, the analyst would then change the model to reflect the application domain. The development of analysis models is described in Chapter 5, *Analysis*.

Analysis models do not focus on implementation. Concepts such as interface details, network communication, and database storage are not represented. Class diagrams are refined during system design and object design to include classes representing the solution domain. For example, the developer adds classes representing databases, user interface windows, adapters around legacy code, optimizations, and so on. The classes are also grouped into subsystems with well-defined interfaces. The development of design models is described in Chapter 6, *System Design: Decomposing the System*, Chapter 8, *Object Design: Reusing Pattern Solutions*, Chapter 9, *Object Design: Specifying Interfaces*, and Chapter 10, *Mapping Models to Code*.

2.4.3   Interaction Diagrams

Interaction diagrams describe patterns of communication among a set of interacting objects. An object interacts with another object by sending **messages**. The reception of a message by an object triggers the execution of a method, which in turn may send messages to other objects. **Arguments** may be passed along with a message and are bound to the parameters of the executing method in the receiving object. In UML, interaction diagrams can take one of two forms: sequence diagrams or communication diagrams.

Sequence diagrams represent the objects participating in the interaction horizontally and time vertically. For example, consider a watch with two buttons (hereafter called 2Bwatch). Setting the time on 2Bwatch requires the actor 2BWatchOwner to first press both buttons simultaneously, after which 2Bwatch enters the set time mode. In the set time mode, 2Bwatch blinks the number being changed (e.g., the hours, minutes, seconds, day, month, or year). Initially, when the 2BWatchOwner enters the set time mode, the hours blink. If the actor presses the first button, the next number blinks (e.g, if the hours are blinking and the actor presses the first button, the hours stop blinking and the minutes start blinking). If the actor presses the second button, the blinking number is incremented by one unit. If the blinking number reaches the end of its range, it is reset to the beginning of its range (e.g., assume the minutes are blinking and its current value is 59, its new value is set to 0 if the actor presses the second button). The actor exits the set time mode by pressing both buttons simultaneously. Figure 2-34 depicts a sequence diagram for an actor setting his 2Bwatch one minute ahead. Each column represents an object that participates in the interaction. Messages are shown by solid arrows. Labels on solid arrows represent message names and may contain arguments. Activations (i.e., executing methods) are depicted by vertical rectangles. The actor who initiates the interaction is shown in the left-most column. The messages coming from the actor represent the interactions described in the use case diagrams. If other actors communicate with the system during the use case, these actors are represented on the right-hand side and can receive messages. Although for simplicity, interactions among objects and actors are uniformly represented as messages, the modeler should keep in mind that interactions between actors and the system are of a different nature than interactions among objects.

Sequence diagrams can be used to describe either an abstract sequence (i.e., all possible interactions) or concrete sequences (i.e., one possible interaction, as in Figure 2-34). When describing all possible interactions, sequence diagrams provide notations for iterations and conditionals. An iteration is denoted by a combined fragment labeled with the loop operator (see Figure 2-35). An alternative is denoted by a combined fragment containing a partition for each alternative. The alternatives are selected by guards on the first message of the partition ([i>0] and [else] in Figure 2-35). If i is positive, the top alternative of the alt combined fragment is executed and the op1() message is sent. Otherwise, the bottom alternative is executed and the op2() message is sent.

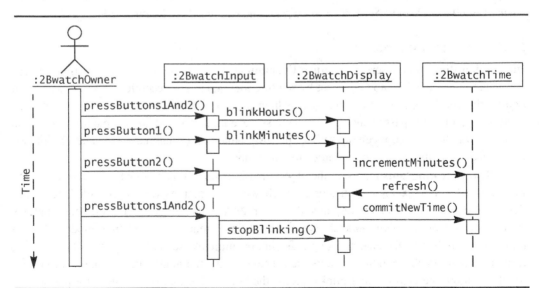

Figure 2-34   Example of a sequence diagram: setting the time on 2Bwatch.

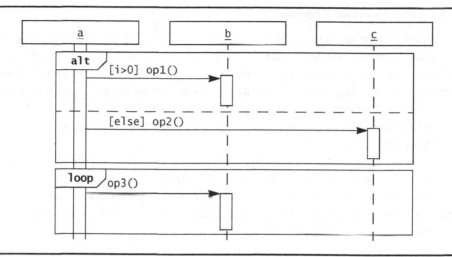

Figure 2-35 Examples of conditions and iterators in sequence diagrams.

Communication diagrams depict the same information as sequence diagrams. Communication diagrams represent the sequence of messages by numbering the interactions. On one hand, this removes the need for geometrical constraints on the objects and results in a more compact diagram. On the other hand, the sequence of messages becomes more difficult to follow. Figure 2-36 depicts the communication diagram that is equivalent to the sequence diagram of Figure 2-34.

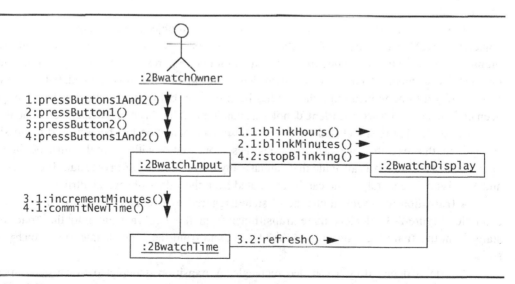

Figure 2-36 Example of a communication diagram: setting the time on 2Bwatch. This diagram represents the same use case as the sequence diagram of Figure 2-34.

Applying interaction diagrams

Interaction diagrams describe interactions among several objects. One of the main reasons for constructing an interaction diagram is to uncover the responsibilities of the classes in the class diagrams and to discover even new classes. In other words, the interaction diagram helps the developer in deciding which objects require particular operations. Typically, there is an interaction diagram for every use case with focus on the event flow. The developer identifies the objects that participate in the use case, and assigns pieces of the use case behavior to the objects in the form of operations.

The class diagram and the associated interaction diagrams are usually constructed in tandem after the initial class diagram has been defined. This process often also leads to refinements in the use case (e.g., correcting ambiguous descriptions, adding missing behavior) and consequently, the discovery of more objects and more services. We describe in detail the use of interaction diagrams in Chapter 5, *Analysis*.

2.4.4   State Machine Diagrams

A UML **state machine** is a notation for describing the sequence of states an object goes through in response to external events. UML state machines are extensions of the finite state machine model. On one hand, state machines provide notation for nesting states and state machines (i.e., a state can be described by a state machine). On the other hand, state machines provide notation for binding transitions with message sends and conditions on objects. UML state machines are largely based on Harel's statecharts [Harel, 1987] and have been adapted for use with object models [Douglass, 1999]. UML state machines can be used to represent any Mealy or Moore state machine.

A **state** is a condition satisfied by the attributes of an object. For example, an Incident object in FRIEND can exist in four states: Active, Inactive, Closed, and Archived (see Figure 2-37). An active Incident denotes a situation that requires a response (e.g., an ongoing fire, a traffic accident). An inactive Incident denotes a situation that was handled, but for which reports are yet to be written (e.g., the fire has been put out, but damage estimates have not yet been completed). A closed Incident denotes a situation that has been handled and documented. An archived Incident is a closed Incident whose documentation has been moved to off-site storage. In this example, we can represent these four states with a single attribute in the Incident class—a status attribute that can take any of four values: Active, Inactive, Closed, and Archived. In general, a state can be computed from the values of several attributes.

A **transition** represents a change of state triggered by events, conditions, or time. For example, Figure 2-37 depicts three transitions: from the Active state into the Inactive state, from the Inactive state to the Closed state, and from the Closed state to the Archived state.

A state is depicted by a rounded rectangle. A transition is depicted by an open arrow connecting two states. States are labeled with their name. A small solid black circle indicates the initial state. A circle surrounding a small solid black circle indicates a final state.

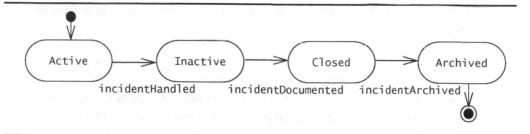

Figure 2-37 A UML state machine diagram for the Incident class.

Figure 2-38 displays another example, a state machine for the 2Bwatch (for which we constructed a sequence diagram in Figure 2-34). At the highest level of abstraction, 2Bwatch has two states, MeasureTime and SetTime. 2Bwatch changes states when the user presses and releases both buttons simultaneously. During the transition from the SetTime state to the MeasureTime state, 2Bwatch beeps. This is indicated by the action /beep on the transition. When 2Bwatch is first powered on, it is in the SetTime state. This is modeled by making SetTime the initial state. When the battery of the watch runs out, the 2Bwatch is permanently out of order. This is indicated with a final state. In this example, transitions can be triggered by an event (e.g., pressBothButtons) or by the passage of time (e.g., after 2 min.).

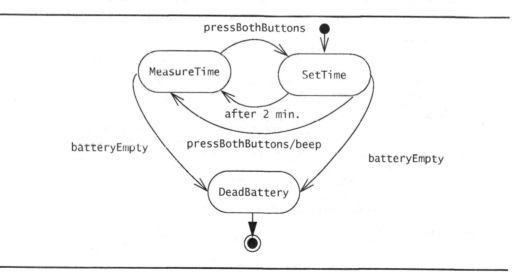

Figure 2-38 State machine diagram for 2Bwatch set time function.

Figure 2-39 depicts a refined state machine diagram for the 2Bwatch depicted in Figure 2-38 using actions to denote the behavior within the states. **Actions** are fundamental units of processing that can take a set of inputs, produce a set of outputs, and can change the state of the system. Actions normally take a short amount of time to execute and are not interruptable.

For example, an action can be realized by an operation call. Actions can occur in three places in a state machine:

- when a transition is taken (e.g., beep when the transition between SetTime and MeasureTime is fired on the pressBothButtons event)
- when a state is entered (e.g., blink hours in the SetTime state in Figure 2-39)
- when a state is exited (e.g., stop blinking in the SetTime state in Figure 2-39).

During a transition, the exit actions of the source state are executed first, then the actions associated with the transition are executed, then the entry actions of the destination state are executed. The exit and entry actions are always executed when a state is exited or entered, respectively. They do not depend on the specific transition that was used to exit or enter the state.

An **internal transition** is a transition that does not leave the state. Internal transitions are triggered by events and can have actions associated with them. However, the firing of an internal transition does not result in the execution of any exit or entry actions. For example, in Figure 2-39, the SetTime state has two internal transitions, one associated with pressing the left button and one associated with pressing the right button.

An **activity** is a coordinated set of actions. A state can be associated an activity that is executed as long as an object resides in this state. While an action is short and non-interruptable, an activity can take a substantial amount of time and is interrupted when a transition exiting the

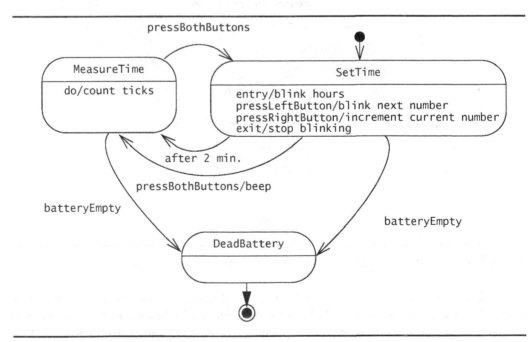

Figure 2-39   Internal transitions associated with the SetTime state (UML state machine diagram).

state is fired. Activities are associated with state using the do label and are placed inside the state where they executed. For example, in Figure 2-39, count ticks is an activity associated with the MeasureTime state

Nested state machines reduce complexity. They can be used instead of internal transitions. In Figure 2-40, the current number is modeled as a **nested state**, whereas actions corresponding to modifying the current number are modeled using internal transitions. Note that each state could be modeled as a nested state machine. For example, the BlinkHours state machine would have 24 substates that correspond to the hours in the day; transitions between these states would correspond to pressing the second button.

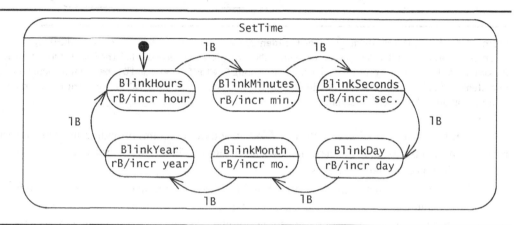

Figure 2-40 Refined state machine associated with the SetTime state (UML state machine diagram). lB and rB correspond to pressing the left and right button, respectively.

Applying state machine diagrams

State machine diagrams are used to represent nontrivial behavior of a subsystem or an object. Unlike interaction diagrams that focus on the events impacting the behavior of a set of objects, state machine diagrams make explicit which attribute or set of attributes have an impact on the behavior of a single object. State machines are used to identify object attributes and to refine the behavior description of an object, and interaction diagrams are used to identify participating objects and the services they provide. State machine diagrams can also be used during system and object design to describe solution domain objects with interesting behavior. We describe the use of state machine diagrams in detail in Chapter 5, *Analysis*, and Chapter 6, *System Design: Decomposing the System*.

2.4.5   Activity Diagrams

UML activity diagrams represent the sequencing and coordination of lower level behaviors. An activity diagram denotes how a behavior is realized in terms of one or several sequences of activities and the object flows needed for coordinating the activities. Activity diagrams are hierarchical: an **activity** is made out of either an action or a graph of subactivities and their associated object flow. Figure 2-41 is an activity diagram corresponding to the state diagram in Figure 2-37. Rounded rectangles represent actions and activities. Edges between activities represent control flow. An activity can be executed only after all predecessor activities completed.

Figure 2-41   A UML activity diagram for `Incident`. During the action `HandleIncident`, the `Dispatcher` receives reports and allocates resources. Once the `Incident` is closed, the `Incident` moves to the `DocumentIncident` activity during which all participating `FieldOfficers` and `Dispatchers` document the `Incident`. Finally, the `ArchiveIncident` activity represents the archival of the `Incident` related information onto slow access medium.

Control nodes coordinate control flows in an activity diagram, providing mechanisms for representing decisions, concurrency, and synchronization. The main control nodes we use are decisions, fork nodes, and join nodes.

Decisions are branches in the control flow. They denote alternatives based on a condition of the state of an object or a set of objects. Decisions are depicted by a diamond with one or more incoming open arrows and two or more outgoing arrows. The outgoing edges are labeled with the conditions that select a branch in the control flow. The set of all outgoing edges from a decision represents the set of all possible outcomes. In Figure 2-42, a decision after the `OpenIncident` action selects between three branches: If the incident is of high priority and if it is a fire, the `FireChief` is notified. If the incident is of high priority and is not a fire, the `PoliceChief` is notified. Finally, if neither condition is satisfied, that is, if the `Incident` is of low priority, no superior is notified and the resource allocation proceeds.

Fork nodes and **join nodes** represent concurrency. Fork nodes denote the splitting of the flow of control into multiple threads, while join nodes denotes the synchronization of multiple threads and their merging of the flow of control into a single thread. For example, in Figure 2-43, the actions `AllocateResources`, `Coordinate-Resources`, and `DocumentIncident` may all occur in parallel. However, they can only be initiated after the `OpenIncident` action, and the `ArchiveIncident` action may only be initiated after all other activities have been completed.

Activities may be grouped into **swimlanes** (also called **activity partitions**) to denote the object or subsystem that implements the actions. Swimlanes are represented as rectangles enclosing a group of actions. Transitions may cross swimlanes. In Figure 2-44, the `Dispatcher` swimlane groups all the actions that are performed by the `Dispatcher` object. The `FieldOfficer` swimlane denotes that the `FieldOfficer` object is responsible for the `DocumentIncident` action.

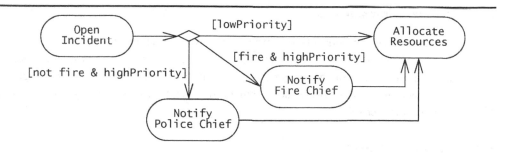

Figure 2-42 Example of decision in the OpenIncident process. If the Incident is a fire and is of high priority, the Dispatcher notifies the FireChief. If it is a high-priority Incident that is not a fire, the PoliceChief is notified. In all cases, the Dispatcher allocates resources to deal with the Incident.

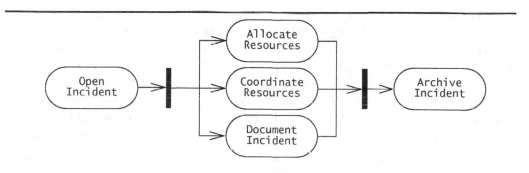

Figure 2-43 An example of fork and join nodes in a UML activity diagram.

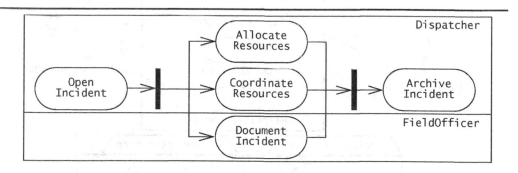

Figure 2-44 An example of swimlanes in a UML activity diagram.

Applying activity diagrams

Activity diagrams provide a task-centric view of the behavior of a set of objects. They can be used: for example, to describe sequencing constraints among use cases, sequential activities among a group of objects, or the tasks of a project. In this book, we use activity diagrams to describe the activities of software development in Chapter 14, *Project Management*, and Chapter 15, *Software Life Cycle*.

2.4.6   Diagram Organization

Models of complex systems quickly become complex as developers refine them. The complexity of models can be dealt with by grouping related elements into **packages**. A package is a grouping of model elements, such as use cases or classes, defining scopes of understanding.

For example, Figure 2-45 depicts use cases of the FRIEND system, grouped by actors. Packages are displayed as rectangles with a tab attached to their upper-left corner. Use cases dealing with incident management (e.g., creating, resource allocation, documentation) are grouped in the IncidentManagement package. Use cases dealing with incident archive (e.g., archiving an incident, generating reports from archived incidents) are grouped in the IncidentArchive package. Use cases dealing with system administration (e.g., adding users, registering end stations) are grouped in the SysAdministration package. This enables the client and the developers to organize use cases into related groups and to focus on only a limited set of use cases at a time.

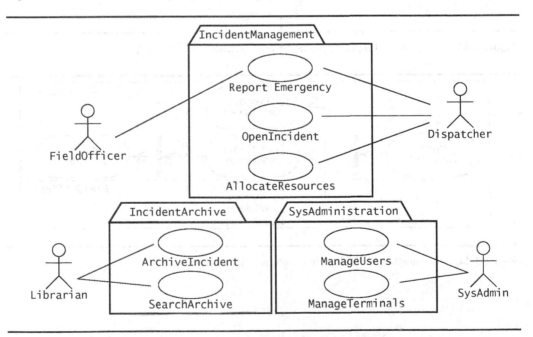

Figure 2-45   Example of packages: use cases of FRIEND organized by actors (UML use case diagram).

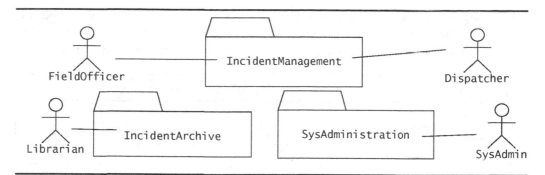

Figure 2-46 Example of packages. This figure displays the same packages as Figure 2-45 except that the details of each packages are suppressed (UML use case diagram).

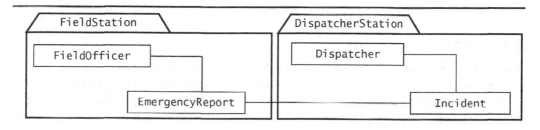

Figure 2-47 Example of packages. The FieldOfficer and EmergencyReport classes are located in the FieldStation package, and the Dispatcher and Incident classes are located on the DispatcherStation package.

Figures 2-46 and 2-47 are examples of class diagrams using packages. Classes from the ReportEmergency use case are organized according to the site where objects are created. FieldOfficer and EmergencyReport are part of the FieldStation package, and Dispatcher and Incident are part of the DispatcherStation. Figure 2-47 displays the packages with the model elements they contain, and Figure 2-46 displays the same information without the contents of each package. Figure 2-46 is a higher-level picture of the system and can be used for discussing system-level issues, whereas Figure 2-47 is a more detailed view that can be used to discuss the content of specific packages.

Packages are used to deal with complexity in the same way a user organizes files and subdirectories into directories. However, packages are not necessarily hierarchical: the same class may appear in more than one package. To reduce inconsistencies, classes (more generally model elements) are owned by exactly one package, whereas the other packages are said to refer to the modeling element. Note that packages are organizing constructs, not objects. They have no associated behavior and cannot send and receive messages.

A **note** is a comment attached to a diagram. Notes are used by developers for attaching information to models and model elements. This is an ideal mechanism for recording outstanding issues relevant to a model, clarifying a complex point, or recording to-dos or reminders. Although notes have no semantics per se, they are sometimes used to express constraints that cannot otherwise be expressed in UML. Figure 2-48 is an example of a note.

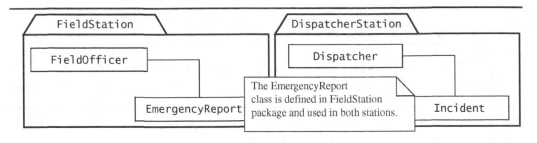

Figure 2-48   An example of a note. Notes can be attached to a specific element in a diagram.

2.4.7   Diagram Extensions

The goal of the UML designers was to provide a set of notations to model a broad class of software systems. They also recognized that a fixed set of notations could not achieve this goal, because it is impossible to anticipate the needs encountered in all application and solution domains. For this reason, UML provides a number of extension mechanisms enabling the modeler to extend the language. In this section, we describe two such mechanisms, **stereotypes** and **constraints**.

A **stereotype** is an extension mechanism that allows developers to classify model elements in UML. A stereotype is represented by string enclosed by guillemets (e.g., «boundary») and attached to the model element to which it applies, such as a class or an association. Formally, attaching a stereotype to a model element is semantically equivalent to creating a new class in the UML meta-model (i.e., the model that represents the constructs of UML). This enables modelers to create new kinds of building blocks that are needed in their domain. For example, during analysis, we classify objects into three types: entity, boundary, and control. Entity, boundary, and control objects have the same structure (i.e., they have attributes, operations, and associations), but serve different purposes. The base UML language only includes one type of object. To represent these three types, we use the stereotypes «entity», «boundary», and «control» (Figure 2-49). The «entity», «boundary», and «control» stereotypes are described in Chapter 5, *Analysis*. Another example is the relationships among use cases. As we saw in Section 2.4.1, include relationships in use case diagrams are denoted with a dashed open arrow and the «include» stereotype.

A **constraint** is a rule that is attached to a UML model element restricting its semantics. This allows us to represent phenomena that cannot otherwise be expressed with UML. For example, in Figure 2-50, an Incident may be associated with one or more EmergencyReports from the field. However, it is important that the Dispatchers are able to view the reports chronologically. We represent the chronological ordering of EmergencyReport to Incident with

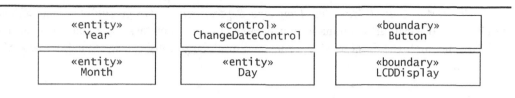

Figure 2-49 Examples of stereotypes (UML class diagram).

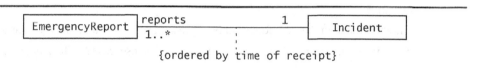

Figure 2-50 An example of constraint (UML class diagram).

the constraint {ordered by time of receipt}. Constraints can be expressed as an informal string or by using a formal language such as OCL (Object Constraint Language, [OMG, 2009]). We describe OCL and the use of constraints in Chapter 9, *Object Design: Specifying Interfaces.*

2.5 Further Readings

The historic roots of modeling notations can be traced back to structured analysis [De Marco, 1978] and structured design [Yourdon & Constantine, 1975], which is based on functional decomposition. These methods were based data flow diagrams [De Marco, 1978]. Data flow diagrams are quite important for software engineers who need to maintain legacy systems designed with structured analysis techniques.

UML came out of the teachings and efforts of many researchers and practitioners, some of whom we cited earlier in this chapter. The efforts of Booch, Jacobson, and Rumbaugh enabled a broadly accepted unified notation. Their earlier works [Booch, 1994], [Jacobson et al., 1992], [Rumbaugh et al., 1991] give much insight into the roots of object-oriented analysis and design and still provide valuable knowledge about object-oriented modeling.

Because it was designed to address a broad range of systems and concern, UML is a complex standard. In this chapter, we focused on the basic elements of UML that you need to understand before proceeding with the next chapters. For further information on UML, refer to the following books:

UML Distilled [Fowler, 2003] is a brief introduction to UML and illustrated with many examples. For readers without any knowledge of UML, this book is a useful overview to get into the notation quickly.

The *Unified Modeling Language User Guide* [Booch et al., 2005] is a comprehensive presentation of UML by its principal designers. It covers much more material than *UML Distilled* and is more appropriate for the advanced modeler. As the *UML User Guide* has fewer examples, *UML Distilled* is more appropriate for novices.

The *OMG Unified Modeling Language Superstructure* [OMG, 2009] is the official specification of UML. It is continuously maintained by a revision task force that is responsible for clarifying ambiguities, correcting errors, and resolving inconsistencies found by the UML community.

2.6 Exercises

2-1 Consider an ATM system. Identify at least three different actors that interact with this system.

2-2 Can the system under consideration be represented as an actor? Justify your answer.

2-3 What is the difference between a scenario and a use case? When do you use each construct?

2-4 Draw a use case diagram for a ticket distributor for a train system. The system includes two actors: a traveler who purchases different types of tickets, and a central computer system that maintains a reference database for the tariff. Use cases should include BuyOneWayTicket, BuyWeeklyCard, BuyMonthlyCard, and UpdateTariff. Also include the following exceptional cases: TimeOut (i.e., traveler took too long to insert the right amount), TransactionAborted (i.e., traveler selected the cancel button without completing the transaction), DistributorOutOfChange, and DistributorOutOfPaper.

2-5 Write the flow of events and specify all fields for the use case UpdateTariff that you drew in Exercise 2-4. Do not forget to specify any relationships.

2-6 Draw a class diagram representing a book defined by the following statement: "A book is composed of a number of parts, which in turn are composed of a number of chapters. Chapters are composed of sections." Focus only on classes and relationships.

2-7 Add multiplicity to the class diagram you produced in Exercise 2-6.

2-8 Draw an object diagram representing the first part of this book (i.e., Part I, *Getting Started*). Make sure that the object diagram you draw is consistent with the class diagram of Exercise 2-6.

2-9 Extend the class diagram of Exercise 2-6 to include the following attributes:
   • a book includes a publisher, publication date, and an ISBN
   • a part includes a title and a number
   • a chapter includes a title, a number, and an abstract
   • a section includes a title and a number.

2-10 Consider the class diagram of Exercise 2-9. Note that the Part, Chapter, and Section classes all include title and number attributes. Add an abstract class and an inheritance relationship to factor out these two attributes into the abstract class.

2-11 Draw a class diagram representing the relationship between parents and children. Take into account that a person can have both a parent and a child. Annotate associations with roles and multiplicities.

2-12 Draw a class diagram for bibliographic references. Use the references in Appendix C, *Bibliography*, to test your class diagram. Your class diagram should be as detailed as possible.

2-13 Draw a sequence diagram for the warehouseOnFire scenario of Figure 2-21. Include the objects bob, alice, john, FRIEND, and instances of other classes you may need. Draw only the first five message sends.

2-14 Draw a sequence diagram for the ReportIncident use case of Figure 2-14. Draw only the first five message sends. Make sure it is consistent with the sequence diagram of Exercise 2-13.

2-15 Consider the process of ordering a pizza over the phone. Draw an activity diagram representing each step of the process, from the moment you pick up the phone to the point where you start eating the pizza. Do not represent any exceptions. Include activities that others need to perform.

2-16 Add exception handling to the activity diagram you developed in Exercise 2-15. Consider at least three exceptions (e.g., delivery person wrote down wrong address, delivery person brings wrong pizza, store out of anchovies).

2-17 Consider the software development activities which we described in Section 1.4 in Chapter 1, *Introduction to Software Engineering*. Draw an activity diagram depicting these activities, assuming they are executed strictly sequentially. Draw a second activity diagram depicting the same activities occurring incrementally (i.e., one part of the system is analyzed, designed, implemented, and tested completely before the next part of the system is developed). Draw a third activity diagram depicting the same activities occurring concurrently.

References

[Booch, 1994]   G. Booch, *Object-Oriented Analysis and Design with Applications*, 2nd ed., Benjamin/Cummings, Redwood City, CA, 1994.

[Booch et al., 2005]   G. Booch, J. Rumbaugh, & I. Jacobson, *The Unified Modeling Language User Guide*, Addison-Wesley, Reading, MA, 2005.

[Coad et al., 1995]   P. Coad, D. North, & M. Mayfield, *Object Models: Strategies, Patterns, & Applications*, Prentice Hall, Englewood Cliffs, NJ, 1995.

[Constantine & Lockwood, 2001]   L.L. Constantine & L.A.D. Lockwood, "Structure and style in use cases for user interface design," in M. van Harmelen (ed.), *Object-Oriented User Interface Design*, 2001.

[De Marco, 1978]   T. De Marco, *Structured Analysis and System Specification*, Yourdon, New York, 1978.

[Douglass, 1999]   B.P. Douglass, *Doing Hard Time: Using Object Oriented Programming and Software Patterns in Real Time Applications*, Addison-Wesley, Reading, MA, 1999.

[Fowler, 2003]   M. Fowler, *UML Distilled: A Brief Guide To The Standard Object Modeling Language*, 3rd ed., Addison-Wesley, Reading, MA, 2003.

[Harel, 1987]   D. Harel, "Statecharts: A visual formalism for complex systems," *Science of Computer Programming*, pp. 231–274, 1987.

[Jacobson et al., 1992]   I. Jacobson, M. Christerson, P. Jonsson, & G. Overgaard, *Object-Oriented Software Engineering—A Use Case Driven Approach,* Addison-Wesley, Reading, MA, 1992.

[Martin & Odell, 1992]   J. Martin & J. J. Odell, *Object-Oriented Analysis and Design*, Prentice Hall, Englewood Cliffs, NJ, 1992.

[Mellor & Shlaer, 1998]   S. Mellor & S. Shlaer, *Recursive Design Approach*, Prentice Hall, Upper Saddle River, NJ, 1998.

[Miller, 1956]   G.A. Miller, "The magical number seven, plus or minus two: Some limits on our capacity for processing information," *Psychological Review*, Vol. 63, pp. 81–97, 1956.

[OMG, 2009]   Object Management Group, *OMG Unified Modeling Language Superstructure. Version 2.2*, http://www.omg.org.

[Popper, 1992]   K. Popper, *Objective Knowledge: An Evolutionary Approach*, Clarendon, Oxford, 1992.

[Rumbaugh et al., 1991]   J. Rumbaugh, M. Blaha, W. Premerlani, F. Eddy, & W. Lorensen, *Object-Oriented Modeling and Design*, Prentice Hall, Englewood Cliffs, NJ, 1991.

[Spivey, 1992]   J. M. Spivey, *The Z Notation, A Reference Manual.* 2nd ed., Prentice Hall International, Hertfordshire, U.K., 1992.

[Wirfs-Brock et al., 1990]   R. Wirfs-Brock, B. Wilkerson, & L. Wiener, *Designing Object-Oriented Software*, Prentice Hall, Englewood Cliffs, NJ, 1990.

[Yourdon & Constantine, 1975]   E. Yourdon & L. Constantine, *Structured Design*, Prentice Hall, Englewood Cliffs, NJ, 1975.

3

Project Organization and Communication

Two electrical boxes for a rocket, manufactured by different contractors, were connected by a pair of wires. Thanks to a thorough preflight check, it was discovered that the wires had been reversed. After the rocket crashed, the inquiry board revealed that the contractors had indeed corrected the reversed wires as instructed.
In fact, both of them had.

Software engineering is a collaborative activity. The development of software brings together participants from different backgrounds, such as domain experts, analysts, designers, programmers, managers, technical writers, graphic designers, and users. No single participant can understand or control all aspects of the system under development, and thus, all participants depend on others to accomplish their work. Moreover, any change in the system or the application domain requires participants to update their understanding of the system. These dependencies make it critical to share information in an accurate and timely manner.

Communication can take many forms depending on the type of activity it is supporting. Participants communicate their status during regular meetings and record it into meeting minutes. Participants communicate project status to the client during client reviews. The communication of requirements and design alternatives is supported by models and their corresponding documents. Crises and misunderstandings are handled through spontaneous information exchanges such as telephone calls, messages, hallway conversations, and ad hoc meetings. As software engineering projects become large, the time each participant must spend in communication increases, thus decreasing the time spent on technical activities. To address these issues, the organization of projects into teams and the sharing of information through formal and informal channels is essential.

We first describe the basic concepts associated with project organization, such as task, work product, and deliverable. We then describe the communication mechanisms available to participants. Finally, we describe the activities associated with project organization and communication. This chapter is written from the perspective of a project participant (e.g., a developer) who needs to *understand* the project organization and communication infrastructure. The *creation* of the project organization and communication infrastructure is the task of the project manager and is the topic of Chapter 14, *Project Management.*

3.1 Introduction: A Rocket Example

When realizing a system, developers focus on constructing a system that behaves according to specifications. When interacting with other project participants, developers focus on communicating information accurately and efficiently. Even if communication may not appear to be a creative or challenging activity, it contributes as much to the success of the project as a good design or efficient implementation, as illustrated by the following example [Lions, 1996].

Ariane 501

June 4, 1996, 30 seconds into lift-off, Ariane 501, the first prototype of the Ariane 5 series, exploded. The main navigational computer experienced an arithmetic overflow, shut down, and handed control over to its twin backup, as it was designed to do. The backup computer, having experienced the same exception a few hundredths of a second earlier, had already shut down. The rocket, without a navigation system, took a fatal sharp turn to correct a deviation that had not occurred.

An independent board of inquiry took less than 2 months to document how a software error resulted in the massive failure. The navigational system of the Ariane 5 design was one of the few components of Ariane 4 that was reused. It had been flight tested and had not failed for Ariane 4.

The navigation system is responsible for calculating course corrections from a specified trajectory based on input from the inertial reference system. An inertial reference system allows a moving vehicle (e.g., a rocket) to compute its position solely based on sensor data from accelerometers and gyroscopes, that is, without reference to the outside world. The inertial system must first be initialized with the starting coordinates and align its axis with the initial orientation of the rocket. The alignment calculations are done by the navigation system before launch and need to be continuously updated to take into account the rotation of the Earth. Alignment calculations are complex and take approximately 45 minutes to complete. Once the rocket is launched, the alignment data are transferred to the flight navigational system. By design, the alignment calculations continue for another 50 seconds after the transfer of data to the navigation system. The decision enables the countdown to be stopped after the transfer of alignment data takes place but before the engines are ignited without having to restart the alignment calculations (that is, without having to restart a 45-minute calculation cycle). In the event the launch succeeds, the alignment module just generates unused data for another 40 seconds after lift-off.

The computer system of Ariane 5 differed from Ariane 4. The electronics were doubled: two inertial reference systems to compute the position of the rocket, two computers to compare the planned trajectory with the actual trajectory, and two sets of control electronics to steer the rocket. If any component would fail, the backup system would take over.

The alignment system, designed for onground calculations only, used 16-bit words to store horizontal velocity (more than enough for displacements due to the wind and to the rotation of the earth). Thirty seconds into flight, the horizontal velocity of Ariane 5 caused an overflow, raised an exception that was handled by shutting down the onboard computer and handing control to the backup system.

Discussion. The alignment software had not been adequately tested. Although it had been subjected to thousands of tests, none included an actual trajectory. The navigation system was tested individually. Tests were specified by the system team and executed by the builders of the navigation system. The system team did not realize that the alignment module could cause the main processor to shut down, especially not in flight. The component team and the system team had failed to communicate.

In this chapter, we discuss organizational and communication issues within a software project. This topic is not specific to software engineering. Communication is, however, pervasive throughout a software development project. Communication failure is costly and can have a high, and sometimes fatal, impact on the project and the quality of the delivered system.

3.2 An Overview of Projects

The techniques and notations we presented in Chapter 2, *Modeling with UML*, enable project participants to build models of the system and communicate about them. However, system models are not the only information needed when communicating in a project. For example, developers need to know

- Who is responsible for which part of the system?
- Which part of the system is due by when?
- Who should be contacted when a problem with a specific version of a component is discovered?
- How should a problem be documented?
- What are the quality criteria for evaluating the system?
- In which form should new requirements be communicated to developers?
- Who should be informed of new requirements?
- Who is responsible for talking to the client?

Although these questions can be relatively easy answered when all participants share a coffee break in the afternoon, the development of large software systems usually does not succeed with such an ad hoc approach. From a developer's perspective, a project consists of four components (Figure 3-1):

- **Work product.** This is any item produced by the project, such as a piece of code, a model, or a document. Work products produced for the client are called **deliverables**.
- **Schedule.** This specifies when work on the project should be accomplished.
- **Participant.** This is any person participating in a project. Sometimes we also call the participant **project member**.

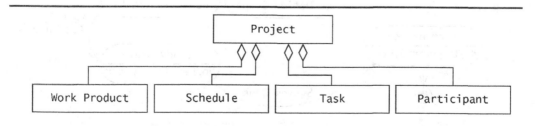

Figure 3-1   Model of a project (UML class diagram).

- **Task.** This is the work to be performed by a project participant to create a work product.

Projects can be defined formally or informally. A signed contract between you and a client requiring the delivery of a software system in three months for one million dollars defines a project; an informal promise you make to your friend to install a new software release on her computer by next week defines a project as well.

Projects come in different types and sizes. Sometimes the characterization of the project type is by the nature of the deliverable. If the outcome is a software system, the project is usually called a software project; building a space shuttle system is called a system project. Projects also come in quite different sizes. Installing a new a space shuttle system, with costs of more than $10 billion and a duration of 10 to 15 years, is a large project, where as changing the furniture of your room is a small project.

From a dynamic point of view, a project can be in any of several phases shown in Figure 3-2. During the **project definition phase**, the project manager, a possible client, and a key project member, the software architect, are involved. The two areas of focus during this phase are an initial understanding of the software architecture, in particular the subsystem decomposition, and the project, in particular the schedule, the work to be performed, and the resources required to do it. This is documented in three documents: the problem statement, the initial software architecture document, and the initial software project management plan. During the **project start phase**, the project manager sets up the project infrastructure, hires participants, organizes them in teams, defines major milestones, and kicks off the project.

During the project definition and project start phases, most decisions are made by the project manager. During the **project steady state phase**, the participants develop the system. They report to their team leader, who is responsible for tracking the status of the developers and identifying problems. The team leaders report the status of their team to the project manager, who then evaluates the status of the complete project. Team leaders respond to deviations from

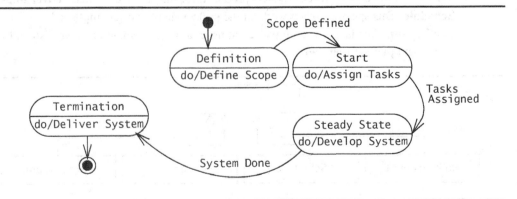

Figure 3-2   States in a software project (UML state machine diagram).

the plan by reallocating tasks to developers or obtaining additional resources from the project manager. The project manager is responsible for the interaction with the client, obtaining formal agreement and renegotiating resources and deadlines.

During the **project termination phase**, the project outcome is delivered to the client and the project history is collected. Most of the developers' involvement with the project ends before this phase. A handful of key developers, the technical writers, and the team leaders are involved with wrapping up the system for installation and acceptance and collecting the project history for future use.

Communication within a project occurs through planned and unplanned events. Planned communication includes:

- **problem inspection**, during which developers gather information from the problem statement, the client, and the user about their needs and the application domain
- **status meetings**, during which teams review their progress
- **peer reviews**, during which team members identify defects and find solutions in preliminary work products
- **client and project reviews**, during which the client or project members review the quality of a work product, in particular deliverables
- **releases**, during which project participants make available to the client and end users versions of the system and its documentation.

Unplanned communication includes:

- **requests for clarification**, during which participants request specific information from others about the system, the application domain, or the project
- **requests for change**, during which participants describe problems encountered in the system or new features that the system should support
- **issue resolution**, during which a conflict between different stakeholders is identified, solutions explored and negotiated, and a resolution agreed upon.

Planned communication helps disseminate information that targeted participants are expected to use. Unplanned communication helps deal with crises and with unexpected information needs. All three communication needs must be addressed for project participants to communicate accurately and efficiently.

When a developer joins a project during the start phase, a problem statement already exists; project management has already written an initial plan to attack the problem, set up a project organization, defined planned communication events, and provided an infrastructure for planned and unplanned communication. Most of the developer's effort when joining a project is to understand these documents and join the existing organizational and communication structures. This is addressed by the following activities:

- *Attend the kick-off meeting.* During this activity, the project participants hear from the client about the problem to be solved and the scope of the system to be developed. This helps them to get a high-level understanding of the problem, which serves as a basis for all other activities.

- *Join a team.* The project manager has decomposed the project into work for individual teams. Participants are assigned to a team based on their skills and interests.

- *Attend training sessions.* Participants who do not have skills for required tasks receive additional training.

- *Join communication infrastructure.* Participants join the project communication infrastructure that supports both planned and unplanned communication events. The infrastructure includes a collection of mechanisms such as groupware, address books, phone books, E-mail services, and video conferencing equipment.

- *Extend communication infrastructure.* Additional bulletin boards and team portals are established specifically for the project.

- *Attend first team status meeting.* During this activity, project participants are taught to conduct status meetings, record status information, and disseminate it to other members of the project.

- *Understand the review schedule.* The review schedule contains a set of high-level milestones to communicate project results in the form of reviews to the project manager and to the client. The objective of project reviews is to inform the project participants of the other teams' status and to identify open issues. The objective of client reviews is to inform the client about the status of the project and to obtain feedback.

In the following sections, we examine these concepts and activities in detail. In Section 3.3, we describe a team-based project organization. In Section 3.4, we discuss the concepts related to project communication. In Section 3.5, we detail the project start activities of a typical team member. In Section 3.6, we provide references to further reading on this topic.

In this chapter, we focus on the perspective of a developer joining a software project, so we do not describe the activities needed to create and manage a project organization and communication infrastructure. We cover these topics in later chapters. Chapter 12, *Rationale Management*, discusses topics related to identifying, negotiating, resolving, and recording issues. Chapter 13, *Configuration Management*, discusses topics related to managing versions, configurations, and releases of documents and system components. In Chapter 14, *Project Management*, we revisit project organization and communication issues from the perspective of the project manager.

3.3 Project Organization Concepts

In this section, we define the following concepts:

- Project Organizations (Section 3.3.1)
- Roles (Section 3.3.2)
- Tasks and Work Products (Section 3.3.3)
- Schedule (Section 3.3.4).

3.3.1   Project Organizations

An important part of any project organization is to define the relationships among participants and between them and tasks, schedule, and work products. In a **team-based organization** (Figure 3-3), the participants are grouped into teams, where a **team** is a small set of participants working on the same activity or task. We distinguish teams from other sets of people, in particular groups and committees. A *group*, for example, is a set of people who are assigned a common task, but they work individually without any need for communication to accomplish their part of the task. A *committee* is comprised of people who come together to review and critique issues and propose actions.

Figure 3-4 shows an instance diagram of an organization for a simple software project consisting of a management team and three developer teams.

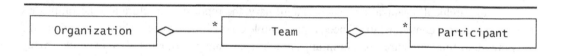

Figure 3-3 A team-based organization consists of organizational units called teams, which consist of participants or other teams (UML class diagram).

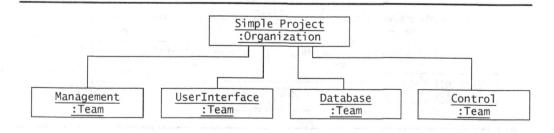

Figure 3-4 Example of a simple project organization (UML instance diagram). Reporting, deciding, and communicating are all made via the aggregation association of the organization.

Project participants interact with each other. The three major types of interaction in a project are:

- **Reporting**. This type of interaction is used for reporting status information. For example, a developer reports to another developer that an API (Application Programmer Interface) is ready, or a team leader reports to a project manager that an assigned task has not yet been completed.

- **Decision**. This type of interaction is used for propagating decisions. For example, a team leader decides that a developer has to publish an API, a project manager decides that a planned delivery must be moved up in time. Another type of decision is the resolution of an issue.

- **Communication**. This type of interaction is used for exchanging all the other types of information needed for decision or status. Communication can take many flavors. Examples are the exchange of requirements or design models or the creation of an argument to support a proposal. An invitation to eat lunch is also a communication.

We call the organization **hierarchical** if both status and decision information are unidirectional; that is, decisions are always made at the root of the organization and passed via the interaction association to the leaves of the organization. Status in hierarchical organizations is generated at the leaves of the organization and reported to the root via the interaction association. The structure of the status and decision information flow is often called the **reporting structure** of the organization. Figure 3-5 illustrates the reporting structure in a hierarchical team-based organization.

In hierarchical organizations, such as a military, the reporting structure also accomplishes the exchange of communication needs. In complex software projects, however, using the existing reporting structure for communication causes many problems. For example, many technical decisions need to be made locally by the developers, but depend on information from developers in other teams. If this information is exchanged via the established reporting

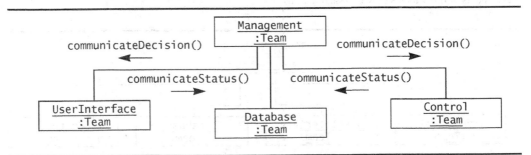

Figure 3-5   Example of reporting structure in a hierarchical organization (UML communication diagram). Status information is reported to the project manager, and corrective decisions are communicated back to the teams by the team leaders. The team leaders and the project manager are called the management team.

structure, the decision-making process can be slowed significantly. Even worse, it often leads to garbling of the information, given its complexity and volume.

The solution to this problem is to exchange information via an additional communication structure that allows participants to communicate directly with each other and in ways different from the reporting structure. Often the communication is delegated to a developer, called a **liaison**, who is responsible for shuttling information back and forth.

Figure 3-6 depicts an example of an organization with liaisons and additional communication lines that deviate from the reporting structure. The documentation team, for example, has a liaison to the user interface team to facilitate information about recent changes made to the appearance of the system. Teams that do not work directly on a subsystem, but rather work on a task that crosses the subsystem team organization, are called **cross-functional teams**. Examples of cross-functional teams include the documentation team, the architecture team, and the testing team.

We call this communication structure, and often also the organization itself, **liaison based**. Liaisons use non-hierarchical communication lines to talk with the liaisons in cross-functional teams. In liaison-based communication structures, the responsibility of team leaders is extended by a new task: not only do they have to make sure that the project manager is aware of the status of the team, but also that team members have all the information they need from other teams. This requires the selection of effective communicators as liaisons to ensure that necessary

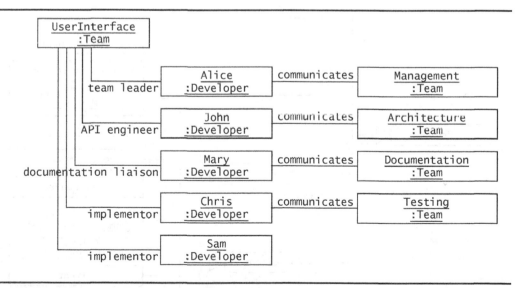

Figure 3-6 Examples of a liaison-based communication structure (UML object diagram). The team is composed of five developers. Alice is the team leader, also called the liaison to the management team. John is the API engineer, also called the liaison to the architecture team. Mary is the liaison to the documentation team. Chris and Sam are implementors and interact with other teams only informally.

communication paths exist. If we allow developers to communicate directly with each other as well, we call the communication structure (and the organization) **peer based**.

3.3.2   Roles

A **role** defines the set of technical and managerial tasks that are expected from a participant or team. In a team-based organization, we assign tasks to a person or a team via a role. For example, the role of tester of a subsystem team consists of the tasks to define the test suites for the subsystem under development, for executing these tests, and for reporting discovered defects back to the developers.

In a software project we distinguish between the following four types of roles: management roles, development roles, cross-functional roles, and consultant roles (Figure 3-7).

Management roles (e.g., project manager, team leader) are concerned with the organization and execution of the project within constraints. We describe this type of role in more detail in Chapter 14, *Project Management.*

Development roles are concerned with specifying, designing, and constructing subsystems. These roles include the analyst, the system architect, the object designer, the implementor, and the tester. Table 3-1 describes examples of development roles in a subsystem team. We describe development roles in more detail in Chapters 5–11.

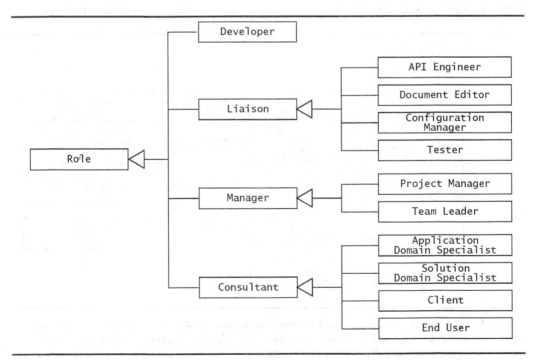

Figure 3-7   Types of roles found in a software engineering project (UML class diagram).

Table 3-1   Examples of roles.

Role	Responsibilities
System architect	The system architect ensures consistency in design decisions and interface styles. The system architect ensures the consistency of the design in the configuration management and testing teams, in particular in the formulation of the configuration management policy as well as the system integration strategy. This is mainly an integration role consuming information from each subsystem team.
Object designer	The object designer is responsible for the interface definition of the assigned subsystem. The interface has to reflect the functionality already assigned to the subsystem and to accommodate the needs of the dependent subsystems. When functionality is traded off with other subsystems, resulting in subsystem changes, the object designer is responsible for propagating changes back to the subsystem team.
Implementor	The implementor is responsible for the coding of a class or a number of classes associated with the subsystem.
Tester	A tester is responsible for evaluating that each subsystem works as specified by the object designer. Often, development projects have a separate team responsible only for testing. Separating the roles of implementor and tester leads to more effective testing.

Cross-functional roles are concerned with coordination among teams. Developers filling these roles are responsible for exchanging information relevant to other teams and negotiating interface details. The cross-functional role is also called **liaison**. The liaison is responsible for disseminating information along the communication structure from one team to another. In some cases (such as the API engineer), a liaison functions as a representative of a subsystem team and may be called to resolve inter-team issues. There are four types of liaisons:

- The **API engineer** is responsible for the interface definition of the assigned subsystem. The interface has to reflect the functionality already assigned to the subsystem and to accommodate the needs of the dependent subsystems. When functionality is traded off with other subsystems, resulting in subsystem changes, the API engineer is responsible for propagating changes back to the subsystem team.

- The **document editor** is responsible for integrating documents produced by a team. A document editor can be seen as a service provider to other teams that depend on a given subsystem team. A document editor also manages information released internally to the team, such as the meeting agendas and minutes.

- The **configuration manager** is responsible for managing different versions of documents, models, and code produced by a team. For simple configuration management policies (e.g., single hardware platform, single branch), this role may be assumed by the team leader.

- A **tester** is responsible for ensuring that each subsystem works as specified by the designer. Often, development projects have a separate team responsible only for testing. Separating the roles of designer, implementor, and tester leads to more effective testing.

Consultant roles are concerned with providing temporary support in areas where the project participants lack expertise. The users and the client act in most projects as consultants on the application domain. Technical consultants may bring expertise on new technologies or methods. Non-technical consultants can help to address legal and marketing issues. We distinguish the following types of consultant roles.

- The **client**, also called customer, is responsible for the formulation of scenarios and the requirements. This includes functional and nonfunctional requirements, as well as constraints. The client is expected to be able to interact with the other developers.

- The **end user** is the person who will be using the delivered system. Sometimes the project does not have access to an end user, or the end user is still unknown. In this case, the end user is represented by the client or even developer of the system.

- The **application domain specialist** is responsible for providing domain knowledge about a specific functional area of the system. Whereas the client has a global view of the required functionality, the application domain specialist has detailed knowledge of a specific problem area.

- The **solution domain specialist** is responsible for providing knowledge about solutions to implement the system. This can include the development method, the process, implementation technology, or the development environment.

3.3.3   Tasks and Work Products

A **task** is a well-defined work assignment for a role. Groups of related tasks are called **activities**. The project manager or team leader assigns a task to a role. The participant who is assigned the role carries out the task, and the manager monitors its progress and completion. A **work product** is a tangible item that results from a task. Examples of work products include an object model, a class diagram, a piece of source code, a document, or parts of documents. Work products result from tasks, are subject to deadlines, and feed into other tasks. For example, the test planning activity for the database subsystem results in a work product including a number of test suites and their expected results. The test suite is then fed to the testing activity of the given subsystem (Figure 3-8 and Table 3-2).

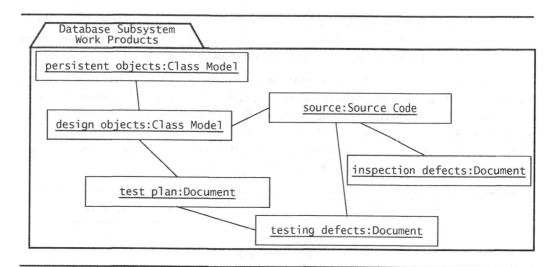

Figure 3-8 Work products for the database subsystem team (UML object diagram). Associations represent dependencies among work products.

Table 3-2 Description of the internal work products depicted in Figure 3-8.

Work product	Type	Description
Persistent Objects	**Class model**	This class model describes completely the objects that are stored by the storage subsystem. For each class, this includes all the attributes, associations, roles, and multiplicities.
Design objects	**Class model**	This class model describes all the objects needed by the storage subsystem that are not described in the persistent object class model.
Subsystem	**Source code**	This is the source code delivered to the testing team.
Test plan	**Document**	This document outlines the test strategy, test criteria, and test cases that are used to find defects in the storage subsystem.
Testing defects	**Document**	This document lists all the defects that have already been found in the storage subsystem through testing.
Inspection defects	**Document**	This document lists all the defects that have already been found in the storage subsystem through peer review, as well as their planned repairs.

Any work product to be delivered to the client is called a **deliverable**. The software system and the accompanying documentation usually constitute a set of deliverables. Work products that are not visible to the client are called **internal work products**.

The specification of work to be accomplished in completing a task or activity is described in a **work package**. A work package includes the task name, the task description, resources needed to perform the task, dependencies on inputs (work products produced by other tasks) and outputs (work products produced by the task in question), as well as dependencies on other tasks. Figure 3-9 depicts the relationships among work packages, activities, tasks, roles, and work products. Table 3-3 provides examples of work packages.

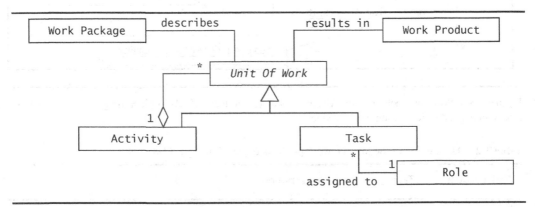

Figure 3-9   Associations among tasks, activities, roles, work products, and work packages (UML class diagram).

Work products are important management artifacts, because we can assess their delivery and the start of the tasks depending on other work products. The late delivery of a testing suite for a subsystem, for example, delays the start of its testing. Note, however, that focusing only on timely delivery is not sufficient: rushing the delivery of test suites meets the project schedule, but can also mean that critical faults are not discovered in time.

3.3.4   Schedule

A schedule is the mapping of tasks onto time: each task is assigned start and end times. This allows us to plan the deadlines for individual deliverables. The two most often used diagrammatic notations for schedules are PERT and Gantt charts [Gantt, 1910]. A **Gantt chart** is a compact way to present the schedule of a software project along the time axis. A Gantt chart is a bar graph on which the horizontal axis represents time and the vertical axis lists the different tasks to be done. Tasks are represented as bars whose length corresponds to the planned duration of the task. A schedule for the database subsystem example is represented as a Gantt chart in Figure 3-10.

Table 3-3   Examples of tasks for the realization of the database subsystem.

Task name	Assigned role	Task description	Input	Output
Database subsystem requirements elicitation	System architect	Elicits requirements from subsystem teams about their storage needs, including persistent objects, their attributes, and relationships	Team liaisons	Database subsystem API, persistent object analysis model (UML class diagram)
Database subsystem design	Object designer	Designs the database subsystem, including the possible selection of a commercial product	Subsystem API	Database subsystem design (UML diagram)
Database subsystem implementation	Implementor	Implements the database subsystem	Subsystem design	Source code
Database subsystem inspection	Implementor, Tester, Object designer	Conducts a code inspection of the database subsystem	Subsystem source code	List of defects
Database subsystem test plan	Tester	Develops a test suite for the database subsystem	Subsystem API, subsystem source code	Tests and test plan
Database subsystem test	Tester	Executes the test suite for the database subsystem	Subsystem, test plan	Test results, list of defects

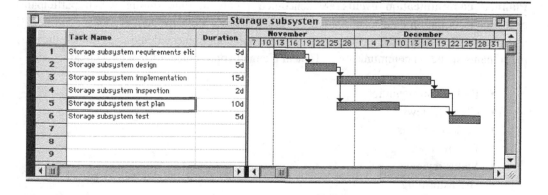

Figure 3-10   An example of schedule for the database subsystem (Gantt chart).

A **PERT chart** represents a schedule as an acyclic graph of tasks. Figure 3-11 is a PERT chart for the database subsystem schedule. The planned start and duration of the tasks are used to compute the critical path, which represents the shortest possible path through the graph. The length of the critical path corresponds to the shortest possible schedule, assuming sufficient resources to accomplish, in parallel, tasks that are independent. Moreover, tasks on the critical path are the most important, as a delay in any of these tasks will result in a delay in the overall project. The tasks and bars represented in thicker lines belong to the critical path.

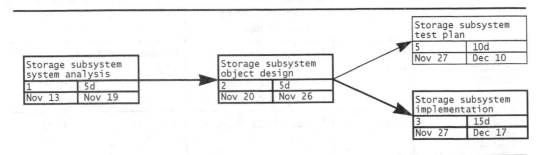

Figure 3-11   Schedule for the database subsystem (PERT chart). Thick lines denote the critical path.

3.4 Project Communication Concepts

So far we have talked about the organization of a project. We now turn to communication in a project. We cover two types of communication that typically occur: planned communication (Section 3.4.1) and unplanned communication (Section 3.4.2). We then survey tools to support project communication (Section 3.4.3). Figure 3-12 shows the interplay between project organization and communication.

3.4.1 Planned Communication

Planned communication events are scheduled points in time during which participants exchange information on a specific topic or review a work product. Such events are formalized and structured to maximize the amount of information communicated and to minimize the time participants spend on communication. Typical planned communication events include

- Problem presentation
- Client reviews
- Project reviews
- Peer reviews
- Status reviews
- Brainstorming
- Releases
- Postmortem reviews.

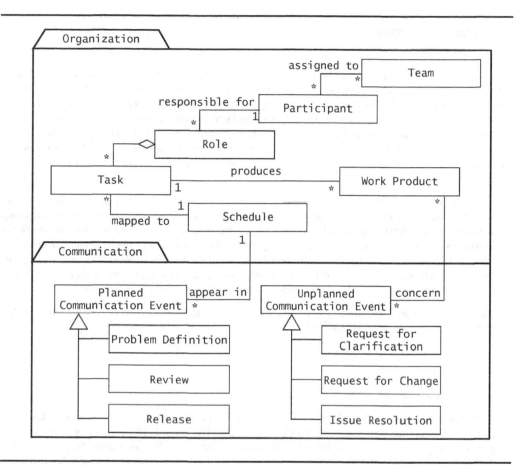

Figure 3-12   Relationships among organizational and communication concepts (UML class diagram).

We describe these communication events in more detail next.

Problem presentation

The focus of **problem presentation** is the presentation of the *Problem Statement* that describes the problem, the application domain, and the desired functionality of the system. It also contains nonfunctional requirements such as platform specification or speed constraints. Figure 3-13 depicts excerpts from an actual problem statement.

The problem statement does not include a complete specification of the system. It is merely a preliminary requirements activity that establishes common ground between the client and the project team. We discuss requirements activities in Chapter 4, *Requirements Elicitation*, and Chapter 5, *Analysis*.

OWL PROBLEM STATEMENT

1. Problem domain

A current trend in the building industry is to provide distributed services and control for the individual occupant as a strategy to correct the overreliance on large centralized systems that characterize office buildings built in the last 30 years. At the Intelligent Workplace, workers will have more control over their environmental conditions—adjusting light level and temperature of their workspace, reducing glare, controlling speed and direction of air flow delivered to workspace. (You can do that in your car—why not in your office?) An energy-efficient facade will allow fresh air ventilation from operable windows and incorporate movable shading devices that adjust to minimize glare and maximize natural lighting of the workspace.

It is desirable to adopt three forms of control in the Intelligent Workplace: responsive, scheduled, and user driven. Responsive control is when the system reacts to a change in sensor reading by actuating some components. Scheduled control can be adopted in the presence of predictable data that allows the components to be directly controlled by a carefully designed schedule. For example, because the position of the sun is predictable, a schedule for the interior shades of the Intelligent Workplace can be adopted. Control system should be flexible enough to respond to the needs of the occupants. If they would like to change the temperature of their local environment, they should be given that opportunity.

In this project, you are asked to build a system called OWL (Object-Oriented Workplace Laboratory) that attempts to improve the way we deal with buildings.

[. . .]

2. Scenarios

2.1 Building control

The building occupant uses a Web browser to access his Personal Environment Module (PEM). He adjusts the temperature and airspeed to cool his workspace. The control information is sent to the PEM equipment. The control actions are logged in the database and the equipment adjusts the heater and the ventilation of the workspace. The system checks neighboring PEMs to check if cooling this particular workspace requires other workspaces heating to be increased.

[. . .]

2.5 Building maintenance

The system monitors the behavior of the controlled devices to detect faults in the system. Faulty light bulbs and unusual parameter readings are reported to the facilities manager, who then plans inspections and repairs. The occurrences of device faults are logged and analyzed for trends, enabling the facilities manager to anticipate faults in the future.

[. . .]

Figure 3-13   Excerpts from the problem statement of OWL [OWL, 1996].

Client review

The goal of **client reviews** is for the client to assess the progress of the development and for the developers to confirm or change the requirements of the system. The client review is used to manage expectations on both sides and to increase the shared understanding among participants. The focus of the review is on what the system does and what constraints are relevant to the client (e.g., performance, platform). In most cases, the review should not focus on the design or implementation of the system unless they affect the client or the user. Exceptions include contracts that impose constraints on the development process, such as those related to safety or regulatory requirements.

A client review is conducted as a formal presentation during which the developers focus on specific functionality with the client. The review is preceded by the release of a work product, such as a specification document, an interface mock-up, or an evaluation prototype. At the outcome of the review, the client provides feedback to the developers. This feedback may consist of a general approval or a request for detailed changes in functionality or schedule. Figure 3-14 depicts an example of an agenda for a client review.

Project review

The goals of a **project review** are for the project manager to assess status and for teams to review subsystem interfaces. Project reviews can also encourage the exchange of operational knowledge across teams, such as common problems encountered with tools or the system. The focus of the review depends on the deliverable under review. For system design, the decomposition and high-level subsystem interfaces are reviewed. For object design, the object interfaces are reviewed. For integration and testing, the tests and their results are reviewed.

A project review is typically conducted as a formal presentation during which each team presents its subsystem to the management or to teams that depend on the subsystem. The review

---

OWL Client acceptance test agenda

Date: 12/5
Time: 3–4:30 P.M.
Location: Forest Hall
Goal: review of the system by the client and identification of open issues
Overview
- Problem statement
- Design goals
- System architecture
- Demo 1: Remote user interface and control
- Demo 2: Site editor
- Demo 3: 3D Visualization and speech user interface
- Questions and answers
- Review wrap up

Figure 3-14   An example of an agenda for a client review.

is usually preceded by the release of a document (e.g., system design document) describing the aspects of the system under review (e.g., the subsystems interfaces). At the close of the review, the developers may negotiate changes in the interfaces and changes in schedule.

Peer review

The objective of code **inspections** and **walkthroughs** is to increase the quality of a subsystem through peer review (as opposed to management or client review). During walkthrough, a developer presents to the other members of her team line-by-line the code she has written. The other team members challenge any suspicious code and attempt to discover as many errors as possible. The role of the developer is to facilitate the presentation and answer the team's questions. During inspections, the members of the team focus on the compliance of the code with a predefined list of criteria. (For example, does the code implement the specified algorithm? Does the code correctly use dependent subsystem interfaces?) During inspections, the team leads the discussion, and the developer answers questions. The focus of the inspection or walkthrough is on the code, not on the programmer or the design.

Communication among participants is code based. The actual code is used as a common frame of reference. Inspections are similar to project reviews in their objective to increase quality and disseminate operational information. They differ from reviews in their formality, their limited audience, and their extended duration. Inspections and walkthroughs are widely used and have been effective at detecting defects early [Fagan, 1976]. We describe walkthroughs more fully in Chapter 11, *Testing*.

Status review

Unlike client and project reviews that focus on the system, **status reviews** focus on tasks. Status reviews are primarily conducted in a team (e.g., weekly) and occasionally conducted in a project (e.g., monthly). The objective of status reviews is to detect deviations from the task plan and to correct them. Status reviews also encourage developers to complete pending tasks. The review of task status encourages the discussion of open issues and unanticipated problems, and, thus, encourages informal communication among team members. Often, solutions to common issues can be shared and operational knowledge disseminated more effectively when discussed within the scope of a team (as opposed to within the scope of the project).

Status reviews represent an investment in person power. Increasing the effectiveness of reviews has a global impact on the team performance. Status meetings should have an agenda, available prior to the meeting, that describes the tasks and issues to be reviewed. This enables meeting participants to prepare for the meeting and redirect the agenda if an urgent issue arises. Minutes for each meeting should be taken by a designated participant in order to capture as much information (mainly status and decisions) as possible. Minutes are made available to the participants for review as early as possible after the meeting. This encourages the minute taker to complete the minutes and for team members who missed the meeting to catch up with team status. Meeting minutes are subsequently referenced when related tasks are discussed or when clarification is needed. Moreover, meeting minutes represent a portion of the project history that can be analyzed after the project is completed.

Brainstorming

The goal of the **brainstorming process** is to generate a large number of solutions to a problem, regardless of their merit, then evaluate them. Brainstorming is usually done in face-to-face meetings, but can also be done via E-mail or groupware. The fundamental idea behind brainstorming is that ideas, however invalid, proposed by any participant can trigger other ideas and proposals from other participants. In particularly difficult problems, the solution often comes from an idea that initially sounded very wrong. Brainstorming encourages thinking "outside the box." When many ideas have been generated, begin evaluating them. Brainstorming also has two beneficial side effects: evaluating proposals within the group will lead to more explicit evaluation criteria, and the brainstorming process itself has the effect of building consensus for the chosen solution.

Release

The goal of a **release** is to make a work product available to other project participants, often replacing an older version of the artifact. A release can be as simple as a two-line electronic message (see Figure 3-15), or it can consist of several pieces of information: the new version of the artifact, a list of changes made since the last release of the artifact, a list of problems or issues yet to be addressed, and an author.

Releases are used to make a large amount of information available in a controlled manner by batching, documenting, and reviewing many changes together. Project and client reviews are typically preceded by a release of one or more deliverables.

```
From: Al
Newsgroups: cs413.f96.architecture.discuss
Subject: SDD
Date: Thu, 25 Nov 03:39:12 -0500
Lines: 6
Message-ID: <3299B30.3507@andrew.cmu.edu>
MimeVersion: 1.0
Content-Type: text/plain; charset=us-ascii
Content-Transfer-Encoding: 7bit

An updated version of the API document for the Notification Subsystem can be found
here: http: //decaf/~al/FRIEND/notifapi.html

--Al
Notification Group Leader
```

Figure 3-15   An example of a release announcement.

We describe the management of versions of documents, models, and subsystems in Chapter 13, *Configuration Management*.

Postmortem review

Postmortem reviews focus on extracting lessons from the development team once the software is delivered. Postmortem reviews need to be conducted shortly after the end of the project so that minimal information is lost or distorted by subsequent experience. The end of the project is usually a good point in time to assess which techniques, methods, and tools have worked and have been critical to the success (or failure) of the system.

A postmortem can be conducted as a brainstorming session, a structured questionnaire followed by interviews, or individual reports written by teams (or participants). In all cases, the areas covered should include the tools, methods, organization, and procedures used by the project. Figure 3-16 is an example of questions that can be used during a postmortem.

Even if the results of post mortems are not disseminated through the company via formal channels (e.g., technical reports), they can still be disseminated indirectly to the project participants. Project participants are frequently reassigned to different projects or functions and often disseminate the lessons learned from the old project to other parts of the company. Hence, postmortem reviews are ideal for crystallizing the lessons learned from a recently completed (or canceled) project.

Question about problems that occurred	What kinds of communication and negotiation problems have emerged in the development of the system?
Question eliciting possible solutions to those problems	Speculate on what kind of information structure is needed for team-based design in conjunction with a model-based object-oriented software engineering methodology.
	Do you feel the forums provided (Discuss, Issues, Documents, Announce, etc.) solved this challenge? Identify issues with the information structure and propose solutions.
Question eliciting other aspects of the project that were either perceived as positive or could be improved	What observations and comments do you have about the project concerning: • your expectations at the beginning of the project and how they evolved • the goals of this project • the use of use cases • the life cycle used in the project • the project management (meetings, communication, etc.) • the documentation process
Open-ended catch-all question	In addition to the above questions, please feel free to discuss any other issues and proposed solutions that you feel are relevant.

Figure 3-16 An example of questions for a postmortem review.

3.4.2 Unplanned Communication

In an ideal project, all communication takes place during planned communication events. In practice, however, it is difficult to anticipate all information needs and plan all communications. Consider the following example:

> *Sunday, March 29, 1998.* Participants of the JAMES project are frantically preparing for the delivery of the system to their client. The client acceptance test is scheduled two days later, at 15:00 CED (Central European Daylight saving time). Daylight saving time has just come into effect, removing an hour of development. The client acceptance test is to be conducted as a high-bandwidth, three-way video conference among the client site in Stuttgart, the German developer site in Munich, and the American developer site in Pittsburgh, PA. The American team will participate in the conference starting at 9 A.M. EDT (Eastern Daylight Time). The agenda has been agreed. Each team has been allocated 12 minutes to present the functionality of its subsystem.
>
> *Later that evening.* The American developer visiting the German team realizes that Germany has switched to daylight saving time one week before the United States. Consequently, the time difference between Munich and Pittsburgh is 7 hours, not 6 hours, as originally thought. Hence, the video conference will actually take place at 8 A.M. EST (Eastern Standard Time). Less than 48 hours before the client acceptance test, the American team realized they were going to miss the deadline by one hour. It takes another day until all members of the American team are notified.

In the above example, basic information about when Germany and the United States switched to daylight saving time was not properly shared among the developer sites; a visiting member accidently stumbled upon this information. Retrospectively, this may appear as a gross oversight. However, in the heat of the preparation activities, JAMES project participants focused mostly on their own tasks, in the context of their own site, and did not step back and anticipate inter-site issues. Generally, issues resulting from a combination of seemingly isolated facts from different areas of the project are difficult to anticipate since no participants have a global overview of all the facts. Consequently, a project should be prepared to deal with unexpected situations, often under pressure. We call the communication resulting from such crises **unplanned communication events**. They include

- Requests for clarification
- Requests for changes
- Issue resolution.

We describe unplanned communication events in more detail next.

Request for clarification

Requests for clarification represent the bulk of the communication among developers, clients, and users. Requests for clarification are unplanned. A participant may request clarification about any aspect of the system that seems ambiguous. Requests for clarification may occur during informal meetings, phone calls, E-mail, or any other communication mechanism available to the project. Situations in which most information needs are handled through requests for clarifications are symptoms of a defective communication infrastructure. Such projects often face serious failures downstream resulting from misunderstandings and missing and misplaced information. Figure 3-17 depicts an example of request for clarification.

```
From: Alice
Newsgroups: cs413.architecture.discuss
Subject: SDD
Date: Thu, 10 Oct 23:12:48 -0400
Message-ID: <325DBB30.4380@andrew.cmu.edu>
MimeVersion: 1.0
Content-Type: text/plain; charset=us-ascii

When exactly would you like the System Design Document? There is some confusion over
the actual deadline: the schedule claims it to be October 22, while the template
says we have until November 7.
Thanks,
    Alice
```

Figure 3-17   An example of a request for clarification.

Request for change

During a **request for change**, a participant reports a problem and, in some cases, proposes solutions. The participant reports a problem with the system itself, its documentation, the development process, or the project organization. Requests for change are often formalized when the number of participants and the system size is substantial. Change requests contain a classification (e.g., severe defect, feature request, comment), a description of the problem, a description of the context in which it occurs, and any supporting material. Change request forms have been popularized by defects-tracking software. They can be applied to other aspects of the project (e.g., task plan, development process, testing procedures). Figure 3-18 depicts an example of change request form.

Issue resolution

Once problems have been reported and solutions proposed and evaluated, a single solution must be selected, communicated, and implemented. A flat organization may select a solution through the brainstorming process. A hierarchical organization or a crisis situation may require a single individual to select and impose a solution. In all cases, the decision needs to be documented and communicated to the relevant participants. Documentation of the resolution allows participants to refer back to the decision later in the project, in case of a misunderstanding. Effective communication of the decision enables participants to remain synchronized.

Header information for identifying the change	Report number: 1291 Date: 5/3 Author: Dave Synopsis: The FRIEND client crashes when empty forms are submitted.
Context information for locating the problem	Subsystem: User interface Version: 3.4.1 Classification: • missing/incorrect functionality • convention violation • **bug** • documentation error Severity: • **severe** • moderate • annoying
Description of the problem and the rationale for change	Description: Rationale:
Description of desired change	Proposed solution:

Figure 3-18   An example of a change request form.

An issue base can serve as a communication mechanism for supporting problem tracking and **issue resolution**. The issue base displayed in Figure 3-19 displays a list of messages exchanged as a result of issue resolutions. The message captions preceded by I: denote issues;

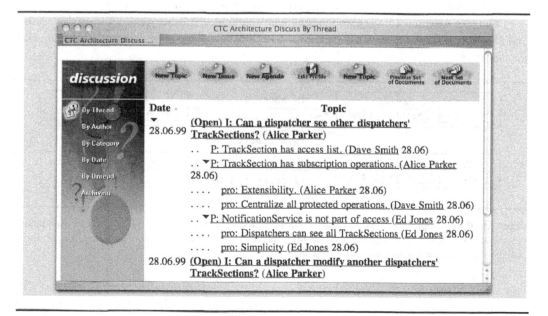

Figure 3-19   An example of an issue base (Domino Lotus Notes database).

those preceded by P: (for proposal) are suggested solutions; A+ and A- denote arguments for and against a solution. Finally, once issues are resolved, a single message, called a resolution, is posted to document the decision that was made on the issue. We describe issue bases and issue modeling in Chapter 12, *Rationale Management*.

3.4.3   Communication Mechanisms

A **communication mechanism** refers to a tool or procedure that can be used to transmit and receive information and support a communication event. Smoke signals and fax machines are communication mechanisms. Communication mechanisms are **synchronous** if they require both sender and receivers to be available at the same time. Otherwise, communication mechanisms are called **asynchronous**. Smoke signals are synchronous, whereas fax machines are asynchronous.

Both synchronous and asynchronous communication mechanisms can be used to support planned communication. For example, in Figure 3-20, either smoke signals or a fax machine can be used for a client review. On the other hand, only asynchronous communication mechanisms can be used for supporting unplanned communication: reporting a problem with smoke signals may lead to loss of information if nobody was scheduled to watch the smoke. Note that a single communication activity can be supported by several communication mechanisms: the requirements analysis document can be faxed to the client, and the client sends back her comments using smoke signals. Similarly, the same mechanism can support many communication events: the fax machine can receive either problem reports or comments from a client review.

Table 3-4 depicts the synchronous communication mechanisms we describe in this section and the communication events they support. Table 3-5 depicts the asynchronous communication mechanisms.

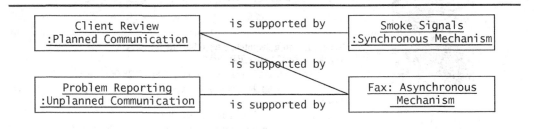

Figure 3-20 Examples of mechanisms (UML class diagram). Both planned and unplanned communication can be supported by asynchronous mechanisms. Unplanned communication, however, can only be supported by asynchronous mechanisms.

Table 3-4 Examples of synchronous mechanisms of communication.

Mechanism	Supported communication events
Hallway conversations	Request for clarification Request for change
Questionnaires and structured interviews	Problem definition Postmortem review
Meetings (face-to-face, telephone, video)	Problem definition Client review Project review Peer review Status review Postmortem review Brainstorming Issue resolution
Synchronous groupware	Client review Project review Peer review Brainstorming Issue resolution

Table 3-5 Examples of asynchronous mechanisms of communication.

Mechanism	Supported communication events
Electronic mail	Change request Brainstorming
Newsgroups	Change request Brainstorming
World Wide Web	Release Asynchronous peer reviews Change request Brainstorming
Lotus Notes	Release Asynchronous peer reviews Change request Brainstorming

Hallway conversations

Hallway conversations are unplanned, informal exchanges of information based on opportunity. Two participants meet by accident and take advantage of the situation to exchange information. The daylight saving time problem we described before was discovered during such a hallway conversation. Below is another example:

> Two project participants, Sally and Bob, meet at the coffee machine. Sally, member of the user interface team, remembers that Bob is a member of the notification team, which is responsible for the communication between the client subsystems and the server. All morning Sally has been experiencing random failures when receiving packets from the server. She is not sure if the problem comes from the server, the communication subsystem, or her code. Bob answers that he was not aware that the server was being used at this time and that he had been testing a new revision of the communication system, explaining the behavior that Sally had observed. Bob had bypassed configuration management policy to save time.

Hallway conversations represent a substantial part in the overall project communication. They are cheap and effective for resolving simple problems that are caused by a lack of coordination between project members. In addition, they are also effective in supporting the exchange of operational knowledge, such as frequently asked questions about tools, procedures, or the location of project information. The drawbacks of hallway conversations include their small audience and lack of history: important information can be lost, and misunderstandings may occur when the content of the conversation is relayed to other participants. Moreover, no document, database, or electronic message can be accessed when referring to a decision that was made and communicated during a hallway conversation. Thus important hallway decisions should be followed up by an E-mail covering the topic of the conversation for the record.

Questionnaires and structured interviews

The objective of a **questionnaire** is to elicit information from one or more persons in a structured manner. Questionnaires are typically used for eliciting domain knowledge from users and experts, understanding user requirements and priorities. They can also be used for extracting lessons learned during a postmortem review. Questionnaires can include both multiple-choice questions and open-ended questions. Questionnaires have the advantage of eliciting reliable information at minimal cost to the user. Questionnaires can be answered by users independently, then reviewed and analyzed by the analyst or developer. Clarifications of ambiguous or incomplete answers are then obtained during a **structured interview**. The drawback of questionnaires is that they are difficult to design. However, the consequences of requirements errors and misunderstandings between the client and the developer often justify their cost. Subsequently, sufficient information is gathered about the domain and a requirements analysis document is written, so that most revisions to the systems and additional issues are addressed in client reviews. [Barone & Switzer, 1995] provides more information about designing questionnaires and interviews.

Meetings

Face-to-face **meetings** enable a number of participants to share, review, and negotiate issues and solutions. To date, meetings are the only mechanism that allow effective resolution of issues and the building of consensus. The drawback of meetings is their cost in resources and the difficulty in managing them. In order to increase the information transfer and the number of decisions made during a meeting, roles are assigned to selected participants:

- The **facilitator** is responsible for organizing the meeting and guiding its execution. The facilitator writes an agenda describing the objective and the scope of the meeting. The agenda is generally released before the meeting for preview by its participants. This allows participants to decide whether the meeting is relevant to them and to allow preparation of support material for the meeting.

- The **minute taker** is responsible for recording the meeting. The minute taker may take notes on paper or on a laptop computer, organize them after the meeting, and release them shortly after the meeting for review by the meeting participants. This enables the participants to reiterate their commitment to the outcome of the meeting. The written record of the meeting also makes it easier for participants to share information with members who were not present at the meeting.

- The **timekeeper** is responsible for keeping track of time and notifying the facilitator if a discussion consumes more time than is allocated by the agenda.

A **meeting agenda** consists of at least three sections: a header identifying the planned meeting location, time, and participants; a list of items participants will report on; and a list of issues to be discussed and resolved in the meeting. Each information-sharing and discussion item is also assigned a time that allows the timekeeper to ensure that the meeting ends on time. Figure 3-21 depicts a meeting agenda. Figure 3-22 depicts a poor one.

A set of **meeting minutes** consists of three sections that correspond to the sections of the agenda. In addition, meeting minutes include a section describing the action items resulting from the meeting; these are items describing actions to be taken by the meeting participants as a consequence of the meeting. The header section contains the actual meeting location, time, and participants. The information-sharing item section contains the information that was shared during the meeting. The decision-item section contains a record of the decisions made and not made. Figure 3-23 is an example of meeting minutes.

Although meetings conducted in a single location are most efficient, it is possible to conduct meetings when participants are distributed geographically by using teleconferencing or video conferencing. This reduces costs at the expense of a lower bandwidth and lower reliability. A well-structured agenda available prior to the meeting becomes crucial as floor control becomes difficult with lower audio and visual quality. Also, knowledge of the individual voices and particularities improves communication among participants.

Header information identifying the meeting and audience	**When and Where** **Date**: 1/30 **Start**: 4:30 P.M. **End**: 5:30 P.M. **Room**: WH, 3420	**Role** **Primary Facilitator**: Peter **Timekeeper**: Dave **Minute Taker**: Ed
Desired outcome of the meeting	**1. Objective** Resolve any requirements issues that prevent us from starting prototyping.	
Action items to be reported on	**2. Status [Allocated Time: 15 minutes]** Dave: State of command parsing code	
Issues scheduled to be discussed (and resolved) during the meeting	**3. Discussion items [Allocated Time: 35 minutes]** 3.1 How to deal with arbitrarily formatted input data sets? 3.2 How to deal with output data? 3.3 Command parsing code (modifiability, backward compatibility)	
The wrap-up period is the same for all meetings	**4. Wrap up [Allocated Time: 5 minutes]** 4.1 Review and assign new action items 4.2 Meeting critique	

Figure 3-21   An example of a meeting agenda.

Open-ended meetings take more time than necessary.	**When and Where** **Date**: 1/30 **Start**: 4:30 P.M. **End**: open **Room**: WH 3420	**Role** **Primary Facilitator**: Peter **Timekeeper**: Dave **Minute Taker**: Ed
This objective is difficult to achieve and cannot be verified.	**1. Objective** Resolve open issues	
Lack of context: what were Dave's action items?	**2. Status [Allocated Time: 15 minutes]** Dave: Dave's action items	
Lack of content: what are the current issues in each of these activities?	**3. Discussion items [Allocated Time: 35 minutes]** 3.1 Requirements issues 3.2 Design issues 3.3 Implementation issues	
	4. Wrap up [Allocated Time: 5 minutes] 4.1 Review and assign new action items 4.2 Meeting critique	

Figure 3-22   An example of poor meeting agenda.

Header information identifying the meeting and audience	**When and Where**	**Role**
	Date: 1/30	**Primary Facilitator**: Peter
	Start: 4:30 P.M.	**Timekeeper**: Dave
	End: 6:00 P.M.	**Minute Taker**: Ed
	Room: WH 3420	**Attending**: Ed, Dave, Mary, Peter, Alice

Verbatim from agenda

1. Objective

...

Summary of the information that was exchanged

2. Status

...

Record of issue discussion and resolution

3. Discussion

3.1 Command parsing code is a 1200–1300 line if statement. This makes it fairly hard to add new commands or to modify existing commands without breaking backward compatibility with existing clients.

Proposals: 1) Restructure the command parsing code by assigning one object per kind of command. 2) Pass all command arguments by name. The latter would make it easier to maintain backward compatibility. On the other hand, this would increase the size of the commands, thus increasing the size of the command file.

Resolution: Restructure code for now. Revisit this issue if backward compatibility is really an issue (the calling code might be rewritten anyway). See AI[1].

...

Discussion of the other issues omitted for brevity

Additions and modifications to the task plan

4. Wrap up

AI[1] For: Dave.

Revisit command parsing code. Emphasis on modularity. Coordinate with Bill from the database group (who might assume backward compatibility).

...

Other action items and meeting critique omitted for brevity

...

Figure 3-23   An example of meeting minutes.

When writing a meeting agenda, the facilitator should be as concrete as possible without adding to the length of the agenda. It is often tempting to develop a generic template agenda and reuse it systematically without modifications. This has the drawback of taking the substance out of the meeting process, turning it into a bureaucratic procedure. Figure 3-22 is an example of contentless agenda. By only modifying the header, this agenda could apply to most subsystem meetings, and thus, does not convey any new information to the participants.

Groupware

Same time, different place groupware are tools that allow distributed users to collaborate synchronously. For a long time, these tools were only available in the realm of research [Grudin, 1988], [Borghoff & Schlichter, 2000], but they become more common in the commercial world with the popularization of Internet chatrooms. Tools such as Netmeeting [Microsoft] enable a group of participants to collaborate synchronously over a shared workspace. They provide a meeting metaphor: users "enter" a chat room, which then allows them to view a graphic or a text under consideration. All users see the same state. Usually only one can modify it at any one time. Floor control can be anarchic (whoever takes the floor has it) or sequential (whoever has the floor relinquishes it to the next user).

A weakness of same-time groupware is the difficulty in coordinating users. Typing takes more time than users are prepared to invest. Written words need to be chosen more carefully, given that nonverbal information is lost. Moreover, slight glitches in the network connection may represent enough interference for user coordination to be lost. While video-based Internet conferencing tools such as Lotus Sametime [Lotus] and increases in network bandwidth promise to alleviate these problems, synchronous groupware tools have not quite reached a level of maturity sufficient for everyday use in the workplace.

In all cases, different-place collaboration is still a nontrivial exercise that must be scripted and planned in advance. Collaborative development of procedures for supporting collaboration is a challenging task when proximity and nonverbal communication are not available.

Different time, different place groupware, or simply, **asynchronous groupware**, has had more success during the past two decades. In its simplest form, newsgroups enable users to discuss issues publicly by contributing messages to discussion threads. The World Wide Web enables the quick access to large repositories of documents acquired from various sources.

Currently, in any software engineering project including more than a couple of people, participants use a combination of forums, repositories, calendars, and address books ranging from free tools for small projects to commercial tools supporting large organizations. A free tool such as Yahoo Groups [Yahoo] allows a team to set up a place quickly to share photos and files, plan events, send newsletters, and discuss topics. BSCW (Basic Support for Cooperative Work) [BSCW] also enables collaboration over the Web and supports document upload, event notification, and team management. Wiki [Wiki] is another simple but powerful Web-based collaboration platform. An interesting feature in Wiki is that all the pages are open for anyone to edit. The system creates cross-reference hyperlinks between web pages automatically. Commercial tools such as Microsoft's Sharepoint Team Services [Microsoft] provide groupware support for Microsoft Office users. Workflow engines such as Lotus Notes [Lotus] provide replication mechanisms, repository features, and an address book making public organizational structures. Repetitive procedures can be automated. Formalized activities, such as the asynchronous review of a document by different stakeholders, can be effectively supported by sending notices to each participant as the document advances through the review pipeline.

3.5   Organizational Activities

We now examine the activities of a developer when joining a project organization and its communication infrastructure. The activities include

- Joining a Team (Section 3.5.1)
- Joining the Communication Infrastructure (Section 3.5.2)
- Attending Team Status Meetings (Section 3.5.3)
- Organizing Client and Project Reviews (Section 3.5.4).

We describe these activities for an example project, focusing on the development of a new system with multiple teams.

3.5.1   Joining a Team

During the project definition phase, the project manager identified a **subsystem team** for each subsystem in the initial decomposition of the software architecture. Additionally, **cross-functional teams** (e.g., architecture team, integration team) are formed to support the subsystem teams. Each team has a team leader who was also already selected during the project definition phase. An important activity during the project start phase is now the assignments of participants to teams.

Based on the interests and skills of the team members, the project manager and team leaders assign them to a team. Each subsystem team also has to nominate a liaison to the cross-functional teams to facilitate information transfer among teams. Table 3-6 depicts an example of role assignment to participants for the database team of the OWL project. The project manager and team leader also determine the training needs for the participants and teams.

3.5.2   Joining the Communication Infrastructure

Two sets of forums are created to support project and team communication, respectively. Members subscribe to all project forums and to their team's forums. Project forums include

- *Announce*. Major events (e.g., review agendas, releases) are announced by management by posting to this forum. Only management can post announcements to this forum; project members can post replies and read all documents.
- *Discuss*. Project-level requests for clarification and requests for change are posted in this forum. Discussion about the requests (e.g., arguments and alternate solutions) are posted as replies to the original messages. All project members can post to this forum and read its documents.
- *Issues*. Open issues and their current state are posted in this forum. All project members can post to this forum and read its documents.

Table 3-6   Role assignment, skills, and training needs for the database team of OWL.

Participant	Roles	Skills	Training needs
Alice	Team leader	Management: team leader Programming: C Configuration management	UML Communication skills
John	Architecture liaison Implementor	Programming: C++ Modeling: UML	Java
Mary	Configuration manager Implementor	Programming: C++, Java Modeling: Entity relationship Databases: relational Configuration management	Object-oriented databases UML modeling
Chris	Implementor	Programming: C++, Java Modeling: Entity relationship Databases: object-oriented	UML modeling
Sam	Facilities management liaison Tester	Programming: C++ Testing: whitebox, blackbox	Inspections Java

- *Documents.* The latest versions of the project deliverables (e.g., Requirements Analysis Document, System Design Document) and other internal project documents (e.g., Software Project Management Plan) are posted in this forum. Only the documentation team can post documents to this forum. All project members can post replies (i.e., annotations to the documents) and read the documents.
- *Equipment list.* This forum contains descriptions of equipment and its status (e.g., availability, current borrower). Only the equipment manager can post to this forum.

The team forums are similar to the project forums, except that they support team communication. Team forums include team discussion, team issues, and team documents. Each project member may read any other team's forum. Team members can post only to their own team's forum. Note that the forums can be created as soon as the subsystem decomposition is relatively stable. Once forums and group accesses are set up, accounts for individual members can be created as the project is staffed.

3.5.3   Attending Team Status Meetings

An important part of a software project is the weekly team meeting. It allows all teams to participate in status reviews, brainstorming, and issue resolution. The weekly team meeting is organized and captured as described in Section 3.4.1. Particularly important is the first time the team meets. Few members will know each other socially or professionally. Moreover, few of them are familiar with formal meeting roles and procedures. Management takes the opportunity of the first weekly team meeting to introduce meeting procedures, explain the importance of these procedures, and motivate team members in their use. Figure 3-24 displays the agenda posted by the management for the first meeting.

The goal of the first meeting is to train participants by example. Discussion about the procedures is encouraged. The meeting and group roles are explained to the participants and assigned by the team for the rest of the project. The role of facilitator is emphasized in that its purpose is to increase the efficiency of the meeting, not to impose decisions. Team members are taught that any meeting participant can take the role of secondary facilitator; that is, any participant can intervene in the discussion in order to put the meeting back within the scope of the agenda. Participants are taught keyword phrases for standard situations. For example, "Let me play the role of secondary facilitator" stands for *The scope of the current discussion is outside the agenda. Let us get back on track.* "Can we pop up a level?" stands for *The discussion has delved into a level of detail that is unnecessary for this audience. Actually, most of us are already lost.* More generally, team members are taught that it is easy to waste time during a meeting, and that the primary goal of any meeting is to communicate efficiently and accurately so that they can go back to their respective tasks.

Management rotates roles on a regular basis so that all participants have the opportunity to fill every role. This has the advantage of creating redundant skills in the project team and increases information sharing. The drawback is that, in the short term, participants will not have time to mature into their roles and thus will not become highly effective at any given task. Requiring early role assignment, role rotation, and fixed meeting procedures may introduce turbulence at the beginning of the project, but represents a healthy investment in the long term. Everyday meeting and communication skills should be well in place before crisis-driven communication needs surface during the implementation and code activities.

The teams are responsible for assigning meeting roles and posting them in their respective team's *Announce* forum. One day before the status meeting, the meeting facilitator is required to post in the team's *Announce* forum the initial draft of the agenda, composed of action items taken from the previous meeting's minutes and issues taken from the *Issues* forum. The minute taker is required to post the minutes within a day of the meeting, as a reply to the corresponding agenda. Other team members may comment on the agenda and minutes by posting replies. The facilitator or the minute taker may then amend the corresponding document.

Meeting roles and procedures are often perceived as overhead. Management is aware of that perception and invests time in the beginning of the project to illustrate the benefits of the meeting procedures. In the first weeks of the project, management systematically reviews the agendas and minutes of the first few weekly meetings, suggests time-saving improvements to the facilitators (e.g., keeping an active document containing open issues and active action items from which the agenda can be cut and pasted), and to the minute takers (e.g., focusing on capturing the action items and unresolved issues first, then focusing on the discussion).

When and Where	Role
Date: 1/9	**Primary Facilitator**: Alice
Start: 4:30 P.M.	**Timekeeper**: Dave
End: 5:30 P.M.	**Minute Taker**: Ed
Building: Wean Hall	
Room: 3420	

1. Objective

Become familiar with project management roles for a medium-scale project with a two-level hierarchy. In particular:

- Understand the difference between a role and a person
- Group roles are assigned to people
- Meeting times are finalized
- First set of action items for next meeting

2. Status and information sharing [Allocated time: 40 minutes]

2.1. How to organize a meeting

Meeting ground rules:

- Active listening
- Active participating
- Punctual attendance
- No one-on-one or side meetings
- Respect the agenda
- Keep time
- Willingness to reach consensus
- Freedom to check process and ground rules

Meeting roles:

- Primary Facilitator
- Timekeeper
- Minute taker
- Scribe

2.2 Following the agenda

Omitted for brevity

3. Discussion items [Allocated time: 15 minutes]

3.1 Team address book

3.2 Meeting roles assignments

3.3 Group roles assignment

4. Wrap up [Allocated time: 5 minutes]

4.1 Review and assign new action items

4.2 Meeting critique

Figure 3-24   First weekly team meeting agenda.

3.5.4   Organizing Client and Project Reviews

Client reviews are conducted after the release of the requirements analysis document and after the delivery of the system. Project reviews are conducted to review the system design documents, the detailed object design, and the test. A project review may also be conducted before delivery as a dry run for the client acceptance test.

Project management schedules all reviews during the planning phase (Table 3-7).

Table 3-7   An example of a review schedule.

Review	Date	Deliverable (release due 1 week before review)
Client review	week 7	Requirements Analysis Document
System design review	week 9	System Design Document
Object design review	week 13 (2 sessions)	Object Design Document
Internal review	week 16	Unit and integration tests
Client acceptance test dry run	week 17	All project deliverables
Client acceptance test	week 17	All project deliverables

Management also introduces procedures for organizing reviews:

1. The deliverables being reviewed are released one week[1] prior to the review.
2. Shortly after the release, management publishes a draft agenda listing presentation topics for each team. The initial draft of the agenda is posted in the *Announce* forum.
3. Candidate presenters reply to the original agendas and refine the presentation topic. Management modifies the agenda based on the replies.
4. Presenters submit their slides by replying to the agenda and including the slides in the reply. The management collates the slides before the presentation and updates the agenda.

The management also assigns the responsibility of minute taker, using the same procedure, to a project member, who will be briefed on how to take minutes by management. During the review, the minute taker uses a laptop and carefully records all the questions and

---

1. This leaves slack time for late documents. Realistically, some deliverables are delivered as late as one day before the review. The critical issues here are: (1) Can the deliverable be made available to all review participants? and (2) Do they have enough time to review them?

answers from the audience. Finally, within a day of the review, the minute taker and management merge their notes and generate a list of action items to be completed as a result of the review and a list of open issues that could not be resolved during the review. These post-processed minutes are posted on the *Announce* forum.

The emphasis on using the communication infrastructure for coordinating the organization of the review and the submission of slides enables more information to be captured, and thus, more information is accessible to all participants in the long run.

3.6 Further Readings

Researchers and practitioners have long noted the importance of communication in software engineering. As projects grow larger and more complex, however, communication becomes increasingly more critical.

[Curtis et al., 1988] is a landmark paper identifying and classifying communication problems in software development. In a field study of 17 large government projects, researchers observe that documentation does not reduce the need for communication, in particular; during the early phases of the project, when stakeholders define terms, coordinate their representational conventions, and create informal communication networks. The study also shows that obstacles to informal communication (e.g., organizational barriers and geographical distance) can lead to misunderstandings in design conventions and rationale.

[Kraut & Streeter, 1995], another landmark paper in the field, observe that communication (e.g., meeting, formal specifications, peer reviews) is useful for routine coordination, whereas informal communication (e.g., hallway conversations, telephone calls, brainstorming) is needed in the face of uncertainty and unanticipated problems, which are typical of software development. In their study, they observe that the need for informal communication increases dramatically as the size and complexity of the software increases.

As face-to-face (or video conference) meetings are still the principal means of communication among project participants—for communicating status, identifying conflicts, and resolving issues—meeting skills are required of all software engineers in order to conduct meetings efficiently and to avoid information loss. However, meeting procedures and meeting skills are usually not included in standard software engineering curricula. *How to make meetings work* [Doyle & Straus, 1982] and *Mining Group Gold* [Kayser, 1990] (from which we derived the agenda and minutes templates for this chapter) describe many useful procedures and heuristics for conducting efficient meetings.

Getting To Yes [Fischer et al., 1991] explains the mechanisms of negotiation and proposes approaches to avoid deadlocks while addressing the conflicts that prompted the negotiation. *Interviewing: Art and Skill* [Barone & Switzer, 1995] provides guidance on how to design a questionnaire and conduct an interview.

Computer-Supported Collaborative Work [Borghoff & Schlichter, 2000] provides a good introduction to the discipline and to groupware in general. Moreover, it can serve as a guide for users and software engineers interested in addressing communication issues with groupware.

3.7 Exercises

3-1 What is the difference between a role and a participant?

3-2 Can a role be shared between two or more participants? Why or why not?

3-3 What is the difference between a client and an end user?

3-4 To which roles would you assign the following tasks?

- Change a subsystem interface to accommodate a new requirement.
- Communicate the subsystem interface change to other teams.
- Change the documentation as a result of the interface change.
- Design a test suite to find defects introduced by the change.
- Ensure that the change is completed on schedule.

3-5 You are responsible for coordinating the development of a system for processing credit applications for a bank. In what roles would the following project participants be able to contribute most to the project?

- a bank employee responsible for processing credit applications
- the manager of the information technology group at the bank, who contracted the system
- a freelancer who developed similar systems in the past
- a technical writer
- you.

3-6 Draw a UML activity diagram representing the meeting process described in Section 3.4.1. Focus in particular on the work products generated before and after the meeting, such as the agenda and the meeting minutes. Use swimlanes to represent roles.

3-7 What is the difference between a work package and a work product? When is a work package defined? When is a work product defined? Consider an assignment where two students collaborate to plan and develop a system for sorting lists of names using two different sort algorithms. The deliverables for the assignment are the source code, the system documentation, and a manual for other developers explaining how new sorting algorithms can be integrated into the code. Give examples of work packages and work products in this project.

3-8 What is the difference between a cross-functional team and a subsystem team? Provide examples and justify your choices.

3-9 As many critical communication events are planned (e.g., client reviews, project reviews, peer reviews), why is there still a need for unplanned communication events (e.g., request for clarification, request for change, issue resolution)?

3-10 Select at random a working day in your work week. Log all activities that qualify as communication activities (e.g., taking to friends over coffee, obtaining information from a fellow student, providing information, negotiating, advertising, browsing the web). Which fraction of your working day does communication represent?

3-11   You are a member of the user interface team. You are responsible for designing and implementing forms that collect information about users of the system (e.g., first name, last name, address, E-mail address, level of expertise). The information you are collecting is stored in the database and used by the reporting subsystem. You are not sure which fields are required information and which are optional. How do you find out?

3-12   You have been reassigned from the user interface team to the database team due to staff shortages and replanning. The implementation phase is well underway. In which role would you be most proficient, given your knowledge of the user interface design and implementation?

3-13   Assume the development platform is Unix and the documentation team writes on the Macintosh platform. The client requires the documents to be available on the Windows platform. Developers produce the design documentation using Adobe FrameMaker. The documentation team uses Microsoft Word for the user-level documentation. The client submits corrections on hardcopies and does not need to modify the delivered documents. How could the information flow between the developers, the technical writers, and the client be set up (e.g., format, tools, etc.) such that duplication of files is minimized, while everybody's tool preferences and platform requirements are still satisfied?

3-14   Which changes in the organization and communication infrastructure would you recommend for a successor of the Ariane 5 project as a consequence of the Ariane 501 failure described at the beginning of this chapter?

References

[Barone & Switzer, 1995]   J.T.T. Barone & J. Switzer, *Interviewing: Art and Skill*, Allyn & Bacon, 1995.

[Borghoff & Schlichter, 2000]   U.W. Borghoff & J. Schlichter, *Computer Supported Cooperative Work: An Introduction into Distributed Applications*, Springer-Verlag. 2000.

[BSCW]   Basic Support for Cooperative Work, http://bscw.gmd.de.

[Curtis et al., 1988]   B. Curtis, H. Krasner, & N. Iscoe, "A field study of the software design process for large systems," *Communications of the ACM*, Vol. 31, No. 11, 1268–87, 1988.

[Doyle & Straus, 1982]   M. Doyle & D. Straus, *How to make meetings work*, The Berkeley Publishing Group, New York, NY, 1982.

[Fagan, 1976]   M. E. Fagan, "Design and code inspections to reduce errors in program development," *IBM System Journal*, Vol. 15, No. 3, pp. 182–211, 1976.

[Fischer et al., 1991]   R. Fisher, W. Ury, & B. Patton, *Getting to Yes: Negotiating Agreement Without Giving In*, 2nd ed., Penguin Books, 1991.

[Gantt, 1910]   H. L. Gantt, "Work, wages, and profits," *The Engineering Magazine*, New York, 1910.

[Grudin, 1988]   J. Grudin, "Why CSCW applications fail: Problems in design and evaluation of organization interfaces," in *Proceedings CSCW'88*, Portland, OR, 1988.

[Kayser, 1990]   T. A. Kayser, *Mining Group Gold*, Serif, El Segundo, CA, 1990.

[Kraut & Streeter, 1995]   R.E. Kraut & L.A. Streeter, "Coordination in software development," *Communications of the ACM*, Vol. 38, No. 3, March 1995.

[Lions, 1996]   J.-L. Lions, *ARIANE 5 Flight 501 Failure: Report by the Inquiry Board*, http://www.esrin.esa.it/htdocs/tidc/Press/Press96/ariane5rep.html, 1996.

[Lotus]   Lotus, http://www.lotus.com/.

[Microsoft]   Microsoft, http://www.microsoft.com/.

[OWL, 1996]   *OWL Project Documentation*, School of Computer Science, Carnegie Mellon University, Pittsburgh, PA, 1996.

[Wiki]   Wiki, http://c2.com/cgi/wiki?WikiWikiWeb.

[Yahoo]   Yahoo, http://groups.yahoo.com/.

PART II
Dealing with Complexity

4

Requirements Elicitation

A common mistake that people make when trying to design something completely foolproof is to underestimate the ingenuity of complete fools.

—Douglas Adams, in *Mostly Harmless*

A **requirement** is a feature that the system must have or a constraint that it must satisfy to be accepted by the client. **Requirements engineering** aims at defining the requirements of the system under construction. Requirements engineering includes two main activities; *requirements elicitation*, which results in the specification of the system that the client understands, and *analysis*, which results in an analysis model that the developers can unambiguously interpret. Requirements elicitation is the more challenging of the two because it requires the collaboration of several groups of participants with different backgrounds. On the one hand, the client and the users are experts in their domain and have a general idea of what the system should do, but they often have little experience in software development. On the other hand, the developers have experience in building systems, but often have little knowledge of the everyday environment of the users.

Scenarios and use cases provide tools for bridging this gap. A *scenario* describes an example of system use in terms of a series of interactions between the user and the system. A *use case* is an abstraction that describes a class of scenarios. Both scenarios and use cases are written in natural language, a form that is understandable to the user.

In this chapter, we focus on scenario-based requirements elicitation. Developers elicit requirements by observing and interviewing users. Developers first represent the user's current work processes as as-is scenarios, then develop visionary scenarios describing the functionality to be provided by the future system. The client and users validate the system description by reviewing the scenarios and by testing small prototypes provided by the developers. As the definition of the system matures and stabilizes, developers and the client agree on a requirements specification in the form of functional requirements, nonfunctional requirements, use cases, and scenarios.

4.1 Introduction: Usability Examples

Feet or miles?[a]

During a laser experiment, a laser beam was directed at a mirror on the Space Shuttle Discovery. The test called for the laser beam to be reflected back toward a mountain top. The user entered the elevation of the mountain as "10,023," assuming the units of the input were in feet. The computer interpreted the number in miles and the laser beam was reflected away from Earth, toward a hypothetical mountain 10,023 miles high.

Decimal point versus thousand separator

In the United States, decimal points are represented by a period (".") and thousand separators are represented by a comma (","). In Germany, the decimal point is represented by a comma and the thousand separator by a period. Assume a user in Germany, aware of both conventions, is viewing an online catalog with prices listed in dollars. Which convention should be used to avoid confusion?

Standard patterns

In the Emacs text editor, the command <Control-x><Control-c> exits the program. If any files need to be saved, the editor will ask the user, "Save file myDocument.txt? (y or n)". If the user answers y, the editor saves the file prior to exiting. Many users rely on this pattern and systematically type the sequence <Control-x><Control-c> followed by a "y" when exiting an editor. Other editors, however, ask when exiting the question: "Are you sure you want to exit? (y or n)". When users switch from Emacs to such an editor, they will fail to save their work until they manage to break this pattern.

---

a.   Examples from [Nielsen, 1993] and [Neumann, 1995].

Requirements elicitation is about communication among developers, clients, and users to define a new system. Failure to communicate and understand each others' domains results in a system that is difficult to use or that simply fails to support the user's work. Errors introduced during requirements elicitation are expensive to correct, as they are usually discovered late in the process, often as late as delivery. Such errors include missing functionality that the system should have supported, functionality that was incorrectly specified, user interfaces that are misleading or unusable, and obsolete functionality. Requirements elicitation methods aim at improving communication among developers, clients, and users. Developers construct a model of the application domain by observing users in their environment. Developers select a representation that is understandable by the clients and users (e.g., scenarios and use cases). Developers validate the application domain model by constructing simple prototypes of the user interface and collecting feedback from potential users. An example of a simple prototype is the layout of a user interface with menu items and buttons. The potential user can manipulate the menu items and buttons to get a feeling for the usage of the system, but there is no actual response after buttons are clicked, because the required functionality is not implemented.

Section 4.2 provides an overview of requirements elicitation and its relationship to the other development activities. Section 4.3 defines the concepts used in this chapter. Section 4.4 discusses the activities of requirements elicitation. Section 4.5 discusses the management activities related to requirements elicitation. Section 4.6 discusses the ARENA case study.

4.2 An Overview of Requirements Elicitation

Requirements elicitation focuses on describing the purpose of the system. The client, the developers, and the users identify a problem area and define a system that addresses the problem. Such a definition is called a **requirements specification** and serves as a contract between the client and the developers. The requirements specification is structured and formalized during analysis (Chapter 5, *Analysis*) to produce an **analysis model** (see Figure 4-1). Both requirements specification and analysis model represent the same information. They differ only in the language and notation they use; the requirements specification is written in natural language, whereas the analysis model is usually expressed in a formal or semiformal notation. The requirements specification supports the communication with the client and users. The analysis model supports the communication among developers. They are both models of the system in the sense that they attempt to represent accurately the external aspects of the system. Given that both models represent the same aspects of the system, requirements elicitation and analysis occur concurrently and iteratively.

Requirements elicitation and analysis focus only on the user's view of the system. For example, the system functionality, the interaction between the user and the system, the errors that the system can detect and handle, and the environmental conditions in which the system functions are part of the requirements. The system structure, the implementation technology selected to build the system, the system design, the development methodology, and other aspects not directly visible to the user are not part of the requirements.

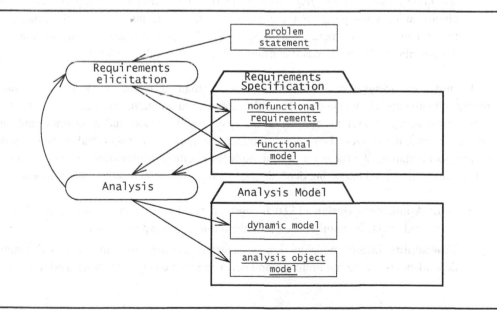

Figure 4-1   Products of requirements elicitation and analysis (UML activity diagram).

Requirements elicitation includes the following activities:

- *Identifying actors*. During this activity, developers identify the different types of users the future system will support.

- *Identifying scenarios*. During this activity, developers observe users and develop a set of detailed scenarios for typical functionality provided by the future system. Scenarios are concrete examples of the future system in use. Developers use these scenarios to communicate with the user and deepen their understanding of the application domain.

- *Identifying use cases*. Once developers and users agree on a set of scenarios, developers derive from the scenarios a set of use cases that completely represent the future system. Whereas scenarios are concrete examples illustrating a single case, use cases are abstractions describing all possible cases. When describing use cases, developers determine the scope of the system.

- *Refining use cases*. During this activity, developers ensure that the requirements specification is complete by detailing each use case and describing the behavior of the system in the presence of errors and exceptional conditions.

- *Identifying relationships among use cases*. During this activity, developers identify dependencies among use cases. They also consolidate the use case model by factoring out common functionality. This ensures that the requirements specification is consistent.

- *Identifying nonfunctional requirements*. During this activity, developers, users, and clients agree on aspects that are visible to the user, but not directly related to functionality. These include constraints on the performance of the system, its documentation, the resources it consumes, its security, and its quality.

During requirements elicitation, developers access many different sources of information, including client-supplied documents about the application domain, manuals and technical documentation of legacy systems that the future system will replace, and most important, the users and clients themselves. Developers interact the most with users and clients during requirements elicitation. We focus on two methods for eliciting information, making decisions with users and clients, and managing dependencies among requirements and other artifacts:

- **Joint Application Design (JAD)** focuses on building consensus among developers, users, and clients by jointly developing the requirements specification.[1]

- **Traceability** focuses on recording, structuring, linking, grouping, and maintaining dependencies among requirements and between requirements and other work products.

---

1. Note that the use of the term "design" in JAD is a misnomer: it has nothing to do with our use of the term in the subsequent chapters on system and object design.

4.3 Requirements Elicitation Concepts

In this section, we describe the main requirements elicitation concepts used in this chapter. In particular, we describe

- Functional Requirements (Section 4.3.1)
- Nonfunctional Requirements (Section 4.3.2)
- Completeness, Consistency, Clarity, and Correctness (Section 4.3.3)
- Realism, Verifiability, and Traceability (Section 4.3.4)
- Greenfield Engineering, Reengineering, and Interface Engineering (Section 4.3.5).

We describe the requirements elicitation activities in Section 4.4.

4.3.1 Functional Requirements

Functional requirements describe the interactions between the system and its environment independent of its implementation. The environment includes the user and any other external system with which the system interacts. For example, Figure 4-2 is an example of functional requirements for SatWatch, a watch that resets itself without user intervention:

SatWatch is a wrist watch that displays the time based on its current location. SatWatch uses GPS satellites (Global Positioning System) to determine its location and internal data structures to convert this location into a time zone.

The information stored in SatWatch and its accuracy measuring time is such that the watch owner never needs to reset the time. SatWatch adjusts the time and date displayed as the watch owner crosses time zones and political boundaries. For this reason, SatWatch has no buttons or controls available to the user.

SatWatch determines its location using GPS satellites and, as such, suffers from the same limitations as all other GPS devices (e.g., inability to determine location at certain times of the day in mountainous regions). During blackout periods, SatWatch assumes that it does not cross a time zone or a political boundary. SatWatch corrects its time zone as soon as a blackout period ends.

SatWatch has a two-line display showing, on the top line, the time (hour, minute, second, time zone) and on the bottom line, the date (day, date, month, year). The display technology used is such that the watch owner can see the time and date even under poor light conditions.

When political boundaries change, the watch owner may upgrade the software of the watch using the WebifyWatch device (provided with the watch) and a personal computer connected to the Internet.

Figure 4-2 Functional requirements for SatWatch.

The above functional requirements focus only on the possible interactions between SatWatch and its external world (i.e., the watch owner, GPS, and WebifyWatch). The above description does not focus on any of the implementation details (e.g., processor, language, display technology).

4.3.2　Nonfunctional Requirements

Nonfunctional requirements describe aspects of the system that are not directly related to the functional behavior of the system. Nonfunctional requirements include a broad variety of requirements that apply to many different aspects of the system, from usability to performance. The FURPS+ model[2] used by the Unified Process [Jacobson et al., 1999] provides the following categories of nonfunctional requirements:

- **Usability** is the ease with which a user can learn to operate, prepare inputs for, and interpret outputs of a system or component. Usability requirements include, for example, conventions adopted by the user interface, the scope of online help, and the level of user documentation. Often, clients address usability issues by requiring the developer to follow user interface guidelines on color schemes, logos, and fonts.

- **Reliability** is the ability of a system or component to perform its required functions under stated conditions for a specified period of time. Reliability requirements include, for example, an acceptable mean time to failure and the ability to detect specified faults or to withstand specified security attacks. More recently, this category is often replaced by **dependability**, which is the property of a computer system such that reliance can justifiably be placed on the service it delivers. Dependability includes reliability, **robustness** (the degree to which a system or component can function correctly in the presence of invalid inputs or stressful environment conditions), and **safety** (a measure of the absence of catastrophic consequences to the environment).

- **Performance** requirements are concerned with quantifiable attributes of the system, such as **response time** (how quickly the system reacts to a user input), **throughput** (how much work the system can accomplish within a specified amount of time), **availability** (the degree to which a system or component is operational and accessible when required for use), and **accuracy**.

- **Supportability** requirements are concerned with the ease of changes to the system after deployment, including for example, **adaptability** (the ability to change the system to deal with additional application domain concepts), **maintainability** (the ability to change the system to deal with new technology or to fix defects), and internationalization (the ability to change the system to deal with additional international conventions, such as languages, units, and number formats). The ISO 9126 standard on software quality [ISO Std. 9126], similar to the FURPS+ model, replaces this category with two categories: **maintainability** and **portability** (the ease with which a system or component can be transferred from one hardware or software environment to another).

2. FURPS+ is an acronym using the first letter of the requirements categories: Functionality, Usability, Reliability, Performance, and Supportability. The + indicates the additional subcategories. The FURPS model was originally proposed by [Grady, 1992]. The definitions in this section are quoted from [IEEE Std. 610.12-1990].

The FURPS+ model provides additional categories of requirements typically also included under the general label of nonfunctional requirements:

- **Implementation requirements** are constraints on the implementation of the system, including the use of specific tools, programming languages, or hardware platforms.

- **Interface requirements** are constraints imposed by external systems, including legacy systems and interchange formats.

- **Operations requirements** are constraints on the administration and management of the system in the operational setting.

- **Packaging requirements** are constraints on the actual delivery of the system (e.g., constraints on the installation media for setting up the software).

- **Legal requirements** are concerned with licensing, regulation, and certification issues. An example of a legal requirement is that software developed for the U.S. federal government must comply with Section 508 of the Rehabilitation Act of 1973, requiring that government information systems must be accessible to people with disabilities.

Nonfunctional requirements that fall into the URPS categories are called **quality requirements** of the system. Nonfunctional requirements that fall into the implementation, interface, operations, packaging, and legal categories are called **constraints** or **pseudo requirements**. Budget and schedule requirements are usually not treated as nonfunctional requirements, as they constrain attributes of the projects (see Chapter 14, *Project Management*). Figure 4-3 depicts the nonfunctional requirements for SatWatch.

Quality requirements for SatWatch

- Any user who knows how to read a digital watch and understands international time zone abbreviations should be able to use SatWatch without the user manual. [Usability requirement]
- As the SatWatch has no buttons, no software faults requiring the resetting of the watch should occur. [Reliability requirement]
- SatWatch should display the correct time zone within 5 minutes of the end of a GPS blackout period. [Performance requirement]
- SatWatch should measure time within 1/100th second over 5 years. [Performance requirement]
- SatWatch should display time correctly in all 24 time zones. [Performance requirement]
- SatWatch should accept upgrades to its onboard via the Webify Watch serial interface. [Supportability requirement]

Constraints for SatWatch

- All related software associated with SatWatch, including the onboard software, will be written using Java, to comply with current company policy. [Implementation requirement]
- SatWatch complies with the physical, electrical, and software interfaces defined by WebifyWatch API 2.0. [Interface requirement]

Figure 4-3   Nonfunctional requirements for SatWatch.

4.3.3   Completeness, Consistency, Clarity, and Correctness

Requirements are continuously validated with the client and the user. Validation is a critical step in the development process, given that both the client and the developer depend on the requirements specification. Requirement validation involves checking that the specification is complete, consistent, unambiguous, and correct. It is **complete** if all possible scenarios through the system are described, including exceptional behavior (i.e., all aspects of the system are represented in the requirements model). The requirements specification is **consistent** if it does not contradict itself. The requirements specification is **unambiguous** if exactly one system is defined (i.e., it is not possible to interpret the specification two or more different ways). A specification is **correct** if it represents accurately the system that the client needs and that the developers intend to build (i.e., everything in the requirements model accurately represents an aspect of the system to the satisfaction of both client and developer). These properties are illustrated in Table 4-1.

The correctness and completeness of a requirements specification are often difficult to establish, especially before the system exists. Given that the requirements specification serves as a contractual basis between the client and the developers, the requirements specification must be

Table 4-1   Specification properties checked during validation.

Complete—All features of interest are described by requirements.

Example of incompleteness: The SatWatch specification does not specify the boundary behavior when the user is standing within GPS accuracy limitations of a state's boundary.

Solution: Add a functional requirement stating that the time depicted by SatWatch should not change more often than once very 5 minutes.

Consistent—No two requirements of the specification contradict each other.

Example of inconsistency: A watch that does not contain any software faults need not provide an upgrade mechanism for downloading new versions of the software.

Solution: Revise one of the conflicting requirements from the model (e.g., rephrase the requirement about the watch not containing any faults, as it is not verifiable anyway).

Unambiguous—A requirement cannot be interpreted in two mutually exclusive ways.

Example of ambiguity: The SatWatch specification refers to time zones and political boundaries. Does the SatWatch deal with daylight saving time or not?

Solution: Clarify the ambiguous concept to select one of the mutually exclusive phenomena (e.g., add a requirement that SatWatch should deal with daylight saving time).

Correct—The requirements describe the features of the system and environment of interest to the client and the developer, but do not describe other unintended features.

Example of fault: There are more than 24 time zones. Several countries and territories (e.g, India) are half an hour ahead of a neighboring time zone.

---

carefully reviewed by both parties. Additionally, parts of the system that present a high risk should be prototyped or simulated to demonstrate their feasibility or to obtain feedback from the user. In the case of SatWatch described above, a mock-up of the watch would be built using a traditional watch and users surveyed to gather their initial impressions. A user may remark that she wants the watch to be able to display both American and European date formats.

4.3.4   Realism, Verifiability, and Traceability

Three more desirable properties of a requirements specification are that it be realistic, verifiable, and traceable. The requirements specification is **realistic** if the system can be implemented within constraints. The requirements specification is **verifiable** if, once the system is built, repeatable tests can be designed to demonstrate that the system fulfills the requirements specification. For example, a mean time to failure of a hundred years for SatWatch would be difficult to verify (assuming it is realistic in the first place). The following requirements are additional examples of nonverifiable requirements:

- *The product shall have a good user interface.*—Good is not defined.
- *The product shall be error free.*—Requires large amount of resources to establish.
- *The product shall respond to the user with 1 second for most cases.*—"Most cases" is not defined.

A requirements specification is **traceable** if each requirement can be traced throughout the software development to its corresponding system functions, and if each system function can be traced back to its corresponding set of requirements. Traceability includes also the ability to track the dependencies among requirements, system functions, and the intermediate design artifacts, including system components, classes, methods, and object attributes. Traceability is critical for developing tests and for evaluating changes. When developing tests, traceability enables a tester to assess the coverage of a test case, that is, to identify which requirements are tested and which are not. When evaluating changes, traceability enables the analyst and the developers to identify all components and system functions that the change would impact.

4.3.5   Greenfield Engineering, Reengineering, and Interface Engineering

Requirements elicitation activities can be classified into three categories, depending on the source of the requirements. In **greenfield engineering**, the development starts from scratch—no prior system exists—so the requirements are extracted from the users and the client. A greenfield engineering project is triggered by a user need or the creation of a new market. SatWatch is a greenfield engineering project.

A **reengineering** project is the redesign and reimplementation of an existing system triggered by technology enablers or by business processes [Hammer & Champy, 1993]. Sometimes, the functionality of the new system is extended, but the essential purpose of the system remains the same. The requirements of the new system are extracted from an existing system.

An **interface engineering** project is the redesign of the user interface of an existing system. The legacy system is left untouched except for its interface, which is redesigned and reimplemented. This type of project is a reengineering project in which the legacy system cannot be discarded without entailing high costs.

In both reengineering and greenfield engineering, the developers need to gather as much information as possible from the application domain. This information can be found in procedures manuals, documentation distributed to new employees, the previous system's manual, glossaries, cheat sheets and notes developed by the users, and user and client interviews. Note that although interviews with users are an invaluable tool, they fail to gather the necessary information if the relevant questions are not asked. Developers must first gain a solid knowledge of the application domain before the direct approach can be used.

Next, we describe the activities of requirements elicitation.

4.4 Requirements Elicitation Activities

In this section, we describe the requirements elicitation activities. These map a problem statement (see Chapter 3, *Project Organization and Communication*) into a requirements specification that we represent as a set of actors, scenarios, and use cases (see Chapter 2, *Modeling with UML*). We discuss heuristics and methods for eliciting requirements from users and modeling the system in terms of these concepts. Requirements elicitation activities include

- Identifying Actors (Section 4.4.1)
- Identifying Scenarios (Section 4.4.2)
- Identifying Use Cases (Section 4.4.3)
- Refining Use Cases (Section 4.4.4)
- Identifying Relationships Among Actors and Use Cases (Section 4.4.5)
- Identifying Initial Analysis Objects (Section 4.4.6)
- Identifying Nonfunctional Requirements (Section 4.4.7).

The methods described in this section are adapted from OOSE [Jacobson et al., 1992], the Unified Software Development Process [Jacobson et al., 1999], and responsibility-driven design [Wirfs-Brock et al., 1990].

4.4.1   Identifying Actors

Actors represent external entities that interact with the system. An actor can be human or an external system. In the SatWatch example, the watch owner, the GPS satellites, and the WebifyWatch serial device are actors (see Figure 4-4). They all exchange information with the SatWatch. Note, however, that they all have specific interactions with SatWatch: the watch

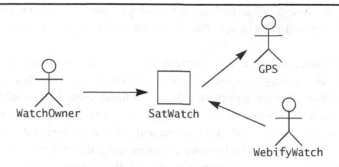

Figure 4-4 Actors for the SatWatch system. WatchOwner moves the watch (possibly across time zones) and consults it to know what time it is. SatWatch interacts with GPS to compute its position. WebifyWatch upgrades the data contained in the watch to reflect changes in time policy (e.g., changes in daylight savings time start and end dates).

owner wears and looks at her watch; the watch monitors the signal from the GPS satellites; the WebifyWatch downloads new data into the watch. Actors define classes of functionality.

Consider a more complex example, FRIEND, a distributed information system for accident management [Bruegge et al., 1994]. It includes many actors, such as FieldOfficer, who represents the police and fire officers who are responding to an incident, and Dispatcher, the police officer responsible for answering 911 calls and dispatching resources to an incident. FRIEND supports both actors by keeping track of incidents, resources, and task plans. It also has access to multiple databases, such as a hazardous materials database and emergency operations procedures. The FieldOfficer and the Dispatcher actors interact through different interfaces: FieldOfficers access FRIEND through a mobile personal assistant, Dispatchers access FRIEND through a workstation (see Figure 4-5).

Actors are role abstractions and do not necessarily directly map to persons. The same person can fill the role of FieldOfficer or Dispatcher at different times. However, the functionality they access is substantially different. For that reason, these two roles are modeled as two different actors.

The first step of requirements elicitation is the identification of actors. This serves both to define the boundaries of the system and to find all the perspectives from which the developers

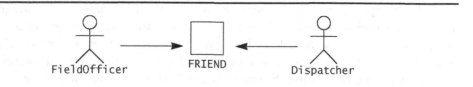

Figure 4-5 Actors of the FRIEND system. FieldOfficers not only have access to different functionality, they use different computers to access the system.

need to consider the system. When the system is deployed into an existing organization (such as a company), most actors usually exist before the system is developed: they correspond to roles in the organization.

During the initial stages of actor identification, it is hard to distinguish actors from objects. For example, a database subsystem can at times be an actor, while in other cases it can be part of the system. Note that once the system boundary is defined, there is no trouble distinguishing between actors and such system components as objects or subsystems. Actors are outside of the system boundary; they are external. Subsystems and objects are inside the system boundary; they are internal. Thus, any external software system using the system to be developed is an actor. When identifying actors, developers can ask the following questions:

Questions for identifying actors

- Which user groups are supported by the system to perform their work?
- Which user groups execute the system's main functions?
- Which user groups perform secondary functions, such as maintenance and administration?
- With what external hardware or software system will the system interact?

In the FRIEND example, these questions lead to a long list of potential actors: fire fighter, police officer, dispatcher, investigator, mayor, governor, an EPA hazardous material database, system administrator, and so on. We then need to consolidate this list into a small number of actors, who are different from the point of view of the usage of the system. For example, a fire fighter and a police officer may share the same interface to the system, as they are both involved with a single incident in the field. A dispatcher, on the other hand, manages multiple concurrent incidents and requires access to a larger amount of information. The mayor and the governor will not likely interact directly with the system, but will use the services of a trained operator instead.

Once the actors are identified, the next step in the requirements elicitation activity is to determine the functionality that will be accessible to each actor. This information can be extracted using scenarios and formalized using use cases.

4.4.2   Identifying Scenarios

A scenario is "a narrative description of what people do and experience as they try to make use of computer systems and applications" [Carroll, 1995]. A scenario is a concrete, focused, informal description of a single feature of the system from the viewpoint of a single actor. Scenarios cannot (and are not intended to) replace use cases, as they focus on specific instances and concrete events (as opposed to complete and general descriptions). However, scenarios enhance requirements elicitation by providing a tool that is understandable to users and clients.

Figure 4-6 is an example of scenario for the FRIEND system, an information system for incident response. In this scenario, a police officer reports a fire and a Dispatcher initiates the incident response. Note that this scenario is concrete, in the sense that it describes a single

Scenario name	warehouseOnFire
Participating actor instances	bob, alice:FieldOfficer john:Dispatcher
Flow of events	1. Bob, driving down main street in his patrol car, notices smoke coming out of a warehouse. His partner, Alice, activates the "Report Emergency" function from her FRIEND laptop. 2. Alice enters the address of the building, a brief description of its location (i.e., northwest corner), and an emergency level. In addition to a fire unit, she requests several paramedic units on the scene, given that the area appears to be relatively busy. She confirms her input and waits for an acknowledgment. 3. John, the Dispatcher, is alerted to the emergency by a beep of his workstation. He reviews the information submitted by Alice and acknowledges the report. He allocates a fire unit and two paramedic units to the Incident site and sends their estimated arrival time (ETA) to Alice. 4. Alice receives the acknowledgment and the ETA.

Figure 4-6 warehouseOnFire scenario for the ReportEmergency use case.

instance. It does not attempt to describe all possible situations in which a fire incident is reported. In particular, scenarios cannot contain descriptions of decisions. To describe the outcome of a decision, two scenarios would be needed, one for the "true" path, and another one for the "false" path.

Scenarios can have many different uses during requirements elicitation and during other activities of the life cycle. Below is a selected number of scenario types taken from [Carroll, 1995]:

- **As-is scenarios** describe a current situation. During reengineering, for example, the current system is understood by observing users and describing their actions as scenarios. These scenarios can then be validated for correctness and accuracy with the users.

- **Visionary scenarios** describe a future system. Visionary scenarios are used both as a point in the modeling space by developers as they refine their ideas of the future system and as a communication medium to elicit requirements from users. Visionary scenarios can be viewed as an inexpensive prototype.

- **Evaluation scenarios** describe user tasks against which the system is to be evaluated. The collaborative development of evaluation scenarios by users and developers also improves the definition of the functionality tested by these scenarios.

- **Training scenarios** are tutorials used for introducing new users to the system. These are step-by-step instructions designed to hand-hold the user through common tasks.

In requirements elicitation, developers and users write and refine a series of scenarios in order to gain a shared understanding of what the system should be. Initially, each scenario may be high level and incomplete, as the warehouseOnFire scenario is. The following questions can be used for identifying scenarios.

Questions for identifying scenarios

- What are the tasks that the actor wants the system to perform?
- What information does the actor access? Who creates that data? Can it be modified or removed? By whom?
- Which external changes does the actor need to inform the system about? How often? When?
- Which events does the system need to inform the actor about? With what latency?

Developers use existing documents about the application domain to answer these questions. These documents include user manuals of previous systems, procedures manuals, company standards, user notes and cheat sheets, user and client interviews. Developers should always write scenarios using application domain terms, as opposed to their own terms. As developers gain further insight into the application domain and the possibilities of the available technology, they iteratively and incrementally refine scenarios to include increasing amounts of detail. Drawing user interface mock-ups often helps to find omissions in the specification and to build a more concrete picture of the system.

In the FRIEND example, we identify four scenarios that span the type of tasks the system is expected to support:

- warehouseOnFire (Figure 4-6): A fire is detected in a warehouse; two field officers arrive at the scene and request resources.

- fenderBender: A car accident without casualties occurs on the highway. Police officers document the incident and manage traffic while the damaged vehicles are towed away.

- catInATree: A cat is stuck in a tree. A fire truck is called to retrieve the cat. Because the incident is low priority, the fire truck takes time to arrive at the scene. In the meantime, the impatient cat owner climbs the tree, falls, and breaks a leg, requiring an ambulance to be dispatched.

- earthQuake: An unprecedented earthquake seriously damages buildings and roads, spanning multiple incidents and triggering the activation of a statewide emergency operations plan. The governor is notified. Road damage hampers incident response.

The emphasis for developers during actor identification and scenario identification is to understand the application domain. This results in a shared understanding of the scope of the system and of the user work processes to be supported. Once developers have identified and described actors and scenarios, they formalize scenarios into use cases.

4.4.3   Identifying Use Cases

A **scenario** is an instance of a **use case**; that is, a use case specifies all possible scenarios for a given piece of functionality. A use case is initiated by an actor. After its initiation, a use case may interact with other actors, as well. A use case represents a complete flow of events through the system in the sense that it describes a series of related interactions that result from its initiation.

Figure 4-7 depicts the use case ReportEmergency of which the scenario warehouseOnFire (see Figure 4-6) is an instance. The FieldOfficer actor initiates this use case by activating the "Report Emergency" function of FRIEND. The use case completes when the FieldOfficer actor receives an acknowledgment that an incident has been created. The steps in the flow of events are indented to denote who initiates the step. Steps 1 and 3 are initiated by the actor, while steps

Use case name	ReportEmergency
Participating actors	Initiated by FieldOfficer Communicates with Dispatcher

Flow of events	1. The FieldOfficer activates the "Report Emergency" function of her terminal.
	
	    2. FRIEND responds by presenting a form to the FieldOfficer.
	
	3. The FieldOfficer completes the form by selecting the emergency level, type, location, and brief description of the situation. The FieldOfficer also describes possible responses to the emergency situation. Once the form is completed, the FieldOfficer submits the form.
	
	    4. FRIEND receives the form and notifies the Dispatcher.
	
	5. The Dispatcher reviews the submitted information and creates an Incident in the database by invoking the OpenIncident use case. The Dispatcher selects a response and acknowledges the report.
	
	    6. FRIEND displays the acknowledgment and the selected response to the FieldOfficer.

Entry condition	• The FieldOfficer is logged into FRIEND.
Exit conditions	• The FieldOfficer has received an acknowledgment and the selected response from the Dispatcher, OR • The FieldOfficer has received an explanation indicating why the transaction could not be processed.
Quality requirements	• The FieldOfficer's report is acknowledged within 30 seconds. • The selected response arrives no later than 30 seconds after it is sent by the Dispatcher.

Figure 4-7   An example of a use case, ReportEmergency. Under ReportEmergency, the left column denotes actor actions, and the right column denotes system responses.

2 and 4 are initiated by the system. This use case is general and encompasses a range of scenarios. For example, the ReportEmergency use case could also apply to the fenderBender scenario. Use cases can be written at varying levels of detail as in the case of scenarios.

Generalizing scenarios and identifying the high-level use cases that the system must support enables developers to define the scope of the system. Initially, developers name use cases, attach them to the initiating actors, and provide a high-level description of the use case as in Figure 4-7. The name of a use case should be a verb phrase denoting what the actor is trying to accomplish. The verb phrase "Report Emergency" indicates that an actor is attempting to report an emergency to the system (and hence, to the Dispatcher actor). This use case is not called "Record Emergency" because the name should reflect the perspective of the actor, not the system. It is also not called "Attempt to Report an Emergency" because the name should reflect the goal of the use case, not the actual activity.

Attaching use cases to initiating actors enables developers to clarify the roles of the different users. Often, by focusing on who initiates each use case, developers identify new actors that have been previously overlooked.

Describing a use case entails specifying four fields. Describing the entry and exit conditions of a use case enables developers to understand the conditions under which a use case is invoked and the impact of the use case on the state of the environment and of the system. By examining the entry and exit conditions of use cases, developers can determine if there may be missing use cases. For example, if a use case requires that the emergency operations plan dealing with earthquakes should be activated, the requirements specification should also provide a use case for activating this plan. Describing the flow of events of a use case enables developers and clients to discuss the interaction between actors and system. This results in many decisions about the boundary of the system, that is, about deciding which actions are accomplished by the actor and which actions are accomplished by the system. Finally, describing the quality requirements associated with a use case enables developers to elicit nonfunctional requirements in the context of a specific functionality. In this book, we focus on these four fields to describe use cases as they describe the most essential aspects of a use case. In practice, many additional fields can be added to describe an exceptional flow of events, rules, and invariants that the use case must respect during the flow of events.

Writing use cases is a craft. An analyst learns to write better use cases with experience. Consequently, different analysts tend to develop different styles, which can make it difficult to produce a consistent requirements specification. To address the issue of learning how to write use cases and how to ensure consistency among the use cases of a requirements specification, analysts adopt a use case writing guide. Figure 4-8 is a simple writing guide adapted from [Cockburn, 2001] that can be used for novice use case writers. Figure 4-9 provides an example of a poor use case that violates the writing guideline in several ways.

The ReportEmergency use case in Figure 4-7 may be illustrative enough to describe how FRIEND supports reporting emergencies and to obtain general feedback from the user, but it does not provide sufficient detail for a requirements specification. Next, we discuss how use cases are refined and detailed.

Simple Use Case Writing Guide

- Use cases should be named with verb phrases. The name of the use case should indicate what the user is trying to accomplish (e.g., ReportEmergency, OpenIncident).
- Actors should be named with noun phrases (e.g., FieldOfficer, Dispatcher, Victim).
- The boundary of the system should be clear. Steps accomplished by the actor and steps accomplished by the system should be distinguished (e.g., in Figure 4-7, system actions are indented to the right).
- Use case steps in the flow of events should be phrased in the active voice. This makes it explicit who accomplished the step.
- The causal relationship between successive steps should be clear.
- A use case should describe a complete user transaction (e.g., the ReportEmergency use case describes all the steps between initiating the emergency reporting and receiving an acknowledgment).
- Exceptions should be described separately.
- A use case should not describe the user interface of the system. This takes away the focus from the actual steps accomplished by the user and is better addressed with visual mock-ups (e.g., the ReportEmergency only refers to the "Report Emergency" function, not the menu, the button, nor the actual command that corresponds to this function).
- A use case should not exceed two or three pages in length. Otherwise, use include and extend relationships to decompose it in smaller use cases, as explained in Section 4.4.5.

Figure 4-8   Example of use case writing guide.

Use case name	Accident	Bad name: What is the user trying to accomplish?
Initiating actor	Initiated by FieldOfficer	
Flow of events	1. The FieldOfficer reports the accident.	
	2. An ambulance is dispatched.	Causality: Which action caused the FieldOfficer to receive an acknowledgment?
		Passive voice: Who dispatches the ambulance?
	3. The Dispatcher is notified when the ambulance arrives on site.	Incomplete transaction: What does the FieldOfficer do after the ambulance is dispatched?

Figure 4-9   An example of a poor use case. Violations of the writing guide are indicated in *italics* in the right column.

4.4.4   Refining Use Cases

Figure 4-10 is a refined version of the ReportEmergency use case. It has been extended to include details about the type of incidents known to FRIEND and detailed interactions indicating how the Dispatcher acknowledges the FieldOfficer.

Use case name	ReportEmergency
Participating actors	Initiated by FieldOfficer Communicates with Dispatcher
Flow of events	1. The FieldOfficer activates the "Report Emergency" function of her terminal. 2. FRIEND responds by presenting a form to the officer. *The form includes an emergency type menu (general emergency, fire, transportation) and location, incident description, resource request, and hazardous material fields.* 3. The FieldOfficer completes the form by *specifying minimally the emergency type and description fields.* The FieldOfficer may also describe possible responses to the emergency situation *and request specific resources.* Once the form is completed, the FieldOfficer submits the form. 4. FRIEND receives the form and notifies the Dispatcher *by a pop-up dialog.* 5. The Dispatcher reviews the submitted information and creates an Incident in the database by invoking the OpenIncident use case. *All the information contained in the FieldOfficer's form is automatically included in the Incident. The Dispatcher selects a response by allocating resources to the Incident (with the AllocateResources use case) and acknowledges the emergency report by sending a short message to the FieldOfficer.* 6. FRIEND displays the acknowledgment and the selected response to the FieldOfficer.
Entry condition	• ...

Figure 4-10   Refined description for the ReportEmergency use case. Additions emphasized in *italics.*

The use of scenarios and use cases to define the functionality of the system aims at creating requirements that are validated by the user early in the development. As the design and implementation of the system starts, the cost of changing the requirements specification and adding new unforeseen functionality increases. Although requirements change until late in the development, developers and users should strive to address most requirements issues early. This entails many changes and much validation during requirements elicitation. Note that many use cases are rewritten several times, others substantially refined, and yet others completely dropped. To save time, much of the exploration work can be done using scenarios and user interface mock-ups.

The following heuristics can be used for writing scenarios and use cases:

Heuristics for developing scenarios and use cases

- Use scenarios to communicate with users and to validate functionality.
- First, refine a single scenario to understand the user's assumptions about the system. The user may be familiar with similar systems, in which case, adopting specific user interface conventions would make the system more usable.
- Next, define many not-very-detailed scenarios to define the scope of the system. Validate with the user.
- Use mock-ups as visual support only; user interface design should occur as a separate task after the functionality is sufficiently stable.
- Present the user with multiple and very different alternatives (as opposed to extracting a single alternative from the user). Evaluating different alternatives broadens the user's horizon. Generating different alternatives forces developers to "think outside the box."
- Detail a broad vertical slice when the scope of the system and the user preferences are well understood. Validate with the user.

The focus of this activity is on completeness and correctness. Developers identify functionality not covered by scenarios, and document it by refining use cases or writing new ones. Developers describe seldom occurring cases and exception handling as seen by the actors. Whereas the initial identification of use cases and actors focused on establishing the boundary of the system, the refinement of use cases yields increasingly more details about the features provided by the system and the constraints associated with them. In particular, the following aspects of the use cases, initially ignored, are detailed during refinement:

- The elements that are manipulated by the system are detailed. In Figure 4-10, we added details about the attributes of the emergency reporting form and the types of incidents.

- The low-level sequence of interactions between the actor and the system are specified. In Figure 4-10, we added information about how the Dispatcher generates an acknowledgment by selecting resources.

- Access rights (which actors can invoke which use cases) are specified.

- Missing exceptions are identified and their handling specified.

- Common functionality among use cases are factored out.

In the next section, we describe how to reorganize actors and use cases with relationships, which addresses the last three bullets points above.

4.4.5   Identifying Relationships among Actors and Use Cases

Even medium-sized systems have many use cases. Relationships among actors and use cases enable the developers and users to reduce the complexity of the model and increase its understandability. We use communication relationships between actors and use cases to describe the system in layers of functionality. We use extend relationships to separate exceptional and common flows of events. We use include relationships to reduce redundancy among use cases.

Communication relationships between actors and use cases

Communication relationships between actors and use cases represent the flow of information during the use case. The actor who initiates the use case should be distinguished from the other actors with whom the use case communicates. By specifying which actor can invoke a specific use case, we also implicitly specify which actors cannot invoke the use case. Similarly, by specifying which actors communicate with a specific use case, we specify which actors can access specific information and which cannot. Thus, by documenting initiation and communication relationships among actors and use cases, we specify access control for the system at a coarse level.

The relationships between actors and use cases are identified when use cases are identified. Figure 4-11 depicts an example of communication relationships in the case of the FRIEND system. The «initiate» stereotype denotes the initiation of the use case by an actor, and the «participate» stereotype denotes that an actor (who did not initiate the use case) communicates with the use case.

Extend relationships between use cases

A use case extends another use case if the extended use case may include the behavior of the extension under certain conditions. In the FRIEND example, assume that the connection between the FieldOfficer station and the Dispatcher station is broken while the

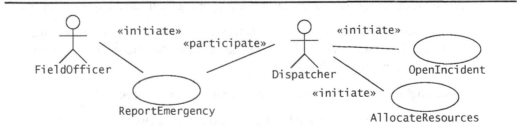

Figure 4-11   Example of communication relationships among actors and use cases in FRIEND (UML use case diagram). The FieldOfficer initiates the ReportEmergency use case, and the Dispatcher initiates the OpenIncident and AllocateResources use cases. FieldOfficers cannot directly open an incident or allocate resources on their own.

FieldOfficer is filling the form (e.g., the FieldOfficer's car enters a tunnel). The FieldOfficer station needs to notify the FieldOfficer that his form was not delivered and what measures he should take. The ConnectionDown use case is modeled as an extension of ReportEmergency (see Figure 4-12). The conditions under which the ConnectionDown use case is initiated are described in ConnectionDown as opposed to ReportEmergency. Separating exceptional and optional flows of events from the base use case has two advantages. First, the base use case becomes shorter and easier to understand. Second, the common case is distinguished from the exceptional case, which enables the developers to treat each type of functionality differently (e.g., optimize the common case for response time, optimize the exceptional case for robustness). Both the extended use case and the extensions are complete use cases of their own. They each must have entry and end conditions and be understandable by the user as an independent whole.

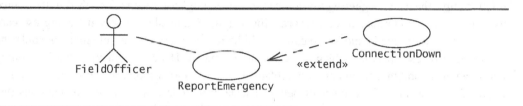

Figure 4-12   Example of use of extend relationship (UML use case diagram). ConnectionDown extends the ReportEmergency use case. The ReportEmergency use case becomes shorter and solely focused on emergency reporting.

Include relationships between use cases

Redundancies among use cases can be factored out using include relationships. Assume, for example, that a Dispatcher needs to consult the city map when opening an incident (e.g., to assess which areas are at risk during a fire) and when allocating resources (e.g., to find which resources are closest to the incident). In this case, the ViewMap use case describes the flow of events required when viewing the city map and is used by both the OpenIncident and the AllocateResources use cases (Figure 4-13).

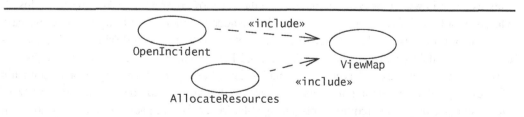

Figure 4-13   Example of include relationships among use cases. ViewMap describes the flow of events for viewing a city map (e.g., scrolling, zooming, query by street name) and is used by both OpenIncident and AllocateResources use cases.

Factoring out shared behavior from use cases has many benefits, including shorter descriptions and fewer redundancies. Behavior should *only* be factored out into a separate use case if it is shared across two or more use cases. Excessive fragmentation of the requirements specification across a large number of use cases makes the specification confusing to users and clients.

Extend versus include relationships

Include and extend are similar constructs, and initially it may not be clear to the developer when to use each one [Jacobson et al., 1992]. The main distinction between these constructs is the direction of the relationship. For include relationships, the event triggering the target (i.e., included) use case is described in the flow of event of the source use case. For extend relationships, the event triggering the source (i.e., extending) use case is described in the source use case as a precondition. In other words, for include relationships, every including use case must specify where the included use case should be invoked. For extend relationships, only the extending use case specifies which use cases are extended. Hence, a behavior that is strongly tied to an event and that occurs only in a relatively few use cases should be represented with an included relationship. These types of behavior usually include common system functions that can be used in several places (e.g., viewing a map, specifying a filename, selecting an element). Conversely, a behavior that can happen anytime or whose occurrence can be more easily specified as an entry condition should be represented with an extend relationship. These types of behavior include exceptional situations (e.g., invoking the online help, canceling a transaction, dealing with a network failure).

Figure 4-14 shows the ConnectionDown example described with an include relationship (left column) and with an extend relationship (right column). In the left column, we need to insert text in two places in the event flow where the ConnectionDown use case can be invoked. Also, if additional exceptional situations are described (e.g., a help function on the FieldOfficer station), the ReportEmergency use case will have to be modified and will become cluttered with conditions. In the right column, we need to describe only the conditions under which the exceptional use case is invoked, which can include a large number of use cases (e.g., "any use case in which the connection between the FieldOfficer and the Dispatcher is lost"). Moreover, additional exceptional situations can be added without modifying the base use case (e.g., ReportEmergency). The ability to extend the system without modifying existing parts is critical, as it allows us to ensure that the original behavior is left untouched. The distinction between include and extend is a documentation issue: using the correct type of relationship reduces dependencies among use cases, reduces redundancy, and lowers the probability of introducing errors when requirements change. However, the impact on other development activities is minimal.

In summary, the following heuristics can be used for selecting an extend or an include relationship.

Heuristics for extend and include relationships

- Use extend relationships for exceptional, optional, or seldom-occurring behavior. An example of seldom-occurring behavior is the breakdown of a resource (e.g., a fire truck). An example of optional behavior is the notification of nearby resources responding to an unrelated incident.
- Use include relationships for behavior that is shared across two or more use cases.
- However, use discretion when applying the above two heuristics and do not overstructure the use case model. A few longer use cases (e.g., two pages long) are easier to understand and review than many short ones (e.g., ten lines long).

In all cases, the purpose of adding include and extend relationships is to reduce or remove redundancies from the use case model, thus eliminating potential inconsistencies.

4.4.6   Identifying Initial Analysis Objects

One of the first obstacles developers and users encounter when they start collaborating with each other is differing terminology. Although developers eventually learn the users' terminology, this problem is likely to be encountered again when new developers are added to the project. Misunderstandings result from the same terms being used in different contexts and with different meanings.

To establish a clear terminology, developers identify the **participating objects** for each use case. Developers should identify, name, and describe them unambiguously and collate them into a glossary.[3] Building this glossary constitutes the first step toward analysis, which we discuss in the next chapter.

The glossary is included in the requirements specification and, later, in the user manuals. Developers keep the glossary up to date as the requirements specification evolves. The benefits of the glossary are manyfold: new developers are exposed to a consistent set of definitions, a single term is used for each concept (instead of a developer term and a user term), and each term has a precise and clear official meaning.

The identification of participating objects results in the initial analysis object model. The identification of participating objects during requirements elicitation only constitutes a first step toward the complete analysis object model. The complete analysis model is usually not used as a means of communication between users and developers, as users are often unfamiliar with object-oriented concepts. However, the description of the objects (i.e., the definitions of the terms in the glossary) and their attributes are visible to the users and reviewed. We describe in detail the further refinement of the analysis model in Chapter 5, *Analysis*.

---

3. The glossary is also called a "data dictionary" [Rumbaugh et al., 1991].

ReportEmergency (include relationship)	ReportEmergency (extend relationship)
1. ... 2. ... 3. The FieldOfficer completes the form by selecting the emergency level, type, location, and brief description of the situation. The FieldOfficer also describes possible responses to the emergency situation. Once the form is completed, the FieldOfficer submits the form, at which point, the Dispatcher is notified. *If the connection with the Dispatcher is broken, the ConnectionDown use case is used.* 4. If the connection is still alive, the Dispatcher reviews the submitted information and creates an Incident in the database by invoking the OpenIncident use case. The Dispatcher selects a response and acknowledges the emergency report. *If the connection is broken, the ConnectionDown use case is used.* 5. ...	1. ... 2. ... 3. The FieldOfficer completes the form by selecting the emergency level, type, location, and brief description of the situation. The FieldOfficer also describes possible responses to the emergency situation. Once the form is completed, the FieldOfficer submits the form, at which point, the Dispatcher is notified. 4. The Dispatcher reviews the submitted information and creates an Incident in the database by invoking the OpenIncident use case. The Dispatcher selects a response and acknowledges the emergency report. 5. ...
ConnectionDown (include relationship)	ConnectionDown (extend relationship)
1. The FieldOfficer and the Dispatcher are notified that the connection is broken. They are advised of the possible reasons why such an event would occur (e.g., "Is the FieldOfficer station in a tunnel?"). 2. The situation is logged by the system and recovered when the connection is reestablished. 3. The FieldOfficer and the Dispatcher enter in contact through other means and the Dispatcher initiates ReportEmergency from the Dispatcher station.	*The ConnectionDown use case extends any use case in which the communication between the FieldOfficer and the Dispatcher can be lost.* 1. The FieldOfficer and the Dispatcher are notified that the connection is broken. They are advised of the possible reasons why such an event would occur (e.g., "Is the FieldOfficer station in a tunnel?"). 2. The situation is logged by the system and recovered when the connection is reestablished. 3. The FieldOfficer and the Dispatcher enter in contact through other means and the Dispatcher initiates ReportEmergency from the Dispatcher station.

Figure 4-14 Addition of ConnectionDown exceptional condition to ReportEmergency. An extend relationship is used for exceptional and optional flow of events because it yields a more modular description.

Many heuristics have been proposed in the literature for identifying objects. Here are a selected few:

Heuristics for identifying initial analysis objects

- Terms that developers or users must clarify to understand the use case
- Recurring nouns in the use cases (e.g., `Incident`)
- Real-world entities that the system must track (e.g., `FieldOfficer`, `Resource`)
- Real-world processes that the system must track (e.g., `EmergencyOperationsPlan`)
- Use cases (e.g., `ReportEmergency`)
- Data sources or sinks (e.g., `Printer`)
- Artifacts with which the user interacts (e.g., `Station`)
- *Always* use application domain terms

During requirements elicitation, participating objects are generated for each use case. If two use cases refer to the same concept, the corresponding object should be the same. If two objects share the same name and do not correspond to the same concept, one or both concepts are renamed to acknowledge and emphasize their difference. This consolidation eliminates any ambiguity in the terminology used. For example, Table 4-2 depicts the initial participating objects we identified for the `ReportEmergency` use case.

Table 4-2 Participating objects for the `ReportEmergency` use case.

`Dispatcher`	Police officer who manages `Incidents`. A `Dispatcher` opens, documents, and closes incidents in response to `EmergencyReports` and other communication with `FieldOfficers`. `Dispatchers` are identified by badge numbers.
`EmergencyReport`	Initial report about an `Incident` from a `FieldOfficer` to a `Dispatcher`. An `EmergencyReport` usually triggers the creation of an `Incident` by the `Dispatcher`. An `EmergencyReport` is composed of an emergency level, a type (fire, road accident, other), a location, and a description.
`FieldOfficer`	Police or fire officer on duty. A `FieldOfficer` can be allocated to at most one `Incident` at a time. `FieldOfficers` are identified by badge numbers.
`Incident`	Situation requiring attention from a `FieldOfficer`. An `Incident` may be reported in the system by a `FieldOfficer` or anybody else external to the system. An `Incident` is composed of a description, a response, a status (open, closed, documented), a location, and a number of `FieldOfficers`.

Once participating objects are identified and consolidated, the developers can use them as a checklist for ensuring that the set of identified use cases is complete.

Heuristics for cross-checking use cases and participating objects

- Which use cases create this object (i.e., during which use cases are the values of the object attributes entered in the system)?
- Which actors can access this information?
- Which use cases modify and destroy this object (i.e., which use cases edit or remove this information from the system)?
- Which actor can initiate these use cases?
- Is this object needed (i.e., is there at least one use case that depends on this information?)

4.4.7   Identifying Nonfunctional Requirements

Nonfunctional requirements describe aspects of the system that are not directly related to its functional behavior. Nonfunctional requirements span a number of issues, from user interface look and feel to response time requirements to security issues. Nonfunctional requirements are defined at the same time as functional requirements because they have as much impact on the development and cost of the system.

For example, consider a mosaic display that an air traffic controller uses to track planes. A mosaic display system compiles data from a series of radars and databases (hence the term "mosaic") into a summary display indicating all aircraft in a certain area, including their identification, speed, and altitude. The number of aircraft such a system can display constrains the performance of the air traffic controller and the cost of the system. If the system can only handle a few aircraft simultaneously, the system cannot be used at busy airports. On the other hand, a system able to handle a large number of aircraft is more costly and more complex to build and to test.

Nonfunctional requirements can impact the work of the user in unexpected ways. To accurately elicit all the essential nonfunctional requirements, both client and developer must collaborate so that they identify (minimally) which attributes of the system that are difficult to realize are critical for the work of the user. In the mosaic display example above, the number of aircraft that a single mosaic display must be able to handle has implications on the size of the icons used for displaying aircraft, the features for identifying aircraft and their properties, the refresh rate of the data, and so on.

The resulting set of nonfunctional requirements typically includes conflicting requirements. For example, the nonfunctional requirements of the SatWatch (Figure 4-3) call for an accurate mechanism, so that the time never needs to be reset, and a low unit cost, so that it is acceptable to the user to replace the watch with a new one when it breaks. These two nonfunctional requirements conflict as the unit cost of the watch increases with its accuracy. To deal with such conflicts, the client and the developer prioritize the nonfunctional requirements, so that they can be addressed consistently during the realization of the system.

Table 4-3   Example questions for eliciting nonfunctional requirements.

Category	Example questions
Usability	• What is the level of expertise of the user? • What user interface standards are familiar to the user? • What documentation should be provided to the user?
Reliability *(including robustness,* *safety, and security)*	• How reliable, available, and robust should the system be? • Is restarting the system acceptable in the event of a failure? • How much data can the system loose? • How should the system handle exceptions? • Are there safety requirements of the system? • Are there security requirements of the system?
Performance	• How responsive should the system be? • Are any user tasks time critical? • How many concurrent users should it support? • How large is a typical data store for comparable systems? • What is the worse latency that is acceptable to users?
Supportability *(including* *maintainability and* *portability)*	• What are the foreseen extensions to the system? • Who maintains the system? • Are there plans to port the system to different software or hardware environments?
Implementation	• Are there constraints on the hardware platform? • Are constraints imposed by the maintenance team? • Are constraints imposed by the testing team?
Interface	• Should the system interact with any existing systems? • How are data exported/imported into the system? • What standards in use by the client should be supported by the system?
Operation	• Who manages the running system?
Packaging	• Who installs the system? • How many installations are foreseen? • Are there time constraints on the installation?
Legal	• How should the system be licensed? • Are any liability issues associated with system failures? • Are any royalties or licensing fees incurred by using specific algorithms or components?

There are unfortunately few systematic methods for eliciting nonfunctional requirements. In practice, analysts use a taxonomy of nonfunctional requirements (e.g., the FURPS+ scheme described previously) to generate check lists of questions to help the client and the developers focus on the nonfunctional aspects of the system. As the actors of the system have already been identified at this point, this check list can be organized by role and distributed to representative users. The advantage of such check lists is that they can be reused and expanded for each new system in a given application domain, thus reducing the number of omissions. Note that such check lists can also result in the elicitation of additional functional requirements. For example, when asking questions about the operation of the system, the client and developers may uncover a number of use cases related with the administration of the system. Table 4-3 depicts example questions for each of the FURPS+ category.

Once the client and the developers identify a set of nonfunctional requirements, they can organize them into refinement and dependency graphs to identify further nonfunctional requirements and identify conflicts. For more material on this topic, the reader is referred to the specialized literature (e.g., [Chung et al., 1999]).

4.5 Managing Requirements Elicitation

In the previous section, we described the technical issues of modeling a system in terms of use cases. Use case modeling by itself, however, does not constitute requirements elicitation. Even after they become expert use case modelers, developers still need to elicit requirements from the users and come to an agreement with the client. In this section, we describe methods for eliciting information from the users and negotiating an agreement with a client. In particular, we describe:

- Negotiating Specifications with Clients: Joint Application Design (Section 4.5.1)
- Maintaining Traceability (Section 4.5.2)
- Documenting Requirements Elicitation (Section 4.5.3).

4.5.1 Negotiating Specifications with Clients: Joint Application Design

Joint Application Design (JAD) is a requirements method developed at IBM at the end of the 1970s. Its effectiveness lies in that the requirements elicitation work is done in one single workshop session in which all stakeholders participate. Users, clients, developers, and a trained session leader sit together in one room to present their viewpoints, listen to other viewpoints, negotiate, and come to a mutually acceptable solution. The outcome of the workshop, the final JAD document, is a complete requirements specification document that includes definitions of data elements, work flows, and interface screens. Because the final document is jointly developed by the stakeholders (that is, the participants who not only have an interest in the success of the project, but also can make substantial decisions), the final JAD document represents an agreement among users, clients, and developers, and thus minimizes requirements changes later in the development process. JAD is composed of five activities (Figure 4-15):

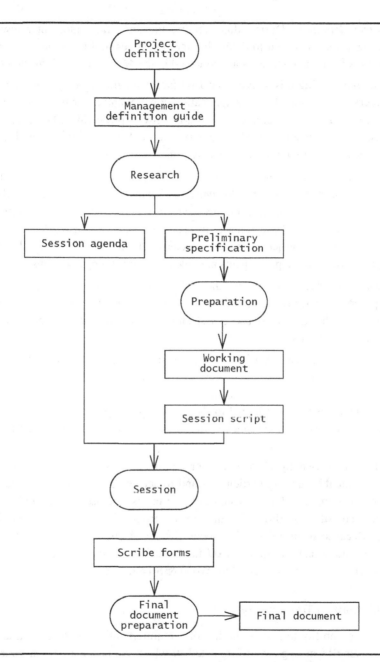

Figure 4-15 Activities of JAD (UML activity diagram). The heart of JAD is the Session activity during which all stakeholders design and agree to a requirements specification. The activities prior to the Session maximize its efficiency. The production of the final document captures the decisions made during the Session.

1. *Project definition.* During this activity, the JAD facilitator interviews the project manager and the client to determine the objectives and the scope of the project. The findings from the interviews are collected in the *Management Definition Guide.*

2. *Research.* During this activity, the JAD facilitator interviews present and future users, gathers information about the application domain, and describes a first set of high-level use cases. The JAD facilitator also starts a list of problems to be addressed during the session. The results of this activity are a *Session Agenda* and a *Preliminary Specification* listing work flow and system information.

3. *Preparation.* During this activity, the JAD facilitator prepares the session. The JAD facilitator creates a *Working Document*, which is the first draft of the final document, an agenda for the session, and any overhead slides or flip charts representing information gathered during the Research activity. The JAD facilitator also selects a team composed of the client, the project manager, selected users, and developers. All stakeholders are represented, and the participants are able to make binding decisions.

4. *Session.* During this activity, the JAD facilitator guides the team in creating the requirements specification. A JAD session lasts for 3 to 5 days. The team defines and agrees on the scenarios, use cases, and user interface mock-ups. All decisions are documented by a scribe.

5. *Final document.* The JAD facilitator prepares the *Final Document*, revising the working document to include all decisions made during the session. The Final Document represents a complete specification of the system agreed on during the session. The Final Document is distributed to the session participants for review. The participants then attend a 1- to 2-hour meeting to discuss the reviews and finalize the document.

JAD has been used by IBM and other companies. JAD leverages group dynamics to improve communication among participants and to accelerate consensus. At the end of a JAD session, developers are more knowledgeable of user needs, and users are more knowledgeable of development trade-offs. Additional gains result from a reduction of redesign activities downstream. Because of its reliance on social dynamics, the success of a JAD session often depends on the qualifications of the JAD facilitator as a meeting facilitator. For a detailed overview of JAD, the reader is referred to [Wood & Silver, 1989].

4.5.2   Maintaining Traceability

Traceability is the ability to follow the life of a requirement. This includes tracing where the requirements came from (e.g., who originated it, which client need does it address) to which aspects of the system and the project it affects (e.g., which components realize the requirement, which test case checks its realization). Traceability enables developers to show that the system is complete, testers to show that the system complies with its requirements, designers to record the rationale behind the system, and maintainers to assess the impact of change.

Consider the SatWatch system we introduced at the beginning of the chapter. Currently, the specification calls for a two-line display that includes time and date. After the client decides that the digit size is too small for comfortable reading, developers change the display requirement to a single-line display combined with a button to switch between time and date. Traceability would enable us to answer the following questions:

- Who originated the two-line display requirement?
- Did any implicit constraints mandate this requirement?
- Which components must be changed because of the additional button and display?
- Which test cases must be changed?

The simplest approach to maintaining traceability is to use cross-references among documents, models, and code artifacts. Each individual element (e.g., requirement, component, class, operation, test case) is identified by a unique number. Dependencies are then documented manually as a textual cross-reference containing the number of the source element and the number of the target element. Tool support can be as simple as a spreadsheet or a word processing tool. This approach is expensive in time and personpower, and it is error prone. However, for small projects, developers can observe benefits early.

For large-scale projects, specialized database tools enable the partial automation of the capture, editing, and linking of traceability dependencies at a more detailed level (e.g., DOORS [Telelogic] or RequisitePro [Rational]). Such tools reduce the cost of maintaining traceability, but they require the buy-in and training of most stakeholders and impose restrictions on other tools in the development process.

4.5.3 Documenting Requirements Elicitation

The results of the requirements elicitation and the analysis activities are documented in the **Requirements Analysis Document (RAD)**. This document completely describes the system in terms of functional and nonfunctional requirements. The audience for the RAD includes the client, the users, the project management, the system analysts (i.e., the developers who participate in the requirements), and the system designers (i.e., the developers who participate in the system design). The first part of the document, including use cases and nonfunctional requirements, is written during requirements elicitation. The formalization of the specification in terms of object models is written during analysis. Figure 4-16 is an example template for a RAD used in this book.

The first section of the RAD is an *Introduction*. Its purpose is to provide a brief overview of the function of the system and the reasons for its development, its scope, and references to the development context (e.g., reference to the problem statement written by the client, references to existing systems, feasibility studies). The introduction also includes the objectives and success criteria of the project.

The second section, *Current system,* describes the current state of affairs. If the new system will replace an existing system, this section describes the functionality and the problems

Requirements Analysis Document

1. Introduction
    1.1 Purpose of the system
    1.2 Scope of the system
    1.3 Objectives and success criteria of the project
    1.4 Definitions, acronyms, and abbreviations
    1.5 References
    1.6 Overview
2. Current system
3. Proposed system
    3.1 Overview
    3.2 Functional requirements
    3.3 Nonfunctional requirements
        3.3.1 Usability
        3.3.2 Reliability
        3.3.3 Performance
        3.3.4 Supportability
        3.3.5 Implementation
        3.3.6 Interface
        3.3.7 Packaging
        3.3.8 Legal
    3.4 System models
        3.4.1 Scenarios
        3.4.2 Use case model
        3.4.3 Object model
        3.4.4 Dynamic model
        3.4.5 User interface—navigational paths and screen mock-ups
4. Glossary

Figure 4-16   Outline of the Requirements Analysis Document (RAD). Sections in *italics* are completed during analysis (see next chapter).

of the current system. Otherwise, this section describes how the tasks supported by the new system are accomplished now. For example, in the case of SatWatch, the user currently resets her watch whenever she travels across a time zone. Because of the manual nature of this operation, the user occasionally sets the wrong time and occasionally neglects to reset. In contrast, the SatWatch will continually ensure accurate time within its lifetime. In the case of FRIEND, the current system is paper based: dispatchers keep track of resource assignments by filling out forms. Communication between dispatchers and field officers is by radio. The current system requires a high documentation and management cost that FRIEND aims to reduce.

The third section, *Proposed system,* documents the requirements elicitation and the analysis model of the new system. It is divided into four subsections:

- *Overview* presents a functional overview of the system.

- *Functional requirements* describes the high-level functionality of the system.

- *Nonfunctional requirements* describes user-level requirements that are not directly related to functionality. This includes usability, reliability, performance, supportability, implementation, interface, operational, packaging, and legal requirements.

- *System models* describes the scenarios, use cases, object model, and dynamic models for the system. This section contains the complete functional specification, including mock-ups illustrating the user interface of the system and navigational paths representing the sequence of screens. The subsections *Object model* and *Dynamic model* are written during the Analysis activity, described in the next chapter.

The RAD should be written after the use case model is stable, that is, when the number of modifications to the requirements is minimal. The requirements, however, are updated throughout the development process when specification problems are discovered or when the scope of the system is changed. The RAD, once published, is baselined and put under configuration management.[4] The revision history section of the RAD will provide a history of changes include the author responsible for each change, the date of the change, and a brief description of the change.

4.6 ARENA Case Study

In this section, we apply the concepts and methods described in this chapter to the ARENA system. We start with the initial problem statement provided by the client, and develop a use case model and an initial analysis object model. In previous sections, we selected examples for their illustrative value. In this section, we focus on a realistic example, describe artifacts as they are created and refined. This enables us to discuss more realistic trade-offs and design decisions and focus on operational details that are typically not visible in illustrative examples. In this discussion, "ARENA" denotes the system in general, whereas "arena" denotes a specific instantiation of the system.

4.6.1 Initial Problem Statement

After an initial meeting with the client, the problem statement is written (Figure 4-17).

Note that this brief text describes the problem and the requirements at a high level. This is not typically the stage at which we commit to a budget or a delivery date. First, we start developing the use case model by identifying actors and scenarios.

---

4. A **baseline** is a version of a work product that has been reviewed and formally approved. **Configuration management** is the process of tracking and approving changes to the baseline. We discuss configuration management in Chapter 13, *Configuration Management*.

ARENA Problem Statement

1. Problem

The popularity of the Internet and the World Wide Web has enabled the creation of a variety of virtual communities, groups of people sharing common interests, but who have never met each other in person. Such virtual communities can be short lived (e.g., a group of people meeting in a chat room or playing a tournament) or long lived (e.g., subscribers to a mailing list). They can include a small group of people or many thousands.

Many multi-player computer games now include support for the virtual communities that are players of the given game. Players can receive news about game upgrades, new game maps and characters; they can announce and organize matches, compare scores and exchange tips. The game company takes advantage of this infrastructure to generate revenue or to advertise its products.

Currently, however, each game company develops such community support in each individual game. Each company uses a different infrastructure, different concepts, and provides different levels of support. This redundancy and inconsistency results in many disadvantages, including a learning curve for players when joining each new community, for game companies who need to develop the support from scratch, and for advertisers who need to contact each individual community separately. Moreover, this solution does not provide much opportunity for cross-fertilization among different communities.

2. Objectives

The objectives of the ARENA project are to:

- provide an infrastructure for operating an arena, including registering new games and players, organizing tournaments, and keeping track of the players scores.
- provide a framework for league owners to customize the number and sequence of matches and the accumulation of expert rating points.
- provide a framework for game developers for developing new games, or for adapting existing games into the ARENA framework.
- provide an infrastructure for advertisers.

3. Functional requirements

ARENA supports five types of users:

- The *operator* should be able to define new games, define new tournament styles (e.g., knock-out tournaments, championships, best of series), define new expert rating formulas, and manage users.
- *League owners* should be able to define a new league, organize and announce new tournaments within a league, conduct a tournament, and declare a winner.
- *Players* should be able to register in an arena, apply for a league, play the matches that are assigned to the player, or drop out of the tournament.
- *Spectators* should be able to monitor any match in progress and check scores and statistics of past matches and players. Spectators do not need to register in an arena.
- The *advertiser* should be able to upload new advertisements, select an advertisement scheme (e.g., tournament sponsor, league sponsor), check balance due, and cancel advertisements.

Figure 4-17   Initial ARENA problem statement.

4. Nonfunctional requirements

- *Low operating cost.* The operator must be able to install and administer an arena without purchasing additional software components and without the help of a full-time system administrator.
- *Extensibility.* The operator must be able to add new games, new tournament styles, and new expert rating formulas. Such additions may require the system to be temporarily shut down and new modules (e.g., Java classes) to be added to the system. However, no modifications of the existing system should be required.
- *Scalability.* The system must support the kick-off of many parallel tournaments (e.g., 10), each involving up to 64 players and several hundreds of simultaneous spectators.
- *Low-bandwidth network.* Players should be able to play matches via a 56K analog modem or faster.

5. Target environment

- All users should be able to access any arena with a web browser supporting cookies, Javascript, and Java applets. Administration functions (e.g., adding new games, tournament styles, and users) used by the operator should not be available through the web.
- ARENA should run on any Unix operating system (e.g., MacOS X, Linux, Solaris).

Figure 4-17   *Continued.*

4.6.2   Identifying Actors and Scenarios

We identify five actors, one for each type of user in the problem statement (Operator, LeagueOwner, Player, Spectator, and Advertiser). As the core functionality of the system is to organize and play tournaments, we first develop an example scenario, organize-TicTacToeTournament (Figure 4-18) to elicit and explore this functionality in more detail. By first focusing on a narrow vertical slice of the system, we understand better the client's expectation of the system, including the boundary of the system and the kinds of interactions between the user and the system. Using the organizeTicTacToeTournament scenario of Figure 4-18, we produce a series of questions for the client depicted in (Figure 4-19). Based on the answers from the client, we refine the scenario accordingly.

Note that when asking questions of a client, our primary goal is to understand the client's needs and the application domain. Once we understand the domain and produce a first version of the requirements specification, we can start trading off features and cost with the client and prioritizing requirements. However, intertwining elicitation and negotiation too early is usually counterproductive.

After we refine the first scenario to the point that both we agree with the client on the system boundary (for that scenario), we focus on the overall scope of the system. This is done by identifying a number of shorter scenarios for each actor. Initially, these scenarios are not detailed, but instead, cover a broad range of functionality (Figure 4-20).

When we encounter disagreements or ambiguities, we detail specific scenarios further. In this example, the scenarios defineKnockOutStyle and installTicTacToeGame would be refined to a comparable level of detail as the organizeTicTacToeTournament (Figure 4-18).

Scenario name	organizeTicTacToeTournament
Participating actor instances	alice:Operator, joe:LeagueOwner, bill:Spectator, mary:Player
Flow of events	1. Joe, a friend of Alice, is a Tic Tac Toe aficionado and volunteers to organize a tournament.
	2. Alice registers Joe in the arena as a league owner.
	3. Joe first defines a Tic Tac Toe beginners league, in which any players can be admitted. This league, dedicated to Tic Tac Toe games, stipulates that tournaments played in this league will follow the knockout tournament style and "Winner Takes All" formula.
	4. Joe schedules the first tournament in the league for 16 players starting the next day.
	5. Joe announces the tournament in a variety of forums over the Web and sends mail to other Tic Tac Toe community members.
	6. Bill and Mary receive the E-mail notification.
	7. Mary is interested in playing the tournament and registers. 19 others apply.
	8. Joe schedules 16 players for the tournament and rejects the 4 that applied last.
	9. The 16 players, including Mary, receive an electronic token for entering the tournament and the time of their first match.
	10. Other subscribers to the Tic Tac Toe mailing list, including Bill, receive a second notice about the Tournament, including the name of the players and the schedule of matches.
	11. As Joe kicks off the tournament, the players have a limited amount of time to enter the match. If a player fails to show up, he loses the game.
	12. Mary plays her first match and wins. She advances in the tournament and is scheduled for the next match against another winner of the first round.
	13. After visiting the Tic Tac Toe Tournament's home page, Bill notices Mary's victory and decides to watch her next match. He selects the match, and sees the sequence of moves of each player as they occur. He also sees an advertisement banner at the bottom of his browser, advertising other tournaments and tic tac toe products.
	14. The tournament continues until the last match, at which point the winner of the tournament is declared and his league record is credited with all the points associated with the tournament.
	15. Also, the winner of the tournament accumulates expert rating points.
	16. Joe can choose to schedule more tournaments in the league, in which case, known players are notified about the date and given priority over new players.

Figure 4-18 organizeTicTacToeTournament scenario for ARENA.

Typical scenarios, once refined, span several pages of text. We also start to maintain a glossary of important terms, to ensure consistency in the specification and to ensure that we use the client's terms. We quickly realize that the terms Match, Game, Tournament, and League represent application domain concepts that need to be defined precisely, as these terms could have a different interpretation in other gaming contexts. To accomplish this, we maintain a working glossary and revise our definitions as our exploratory work progresses (Table 4-4).

Steps 2, 7: Different actors register with the system. In the first case, the administrator registers Joe as a league owner; in the second case, a player registers herself with the system.

- Registration of users should follow the same paradigm. Who provides the registration information and how is the information reviewed, validated, and accepted?
- *Client: Two processes are confused in steps 2 & 7, the registration process, during which new users (e.g., a player or a league owner) establish their identity, and the application process, during which players indicate they want to take part in a specific tournament. During the registration process, the user provides information about themselves (name, nickname, E-mail) and their interests (types of games and tournaments they want to be informed about). The information is validated by the operator. During the application process, players indicate which tournament they want to participate in. This is used by the league owner during match scheduling.*
- Since the player information has already been validated by the operator, should the match scheduling be completely automated?
- *Client: Yes, of course.*

Step 5: Joe sends mail to the Tic Tac Toe community members:

- Does ARENA provide the opportunity to users to subscribe to individual mailing lists?
- *Client: Yes. There should be mailing lists for announcing new games, new leagues, new tournaments, etc.*
- Does ARENA store a user profile (e.g., game watched, games played, interests specified by a user survey) for the purpose of advertisement?
- *Client: Yes, but users should still be able to register without completing a user survey, if they want to. They should be encouraged to enter the survey, but this should not prevent them from entering. They will be exposed to advertisements anyway.*
- Should the profile be used to automatically subscribe to mailing lists?
- *Client: No, we think users in our community would prefer having complete control over their mailing list subscriptions. Guessing subscriptions would not give them the impression they are in control.*

Step 13: Bill browses match statistics and decides to see the next match in real time.

- How are players identified to the spectators? By real name, by E-mail, by nickname?
- *Client: This should be left to the user during the registration.*
- Can a spectator replay old matches?
- *Client: Games should be able to provide this ability, but some games (e.g., real-time, 3D action games) may choose not to do so because of resource constraints.*
- ARENA should support real-time games?
- *Client: Yes, these represent the largest share of our market. In general, ARENA should support as broad a range of games as possible.*
- ...

Figure 4-19 Questions generated from the scenario of Figure 4-18. Answers from the client emphasized in *italics*. The interviewer can ask follow-up questions as new knowledge is accidentally stumbled upon.

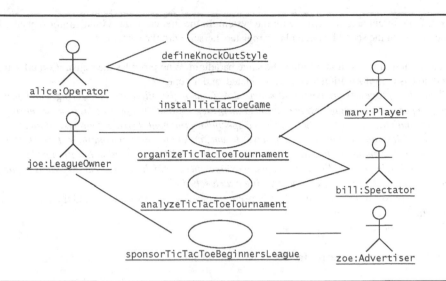

Figure 4-20   High-level scenarios identified for ARENA. Clients and developers initially briefly describe scenarios. They refine them further to clarify ambiguities or uncover disagreements.

Table 4-4   Working glossary for ARENA. Keeping track of important terms and their definitions ensures consistency in the specification and ensures that developers use the language of the client.

Game	A Game is a competition among a number of Players that is conducted according to a set of rules. In ARENA, the term Game refers to a piece of software that enforces the set of rules, tracks the progress of each Player, and decides the winner. For example, tic tac toe and chess are Games.
Match	A Match is a contest between two or more Players following the rules of a Game. The outcome of a Match can be a single winner and a set of losers or a tie (in which their are no winners or losers). Some Games may disallow ties.
Tournament	A Tournament is a series of Matches among a set of Players. Tournaments end with a single winner. The way Players accumulate points and Matches are scheduled is dictated by the League in which the Tournament is organized.
League	A League represents a community for running Tournaments. A League is associated with a specific Game and TournamentStyle. Players registered with the League accumulate points according to the ExpertRating defined in the League. For example, a novice chess League has a different ExpertRating formula than an expert League.
TournamentStyle	The TournamentStyle defines the number of Matches and their sequence for a given set of Players. For example, Players face all other Players in the Tournament exactly once in a round robin TournamentStyle.

Once we agree with the client on a general scope of the system, we formalize the knowledge acquired so far in the form of high-level use cases.

4.6.3   Identifying Use Cases

Generalizing scenarios into use cases enables developers to step back from concrete situations and consider the general case. Developers can then consolidate related functionality into single use cases and split unrelated functionality into several use cases.

When inspecting the `organizeTicTacToeTournament` scenario closely, we realize that it covers a broad range of functionality initiated by many actors. We anticipate that generalizing this scenario would result in a use case of several dozen pages long, and attempt to split it into self-contained and independent use cases initiated by single actors. We first decide to split the functionality related to user accounts into two use cases, `ManageUserAccounts`, initiated by the `Operator`, and `Register`, initiated by potential players and league owners (Figure 4-21). We identify a new actor, `Anonymous`, representing these potential users who do not yet have an account. Similarly, we split the functionality with browsing past matches and with managing user profiles into separate use cases (`BrowseTournamentHistory` and `ManageOwnProfile`, initiated by the `Spectator` and the `Player`, respectively). Finally, to further shorten the use case `OrganizeTournament`, we split off the functionality for creating new leagues into the `DefineLeague` use case, as a `LeagueOwner` may create many tournaments within the scope of a single league. Conversely, we anticipate that the installation of new games and new styles requires similar steps from the `Operator`. Hence, we consolidate all functionality related to installing new components into the `ManageComponents` use case initiated by the `Operator`.

We capture these decisions by drawing an overview use case diagram and by briefly describing each use case (Figure 4-21). Note that a use case diagram alone does not describe much functionality. Instead, it is an index into the many descriptions produced during this phase.

Next, we describe the fields of each high-level use case, including the participating actors, entry and exit conditions, and a flow of events. Figure 4-22 depicts the high-level `OrganizeTournament` use case.

Note that all steps in this flow of events describe actor actions. High-level use cases focus primarily on the task accomplished by the actor. The detailed interaction with the system, and decisions about the boundaries of the system, are initially postponed to the refinement phase. This enables us to first describe the application domain with use cases, capturing, in particular, how different actors collaborate to accomplish their goals.

In Figure 4-22, we describe the sequence of actions that are performed by four actors to organize a tournament: the `LeagueOwner`, who facilitates the complete activity, the `Advertiser`, to resolve exclusive sponsorship issues, the potential `Players` who want to participate, and the `Spectators`. In the first step, we describe the handling of the sponsorship issue, thus making clear that any sponsorship issue needs to be resolved before the tournament is advertised and before the players apply for the tournament. Originally, the sponsorship issue was not described clearly in the scenarios of Figure 4-20 (which only described the sponsorships of leagues). After

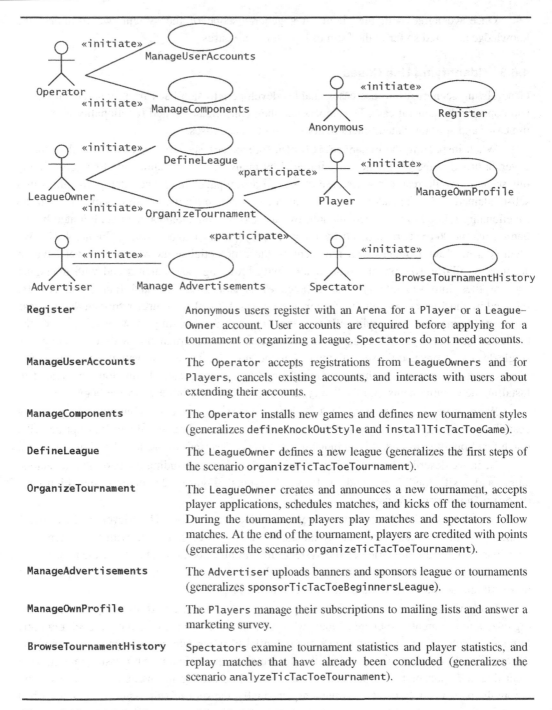

Register	Anonymous users register with an Arena for a Player or a League-Owner account. User accounts are required before applying for a tournament or organizing a league. Spectators do not need accounts.
ManageUserAccounts	The Operator accepts registrations from LeagueOwners and for Players, cancels existing accounts, and interacts with users about extending their accounts.
ManageComponents	The Operator installs new games and defines new tournament styles (generalizes defineKnockOutStyle and installTicTacToeGame).
DefineLeague	The LeagueOwner defines a new league (generalizes the first steps of the scenario organizeTicTacToeTournament).
OrganizeTournament	The LeagueOwner creates and announces a new tournament, accepts player applications, schedules matches, and kicks off the tournament. During the tournament, players play matches and spectators follow matches. At the end of the tournament, players are credited with points (generalizes the scenario organizeTicTacToeTournament).
ManageAdvertisements	The Advertiser uploads banners and sponsors league or tournaments (generalizes sponsorTicTacToeBeginnersLeague).
ManageOwnProfile	The Players manage their subscriptions to mailing lists and answer a marketing survey.
BrowseTournamentHistory	Spectators examine tournament statistics and player statistics, and replay matches that have already been concluded (generalizes the scenario analyzeTicTacToeTournament).

Figure 4-21   High-level use cases identified for ARENA.

Use case name	OrganizeTournament
Participating actors	Initiated by LeagueOwner Communicates with Advertiser, Player, and Spectator
Flow of events	1. The LeagueOwner creates a Tournament, solicits sponsorships from Advertisers, and announces the Tournament (include use case AnnounceTournament). 2. The Players apply for the Tournament (include use case ApplyForTournament). 3. The LeagueOwner processes the Player applications and assigns them to matches (include use case ProcessApplications). 4. The LeagueOwner kicks off the Tournament (include use case KickoffTournament). 5. The Players compete in the matches as scheduled and Spectators view the matches (include use case PlayMatch). 6. The LeagueOwner declares the winner and archives the Tournament (include use case ArchiveTournament).
Entry condition	• The LeagueOwner is logged into ARENA.
Exit conditions	• The LeagueOwner archived a new tournament in the ARENA archive and the winner has accumulated new points in the league, OR • The LeagueOwner cancelled the tournament and the players' standing in the league is unchanged.

Figure 4-22   An example of a high-level use case, OrganizeTournament.

discussions with the client, we decided to handle also tournament sponsorship, and to handle it at the beginning of each tournament. On the one hand, this enables new sponsors to be added to the system, and on the other hand, it allows the sponsor, in exchange, to advertise the tournament using his or her own resources. Finally, this enables the system to better select advertisement banners during the application process.

In this high-level use case, we boiled down the essentials of the organize-TicTacToeTournament scenario into six steps and left the details to the detailed use case. By describing each high-level use case in this manner, we capture all relationships among actors that the system must be aware of. This also results in a summary description of the system that is understandable to any newcomer to the project.

Next, we write the detailed use cases to specify the interactions between the actors and the system.

4.6.4   Refining Use Cases and Identifying Relationships

Refining use cases enables developers to define precisely the information exchanged among the actors and between the actors and the system. Refining use cases also enables the discovery of alternative flows of events and exceptions that the system should handle.

To keep the case study manageable, we do not show the complete refinement. We start by identifying one detailed use case for each step of the flow of events in the high-level OrganizeTournament use case. The resulting use case diagram is shown in Figure 4-23. We then focus on the use case, AnnounceTournament: Figure 4-24 contains a description of the flow of events, and Figure 4-25 identifies the exceptions that could occur in AnnounceTournament. The remaining use cases will be developed similarly.

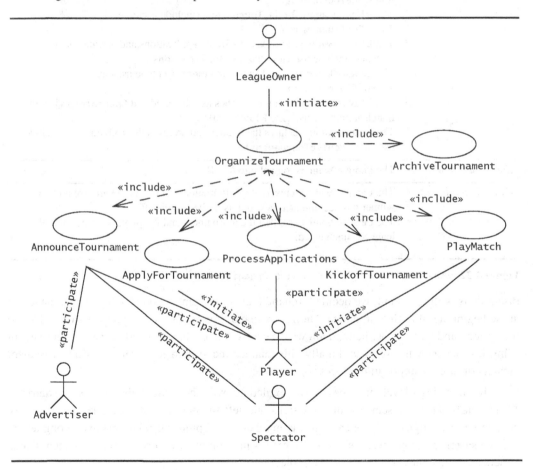

Figure 4-23   Detailed use cases refining the OrganizeTournament high-level use case.

All of the use cases in Figure 4-23 are initiated by the LeagueOwner, except that the ApplyForTournament and PlayMatch are initiated by the Player. The Advertiser participates in AnnounceTournament and the Spectator participates in AnnounceTournament and PlayMatch use cases. The Player participates in all use cases that refine OrganizeTournament. To keep the use case diagram readable, we omitted the «initiate» relationships between the LeagueOwner and the refined use cases. When using a UML modeling tool, we would include those

Name	AnnounceTournament
Participating actors	Initiated by LeagueOwner Communicates with Player, Advertiser, Spectator
Flow of events	1. The LeagueOwner requests the creation of a tournament.

2. The system checks if the LeagueOwner has exceeded the number of tournaments in the league or in the arena. If not, the system presents the LeagueOwner with a form.

3. The LeagueOwner specifies a name, application start and end dates during which Players can apply to the tournament, start and end dates for conducting the tournament, and a maximum number of Players.

4. The system asks the LeagueOwner whether an exclusive sponsorship should be sought and, if yes, presents a list of Advertisers who expressed the desire to be exclusive sponsors.

5. If the LeagueOwner decides to seek an exclusive sponsor, he selects a subset of the names of the proposed sponsors.

6. The system notifies the selected sponsors about the upcoming tournament and the flat fee for exclusive sponsorships.

7. The system communicates their answers to the LeagueOwner.

8. If there are interested sponsors, the LeagueOwner selects one of them.

9. The system records the name of the exclusive sponsor and charges the flat fee for sponsorships to the Advertiser's account. From now on, all advertisement banners associated with the tournament are provided by the exclusive sponsor only.

10. Otherwise, if no sponsors were selected (either because no Advertiser was interested or the LeagueOwner did not select one), the advertisement banners are selected at random and charged to the Advertiser's account on a per unit basis.

11. Once the sponsorship issue is closed, the system prompts the LeagueOwner with a list of groups of Players, Spectators, and Advertisers that could be interested in the new tournament.

12. The LeagueOwner selects which groups to notify.

13. The system creates a home page in the arena for the tournament. This page is used as an entry point to the tournament (e.g., to provide interested Players with a form to apply for the tournament, and to interest Spectators in watching matches).

14. On the application start date, the system notifies each interested user by sending them a link to the main tournament page. The Players can then apply for the tournament with the ApplyForTournament use case until the application end date.

Figure 4-24 An example of a detailed use case, AnnounceTournament.

Entry condition	• The LeagueOwner is logged into ARENA.
Exit conditions	• The sponsorship of the tournament is settled: either a single exclusive Advertiser paid a flat fee or banners are drawn at random from the common advertising pool of the Arena. • Potential Players received a notice concerning the upcoming tournament and can apply for participation. • Potential Spectators received a notice concerning the upcoming tournament and know when the tournament is about to start. • The tournament home page is available for any to see, hence, other potential Spectators can find the tournament home page via web search engines, or by browsing the Arena home page.
Quality requirements	• Offers to and replies from Advertisers require secure authentication, so that Advertisers can be billed solely on their replies. • Advertisers should be able to cancel sponsorship agreements within a fixed period, as required by local laws.

Figure 4-24   *Continued.*

relationships as well. We start by writing out the flow of events for the AnnounceTournament use case (Figure 4-24).

The steps in Figure 4-24 describe in detail the information exchanged between the actor and the system. Note, however, that we did not describe any details of the user interface (e.g., forms, buttons, layout of windows or web pages). It is much easier to design a usable user interface later, after we know the intent and responsibility of each actor. Hence, the focus on the refinement phase is to assign (or discover) the detailed intent and responsibilities of each actor.

When describing the steps of the detailed AnnounceTournament use case, we and the client made more decisions about the boundaries of the system:

- We introduced start and end dates for the application process and for executing the tournament (Step 3 in Figure 4-24). This enables us to communicate deadlines to all actors involved to ensure that the tournament happens within a reasonable time frame.

- We decided that advertisers indicate in their profile whether they are interested in exclusive sponsorships or not. This enables the LeagueOwner to target Advertisers more specifically (Step 4 in Figure 4-24).

- We also decided to enable advertisers to commit to sponsorship deals through the system and automated the accounting of advertisement and the billing. This entails security and legal requirements on the system, which we document in the "quality requirements" field of the use case (Step 9 and 10 in Figure 4-24).

Note that these decisions are validated with the client. Different clients and environments can lead to evaluating trade-offs differently for the same system. For example, the decision about soliciting Advertisers and obtaining a commitment through the system results in a more complex and expensive system. An alternative would have been to solicit Advertisers via E-mail, but obtain their commitment via phone. This would have resulted in a simpler system, but more work on the part of the LeagueOwner. The client is the person who decides between such alternatives, understanding, of course, that these decisions have an impact on the cost and the delivery date of the system.

Next, we identify the exceptions that could occur during the detailed use case. This is done by reviewing every step in the use case and identifying all the events that could go wrong. We briefly describe the handling of each exception and depict the exception handling use cases as extensions of the AnnounceTournament use case (Figure 4-25).

Note that not all exceptions are equal, and different kinds of exceptions are best addressed at different stages of development. In Figure 4-25, we identify exceptions caused by resource constraints (MaxNumberOfTournamentsExceeded), invalid user input (InvalidDate, NameInUse), or application domain constraints (AdvertiserCreditExceeded, NoMatchingSponsorFound). Exceptions associated with resource constraints are best handled during system design. Only during system design will it become clear which resources are limited and how to best share

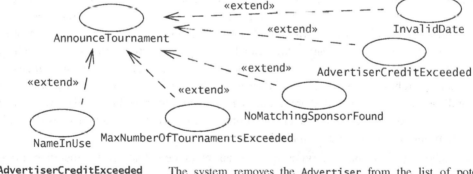

AdvertiserCreditExceeded	The system removes the Advertiser from the list of potential sponsors.
InvalidDate	The system informs the LeagueOwner and prompts for a new date.
MaxNumberOfTournaments Exceeded	The AnnounceTournament use case is terminated.
NameInUse	The system informs the LeagueOwner and prompts for a new name.
NoMatchingSponsorFound	The system skips the exclusive sponsor steps and chooses random advertisements from the advertisement pool.

Figure 4-25 Exceptions occurring in AnnounceTournament represented as extending use cases. (Note that AnnounceTournament in this figure is the same as the use case in Figure 4-23).

them among different users which may, in turn, trigger further requirements activities during system design to validate with the client the handling of such exceptions. Exceptions associated with invalid user input are best handled during user interface design, when developers will be able to decide at which point to check for invalid input, how to display error messages, and how to prevent invalid inputs in the first place. The third category of exceptions—application domain constraints—should receive the focus of the client and developer early. These are exceptions that are usually not obvious to the developer. When missed, they require substantial rework and changes to the system. A systematic way to elicit those exceptions is to walk through the use case step by step with the client or a domain expert.

Many exceptional events can be represented either as an exception (e.g., AdvertiserCreditExceeded) or as a nonfunctional requirement (e.g., "An Advertiser should not be able to spend more advertisement money than a fixed limit agreed beforehand with the Operator during the registration"). The latter representation is more appropriate for global constraints that apply to several use cases. Conversely, the former is more appropriate for events that can occur only in one use case (e.g., "NoMatchingSponsorFound").

Writing each detailed use case, including their exceptions, constitutes the lion's share of the requirements elicitation effort. Ideally, developers write every detailed use case and address all application domain issues before committing to the project and initiating the realization of the system. In practice, this never happens. For large systems, the developers produce a large amount of documentation in which it is difficult, if not impossible, to maintain consistency. Worse, the requirements elicitation activity of large projects should already be financed, as this phase requires a lot of resources from both the client and the development organization. Moreover, completeness at an early stage can be counterproductive: use case steps change during development as new domain facts are discovered. The decision about how many use cases to detail and how much to leave implicit is as much a question of trust as of economics: the client and the developers should share a sufficiently good understanding of the system to be ready to commit to a schedule, a budget, and a process for handling future changes (including changes in requirements, schedule, and budget).

In ARENA, we focus on specifying in detail the interactions that involve the Advertisers and the Players, since they have critical roles in generating revenue. Use cases associated with the administration of the system or the installation of new games or tournament styles are left for later, since they also include more technical issues that are dependent on the solution domain.

4.6.5   Identifying Nonfunctional Requirements

Nonfunctional requirements come from a variety of sources during the elicitation. The problem statement we started with in Figure 4-17 already specified performance and implementation requirements. When detailing the AnnounceTournament use case, we identified further legal requirements for billing Advertisers. When reviewing exceptions in the previous section, we identified a constraint on the amount of money Advertisers can spend. Although we encounter many nonfunctional requirements while writing use cases and refining them, we cannot ensure that we identify all the essential nonfunctional requirements. To ensure completeness, we use the FURPS+ categories we described in Section 4.3.2 (or any other systematic taxonomy of nonfunctional requirements) as a checklist for asking questions of the client. Table 4-5 depicts the nonfunctional requirements we identified in ARENA after detailing the AnnounceTournament use case.

Table 4-5 Consolidated nonfunctional requirements for ARENA, after the first version of the detailed AnnounceTournament use case.

Category	Nonfunctional requirements
Usability	• Spectators must be able to access games in progress without prior registration and without prior knowledge of the Game.
Reliability	• Crashes due to software bugs in game components should interrupt at most one Tournament using the Game. The other Tournaments in progress should proceed normally. • When a Tournament is interrupted because of a crash, its LeagueOwner should be able to restart the Tournament. At most, only the last move of each interrupted Match can be lost.
Performance	• The system must support the kick-off of many parallel Tournaments (e.g., 10), each involving up to 64 Players and several hundreds of simultaneous Spectators. • Players should be able to play matches via an analog modem.
Supportability	• The Operator must be able to add new Games and new TournamentStyles. Such additions may require the system to be temporarily shut down and new modules (e.g., Java classes) to be added to the system. However, no modifications of the existing system should be required.
Implementation	• All users should be able to access an Arena with a web browser supporting cookies, Javascript, and Java applets. Administration functions used by the operator are not available through the web. • ARENA should run on any Unix operating system (e.g., MacOS X, Linux, Solaris).
Operation	• An Advertiser should not be able to spend more advertisement money than a fixed limit agreed beforehand with the Operator during the registration.
Legal	• Offers to and replies from Advertisers require secure authentication, so that agreements can be built solely on their replies. • Advertisers should be able to cancel sponsorship agreements within a fixed period, as required by local laws.

4.6.6   Lessons Learned

In this section, we developed an initial use case and analysis object model based on a problem statement provided by the client. We used scenarios and questions as elicitation tools to clarify ambiguous concepts and uncover missing information. We also elicited a number of nonfunctional requirements. We learned that

- Requirements elicitation involves constant switching between perspectives (e.g., high-level vs. detailed, client vs. developer, activity vs. entity).

- Requirements elicitation requires a substantial involvement from the client.

- Developers should not assume that they know what the client wants.

- Eliciting nonfunctional requirements forces stakeholders to make and document trade-offs.

4.7 Further Readings

The concept of use case was made popular by Ivar Jacobson in his landmark book, *Object-Oriented Software Engineering: A Use Case Approach* [Jacobson et al., 1992]. For an account of the early research on scenario-based requirements and, more generally, on participatory design, *Scenario-Based Design* [Carroll, 1995] includes many papers by leading researchers about scenarios and use cases. This book also describes limitations and pitfalls of scenario-based requirements and participatory design, which are still valid today.

For specific method guidance, *Software for Use* [Constantine & Lockwood, 1999] contains much material on specifying usable systems with use cases, including eliciting imprecise knowledge from users and clients, a soft topic that is usually not covered in software engineering text books. *Writing Effective Use Cases* [Cockburn, 2001] and its accompanying website http://www.usecases.org provide many practical heuristics for writing use cases textually (as opposed to just drawing them).

End users play a critical role during requirements elicitation. Norman illustrates this by using examples from everyday objects such as doors, stoves, and faucets [Norman, 2002]. He argues that users should not be expected to read a user manual and learn new skills for every product to which they are exposed. Instead, knowledge about the use of the product, such as hints indicating in which direction a door opens, should be embedded in its design. He takes examples from everyday objects, but the same principles are applicable to computer systems and user interface design.

The world of requirements engineering is much poorer when it comes to dealing with nonfunctional requirements. The NFR Framework, described in *Non-Functional Requirements in Software Engineering* [Chung et al., 1999], is one of the few methods that addresses this topic systematically and thoroughly.

The RAD template introduced in this chapter is just one example of how to organize a requirements document. IEEE published the documentation standard IEEE-Std 830-1998 for software requirements specifications [IEEE Std. 830-1998]. The appendix of the standard contains several sample outlines for the description of specific requirements.

The examples in this chapter followed a dialectic approach to requirements elicitation, a process of discussion and negotiation among developers, the client, and the end users. This approach works well when the client is the end user, or when the client has a sufficiently detailed knowledge of the application domain. In large systems, such as an air traffic control system, no single user or client has a complete perspective of the system. In these situations, the dialectic approach breaks down, as much implicit knowledge about the users' activities is not encountered until too late. In the past decade, ethnography, a field method from anthropology, has gained popularity in requirements engineering. Using this approach, analysts immerse themselves in the world of users, observe their daily work, and participate in their meetings. Analysts record their observations from a neutral point of view. The goal of such an approach is to uncover implicit knowledge. The coherence method, reported in *Social analysis in the requirements engineering process: from ethnography to method* [Viller & Sommerville, 1999], provides a practical example of ethnography applied to requirements engineering.

Managing traceability beyond requirements is still a research topic, the reader is referred to the specialized literature [Jarke, 1998].

Finally, *Software Requirements & Specifications: A Lexicon of Practice, Principles and Prejudices* [Jackson, 1995] is a concise, incisive, and entertaining piece that provides many insights into principles and methods of requirements engineering.

4.8 Exercises

4-1 Consider your watch as a system and set the time 2 minutes ahead. Write down each interaction between you and your watch as a scenario. Record all interactions, including any feedback the watch provides you.

4-2 Consider the scenario you wrote in Exercise 4-1. Identify the actor of the scenario. Next, write the corresponding use case SetTime. Include all cases, and include setting the time forward and backward, and setting hours, minutes, and seconds.

4-3 Assume the watch system you described in Exercises 4-1 and 4-2 also supports an alarm feature. Describe setting the alarm time as a self-contained use case named SetAlarmTime.

4-4 Examine the SetTime and SetAlarmTime use cases you wrote in Exercises 4-2 and 4-3. Eliminate any redundancy by using an include relationship. Justify why an include relationship is preferable to an extend relationship in this case.

4-5 Assume the FieldOfficer can invoke a Help feature when filling an EmergencyReport. The HelpReportEmergency feature provides a detailed description for each field and specifies which fields are required. Modify the ReportEmergency use case (described in Figure 4-10) to include this help functionality. Which relationship should you use to relate the ReportEmergency and HelpReportEmergency?

4-6   Below are examples of nonfunctional requirements. Specify which of these requirements are verifiable and which are not:

- "The system must be usable."
- "The system must provide visual feedback to the user within one second of issuing a command."
- "The availability of the system must be above 95 percent."
- "The user interface of the new system should be similar enough to the old system that users familiar with the old system can be easily trained to use the new system."

4-7   The need for developing a complete specification may encourage an analyst to write detailed and lengthy documents. Which competing quality of specification (see Table 4-1) may encourage an analyst to keep the specification short?

4-8   Maintaining traceability during requirements and subsequent activities is expensive, because of the additional information that must be captured and maintained. What are the benefits of traceability that outweigh this overhead? Which of those benefits are directly beneficial to the analyst?

4-9   Explain why multiple-choice questionnaires, as a primary means of extracting information from the user, are not effective for eliciting requirements.

4-10 From your point of view, describe the strengths and weaknesses of users during the requirements elicitation activity. Describe also the strengths and weaknesses of developers during the requirements elicitation activity.

4-11 Briefly define the term "menu." Write your answer on a piece of paper and put it upside down on the table together with the definitions of four other students. Compare all five definitions and discuss any substantial difference.

4-12 Write the high-level use case ManageAdvertisement initiated by the Advertiser, and write detailed use cases refining this high-level use case. Consider features that enable an Advertiser to upload advertisement banners, to associate keywords with each banner, to subscribe to notices about new tournaments in specific leagues or games, and to monitor the charges and payments made on the advertisement account. Make sure that your use cases are also consistent with the ARENA problem statement provided in Figure 4-17.

4-13 Considering the AnnounceTournament use case in Figure 4-24, write the event flow, entry conditions, and exit conditions for the use case ApplyForTournament, initiated by a Player interested in participating in the newly created tournament. Consider also the ARENA problem statement provided in Figure 4-17. Write a list of questions for the client when you encounter any alternative.

4-14 Write the event flows, entry conditions, and exit conditions for the exceptional use cases for AnnounceTournament depicted in Figure 4-25. Use include relationships if necessary to remove redundancy.

References

[Bruegge et al., 1994]   B. Bruegge, K. O'Toole, & D. Rothenberger, "Design considerations for an accident management system," in M. Brodie, M. Jarke, M. Papazoglou (eds.), *Proceedings of the Second International Conference on Cooperative Information Systems*, pp. 90–100, University of Toronto Press, Toronto, Canada, May 1994.

[Carroll, 1995]   J. M. Carroll (ed.), *Scenario-Based Design: Envisioning Work and Technology in System Development*. Wiley, New York, 1995.

[Chung et al., 1999]   L. Chung, B. A. Nixon, E. Yu & J. Mylopoulos, *Non-Functional Requirements in Software Engineering*, Kluwer Academic, Boston, 1999.

[Cockburn, 2001]   A. Cockburn, *Writing Effective Use Cases*, Addison-Wesley, Reading, MA, 2001.

[Constantine & Lockwood, 1999] L. L Constantine & L. A. D. Lockwood, *Software for Use*, Addison-Wesley, Reading, MA, 1999

[Grady, 1992]   R. Grady, *Practical Software Metrics for Project Management and Process Improvement*, Prentice Hall, Englewood Cliffs, NJ, 1992.

[Hammer & Champy, 1993]   M. Hammer & J. Champy, *Reengineering The Corporation: a Manifesto For Business Revolution*, Harper Business, New York, 1993.

[IEEE Std. 610.12-1990]   IEEE, *IEEE Standard Computer Dictionary: A Compilation of IEEE Standard Computer Glossaries*, New York, NY, 1990.

[IEEE Std. 830-1998]   *IEEE Standard for Software Requirements Specification*, IEEE Standards Board, 1998.

[ISO Std. 9126]   International Standards Organization. *Software engineering—Product quality*. ISO/IEC-9126, Geneva, Switzerland, 2001.

[Jackson, 1995]   M. Jackson, *Software Requirements & Specifications: A Lexicon of Practice, Principles and Prejudices*, Addison-Wesley, Reading, MA, 1995.

[Jacobson et al., 1992]   I. Jacobson, M. Christerson, P. Jonsson, & G. Overgaard, *Object-Oriented Software Engineering—A Use Case Driven Approach*, Addison-Wesley, Reading, MA, 1992.

[Jacobson et al., 1999]   I. Jacobson, G. Booch, & J. Rumbaugh, *The Unified Software Development Process*, Addison-Wesley, Reading, MA, 1999.

[Jarke, 1998]   M. Jarke, "Requirements tracing," *Communications of the ACM*, Vol. 41, No. 12, December 1998.

[Neumann, 1995]   P. G. Neumann, *Computer-Related Risks*, Addison-Wesley, Reading, MA, 1995.

[Nielsen, 1993]   J. Nielsen, *Usability Engineering*, Academic, New York, 1993.

[Norman, 2002]   D. A. Norman, *The Design of Everyday Things*, Basic Books, New York, 2002.

[Rational]   Rationale, http://www.rational.com.

[Rumbaugh et al., 1991]   J. Rumbaugh, M. Blaha, W. Premerlani, F. Eddy, & W. Lorensen, *Object-Oriented Modeling and Design*, Prentice Hall, Englewood Cliffs, NJ, 1991.

[Telelogic]   Telelogic, http://www.telelogic.se.

[Viller & Sommerville, 1999] S. Viller & I. Sommerville, "Social analysis in the requirements engineering process: from ethnography to method," *International Symposium on Requirements Engineering (ISRE'99)*, Limerick, Ireland, June 1999.

[Wirfs-Brock et al., 1990]   R. Wirfs-Brock, B. Wilkerson, & L. Wiener, *Designing Object-Oriented Software*, Prentice Hall, Englewood Cliffs, NJ, 1990.

[Wood & Silver, 1989]   J. Wood & D. Silver, *Joint Application Design*®, Wiley, New York, 1989.

5

Analysis

I am Foo with a name, if I could only remember it.

—A programmer of very little brain

A nalysis results in a model of the system that aims to be correct, complete, consistent, and unambiguous. Developers formalize the requirements specification produced during requirements elicitation and examine in more detail boundary conditions and exceptional cases. Developers validate, correct and clarify the requirements specification if any errors or ambiguities are found. The client and the user are usually involved in this activity when the requirements specification must be changed and when additional information must be gathered.

In object-oriented analysis, developers build a model describing the application domain. For example, the analysis model of a watch describes how the watch represents time: Does the watch know about leap years? Does it know about the day of the week? Does it know about the phases of the moon? The analysis model is then extended to describe how the actors and the system interact to manipulate the application domain model: How does the watch owner reset the time? How does the watch owner reset the day of the week? Developers use the analysis model, together with nonfunctional requirements, to prepare for the architecture of the system developed during high-level design (Chapter 6, *System Design: Decomposing the System*).

In this chapter, we discuss the analysis activities in more detail. We focus on the identification of objects, their behavior, their relationships, their classification, and their organization. We describe management issues related to analysis in the context of a multi-team development project. Finally, we discuss in more detail analysis issues and trade-offs using the ARENA case study.

5.1 Introduction: An Optical Illusion

In 1915, Rubin exhibited a drawing similar to Figure 5-1 to illustrate the concept of multi-stable images. What do you see? Two faces looking at each other? If you focus more closely on the white area, you can see a vase instead. Once you are able to perceive both shapes individually, it is easier to switch back and forth between the vase and the faces.

Figure 5-1 Ambiguity: what do you see?

If the drawing in Figure 5-1 had been a requirements specification, which models should you have constructed? Specifications, like multi-stable images, contain ambiguities caused by the inaccuracies inherent to natural language and by the assumptions of the specification authors. For example, a quantity specified without a unit is ambiguous (e.g., the "Feet or Miles?" example in Section 4.1), a time without time zone is ambiguous (e.g., scheduling a phone call between different countries).

Formalization helps identify areas of ambiguity as well as inconsistencies and omissions in a requirements specification. Once developers identify problems with the specification, they address them by eliciting more information from the users and the client. Requirements elicitation and analysis are iterative and incremental activities that occur concurrently.

5.2 An Overview of Analysis

Analysis focuses on producing a model of the system, called the analysis model, which is correct, complete, consistent, and verifiable. Analysis is different from requirements elicitation in that developers focus on structuring and formalizing the requirements elicited from users (Figure 5-2). This formalization leads to new insights and the discovery of errors in the

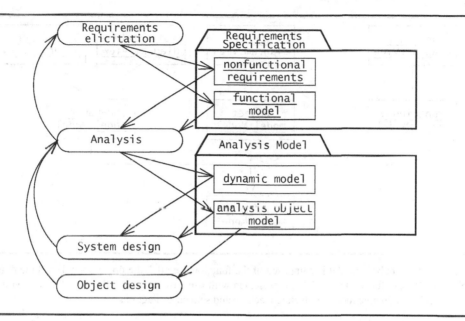

Figure 5-2   Products of requirements elicitation and analysis (UML activity diagram).

requirements. As the analysis model may not be understandable to the users and the client, developers need to update the requirements specification to reflect insights gained during analysis, then review the changes with the client and the users. In the end, the requirements, however large, should be understandable by the client and the users.

There is a natural tendency for users and developers to postpone difficult decisions until later in the project. A decision may be difficult because of lack of domain knowledge, lack of technological knowledge, or simply because of disagreements among users and developers. Postponing decisions enables the project to move on smoothly and avoids confrontation with reality or peers. Unfortunately, difficult decisions eventually must be made, often at higher cost when intrinsic problems are discovered during testing, or worse, during user evaluation. Translating a requirements specification into a formal or semiformal model forces developers to identify and resolve difficult issues early in the development.

The **analysis model** is composed of three individual models: the **functional model**, represented by use cases and scenarios, the **analysis object model**, represented by class and object diagrams, and the **dynamic model**, represented by state machine and sequence diagrams (Figure 5-3). In the previous chapter, we described how to elicit requirements from the users and describe them as use cases and scenarios. In this chapter, we describe how to refine the functional model and derive the object and the dynamic model. This leads to a more precise and complete specification as details are added to the analysis model. We conclude the chapter by describing management activities related to analysis. In the next section, we define the main concepts of analysis.

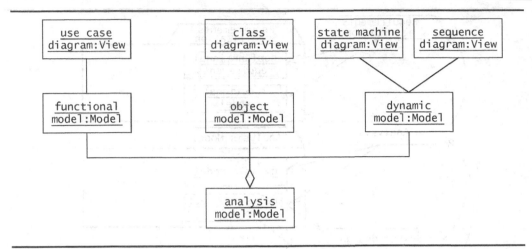

Figure 5-3   The analysis model is composed of the functional model, the object model, and the dynamic model. In UML, the functional model is represented with use case diagrams, the object model with class diagrams, and the dynamic model with state machine and sequence diagrams.

5.3   Analysis Concepts

In this section, we describe the main analysis concepts used in this chapter. In particular, we describe

- Analysis Object Models and Dynamic Models (Section 5.3.1)
- Entity, Boundary, and Control Objects (Section 5.3.2)
- Generalization and Specialization (Section 5.3.3).

5.3.1   Analysis Object Models and Dynamic Models

The analysis model represents the system under development from the user's point of view. The **analysis object model** is a part of the analysis model and focuses on the individual concepts that are manipulated by the system, their properties and their relationships. The analysis object model, depicted with UML class diagrams, includes classes, attributes, and operations. The analysis object model is a visual dictionary of the main concepts visible to the user.

The **dynamic model** focuses on the behavior of the system. The dynamic model is depicted with sequence diagrams and with state machines. Sequence diagrams represent the interactions among a set of objects during a single use case. State machines represent the behavior of a single object (or a group of very tightly coupled objects). The dynamic model serves to assign responsibilities to individual classes and, in the process, to identify new classes, associations, and attributes to be added to the analysis object model.

When working with either the analysis object model or the dynamic model, it is essential to remember that these models represent user-level concepts, not actual software classes or components. For example, classes such as `Database`, `Subsystem`, `SessionManager`, `Network`, should not appear in the analysis model as the user is completely shielded from those concepts. Note that most classes in the analysis object model will correspond to one or more software classes in the source code. However, the software classes will include many more attributes and associations than their analysis counterparts. Consequently, analysis classes should be viewed as high-level abstractions that will be realized in much more detail later. Figure 5-4 depicts good and bad examples of analysis objects for the `SatWatch` example.

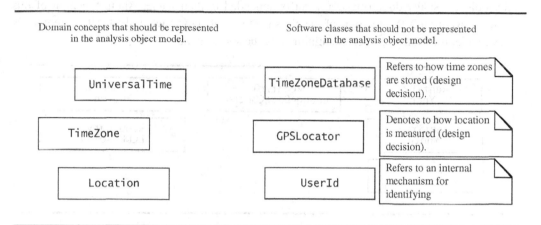

Figure 5-4 Examples and counterexamples of classes in the analysis object model of `SatWatch`.

5.3.2 Entity, Boundary, and Control Objects

The analysis object model consists of entity, boundary, and control objects [Jacobson et al., 1999]. **Entity objects** represent the persistent information tracked by the system. **Boundary objects** represent the interactions between the actors and the system. **Control objects** are in charge of realizing use cases. In the `2Bwatch` example, `Year`, `Month`, and `Day` are entity objects; `Button` and `LCDDisplay` are boundary objects; `ChangeDateControl` is a control object that represents the activity of changing the date by pressing combinations of buttons.

Modeling the system with entity, boundary, and control objects provides developers with simple heuristics to distinguish different, but related concepts. For example, the time that is tracked by a watch has different properties than the display that depicts the time. Differentiating between boundary and entity objects forces that distinction: The time that is tracked by the watch is represented by the `Time` object. The display is represented by the `LCDDisplay`. This approach with three object types results in smaller and more specialized objects. The three-object-type approach also leads to models that are more resilient to change: the interface to the system (represented by the boundary objects) is more likely to change than its basic functionality (represented by the entity and control objects). By separating the interface from the basic functionality, we are able to keep most of a model untouched when, for example, the user interface changes, but the entity objects do not.

To distinguish between different types of objects, UML provides the stereotype mechanism to enable the developer to attach such meta-information to modeling elements. For example, in Figure 5-5, we attach the «control» stereotype to the ChangeDateControl object. In addition to stereotypes, we may also use naming conventions for clarity and recommend distinguishing the three different types of objects on a syntactical basis: control objects may have the suffix Control appended to their name; boundary objects may be named to clearly denote an interface feature (e.g., by including the suffix Form, Button, Display, or Boundary); entity objects usually do not have any suffix appended to their name. Another benefit of this naming convention is that the type of the class is represented even when the UML stereotype is not available, for example, when examining only the source code.

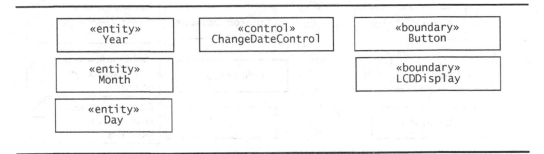

Figure 5-5   Analysis classes for the 2Bwatch example.

5.3.3   Generalization and Specialization

As we saw in Chapter 2, *Modeling with UML*, **inheritance** enables us to organize concepts into hierarchies. At the top of the hierarchy is a general concept (e.g., an Incident, Figure 5-6), and at the bottom of the hierarchy are the most specialized concepts (e.g., CatInTree, TrafficAccident, BuildingFire, EarthQuake, ChemicalLeak). There may be any number of intermediate levels in between, covering more-or-less generalized concepts (e.g., LowPriorityIncident, Emergency, Disaster). Such hierarchies allow us to refer to many concepts precisely. When we use the term Incident, we mean all instances of all types of Incidents. When we use the term Emergency, we only refer to an Incident that requires an immediate response.

Generalization is the modeling activity that identifies abstract concepts from lower-level ones. For example, assume we are reverse-engineering an emergency management system and discover screens for managing traffic accidents and fires. Noticing common features among these three concepts, we create an abstract concept called Emergency to describe the common (and general) features of traffic accidents and fires.

Specialization is the activity that identifies more specific concepts from a high-level one. For example, assume that we are building an emergency management system from scratch and that we are discussing its functionality with the client. The client first introduces us with the

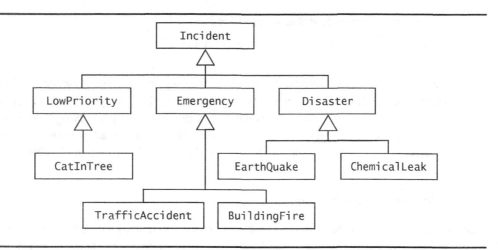

Figure 5-6   An example of a generalization hierarchy (UML class diagram). The top of the hierarchy represents the most general concept, whereas the bottom nodes represent the most specialized concepts.

concept of an incident, then describes three types of Incidents: Disasters, which require the collaboration of several agencies, Emergencies, which require immediate handling but can be handled by a single agency, and LowPriorityIncidents, that do not need to be handled if resources are required for other, higher-priority Incidents.

In both cases, generalization and specialization result in the specification of inheritance relationships between concepts. In some instances, modelers call inheritance relationships **generalization-specialization** relationships. In this book, we use the term "inheritance" to denote the relationship and the terms "generalization" and "specialization" to denote the activities that find inheritance relationships.

5.4 Analysis Activities: From Use Cases to Objects

In this section, we describe the activities that transform the use cases and scenarios produced during requirements elicitation into an analysis model. Analysis activities include:

- Identifying Entity Objects (Section 5.4.1)
- Identifying Boundary Objects (Section 5.4.2)
- Identifying Control Objects (Section 5.4.3)
- Mapping Use Cases to Objects with Sequence Diagrams (Section 5.4.4)
- Modeling Interactions among Objects with CRC Cards (Section 5.4.5)
- Identifying Associations (Section 5.4.6)
- Identifying Aggregates (Section 5.4.7)
- Identifying Attributes (Section 5.4.8)
- Modeling State-Dependent Behavior of Individual Objects (Section 5.4.9)

- Modeling Inheritance Relationships (Section 5.4.10)

- Reviewing the Analysis Model (Section 5.4.11).

We illustrate each activity by focusing on the ReportEmergency use case of FRIEND described in Chapter 4, *Requirements Elicitation*. These activities are guided by heuristics. The quality of their outcome depends on the experience of the developer in applying these heuristics and methods. The methods and heuristics presented in this section are adapted from [De Marco, 1978], [Jacobson et al., 1999], [Rumbaugh et al., 1991], and [Wirfs-Brock et al., 1990].

5.4.1   Identifying Entity Objects

Participating objects (see Section 4.4.6) form the basis of the analysis model. As described in Chapter 4, *Requirements Elicitation*, participating objects are found by examining each use case and identifying candidate objects. Natural language analysis [Abbott, 1983] is an intuitive set of heuristics for identifying objects, attributes, and associations from a requirements specification. Abbott's heuristics maps parts of speech (e.g., nouns, having verbs, being verbs, adjectives) to model components (e.g., objects, operations, inheritance relationships, classes). Table 5-1 provides examples of such mappings by examining the ReportEmergency use case (Figure 5-7).

Natural language analysis has the advantage of focusing on the users' terms. However, it suffers from several limitations. First, the quality of the object model depends highly on the style of writing of the analyst (e.g., consistency of terms used, verbification of nouns). Natural language is an imprecise tool, and an object model derived literally from text risks being imprecise. Developers can address this limitation by rephrasing and clarifying the requirements specification as they identify and standardize objects and terms. A second limitation of natural

Table 5-1   Abbott's heuristics for mapping parts of speech to model components [Abbott, 1983].

Part of speech	Model component	Examples
Proper noun	Instance	Alice
Common noun	Class	Field officer
Doing verb	Operation	Creates, submits, selects
Being verb	Inheritance	Is a kind of, is one of either
Having verb	Aggregation	Has, consists of, includes
Modal verb	Constraints	Must be
Adjective	Attribute	Incident description

Use case name	ReportEmergency
Entry condition	1. The FieldOfficer activates the "Report Emergency" function of her terminal.
Flow of events	2. FRIEND responds by presenting a form to the officer. The form includes an emergency type menu (general emergency, fire, transportation), a location, incident description, resource request, and hazardous material fields.
	3. The FieldOfficer completes the form by specifying minimally the emergency type and description fields. The FieldOfficer may also describe possible responses to the emergency situation and request specific resources. Once the form is completed, the FieldOfficer submits the form by pressing the "Send Report" button, at which point, the Dispatcher is notified.
	4. The Dispatcher reviews the information submitted by the FieldOfficer and creates an Incident in the database by invoking the OpenIncident use case. All the information contained in the FieldOfficer's form is automatically included in the incident. The Dispatcher selects a response by allocating resources to the incident (with the AllocateResources use case) and acknowledges the emergency report by sending a FRIENDgram to the FieldOfficer.
Exit condition	5. The FieldOfficer receives the acknowledgment and the selected response.

Figure 5-7   An example of use case, ReportEmergency (one-column format).

language analysis is that there are many more nouns than relevant classes. Many nouns correspond to attributes or synonyms for other nouns. Sorting through all the nouns for a large requirements specification is a time-consuming activity. In general, Abbott's heuristics work well for generating a list of initial candidate objects from short descriptions, such as the flow of events of a scenario or a use case. The following heuristics can be used in conjunction with Abbott's heuristics:

Heuristics for identifying entity objects

- Terms that developers or users need to clarify in order to understand the use case
- Recurring nouns in the use cases (e.g., Incident)
- Real-world entities that the system needs to track (e.g., FieldOfficer, Dispatcher, Resource)
- Real-world activities that the system needs to track (e.g., EmergencyOperationsPlan)
- Data sources or sinks (e.g., Printer).

Developers name and briefly describe the objects, their attributes, and their responsibilities as they are identified. Uniquely naming objects promotes a standard terminology. For entity objects we recommend *always* to start with the names used by end users and application domain specialists. Describing objects, even briefly, allows developers to clarify the concepts they use and avoid misunderstandings (e.g., using one object for two different but related concepts). Developers need not, however, spend a lot of time detailing objects or attributes given that the analysis model is still in flux. Developers should document attributes and responsibilities if they are not obvious; a tentative name and a brief description for each object is sufficient otherwise. There will be plenty of iterations during which objects can be revised. However, once the analysis model is stable, the description of each object should be as detailed as necessary (see Section 5.4.11).

For example, after a first examination of the ReportEmergency use case (Figure 5-7), we use application domain knowledge and interviews with the users to identify the objects Dispatcher, EmergencyReport, FieldOfficer, and Incident. Note that the EmergencyReport object is not mentioned explicitly by name in the ReportEmergency use case. Step 4 of the use case refers to the emergency report as the "information submitted by the FieldOfficer." After review with the client, we discover that this information is usually referred to as the "emergency report" and decide to name the corresponding object EmergencyReport.

The definition of entity objects leads to the initial analysis model described in Table 5-2. Note that this model is far from a complete description of the system implementing the ReportEmergency use case. In the next section, we describe the identification of boundary objects.

Table 5-2   Entity objects for the ReportEmergency use case.

Dispatcher	Police officer who manages Incidents. A Dispatcher opens, documents, and closes Incidents in response to Emergency Reports and other communication with FieldOfficers. Dispatchers are identified by badge numbers.
EmergencyReport	Initial report about an Incident from a FieldOfficer to a Dispatcher. An EmergencyReport usually triggers the creation of an Incident by the Dispatcher. An EmergencyReport is composed of an emergency level, a type (fire, road accident, other), a location, and a description.
FieldOfficer	Police or fire officer on duty. A FieldOfficer can be allocated to, at most, one Incident at a time. FieldOfficers are identified by badge numbers.
Incident	Situation requiring attention from a FieldOfficer. An Incident may be reported in the system by a FieldOfficer or anybody else external to the system. An Incident is composed of a description, a response, a status (open, closed, documented), a location, and a number of FieldOfficers.

5.4.2   Identifying Boundary Objects

Boundary objects represent the system interface with the actors. In each use case, each actor interacts with at least one boundary object. The boundary object collects the information from the actor and translates it into a form that can be used by both entity and control objects.

Boundary objects model the user interface at a coarse level. They do not describe in detail the visual aspects of the user interface. For example, boundary objects such as "menu item" or "scroll bar" are too detailed. First, developers can discuss user interface details more easily with sketches and mock-ups. Second, the design of the user interface continues to evolve as a consequence of usability tests, even after the functional specification of the system becomes stable. Updating the analysis model for every user interface change is time consuming and does not yield any substantial benefit.

Heuristics for identifying boundary objects

- Identify user interface controls that the user needs to initiate the use case (e.g., ReportEmergencyButton).
- Identify forms the users needs to enter data into the system (e.g., EmergencyReportForm).
- Identify notices and messages the system uses to respond to the user (e.g., AcknowledgmentNotice).
- When multiple actors are involved in a use case, identify actor terminals (e.g., DispatcherStation) to refer to the user interface under consideration.
- Do not model the visual aspects of the interface with boundary objects (user mock-ups are better suited for that).
- *Always* use the end user's terms for describing interfaces; do not use terms from the solution or implementation domains.

We find the boundary objects of Table 5-3 by examining the ReportEmergency use case.

Table 5-3   Boundary objects for the ReportEmergency use case.

AcknowledgmentNotice	Notice used for displaying the Dispatcher's acknowledgment to the FieldOfficer.
DispatcherStation	Computer used by the Dispatcher.
ReportEmergencyButton	Button used by a FieldOfficer to initiate the ReportEmergency use case.
EmergencyReportForm	Form used for the input of the ReportEmergency. This form is presented to the FieldOfficer on the FieldOfficerStation when the "Report Emergency" function is selected. The EmergencyReportForm contains fields for specifying all attributes of an emergency report and a button (or other control) for submitting the completed form.
FieldOfficerStation	Mobile computer used by the FieldOfficer.
IncidentForm	Form used for the creation of Incidents. This form is presented to the Dispatcher on the DispatcherStation when the EmergencyReport is received. The Dispatcher also uses this form to allocate resources and to acknowledge the FieldOfficer's report.

Note that the IncidentForm is not explicitly mentioned anywhere in the ReportEmergency use case. We identified this object by observing that the Dispatcher needs an interface to view the emergency report submitted by the FieldOfficer and to send back an acknowledgment. The terms used for describing the boundary objects in the analysis model should follow the user terminology, even if it is tempting to use terms from the implementation domain.

We have made progress toward describing the system. We now have included the interface between the actor and the system. We are, however, still missing some significant pieces of the description, such as the order in which the interactions between the actors and the system occur. In the next section, we describe the identification of control objects.

5.4.3 Identifying Control Objects

Control objects are responsible for coordinating boundary and entity objects. Control objects usually do not have a concrete counterpart in the real world. Often a close relationship exists between a use case and a control object; a control object is usually created at the beginning of a use case and ceases to exist at its end. It is responsible for collecting information from the boundary objects and dispatching it to entity objects. For example, control objects describe the behavior associated with the sequencing of forms, undo and history queues, and dispatching information in a distributed system.

Initially, we model the control flow of the ReportEmergency use case with a control object for each actor: ReportEmergencyControl for the FieldOfficer and ManageEmergency-Control for the Dispatcher, respectively (Table 5-4).

The decision to model the control flow of the ReportEmergency use case with two control objects stems from the knowledge that the FieldOfficerStation and the DispatcherStation are actually two subsystems communicating over an asynchronous link. This decision could have been postponed until the system design activity. On the other hand, making this concept visible in the analysis model allows us to focus on such exception behavior as the loss of communication between both stations.

Heuristics for identifying control objects
- Identify one control object per use case.
- Identify one control object per actor in the use case.
- The life span of a control object should cover the extent of the use case or the extent of a user session. If it is difficult to identify the beginning and the end of a control object activation, the corresponding use case probably does not have well-defined entry and exit conditions.

In modeling the ReportEmergency use case, we modeled the same functionality by using entity, boundary, and control objects. By shifting from the event flow perspective to a structural perspective, we increased the level of detail of the description and selected standard terms to refer to the main entities of the application domain and the system. In the next section, we

Table 5-4   Control objects for the ReportEmergency use case.

ReportEmergencyControl	Manages the ReportEmergency reporting function on the FieldOfficerStation. This object is created when the FieldOfficer selects the "Report Emergency" button. It then creates an EmergencyReportForm and presents it to the FieldOfficer. After submitting the form, this object then collects the information from the form, creates an EmergencyReport, and forwards it to the Dispatcher. The control object then waits for an acknowledgment to come back from the DispatcherStation. When the acknowledgment is received, the ReportEmergencyControl object creates an AcknowledgmentNotice and displays it to the FieldOfficer.
ManageEmergencyControl	Manages the ReportEmergency reporting function on the DispatcherStation. This object is created when an EmergencyReport is received. It then creates an IncidentForm and displays it to the Dispatcher. Once the Dispatcher has created an Incident, allocated Resources, and submitted an acknowledgment, ManageEmergencyControl forwards the acknowledgment to the FieldOfficerStation.

construct a sequence diagram using the ReportEmergency use case and the objects we discovered to ensure the completeness of our model.

5.4.4   Mapping Use Cases to Objects with Sequence Diagrams

A **sequence diagram** ties use cases with objects. It shows how the behavior of a use case (or scenario) is distributed among its participating objects. Sequence diagrams are usually not as good a medium for communication with the user as use cases are, since sequence diagrams require more background about the notation. For computer savvy clients, they are intuitive and can be more precise than use cases. In all cases, however, sequence diagrams represent another shift in perspective and allow the developers to find missing objects or grey areas in the requirements specification.

In this section, we model the sequence of interactions among objects needed to realize the use case. Figures 5-8 through 5-10 are sequence diagrams associated with the ReportEmergency use case. The columns of a sequence diagram represent the objects that participate in the use case. The left-most column is the actor who initiates the use case. Horizontal arrows across columns represent messages, or stimuli, that are sent from one object to the other. Time proceeds vertically from top to bottom. For example, the first arrow in Figure 5-8 represents the press message sent by a FieldOfficer to an ReportEmergencyButton. The receipt of a message triggers the activation of an operation. The activation is represented by a vertical rectangle from which other messages can originate. The length of the rectangle represents the time the operation is active. In Figure 5-8, the operation triggered by the press message sends a create message to the ReportEmergencyControl class. An operation can be thought of as a service that the object provides to other objects. Sequence diagrams also depict the lifetime of objects. Objects that already exist before the first stimuli in the sequence diagram are depicted at the top of the diagram. Objects that are created during the interaction are depicted with the «create» message pointing to the object. Instances that are destroyed during the interaction have a cross indicating when the object ceases to exist. Between the rectangle representing the object and the cross (or the bottom of the diagram, if the object survives the interaction), a dashed line represents the time span when the object can receive messages. The object cannot receive messages below the cross sign. For example, in Figure 5-8 an object of class ReportEmergencyForm is created when object of ReportEmergencyControl sends the «create» message and is destroyed once the EmergencyReportForm has been submitted.

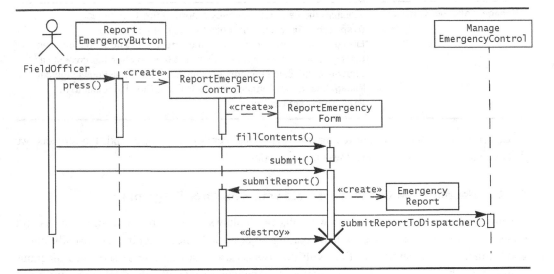

Figure 5-8   Sequence diagram for the ReportEmergency use case.

In general, the second column of a sequence diagram represents the boundary object with which the actor interacts to initiate the use case (e.g., ReportEmergencyButton). The third column is a control object that manages the rest of the use case (e.g., ReportEmergency-Control). From then on, the control object creates other boundary objects and may interact with other control objects as well (e.g., ManageEmergencyControl).

In Figure 5-9, we discover the entity object Acknowledgment that we forgot during our initial examination of the ReportEmergency use case (in Table 5-2). The Acknowledgment object is different from an AcknowledgmentNotice: Acknowledgment holds the information associated with an Acknowledgment and is created before the AcknowledgmentNotice boundary object. When describing the Acknowledgment object, we also realize that the original ReportEmergency use case (described in Figure 5-7) is incomplete. It only mentions the existence of an Acknowledgment and does not describe the information associated with it. In this case, developers need clarification from the client to define what information is needed in the

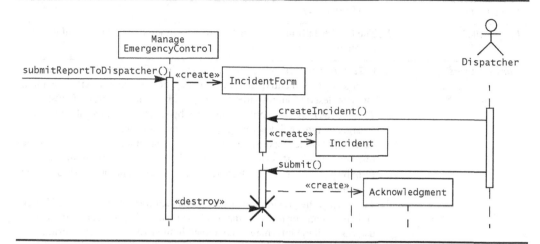

Figure 5-9 Sequence diagram for the ReportEmergency use case (continued from Figure 5-8).

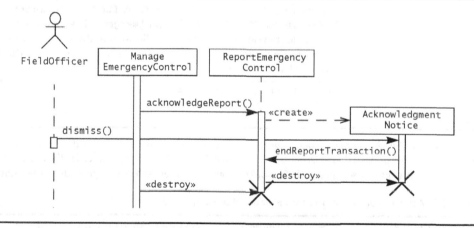

Figure 5-10 Sequence diagram for the ReportEmergency use case (continued from Figure 5-9).

Acknowledgment. After obtaining such clarification, the Acknowledgment object is added to the analysis model (Table 5-5), and the ReportEmergency use case is clarified to include the additional information (Figure 5-11).

By constructing sequence diagrams, we not only model the order of the interaction among the objects, we also distribute the behavior of the use case. That is, we assign responsibilities to each object in the form of a set of operations. These operations can be shared by any use case in which a given object participates. Note that the definition of an object that is shared across two or more use cases should be identical; that is, if an operation appears in more than one sequence diagram, its behavior should be the same.

Use case name	ReportEmergency
Entry condition	1. The FieldOfficer activates the "Report Emergency" function of her terminal.
Flow of events	2. FRIEND responds by presenting a form to the officer. The form includes an emergency type menu (general emergency, fire, transportation), a location, incident description, resource request, and hazardous material fields.
	3. The FieldOfficer completes the form by specifying minimally the emergency type and description fields. The FieldOfficer may also describe possible responses to the emergency situation and request specific resources. Once the form is completed, the FieldOfficer submits the form by pressing the "Send Report" button, at which point the Dispatcher is notified.
	4. The Dispatcher reviews the information submitted by the FieldOfficer and creates an Incident in the database by invoking the OpenIncident use case. All the information contained in the FieldOfficer's form is automatically included in the Incident. The Dispatcher selects a response by allocating resources to the Incident (with the AllocateResources use case) and acknowledges the emergency report by sending a FRIENDgram to the FieldOfficer. **The Acknowledgment indicates to the FieldOfficer that the EmergencyReport was received, an Incident created, and resources allocated to the Incident. The Acknowledgment includes the resources (e.g., a fire truck) and their estimated arrival time.**
Exit condition	5. The FieldOfficer receives the Acknowledgment and the selected response.

Figure 5-11 Refined ReportEmergency use case. The discovery and addition of the Acknowledgment object to the analysis model revealed that the original ReportEmergency use case did not accurately describe the information associated with Acknowledgments. The refinements are indicated in **boldface**.

Table 5-5 Acknowledgment object for the ReportEmergency use case.

Acknowledgment	Response of a dispatcher to a FieldOfficer's EmergencyReport. By sending an Acknowledgment, the Dispatcher communicates to the FieldOfficer that she has received the EmergencyReport, created an Incident, and assigned resources to it. The Acknowledgment contains the assigned resources and their estimated arrival time.

Sharing operations across use cases allows developers to remove redundancies in the requirements specification and to improve its consistency. Note that clarity should always be given precedence to eliminating redundancy. Fragmenting behavior across many operations unnecessarily complicates the requirements specification.

In analysis, sequence diagrams are used to help identify new participating objects and missing behavior. Because sequence diagrams focus on high-level behavior, implementation issues such as performance should not be addressed at this point. Given that building interaction diagrams can be time consuming, developers should focus on problematic or underspecified functionality first. Drawing interaction diagrams for parts of the system that are simple or well defined might not look like a good investment of analysis resources, but it should also be done to avoid overlooking some key decisions.

Heuristics for drawing sequence diagrams

- The first column should correspond to the actor who initiated the use case.
- The second column should be a boundary object (that the actor used to initiate the use case).
- The third column should be the control object that manages the rest of the use case.
- Control objects are created by boundary objects initiating use cases.
- Boundary objects are created by control objects.
- Entity objects are accessed by control and boundary objects.
- Entity objects *never* access boundary or control objects; this makes it easier to share entity objects across use cases.

5.4.5   Modeling Interactions among Objects with CRC Cards

An alternative for identifying interactions among objects are **CRC cards** [Beck & Cunningham, 1989]. CRC cards (CRC stands for class, responsibilities, and collaborators) were initially introduced as a tool for teaching object-oriented concepts to novices and to experienced developers unfamiliar with object-orientation. Each class is represented with an index card (called the CRC card). The name of the class is depicted on the top, its responsibilities in the left column, and the names of the classes it needs to accomplish its responsibilities are depicted in the right column. Figure 5-12 depicts two cards for the ReportEmergencyControl and the Incident classes.

CRC cards can be used during modeling sessions with teams. Participants, typically a mix of developers and application domain experts, go through a scenario and identify the classes that are involved in realizing the scenario. One card per instance is put on the table. Responsibilities

ReportEmergencyControl		Incident	
Responsibilities	**Collaborators**	**Responsibilities**	**Collaborators**
Collects input from Field-officer	EmergencyReportForm EmergencyReport AcknowledgementNotic	Track all information related to a single incident.	Resource
Controls sequence of forms during emergency reporting			

Figure 5-12   Examples of CRC cards for the ReportEmergencyControl and the Incident classes.

are then assigned to each class as the scenario unfolds and participants negotiate the responsibilities of each object. The collaborators column is filled as the dependencies with other cards are identified. Cards are modified or pushed to the side as new alternatives are explored. Cards are never thrown away, because building blocks for past alternatives can be reused when new ideas are put on the table.

CRC cards and sequence diagrams are two different representations for supporting the same type of activity. Sequence diagrams are a better tool for a single modeler or for documenting a sequence of interactions, because they are more precise and compact. CRC cards are a better tool for a group of developers refining and iterating over an object structure during a brainstorming session, because they are easier to create and to modify.

5.4.6   Identifying Associations

Whereas sequence diagrams allow developers to represent interactions among objects over time, class diagrams allow developers to describe the interdependencies of objects. We described the UML class diagram notation in Chapter 2, *Modeling with UML*, and use it throughout the book to represent various project artifacts (e.g., activities, deliverables). In this section, we discuss the use of class diagrams for representing associations among objects. In Section 5.4.8, we discuss the use of class diagrams for representing object attributes.

An **association** shows a relationship between two or more classes. For example, a FieldOfficer writes an EmergencyReport (see Figure 5-13). Identifying associations has two advantages. First, it clarifies the analysis model by making relationships between objects explicit (e.g., an EmergencyReport can be created by a FieldOfficer or a Dispatcher). Second, it enables the developer to discover boundary cases associated with links. Boundary cases are exceptions that must be clarified in the model. For example, it is intuitive to assume that most EmergencyReports are written by one FieldOfficer. However, should the system support EmergencyReports written by more than one? Should the system allow for anonymous EmergencyReports? Those questions should be investigated during analysis by discussing them with the client or with end users.

Associations have several properties:

- A **name** to describe the association between the two classes (e.g., Writes in Figure 5-13). Association names are optional and need not be unique globally.

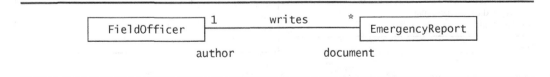

Figure 5-13   An example of association between the EmergencyReport and the FieldOfficer classes.

- A **role** at each end, identifying the function of each class with respect to the associations (e.g., author is the role played by FieldOfficer in the Writes association).

- A **multiplicity** at each end, identifying the possible number of instances (e.g., * indicates a FieldOfficer may write zero or more EmergencyReports, whereas 1 indicates that each EmergencyReport has exactly one FieldOfficer as author).

Initially, the associations between entity objects are the most important, as they reveal more information about the application domain. According to Abbott's heuristics (see Table 5-1), associations can be identified by examining verbs and verb phrases denoting a state (e.g., *has, is part of, manages, reports to, is triggered by, is contained in, talks to, includes*). Every association should be named, and roles should be assigned to each end.

Heuristics for identifying associations

- Examine verb phrases.
- Name associations and roles precisely.
- Use qualifiers as often as possible to identify namespaces and key attributes.
- Eliminate any association that can be derived from other associations.
- Do not worry about multiplicity until the set of associations is stable.
- Too many associations make a model unreadable.

The object model will initially include too many associations if developers include all associations identified after examining verb phrases. In Figure 5-14, for example, we identify two relationships: the first between an Incident and the EmergencyReport that triggered its creation; the second between the Incident and the reporting FieldOfficer. Given that the EmergencyReport and FieldOfficer already have an association modeling authorship, the association between Incident and FieldOfficer is not necessary. Adding unnecessary associations complicates the model, leading to incomprehensible models and redundant information.

Most entity objects have an identifying characteristic used by the actors to access them. FieldOfficers and Dispatchers have a badge number. Incidents and Reports are assigned numbers and are archived by date. Once the analysis model includes most classes and associations, the developers should go through each class and check how it is identified by the actors and in which context. For example, are FieldOfficer badge numbers unique across the universe? Across a city? A police station? If they are unique across cities, can the FRIEND system know about FieldOfficers from more than one city? This approach can be formalized by examining each individual class and identifying the sequence of associations that need to be traversed to access a specific instance of that class.

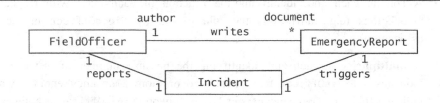

Figure 5-14 Eliminating redundant association. The receipt of an EmergencyReport triggers the creation of an Incident by a Dispatcher. Given that the EmergencyReport has an association with the FieldOfficer that wrote it, it is not necessary to keep an association between FieldOfficer and Incident.

5.4.7   Identifying Aggregates

Aggregations are special types of associations denoting a whole–part relationship. For example, a FireStation consists of a number of FireFighters, FireEngines, Ambulances, and a LeadCar. A State is composed of a number of Counties that are, in turn, composed of a number of Townships (Figure 5-15). An aggregation is shown as a association with a diamond on the side of the whole part.

There are two types of aggregation, composition and shared. A solid diamond denotes composition. A **composition aggregation** indicates that the existence of the parts depends on the whole. For example, a County is always part of exactly one State, a Township is always part of a County. As political boundaries do not change often, a Township will not be part of or shared with another County (at least, in the life time of the emergency response system).

A hollow diamond denotes a **shared aggregation** relationship, indicating the whole and the part can exist independently. For example, although a FireEngine is part of at most one FireStation at the time, it can be reassigned to a different FireStation during its life time.

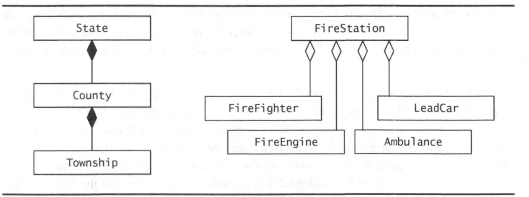

Figure 5-15 Examples of aggregations and compositions (UML class diagram). A State is composed of many Counties, which in turn is composed of many Townships. A FireStation includes FireFighters, FireEngines, Ambulances, and a LeadCar.

Aggregation associations are used in the analysis model to denote whole–part concepts. Aggregation associations add information to the analysis model about how containment concepts in the application domain can be organized in a hierarchy or in a directed graph. Aggregations are often used in the user interface to help the user browse through many instances. For example, in Figure 5-15, FRIEND could offer a tree representation for Dispatchers to find Counties within a State or Townships with a specific County. However, as with many modeling concepts, it is easy to over-structure the model. If you are not sure that the association you are describing is a whole–part concept, it is better to model it as a one-to-many association, and revisit it later when you have a better understanding of the application domain.

5.4.8   Identifying Attributes

Attributes are properties of individual objects. For example, an EmergencyReport, as described in Table 5-2, has an emergency type, a location, and a description property (see Figure 5-16). These are entered by a FieldOfficer when she reports an emergency and are subsequently tracked by the system. When identifying properties of objects, only the attributes relevant to the system should be considered. For example, each FieldOfficer has a social security number that is not relevant to the emergency information system. Instead, FieldOfficers are identified by badge number, which is represented by the badgeNumber property.

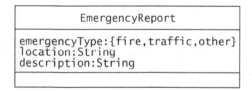

Figure 5-16   Attributes of the EmergencyReport class.

Properties that are represented by objects are not attributes. For example, every EmergencyReport has an author that is represented by an association to the FieldOfficer class. Developers should identify as many associations as possible before identifying attributes to avoid confusing attributes and objects. Attributes have:

- A **name** identifying them within an object. For example, an EmergencyReport may have a reportType attribute and an emergencyType attribute. The reportType describes the kind of report being filed (e.g., initial report, request for resource, final report). The emergencyType describes the type of emergency (e.g., fire, traffic, other). To avoid confusion, these attributes should not both be called type.

- A brief description.

- A **type** describing the legal values it can take. For example, the `description` attribute of an `EmergencyReport` is a string. The `emergencyType` attribute is an enumeration that can take one of three values: `fire`, `traffic`, `other`. Attribute types are based on predefined basic types in UML.

Attributes can be identified using Abbott's heuristics (see Table 5-1). In particular, a noun phrase followed by a possessive phrase (e.g., the description of an emergency) or an adjective phrase (e.g., the emergency description) should be examined. In the case of entity objects, any property that must be stored by the system is a candidate attribute.

Note that attributes represent the least stable part of the object model. Often, attributes are discovered or added late in the development when the system is evaluated by the users. Unless the added attributes are associated with additional functionality, the added attributes do not entail major changes in the object (and system) structure. For these reasons, the developers need not spend excessive resources in identifying and detailing attributes that represent less important aspects of the system. These attributes can be added later when the analysis model or the user interface sketches are validated.

Heuristics for identifying attributes[a]

- Examine possessive phrases.
- Represent stored state as an attribute of the entity object.
- Describe each attribute.
- Do not represent an attribute as an object; use an association instead (see Section 5.4.6).
- Do not waste time describing fine details before the object structure is stable.

---

a.   Adapted from [Rumbaugh et al., 1991].

5.4.9   Modeling State-Dependent Behavior of Individual Objects

Sequence diagrams are used to distribute behavior across objects and to identify operations. Sequence diagrams represent the behavior of the system from the perspective of a single use case. State machine diagrams represent behavior from the perspective of a single object. Viewing behavior from the perspective of each object enables the developer to build a more formal description of the behavior of the object, and consequently, to identify missing use cases. By focusing on individual states, developers may identify new behavior. For example, by examining each transition in the state machine diagram that is triggered by a user action, the developer should be able to identify a flow step in a use case that describes the actor action that triggers the transition. Note that it is not necessary to build state machines for every class in the system. Only objects with an extended lifespan and state-dependent behavior are worth considering. This is almost always the case for control objects, less often for entity objects, and almost never for boundary objects.

Figure 5-17 displays a state machine for the Incident class. The examination of this state machine may help the developer to check if there are use cases for documenting, closing, and archiving Incidents. By further refining each state, the developer can add detail to the different user actions that change the state of an incident. For example, during the Active state of an indicate, FieldOfficers should be able to request new resources, and Dispatchers should be able to allocate resource to existing incidents.

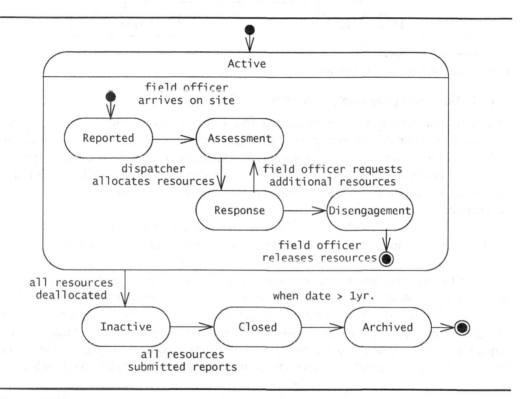

Figure 5-17   UML state machine for Incident.

5.4.10 Modeling Inheritance Relationships between Objects

Generalization is used to eliminate redundancy from the analysis model. If two or more classes share attributes or behavior, the similarities are consolidated into a superclass. For example, Dispatchers and FieldOfficers both have a badgeNumber attribute that serves to identify them within a city. FieldOfficers and Dispatchers are both PoliceOfficers who are assigned different functions. To model explicitly this similarity, we introduce an abstract *PoliceOfficer* class from which the FieldOfficer and Dispatcher classes inherit (see Figure 5-18).

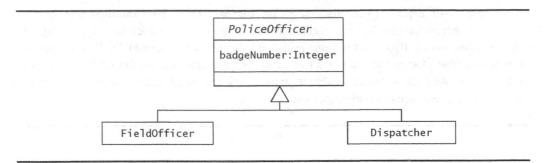

Figure 5-18   An example of inheritance relationship (UML class diagram).

5.4.11 Reviewing the Analysis Model

The analysis model is built incrementally and iteratively. The analysis model is seldom correct or even complete on the first pass. Several iterations with the client and the user are necessary before the analysis model converges toward a correct specification usable by the developers for design and implementation. For example, an omission discovered during analysis will lead to adding or extending a use case in the requirements specification, which may lead to eliciting more information from the user.

Once the number of changes to the model are minimal and the scope of the changes localized, the analysis model becomes stable. Then the analysis model is reviewed, first by the developers (i.e., internal reviews), then jointly by the developers and the client. The goal of the review is to make sure that the requirements specification is correct, complete, consistent, and unambiguous. Moreover, developers and client also review if the requirements are realistic and verifiable. Note that developers should be prepared to discover errors downstream and make changes to the specification. It is, however, a worthwhile investment to catch as many requirements errors upstream as possible. The review can be facilitated by a checklist or a list of questions. Below are example questions adapted from [Jacobson et al., 1999] and [Rumbaugh et al., 1991].

The following questions should be asked to ensure that the model is *correct*:
- Is the glossary of entity objects understandable by the user?
- Do abstract classes correspond to user-level concepts?
- Are all descriptions in accordance with the users' definitions?
- Do all entity and boundary objects have meaningful noun phrases as names?
- Do all use cases and control objects have meaningful verb phrases as names?
- Are all error cases described and handled?

The following questions should be asked to ensure that the model is *complete*:
- For each object: Is it needed by any use case? In which use case is it created? modified? destroyed? Can it be accessed from a boundary object?

- For each attribute: When is it set? What is its type? Should it be a qualifier?
- For each association: When is it traversed? Why was the specific multiplicity chosen? Can associations with one-to-many and many-to-many multiplicities be qualified?
- For each control object: Does it have the necessary associations to access the objects participating in its corresponding use case?

The following questions should be asked to ensure that the model is *consistent*:
- Are there multiple classes or use cases with the same name?
- Do entities (e.g., use cases, classes, attributes) with similar names denote similar concepts?
- Are there objects with similar attributes and associations that are not in the same generalization hierarchy?

The following questions should be asked to ensure that the system described by the analysis model is *realistic*:
- Are there any novel features in the system? Were any studies or prototypes built to ensure their feasibility?
- Can the performance and reliability requirements be met? Were these requirements verified by any prototypes running on the selected hardware?

5.4.12 Analysis Summary

The requirements elicitation activity is highly iterative and incremental. Chunks of functionality are sketched and proposed to the users and the client. The client adds requirements, criticizes existing functionality, and modifies existing requirements. The developers investigate nonfunctional requirements through prototyping and technology studies and challenge each proposed requirement. Initially, requirements elicitation resembles a brainstorming activity. As the description of the system grows and the requirements become more concrete, developers need to extend and modify the analysis model in a more orderly manner to manage the complexity of information.

Figure 5-19 depicts a typical sequence of the analysis activities. The users, developers, and client are involved in developing an initial use case model. They identify a number of concepts and build a glossary of participating objects. These first two activities were discussed in the previous chapter. The remaining activities were covered in this section. The developers classify the participating objects into entity, boundary, and control objects (in *Define entity objects*, Section 5.4.1, *Define boundary objects*, Section 5.4.2, and *Define control objects*, Section 5.4.3). These activities occur in a tight loop until most of the functionality of the system has been identified as use cases with names and brief descriptions. Then the developers construct sequence diagrams to identify any missing objects (*Define interactions*, Section 5.4.4). When all entity objects have been named and briefly described, the analysis model should remain fairly stable as it is refined.

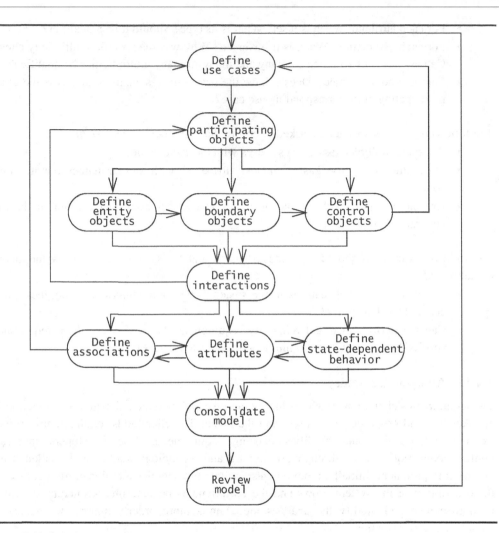

Figure 5-19   Analysis activities (UML activities diagram).

Define associations (Section 5.4.6), *Define attributes* (Section 5.4.8) and *Define state-dependent behavior* (Section 5.4.9) constitute the refinement of the analysis model. These three activities occur in a tight loop during which the state of the objects and their associations are extracted from the sequence diagrams and detailed. The use cases are then modified to account for any changes in functionality. This phase may lead to the identification of an additional chunk of functionality in the form of additional use cases. The overall process is then repeated incrementally for these new use cases.

During *Consolidate model* (Section 5.4.10), the developers solidify the model by introducing qualifiers and generalization relationships and suppressing redundancies. During *Review model* (Section 5.4.11), the client, users, and developers examine the model for correctness, consistency, completeness, and realism. The project schedule should plan for multiple reviews to ensure high-quality requirements and to provide opportunities to learn the requirements activity. However, once the model reaches the point where most modifications are cosmetic, system design should proceed. There will come a point during requirements where no more problems can be anticipated without further information from prototyping, usability studies, technology surveys, or system design. Getting every detail right becomes a wasteful exercise: some of these details will become irrelevant by the next change. Management should recognize this point and initiate the next phase in the project.

5.5 Managing Analysis

In this section, we discuss issues related to managing the analysis activities in a multi-team development project. The primary challenge in managing the requirements in such a project is to maintain consistency while using so many resources. In the end, the requirements analysis document should describe a single coherent system understandable to a single person.

We first describe a document template that can be used to document the results of analysis (Section 5.5.1). Next, we describe the role assignment to analysis (Section 5.5.2). We then address communication issues during analysis. Next, we address management issues related to the iterative and incremental nature of requirements (Section 5.5.4).

5.5.1 Documenting Analysis

As we saw in the previous chapter, the requirements elicitation and analysis activities are documented in the Requirements Analysis Document (RAD, Figure 5-20). RAD Sections 1 through 3.5.2 have already been written during requirements elicitation. During analysis, we revise these sections as ambiguities and new functionality are discovered. The main effort, however, focuses on writing the sections documenting the analysis object model (RAD Sections 3.5.3 and 3.5.4).

RAD Section 3.5.3, *Object models*, documents in detail all the objects we identified, their attributes, and, when we used sequence diagrams, operations. As each object is described with textual definitions, relationships among objects are illustrated with class diagrams.

RAD Section 3.5.4, *Dynamic models*, documents the behavior of the object model in terms of state machine diagrams and sequence diagrams. Although this information is redundant with the use case model, dynamic models enable us to represent more precisely complex behaviors, including use cases involving many actors.

The RAD, once completed and published, will be baselined and put under configuration management. The revision history section of the RAD will provide a history of changes including the author responsible for each change, the date of the change, and brief description of the change.

Requirements Analysis Document

1. Introduction
2. Current system
3. Proposed system
    3.1 Overview
    3.2 Functional requirements
    3.3 Nonfunctional requirements
    3.4 System models
        3.4.1 Scenarios
        3.4.2 Use case model
        3.4.3 Object model
            3.4.3.1 Data dictionary
            3.4.3.2 Class diagrams
        3.4.4 Dynamic models
        3.4.5 User interface—navigational paths and screen mock-ups
4. Glossary

Figure 5-20 Overview outline of the Requirements Analysis Document (RAD). See Figure 4-16 for a detailed outline.

5.5.2 Assigning Responsibilities

Analysis requires the participation of a wide range of individuals. The target user provides application domain knowledge. The client funds the project and coordinates the user side of the effort. The analyst elicits application domain knowledge and formalizes it. Developers provide feedback on feasibility and cost. The project manager coordinates the effort on the development side. For large systems, many users, analysts, and developers may be involved, introducing additional challenges during for integration and communication requirements of the project. These challenges can be met by assigning well-defined roles and scopes to individuals. There are three main types of roles: generation of information, integration, and review.

- The **end user** is the application domain expert who generates information about the current system, the environment of the future system, and the tasks it should support. Each user corresponds to one or more actors and helps identify their associated use cases.

- The **client**, an integration role, defines the scope of the system based on user requirements. Different users may have different views of the system, either because they will benefit from different parts of the system (e.g., a dispatcher vs. a field officer) or because the users have different opinions or expectations about the future system. The client serves as an integrator of application domain information and resolves inconsistencies in user expectations.

- The **analyst** is the application domain expert who models the current system and generates information about the future system. Each analyst is initially responsible for detailing one or more use cases. For a set of use cases, the analysis will identify a number of objects, their associations, and their attributes using the techniques outlined in Section 5.4. The analyst is typically a developer with broad application domain knowledge.

- The **architect**, an integration role, unifies the use case and object models from a system point of view. Different analysts may have different styles of modeling and different views of the parts of the systems for which they are not responsible. Although analysts work together and will most likely resolve differences as they progress through analysis, the role of the architect is necessary to provide a system philosophy and to identify omissions in the requirements.

- The **document editor** is responsible for the low-level integration of the document and for the overall format of the document and its index.

- The **configuration manager** is responsible for maintaining a revision history of the document as well as traceability information relating the RAD with other documents (such as the System Design Document; see Chapter 6, *System Design: Decomposing the System*).

- The **reviewer** validates the RAD for correctness, completeness, consistency, and clarity. Users, clients, developers, or other individuals may become reviewers during requirements validation. Individuals that have not yet been involved in the development represent excellent reviewers, because they are more able to identify ambiguities and areas that need clarification.

The size of the system determines the number of different users and analysts that are needed to elicit and model the requirements. In all cases, there should be one integrating role on the client side and one on the development side. In the end, the requirements, however large the system, should be understandable by a single individual knowledgeable in the application domain.

5.5.3   Communicating about Analysis

The task of communicating information is most challenging during requirements elicitation and analysis. Contributing factors include

- *Different backgrounds of participants.* Users, clients, and developers have different domains of expertise and use different vocabularies to describe the same concepts.

- *Different expectations of stakeholders.* Users, clients, and managements have different objectives when defining the system. Users want a system that supports their current work processes, with no interference or threat to their current position (e.g., an improved system often translates into the elimination of current positions). The client wants to maximize return on investment. Management wants to deliver the system on time. Different expectations and different stakes in the project can lead to a reluctance to share information and to report problems in a timely manner.

- *New teams.* Requirements elicitation and analysis often marks the beginning of a new project. This translates into new participants and new team assignments, and, thus, into a ramp-up period during which team members must learn to work together.

- *Evolving system.* When a new system is developed from scratch, terms and concepts related to the new system are in flux during most of the analysis and the system design. A term may have a different meaning tomorrow.

No requirements method or communication mechanism can address problems related to internal politics and information hiding. Conflicting objectives and competition will always be part of large development projects. A few simple guidelines, however, can help in managing the complexity of conflicting views of the system:

- *Define clear territories.* Defining roles as described in Section 5.5.2 is part of this activity. This also includes the definition of private and public discussion forums. For example, each team may have a discussion database as described in Chapter 3, *Project Organization and Communication*, and discussion with the client is done on a separate client database. The client should not have access to the internal database. Similarly, developers should not interfere with client/user internal politics.

- *Define clear objectives and success criteria.* The codefinition of clear, measurable, and verifiable objectives and success criteria by both the client and the developers facilitates the resolution of conflicts. Note that defining a clear and verifiable objective is a nontrivial task, given that it is easier to leave objectives open-ended. The objectives and the success criteria of the project should be documented in Section 1.3 of the RAD.

- *Brainstorm.* Putting all the stakeholders in the same room and to quickly generate solutions and definitions can remove many barriers in communication. Conducting reviews as a reciprocal activity (i.e., reviewing deliverables from both the client and the developers during the same session) has a similar effect.

Brainstorming, and more generally the cooperative development of requirements, can lead to the definition of shared, ad hoc notations for supporting the communication. Storyboards, user interface sketches, and high-level dataflow diagrams often appear spontaneously. As the information about the application domain and the new system accrue, it is critical that a precise and structured notation be used. In UML, developers employ use cases and scenarios for communicating with the client and the users, and use object diagrams, sequence diagrams, and state machines to communicate with other developers (see Sections 4.4 and 5.4). Moreover, the latest release of the requirements should be available to all participants. Maintaining a live online version of the requirements analysis document with an up-to-date change history facilitates the timely propagation of changes across the project.

5.5.4 Iterating over the Analysis Model

Analysis occurs iteratively and incrementally, often in parallel with other development activities such as system design and implementation. Note, however, that the unrestricted modification and extension of the analysis model can only result in chaos, especially when a large number of participants are involved. Iterations and increments must be carefully managed and requests for changes tracked once the requirements are baselined. The requirements activity can be viewed as several steps (brainstorming, solidification, maturity) converging toward a stable model.

Brainstorming

Before any other development activity is initiated, requirements is a brainstorming process. Everything—concepts and the terms used to refer to them—changes. The objective of a brainstorming process is to generate as many ideas as possible without necessarily organizing them. During this stage, iterations are rapid and far reaching.

Solidification

Once the client and the developers converge on a common idea, define the boundaries of the system, and agree on a set of standard terms, solidification starts. Functionality is organized into groups of use cases with their corresponding interfaces. Groups of functionality are allocated to different teams that are responsible for detailing their corresponding use cases. During this stage, iterations are rapid but localized.

Maturity

Changes at the higher level are still possible but more difficult, and thus, are made more carefully. Each team is responsible for the use cases and object models related to the functionality they have been assigned. A cross-functional team, the architecture team, made of representatives of each team, is responsible for ensuring the integration of the requirements (e.g., naming).

Once the client signs off on the requirements, modification to the analysis model should address omissions and errors. Developers, in particular the architecture team, need to ensure that the consistency of the model is not compromised. The requirements model is under configuration management and changes should be propagated to existing design models. Iterations are slow and often localized.

The number of features and functions of a system will always increase with time. Each change, however, can threaten the integrity of the system. The risk of introducing more problems with late changes results from the loss of information in the project. The dependencies across functions are not all captured; many assumptions may be implicit and forgotten by the time the change is made. Often the change responds to a problem, in which case there is a lot of pressure to implement it, resulting in only a superficial examination of the consequence of the change. When new features and functions are added to the system, they should be challenged with the following questions: Were they requested by the client? Are they necessary, or are they embellishments? Should they be part of a separate, focused utility program instead of part of the base system? Are the changes core requirements or optional features? What is the impact of the changes to existing functions in terms of consistency, interface, reliability?

When changes are necessary, the client and developer define the scope of the change and its desired outcome and change the analysis model. Given that a complete analysis model exists for the system, specifying new functionality is easier (although implementing it is more difficult).

5.5.5   Client Sign-Off

The client sign-off represents the acceptance of the analysis model (as documented by the requirements analysis document) by the client. The client and the developers converge on a single idea and agree about the functions and features that the system will have. In addition, they agree on:

- a list of priorities
- a revision process
- a list of criteria that will be used to accept or reject the system
- a schedule and a budget.

Prioritizing system functions allows the developers to understand better the client's expectations. In its simplest form, it allows developers to separate bells and whistles from essential features. It also allows developers to deliver the system in incremental chunks: essential functions are delivered first, additional chunks are delivered depending on the evaluation of the previous chunk. Even if the system is to be delivered as a single, complete package, prioritizing functions enables the client to communicate clearly what is important to her and where the emphasis of the development should be. Figure 5-21 provides an example of a priority scheme.

Each function shall be assigned one of the following priorities

- **High priority**—A high-priority feature must be demonstrated successfully during client acceptance.
- **Medium priority**—A medium-priority feature must be taken into account in the system design and the object design. It will be implemented and demonstrated in the second iteration of the system development.
- **Low priority**—A low-priority feature illustrates how the system can be extended in the longer term.

Figure 5-21   An example of a priority scheme for requirements.

After the client sign off, the requirements are baselined and are used for refining the cost estimate of the project. Requirements continue to change after the sign-off, but these changes are subject to a more formal revision process. The requirements change, whether because of errors, omissions, changes in the operating environment, changes in the application domain, or changes in technology. Defining a revision process up front encourages changes to be communicated across the project and reduces the number of surprises in the later stages. Note that a change process need not be bureaucratic or require excessive overhead. It can be as simple as naming a person responsible for receiving change requests, approving changes, and tracking their implementation. Figure 5-22 depicts a more complex example in which changes are designed

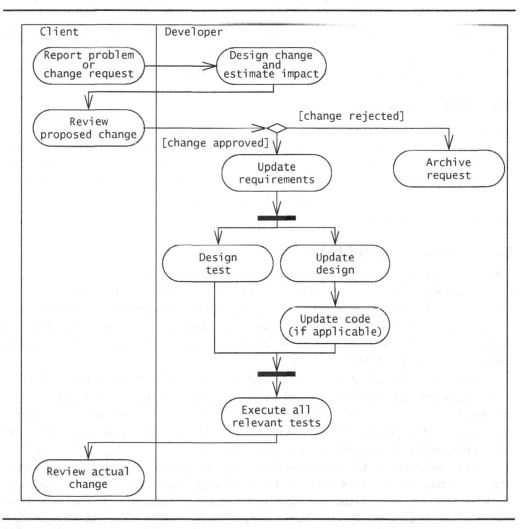

Figure 5-22 An example of a revision process (UML activity diagram).

and reviewed by the client before they are implemented in the system. In all cases, acknowledging that requirements cannot be frozen (but only baselined) will benefit the project.

The list of acceptance criteria is revised prior to sign-off. The requirements elicitation and analysis activity clarifies many aspects of the system, including the nonfunctional requirements with which the system should comply and the relative importance of each function. By restating the acceptance criteria at sign-off, the client ensures that the developers are updated about any changes in client expectations.

The budget and schedule are revisited after the analysis model becomes stable. We describe in Chapter 14, *Project Management*, issues related to cost estimation.

Whether the client sign-off is a contractual agreement or whether the project is already governed by a prior contract, it is an important milestone in the project. It represents the convergence of client and developer on a single set of functional definitions of the system and a single set of expectations. The acceptance of the requirements analysis document is more critical than any other document, given that many activities depend on the analysis model.

5.6 ARENA Case Study

In this section, we apply the concepts and methods described in this chapter to the ARENA system. We start with the use case model and the glossary developed in the previous chapter. We identify participating entity, boundary, and control objects, and refine them by adding attributes and associations to the analysis object model. Finally, we identify inheritance relationships and consolidate the analysis object model. In this section, we focus primarily on the AnnounceTournament use case.

5.6.1 Identifying Entity Objects

Entity objects represent concepts in the application domain that are tracked by the system. We use the glossary produced during elicitation as a starting point for identifying entity objects in ARENA. We identify additional entity objects and their attributes by applying Abbott's heuristics on the use cases. We initially focus only on noun phrases that denote concepts of the application domain. Figure 5-23 depicts the AnnounceTournament use case with the first occurrence of noun phrases we identified in **bold**.

Note that we identify entity objects corresponding to actors in the use case model. Actors are concepts in the application domain and are relevant to the system (e.g., for access control or for documenting responsibilities or authorship). In ARENA, each legitimate LeagueOwner is represented with an object that is used to store data specific to that LeagueOwner, such as her contact information, the leagues that she manages, and so on.

Note, also, that not all noun phrases we identified correspond to classes. For example, name of a tournament is a noun phrase referring to an attribute of the Tournament class. List of Advertisers is an association, in this case, between the League class and the Advertiser class. We can use a few simple heuristics to distinguish between noun phrases that correspond to objects, attributes, and associations:

Name	AnnounceTournament

Flow of events   1. The **LeagueOwner** requests the creation of a **tournament**.

2. The system checks if the LeagueOwner has exceeded the **number of tournaments** in the **league** or in the **arena**. If not, the system presents the LeagueOwner with a form.

3. The LeagueOwner specifies a **name**, **application start and end dates** during which Players can apply to the tournament, **start and end dates** for conducting the tournament, and a **maximum number of Players**.

4. The system asks the LeagueOwner whether an exclusive sponsorship should be sought and, if yes, presents a **list of Advertisers** who expressed the desire to be **exclusive sponsors**.

5. If the LeagueOwner decides to seek an exclusive sponsor, he selects a subset of the **names** of the **proposed sponsors**.

6. The system notifies the selected sponsors about the upcoming tournament and the **flat fee** for exclusive sponsorships.

7. The system communicates their **answers** to the LeagueOwner.

8. If there are interested sponsors, the LeagueOwner selects one of them.

9. The system records the **name** of the exclusive sponsor and charges the flat fee for sponsorships to the **Advertiser's account**. From now on, all **advertisement banners** associated with the tournament are provided by the exclusive sponsor only.

10. If no sponsors were selected (either because no Advertisers were interested or the LeagueOwner did not select any), the advertisement banners are selected at random and charged to each Advertiser's account on a per unit basis.

11. Once the sponsorship issues is closed, the system prompts the LeagueOwner with a **list of groups of Players, Spectators, and Advertisers** that could be interested in the new tournament.

12. The LeagueOwner selects which groups to notify.

13. The system creates a home page in the arena for the tournament. This page is used as an entry point to the tournament (e.g., to provide interested Players with a form to apply for the tournament, and to interest Spectators into watching **matches**).

14. At the **application start date**, the system notifies each interested user by sending them a link to the main tournament page. The Players can then apply for the tournament with the ApplyForTournament use case until the **application end date**.

Figure 5-23   Applying Abbott's heuristics for identifying entity objects in the AnnounceTournament use case. The first occurrence of a noun phrase is emphasized in **bold**.

- *Attributes are properties.* Attributes represent a single property of an object. They represent a partial aspect of an object and are incomplete. For example, the name of an Advertiser is an attribute that identifies an Advertiser. However, it does not include other relevant information about the Advertiser (e.g., her current account balance, the type of banners she advertises, etc.) that are represented by other attributes or associations of the Advertiser class.

- *Attributes have simple types.* Attributes are properties that often have types such as a number (e.g., maximum number of Tournaments), string (e.g., the name of an Advertiser), dates (e.g., the application start and end date of a Tournament). Properties such as an address, a social security number, and a vehicle identification number are also usually considered as simple types (and hence represented as attributes) because users treat those as simple, atomic concepts. Complex concepts are represented as objects that are related to other objects with associations. For example, an Account is an object that is related to the corresponding Advertiser and can include a balance, a history of transactions, a credit limit, and other similar properties.

- *Nouns referring to collections are associations, often with implicit ends.* Lists, groups, tables, and sets are represented by associations. For example, ARENA prompts the LeagueOwner with a list of Advertisers that are potentially interested in exclusive sponsorships. This concept can be represented with an association between the Arena class and the Advertiser class, denoting which Advertisers are interested in exclusive sponsorships. Often, the association end is implicit. For example, when sponsorship issues are closed, ARENA prompts the LeagueOwner with a list of groups of Players, Spectators, and Advertisers. We identify a new class, InterestGroup, representing collections of users interested in new events about a league or a game. Then, we identify an association between the Arena class and the InterestGroup class (corresponding to the word "list") representing all InterestGroups. Then, we identify an association between the InterestGroup class and the Player, Spectator, and Advertisers classes (corresponding to the word "group"). Finally, we identify additional associations originating from the InterestGroup class to other classes representing the interest of the users in the InterestGroup (i.e., League, Game).

Table 5-6 lists the entity objects, their attributes, and their associations that we identified so far from the AnnounceTournament use case. We attach the attributes and associations to their relevant classes and write definitions for new classes. Writing definitions has several purposes. First, a name is not specific enough for all stakeholders to share the same understanding about the concept. For example, terms such as Game and Match can be interchanged in many contexts. In ARENA, however, they refer to distinct concepts (i.e., a Game represents a set of rules enforced by a piece of software, a Match represent a competition among a set of Players). Second, objects identified during analysis correspond also to terms in the glossary we started during elicitation. Stakeholders use the glossary throughout development to resolve ambiguities and establish a standard terminology. Writing short definitions as classes are identified is the best way to prevent ambiguities and misunderstandings. Postponing the writing of definitions results in loss of information and in incomplete definitions.

Table 5-6   Entity objects participating in the AnnounceTournament use case identified from noun phrases in the use case. "(?)" denote areas of uncertainty that lead to the questions in Figure 5-24.

Entity Object	Attributes & Associations	Definition
Account	• balance • history of charges (?) • history of payments (?)	An Account represents the amount currently owed by an Advertiser, a history of charges, and payments.
Advertiser	• name • leagues of interest for exclusive sponsorships (?) • sponsored tournaments • account	Actor interested in displaying advertisement banners during the Matches.
Advertisement	• associated game (?)	Image provided by an Advertiser for display during matches.
Arena	• max number of tournaments • flat fee for sponsorships (?) • leagues *(implied)* • interest groups *(implied)*	An instantiation of the ARENA system.
Game		A Game is a competition among a number of Players that is conducted according to a set of rules. In ARENA, the term Game refers to a piece of software that enforces the set of rules, tracks the progress of each Player, and decides the winner.
InterestGroup	• list of players, spectators, or advertisers • games and leagues of interests *(implied)*	InterestGroups are lists of users in the ARENA which share an interest (e.g, for a game or a league). InterestGroups are used as mailing lists for notifying potential actors of new events.
League	• max number of tournament • game	A League represents a community for running Tournaments. A League is associated with a specific Game and TournamentStyle. Players registered with the League accumulate points according to the ExpertRating of the League.

Table 5-6 *Continued.*

Entity Object	Attributes & Associations	Definition
LeagueOwner	• name *(implied)*	The actor creating a League and responsible for organizing Tournaments within the League.
Match	• tournament • players	A Match is a contest between two or more Players within the scope of a Game. The outcome of a Match can be a single winner and a set of losers or a tie (in which their are no winners or losers). Some TournamentStyles may disallow ties.
Player	• name *(implied)*	
Tournament	• name • application start date • application end date • play start date • play end date • max number of players • exclusive sponsor	A Tournament is a series of Matches among a set of Players. Tournaments end with a single winner. The way Players accumulate points and Matches are scheduled is dictated by the League in which the Tournament is organized.

The identification of entity objects and their related attributes usually triggers additional questions for the client. For example, when we identify implicit attributes and associations, we should double-check with the client to confirm whether our intuition was correct. In other cases, the ends of an association are ambiguous. We collect all the questions generated by the identification of objects and go back to the client (or the domain expert). Figure 5-24 depicts the questions we have after identifying entity objects participating in the AnnounceTournament use case.

Questions for the ARENA client

- What information should be recorded in the advertisers' accounts? For example, should a complete log of the display of each advertisement banner be recorded?
- Do advertisers express the interest for exclusive sponsorships for specific leagues or for the complete arena?
- Should advertisement banners be associated to games (to enable a more intelligent selection of banners when there is no exclusive sponsorship)?
- Does the flat fee for exclusive sponsorship vary across leagues or tournaments?

Figure 5-24 Questions triggered by the identification of entity objects.

5.6.2   Identifying Boundary Objects

Boundary objects represent the interface between the system and the actors. They are identified from the use cases and usually represent the user interface at a coarse level. Do not represent layout information or user interface details such as menus and buttons. User interface mock-ups are much better suited for this type of information. Instead, boundary objects represent concepts such as windows, forms, or hardware artifacts such as workstations. This enables stakeholders to visualize where functionality is available in the system.

Abbott's heuristics do not identify many boundary objects, as they are often left implicit initially. Instead, we scan the AnnounceTournament use case (Figure 5-23) and identify where information is exchanged between the actors and the system. We focus both on forms in which actors provide information to the system (e.g., the form used by the LeagueOwner to create a Tournament) and on notices in which the system provides information to the actors (e.g., a notice received by Advertisers requesting sponsorship). As with other objects, we briefly define each class as we identify it. Table 5-7 depicts the boundary objects we identified for AnnounceTournament with their definitions. Figure 5-25 depicts our additional questions.

Note that AnnounceTournament is a relatively complex use case involving several actors. This yields a relatively large number boundary objects. In practice, a use case can have as few as a single boundary object to represent the interface between the initiating actor and the system. In all cases, however, each use case should have at least one participating boundary object (possibly shared with other use cases).

Table 5-7   Boundary objects participating in the AnnounceTournament use case.

Boundary Object	Definition
TournamentForm	Form used by the LeagueOwner to specify the properties of a Tournament during creation or editing.
RequestSponsorshipForm	Form used by the LeagueOwner to request sponsorships from interested Advertisers.
SponsorshipRequest	Notice received by Advertisers requesting sponsorship.
SponsorshipReply	Notice received by LeagueOwner indicating whether an Advertiser wants the exclusive sponsorship of the tournament.
SelectExclusiveSponsorForm	Form used by the LeagueOwner to close the sponsorship issue.
NotifyInterestGroupsForm	Form used by the LeagueOwner to notify interested users.
InterestGroupNotice	Notice received by interested users about the creation of a new Tournament.

More questions for the ARENA client

- What should we do about sponsors who do not answer?
- How should we advertise a new tournament if there are no relevant interest groups?
- How should users be notified (e.g., E-mail, cell phone, ARENA notice box)?

Figure 5-25   Questions triggered by the identification of boundary objects.

5.6.3   Identifying Control Objects

Control objects represent the coordination among boundary and entity objects. In the common case, a single control object is created at the beginning of the use case and accumulates all the information needed to complete the use case. The control object is then destroyed with the completion of the use case.

In AnnounceTournament, we identify a single control object called AnnounceTournamentControl, which is responsible for sending and collecting notices to Advertisers, checking resource availability, and, finally, notifying interested users. Note that, in the general case, several control objects could participate in the same use case, if, for example, there are alternate flows of events to be coordinated, multiple workstations operating asynchronously, or if some control information survives the completion of the use case.

5.6.4   Modeling Interactions Among Objects

We have identified a number of entity, boundary, and control objects participating in the AnnounceTournament use case. Along the way, we also identified some of their attributes and associations. We represent these objects in a sequence diagram, depicting the interactions that occur during the use case to identify additional associations and attributes.

In the sequence diagram, we arrange the objects we identified along the top row. We place left-most the initiating actor (i.e., LeagueOwner), followed by the boundary object responsible for initiating the use case (i.e., TournamentForm), followed by the main control object (i.e., AnnounceTournamentControl), and the entity objects (i.e., Arena, League, and Tournament). Any other participating actors and their corresponding boundary objects are on the right of the diagram. We split the sequence diagram associated with AnnounceTournament into three figures for space reasons. Figure 5-26 depicts the sequence of interactions leading to the creation of a tournament. Figure 5-27 depicts the workflow for requesting and selecting an exclusive sponsor. Figure 5-28 focuses on the notification of interest groups.

The sequence diagram in Figure 5-26 is straightforward. The LeagueOwner requests the creation of the tournament and specifies its initial parameter (e.g., name, maximum number of players). The AnnounceTournamentControl instance is created and, if resources allow, a Tournament entity instance is created.

The sequence diagram in Figure 5-27 is more interesting as it leads to the identification of additional associations and attributes. When requesting sponsorships, the control object must

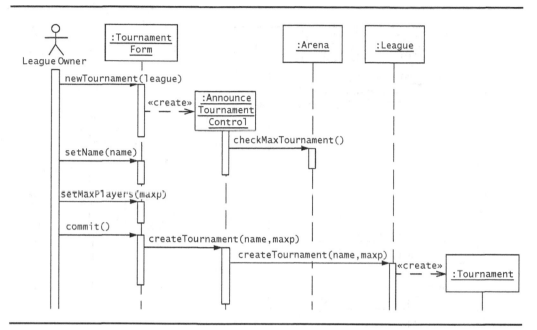

Figure 5-26 UML sequence diagram for AnnounceTournament, tournament creation workflow.

first obtain a list of interested sponsors. It requests it from the Arena class, which maintains the list of interested sponsors. This entails that the Arena class maintains at all times the list of all Advertisers, so that it can return this list to the AnnounceTournamentControl object (or control objects for other use cases that require the list of all Advertisers). To notify an Advertiser, we also may need contact information, such as E-mail address, or we may need to create a mailbox for notices within ARENA. Consequently, we add an contact attribute to the Advertiser class, which initially stores the E-mail address of the Advertiser until further devices are supported. Anticipating similar needs for other actors, we also add contact attributes to the LeagueOwner and Player classes.

When constructing the sequence diagram for notifying interest groups (Figure 5-28), we realize that the use case does not specify how the selected sponsor is notified. Consequently, we add a step in the use case to notify all sponsors who replied about the sponsorship decisions before interest groups are notified. This requires the identification of a new boundary object, SponsorNotice. The rest of the interaction does not yield any new discovery, as we already anticipated the need for the InterestGroup and the InterestGroupNotice classes.

5.6.5 Reviewing and Consolidating the Analysis Model

Now that we have identified most participating objects, their associations, and their attributes, we draw UML class diagrams documenting the results of our analysis so far. As we have identified many objects, we use several class diagrams to depict the analysis object model. We

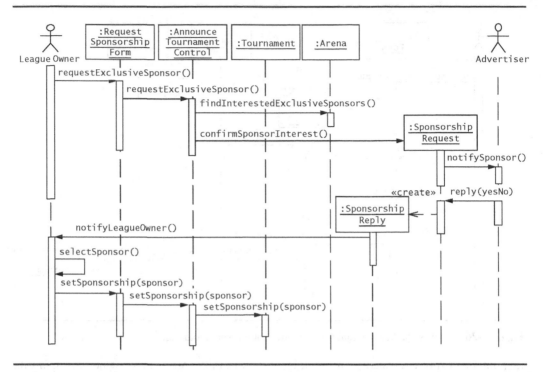

Figure 5-27 UML sequence diagram for AnnounceTournament use case, sponsorship workflow.

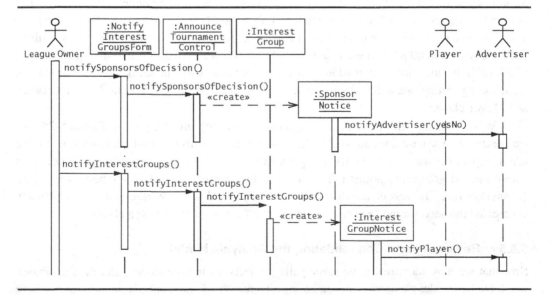

Figure 5-28 UML sequence diagram for AnnounceTournament use case, interest group workflow.

use these class diagrams as a visual index into the glossary we developed. Although we should not expect the client or the users to be able to review class diagrams, we can use class diagrams for generating more questions for interviews with the client.

We first focus on the entity objects, since these need to be carefully reviewed by the client as they represent application domain concepts (Figure 5-29). Note that we use the Arena class as a root object in the system; the Arena class represents a specific instantiation. For example, given an instantiation, it is possible to get a list of all InterestGroups, Advertisers, LeagueOwners, Games, and TournamentStyles by querying the Arena class. Moreover, note that objects are not shared among instantiations. For example, LeagueOwners belong to exactly one instantiation of the system. If a user is a LeagueOwner in several ARENA instantiations of the system, she holds a LeagueOwner account in each instantiation. We make these type of choices during analysis based on our interpretation of the problem statement, based on our experience, and based on resources available to build in the system. In all cases, these decisions need to be reviewed and confirmed by the client.

Next, we draw a class diagram depicting the inheritance hierarchies (Figure 5-30). Although UML allows inheritance relationships and associations to coexist in the same diagram, it is good practice during analysis to draw two separate diagrams to depict each type of

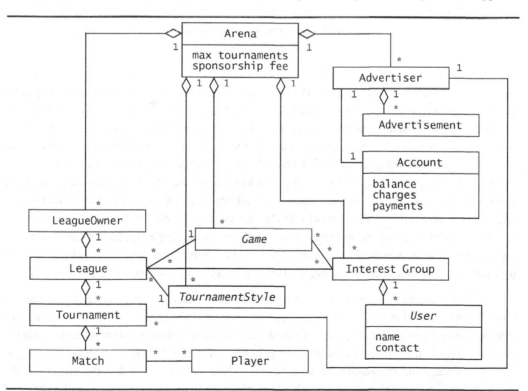

Figure 5-29   Entity objects identified after analyzing the AnnounceTournament use case.

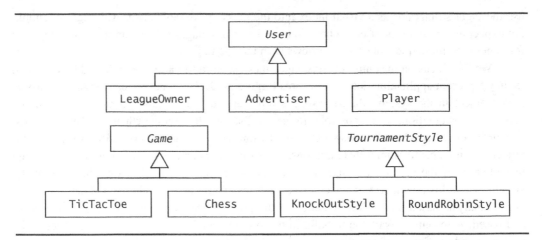

Figure 5-30   Inheritance hierarchy among entity objects of the AnnounceTournament use case.

relationship. First, the UML symbols used to denote each type are similar and easily confused. Second, analysts usually focus on inheritance and associations at different times. We will see later, in Chapters 6 through 10, that this is not the case during system design and object design, where it is often necessary to consider both relationships to understand how different classes are related.

Figure 5-30 shows three inheritance hierarchies. First, we identified an abstract class User through generalization. This enables us to treat common attributes of various users in a more general fashion, including contact information and registration procedures. Note that in the problem statement and in the use cases, we already used the term "user," so we are simply formalizing a concept that was already in use. We identified two other inheritance hierarchies, Game and TournamentStyle, identified through specialization to provide examples for both concepts and to provide traceability to the problem statement. The TicTacToe and the Chess classes are concrete specializations of Game that embody rules for the games called "tic tac toe" and "chess," respectively. The KnockOutStyle and the RoundRobinStyle classes are concrete specializations of the TournamentStyle that provide algorithms for assigning Players to knockout tournaments (in which players need to win to remain in the tournament) and round robin tournaments (in which each player plays all other players exactly once), respectively.

Finally, we draw a class diagram that depicts the associations among the boundary, control, and selected entity objects associated with the use case (Figure 5-31). To generate this diagram from the sequence diagrams, we draw the equivalent communication diagram, with the control object to the left, the boundary objects in the center, and the entity objects on the right. We then replace the iterations with associations, where necessary, so that the objects in the workflow can carry send messages to objects depicted in the sequence diagrams. We then add navigation to the associations to denote the direction of the dependencies: control and boundary objects usually know about each other, but entity objects do not depend on any control or boundary objects.

Whereas the class diagram in Figure 5-29 focused primarily on the relationships among application domain concepts, the class diagram of Figure 5-31 focuses on the concepts associated with workflow of the use case at a coarse level. The control object acts as the glue among boundary and entity objects, since it represents the coordination and the sequencing among the forms and notices. As indicated in the sequence diagrams in Figures 5-26 through 5-28, the control object also creates several of the boundary objects. The class diagram in Figure 5-31 provides a summary of the objects participating in the use case and the associations traversed during the use case. However, the sequence diagrams provide the complete sequencing information of the workflow.

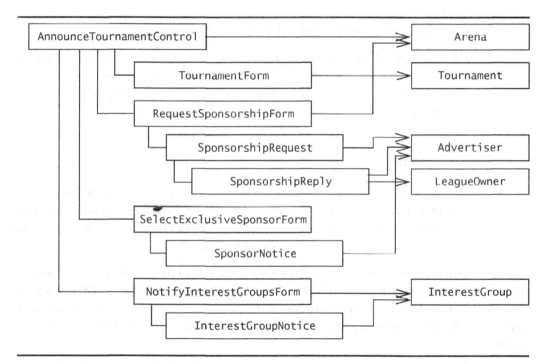

Figure 5-31   Associations among boundary, control, and selected entity objects participating in the AnnounceTournament use case.

5.6.6   Lessons Learned

In this section, we developed the part of the analysis object model relevant to the AnnounceTournament use case of ARENA. We started by identifying entity objects using Abbott's heuristics, then identified boundary and control objects, and used sequence diagrams to find additional associations, attributes, and objects. Finally, we consolidated the object model and depicted it with a series of class diagrams. We learned that:

- Identifying objects, their attributes and associations, takes many iterations, often with the client.

- Object identification uses many sources, including the problem statement, use case model, the glossary, and the event flows of the use cases.

- A nontrivial use case can require many sequence diagrams and several class diagrams. It is unrealistic to represent all discovered objects in a single diagram. Instead, each diagram serves a specific purpose—for example, depicting associations among entity objects, or depicting associations among participating objects in one use case.

- Key deliverables, such as the glossary, should be kept up to date as the analysis model is revised. Others, such as sequence diagrams, can be redone later if necessary. Maintaining consistency at all times, however, is unrealistic.

- There are many different ways to model the same application domain or the same system, based on the personal style and experience of the analyst. This calls for developing style guides and conventions within a project, so that all analysts can communicate effectively.

5.7 Further Readings

The classification of analysis objects into entity, boundary, and control objects has been made popular by the Objectory method [Jacobson et al., 1992]. These concepts originated from the model/view/controller (MVC) paradigm used in the Smalltalk-80 environment and also found their way into the Java Swing user interface framework [JFC, 2009].

CRC cards were introduced by Beck and Cunningham for teaching object-oriented thinking to novices and experienced developers in an OOPSLA paper entitled *A Laboratory For Teaching Object-Oriented Thinking* [Beck & Cunningham, 1989]. CRC cards are used extensively in the responsibility-driven design method from Wirfs-Brock [Wirfs-Brock et al., 1990].

Object-oriented analysis and design has evolved from many different sets of heuristics and terminologies. Modeling, like programming, is a craft, and requires much experience and willingness to make mistakes (hence the importance of client and user feedback). *Object-Oriented Modeling and Design* [Rumbaugh et al., 1991] provides an excellent guide to novices for class modeling. A more recent book, *Applying UML and Patterns* [Larman, 2005], provides a comprehensive treatment of object-oriented analysis and design, including use case modeling and reusing design patterns. For dynamic modeling with state machines, *Doing Hard Time: Using Object Oriented Programming and Software Patterns in Real Time Applications* [Douglass, 1999] provides detailed information and modeling heuristics on the topic.

5.8 Exercises

5-1   Consider a file system with a graphical user interface, such as Macintosh's Finder, Microsoft's Windows Explorer, or Linux's KDE. The following objects were identified from a use case describing how to copy a file from a floppy disk to a hard disk: File, Icon, TrashCan, Folder, Disk, Pointer. Specify which are entity objects, which are boundary objects, and which are control objects.

5-2   Assuming the same file system as before, consider a scenario consisting of selecting a File on a floppy, dragging it to Folder and releasing the mouse. Identify and define at least one control object associated with this scenario.

5-3   Arrange the objects listed in Exercises 5-1 and 5-2 horizontally on a sequence diagram, the boundary objects to the left, then the control object you identified, and finally, the entity objects. Draw the sequence of interactions resulting from dropping the file into a folder. For now, ignore the exceptional cases.

5-4   Examining the sequence diagram you produced in Exercise 5-3, identify the associations between these objects.

5-5   Identify the attributes of each object that are relevant to this scenario (copying a file from a floppy disk to a hard disk). Also consider the exception cases "There is already a file with that name in the folder" and "There is no more space on disk."

5-6   Consider the object model in Figure 5-32 (adapted from [Jackson, 1995]):

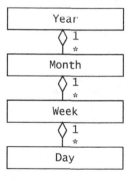

Figure 5-32   A naive model of the Gregorian calendar (UML class diagram).

Given your knowledge of the Gregorian calendar, list all the problems with this model. Modify it to correct each of them.

5-7   Consider the object model of Figure 5-32. Using association multiplicity only, can you modify the model such that a developer unfamiliar with the Gregorian calendar could deduce the number of days in each month? Identify additional classes if necessary.

5-8   Consider a traffic light system at a four-way crossroads (two roads intersecting at right
       angles). Assume the simplest algorithm for cycling through the lights (e.g., all traffic on
       one road is allowed to go through the crossroad, while the other traffic is stopped).
       Identify the states of this system and draw a state machine describing them. Remember
       that each individual traffic light has three states (green, yellow, and red).

5-9   From the sequence diagram Figure 2-34, draw the corresponding class diagram. Hint:
       Start with the participating objects in the sequence diagram.

5-10   Consider the addition of a nonfunctional requirement stipulating that the effort needed
       by Advertisers to obtain exclusive sponsorships should be minimized. Change the
       AnnounceTournament (Figure 5-23) and the ManageAdvertisements use case (solution
       of Exercise 4-12) so that the Advertiser can specify preferences in her profile so that
       exclusive sponsorships can be decided automatically by the system.

5-11   Identify and write definitions for any additional entity, boundary, and control objects
       participating in the AnnounceTournament use case that were introduced by realizing the
       change specified in Exercise 5-10.

5-12   Update the class diagrams of Figure 5-29 and Figure 5-31 to include the new objects
       you identified in Exercise 5-11.

5-13   Draw a state machine describing the behavior of the AnnounceTournamentControl
       object based on the sequence diagrams of Figures 5-26 through 5-28. Treat the sending
       and receiving of each notice as an event that triggers a change of state.

References

[Abbott, 1983] R. Abbott, "Program design by informal English descriptions," *Communications of the ACM*, Vol. 26, No. 11, 1983.

[Beck & Cunningham, 1989] K. Beck & W. Cunningham, "A laboratory for teaching object-oriented thinking," *OOPSLA'89 Conference Proceedings*, New Orleans, LA, Oct. 1–6, 1989.

[De Marco, 1978] T. De Marco, *Structured Analysis and System Specification*, Yourdon, New York, 1978.

[Douglass, 1999] B. P. Douglass, *Doing Hard Time: Using Object Oriented Programming and Software Patterns in Real Time Applications*, Addison-Wesley, Reading, MA, 1999.

[Jackson, 1995] M. Jackson, *Software Requirements & Specifications: A Lexicon of Practice, Principles and Prejudices*, Addison-Wesley, Reading, MA, 1995.

[Jacobson et al., 1992] I. Jacobson, M. Christerson, P. Jonsson, & G. Overgaard, *Object-Oriented Software Engineering—A Use Case Driven Approach*, Addison-Wesley, Reading, MA, 1992.

[Jacobson et al., 1999] I. Jacobson, G. Booch, & J. Rumbaugh, *The Unified Software Development Process*, Addison-Wesley, Reading, MA, 1999.

[JFC, 2009] *Java Foundation Classes*, JDK Documentation, Javasoft, 2009.

[Larman, 2005] C. Larman, *Applying UML and Patterns: An Introduction to Object-Oriented Analysis and Design*, 3rd ed., Prentice Hall, Upper Saddle River, NJ, 2005.

[Rumbaugh et al., 1991] J. Rumbaugh, M. Blaha, W. Premerlani, F. Eddy, & W. Lorensen, *Object-Oriented Modeling and Design*, Prentice Hall, Englewood Cliffs, NJ, 1991.

[Wirfs-Brock et al., 1990] R. Wirfs-Brock, B. Wilkerson, & L. Wiener, *Designing Object-Oriented Software*, Prentice Hall, Englewood Cliffs, NJ, 1990.

6

System Design: Decomposing the System

There are two ways of constructing a software design: One way is to make it so simple that there are obviously no deficiencies, and the other way is to make it so complicated that there are no obvious deficiencies.
—C.A.R. Hoare, in *The Emperor's Old Clothes*

System design is the transformation of an analysis model into a system design model. During system design, developers define the design goals of the project and decompose the system into smaller subsystems that can be realized by individual teams. Developers also select strategies for building the system, such as the hardware/software strategy, the persistent data management strategy, the global control flow, the access control policy, and the handling of boundary conditions. The result of system design is a model that includes a subsystem decomposition and a clear description of each of these strategies.

System design is not algorithmic. Developers have to make trade-offs among many design goals that often conflict with each other. They also cannot anticipate all design issues that they will face because they do not yet have a clear picture of the solution domain. System design is decomposed into several activities, each addressing part of the overall problem of decomposing the system:

- *Identify design goals.* Developers identify and prioritize the qualities of the system that they should optimize.
- *Design the initial subsystem decomposition.* Developers decompose the system into smaller parts based on the use case and analysis models. Developers use standard architectural styles as a starting point during this activity.
- *Refine the subsystem decomposition to address the design goals.* The initial decomposition usually does not satisfy all design goals. Developers refine it until all goals are satisfied.

In this chapter, we focus on the first two activities. In the next chapter, we refine the system decomposition and provide an in-depth example with the ARENA case study.

6.1 Introduction: A Floor Plan Example

System design, object design, and implementation constitute the construction of the system. During these three activities, developers bridge the gap between the requirements specification, produced during requirements elicitation and analysis, and the system that is delivered to the users. System design is the first step in this process and focuses on decomposing the system into manageable parts. During requirements elicitation and analysis, we concentrated on the purpose and the functionality of the system. During system design, we focus on the processes, data structures, and software and hardware components necessary to implement it. The challenge of system design is that many conflicting criteria and constraints must be met when decomposing the system.

Consider, for example, the task of designing a residential house. After agreeing with the client on the number of rooms and floors, the size of the living area, and the location of the house, the architect must design the floor plan, that is, where the walls, doors, and windows should be located. He must do so according to a number of functional requirements: the kitchen should be close to the dining room and the garage, the bathroom should be close to the bedrooms, and so on. The architect can also rely on a number of standards when establishing the dimensions of each room and the location of the door: kitchen cabinets come in fixed increments and beds come in standard sizes. Note, however, that the architect does not need to know the exact contents of each room and the layout of the furniture; on the contrary, these decisions should be delayed and left to the client.

Figure 6-1 shows three successive revisions to a floor plan for a residential house. We set out to satisfy the following constraints:

1. This house should have two bedrooms, a study, a kitchen, and a living room area.
2. The overall distance the occupants walk every day should be minimized.
3. The use of daylight should be maximized.

To satisfy the above constraints, we assume that most of the walking will be done between the entrance door and the kitchen, when groceries are unloaded from the car, and between the kitchen and the living/dining area, when dishes are carried before and after the meals. The next walking path to minimize is the path from the bedrooms to the bathrooms. We assume that the occupants of the house will spend most of their time in the living/dining area and in the master bedroom.

In the first version of our floor plan (at the top of Figure 6-1), we find that the dining room is too far from the kitchen. To address this problem, we exchange it with bedroom 2 (see gray arrows in Figure 6-1). This also has the advantage of moving the living room to the south wall of the house. In the second revision, we find that the kitchen and the stairs are too far from the entrance door. To address this problem, we move the entrance door to the north wall. This allows us to reorient bedroom 2 and move the bathroom closer to both bedrooms. The living area is increased, and we satisfied all original constraints.

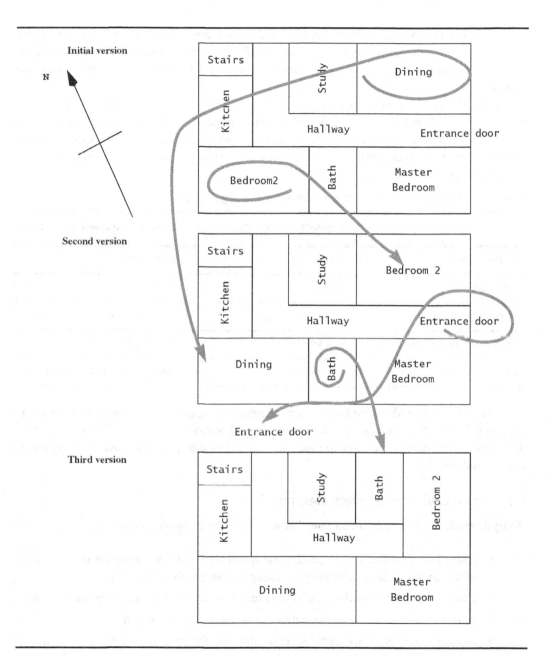

Figure 6-1 Example of floor plan design. Three successive versions show how we minimize walking distance and take advantage of sunlight.

At this point, we can position the doors and the windows of each room to meet localized requirements. Once this is done, we have completed the design without detailed knowledge of the layout of each individual room. Plans for plumbing, electrical lines, and heating ducts can proceed.

The design of a floor plan in architecture is similar to system design in software engineering (Table 6-1). The whole is divided into simpler components and interfaces, while taking into account nonfunctional and functional requirements. System design impacts implementation activities and results in costly rework if changed later. The design of individual components is delayed until later.

Table 6-1   Mapping of architectural and software engineering concepts.

	Architectural concept	Software engineering concept
Components	Rooms	Subsystems
Interfaces	Doors	Services
Nonfunctional requirements	Living area	Response time
Functional requirements	Residential house	Use cases
Costly rework	Moving walls	Change of subsystem interfaces

Section 6.2 provides a bird's-eye view of system design and its relationship to analysis. Section 6.3 describes the concept of subsystems and subsystem decomposition. Section 6.4 describes system design activities and uses an example to illustrate how these building blocks can be used together.

6.2 An Overview of System Design

Analysis results in the requirements model described by the following products:

- a set of *nonfunctional requirements* and *constraints,* such as maximum response time, minimum throughput, reliability, operating system platform, and so on
- a *use case model,* describing the system functionality from the actors' point of view
- an *object model,* describing the entities manipulated by the system
- a *sequence diagram* for each use case, showing the sequence of interactions among objects participating in the use case.

The analysis model describes the system completely from the actors' point of view and serves as the basis of communication between the client and the developers. The analysis model, however, does not contain information about the internal structure of the system, its hardware configuration, or more generally, how the system should be realized. System design is the first step in this direction. System design results in the following products:

- *design goals*, describing the qualities of the system that developers should optimize
- *software architecture*, describing the subsystem decomposition in terms of subsystem responsibilities, dependencies among subsystems, subsystem mapping to hardware, and major policy decisions such as control flow, access control, and data storage
- *boundary use cases*, describing the system configuration, startup, shutdown, and exception handling issues.

The design goals are derived from the nonfunctional requirements. Design goals guide the decisions to be made by the developers when trade-offs are needed. The subsystem decomposition constitutes the bulk of system design. Developers divide the system into manageable pieces to deal with complexity: each subsystem is assigned to a team and realized independently. For this to be possible, developers need to address system-wide issues when decomposing the system. In this chapter, we describe the concept of subsystem decomposition and discuss examples of generic system decompositions called "architectural styles." In the next chapter, we describe how the system decomposition is refined to meet specific design goals. Figure 6-2 depicts the relationship of system design with other software engineering activities.

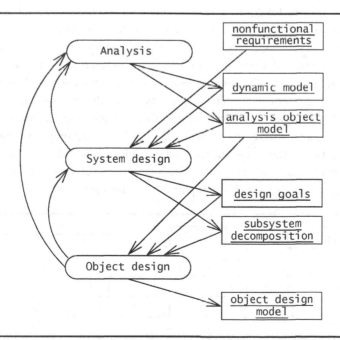

Figure 6-2   The activities of system design (UML activity diagram).

6.3 System Design Concepts

In this section, we describe subsystem decompositions and their properties in more detail. First, we define the concept of **subsystem** and its relationship to classes (Section 6.3.1). Next, we look at the interface of subsystems (Section 6.3.2): subsystems provide services to other subsystems. A **service** is a set of related operations that share a common purpose. During system design, we define the subsystems in terms of the services they provide. Later, during object design, we define the subsystem interface in terms of the operations it provides. Next, we look at two properties of subsystems, coupling and cohesion (Section 6.3.3). **Coupling** measures the dependencies between two subsystems, whereas **cohesion** measures the dependencies among classes within a subsystem. Ideal subsystem decomposition should minimize coupling and maximize cohesion. Then, we look at layering and partitioning, two techniques for relating subsystems to each other (Section 6.3.4). **Layering** allows a system to be organized as a hierarchy of subsystems, each providing higher-level services to the subsystem above it by using lower-level services from the subsystems below it. **Partitioning** organizes subsystems as peers that mutually provide different services to each other. In Section 6.3.5, we describe a number of typical software architectures that are found in practice.

6.3.1 Subsystems and Classes

In Chapter 2, *Modeling with UML*, we introduced the distinction between application domain and solution domain. In order to reduce the complexity of the application domain, we identified smaller parts called "classes" and organized them into packages. Similarly, to reduce the complexity of the solution domain, we decompose a system into simpler parts, called "subsystems," which are made of a number of solution domain classes. A **subsystem** is a replaceable part of the system with well-defined interfaces that encapsulates the state and behavior of its contained classes. A subsystem typically corresponds to the amount of work that a single developer or a single development team can tackle. By decomposing the system into relatively independent subsystems, concurrent teams can work on individual subsystems with minimal communication overhead. In the case of complex subsystems, we recursively apply this principle and decompose a subsystem into simpler subsystems (see Figure 6-3).

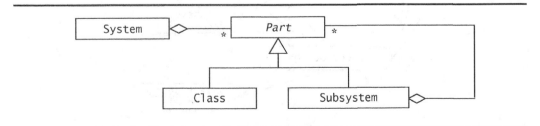

Figure 6-3   Subsystem decomposition (UML class diagram).

For example, the accident management system we previously described can be decomposed into a `DispatcherInterface` subsystem, realizing the user interface for the `Dispatcher`; a `FieldOfficerInterface` subsystem, realizing the user interface for the `FieldOfficer`; an `IncidentManagement` subsystem, responsible for the creation, modification, and storage of `Incidents`; a `ResourceManagement` subsystem, responsible for tracking available `Resources` (e.g., `FireTrucks` and `Ambulances`); a `MapManagement` for depicting `Maps` and `Locations`; and a `Notification` subsystem, implementing the communication between `FieldOfficer` terminals and `Dispatcher` stations.

This subsystem decomposition is depicted in Figure 6-4 using UML components. Components are depicted as rectangles with the component icon in the upper right corner. Dependencies among components can be depicted with dashed stick arrows. In UML, components can represent both logical and physical components. A **logical component** corresponds to a subsystem that has no explicit run-time equivalent, for example, individual business components that are composed together into a single run-time application logic layer. A **physical component** corresponds to a subsystem that as an explicit run-time equivalent, for example, a database server.

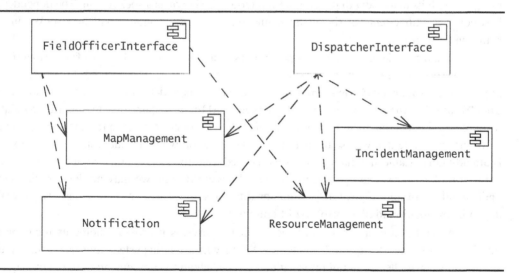

Figure 6-4 Subsystem decomposition for an accident management system (UML component diagram). Subsystems are shown as UML components. Dashed arrows indicate dependencies between subsystems.

Several programming languages (e.g., Java and Modula-2) provide constructs for modeling subsystems (packages in Java, modules in Modula-2). In other languages, such as C or C++, subsystems are not explicitly modeled, so developers use conventions for grouping classes (e.g., a subsystem can be represented as a directory containing all the files that implement the subsystem). Whether or not subsystems are explicitly represented in the programming language, developers need to document carefully the subsystem decomposition as subsystems are usually realized by different teams.

6.3.2 Services and Subsystem Interfaces

A subsystem is characterized by the services it provides to other subsystems. A **service** is a set of related operations that share a common purpose. A subsystem providing a notification service, for example, defines operations to send notices, look up notification channels, and subscribe and unsubscribe to a channel. The set of operations of a subsystem that are available to other subsystems form the **subsystem interface**. The subsystem interface includes the name of the operations, their parameters, their types, and their return values. System design focuses on defining the services provided by each subsystem, that is, enumerating the operations, their parameters, and their high-level behavior. Object design will focus on the **application programmer interface** (API), which refines and extends the subsystem interfaces. The API also includes the type of the parameters and the return value of each operation.

Provided and required interfaces can be depicted in UML with **assembly connectors**, also called **ball-and-socket connectors**. The provided interface is shown as a ball icon (also called lollipop) with its name next to it. A required interface is shown as a socket icon. The dependency between two subsystems is shown by connecting the corresponding ball and socket in the component diagram.

Figure 6-5 depicts the dependencies among the `FieldOfficerInterface`, `DispatchterInterface` and `ResourceManagement` subsystems. The `FieldOfficerInterface` requires the `ResourceUpdateService` to update the status and location of the `FieldOfficer`. The `DispatcherInterface` requires the `ResourceAllocationService` to identify available resources and allocating them to new `Incidents`. The `ResourceManagement` subsystem provides both services. Note that we use the ball-and-socket notation when the subsystem decomposition is already fairly stable and that our focus has shifted from the identification of subsystems to the definition of services. During the early stages of system design, we may not have such a clear understanding of the allocation of functionality to subsystems, in which case we use the dependency notation (dashed arrows) of Figure 6-4

The definition of a subsystem in terms of the services it provides helps us focus on its interface as opposed to its implementation. When writing a subsystem interface, one should strive to minimize the amount of information provided about the implementation. For example, a subsystem interface should not refer to internal data structures, such as linked lists, arrays, or hash tables. This allows us to minimize the impact of change when we revise the implementation of a subsystem. More generally, we want to minimize the impact of change by minimizing the dependencies among subsystems.

6.3.3 Coupling and Cohesion

Coupling is the number of dependencies between two subsystems. If two subsystems are loosely coupled, they are relatively independent, so modifications to one of the subsystems will

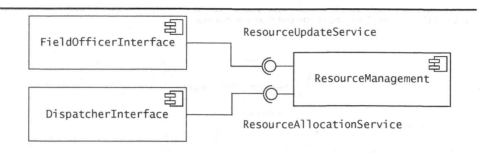

Figure 6-5 Services provided by the ResourceManagement subsystem (UML component diagram, ball-and-socket notation depicting provided and required interfaces).

have little impact on the other. If two subsystems are strongly coupled, modifications to one subsystem is likely to have impact on the other. A desirable property of a subsystem decomposition is that subsystems are as loosely coupled as reasonable. This minimizes the impact that errors or future changes in one subsystem have on other subsystems.

Consider, for example, the emergency response system depicted in Figure 6-4. During system design, we decide to store all persistent data (i.e., all data that outlive a single execution of the system) in a relational database. This leads to an additional subsystem called Database (Figure 6-6). Initially, we design the interface of the database subsystem so that subsystems that need to store data simply issue commands in the native query language of the database, such as SQL. For example, the IncidentManagement subsystem issues SQL queries to store and retrieve records representing Incidents in the database. This leads to a situation with a high coupling among the Database subsystem and the three client subsystems (i.e., IncidentManagement, ResourceManagement, and MapManagement) that need to store and retrieve data, as any change in the way the data is stored will require changes in the client subsystems. For example, if we change database vendors we will have to change the subsystems to use a different dialect of the query language. To reduce the coupling among these four subsystems, we decide to create a new subsystem, called Storage, which shields the Database from the other subsystems. In this alternative, the three client subsystems use services provided by the Storage subsystem, which is then responsible for issuing queries in SQL to the Database subsystem. If we decide to change database vendors or to use a different storage mechanism (e.g., flat files), we only need to change the Storage subsystem. Hence, the overall coupling of the subsystem decomposition has been decreased.

Note that reducing coupling is not an end in itself. In the example above, reducing the coupling resulted in additional complexity. By reducing coupling, developers can introduce many unnecessary layers of abstraction that consume development time and processing time. High coupling is an issue only if it is likely that any subsystem changes.

Cohesion is the number of dependencies within a subsystem. If a subsystem contains many objects that are related to each other and perform similar tasks, its cohesion is high. If a

Alternative 1: Direct access to the Database subsystem

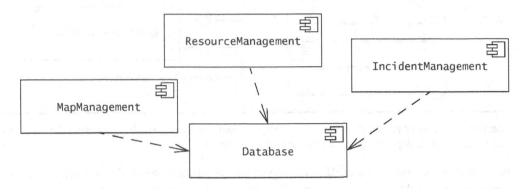

Alternative 2: Indirect access to the Database through a Storage subsystem

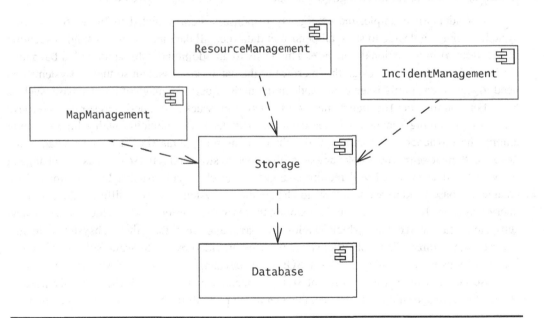

Figure 6-6   Example of reducing the coupling of subsystems (UML component diagram, subsystems `FieldOfficerInterface`, `DispatcherInterface`, and `Notification` omitted for clarity). Alternative 1 depicts a situation where all subsystems access the database directly, making them vulnerable to changes in the interface of the `Database` subsystem. Alternative 2 shields the database with an additional subsystem (`Storage`). In this situation, only one subsystem will need to change if there are changes in the interface of the `Database` subsystem. The assumption behind this design change is that the `Storage` subsystem has a more stable interface than the `Database` subsystem.

subsystem contains a number of unrelated objects, its cohesion is low. A desirable property of a subsystem decomposition is that it leads to subsystems with high cohesion.

For example, consider a decision tracking system for recording design problems, discussions, alternative evaluations, decisions, and their implementation in terms of tasks (Figure 6-7). DesignProblem and Option represent the exploration of the design space: we formulate the system in terms of a number of DesignProblems and document each Option they explore. The Criterion class represents the qualities in which we are interested. Once we assessed the explored Options against desirable Criteria, we implement Decisions in terms of Tasks. Tasks are recursively decomposed into Subtasks small enough to be assigned to individual developers. We call atomic tasks ActionItems.

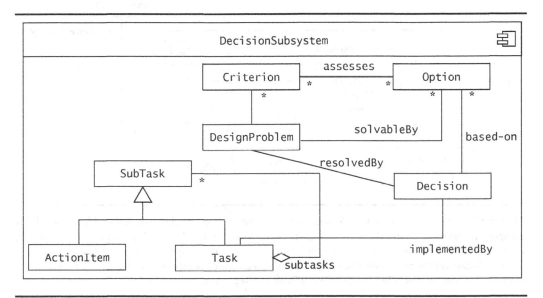

Figure 6-7 Decision tracking system (UML component diagram). The DecisionSubsystem has a low cohesion: The classes Criterion, Option, and DesignProblem have no relationships with Subtask, ActionItem, and Task.

The decision tracking system is small enough that we could lump all these classes into one subsystem called DecisionSubsystem (see Figure 6-7). However, we observe that the class model can be partitioned into two subgraphs. One, called the RationaleSubsystem, contains the classes DesignProblem, Option, Criterion, and Decision. The other, called the PlanningSubsystem, contains Task, Subtask, and ActionItem (see Figure 6-8). Both subsystems have a higher cohesion than the original DecisionSubsystem. This enables us to reuse each part independently, as other subsystems need only the planning part or the rationale part. Moreover, the resulting subsystems are smaller than the original subsystem, enabling us to

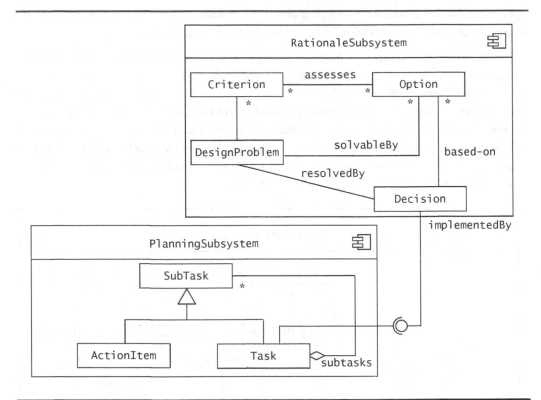

Figure 6-8 Alternative subsystem decomposition for the decision tracking system of Figure 6-7 (UML component diagram, ball-and-socket notation). The cohesion of the RationaleSubsystem and the PlanningSubsystem is higher than the cohesion of the original DecisionSubsystem. The RationaleSubsystem and PlanningSubsystem subsystems are also simpler. However, we introduced an interface for realizing the relationship between Task and Decision.

assign each of them to a single developer. The coupling between the subsystems is relatively low, with only one association between the two subsystems.

In general, there is a trade-off between cohesion and coupling. We can often increase cohesion by decomposing the system into smaller subsystems. However, this also increases coupling as the number of interfaces increases. A good heuristic is that developers can deal with 7 ± 2 concepts at any one level of abstraction. If there are more than nine subsystems at any given level of abstraction, or if a subsystem provides more than nine services, you should consider revising the decomposition. By the same token, the number of layers should not be more than 7 ± 2. In fact, good systems design can often be accomplished with just three layers.

6.3.4   Layers and Partitions

A **hierarchical decomposition** of a system yields an ordered set of layers. A **layer** is a grouping of subsystems providing related services, possibly realized using services from another layer. Layers are ordered in that each layer can depend only on lower level layers and has no knowledge of the layers above it. The layer that does not depend on any other layer is called the bottom layer, and the layer that is not used by any other is called the top layer (Figure 6-9). In a **closed architecture**, each layer can access only the layer immediately below it. In an **open architecture**,[1] a layer can also access layers at deeper levels.

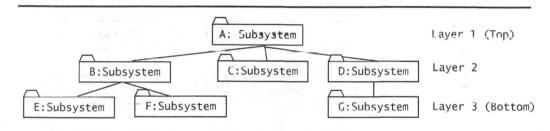

Figure 6-9   Subsystem decomposition of a system into three layers (UML object diagram, layers depicted as packages). A subset from a layered decomposition that includes at least one subsystem from each layer is called a vertical slice. For example, the subsystems A, B, and E constitute a vertical slice, whereas the subsystems D and G do not.

An example of a closed architecture is the Reference Model of Open Systems Interconnection (in short, the OSI model), which is composed of seven layers [Day & Zimmermann, 1983]. Each layer is responsible for performing a well-defined function. In addition, each layer provides its services by using services of the layer below (Figure 6-10).

The `Physical` layer represents the hardware interface to the network. It is responsible for transmitting bits over a communication channel. The `DataLink` layer is responsible for transmitting data frames without error using the services of the `Physical` layer. The `Network` layer is responsible for transmitting and routing packets within a network. The `Transport` layer is responsible for ensuring that the data are reliably transmitted from end to end. The `Transport` layer is the interface Unix programmers see when transmitting information over TCP/IP sockets between two processes. The `Session` layer is responsible for initializing and authenticating a connection. The `Presentation` layer performs data transformation services, such as byte swapping and encryption. The `Application` layer is the system you are designing (unless you are building an operating system or protocol stack). The `Application` layer can also consist of layered subsystems.

---

1. In the software engineering community, the term *open* usually means *non-proprietary*. We use the term *open architecture* as defined by [Rumbaugh et al., 1991], not to imply non-proprietary architecture.

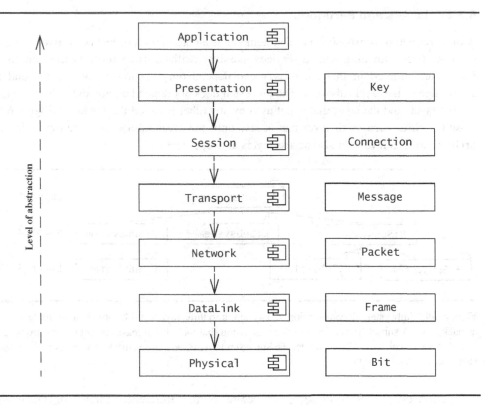

Figure 6-10   An example of closed architecture: the OSI model (UML component diagram). The OSI model decomposes network services into seven layers, each responsible for a different level of abstraction.

Until recently, only the four bottom layers of the OSI model were well standardized. Unix and many desktop operating systems, for example, provide interfaces to TCP/IP that implemented the Transport, Network, and Datalink layers. The application developer still needed to fill the gap between the Transport layer and the Application layer. With the growing number of distributed applications, this gap motivated the development of middleware such as CORBA [OMG, 2008] and Java RMI [RMI, 2009]. CORBA and Java RMI allow us to access remote objects transparently by sending messages to them as messages are sent to local objects, effectively implementing the Presentation and Session layers (see Figure 6-11).

An example of an open architecture is the Swing user interface toolkit for Java [JFC, 2009]. The lowest layer is provided by the operating system or by a windowing system, such as X11, and provides basic window management. AWT is an abstract window interface provided by Java to shield applications from specific window platforms. Swing is a library of user interface objects that provides a wide range of facilities, from buttons to geometry management. An Application usually accesses only the Swing interface. However, the Application layer may

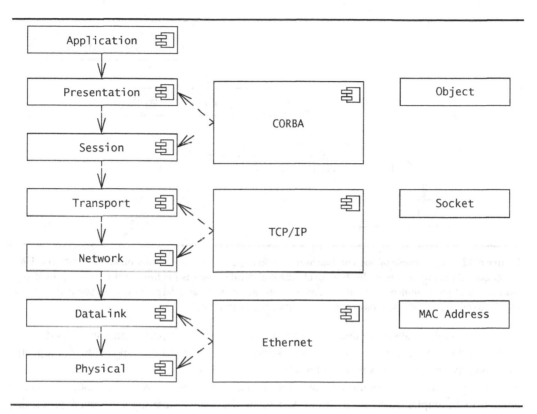

Figure 6-11 An example of closed architecture (UML component diagram). CORBA enables the access of objects implemented in different languages on different hosts. CORBA effectively implements the Presentation and Session layers of the OSI stack.

bypass the Swing layer and directly access AWT. In general, the openness of the architecture allows developers to bypass the higher layers to address performance bottlenecks (Figure 6-12).

Closed, layered architectures have desirable properties: they lead to low coupling between subsystems, and subsystems can be integrated and tested incrementally. Each level, however, introduces a speed and storage overhead that may make it difficult to meet nonfunctional requirements. Also, adding functionality to the system in later revisions may prove difficult, especially when the additions were not anticipated. In practice, a system is rarely decomposed into more than three to five layers.

Another approach to dealing with complexity is to **partition** the system into peer subsystems, each responsible for a different class of services. For example, an onboard system for a car could be decomposed into a travel service that provides real-time directions to the driver, an individual preferences service that remembers a driver's seat position and favorite radio station, and vehicle service that tracks the car's gas consumption, repairs, and scheduled maintenance. Each subsystem depends loosely on the others, but can often operate in isolation.

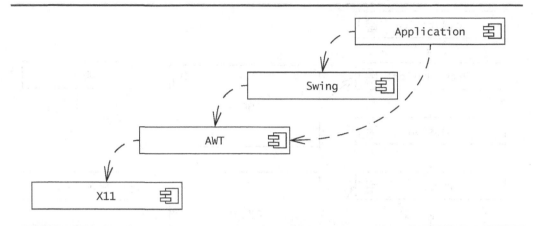

Figure 6-12   An example of open architecture: the Swing user interface library on an X11 platform (UML component diagram). X11 provides low-level drawing facilities. AWT is the low-level interface provided by Java to shield programmers from the window system. Swing provides a large number of sophisticated user interface objects. Some Applications often bypass the Swing layer.

In general, a subsystem decomposition is the result of both partitioning and layering. We first partition the system into top-level subsystems, which are responsible for specific functionality or run on a specific hardware node. Each of the resulting subsystems are, if complexity justifies it, decomposed into lower- and lower-level layers until they are simple enough to be implemented by a single developer. Each subsystem adds a certain processing overhead because of its interface with other systems. Excessive partitioning or layering can increase complexity.

6.3.5   Architectural Styles

As the complexity of systems increases, the specification of system decomposition is critical. It is difficult to modify or correct weak decomposition once development has started, as most subsystem interfaces would have to change. In recognition of the importance of this problem, the concept of **software architecture** has emerged. A software architecture includes system decomposition, global control flow, handling of boundary conditions, and intersubsystem communication protocols [Shaw & Garlan, 1996].

In this section, we describe several architectural styles that can be used as a basis for the architecture of different systems. This is by no means a systematic or thorough exposition of the subject. Rather, we aim to provide a few representative examples and refer the reader to the literature for more details.

Repository

In the **repository architectural style** (see Figure 6-13), subsystems access and modify a single data structure called the central **repository**. Subsystems are relatively independent and interact only through the repository. Control flow can be dictated either by the central repository (e.g., triggers on the data invoke peripheral systems) or by the subsystems (e.g., independent flow of control and synchronization through locks in the repository).

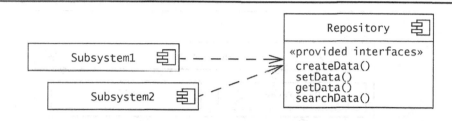

Figure 6-13   Repository architectural style (UML component diagram). Every Subsystem depends only on a central data structure called the Repository. The Repository has no knowledge of the other Subsystems.

Repositories are typically used for database management systems, such as a payroll system or a bank system. The central location of the data makes it easier to deal with concurrency and integrity issues between subsystems. Compilers and software development environments also follow a repository architectural style (Figure 6-14). The different subsystems of a compiler access and update a central parse tree and a symbol table. Debuggers and syntax editors access the symbol table as well.

The repository subsystem can also be used for implementing the global control flow. In the compiler example of Figure 6-14, each individual tool (e.g., the compiler, the debugger, and the editor) is invoked by the user. The repository only ensures that concurrent accesses are serialized. Conversely, the repository can be used to invoke the subsystems based on the state of the central data structure. These systems are called "blackboard systems." The HEARSAY II speech understanding system [Erman et al., 1980], one of the first blackboard systems, invoked tools based on the current state of the blackboard.

Repositories are well suited for applications with constantly changing, complex data-processing tasks. Once a central repository is well defined, we can easily add new services in the form of additional subsystems. The main disadvantage of repository systems is that the central repository can quickly become a bottleneck, both from a performance aspect and a modifiability aspect. The coupling between each subsystem and the repository is high, thus making it difficult to change the repository without having an impact on all subsystems.

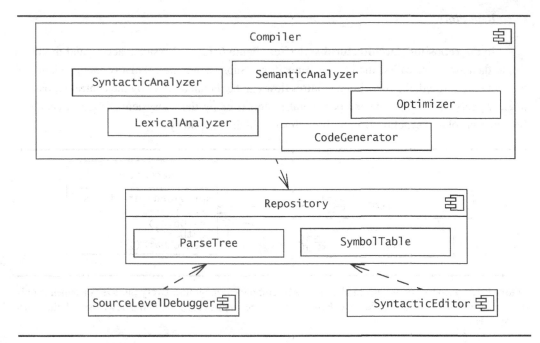

Figure 6-14 An instance of the repository architectural style (UML component diagram). A `Compiler` incrementally generates a `ParseTree` and a `SymbolTable` that can be used by `SourceLevelDebuggers` and `SyntaxEditors`.

Model/View/Controller

In the **Model/View/Controller** (MVC) architectural style (Figure 6-15), subsystems are classified into three different types: **model** subsystems maintain domain knowledge, **view** subsystems display it to the user, and **controller** subsystems manage the sequence of interactions with the user. The model subsystems are developed such that they do not depend on any view or controller subsystem. Changes in their state are propagated to the view subsystem via a subscribe/notify protocol. The MVC is a special case of the repository where `Model` implements the central data structure and control objects dictate the control flow.

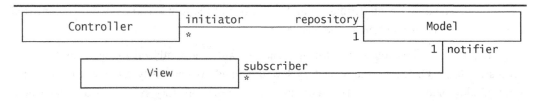

Figure 6-15 Model/View/Controller architectural style (UML class diagram). The `Controller` gathers input from the user and sends messages to the `Model`. The `Model` maintains the central data structure. The `Views` display the `Model` and are notified (via a subscribe/notify protocol) whenever the `Model` is changed.

For example, Figures 6-16 and 6-17 illustrate the sequence of events that occur in an MVC architectural style. Figure 6-16 displays two views of a file system. The bottom window lists the content of the `Comp-Based Software Engineering` folder, including the file `9DesignPatterns2.ppt`. The top window displays information about this file. The name of the file `9DesignPatterns2.ppt` appears in three places: in both windows and in the title of the top window. Assume now that we change the name of the file to `9DesignPatterns.ppt`. Figure 6-17 shows the sequence of events:

1. The `InfoView` and the `FolderView` both subscribe for changes to the `File` models they display (when they are created).

2. The user types the new name of the file.

3. The `Controller`, the object responsible for interacting with the user during file name changes, sends a request to the `Model`.

4. The `Model` changes the file name and notifies all subscribers of the change.

5. Both `InfoView` and `FolderView` are updated, so the user sees a consistent change.

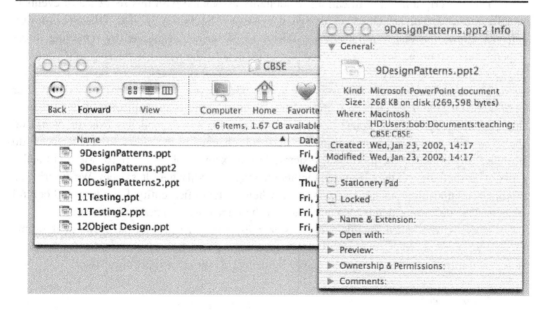

Figure 6-16 An example of MVC architectural style. The "model" is the filename `9DesignPAtterns2.ppt`. One "view" is a window titled `CBSE`, which displays the contents of a folder containing the file `9DesignPatterns2.ppt`. The other "view" is window called `9DesignPatterns2.ppt Info`, which displays information related to the file. If the file name is changed, both views are updated by the "controller."

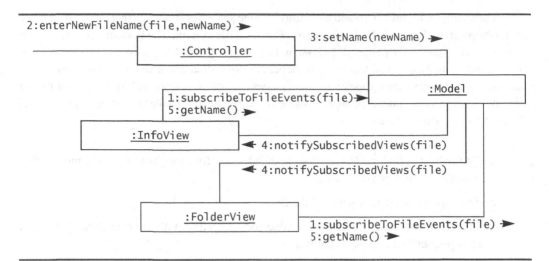

Figure 6-17   Sequence of events in the Model/View/Control architectural style (UML communication diagram).

The subscription and notification functionality associated with this sequence of events is usually realized with an Observer design pattern (see Section A.7). The **Observer design pattern** allows the Model and the View objects to be further decoupled by removing direct dependencies from the Model to the View. For more details, the reader is referred to [Gamma et al., 1994] and to Section A.7.

The rationale between the separation of Model, View, and Controller is that user interfaces, i.e., the View and the Controller, are much more often subject to change than is domain knowledge, i.e., the Model. Moreover, by removing any dependency from the Model on the View with the subscription/notification protocol, changes in the views (user interfaces) do not have any effect on the model subsystems. In the example of Figure 6-16, we could add a Unix-style shell view of the file system without having to modify the file system. We described a similar decomposition in Chapter 5, *Analysis*, when we identified entity, boundary, and control objects. This decomposition is also motivated by the same considerations about change.

MVC is well suited for interactive systems, especially when multiple views of the same model are needed. MVC can be used for maintaining consistency across distributed data; however it introduces the same performance bottleneck as for other repository styles.

Client/server

In the **client/server architectural style** (Figure 6-18), a subsystem, the **server**, provides services to instances of other subsystems called the **clients**, which are responsible for interacting with the user. The request for a service is usually done via a remote procedure call mechanism or a common object broker (e.g., CORBA, Java RMI, or HTTP). Control flow in the clients and the servers is independent except for synchronization to manage requests or to receive results.

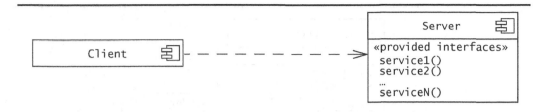

Figure 6-18 Client/server architectural style (UML component diagram). `Clients` request services from one or more `Servers`. The `Server` has no knowledge of the `Client`. The client/server architectural style is a specialization of the repository architectural style.

An information system with a central database is an example of a client/server architectural style. The clients are responsible for receiving inputs from the user, performing range checks, and initiating database transactions when all necessary data are collected. The server is then responsible for performing the transaction and guaranteeing the integrity of the data. In this case, a client/server architectural style is a special case of the repository architectural style in which the central data structure is managed by a process. Client/server systems, however, are not restricted to a single server. On the World Wide Web, a single client can easily access data from thousands of different servers (Figure 6-19).

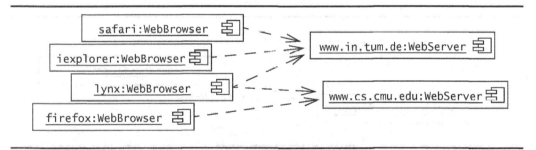

Figure 6-19 The Web as an instance of the client/server architectural style (UML deployment diagram).

Client/server architectural styles are well suited for distributed systems that manage large amounts of data.

Peer-to-peer

A **peer-to-peer architectural style** (see Figure 6-20) is a generalization of the client/server architectural style in which subsystems can act both as client or as servers, in the sense that each subsystem can request and provide services. The control flow within each subsystem is independent from the others except for synchronizations on requests.

An example of a peer-to-peer architectural style is a database that both accepts requests from the application and notifies to the application whenever certain data are changed

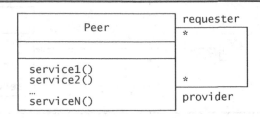

Figure 6-20   Peer-to-peer architectural style (UML class diagram). Peers can request services from and provide services to other peers.

(Figure 6-21). Peer-to-peer systems are more difficult to design than client/server systems because they introduce the possibility of deadlocks and complicate the control flow.

Callbacks are operations that are temporary and customized for a specific purpose. For example, a DBUser peer in Figure 6-21 can tell the DBMS peer which operation to invoke upon a change notification. The DBUser then uses the callback operation specified by each DBUser for notification when a change occurs. Peer-to-peer systems in which a "server" peer invokes "client" peers only through callbacks are often referred to as client/server systems, even though this is inaccurate since the "server" can also initiate the control flow.

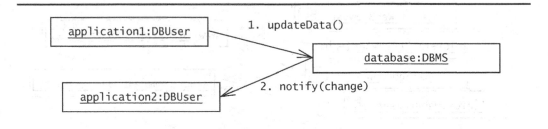

Figure 6-21   An example of peer-to-peer architectural style (UML communication diagram). The database server can both process requests from and send notifications to applications.

Three-tier

The **three-tier architectural style** organizes subsystems into three layers (Figure 6-22):

- The *interface layer* includes all boundary objects that deal with the user, including windows, forms, web pages, and so on.

- The *application logic layer* includes all control and entity objects, realizing the processing, rule checking, and notification required by the application.

- The *storage layer* realizes the storage, retrieval, and query of persistent objects.

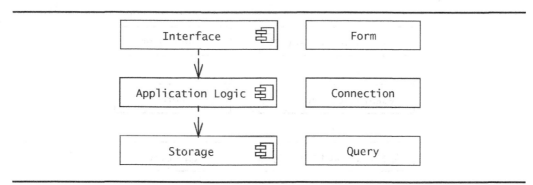

Figure 6-22 Three-tier architectural style (UML component diagram). Objects are organized into three layers realizing the user interface, the processing, and the storage.

The three-tier architectural style was initially described in the 1970s for information systems. The storage layer, an analog to the `Repository` subsystem in the repository architectural style, can be shared by several different applications operating on the same data. In turn, the separation between the interface layer and the application logic layer enables the development or modification of different user interfaces for the same application logic.

Four-tier

The **four-tier architectural style** is a three-tier architecture in which the Interface layer is decomposed into a `Presentation Client` layer and a `Presentation Server` layer (Figure 6-23). The `Presentation Client` layer is located on the user machines, whereas the `Presentation Server` layer can be located on one or more servers. The four-tier architecture enables a wide range of different presentation clients in the application, while reusing some of the presentation objects across clients. For example, a banking information system can include a host of different clients, such as a Web browser interface for home users, an Automated Teller Machine, and an application client for bank employees. Forms shared by all three clients can then be defined and processed in the `Presentation Server` layer, thus removing redundancy across clients.

Pipe and filter

In the **pipe and filter architectural style** (Figure 6-24), subsystems process data received from a set of inputs and send results to other subsystems via a set of outputs. The subsystems are called "filters," and the associations between the subsystems are called "pipes." Each filter knows only the content and the format of the data received on the input pipes, not the filters that

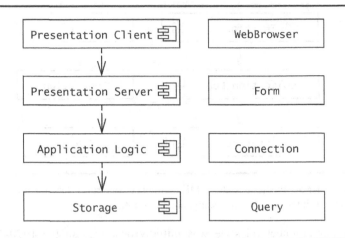

Figure 6-23   Four-tier architectural style (UML component diagram). The `Interface` layer of the three-tier style is split into two layers to enable more variability on the user interface style.

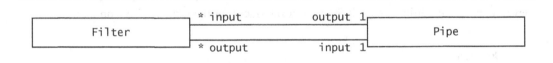

Figure 6-24   Pipe and filter architectural style (UML class diagram). A `Filter` can have many inputs and outputs. A `Pipe` connects one of the outputs of a `Filter` to one of the inputs of another `Filter`.

produced them. Each filter is executed concurrently, and synchronization is accomplished via the pipes. The pipe and filter architectural style is modifiable: filters can be substituted for others or reconfigured to achieve a different purpose.

The best known example of a pipe and filter architectural style is the Unix shell [Ritchie & Thompson, 1974]. Most filters are written such that they read their input and write their results on standard pipes. This enables a Unix user to combine them in many different ways. Figure 6-25 shows an example made of four filters. The output of ps (process status) is fed into grep (search for a pattern) to remove all the processes that are not owned by a specific user. The output of grep (i.e., the processes owned by the user) is then sorted by sort and sent to more, which is a filter that displays its input to a terminal, one screen at a time.

Pipe and filter styles are suited for systems that apply transformations to streams of data without intervention by users. They are not suited for systems that require more complex interactions between components, such as an information management system or an interactive system.

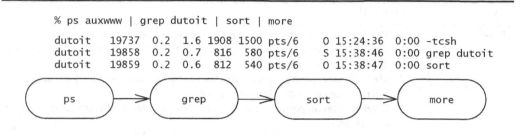

```
% ps auxwww | grep dutoit | sort | more
dutoit    19737   0.2   1.6  1908  1500  pts/6      0  15:24:36   0:00  -tcsh
dutoit    19858   0.2   0.7   816   580  pts/6      S  15:38:46   0:00  grep dutoit
dutoit    19859   0.2   0.6   812   540  pts/6      0  15:38:47   0:00  sort
```

Figure 6-25 Unix command line as an instance of the pipe and filter style (UML activity diagram).

6.4 System Design Activities: From Objects to Subsystems

System design consists of transforming the analysis model into the design model that takes into account the nonfunctional requirements described in the requirements analysis document. We illustrate these activities with an example, MyTrip, a route planning system for car drivers. We start with the analysis model from MyTrip; then we describe the identification of design goals (Section 6.4.2) and the design of an initial system decomposition (Section 6.4.3).

6.4.1 Starting Point: Analysis Model for a Route Planning System

Using MyTrip, a driver can plan a trip from a home computer by contacting a trip-planning service on the Web (PlanTrip in Figure 6-26). The trip is saved for later retrieval on the server. The trip-planning service must support more than one driver.

Use case name	PlanTrip
Flow of events	1. The Driver activates her computer and logs into the trip-planning Web service.
	2. The Driver enters constraints for a trip as a sequence of destinations.
	3. Based on a database of maps, the planning service computes the shortest way of visiting the destinations in the order specified. The result is a sequence of segments binding a series of crossings and a list of directions.
	4. The Driver can revise the trip by adding or removing destinations.
	5. The Driver saves the planned trip by name in the planning service database for later retrieval.

Figure 6-26 PlanTrip use case of the MyTrip system.

The driver then goes to the car and starts the trip, while the onboard computer gives directions based on trip information from the planning service and her current position indicated by an onboard GPS system (ExecuteTrip in Figure 6-27).

We perform the analysis for the MyTrip system following the techniques outlined in Chapter 5, *Analysis*, and obtain the model in Figure 6-28.

Use case name	ExecuteTrip
Flow of events	1. The Driver starts her car and logs into the onboard route assistant.
	2. Upon successful login, the Driver specifies the planning service and the name of the trip to be executed.
	3. The onboard route assistant obtains the list of destinations, directions, segments, and crossings from the planning service.
	4. Given the current position, the route assistant provides the driver with the next set of directions.
	5. The Driver arrives to destination and shuts down the route assistant.

Figure 6-27   ExecuteTrip use case of the MyTrip system.

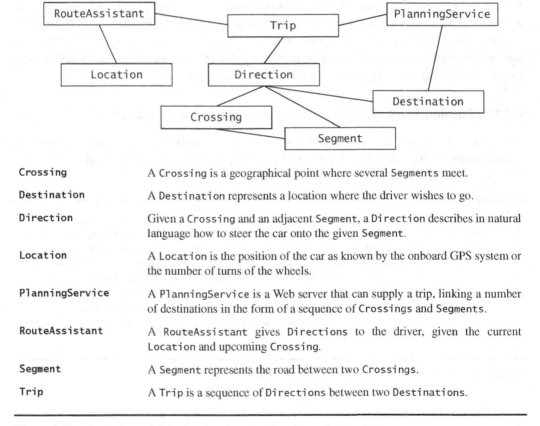

Crossing	A Crossing is a geographical point where several Segments meet.
Destination	A Destination represents a location where the driver wishes to go.
Direction	Given a Crossing and an adjacent Segment, a Direction describes in natural language how to steer the car onto the given Segment.
Location	A Location is the position of the car as known by the onboard GPS system or the number of turns of the wheels.
PlanningService	A PlanningService is a Web server that can supply a trip, linking a number of destinations in the form of a sequence of Crossings and Segments.
RouteAssistant	A RouteAssistant gives Directions to the driver, given the current Location and upcoming Crossing.
Segment	A Segment represents the road between two Crossings.
Trip	A Trip is a sequence of Directions between two Destinations.

Figure 6-28   Analysis model for the MyTrip route planning and execution.

In addition, during requirements elicitation, our client specified the following nonfunctional requirements for MyTrip:

Nonfunctional requirements for MyTrip

1. MyTrip is in contact with the PlanningService via a wireless modem. Assume that the wireless modem functions properly at the initial destination.
2. Once the trip has been started, MyTrip should give correct directions even if modem fails to maintain a connection with the PlanningService.
3. MyTrip should minimize connection time to reduce operation costs.
4. Replanning is possible only if the connection to the PlanningService is possible.
5. The PlanningService can support at least 50 different drivers and 1,000 trips.

6.4.2 Identifying Design Goals

The definition of design goals is the first step of system design. It identifies the qualities that our system should focus on. Many design goals can be inferred from the nonfunctional requirements or from the application domain. Others will have to be elicited from the client. It is, however, necessary to state them explicitly such that every important design decision can be made consistently following the same set of criteria.

For example, in the light of the nonfunctional requirements for MyTrip described in Section 6.4.1, we identify *reliability* and *fault tolerance to connectivity loss* as design goals. We then identify *security* as a design goal, as numerous drivers will have access to the same trip planning server. We add *modifiability* as a design goal, as we want to provide the ability for drivers to select a trip planning service of their choice. The following box summarizes the design goals we identified.

Design goals for MyTrip

- **Reliability:** MyTrip should be reliable [generalization of nonfunctional requirement 2].
- **Fault Tolerance:** MyTrip should be fault tolerant to loss of connectivity with the routing service [rephrased nonfunctional requirement 2].
- **Security:** MyTrip should be secure, i.e., not allow other drivers or nonauthorized users to access a driver's trips [deduced from application domain].
- **Modifiability:** MyTrip should be modifiable to use different routing services [anticipation of change by developers].

In general, we can select design goals from a long list of highly desirable qualities. Tables 6-2 through 6-6 list a number of possible design criteria. These criteria are organized into five groups: *performance, dependability, cost, maintenance,* and *end user criteria.* Performance, dependability, and end user criteria are usually specified in the requirements or inferred from the application domain. Cost and maintenance criteria are dictated by the customer and the supplier.

Performance criteria (Table 6-2) include the speed and space requirements imposed on the system. Should the system be responsive, or should it accomplish a maximum number of tasks? Is memory space available for speed optimizations, or should memory be used sparingly?

Table 6-2   Performance criteria.

Design criterion	Definition
Response time	How soon is a user request acknowledged after the request has been issued?
Throughput	How many tasks can the system accomplish in a fixed period of time?
Memory	How much space is required for the system to run?

Dependability criteria (Table 6-3) determine how much effort should be expended in minimizing system crashes and their consequences. How often can the system crash? How available to the user should the system be? Should the system tolerate errors and failures? Are security risks associated with the system environment? Are safety issues associated with system crashes?

Table 6-3   Dependability criteria.

Design criterion	Definition
Robustness	Ability to survive invalid user input
Reliability	Difference between specified and observed behavior
Availability	Percentage of time that system can be used to accomplish normal tasks
Fault tolerance	Ability to operate under erroneous conditions
Security	Ability to withstand malicious attacks
Safety	Ability to avoid endangering human lives, even in the presence of errors and failures

Cost criteria (Table 6-4) include the cost to develop the system, to deploy it, and to administer it. Note that cost criteria not only include design considerations but managerial ones, as well. When the system is replacing an older one, the cost of ensuring backward compatibility or transitioning to the new system has to be taken into account. There are also trade-offs between different types of costs such as development cost, end user training cost, transition costs, and maintenance costs. Maintaining backward compatibility with a previous system can add to the development cost while reducing the transition cost.

Table 6-4   Cost criteria.

Design criterion	Definition
Development cost	Cost of developing the initial system
Deployment cost	Cost of installing the system and training the users
Upgrade cost	Cost of translating data from the previous system. This criteria results in backward compatibility requirements
Maintenance cost	Cost required for bug fixes and enhancements to the system
Administration cost	Cost required to administer the system

Maintenance criteria (Table 6-5) determine how difficult it is to change the system after deployment. How easily can new functionality be added? How easily can existing functions be revised? Can the system be adapted to a different application domain? How much effort will be required to port the system to a different platform? These criteria are harder to optimize and plan for, as it is seldom clear how successful the project will be and how long the system will be operational.

Table 6-5   Maintenance criteria.

Design criterion	Definition
Extensibility	How easy is it to add functionality or new classes to the system?
Modifiability	How easy is it to change the functionality of the system?
Adaptability	How easy is it to port the system to different application domains?
Portability	How easy is it to port the system to different platforms?
Readability	How easy is it to understand the system from reading the code?
Traceability of requirements	How easy is it to map the code to specific requirements?

End user criteria (Table 6-6) include qualities that are desirable from a users' point of view, but have not yet been covered under the performance and dependability criteria. Is the software difficult to use and to learn? Can the users accomplish needed tasks on the system? Often these criteria do not receive much attention, especially when the client contracting the system is different from its users.

Table 6-6   End user criteria.

Design criterion	Definition
Utility	How well does the system support the work of the user?
Usability	How easy is it for the user to use the system?

When defining design goals, only a small subset of these criteria can be simultaneously taken into account. It is, for example, unrealistic to develop software that is safe, secure, and cheap. Typically, developers need to prioritize design goals and trade them off against each other as well as against managerial goals as the project runs behind schedule or over budget. Table 6-7 lists several possible trade-offs.

Table 6-7   Examples of design goal trade-offs.

Trade-off	Rationale
Space vs. speed	If the software does not meet response time or throughput requirements, more memory can be expended to speed up the software (e.g., caching, more redundancy). If the software does not meet memory space constraints, data can be compressed at the cost of speed.
Delivery time vs. functionality	If development runs behind schedule, a project manager can deliver less functionality than specified on time, or deliver the full functionality at a later time. Contract software usually puts more emphasis on functionality, whereas off-the-shelf software projects put more emphasis on delivery date.
Delivery time vs. quality	If testing runs behind schedule, a project manager can deliver the software on time with known bugs (and possibly provide a later patch to fix any serious bugs), or deliver the software later with fewer bugs.
Delivery time vs. staffing	If development runs behind schedule, a project manager can add resources to the project to increase productivity. In most cases, this option is only available early in the project; adding resources usually decreases productivity while new personnel are trained or brought up to date. Note that adding resources will also raise the cost of development.

Managerial goals can be traded off against technical goals (e.g., delivery time vs. functionality). Once we have a clear idea of the design goals, we can proceed to design an initial subsystem decomposition.

6.4.3   Identifying Subsystems

Finding subsystems during system design is similar to finding objects during analysis. For example, some of the object identification techniques we described in Chapter 5, *Analysis*, such as Abbotts's heuristics, are applicable to subsystem identification. Moreover, subsystem decomposition is constantly revised whenever new issues are addressed: several subsystems are merged into one subsystem, a complex subsystem is split into parts, and some subsystems are added to address new functionality. The first iterations over subsystem decomposition can introduce drastic changes in the system design model. These are often best handled through brainstorming.

The initial subsystem decomposition should be derived from the functional requirements. For example, in the MyTrip system, we identify two major groups of objects: those that are involved during the PlanTrip use case and those that are involved during the ExecuteTrip use case. The Trip, Direction, Crossing, Segment, and Destination classes are shared between both use cases. This set of classes is tightly coupled as it is used as a whole to represent a Trip. We decide to assign them with PlanningService to the PlanningSubsystem, and the remainder of the classes are assigned to the RoutingSubsystem (Figure 6-29). This leads to only one association crossing subsystem boundaries. Note that this subsystem decomposition is a repository in which the PlanningSubsystem is responsible for the central data structure.

Another heuristic for subsystem identification is to keep functionally related objects together. A starting point is to assign the participating objects that have been identified in each use case to the subsystems. Some group of objects, as the Trip group in MyTrip, are shared and used for communicating information from one subsystem to another. We can either create a new subsystem to accommodate them or assign them to the subsystem that creates these objects.

Heuristics for grouping objects into subsystems

- Assign objects identified in one use case into the same subsystem.
- Create a dedicated subsystem for objects used for moving data among subsystems.
- Minimize the number of associations crossing subsystem boundaries.
- All objects in the same subsystem should be functionally related.

Encapsulating subsystems with the Facade design pattern

Subsystem decomposition reduces the complexity of the solution domain by minimizing coupling among subsystems. The **Facade design pattern** (see Appendix A.6 and [Gamma et al., 1994]) allows us to further reduce dependencies between classes by encapsulating a subsystem with a simple, unified interface. For example, in Figure 6-30, the Compiler class is a façade hiding the classes CodeGenerator, Optimizer, ParseNode, Parser, and Lexer. The façade provides access only to the public services offered by the subsystem and hides all other details, effectively reducing coupling between subsystems.

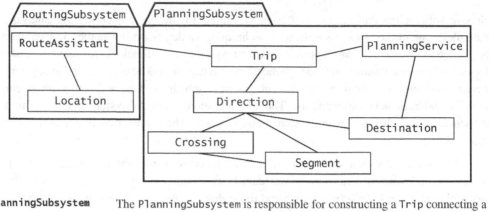

PlanningSubsystem   The PlanningSubsystem is responsible for constructing a Trip connecting a sequence of Destinations. The PlanningSubsystem is also responsible for responding to replan requests from RoutingSubsystem.

RoutingSubsystem   The RoutingSubsystem is responsible for downloading a Trip from the PlanningService and executing it by giving Directions to the driver based on its Location.

Figure 6-29   Initial subsystem decomposition for MyTrip (UML class diagram).

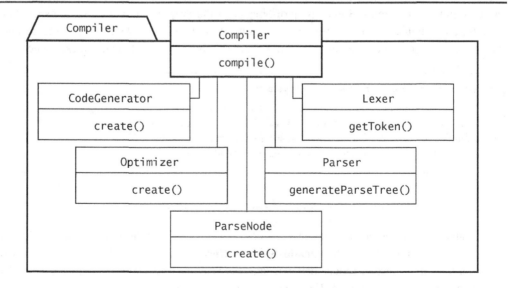

Figure 6-30   An example of the Facade design pattern (UML class diagram).

Subsystems identified during the initial subsystem decomposition often result from grouping several functionally related classes. These subsystems are good candidates for the Facade design pattern and should be encapsulated under one class.

6.5 Further Readings

Historically, the discipline of software architecture originated with Dijkstra and Parnas. They pointed out that the structure of a piece of software is as critical as its ability to compute correct results. Dijkstra introduced the concept of a layered architecture and discussed its application to the design of the operating system T.H.E. [Dijkstra, 1968]. Parnas introduced the concept of information hiding and discussed the criteria that should be used when decomposing a system [Parnas, 1972].

The *Structured Design* method [Yourdon & Constantine, 1979] introduced the concepts of cohesion and coupling metrics to design a software architecture.

Although the need and advantages for software architectures have been well understood since then, the field of software architecture has continued to evolve for several decades. The main barriers so far have been a lack of common language to describe architectures and a lack of analysis methods for comparing architectures and predicting whether they can meet the specified requirements of the system.

Software Architecture: Perspectives on an Emerging Discipline [Shaw & Garlan, 1996] and *Pattern-Oriented Software Architecture* [Buschmann et al., 1996] are the first widely cited systematic efforts to provide a catalog of architectures. Shaw and Garlan introduced the concept of architectural styles; Buschmann et al. used architectural patterns as a description language.

In the 1990s, more case studies in product line engineering provided concrete examples of the benefits of reusing of software architectures, not only from a technical point of view (design decisions about structure and components are reused), but also from a management point of view (team organizations and methods of communication are reused). The Software Engineering Institute at Carnegie Mellon University has collected, maintained, and developed extensive material on software architecture and product lines. For example, *Software Architecture in Practice* [Bass et al., 2003] and *Evaluating Software Architectures* [Clements et al., 2002] describe methods and case studies for selecting and evaluating software architecture.

Also relevant to software architecture is *Applied Software Architecture* [Hofmeister, 2000], which focuses on practical industrial applications of software architecture.

6.6 Exercises

6-1 Decomposing a system into subsystems reduces the complexity developers have to deal with by simplifying the parts and increasing their coherence. Decomposing a system into simpler parts usually increases a different kind of complexity: simpler parts also means more parts and more interfaces. If cohesion is the guiding principle driving developers to decompose a system into small parts, which competing principle drives them to keep the total number of parts small?

6-2   In Section 6.4.2, we classified design goals into five categories: performance, dependability, cost, maintenance, and end user. Assign one or more categories to each of the following goals:

- Users must be given feedback within one second after they issue any command.

- The TicketDistributor must be able to issue train tickets, even in the event of a network failure.

- The housing of the TicketDistributor must allow for new buttons to be installed in case the number of fares increases.

- The AutomatedTellerMachine must withstand brute force attacks (i.e., users attempting to discover a identification number by systematic trial).

6-3   You are developing a system that stores its data on a Unix file system. You anticipate that you will port future versions of the system to other operating systems that provide different file systems. Propose a subsystem decomposition that anticipates this change.

6-4   Older compilers were designed according to a pipe and filter architecture, in which each stage would transform its input into an intermediate representation passed to the next stage. Modern development environments, including compilers integrated into interactive development environments with syntactical text editors and source-level debuggers, use a repository architecture. Identify the design goals that may have triggered the shift from pipe and filter to repository architecture.

6-5   Consider the model/view/control example depicted in Figures 6-17 and 6-16

a. Redraw the communication diagram of Figure 6-17 as a sequence diagram.

b. Discuss how the MVC architecture helps or hurts the following design goals:

- Extensibility (e.g., the addition of new types of views)

- Response time (e.g., the time between a user input and the time all views have been updated)

- Modifiability (e.g., the addition of new attributes in the model)

- Access control (i.e., the ability to ensure that only legitimate users can access specific parts of the model).

6-6   List design goals that would be difficult to meet when using a closed architecture with many layers, such as the OSI example depicted in Figure 6-11.

6-7   In many architectures, such as the three- and four-tier architectures (Figures 6-22 and 6-23), the storage of persistent objects is handled by a dedicated layer. In your opinion, which design goals have lead to this decision?

References

[Bass et al., 2003]   L. Bass, P. Clements, & R. Kazman, *Software Architecture in Practice*, 2nd ed., Addison-Wesley, Reading, MA, 2003.

[Buschmann et al., 1996]   F. Buschmann, R. Meunier, H. Rohnert, P. Sommerlad, & M. Stal. *Pattern-Oriented Software Architecture*, John Wiley & Sons, Chichester, 1996.

[Clements et al., 2002]   P. Clements, R. Kazam, & M. Klein. *Evaluating Software Architectures: Methods and Case Studies*, SEI Series in Software Engineering, Addison-Wesley, 2002.

[Day & Zimmermann, 1983]   J.D. Day & H. Zimmermann, "The OSI Reference Model," *Proceedings of the IEEE*, vol. 71, pp. 1334–1340, December 1983.

[Dijkstra, 1968]   E.W. Dijkstra, "The Structure of the 'T.H.E' Multiprogramming System," *Communication of the ACM* 18(8), pp. 453–457, 1968.

[Erman et al., 1980]   L. D. Erman, F. Hayes-Roth, et al., "The Hearsay-II Speech-Understanding System: Integrating knowledge to resolve uncertainty." *ACM Computing Surveys*, vol. 12, no. 2, pp. 213–253, 1980.

[Gamma et al., 1994]   E. Gamma, R. Helm, R. Johnson, & J. Vlissides, *Design Patterns: Elements of Reusable Object-Oriented Software*, Addison-Wesley, Reading, MA, 1994.

[Hofmeister, 2000]   C. Hofmeister, R. Nord, & D. Soni, *Applied Software Architecture*, Object Technology Series, Addison-Wesley, 2000.

[JFC, 2009]   *Java Foundation Classes*, JDK Documentation, Javasoft, 2009.

[OMG, 2008]   Object Management Group, *Common Object Request Broker Architecture (CORBA) Specification: Version 3.1*, http://www.omg.org 2008.

[Parnas, 1972]   D. Parnas, "On the Criteria to Be Used in Decomposing Systems into Modules," *Communications of the ACM*, 15(12), pp. 1053–1058, 1972.

[Ritchie & Thompson, 1974] D. M. Ritchie 7 K. Thompson, "The Unix Time-sharing System," *Communications of the ACM*, Vol. 17, No. 7, pp 365–37, July 1974.

[RMI, 2009]   *Java Remote Method Invocation*, JDK Documentation, Javasoft, 2009.

[Rumbaugh et al., 1991]   J. Rumbaugh, M. Blaha, W. Premerlani, F. Eddy, & W. Lorensen. *Object-Oriented Modeling and Design*, Prentice Hall, Englewood Cliffs, NJ, 1991.

[Shaw & Garlan, 1996]   M. Shaw & D. Garlan, *Software Architecture: Perspectives on an Emerging Discipline*, Prentice Hall, Upper Saddle River, NJ, 1996.

[Yourdon & Constantine, 1979] E. Yourdon & L. L. Constantine, *Structured Design*, Prentice-Hall, Englewood Cliffs, NJ, 1979.

7

System Design: Addressing Design Goals

Good, fast, cheap. Pick any two.
    —Old software engineering aphorism

During system design, we identify design goals, decompose the system into subsystems, and refine the subsystem decomposition until all design goals are addressed. In the previous chapter, we described the concepts of design goals and system decomposition. In this chapter, we introduce the system design activities that address the design goals. In particular, we examine

- *Selection of off-the-shelf and legacy components.* Off-the-shelf or legacy components realize specific subsystems more economically. The initial subsystem decomposition is adjusted to accommodate them.
- *Mapping of subsystem to hardware.* When the system is deployed on several nodes, additional subsystems are required for addressing reliability or performance issues.
- *Design of a persistent data management infrastructure.* Managing the states that outlives a single execution of the system has an impact on overall system performance and leads to the identification of one or more storage subsystems.
- *Specification of an access control policy.* Shared objects are protected so that user access to them is controlled. Access control impacts how objects are distributed within subsystems.
- *Design of the global control flow.* Determining the sequence of operations impacts the interface of the subsystems.
- *Handling of boundary conditions.* Once all subsystems have been identified, developers decide on the order in which individual components are started and shutdown.

We then describe the management issues related to system design, such as documentation, responsibilities, and communication. We conclude this chapter by discussing in more detail system design issues and trade-offs using the ARENA case study.

7.1 Introduction: A Redundancy Example

Redundancy in the Space Shuttle computer system

Unlike previous spacecraft, the space shuttle was designed to be autonomous. Space shuttle missions would be longer and crews larger than on Apollo or Gemini missions. It was also expected that multiple missions would be in space at the same time. Hence, the space shuttle would need to tolerate several failures before aborting the mission, and its design included many redundant features, including a fault-tolerant computer system responsible for guidance, navigation, and altitude control.

Using redundancy in spacecraft computer systems was not new. The Saturn rocket that launched the Apollo spacecraft used triple modular redundancy for the guidance system; that is, each of the components in the computer was tripled. The failure of a single component was detected when it produced a different output than the other two. A voting component would compare these outputs at all times and mask single failures. This type of computer was expensive to manufacture and could only address local single failures. It would not have survived a massive failure, such as the explosion on Apollo 13.

The Skylab space station took a different approach. The computer systems were completely duplicated and located at different ends of the station. When one computer failed, the other would be switched on to take over. Whereas a slow switch-over was acceptable for a space station (i.e., the space station could loose some altitude before safety became an issue), it would not be acceptable for the space shuttle, whose computer system was responsible for high-frequency tasks such as guidance during take-off and landing.

Hence, the space shuttle needed a computer system that was duplicated at the system level, as in the Skylab, but that functioned simultaneously so that switch-over could happen in a short time, as in the Saturn rocket. The initial requirements by NASA were that the Shuttle should be able to experience two consecutive failures before the mission was aborted. This lead to a system design with five identical computers running the same software. If two individual computers failed, the last three would constitute a triple redundancy system for landing. If a third computer failed during the decent, the last two would be enough to ensure a safe landing.

Due to cost consideration, NASA later decided to lower its requirement to one failure before mission abort. However, since the procurement for the five computers was already completed and the five computers had been factored into the design, the fifth computer evolved into a back-up system. While the quadruple redundancy protects against hardware failures, it does not increase reliability against software faults, as all four main computers run the same software. The back-up system, however, runs a simpler version of the software that is only able to guide the shuttle during take-off and landing.

The example above illustrates how architectural decisions were made during the design of a complex computer system. While some decisions are historical, most are driven by design goals and nonfunctional requirements. Addressing design goals for software systems entails different approaches than a hardware system such as the space shuttle. However, the impact is similar: one design goal is examined at the time, influencing the system decomposition and resulting in the change of the subsystem decomposition or its interfaces. By the end of system design, all design goals should have been addressed. Section 7.2 provides a bird's-eye view of the activities of system design for addressing design goals. Section 7.3 describes the concept of UML deployment diagram. Section 7.4 describes system design activities and uses an example to illustrate how these building blocks can be used together. Section 7.5 describes management issues related to system design. Section 7.6 discusses these concepts in more detail with the ARENA case study.

7.2 An Overview of System Design Activities

Design goals guide the decisions to be made by the developers especially when trade-offs are needed. Developers divide the system into manageable pieces to deal with complexity: each subsystem is assigned to a team and realized independently. In order for this to be possible, though, developers need to address system-wide issues when decomposing the system. In particular, they need to address the following issues:

- *Hardware/software mapping:* What is the hardware configuration of the system? Which node is responsible for which functionality? How is communication between nodes realized? Which services are realized using existing software components? How are these components encapsulated? Addressing hardware/software mapping issues often leads to the definition of *additional subsystems* dedicated to moving data from one node to another, dealing with concurrency, and reliability issues. Off-the-shelf components enable developers to realize complex services more economically. User interface packages and database management systems are prime examples of off-the-shelf components. Components, however, should be encapsulated to minimize dependency on a particular component; a competing vendor may offer a better product in the future, and you want the option to switch.

- *Data management:* Which data should be persistent? Where should persistent data be stored? How are they accessed? Persistent data represents a bottleneck in the system on many different fronts: most functionality in system is concerned with creating or manipulating persistent data. For this reason, access to the data should be fast and reliable. If retrieving data is slow, the whole system will be slow. If data corruption is likely, complete system failure is likely. These issues must be addressed consistently at the system level. Often, this leads to the selection of a database management system and of an *additional subsystem* dedicated to the management of persistent data.

- *Access control:* Who can access which data? Can access control change dynamically? How is access control specified and realized? Access control and security are system-wide issues. The access control must be consistent across the system; in other words, the policy used to specify who can and cannot access certain data should be the same *across all subsystems.*

- *Control flow:* How does the system sequence operations? Is the system event driven? Can it handle more than one user interaction at a time? The choice of control flow has an impact on the interfaces of subsystems. If an event-driven control flow is selected, subsystems will provide event handlers. If threads are selected, subsystems must guarantee mutual exclusion in critical sections.

- *Boundary conditions:* How is the system initialized and shut down? How are exceptional cases handled? System initialization and shutdown often represent much of the complexity of a system, especially in a distributed environment. Initialization, shutdown, and exception handling have an impact on the interface of *all subsystems*.

Figure 7-1 depicts the activities of system design. Each activity addresses one of the issues we described above. Addressing any one of these issues can lead to changes in subsystem decomposition and raising new issues. As you will see in this chapter, system design is a highly iterative activity that likely results in the identification of new subsystems, the modification of existing subsystems, and system-wide revisions that impact all subsystems.

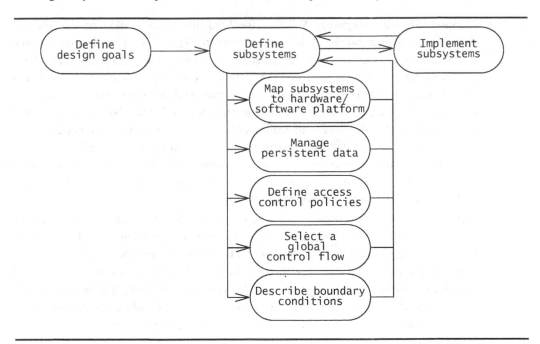

Figure 7-1   The activities of system design (UML activity diagram).

7.3 Concepts: UML Deployment Diagrams

UML **deployment diagrams** are used to depict the relationship among run-time components and nodes. Components are self-contained entities that provide services to other components or actors. A Web server, for example, is a component that provides services to Web browsers. A Web browser such as Safari is a component that provides services to a user. A node is a physical device or an execution environment in which components are executed. A system is composed of interacting run-time components that can be distributed among several nodes. Furthermore a node can contain another node, for example, a device can contain an execution environment.

In UML deployment diagrams, nodes are represented by boxes containing component icons. Nodes can be stereotyped to denote physical devices or execution environments. Communication paths between nodes are represented by solid lines. The protocol used by two nodes to communicate can be indicated with a stereotype on the communication path. Figure 7-2 depicts an example of a deployment diagram with two Web browsers accessing a Web server. The Web server in turns accesses a database server. We can see from the diagram that the Web browsers do not directly access the database at any time.

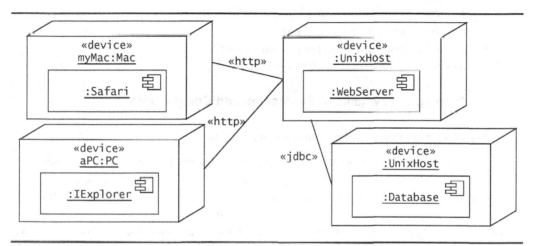

Figure 7-2 A UML deployment diagram representing the allocation of components to different nodes. Web browsers on PCs and Macs can access a WebServer that provides information from a Database.

The deployment diagram in Figure 7-2 focuses on the allocation of components to nodes and provides a high-level view of each component. Components can be refined to include information about the interfaces they provide and the classes they contain. Figure 7-3 illustrates the WebServer component and its containing classes.

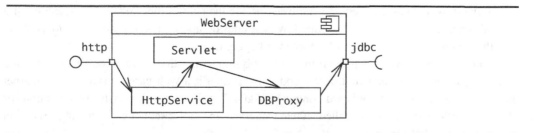

Figure 7-3 Refined view of the WebServer component (UML component diagram). WebServer provides an http interface and requires a jdbc interface. The http interface is realized by the HttpService class.

7.4 System Design Activities: Addressing Design Goals

In this section, we describe the activities needed to ensure that subsystem decomposition addresses all the nonfunctional requirements and can account for any constraints during the implementation phase. In Section 6.4, we identified a set of design goals and designed an initial subsystem decomposition for MyTrip. Here, we refine the subsystem decomposition by

- Mapping Subsystems to Processors and Components (Section 7.4.1)
- Identifying and Storing Persistent Data (Section 7.4.2)
- Providing Access Control (Section 7.4.3)
- Designing the Global Control Flow (Section 7.4.4)
- Identifying Services (Section 7.4.5)
- Identifying Boundary Conditions (Section 7.4.6)
- Reviewing the System Design Model (Section 7.4.7).

7.4.1 Mapping Subsystems to Processors and Components

Selecting a hardware configuration and a platform

Many systems run on more than one computer and depend on access to an intranet or to the Internet. The use of multiple computers can address high-performance needs and interconnect multiple distributed users. Consequently, we need to examine carefully the allocation of subsystems to computers and the design of the infrastructure for supporting communication between subsystems. These computers are modeled as nodes in UML deployment diagrams. Because the hardware mapping activity has significant impact on the performance and complexity of the system, we perform it early in system design.

Selecting a hardware configuration also includes selecting a virtual machine onto which the system should be built. The virtual machine includes the operating system and any software components that are needed, such as a database management system or a communication package. The selection of a virtual machine reduces the distance between the system and the hardware platform on which it will run. The more functionality the components provide, the less development work is involved. The selection of the virtual machine, however, may be constrained by a client who acquires hardware before the start of the project. The selection of a virtual machine may also be constrained by cost considerations: it can be difficult to estimate whether building a component costs more than buying it.

In MyTrip, we deduce from the requirements that PlanningSubsystem and RoutingSubsystem run on two different nodes: the former is a Web-based service on an Internet host, the latter runs on the onboard computer. Figure 7-4 illustrates the hardware allocation for MyTrip with two devices called :OnBoardComputer and :WebHost, and an execution environment called :Apache.

We select a Unix machine as the virtual machine for the :WebServer, and the Web browsers Safari and Internet Explorer as the virtual machines for the :OnBoardComputer.

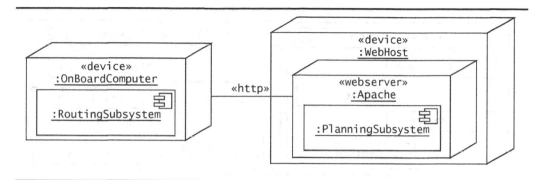

Figure 7-1 Allocation of MyTrip subsystems to devices and execution environments (UML deployment diagram). RoutingSubsystem runs on the OnBoardComputer; PlanningSubsystem runs on an Apache server.

Allocating objects and subsystems to nodes

Once the hardware configuration has been defined and the virtual machines selected, objects and subsystems are assigned to nodes. This often triggers the identification of new objects and subsystems for transporting data among the nodes.

In the MyTrip system, both RoutingSubsystem and PlanningSubsystem share the objects Trip, Destination, Crossing, Segment, and Direction. Instances of these classes need to communicate via a wireless modem using some communication protocol. We create a new subsystem to support this communication: CommunicationSubsystem, a subsystem located on both nodes for managing the communication between them.

We also notice that only segments constituting the planned trip are stored in RoutingSubsystem. Adjacent segments not part of the trip are stored only in the PlanningSubsystem. To take this into account, we need objects in the RoutingSubsystem that can act as surrogates to Segments and Trips in the PlanningSubsystem. An object that acts on the behalf of another one is called a "proxy." We therefore create two new classes, SegmentProxy and TripProxy, and make them part of the RoutingSubsystem. These proxies are examples of the **Proxy design pattern** (see Appendix A.8 and [Gamma et al., 1994]).

In case of replanning by the driver, this class will transparently request the CommunicationSubsystem to retrieve the information associated with its corresponding Segments on the PlanningSubsystem. Finally, the CommunicationSubsystem is used for transferring a complete trip from PlanningSubsystem to RouteAssistant. The revised design model and the additional class descriptions are depicted in Figure 7-5.

In general, allocating subsystems to hardware nodes enables us to distribute functionality and processing power where it is most needed. Unfortunately, it also introduces issues related to storing, transferring, replicating, and synchronizing data among subsystems. For this reason, developers also select the components they will use for developing the system.

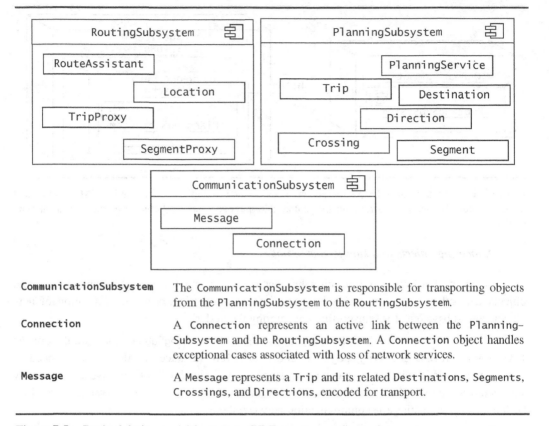

CommunicationSubsystem	The CommunicationSubsystem is responsible for transporting objects from the PlanningSubsystem to the RoutingSubsystem.
Connection	A Connection represents an active link between the Planning-Subsystem and the RoutingSubsystem. A Connection object handles exceptional cases associated with loss of network services.
Message	A Message represents a Trip and its related Destinations, Segments, Crossings, and Directions, encoded for transport.

Figure 7-5   Revised design model for MyTrip (UML component diagram).

7.4.2   Identifying and Storing Persistent Data

Persistent data outlive a single execution of the system. For example, at the end of the day, an author saves his work into a file on a word processor. The file can then be reopened later. The word processor need not run for the file to exist. Similarly, information related to employees, their employment status, and their paychecks live in a database management system. This allows all the programs that operate on employee data to do so consistently. Moreover, storing data in a database enables the system to perform complex queries on a large data set (e.g., the records of several thousand employees).

Where and how data is stored in the system affects system decomposition. In some cases, for example, in a repository architectural style (see Section 6.3.5), a subsystem can be completely dedicated to the storage of data. The selection of a specific database management system can also have implications on the overall control strategy and concurrency management.

For example, in MyTrip, we decide to store the current Trip in a file on a removable disk to allow the recovery of the Trip in case the driver shuts off the car before reaching the final

Destination. Using a file is the simplest and most efficient solution in this case, given that the RoutingSubsystem will only store complete Trips to the file before shutdown and load the file at start-up. In the PlanningSubsystem, however, the Trips will be stored in a database. This subsystem can then be used to manage all Trips for many drivers, as well as the maps needed to generate the Trips. Using a database for this subsystem allows us to perform complex queries on these data. We add the TripFileStoreSubsystem and the MapDBStoreSubsystem subsystems to MyTrip to reflect these decisions, as illustrated in Figure 7-6.

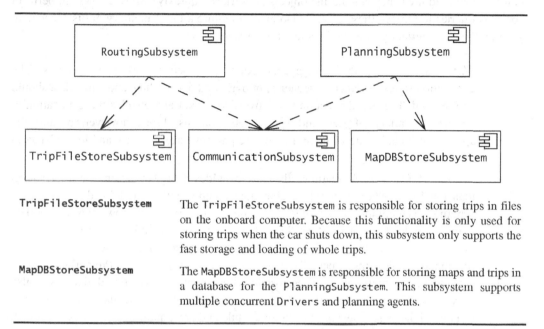

TripFileStoreSubsystem   The TripFileStoreSubsystem is responsible for storing trips in files on the onboard computer. Because this functionality is only used for storing trips when the car shuts down, this subsystem only supports the fast storage and loading of whole trips.

MapDBStoreSubsystem   The MapDBStoreSubsystem is responsible for storing maps and trips in a database for the PlanningSubsystem. This subsystem supports multiple concurrent Drivers and planning agents.

Figure 7-6   Subsystem decomposition of MyTrip after deciding on the issue of data stores (UML component diagram).

Identifying persistent objects

First, we identify which data must be persistent. The entity objects identified during analysis are obvious candidates for persistency. In MyTrip, Trips and their related classes (Crossing, Destination, PlanningService, and Segment) must be stored. Note that not all entity objects must be persistent. For example, Location and Direction are constantly recomputed as the car moves. Persistent objects are not limited to entity objects, however. In a multi-user system, information related to users (e.g., Drivers) is persistent, as well as some attributes of the boundary objects (e.g., window positions, user interface preferences, state of long-running control objects). In general, we can identify persistent objects by examining all the classes that must survive system shutdown, either in case of a controlled shutdown or an unexpected crash. The system will then restore these long-lived objects by retrieving their attributes from storage during system initialization or on demand as the persistent objects are needed.

Selecting a storage management strategy

Once all persistent objects are identified, we need to decide how these objects should be stored. The decision for storage management is more complex and is usually dictated by nonfunctional requirements: Should the objects be retrieved quickly? Must the system perform complex queries to retrieve these objects? Do objects require a lot of memory or disk space? In general, there are currently three options for storage management:

- *Flat files.* Files are the storage abstractions provided by operating systems. The application stores its data as a sequence of bytes and defines how and when data should be retrieved. The file abstraction is relatively low level and enables the application to perform a variety of size and speed optimizations. Files, however, require the application to take care of many issues, such as concurrent access and loss of data in case of system crash.

- *Relational database.* A relational database provides data abstraction at a higher level than flat files. Data are stored in tables that comply with a predefined type called a **schema**. Each column in the table represents an attribute. Each row represents a data item as a tuple of attribute values. Several tuples in different tables are used to represent the attributes of an individual object. Mapping complex object models to a relational schema is challenging. Specialized methods, such as [Blaha & Premerlani, 1998], provide a systematic way of performing this mapping. Relational databases also provide services for concurrency management, access control, and crash recovery. Relational databases have been used for a while and are a mature technology. Although scalable and ideal for large data sets, they are relatively slow for small data sets and for unstructured data (e.g., images, natural language text).

- *Object-oriented database.* An object-oriented database provides services similar to a relational database. Unlike a relational database, it stores data as objects and associations. In addition to providing a higher level of abstraction (and thus reducing the need to translate between objects and storage entities), object-oriented databases provide developers with inheritance and abstract data types. Object-oriented databases significantly reduce the time for the initial development of the storage subsystem. However, they are slower than relational databases for typical queries and are more difficult to tune.

Figure 7-7 summarizes trade-offs when selecting a storage management system. Note that within a complex system, hybrid solutions mixing flat files and a database management system can be used for different sets of persistent objects. In Chapter 10, *Mapping Models to Code*, we examine how persistent objects are mapped into database tables and flat files.

Trade-off between flat files, relational databases, and object-oriented databases

When should you choose flat files?

- Voluminous data (e.g., images)
- Temporary data (e.g., core file)
- Low information density (e.g., archival files, history logs)

When should you choose a relational or an object-oriented database?

- Concurrent accesses
- Access at finer levels of detail
- Multiple platforms or applications for the same data

When should you choose a relational database?

- Complex queries over attributes
- Large data set

When should you choose an object-oriented database?

- Extensive use of associations to retrieve data
- Medium-sized data set
- Irregular associations among objects

Figure 7-7 Trade-off between files and databases for storage management.

7.4.3 Providing Access Control

In multi-user systems, different actors have access to different functionality and data. For example, an everyday actor may only access the data it creates, whereas a system administrator actor may have unlimited access to system data and to other users' data. During analysis, we modeled these distinctions by associating different use cases to different actors. During system design, we model access by determining which objects are shared among actors, and by defining how actors can control access. Depending on the security requirements of the system, we also define how actors are authenticated to the system (i.e., how actors prove to the system who they are) and how selected data in the system should be encrypted.

For example, in MyTrip, storing maps and Trips for many drivers in the same database introduces security issues. We must ensure that Trips are sent only to the driver who created them. This is consistent with the security design goal we defined in Section 6.4.2 for MyTrip. Consequently, we model a driver with the Driver class and associate it with the Trip class. The PlanningSubsystem also becomes responsible for authenticating Drivers before sending Trips. Finally, we decide to encrypt the communication traffic between the RoutingSubsystem and the PlanningSubsystem. This will be done by the CommunicationSubsystem. The descriptions for the Driver class and the revised descriptions for the PlanningSubsystem and the CommunicationSubsystem are displayed in Table 7-1. The revisions to the design model are indicated in italics.

Table 7-1   Revisions to the design model stemming from the decision to authenticate `Drivers` and encrypt communication traffic. The text added to the model is in *italics*.

Communication Subsystem	The `CommunicationSubsystem` is responsible for transporting `Trips` from the `PlanningSubsystem` to the `RoutingSubsystem`. *The CommunicationSubsystem uses the Driver associated with the Trip being transported for selecting a key and encrypting the communication traffic.*
Planning Subsystem	The `PlanningSubsystem` is responsible for constructing a `Trip` connecting a sequence of `Destinations`. The `PlanningSubsystem` is also responsible for responding to replan requests from `RoutingSubsystem`. *Prior to processing any requests, the PlanningSubsystem authenticates the Driver from the RoutingSubsystem. The authenticated Driver is used to determine which Trips can be sent to the corresponding RoutingSubsystem.*
Driver	*A Driver represents an authenticated user. It is used by the CommunicationSubsystem to remember keys associated with a user and by the PlanningSubsystem to associate Trips with users.*

Defining access control for a multi-user system is usually more complex than in `MyTrip`. In general, we need to define for each actor which operations they can access on each shared object. For example, a bank teller may post credits and debits up to a predefined amount. If the transaction exceeds the predefined amount, a manager must approve the transaction. Managers can examine the branch statistics; but cannot access the statistics of other branches. Analysts can access information across all branches of the corporation, but cannot post transactions on individual accounts. We model access on classes with an access matrix. The rows of the matrix represent the actors of the system. The columns represent classes whose access we control. An entry (`class`, `actor`) in the access matrix is called an **access right** and lists the operations (e.g., `postSmallDebit()`, `postLargeDebit()`, `examineGlobalStats()`) that can be executed on instances of the `class` by the `actor`. Table 7-2 depicts the access matrix for our bank.

We can represent the access matrix using one of three different approaches: global access table, access control list, and capabilities.

- A **global access table** represents explicitly every cell in the matrix as a (`actor`, `class`, `operation`) tuple. Determining if an actor has access to a specific object requires looking up the corresponding tuple. If no such tuple is found, access is denied.

- An **access control list** associates a list of (`actor`, `operation`) pairs with each `class` to be accessed. Empty cells are discarded. Every time an object is accessed, its access list is checked for the corresponding actor and operation. An example of an access control list is the guest list for a party. A butler checks the arriving guests by comparing their names against names on the guest list. If there is a match, the guests can enter; otherwise, they are turned away.

- A **capability** associates a (class, operation) pair with an actor. A capability allows an actor access to an object of the class described in the capability. Denying a capability is equivalent to denying access. An example of a capability is an invitation card for a party. In this case, the butler checks if the arriving guests hold an invitation for the party. If the invitation is valid, the guests are admitted; otherwise, they are turned away. No other checks are necessary.

The representation of the access matrix is also a performance issue. Global access tables require a lot of space. Access control lists make it faster to answer the question, "Who has access to this object?", whereas capability lists make it faster to answer the question, "Which objects has this actor access to?"

Each row in the global access matrix represents a different access view of the classes listed in the columns. All of these access views should be consistent. Usually, however, access views are implemented by defining a subclass for each different type of (actor, operation) tuple. For example, in our banking system, we would implement an AccountViewedByTeller and AccountViewedByManager class as subclasses of Account. Only the appropriate classes are available to the corresponding actor. For example, the Analyst client software would not include an Account class, because the Analyst has no access to any operation in this class. This reduces the risk that an error in the system results in the possibility of unauthorized access.

Often, the number of actors and the number of protected objects are too large for either the capability or the access control list representations. In such cases, rules can be used as a compact representation of the global access matrix. For example, **firewalls** protect services located on Intranet Hosts from other hosts on the Internet. Based on the source host and port, destination host and port, and packet size, the firewall allows or denies packets to reach their destination.

Table 7-2 Access matrix for a banking system. Tellers can perform small transactions and inquire balances. Managers can perform larger transactions and access branch statistics in addition to the operations accessible to the Tellers. Analysts can access statistics for all branches, but cannot perform operations at the account level.

Objects Actors	Corporation	LocalBranch	Account
Teller			postSmallDebit() postSmallCredit() examineBalance()
Manager		examineBranchStats()	postSmallDebit() postSmallCredit() postLargeDebit() postLargeCredit() examineBalance() examineHistory()
Analyst	examineGlobalStats()	examineBranchStats()	

As there are potentially many different combinations of source and destination hosts and ports, firewall access is specified in terms of a list of rules. For a given packet, the list is searched sequentially until a matching rule is found. The action of the matching rule then dictates whether the current packet should be filtered or not. For completeness, the last rule of the list matches any packet and has a deny action, thus filtering out packets that do not match any of the other rules. Table 7-3 depicts an example list of rules for the firewall depicted in Figure 7-8. The first two rules allow any host (located in the internet or in the intranet) to access the http service on the `Web Server` and to deliver mail to the `Mail Server`. The next two rules allow Intranet hosts to update the pages of the `Web Server` and to retrieve mail from the `Mail Server`. Consequently, since these are the last two rules that allow packets through, all Internet hosts are denied access to modify web pages on the Web Server, read mail from the Mail Server, or any other service on any of the Intranet hosts. For readability and robustness purposes, these can also have been specified with deny rules (rows 5–7 in Table 7-3).

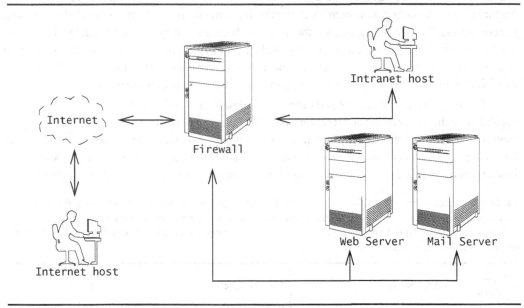

Figure 7-8   Packet filtering firewall: a filter, located at the router, allows or denies individual packets based on header information, such as source and destination.

When the number of actors and objects is large, a rule-based representation is more compact than either access control lists or capabilities. Moreover, a small set of rules is more readable, and hence, more easily proofed by a human reader, which is a critical aspect when setting up a secure environment.

An access matrix only represents **static access control**. This means that access rights can be modeled as attributes of the objects of the system. In the bank information system example,

Table 7-3 Simplified example of packet filtering rules for firewall of Figure 7-8.

Source Host	Destination Host	Destination Port	Action
any[a]	Web Server	http	allow
any	Mail Server	smtp	allow
Intranet host	Web Server	rsync	allow
Intranet host	Mail Server	pop	allow
Internet host	Web Server	rsync	deny
Internet host	Mail Server	pop	deny
Internet host	Intranet host	any	deny
any	any	any	deny

a. **any** means any one of Intranet host, Internet host, Web Server, or Mail Server.

consider a broker actor who is assigned a set of portfolios. By policy, a broker cannot access portfolios managed by another broker. In this case, we need to model access rights dynamically in the system, and, hence, this type of access is called **dynamic access control**. For example, Figure 7-9 shows how this access can be implemented with a protection **Proxy design pattern** (Appendix A.8, [Gamma et al., 1994]). For each Portfolio, we create a PortfolioProxy to protect the Portfolio and check for access. An Access association between a legitimate Broker and a PortfolioProxy indicates which Portfolio the Broker has access to. To access a Portfolio, the Broker sends a message to the corresponding PortfolioProxy. The PortfolioProxy first checks if the invoking Broker has the appropriate association with the PortfolioProxy. If access is granted, the PortfolioProxy delegates the message to the Portfolio. Otherwise, the operation fails.

In both static and dynamic access control, we assume that we know the actor: either the user behind the keyboard or the calling subsystem. This process of verifying the association between the identity of the user or subsystem and the system is called **authentication**. A widely used authentication mechanism, for example, is for the user to specify a user name, known by everybody, and a corresponding password, only known to the system and stored in an access control list. The system protects its users' passwords by encrypting them before storing or transmitting them. If only a single user knows this user name–password combination, then we can assume that the user behind the keyboard is legitimate. Although password authentication can be made secure with current technology, it suffers from many usability disadvantages: users choose passwords that are easy to remember and, thus, easy to guess. They also tend to write their password on notes that they keep close to their monitor, and thus, visible to many other users, authorized or not. Fortunately, other, more secure authentication mechanisms are

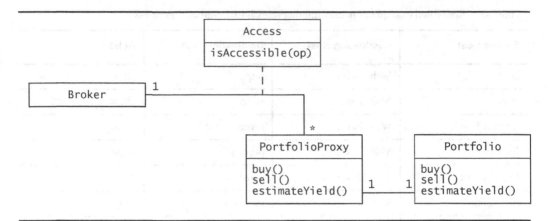

Figure 7-9 Dynamic access implemented with a protection Proxy. The Access association class contains a set of operations that a Broker can use to access a Portfolio. Every operation in the PortfolioProxy first checks with the isAccessible() operation if the invoking Broker has legitimate access. Once access has been granted, PortfolioProxy delegates the operation to the actual Portfolio object. One Access association can be used to control access to many Portfolios.

available. For example, a smart card can be used in conjunction with a password: an intruder would need both the smart card and the password to gain access to the system. Better, we can use a biometric sensor for analyzing patterns of blood vessels in a person's fingers or eyes. An intruder would then need the physical presence of the legitimate user to gain access to the system, which is much more difficult than just stealing a smart card.

In an environment where resources are shared among multiple users, authentication is usually not sufficient. In the case of a network, for example, it is relatively easy for an intruder to find tools to snoop the network traffic, including packets generated by other users (see Figure 7-10). Worse, protocols such as TCP/IP were not designed with security in mind: an intruder can forge packets such that they appear as if they were coming from legitimate users.

Encryption is used to prevent such unauthorized access. Using an encryption algorithm, we can translate a message, called "plaintext," into an encrypted message, called a "ciphertext," such that even if intercepted, it cannot be understood. Only the receiver has sufficient knowledge to correctly decrypt the message, that is, to reverse the original process. The encryption process is parameterized by a "key," such that the method of encryption and decryption can be switched quickly in case the intruder manages to obtain sufficient knowledge to decrypt the message.

Secure authentication and encryption are fundamentally difficult problems. You should always select one or more off-the-shelf algorithms or packages instead of designing your own (unless you are in the business of building such packages). Many such packages are based on public standards that are widely reviewed by academia and the industry, thus ensuring a relatively high level of reliability and security.

Once authentication and encryption are provided, application-specific access control can be more easily implemented on top of these building blocks. In all cases, addressing security

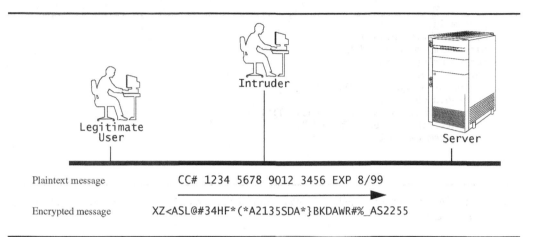

Figure 7-10 Passive attack. Given current technology, a passive intruder can listen to all network traffic. To prevent this kind of attack, encryption makes the information in transit difficult to understand.

issues is a difficult topic. When addressing these issues, developers should record their assumptions and describe the intruder scenarios they are considering. When several alternatives are explored, developers should state the design problems they are attempting to solve and record the results of the evaluation. We describe in the next chapter how to do this systematically using issue modeling.

7.4.4   Designing the Global Control Flow

Control flow is the sequencing of actions in a system. In object-oriented systems, sequencing actions includes deciding which operations should be executed and in which order. These decisions are based on external events generated by an actor or on the passage of time.

Control flow is a design problem. During analysis control flow is not an issue, because we assume that all objects are running simultaneously executing operations any time they need to. During system design, we need to take into account that not every object has the luxury of running on its own processor. There are three possible control flow mechanisms:

- **Procedure-driven control.** Operations wait for input whenever they need data from an actor. This kind of control flow is mostly used in legacy systems and systems written in procedural languages. It introduces difficulties when used with object-oriented languages. As the sequencing of operations is distributed among a large set of objects, it becomes increasingly difficult to determine the order of inputs by looking at the code (Figure 7-11).

```
    Stream in, out;
    String userid, passwd;
/* Initialization omitted */
    out.println("Login:");
    in.readln(userid);
    out.println("Password:");
    in.readln(passwd);
    if (!security.check(userid, passwd)) {
        out.println("Login failed.");
        system.exit(-1);
    }
/* ...*/
```

Figure 7-11 An example of procedure driven control (Java). The code prints out messages and waits for input from the user.

- **Event-driven control**. A main loop waits for an external event. Whenever an event becomes available, it is dispatched to the appropriate object, based on information associated with the event. This kind of control flow has the advantage of leading to a simpler structure and to centralizing all input in the main loop. However, it makes the implementation of multi-step sequences more difficult to implement (Figure 7-12).

```
Iterator subscribers, eventStream;
Subscriber subscriber;
Event event;
EventStream eventStream;
/* ... */
while (eventStream.hasNext()) {
    event = eventStream.next();
    subscribers = dispatchInfo.getSubscribers(event);
    while (subscribers.hasNext()) {
        subscriber = subscribers.next()) {
        subscriber.process(event);
    }
}
/* ... */
```

Figure 7-12 An example of main loop for event-driven control (Java). An event is taken from an eventStream and sent to objects interested in it.

- **Threads.** Threads are the concurrent variation of procedure-driven control: The system can create an arbitrary number of threads, each responding to a different event. If a thread needs additional data, it waits for input from a specific actor. This kind of control flow is the most intuitive of the three mechanisms. However, debugging threaded software requires good tools: preemptive thread schedulers introduce nondeterminism and, thus, make testing harder (Figure 7-13).

```
Thread thread;
Event event;
EventHandler eventHandler;
boolean done;
/* ...*/
while (!done) {
    event = eventStream.getNextEvent();
    eventHandler = new EventHandler(event)
    thread = new Thread(eventHandler);
    thread.start();
}
/* ...*/
```

Figure 7-13 An example of event processing with threads (Java). eventHandler is an object dedicated to handling event. It implements the run() operation, which is invoked when thread is started.

Procedure-driven control is useful for testing subsystems. A driver makes specific calls to methods offered by the subsystem. For the control flow of the final system, though, procedure-driven control should be avoided.

The trade-off between event-driven control and threads is more complicated. Event-driven control is more mature than threads. Modern languages have only recently started to provide support for thread programming. As more debugging tools become available and experience is accumulated, developing thread-based systems will become easier. Also, many user interface packages supply the infrastructure for dispatching events and impose this kind of control flow on the design. Although threads are more intuitive, they currently introduce many problems during debugging and testing. Until more mature tools and infrastructures are available for developing with threads, event-driven control flow is preferred.

Once a control flow mechanism is selected, we can realize it with a set of one or more control objects. The role of control objects is to record external events, store temporary states about them, and issue the right sequence of operation calls on the boundary and entity objects associated with the external event. Localizing control flow decisions for a use case in a single object not only results in more understandable code, but it also makes the system more resilient to changes in control flow implementation.

7.4.5   Identifying Services

Until this point, we have examined the key system design decisions that impact the subsystem decomposition. We have now identified the main subsystems and we have a rough idea of how to allocate responsibilities to each subsystem. In this activity, we refine the subsystem decomposition by identifying the services provided by each subsystems. We review each dependency between subsystems and define an interface for each service we identified (depicted in UML by a lollipop). In this activity, we name the identified services. During object design, we specify each service precisely in terms of operations, parameters, and constraints (see Chapter 9, *Object Design: Specifying Interfaces*).

By focusing on dependencies between subsystems, we refine the subsystem responsibilities, we find omissions in our decomposition, and we validate the current software architecture. By focusing on services (as opposed to attributes or operations), we remain at the architectural abstraction level, allowing us to reassign responsibilities between subsystems, without changing many modeling elements.

For example, let us focus on the interfaces of the CommunicationSubsystem of MyTrip. The responsibility of the CommunicationSubsystem is to transport trips from the PlanningSubsystem to the RoutingSubsystem. The RoutingSubsystem initiates the connection, as the PlanningSubsystem is a server that is always available, while the RoutingSubsystem runs only while the car is powered. This asymmetry leads us to define three interfaces (Figure 7-14):

- ConnectionManager allows a subsystem to register with the CommunicationSubsystem, to authenticate, find other nodes, and initiate and close connections.
- TripRequester allows a subsystem to request a list of available trips and download selected trips.
- TripProvider allows a subsystem to provide a list of trips that are available for the specified car driver and respond to specific trip requests.

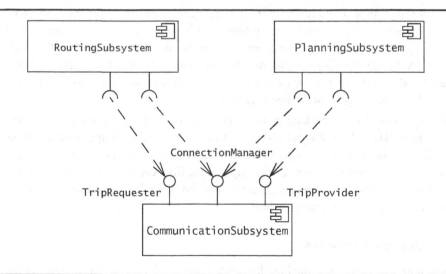

Figure 7-14   Refining the subsystem decompositions by identifying subsystem services (UML component diagram). The CommunicationSubsystem provides three services for managing connections, uploading trips, and downloading trips.

While we have not yet specified any operations of the CommunicationSubsystem, naming services provides us with enough detail for identifying missing functionality and discussing design trade-offs. For example:

- Should the RoutingSubsystem be able to provide data (e.g., average speed on current trip leg, location of traffic jam) back to the PlanningSubsystem in a future use case?

- Should the CommunicationSubsystem only deal with entire trips or should provide the ability to send trips in multiple packages?

These questions lead us to further design decisions. We add service to the CommunicationSubsystem for returning real-time data to the PlanningSubsystem. We can structure the interface of the CommunicationSubsystem so that we could support either downloading policy.

Note that, by convention, we use noun phrases to name services (e.g., TripRequester), as they correspond to an interface including both attributes and operations. Operations provided by the interface are named with verb phrases starting with a lower case (e.g, requestTrip()). Attributes defined by the interface are named with noun phrases starting with a lower case (e.g., connectionStatus).

Once we reviewed the dependencies among subsystems and identified corresponding services, we have a concrete understanding of the subsystem responsibilities for the steady state. We are now ready to examine boundary cases.

7.4.6   Identifying Boundary Conditions

In previous sections, we dealt with designing and refining the system decomposition. We now have a better idea of how to decompose the system, how to distribute use cases among subsystems, where to store data, and how to achieve access control and ensure security. We still need to examine the **boundary conditions** of the system—that is, to decide how the system is started, initialized, and shut down—and we need to define how we deal with major failures such as data corruption and network outages, whether they are caused by a software error or a power outage. Uses cases dealing with these conditions are called **boundary use cases**.

For example, we now have a good idea of how MyTrip should work in steady state. We have, however, not yet addressed how MyTrip is initialized. For example, how are maps loaded into the PlanningService? How is MyTrip installed in the car? How does MyTrip know which PlanningService to connect to? How are drivers added to the PlanningService? We quickly discover use cases that have not been specified.

It is common that boundary use cases are not specified during analysis or that they are treated separately from the common use cases. For example, many system administration functions can be inferred from the everyday user requirements (registering and deleting users, managing access control), whereas, many other functions are consequences of design decisions (cache sizes, location of database server, location of backup server) and not of requirement decisions. In general, we identify boundary use cases by examining each subsystem and each persistent object:

- **Configuration**. For each persistent object, we examine in which use cases it is created or destroyed (or archived). For objects that are not created or destroyed in any of the common use cases (e.g., Maps in the MyTrip system), we add a use case invoked by a system administrator (e.g., ManageMaps in the MyTrip system).
- **Start-up and shutdown**. For each component (e.g., a WebServer), we add three use cases to start, shutdown, and configure the component. Note that a single use case can manage several tightly coupled components.
- **Exception handling**. For each type of component failure (e.g., network outage), we decide how the system should react (e.g., inform users of the failure). We document each of these decisions with an exceptional use case that extends the relevant common uses cases identified during requirements elicitation. Note that, when tolerating the effects of a failure, the handling of an exceptional condition can lead to changing the system design instead of adding an exceptional use case. For example, the RouteAssistant can completely download the Trip onto the car before the start of the trip.

In general, an **exception** is an event or error that occurs during the execution of the system. Exceptions are caused by three different sources:

- *A hardware failure.* Hardware ages and fails. A hard disk crash can lead to the permanent loss of data. The failure of a network link, for example, can momentarily disconnect two nodes of the system.
- *Changes in the operating environment.* The environment also affects the way a system works. A wireless mobile system can loose connectivity if it is out of range of a transmitter. A power outage can bring down the system, unless it is fitted with back-up batteries.
- *A software fault.* An error can occur because the system or one of its components contains a design error. Although writing bug-free software is difficult, individual subsystems can anticipate errors from other subsystems and protect against them.

Exception handling is the mechanism by which a system treats an exception. In the case of a user error, the system should display a meaningful error message to the user so that she can correct her input. In the case of a network link failure, the system should save its temporary state so that it can recover when the network comes back on line.

For example, consider a wireless navigation system in a car that retrieves on-demand traffic information from a central computer. When the car enters a tunnel, the transfer of information will be interrupted in the physical network layer. The network layer will raise an exception (e.g., "socket unexpectedly closed") and forward it to the upper layer. The upper layer has the option of forwarding the exception to a higher layer or of tolerating the exception (e.g., wait for a short time and attempt to retrieve the data again, operate with older traffic data). When identifying boundary conditions, developers examine each component failure and decide how to handle it. They can design components to tolerate the failure or write boundary use cases to specify how the user will experience the failure. Note that during system design, we only examine failures at the level of components. In Chapter 9, *Object Design: Specifying Interfaces*, we will examine how to handle exceptions at the object level.

Developing reliable systems is a difficult topic. Often, trading off some functionality can make system design easier. In MyTrip, we assumed that the connection is always possible at the source destination and that replanning could be affected by communication problems along the trip.

For example (Figure 7-15), we now modify the analysis model for MyTrip to include the boundary use cases. In particular, we add three use cases: ManageDrivers, to add, remove, and edit drivers; ManageMaps, to add, remove, and update maps used to generate trips; and ManageServer, to perform routine configuration, start-up, and shutdown. StartServer, part of ManageServer, is provided as an example in Figure 7-16.

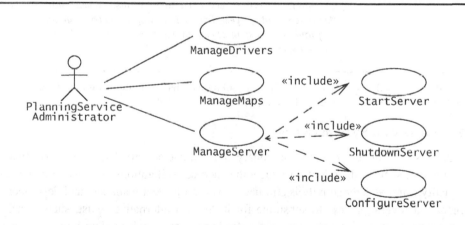

Figure 7-15 Administration use cases for MyTrip (UML use case diagram). ManageDrivers is invoked to add, remove, modify, or read data about drivers (e.g., user name and password, usage log, encryption key generation). ManageMaps is invoked to add, remove, or update maps that are used to generate trips. ManageServer includes all the functions necessary to start up and shutdown the server.

In this case, revising the use case model by adding three use cases does not affect subsystem decomposition. We added, however, new use cases to existing subsystems: The MapDBStoreSubsystem should be able to detect whether or not it was properly shut down and should be able to perform consistency checks and repair corrupted data, as necessary. We revise the description of MapDBStoreSubsystem (Figure 7-17).

Use case name	StartServer
Entry condition	1. The PlanningServiceAdministrator logs into the server machine.
Flow of events	2. Upon successful login, the PlanningServiceAdministrator executes the startPlanningService command.
	3. If the PlanningService was previously shutdown normally, the server reads the list of legitimate Drivers and the index of active Trips and Maps. If the PlanningService had crashed, it notifies the PlanningServiceAdministrator and performs a consistency check on the MapDBStore.
Exit condition	4. The PlanningService is available and waits for connections from RoutingAssistants.

Figure 7-16   StartServer use case of the MyTrip system.

MapDBStoreSubsystem	The MapDBStoreSubsystem is responsible for storing Maps and Trips in a database for the PlanningSubsystem. This subsystem supports multiple concurrent Drivers and planning agents. *When starting up, the MapDBStoreSubsystem detects if it was properly shut down. If not, it performs a consistent check on Maps and Trips and repairs corrupted data if necessary.*

Figure 7-17   Revised description for MapDBStoreSubsystem based on the additional StartServer use case of Figure 7-16. (Changes indicated in *italics*.)

7.4.7   Reviewing System Design

Like analysis, system design is an evolutionary and iterative activity. Unlike analysis, there is no external agent, such as the client, to review the successive iterations and ensure better quality. This quality improvement activity is still necessary, and project managers and developers need to organize a review process to substitute for it. Several alternatives exist, such as using the developers who were not involved in system design to act as independent reviewers, or to use developers from another project to act as a peer review. These review processes work only if the reviewers have an incentive to discover and report problems.

In addition to meeting the design goals that were identified during system design, we need to ensure that the system design model is correct, complete, consistent, realistic, and readable. The system design model is **correct** if the analysis model can be mapped to the system design model. You should ask the following questions to determine if the system design is correct:

- Can every subsystem be traced back to a use case or a nonfunctional requirement?
- Can every use case be mapped to a set of subsystems?
- Can every design goal be traced back to a nonfunctional requirement?

- Is every nonfunctional requirement addressed in the system design model?
- Does each actor have an access policy?
- Is every access policy consistent with the nonfunctional security requirement?

The model is **complete** if every requirement and every system design issue has been addressed. You should ask the following questions to determine if the system design is complete:

- Have the boundary conditions been handled?
- Was there a walkthrough of the use cases to identify missing functionality in the system design?
- Have all use cases been examined and assigned a control object?
- Have all aspects of system design (i.e., hardware allocation, persistent storage, access control, legacy code, boundary conditions) been addressed?
- Do all subsystems have definitions?

The model is **consistent** if it does not contain any contradictions. You should ask the following questions to determine if a system design is consistent:

- Are conflicting design goals prioritized?
- Does any design goal violate a nonfunctional requirement?
- Are there multiple subsystems or classes with the same name?
- Are collections of objects exchanged among subsystems in a consistent manner?

The model is **realistic** if the corresponding system can be implemented. You ask the following questions to determine if a system design is realistic:

- Are any new technologies or components included in the system? Was the appropriateness or robustness of these technologies or components evaluated? How?
- Have performance and reliability requirements been reviewed in the context of subsystem decomposition?
- Have concurrency issues (e.g., contention, deadlocks) been addressed?

The model is **readable** if developers not involved in the system design can understand the model. You should ask the following questions to ensure that the system design is readable:

- Are subsystem names understandable?
- Do entities (e.g., subsystems, classes) with similar names denote similar concepts?
- Are all entities described at the same level of detail?

In many projects, you will find that system design and implementation overlap quite a bit. For example, you may build prototypes of selected subsystems before the architecture is stable in order to evaluate new technologies. This leads to many partial reviews instead of an encompassing review followed by a client sign-off, as for analysis. Although this process yields greater flexibility, it also requires developers to track open issues more carefully. Many difficult issues tend to be resolved late not because they are difficult, but because they fell through the cracks of the process.

7.5 Managing System Design

In this section, we discuss issues related to managing the system design activities. As in analysis, the primary challenge in managing the system design is to maintain consistency while using as many resources as possible. In the end, the software architecture and the system interfaces should describe a single cohesive system understandable by a single person.

We first describe a document template that can be used to document the results of system design (Section 7.5.1). Next, we describe the role assignment during system design (Section 7.5.2) and address communication issues during system design (Section 7.5.3). Next, we address management issues related to the iterative nature of system design (Section 7.5.4).

7.5.1 Documenting System Design

System design is documented in the System Design Document (SDD). It describes design goals set by the project, subsystem decomposition (with UML class diagrams), hardware/software mapping (with UML deployment diagrams), data management, access control, control flow mechanisms, and boundary conditions. The SDD is used to define interfaces between teams of developers and serve as a reference when architecture-level decisions need to be revisited. The audience for the SDD includes the project management, the system architects (i.e., the developers who participate in the system design), and the developers who design and implement each subsystem. Figure 7-18 is an example template for a SDD.

The first section of the SDD is an *Introduction*. Its purpose is to provide a brief overview of the software architecture and the design goals. It also provides references to other documents and traceability information (e.g., related requirements analysis document, references to existing systems, constraints impacting the software architecture).

The second section, *Current software architecture*, describes the architecture of the system being replaced. If there is no previous system, this section can be replaced by a survey of current architectures for similar systems. The purpose of this section is to make explicit the background information that system architects used, their assumptions, and common issues the new system will address.

The third section, *Proposed system architecture*, documents the system design model of the new system. It is divided into seven subsections:

- *Overview* presents a bird's-eye view of the software architecture and briefly describes the assignment of functionality to each subsystem.

System Design Document

1. Introduction
   1.1 Purpose of the system
   1.2 Design goals
   1.3 Definitions, acronyms, and abbreviations
   1.4 References
   1.5 Overview
2. Current software architecture
3. Proposed software architecture
   3.1 Overview
   3.2 Subsystem decomposition
   3.3 Hardware/software mapping
   3.4 Persistent data management
   3.5 Access control and security
   3.6 Global software control
   3.7 Boundary conditions
4. Subsystem services
   Glossary

Figure 7-18   Example outline for the System Design Document (SDD).

- *Subsystem decomposition* describes the decomposition into subsystems and the responsibilities of each. This is the main product of system design.

- *Hardware/software mapping* describes how subsystems are assigned to hardware and off-the-shelf components. It also lists the issues introduced by multiple nodes and software reuse.

- *Persistent data management* describes the persistent data stored by the system and the data management infrastructure required for it. This section typically includes the description of data schemes, the selection of a database, and the description of the encapsulation of the database.

- *Access control and security* describes the user model of the system in terms of an access matrix. This section also describes security issues, such as the selection of an authentication mechanism, the use of encryption, and the management of keys.

- *Global software control* describes how the global software control is implemented. In particular, this section should describe how requests are initiated and how subsystems synchronize. This section should list and address synchronization and concurrency issues.

- *Boundary conditions* describes the start-up, shutdown, and error behavior of the system. (If new use cases are discovered for system administration, these should be included in the requirements analysis document, not in this section.)

The fourth section, *Subsystem services,* describes the services provided by each subsystem. Although this section is usually empty or incomplete in the first versions of the SDD, this section serves as a reference for teams for the boundaries between their subsystems. The interface of each subsystem is derived from this section and detailed in the Object Design Document.

The SDD is written after the initial system decomposition is done; that is, system architects should not wait until all system design decisions are made before publishing the document. The SDD, moreover, is updated throughout the process when design decisions are made or problems are discovered. The SDD, once published, is baselined and put under configuration management. The revision history section of the SDD provides a history of changes as a list of changes, including author responsible for the change, date of change, and brief description of the change.

7.5.2   Assigning Responsibilities

Unlike analysis, system design is the realm of developers. The client and the end user fade into the background. Note, however, that many activities in system design trigger revisions to the analysis model. The client and the user are brought back into the process for such revisions. System design in complex systems is centered around the architecture team. This is a cross-functional team made up of architects who define the subsystem decomposition and selected developers who will implement the subsystem. It is critical that system design include people who are exposed to the consequences of system design decisions. The architecture team starts work as soon as the analysis model is stable and continues to function until the end of the integration phase. This creates an incentive for the architecture team to anticipate problems encountered during integration. Below are the main roles of system design:

- The **architect** takes the main role in system design. The architect ensures consistency in design decisions and interface styles. The architect ensures the consistency of the design in the configuration management and testing teams, in particular in the formulation of the configuration management policy and the system integration strategy. This is mainly an integration role consuming information from each subsystem team. The architect is the leader of the cross-functional architecture team.

- **Architecture liaisons** are the members of the architecture team. They are representatives from the subsystem teams. They convey information from and to their teams and negotiate interface changes. During system design, they focus on the subsystem services; during the implementation phase, they focus on the consistency of the APIs.

- The **document editor**, **configuration manager**, and **reviewer** roles are the same as for analysis (see Section 5.5.2).

The number of subsystems determines the size of the architecture team. For complex systems, an architecture team is introduced for each level of abstraction. In all cases, there should be one integrating role on the team to ensure consistency and the understandability of the architecture by a single individual.

7.5.3   Communicating about System Design

Communication during system design should be less challenging than during analysis: the functionality of the system has been defined, project participants have similar backgrounds and by now should know each other better. Communication is still difficult, due to new sources of complexity:

- *Size.* The number of issues to be dealt with increases as developers start designing. The number of items that developers manipulate increases: each piece of functionality requires many operations on many objects. Moreover, developers investigate, often concurrently, multiple designs and multiple implementation technologies.

- *Change.* The subsystem decomposition and the interfaces of the subsystems are in constant flux. Terms used by developers to name different parts of the system evolve constantly. If the change is rapid, developers may not be discussing the same version of the subsystem, which can lead to much confusion.

- *Level of abstraction.* Discussions about requirements can be made concrete by using interface mock-ups and analogies with existing systems. Discussions about implementation become concrete when integration and test results are available. System design discussions are seldom concrete, as consequences of design decisions are felt only later, during implementation and testing.

- *Reluctance to confront problems.* The level of abstraction of most discussions can also make it easy to delay the resolution of difficult issues. A typical resolution of control issues is often, "Let us revisit this issue during implementation." Whereas it is usually desirable to delay certain design decisions, such as the internal data structures and algorithms used by each subsystem, any decision that has an impact on the system decomposition and the subsystem interfaces should not be delayed.

- *Conflicting goals and criteria.* Individual developers often optimize different criteria. A developer experienced in user interface design will be biased toward optimizing response time. A developer experienced in databases might optimize throughput. These conflicting goals, especially when implicit, result in developers pulling the system decomposition in different directions and lead to inconsistencies.

The same techniques we discussed in analysis (see Section 5.5.3) can be applied during system design:

- *Identify and prioritize the design goals for the system and make them explicit* (see Section 6.4.2). If the developers concerned with system design have input in this process, they will have an easier time committing to these design goals. Design goals also provide an objective framework against which decisions can be evaluated.

- *Make the current version of the system decomposition available to all concerned.* A live document distributed via the Internet is one way to achieve rapid distribution. Using a configuration management tool to maintain the system design documents helps developers in identifying recent changes.

- *Maintain an up-to-date glossary.* As in analysis, defining terms explicitly reduces misunderstandings. When identifying and modeling subsystems, provide definitions in addition to names. A UML diagram with only subsystem names is not sufficient for supporting effective communication. A brief and substantial definition should accompany every subsystem and class name.

- *Confront design problems.* Delaying design decisions can be beneficial when more information is needed before committing to the design decision. This approach, however, can prevent the confrontation of difficult design problems. Before tabling an issue, several possible alternatives should be explored and described, and the delay justified. This ensures that issues can be delayed without serious impact on the system decomposition.

- *Iterate.* Selected excursions into the implementation phase can improve the system design. For example, new features in a vendor-supplied component can be evaluated by implementing a vertical prototype (see Section 7.5.4) for the functionality most likely to benefit from the feature.

Finally, no matter how much effort is expended on system design, the system decomposition and the subsystem interfaces will almost certainly change during implementation. As new information about implementation technologies becomes available, developers have a clearer understanding of the system, and design alternatives are discovered. Developers should anticipate change and reserve some time to update the SDD before system integration.

7.5.4   Iterating over the System Design

As in the case of requirements, system design occurs through successive iteration and change. Change, however, should be controlled to prevent chaos, especially in complex projects including many participants. We distinguish three types of iterations during system design. First, major decisions early in system design affect subsystem decomposition as each of the different activities of system design is initiated. Second, revisions to the interfaces of the subsystems occur when evaluation prototypes are created to evaluate specific issues. Third, errors and oversights that are discovered late trigger changes to the subsystem interfaces and sometimes to the system decomposition itself.

The first set of iterations is best handled in brainstorming sessions (either face-to-face or electronic). Definitions are still in flux, developers do not have yet a grasp of the whole system, and communication should be maximized at the expense of formality or procedure. Often in team-based projects, the initial system decomposition is designed before the analysis is complete. Decomposing the system early allows the responsibility of different subsystems to be assigned to different teams. Change and exploration should be encouraged, if only to broaden the developers' shared understanding or to generate supporting evidence for the current design. For this reason, a bureaucratic formal change process should not be used during this phase.

The second set of iterations aims at solving difficult and focused issues, such as the choice of a specific vendor or technology. The subsystem decomposition is stable (ideally, it should be independent of vendors and technology), and most of these explorations aim at identifying whether a specific package is appropriate for the system. During this period, developers can also create a vertical prototype[1] for a critical use case to test the appropriateness of the decomposition. This enables control flow issues to be discovered and addressed early. Again, a formal change process is not necessary. A list of pending issues and their status can help developers quickly propagate the results of a technology investigation.

The third set of iterations remedies design problems discovered late in the process. Although developers would much rather avoid these iterations, as they tend to be costly and introduce many new bugs in the system, they should anticipate changes late in development. Anticipating late iterations includes documenting dependencies among subsystems, the design rationale for subsystem interfaces, and any workaround that is likely to fail in case of change. Change should be carefully managed, and a change process similar to the one tracking requirements changes should be put in place.

We can achieve the progressive stabilization of subsystem decomposition by using the concept of a design window. To encourage change while controlling it, critical issues are left open only during a specified time. For example, the hardware/software platform on which the system is targeted should be resolved early in the project so that purchasing decisions for the hardware can be done in time for development. Internal data structures and algorithms, however, can be left open until after integration, allowing developers to revise them based on performance testing. Once the design window is closed, the issue must be resolved and can only be reopened in a subsequent iteration.

With the pace of technology innovation quickening, many changes can be anticipated when a dedicated part of the organization is responsible for technology management. Technology managers scan new technologies, evaluate them, and accumulate knowledge that is used during the selection of components. Often, change happens so fast that companies are not aware of which technologies they themselves provide.

---

1. A **vertical prototype** completely implements a restricted functionality, for example, all the interface, control, and entity objects for one use case. A **horizontal prototype** partially implements a broad range of functionality, for example, only the interface objects for a number of use cases.

7.6 ARENA Case Study

In this section, we apply the concepts and methods described in this chapter to the ARENA system. We start with identifying the design goals for ARENA and design an initial subsystem decomposition. We then select a software and hardware platform and define the persistent stores, access control, and global control flow. Finally, we look at the boundary conditions of ARENA.

7.6.1 Identifying Design Goals

Design goals are qualities that enable us to prioritize the development of the system. Design goals originate from the nonfunctional requirements specified during requirements elicitation and from technical and management goals specified by the project.

In ARENA, the main client is the ArenaOperator, who provides the resources for setting up an Arena for a particular community. ArenaOperators are themselves Players who may have system administration or even programming skills. The advertisement features allow them to recoup some of their costs. Moreover, we anticipate that ArenaOperators will form a community and that the integration of new games into ARENA and improvements to ARENA will be mostly contributed by ArenaOperators. However, advertisement is not the main purpose of ARENA. From these observations and from the ARENA problem statement (Figure 4-17), we identify the following design goals:

- *Low operating cost.* To minimize the need for advertisement, the cost of running the system (e.g., hardware resources, network resources, administration costs, etc.) should be minimized. This also leads us to select free or open-source components. This design goal is a refinement of the nonfunctional requirement "low operating cost" of the ARENA problem statement (Figure 4-17).

- *High availability.* The value of an Arena increases with the number of players available for playing tournaments. Unexpected crashes and interruptions in tournaments will create a lot of frustration for the players and discourage them from attending other tournaments. This design goal is not explicitly stated in the problem statement or the requirements, but is necessary if an Arena is to attract and keep a sufficiently large number of players.

- *Scalability in terms of number of players and concurrent tournaments.* The response time of the Arena may not degrade dramatically with the number of Players. When needed, an ArenaOperator should have the option of increasing the capacity of an Arena by adding hardware nodes. This design goal is a refinement of the nonfunctional requirement "scalability" in the ARENA problem statement (Figure 4-17).

- *Ease of adding new games.* Some games, such as chess, are timeless. However, the computer game industry evolves with different fashions and hardware improvements. Consequently, to keep an Arena active, it should be relatively easy to adapt and install new games. This design goal is a refinement of the nonfunctional requirement "extensibility" in the ARENA problem statement (Figure 4-17).

- *Documentation for open source development.* The organization and documentation of the ARENA game framework should then make it easier for new developers to contribute features to the code. This includes source code documentation that supports low-level changes and improvements, as well as a good architecture-level documentation that supports the addition of new features. This design goal originated from the developers and management of ARENA (as opposed to the client). Note that such design goals may require additional interaction with the client, as they might interfere with implicit client goals that have not yet been made explicit.

7.6.2   Identifying Subsystems

We first identify subsystems from the functional requirements of ARENA and from the analysis model. The purpose of this activity is to divide the system in self-contained components that can be managed by individuals. As we address other design issues, such as access control and persistency management, we will refine or modify this initial subsystem decomposition.

We first distinguish two main parts of the ARENA subsystem: the game organization part of the system, which is responsible for coordinating Users when organizing an Arena, a League, or a Tournament, and the game playing part, in which Players conduct individual Matches in the scope of a Tournament.

For the game organization part, we select a three-tier architectural style (Figure 7-19) in which an ArenaClient subsystem provides a front end for users to initiate all organization-related use cases (e.g., AnnounceTournament, ApplyForTournament, RegisterPlayer). The ArenaServer subsystem is responsible for access control and concurrency control, and delegates to nested subsystems for the application logic. Different subsystems are dedicated to the user management of users, advertisements, tournaments, and games. The bottom tier is realized by the ArenaStorage subsystem, responsible for storing any persistent objects, except for those representing Match states.

For the game playing part, the client server architecture may not be sufficient for synchronous games in which the action of one player can trigger events for another player within a relatively short time. Synchronous behavior could be simulated with polling; however, because of scalability and responsiveness goals, we select a peer-to-peer architecture in which MatchFrontEndPeer subsystems provide the user interface and a GamePeer maintains the state of the matches currently under way and enforces the game rules. MatchFrontEndPeers may also communicate directly with each other for real-time games. To achieve the game independence design goal, ARENA provides a framework for both the MatchFrontEndPeer and the GamePeer, while the bulk of the game logic is provided by customized game-dependent components. Adding a game consists of developing adapters for existing games or ARENA-compliant components for new games. The TournamentManagement subsystem uses the GameManagement subsystem to initiate a GamePeer and to collect the results of the individual Matches. The

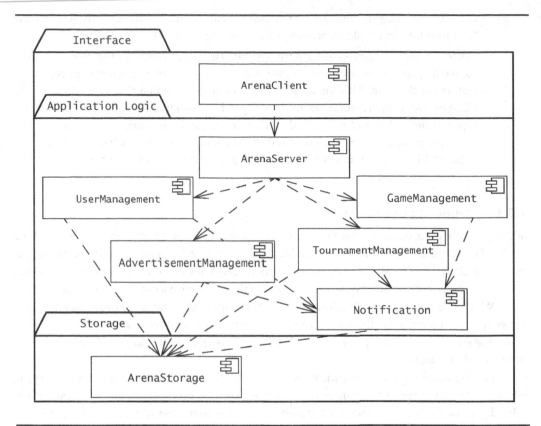

Figure 7-19 ARENA subsystem decomposition, game organization part (UML component diagram, layers shown as UML packages).

MatchFrontEndPeer uses the AdvertisementManagement subsystem to retrieve Advertisements (Figure 7-20). Note that for turn-based games, a client server architectural style would be sufficient, as the response time for such games is less critical. The selection of the peer-to-peer style does not prevent specific games from following a client server style.

7.6.3   Mapping Subsystems to Processors and Components

Mapping subsystems to processors and components enables us to identify potential concurrency among subsystems and to address performance and reliability goals.

ARENA is inherently a distributed system, as users sit in front of different machines, possibly several time zones apart. However, we distinguish only between two types of nodes: the UserMachine to provide a user interface and the ServerMachines to run the application logic and storage and, more generally, to provide the ARENA services. ArenaClient and the MatchFrontEndPeer subsystems run on the UserMachine. In an installation of ARENA with few

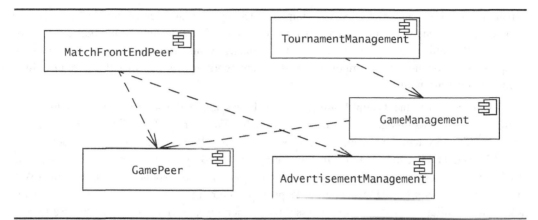

Figure 7-20 ARENA subsystem decomposition, game playing part (UML component diagram).

players, all other subsystems can be collocated onto a single ServerMachine. However, to ensure scalability, we identify an additional subsystem dedicated to send advertisement banners to the browser, and assign the AdvertisementServer, the GamePeer, the ArenaStorage, and the ArenaServer subsystems to different processes that can run on different ServerMachines. The ArenaServer component includes the nested, TournamentManagement, UserManagement, and GameManagement subsystems (Figure 7-21).

For the realization of the game organization part of ARENA, we select the Java EE framework. Java EE is a collection of interfaces and standards developed by Sun Microsystems and community efforts for developing portable web based information systems in Java. The

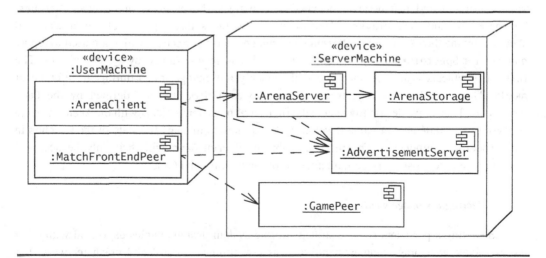

Figure 7-21 ARENA hardware/software mapping (UML deployment diagram). Note that each run-time component may support several subsystems.

advantage of this standard is that it is implemented by several open-source and commercial products, thus enabling an ArenaOperator to trade off scale (e.g., number of players, tournaments, and leagues) for set-up cost (e.g., licensing and run-time costs). Also, in their simplest form, open-source components of this framework are easy to install and require little prior administration knowledge.

Consequently, the ArenaClient is a Web browser and the ArenaServer and the other game organization subsystems are accessed through a Web server. To realize the ArenaServer and related subsystems, we select Java Servlets and Java Server Pages (JSP), components of Java EE, as the main technology for implementing the boundary objects. Servlets are classes that are located on the ServerMachine. Servlets receive, process, and respond to requests from a Web browser by generating an HTML page. JSPs provide a compact way of specifying servlets using a language similar to HTML. A preprocessor then generates a servlet from a JSP. We use JSPs to realize the boundary and control objects of ARENA. JSPs in turn invoke methods on entity objects and storage objects, which are also realized using the Java Foundation classes.

Having identified the subsystems, the concurrency, and the hardware/software mapping, we now turn our attention to persistency management.

7.6.4   Identifying and Storing Persistent Data

Identifying persistent objects

ARENA deals with two sets of objects that must be stored. The first set includes the objects that are created and accessed by the game organization subsystems (e.g., Tournament, Game, Match, Player) and that need to be persistent to track the progress of Leagues, Matches, Tournaments, and their Players. The second set includes the objects that are created and accessed by the GamePeer and the MatchFrontEndPeer during Matches, which are used to replay matches for Spectators and to resume Matches that were interrupted by system crashes. The first set of objects is well defined and will probably not change much during the lifetime of ARENA. The second set of objects are specific to each Game and are defined by the Game developers. Hence, we decide to manage the first set of persistent objects with the ArenaStorage subsystem of ARENA and let game developers decide how to manage the state of the Matches in game-specific components. The persistent objects of each Game will then only be accessed through a generic Game interface implemented by each individual Game.

Selecting a storage strategy

Selecting a persistent storage strategy during system design enables us to deal with other issues related to storage management, such as concurrency control and crash recovery. For example, many database management systems allow concurrent queries and provide transaction mechanisms to ensure data integrity.

Our highest priority design goal in ARENA is to minimize operating costs, so we first consider using flat files for storage. Such a system can be installed easily, since there is no database management system to configure or to manage. However, a system based solely on flat files would not scale to large installations with dozens of games and thousands of players.

To accommodate both goals, we select a mixed strategy. The storage subsystem will provide an abstract interface that enables both a flat file and a relational database implementation. When installing an Arena the first time, the ArenaOperator selects which implementation fits the goals best. The ArenaOperator will not be able to switch strategies at run time, but will be able to convert persistent objects from flat files to the database and back during system reconfiguration. This will increase the development cost of ARENA, but provide more flexibility to the ArenaOperator. To reduce development risks, the initial prototype of ARENA will only use flat files. A second prototype will use a database-independent API (e.g., JDBC [JDBC, 2009]) to store persistent objects in a relational database, thus enabling ArenaOperators to use different relational products.

Game developers will address game storage issues individually. Given the sequential nature of game data, we anticipate games to use flat files for storage as well.

7.6.5   Providing Access Control

As ARENA is a multi-user system, different actors are allowed to view different sets of objects and invoke different types of operations on them. To succinctly document access rights, we draw an access control matrix (Table 7-4) depicting the allowed operations on the entity objects for each actor. In summary, ArenaOperator can create Users and Leagues, LeagueOwners can create Tournaments and Matches. Advertisers can upload and remove advertisements as well as apply for sponsorship of Leagues or Tournaments. Note that the LeagueOwner makes the final sponsorship decision, as documented in the analysis. Players can subscribe to a League (to receive announcements), apply for a Tournament, and play Matches they have been scheduled for. Finally, Spectators can view player statistics, view League and Tournament schedules, and subscribe to receive notifications and view Matches.

Note that most of the access control information is already available in the use case model. The access control matrix, however, presents a more detailed and compact view, thus enabling a client to review access control more easily and a developer to implement it correctly.

Spectators are actors that are not authenticated to the system. All other actors must first authenticate before they can modify any object in the system. We select a user name/password mechanism for initiating sessions. We then use access control lists on each object (e.g., Leagues, Tournaments, and Matches) to check the access privileges of the user. A Session object per authenticated user tracks currently logged in users.

Table 7-4   Access matrix for main ARENA objects.

Objects Actors	Arena	User	League	Tournament	Match
ArenaOperator	«create» createUser	«create» deactivate	«create» archive		
LeagueOwner		getStats getInfo	archive setSponsor	«create» archive setSponsor	«create» end
Advertiser	uploadAds removeAds		apply for sponsorship	apply for sponsorship	
Player	apply for LeagueOwner	setInfo	view subscribe	apply for tournament view subscribe	play end
Spectator	apply for Player apply for Advertiser	getStats	view subscribe	view subscribe	subscribe replay

7.6.6   Designing the Global Control Flow

As described in Section 7.4.4, there are three types of control flow paradigms: procedure-driven, event-driven, or threaded control flow paradigm. The selection of one paradigm over another depends on response time and throughput requirements on the system and development complexity. Moreover, in a system with multiple components, it is possible to select different control paradigms for different components.

In Sections 7.6.3 and 7.6.4, when selecting components for the interface and storage subsystems of ARENA, we effectively restricted the alternatives for control flow mechanisms for the game organization part. The WebServer waits for requests from the WebBrowser. Upon the receipt of a request, the WebServer processes it and dispatches it to the appropriate servlet or JSP, thus resulting in an event-based control flow. The WebServer allocates a new thread for each request, allowing the parallel handling of requests. This results in a more responsive system by enabling the WebServer to respond to individual WebBrowser requests before other requests have been completely processed, and can increase throughput by enabling the processing of one request while another is waiting for the database to respond. The drawback of threads is the higher complexity of the system resulting from synchronizing parallel threads. To ensure a robust design with respect to concurrency, we define the following strategy for dealing with concurrent accesses to shared data:

- *Boundary objects should not define any fields.* Instead, boundary objects hold temporary data associated with the current request in local variables. As boundary objects are shared among threads, this prevents concurrency hazards at that level.

- *Control objects should not be shared among threads.* Instead, there should be at most one control object associated with each session, and users should not be able to issue concurrent requests involving the same control object within the same session. This should especially be enforced when control objects survive the processing of a single request.

- *Entity objects should not provide direct access to their fields.* Instead, all changes and accesses to the object state should be done through dedicated methods. Moreover, these methods should only access the fields of the receiver object (i.e., this), and not of other instances of the same class. If classes are realized as abstract data types (see Section 2.3.2), all fields should already be private.

- *Methods for accessing state in entity objects should be synchronized.* That is, the synchronized mechanism provided by Java should be used so that only one thread at a time can be active in the access method.

- *Nested calls to synchronized methods should be avoided.* Developers of synchronized methods should investigate if a nested method call can result in calling another synchronized method. This could lead to deadlocks and should be avoided. If such nested calls cannot be avoided, developers should either reallocate class behavior among methods to avoid such nested calls, or impose a strict ordering of synchronized method calls.

- *Redundant state should be time-stamped.* The state of an object can occasionally be duplicated. One example of duplication is when the state of an object is stored in a Web form in the WebBrowser and in storage subsystem. To detect situations in which concurrent changes to the same object can lead to a conflict, a time-stamp should be added to the duplicated data to represent the last modification time.

For the game part of ARENA, the MatchFrontEndPeer and the GamePeer run in separate processes. These processes are started by the GameManagement subsystem as required by Tournament schedules and Player attendance. The internal control flow of the MatchFrontEndPeer and the GamePeer can be event driven or threaded, depending on the needs of the specific game.

7.6.7   Identifying Services

We have now defined a subsytem decomposition and decided on the control flow paradgms for each run-time component and for the system as a whole. We are now ready to identify services provided by each subsystem.

In this example, we focus on the dependencies among ArenaServer, UserManagement, AdvertisementManagement, and TournamentManagement, in the context of the Organize-Tournament use case (Figure 4-24).

We first notice that all requests handled by the ArenaServer must be authorized according to the access control policy defined in Section 7.6.5. This leads us to define an Authentication service to check a user's credentials upon login, and an Authorization service to check if the request is allowed for the role of the requesting user. We assign both services to UserManagement.

During the first steps in the OrganizeTournament use case, the LeagueOwner creates a Tournament in the context of a League. TournamentManagement therefore needs to provide services for creating and getting information about Tournaments and Leagues. These services are trivial but are needed for every class in the analysis model. To denote that the TournamentManagement subsystem owns the Tournament and League classes, we define the Tournament and League services. In practice, these types of services are left implicit in the model to avoid overcrowding, as they add little information.

In the next steps, the LeagueOwner invites Advertisers to sponsor the new Tournament. We add the Sponsorship service to AdvertisementManagement, allowing the LeagueOwner to invite Advertisers and Advertisers to respond. Defining both sets of actions in the same service allows us to keep all operations related to sponsorship in one place.

When the LeagueOwner selects Advertisers to sponsor a Tournament, we are presented with the option of defining a new service either in AdvertisementManagement or in TournamentManagement, as each subsystem owns an end of the Advertiser-Tournament association. We decide to assign the responsibility to track the state of the OrganizeTournament activity to TournamentManagement, as the use case centers on the definition of Tournaments. In analysis terms, TournamentManagement owns the control object associated with OrganizeTournament. Consequently, we add a SponsorSelection service to the TournamentManagement subsystem.

In the next steps of OrganizeTournament, the LeagueOwner advertises the Tournament and interested Players apply and are selected. We are faced with the question of allocating the Player service to the UserManagement or the TournamentManagement subsystem. We decide to assign Player to the TournamentManagement, as Player is strongly connected with League and Tournament. As accepting Players in Tournaments goes beyond simply creating Players and getting information about them, we define a PlayerAcceptance service to support this step.

Figure 7-22 depicts the services identified so far. We observe two trends during the above discussion:

- When trading off services between two subsystems, functionality tends to aggregate in the subsystem where the control object corresponding to the use case is defined. While this results in subsystem with high coherence, we need to be careful that the resulting complexity of the subsystem is not too high.

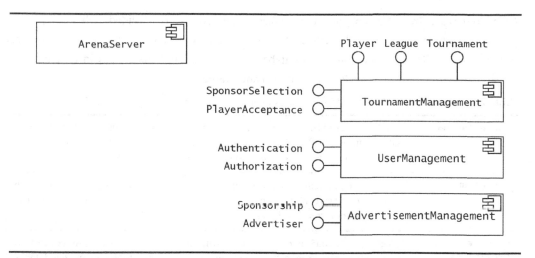

Figure 7-22 ARENA subsystem decomposition, game organization part with services identified (UML component diagram, ball-and-socket notation, dependencies omitted for clarity).

- Defining services based on steps in a use case tend to result in fine grained services. While this allows us to validate the subsystem decomposition, it may result in many interfaces that each define a single operation. This is a sign that we are moving too quickly towards object design. During a second pass, we may choose to consolidate several related services into single services to keep the design at the architectural level of abstraction and the subsystem decomposition understandable. Naming services with noun phrases that denote a collection of operations also helps us in avoiding this pittfall.

7.6.8 Identifying Boundary Conditions

During this activity, we review the design decisions we made so far and identify additional administrator use cases. We first examine the life time of the persistent objects of ARENA, the life time of each run-time component, and the types of system failures.

Configuration use cases

The handling of most persistent objects is already described in the use cases developed during analysis (Figure 4-21) and in the access control matrix (Table 7-4). For example, ArenaOperators create and deactivate Users. LeagueOwners create and archive Leagues and Tournaments. Players initiate and end Matches. Advertisers manage Advertisement Banners. However, the handling of the Arena and Game objects has not been described in the use case model so far, as these objects have been refined during system design. Arena is created with the installation of the system. Games are created and destroyed whenever Games are added or deleted from the system. Hence, we identify two additional use cases invoked by the

ArenaOperator, InstallArena and ManageGames. Moreover, we decided, when discussing persistent storage (Section 7.6.4), that an ArenaOperator could convert the persistent objects between a flat file representation and a database representation. This results in an additional configuration use case, ConvertPersistentStorage (Table 7-5).

Table 7-5   Additional ARENA boundary use cases identified when reviewing persistent objects.

InstallArena	The ArenaOperator creates an Arena, gives it a name, selects a persistent storage subsystem (either flat file or database), and configures resource parameters (e.g., maximum number of concurrent tournaments, file path for storage).
ManageGames	The ArenaOperator installs or removes a Game, including custom code for the GamePeer and MatchFrontEndPeer. The list of Games is updated for the next time a LeagueOwner creates a League.
Convert Persistent Storage	When the ArenaServer is shut down, the ArenaOperator can convert the persistent storage from a flat file storage to a database storage or from a database storage to a flat file storage.

Start-up and shutdown use cases

As depicted in the UML deployment diagram in Figure 7-21, ARENA includes five run-time components: the WebBrowser, the ArenaServer (which includes the subsystems UserManagement, GameManagement, TournamentManagement, Notification, and Arena-Storage), the MatchFrontEndPeer, the GamePeer, and for the second prototype, the DatabaseServer. The WebBrowser and the DatabaseServer are off-the-shelf components and are started and shut down individually. The MatchFrontEndPeer and the GamePeer are started and shut down by the WebBrowser and the ArenaServer, respectively. The start-up and shutdown of ArenaServer is currently not described in the use case model. Hence, we identify two additional use cases invoked by the ArenaOperator (Table 7-6).

Table 7-6   Additional ARENA boundary use cases identified when reviewing runtime components.

StartArenaServer	The ArenaOperator starts the ArenaServer. If the server was not cleanly shut down, this use case invokes the Check Data Integrity use case described in the next section. As soon as the initialization of the server is complete, LeagueOwners, Players, Spectators, and Advertisers can initiate any of their use cases.
ShutDownArenaServer	The ArenaOperator stops the ArenaServer. The server terminates any ongoing Matches and stores any cached data. MatchFrontEndPeers and GamePeers are shut down. Once this use case is completed, the LeagueOwners, Players, Spectators, and Advertisers cannot access or modify the Arena.

Exception use cases

ARENA can experience four major classes of system failures:

- A network failure in which one or more connections among MatchFrontEndPeers and GamePeers are interrupted

- A host or a component failure in which one or more MatchFrontEndPeers or GamePeers are unexpectedly terminated

- A network failure in which one or more connections between a WebBrowser and the ArenaServer are interrupted

- A server failure in which the ArenaServer is unexpectedly terminated.

We decide to handle the first two classes of exceptions in the custom Game components. We will provide generic methods for MatchFrontEndPeers and GamePeers to re-establish connection after a network failure or to restore the state of Matches after a crash. However, the handling of the exception itself depends on the type of game. For example, a real-time simulation game will not tolerate network failures and should be interrupted or restarted, whereas a board game can tolerate short interruptions transparently from its Players. Hence, we leave the flexibility to the game developers to decide how to handle those exceptions.

We handle network failures interrupting connections between the WebBrowser and the ArenaServer by notifying the user of the network failure, similar to current WebBrowsers. We expect the actors to retry later, at the cost of loosing the data that was already entered in a form. Consequently, we will design forms in such a way that little data can be lost in any one failure.

We decide to handle the last type of failure by a use case for checking the integrity of the persistent data after an unexpected termination of the ArenaServer (see Table 7-7). This use case can be invoked automatically by the system upon start-up (see StartArenaServer in Table 7-6) or manually by the ArenaOperator. We also identify an additional use case to restart interrupted GamePeers and notify relevant players.

Table 7-7   Additional ARENA boundary use cases identified when reviewing persistent objects.

CheckDataIntegrity	ARENA checks the integrity of the persistent data. For file-based storage, this may include checking if the last logged transactions were saved to disk. For database storage, this may include invoking tools providing by the database system to re-index the tables.
RestartGamePeers	ARENA starts any interrupted Matches and notifies any running MatchFrontEndPeer that GamePeer is back on-line.

7.6.9   Lessons Learned

In this section, we examined the system design issues for the ARENA system. We identified and prioritized design goals, we decomposed the system into subsystems, we mapped the subsystems to components and platforms, we selected a persistent data storage strategy, we described the access control mechanisms for the system, we examined control flow issues, and we identified use cases for handling boundary cases. We learned that

- Most system design issues are interrelated. For example, selecting a component for boundary or storage objects has implications on the global control flow of the system.

- Some system design issues have different solutions in different parts of the system. For example, we dealt with issues related to architecture, control flow, crash recovery, and storage issues differently for the organization part than for the game playing part of ARENA.

- Some system design issues can be postponed until the object design phase (e.g., decisions about GamePeers) or to a later release (e.g., storage implementation).

- In all cases, design goals serve to prioritize and evaluate different design alternatives.

7.7 Further Readings

Meeting multiple, conflicting design goals is a difficult task that can only be accomplished with experience and practice. Here are a few books related to the material presented in this chapter.

Software Architecture in Practice [Bass et al., 2003] and *Evaluating Software Architectures* [Clements et al., 2002] focus on general methods for evaluating architectures given a set of design goals. Both books also include case studies from the state of the art.

Object-Oriented Modeling and Design for Database Applications [Blaha & Premerlani, 1998] describes methods for realizing database applications, taking into consideration design goals such as performance, extensibility, and modifiability.

Reliable Computer Systems: Design and Evaluation [Siewiorek & Swarz, 1992] is the reference book for reliable system design. It includes a broad survey of techniques and methods for achieving reliability as well as a substantial number of case studies for industry projects.

Safeware: System Safety and Computers [Leveson, 1995] surveys a large number of cases of computer failures and draws several conclusions. It then surveys current approaches to safety and emphasizes the need for comprehensive methods in the design of systems.

Service-Oriented Architectures [Erl, 2005] provides an introduction and tutorial for designing service-oriented web platform. The goal of SOA architectures is to structure the application around business processes, making it easier to evolve or combine services offered to the end user.

7.8 Exercises

7-1   Consider a system that includes a Web server and two database servers. Both database servers are identical: the first acts as a main server, and the second acts as a redundant back-up in case the first one fails. Users use Web browsers to access data through the Web server. They also have the option of using a proprietary client that accesses the databases directly. Draw a UML deployment diagram representing the hardware/software mapping of this system.

7-2   Consider a legacy, fax-based, problem-reporting system for an aircraft manufacturer. You are part of a reengineering project replacing the core of the system with a computer-based system that includes a database and a notification system. The client requires the fax to remain an entry point for problem reports. You propose an E-mail entry point. Describe a subsystem decomposition that would allow both interfaces. Note that such systems are used to process many problem reports per day (e.g., 2000 faxes per day).

7-3   You are designing the access control policies for a Web-based retail store. Customers access the store via the Web, browse product information, input their address and payment information, and purchase products. Suppliers can add new products, update product information, and receive orders.The store owner sets the retail prices, makes tailored offers to customers based on their purchasing profiles, and provides marketing services. You have to deal with three actors: StoreAdministrator, Supplier, and Customer. Design an access control policy for all three actors. Customers can be created via the Web, whereas Suppliers are created by the StoreAdministrator.

7-4   Select a control flow mechanism you find most appropriate for each of the following systems. Because multiple choices are possible in most cases, justify your choices.

- a Web server designed to sustain high loads
- a graphical user interface for a word processor
- a real-time embedded system (e.g., a guidance system on a satellite launcher).

7-5   Why can you not describe boundary use cases during requirements elicitation or analysis?

7-6   You are designing a caching subsystem that temporarily stores data retrieved over the network (e.g., web pages) into a faster access storage (e.g., the hard disk). Due to a change in requirements, you define an additional service in your subsystem for configuring cache parameters (e.g., the maximum amount of hard disk the cache can use). Which project participants do you notify?

References

[Bass et al., 2003]   L. Bass, P. Clements, & R. Kazman, *Software Architecture in Practice*, 2nd ed., Addison-Wesley, Reading, MA, 2003.

[Blaha & Premerlani, 1998]   M. Blaha & W. Premerlani, *Object-Oriented Modeling and Design for Database Applications*, Prentice Hall, Upper Saddle River, NJ, 1998.

[Clements et al., 2002]   P. Clements, R. Kazam, & M. Klein, *Evaluating Software Architectures: Methods and Case Studies*, SEI Series in Software Engineering, Addison-Wesley, Reading, MA, 2002.

[Erl, 2005]   T. Erl, *Service-Oriented Architectures:Concepts, Technology, and Design*, Prentice Hall, Upper Saddle River, NJ, 2005.

[Gamma et al., 1994]   E. Gamma, R. Helm, R. Johnson, & J. Vlissides, *Design Patterns: Elements of Reusable Object-Oriented Software*, Addison-Wesley, Reading, MA, 1994.

[Hofmeister, 2000]   C. Hofmeister, R. Nord, & D. Soni, *Applied Software Architecture*, Object Technology Series, Addison-Wesley, Reading, MA, 2000.

[Jacobson et al., 1999]   I. Jacobson, G. Booch, & J. Rumbaugh, *The Unified Software Development Process*, Addison-Wesley, Reading, MA, 1999.

[JDBC, 2009]   *JDBC^{TM}—Connecting Java and Databases*, JDK Documentation, Javasoft, 2009.

[Leveson, 1995]   N. G. Leveson, *Safeware: System Safety And Computers*, Addison-Wesley, Reading, MA, 1995.

[RMI, 2009]   *Java Remote Method Invocation*, JDK Documentation. Javasoft, 2009.

[Siewiorek & Swarz, 1992]   D. P. Siewiorek & R. S. Swarz, *Reliable Computer Systems: Design and Evaluation*, 2nd ed., Digital, Burlington, MA, 1992.

8

Object Design: Reusing Pattern Solutions

Cheating rule: You cheat if you do not acknowledge the contribution made by others.
— 15-413, Software Engineering,
Carnegie Mellon University

During analysis, we describe the purpose of the system. This results in the identification of application objects. During system design, we describe the system in terms of its architecture, such as its subsystem decomposition, global control flow, and persistency management. During system design, we also define the hardware/software platform on which we build the system. This allows the selection of off-the-shelf components that provide a higher level of abstraction than the hardware. During object design, we close the gap between the application objects and the off-the-shelf components by identifying additional solution objects and refining existing objects. Object design includes

- *reuse*, during which we identify off-the-shelf components and design patterns to make use of existing solutions
- *service specification*, during which we precisely describe each class interface
- *object model restructuring*, during which we transform the object design model to improve its understandability and extensibility
- *object model optimization*, during which we transform the object design model to address performance criteria such as response time or memory utilization.

Object design, like system design, is not algorithmic. The identification of existing patterns and components is central to the problem-solving process. We discuss these building blocks and the activities related to them. In this chapter, we provide an overview of object design and focus on reuse, that is the selection of components and the application of design patterns. In the next chapter, we focus on service specification. In Chapter 10, *Mapping Models to Code*, we focus on the object model restructuring and optimization activities.

8.1 Introduction: Bloopers

Consider the following examples from the movie industry:

Speed **(1994)**

Harry, an LAPD cop, is taken hostage by Howard, a mad bomber. Jack, Harry's partner, shoots Harry in the leg to slow down Howard's advance. Harry is shot in the right leg. Throughout the movie, Harry limps on the left leg.

Star Wars **Trilogy (1977, 1980, & 1983)**

At the end of episode V, *The Empire Strikes Back* (1980), Han Solo is captured and frozen into carbonite for delivery to Jabba. At the beginning of episode VI, *The Return of the Jedi* (1983), the frozen Han Solo is recovered by his friends and thawed back to life. When being frozen, Solo is wearing a jacket. When thawed, he is wearing a white shirt.

Titanic **(1997)**

Jack, a drifter, is teaching Rose, a high-society lady, to spit. He demonstrates by example and encourages Rose to practice as well. During the lesson, Rose's mother arrives impromptu. As Jack starts to turn to face Rose's mother, there is no spit on his face. As he completes his turn, he has spit on his chin.

The budgets for *Speed*, *The Empire Strikes Back*, *The Return of the Jedi*, and *Titanic* were 30, 18, 32.5, and 200 millions dollars, respectively.

Movies are systems that contain (often many) bugs when delivered to the client. It is surprising, considering their cost of production, that any obvious mistakes should remain in the final product. Movies, however, are more complex than they seem.

Many factors conspire to introduce mistakes in a movie: movies require the cooperation of many different people; scenes are shot out of sequence; some scenes are reshot out of schedule; details, such as props and costumes, are changed during production; the pressure of the release date is high during the editing process, when all the pieces are integrated together. When a scene is shot, the state of every object and actor in the scene should be consistent with the scenes preceding and following it. This can include the pose of each actor, the condition of his or her clothes, jewelry, makeup, and hair, the content of their glasses, and so on. When different segments are combined into a single scene, an editor, called the "continuity editor," ensures that such details were restored correctly. When changes occur, such as the addition or removal of a prop, the change must not interfere with other scenes.

Software systems, like movies, are complex, subject to continuous change and integrated under time pressure. During object design, developers close the gap between the application objects identified during analysis and the hardware/software platform selected during system design. Developers identify and build custom solution objects whose purpose is to realize any remaining functionality and to bridge the gap between application objects and the selected hardware/software platform. During object design, developers realize custom objects in a way similar to the shooting of movie scenes. They are implemented out of sequence, by different developers, and change several times before they reach their final form. Often, the caller of an operation has only an informal specification of the operation and makes assumptions about its side effects and its boundary cases. This results in mismatches between caller and callee, missing behavior, or incorrect behavior. To address these issues, developers construct precise specifications of the classes, attributes, and operations in terms of constraints. Similarly, developers adjust and reuse off-the-shelf components that have been annotated with interface specifications. Finally, developers restructure and optimize the object design model to address design goals such as maintainability, extensibility, efficiency, response time, or timely delivery.

Section 8.2 provides an overview of object design. Section 8.3 defines the main object design concepts, such as constraints used to specify interfaces. Section 8.4 describes in more detail the activities of object design. Section 8.5 discusses management issues related with object design. We do not describe activities such as implementing algorithms and data structures or using specific programming languages. First, we assume the reader already has experience in those areas. Second, these activities become less critical as more and more off-the-shelf components become available.

8.2 An Overview of Object Design

Conceptually, software system development fills the gap between a given problem and an existing machine. The activities of system development incrementally close this gap by identifying and defining objects that realize part of the system (Figure 8-1).

Analysis reduces the gap between the problem and the machine by identifying objects representing problem-specific concepts. During analysis the system is described in terms of external behavior such as its functionality (use case model), the application domain concepts it manipulates (object model), its behavior in terms of interactions (dynamic model), and its nonfunctional requirements.

System design reduces the gap between the problem and the machine in two ways. First, system design results in a virtual machine that provides a higher level of abstraction than the machine. This is done by selecting off-the-shelf components for standard services such as middleware, user interface toolkits, application frameworks, and class libraries. Second, system design identifies off-the-shelf components for application domain objects such as reusable class libraries of banking objects.

After several iterations of analysis and system design, the developers are usually left with a puzzle that has a few pieces missing. These pieces are found during object design. This includes identifying new solution objects, adjusting off-the-shelf components, and precisely specifying each subsystem interface and class. The object design model can then be partitioned into sets of classes that can be implemented by individual developers.

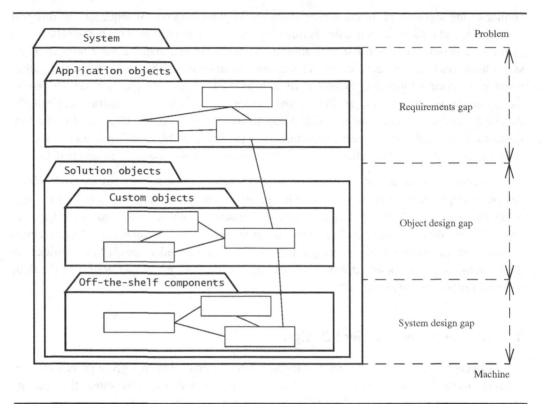

Figure 8-1   Object design closes the gap between application objects identified during requirements and off-the-shelf components selected during system design (stylized UML class diagram).

Object design includes four groups of activities (see Figure 8-2):

• *Reuse*. Off-the-shelf components identified during system design are used to help in the realization of each subsystem. Class libraries and additional components are selected for basic data structures and services. Design patterns are selected for solving common problems and for protecting specific classes from future change. Often, components and design patterns need to be adapted before they can be used. This is done by wrapping custom objects around them or by refining them using inheritance. During all these activities, the developers are faced with the same buy-versus-build trade-offs they encountered during system design.

• *Interface specification*. During this activity, the subsystem services identified during system design are specified in terms of class interfaces, including operations, arguments, type signatures, and exceptions. Additional operations and objects needed to transfer data among subsystems are also identified. The result of service specification is a complete interface specification for each subsystem. The subsystem service specification is often called subsystem **API** (Application Programmer Interface).

* *Restructuring.* Restructuring activities manipulate the system model to increase code reuse or meet other design goals. Each restructuring activity can be seen as a graph transformation on subsets of a particular model. Typical activities include transforming N-ary associations into binary associations, implementing binary associations as references, merging two similar classes from two different subsystems into a single class, collapsing classes with no significant behavior into attributes, splitting complex classes into simpler ones, and/or rearranging classes and operations to increase the inheritance and packaging. During restructuring, we address design goals such as maintainability, readability, and understandability of the system model.

* *Optimization.* Optimization activities address performance requirements of the system model. This includes changing algorithms to respond to speed or memory requirements, reducing multiplicities in associations to speed up queries, adding redundant associations for efficiency, rearranging execution orders, adding derived attributes to improve the access time to objects, and opening up the architecture, that is, adding access to lower layers because of performance requirements.

Object design is not sequential. Although each group of activities described above addresses a specific object design issue, they usually occur concurrently. A specific off-the-shelf component may constrain the number of types of exceptions mentioned in the specification of an operation and thus may impact the subsystem interface. The selection of a component may reduce the implementation work while introducing new "glue" objects, which also need to be specified. Finally, restructuring and optimizing may reduce the number of components to be implemented by increasing the amount of reuse in the system.

Usually, interface specification and reuse activities occur first, yielding an object design model that is then checked against the use cases that exercise the specific subsystem. Restructuring and optimization activities occur next, once the object design model for the subsystem is relatively stable. Focusing on interfaces, components, and design patterns results in an object design model that is much easier to modify. Focusing on optimizations first tends to produce object design models that are rigid and difficult to modify. However, as depicted in Figure 8-2, activities of object design occur iteratively.

Given the variety and breadth of activities in object design, we divided this material into three different chapters. This chapter focuses on activities related to reuse, in particular, components and design patterns. In the next chapter, Chapter 9, *Object Design: Specifying Interfaces*, we examine the activities related to interface specification, in particular, UML's Object Constraint Language and its use for specifying invariants, preconditions, and post conditions. In Chapter 10, *Mapping Models to Code*, we examine the activities related to restructuring and optimization.

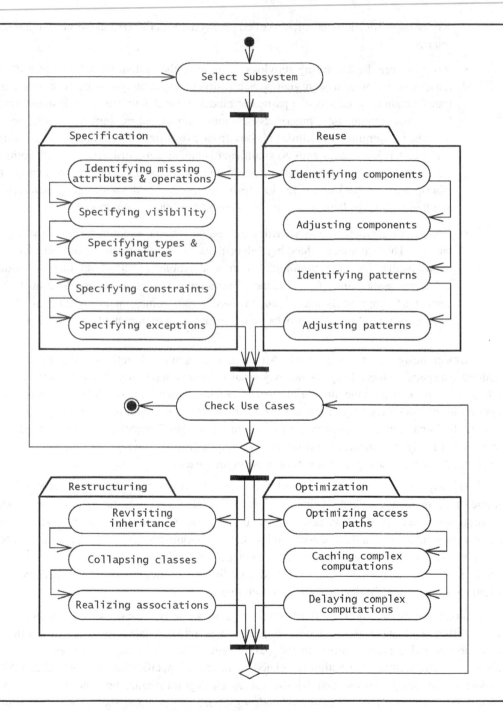

Figure 8-2   Activities of object design (UML activity diagram).

8.3   Reuse Concepts: Solution Objects, Inheritance, and Design Patterns

In this section, we present the object design concepts related to reuse:

- Application Objects and Solution Objects (Section 8.3.1)
- Specification Inheritance and Implementation Inheritance (Section 8.3.2)
- Delegation (Section 8.3.3)
- The Liskov Substitution Principle (Section 8.3.4)
- Delegation and Inheritance in Design Patterns (Section 8.3.5).

8.3.1   Application Objects and Solution Objects

As we saw in Chapter 2, *Modeling with UML*, class diagrams can be used to model both the application domain and the solution domain. **Application objects**, also called "domain objects," represent concepts of the domain that are relevant to the system. **Solution objects** represent components that do not have a counterpart in the application domain, such as persistent data stores, user interface objects, or middleware.

During analysis, we identify entity objects and their relationships, attributes, and operations. Most entity objects are application objects that are independent of any specific system. During analysis, we also identify solution objects that are visible to the user, such as boundary and control objects representing forms and transactions defined by the system. During system design, we identify more solution objects in terms of software and hardware platforms. During object design, we refine and detail both application and solution objects and identify additional solution objects needed to bridge the object design gap.

8.3.2   Specification Inheritance and Implementation Inheritance

During analysis, we use inheritance to classify objects into taxonomies. This allows us to differentiate the common behavior of the general case, that is, the **superclass** (also called the "**base class**"), from the behavior that is specific to specialized objects, that is, the **subclasses** (also called the "**derived classes**"). The focus of generalization (i.e., identifying a common superclass from a number of existing classes) and specialization (i.e., identifying new subclasses given an existing superclass) is to organize analysis objects into an understandable hierarchy. Readers of the analysis model can start from the abstract concepts, grasp the core functionality of the system, and make their way down to concrete concepts and review specialized behavior. For example, when examining the analysis model for the FRIEND emergency response system described in Chapter 4, *Requirements Elicitation*, we first focus on understanding how the system deals with Incidents in general, and then move to the differences in handling Traffic Accidents or Fires.

The focus of inheritance during object design is to reduce redundancy and enhance extensibility. By factoring all redundant behavior into a single superclass, we reduce the risk of introducing inconsistencies during changes (e.g., when repairing a defect) since we have to make changes only once for all subclasses. By providing abstract classes and interfaces that are used by the application, we can write new specialized behavior by writing new subclasses that comply with the abstract interfaces. For example, we can write an application manipulating images in terms of an abstract `Image` class, which defines all the operations that all `Image`s should support, and a series of specialized classes for each image format supported by the application (e.g., `GIFImage`, `JPEGImage`). When we need to extend the application to a new format, we only need to add a new specialized class.

Although inheritance can make an analysis model more understandable and an object design model more modifiable or extensible, these benefits do not occur automatically. On the contrary, inheritance is such a powerful mechanism that novice developers often produce code that is more obfuscated and more brittle than if they had not used inheritance in the first place.

Consider the following example: Assume for a moment that Java does not provide a set abstraction and that we needed to write our own. We decide to reuse the `java.util.Hashtable` class to implement a set abstraction that we call `MySet`. Inserting an element in `MySet` is equivalent to checking if the corresponding key exists in the table and creating an entry if necessary. Checking if an element is in `MySet` is equivalent to checking if an entry is associated with the corresponding key (see Figure 8-3, left column).

Such an implementation of a set allows us to reuse code and provides us with the desired behavior. It also provides us, however, with unwanted behavior. For example, `Hashtable` implements the `containsKey()` operation to check if the specified object exists as a key in the `Hashtable` and the `containsValue()` operation to check if the specified object exists as an entry. `containsKey()` is inherited by `MySet`, but `containsValue()` is overwritten. Given our implementation, the operation `containsValue()` invoked on a `MySet` object has the same behavior as `containsKey()`, which is counterintuitive. Worse, a developer could use both `containsKey()` and `containsValue()`, which would make it difficult to change the internal representation of `MySet` in the future. For example, if we decided to implement `MySet` as a `List` instead of a `Hashtable`, all invocations to `containsKey()` would become invalid. To address this issue, we could overwrite all operations inherited from `Hashtable` that should not be used on `MySet` with methods throwing exceptions. However, this would lead to a `MySet` class that is difficult to understand and reuse.

Inheritance yields its benefits by decoupling the classes using a superclass from the specialized subclasses. In doing so, however, it introduces a strong coupling along the inheritance hierarchy between the superclass and the subclass. Whereas this is acceptable when the inheritance hierarchy represents a taxonomy (e.g., it is acceptable for `Image` and `GIFImage` to be tightly coupled), it introduces unwanted coupling in the other cases. In our example, two previously unrelated concepts, `Hashtable` and `Set`, become tightly coupled as a result of subclassing, introducing many issues when `Hashtable` is modified or when a `Set` is used by a class as a specialized `Hashtable`. The fundamental problem in this example is that, although `Hashtable` provides behavior that we would like to reuse in implementing `Set`, because that would save us time, there is no taxonomy in which the `Set` concept is related to the `Hashtable` concept.

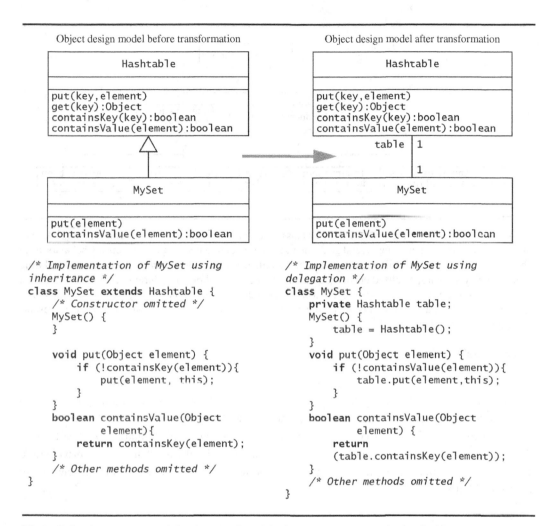

Object design model before transformation

Object design model after transformation

```
/* Implementation of MySet using
inheritance */
class MySet extends Hashtable {
    /* Constructor omitted */
    MySet() {
    }

    void put(Object element) {
        if (!containsKey(element)){
            put(element, this);
        }
    }
    boolean containsValue(Object
            element){
        return containsKey(element);
    }
    /* Other methods omitted */
}
```

```
/* Implementation of MySet using
delegation */
class MySet {
    private Hashtable table;
    MySet() {
        table = Hashtable();
    }
    void put(Object element) {
        if (!containsValue(element)){
            table.put(element,this);
        }
    }
    boolean containsValue(Object
            element) {
        return
            (table.containsKey(element));
    }
    /* Other methods omitted */
}
```

Figure 8-3 An example of implementation inheritance. The left column depicts a questionable implementation of MySet using implementation inheritance. The right column depicts an improved implementation using delegation (UML class diagram and Java).

The use of inheritance for the sole purpose of reusing code is called **implementation inheritance**. With implementation inheritance, developers reuse code quickly by subclassing an existing class and refining its behavior. A Set implemented by inheriting from a Hashtable is an example of implementation inheritance. Conversely, the classification of concepts into type hierarchies is called **specification inheritance** (also called "interface inheritance"). The UML class model of Figure 8-4 summarizes the four different types of inheritance we discussed in this section.

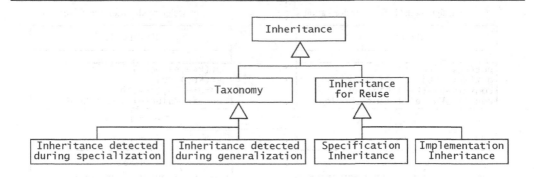

Figure 8-4 Inheritance meta-model (UML class diagram). In object-oriented analysis and design, inheritance is used for achieving several goals, in particular modeling taxonomies and reusing behavior from abstract classes. When modeling taxonomies, the inheritance relationships can be identified either during specializations (when specialized classes are identified after general ones) or during generalizations (when general classes are abstracted out of a number of specialized ones). When using inheritance for reuse, specification inheritance represents subtyping relationships, and implementation inheritance represents reuse among conceptually unrelated classes.

8.3.3   Delegation

Delegation is the alternative to implementation inheritance that should be used when reuse is desired. A class is said to delegate to another class if it implements an operation by resending a message to another class. Delegation makes explicit the dependencies between the reused class and the new class. The right column of Figure 8-3 shows an implementation of MySet using delegation instead of implementation inheritance. The only significant change is the private field table and its initialization in the MySet() constructor. This addresses both problems we mentioned before:

- *Extensibility.* The MySet on the right column does not include the containsKey() method in its interface and the new field table is private. Hence, we can change the internal representation of MySet to another class (e.g., a List) without impacting any clients of MySet.

- *Subtyping.* MySet does not inherit from Hashtable and, hence, cannot be substituted for a Hashtable in any of the client code. Consequently, any code previously using Hashtables still behaves the same way.

Delegation is a preferable mechanism to implementation inheritance as it does not interfere with existing components and leads to more robust code. Note that specification inheritance is preferable to delegation in subtyping situations as it leads to a more extensible design.

8.3.4   The Liskov Substitution Principle

The Liskov Substitution Principle [Liskov, 1988] provides a formal definition for specification inheritance. It essentially states that, if a client code uses the methods provided by a superclass, then developers should be able to add new subclasses without having to change the client code. For example, in the left column of Figure 8-3, this means that, if a client uses a Hashtable, the client should not have to be modified when we substitute the Hashtable for any of its subclasses, for example MySet. Clearly, this is not the case, so the relationship between MySet and Hashtable is not a specification inheritance relationship. Below is the formal definition of the Liskov Substitution Principle:

Liskov Substitution Principle

If an object of type S can be substituted in all the places where an object of type T is expected, then S is a subtype of T.

Interpretation

In object design, the Liskov Substitution Principle means that if all classes are subtypes of their superclasses, all inheritance relationships are specification inheritance relationships. In other words, a method written in terms of a superclass T must be able to use instances of any subclass of T without knowing whether the instances are of a subclass. Consequently, new subclasses of T can be added without modifying the methods of T, hence leading to an extensible system. An inheritance relationship that complies with the Liskov Substitution Principle is called **strict inheritance**.

8.3.5   Delegation and Inheritance in Design Patterns

In general, when to use delegation or inheritance is not always clear and requires some experience and judgement on the part of the developer. Inheritance and delegation, used in different combinations, can solve a wide range of problems: decoupling abstract interfaces from their implementation, wrapping around legacy code, and/or decoupling classes that specify a policy from classes that provide mechanism.

In object-oriented development, **design patterns** are template solutions that developers have refined over time to solve a range of recurring problems [Gamma et al., 1994]. A design pattern has four elements:

1. A *name* that uniquely identifies the pattern from other patterns.
2. A *problem description* that describes the situations in which the pattern can be used. Problems addressed by design patterns are usually the realization of modifiability and extensibility design goals and nonfunctional requirements.
3. A *solution* stated as a set of collaborating classes and interfaces.
4. A set of *consequences* that describes the trade-offs and alternatives to be considered with respect to the design goals being addressed.

For example, we can restate the problem of writing a set class of Figure 8-3 as implementing a new class (i.e., MySet) that complies with an existing interface (i.e., the Java Set interface) reusing the behavior provided by an existing class (i.e., the Hashtable class). Both the Set interface and the Hashtable class are already provided and neither can be modified. The **Adapter design pattern** (Figure 8-5; Appendix A.2) is a template solution for such problems.

The Adapter pattern works as follows: An Adapter class implements each method declared in the ClientInterface in terms of requests to the LegacyClass. Any conversion of data structures or adjustment of behaviors is done in the Adapter class so that Adapter behaves as expected by the Client. The Adapter pattern enables reuse since neither the ClientInterface nor the LegacyClass need to be modified. The Adapter pattern also encourages extensibility, as the same Adapter class can be used for any subtypes of the LegacyClass, as subtypes can be substituted for their supertype, according to the Liskov Substitution Principle. By applying the Adapter pattern to our Set problem (Figure 8-6), we end up with the same delegation relationship between MySet and Hashtable as in Figure 8-3.

Note that the Adapter pattern uses both inheritance and delegation. When studying design patterns, you will notice that many patterns use a mix of inheritance and delegation and therefore look similar. However, the same mechanisms are used in subtly different ways. To clarify the differences, we use the following terms to denote different classes participating in the pattern:

- The **client class** accesses the pattern. In the class diagram of the Adapter pattern (Figure 8-5), this class is simply called Client. Client classes can be either existing classes of a class library or new classes of the system under development.

- The **pattern interface** is the part of the pattern that is visible to the client class. Often, the pattern interface is realized by an abstract class or an interface. In the Adapter pattern, this class is called ClientInterface.

- The **implementor class** provides the lower-level behavior of the pattern. In the Adapter pattern, the LegacyClass and the Adapter are implementor classes. In many patterns, a number of collaborating implementor classes are needed to realize the pattern behavior.

- The **extender class** specializes an implementor class to provide a different implementation or an extended behavior of the pattern. In the Adapter pattern, the subtypes of LegacyClass are extender classes. Note that, often, extender classes represent future classes that developers anticipate.

Since developers have strived to evolve and refine design patterns for maximizing reuse and flexibility, they are usually not solutions that programmers would initially think of. As design patterns capture a great deal of knowledge (e.g., by documenting the context and trade-offs involved in applying a pattern), they also constitute a source of guidance about when to use inheritance and delegation.

In the next section, we examine the use of design patterns and frameworks for solving a range of common object design problems.

Name	Adapter Design Pattern
Problem description	Convert the interface of a legacy class into a different interface expected by the client, so that the client and the legacy class can work together without changes.
Solution	An `Adapter` class implements the `ClientInterface` expected by the client. The `Adapter` delegates requests from the client to the `LegacyClass` and performs any necessary conversion.

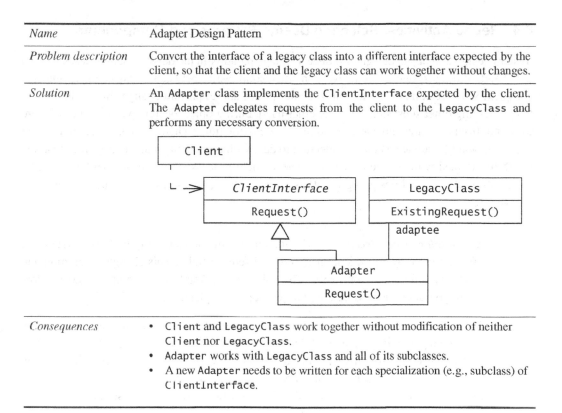

Consequences	• `Client` and `LegacyClass` work together without modification of neither `Client` nor `LegacyClass`. • `Adapter` works with `LegacyClass` and all of its subclasses. • A new `Adapter` needs to be written for each specialization (e.g., subclass) of `ClientInterface`.

Figure 8-5   An example of design pattern, Adapter (adapted from [Gamma et al., 1994]).

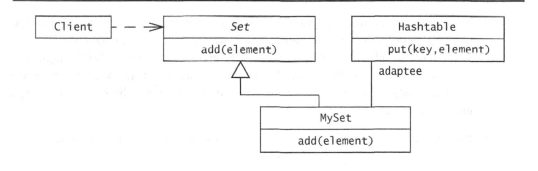

Figure 8-6   Applying the Adapter design pattern to the `Set` problem of Figure 8-3 (UML class diagram).

8.4 Reuse Activities: Selecting Design Patterns and Components

System design and object design introduce a strange paradox in the development process. On the one hand, during system design, we construct solid walls between subsystems to manage complexity by breaking the system into smaller pieces and to prevent changes in one subsystem from affecting other subsystems. On the other hand, during object design, we want the software to be modifiable and extensible to minimize the cost of future changes. These are conflicting goals: we want to define a stable architecture to deal with complexity, but we also want to allow flexibility to deal with change later in the development process. This conflict can be solved by anticipating change and designing for it, as sources of later changes tend to be the same for many systems:

- *New vendor or new technology.* Commercial components used to build the system are often replaced by equivalent ones from a different vendor. This change is common and generally difficult to cope with. The software marketplace is dynamic, and vendors might go out of business before your project is completed.

- *New implementation.* When subsystems are integrated and tested together, the overall system response time is, more often than not, above performance requirements. System performance is difficult to predict and should not be optimized before integration. Developers should focus on the subsystem services first. This triggers the need for more efficient data structures and algorithms—often under time constraints.

- *New views.* Testing the software with real users uncovers many usability problems. These often translate into the need to create additional views on the same data.

- *New complexity of the application domain.* The deployment of a system triggers ideas of new generalizations: a bank information system for one branch may lead to the idea of a multi-branch information system. The application domain itself might also increase in complexity: previously, flight numbers were associated with one plane, and one plane only, but with air carrier alliances, one plane can now have a different flight number from each carrier.

- *Errors.* Many requirements errors are discovered when real users start using the system.

The use of delegation and inheritance in conjunction with abstract classes decouples the interface of a subsystem from its actual implementation. In this section, we provide selected examples of design patterns that can deal with the type of changes mentioned above.

After identifying a design pattern for each type of anticipated change (Table 8-1), we discuss the pattern in the context of an actual situation and, in each case, discuss how inheritance and delegation are used as building blocks to achieve modifiability and extensibility.

Table 8-1   Selected design patterns and the changes they anticipate.

Design Pattern	Anticipated Change	References
Bridge	*New vendor, new technology, new implementation.* This pattern decouples the interface of a class from its implementation. It serves the same purpose as the Adapter pattern except that the developer is not constrained by an existing component.	Section 8.4.1 Appendix A.3
Adapter	*New vendor, new technology, new implementation.* This pattern encapsulates a piece of legacy code that was not designed to work with the system. It also limits the impact of substituting the piece of legacy code for a different component.	Section 8.4.2 Appendix A.2
Strategy	*New vendor, new technology, new implementation.* This pattern decouples an algorithm from its implementation(s). It serves the same purpose as the Adapter and Bridge patterns, except that the encapsulated unit is a behavior.	Section 8.4.3 Appendix A.9
Abstract Factory	*New vendor, new technology.* Encapsulates the creation of families of related objects. This shields the client from the creation process and prevents the use of objects from different (incompatible) families.	Section 8.4.4 Appendix A.1
Command	*New functionality.* This patterns decouples the objects responsible for command processing from the commands themselves. This pattern protects these objects from changes due to new functionality.	Section 8.4.5 Appendix A.4
Composite	*New complexity of application domain.* This pattern encapsulates hierarchies by providing a common superclass for aggregate and leaf nodes. New types of leaves can be added without modifying existing code.	Section 8.4.6 Appendix A.5

8.4.1   Encapsulating Data Stores with the Bridge Pattern

Consider the problem of incrementally developing, testing, and integrating subsystems realized by different developers. Subsystems may be completed at different times, delaying the integration of all subsystems until the last one is completed. To avoid this delay, projects often use a stub implementation in place of a specific subsystem so that the integration tests can start even before the subsystems are completed. In other situations, several implementations of the same subsystem are realized, such as a reference implementation that realizes the specified functionality with the most basic algorithms, or an optimized implementation that delivers better performance at the cost of additional complexity. In short, a solution is needed for dynamically substituting multiple realizations of the same interface for different uses.

This problem can be addressed with the **Bridge design pattern** (Appendix A.3, [Gamma et al., 1994]). For example, consider the storage of Leagues in ARENA. In the early stages of the project, we are interested in a rudimentary storage subsystem based on object serialization for the purpose of debugging and testing the core use cases of the TournamentManagement subsystem. The entity objects will be subject to many changes, and we do not know yet what performance bottlenecks will be encountered during storage. Consequently, an efficient storage subsystem should not be the focus of the first prototype. As discussed during the system design of ARENA (Section 7.6.4), however, we anticipate that both a file-based implementation and a relational database implementation of the storage subsystem should be provided, in the first and second iteration of the system, respectively. In addition, a set of stubs should be provided to allow early integration testing even before the file-based implementation is ready. To solve this problem, we apply the Bridge pattern shown in Figure 8-7. The LeagueStore is the interface class to the pattern, and provides all high-level functionality associated with storage. The LeagueStoreImplementor is an abstract interface that provides the common interface for the three implementations, namely the StubStoreImplementor for the stubs, the XMLStoreImplementor for the file-based implementation, and the JDBCStoreImplementor for the relational database implementation.

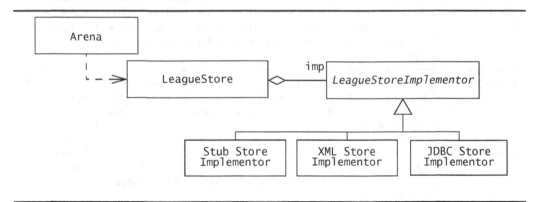

Figure 8-7   Applying the Bridge design pattern for abstracting database vendors (UML class diagram).

Note that even if most LeagueStoreImplementors provide similar services, using a Bridge abstraction reduces performance. The design goals we defined at the beginning of system design (Section 6.4.2) help us decide about performance and modifiability trade-offs.

Inheritance and delegation in the Bridge pattern

The Bridge pattern interface is realized by the Abstraction class, and its behavior by the selected ConcreteImplementor class. The design pattern can be extended by providing new RefinedAbstraction or ConcreteImplementor classes. This pattern is a classic example of combining specification inheritance and delegation to achieve both reuse and flexibility.

On the one hand, specification inheritance is used between the abstract Implementor interface and the classes ConcreteImplementors. As a result, each ConcreteImplementor can be substituted transparently at runtime, from the Abstraction class and RefinedAbstraction classes. This also ensures that, when adding a new ConcreteImplementor, developers will strive to provide the same behavior as all other ConcreteImplementors.

On the other hand, Abstraction and Implementor are decoupled using delegation. This enables the distribution of different behavior in each of the side of the bridge. For example, the LeagueStore class in Figure 8-7 provides the high-level behavior for storing Leagues, whereas the concrete LeagueStoreImplementor provides specific lower-level functionality that differs in its realization from one storage approach to the other. Since LeagueStore and LeagueStoreImplementor provide different behaviors, they cannot be treated as subtypes according to the Liskov Substitution Principle.

8.4.2 Encapsulating Legacy Components with the Adapter Pattern

As the complexity of systems increases and the time to market shortens, the cost of software development significantly exceeds the cost of hardware. Hence, developers have a strong incentive to reuse code from previous projects or to use off-the-shelf components. Interactive systems, for example, are now rarely built from scratch; they are developed with user interface toolkits that provide a wide range of dialogs, windows, buttons, or other standard interface objects. Interface engineering projects focus on reimplementing only part of an existing system. For example, corporate information systems, costly to design and build, must be updated to new client hardware. Often, only the client side of the system is upgraded with new technology; the back end of the system left untouched. Whether dealing with off-the-shelf component or legacy code, developers have to deal with code they cannot modify and which usually was not designed for their system.

We deal with existing components by encapsulating them. This approach has the advantage of decoupling the system from the encapsulated component, thus minimizing the impact of existing software on the new design. This can be done using an Adapter pattern.

The **Adapter design pattern** (Appendix A.2, [Gamma et al., 1994]) converts the interface of a component into an interface that the client expects. This interface is called the *ClientInterface* in Figure 8-5. An Adapter class provides the glue between *ClientInterface* and LegacyClass. For example, assume the client is the static sort() method of the Java Array class (Figures 8-8 and 8-9). This method expects two arguments a, an Array of objects, and c, a Comparator object, which provides a compare() method to define the relative order between elements. Assume we are interested in sorting strings of the class MyString, which defines the greaterThan() and an equals() methods. To sort an Array of MyStrings, we need to define a new comparator, MyStringComparator, which provides a compare() method using greaterThan() and equals(). MyStringComparator is an Adapter class.[1]

---

1. When designing a new system, adaptors are seldom necessary, as the new classes can be defined such that they realize the existing interfaces.

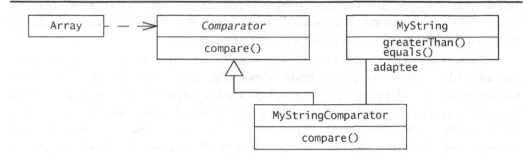

Figure 8-8 Applying the Adapter design pattern for sorting `Strings` in an `Array` (UML class diagram). See also source code in Figure 8-9.

```
/* Existing target interface */
interface Comparator {
    int compare(Object o1, Object o2);
    /* ... */
}
/* Existing client */
class Array {
    static void sort(Object [] a, Comparator c);
    /* ... */
}
/* Existing adaptee class */
class MyString extends String {
    boolean equals(Object o);
    boolean greaterThan(MyString s);
    /* ... */
}
/* New adapter class */
class MyStringComparator implements Comparator {
    /* ... */
    int compare(Object o1, Object o2) {
        int result;
        if (((String)o1).greaterThan(o2)) {
            result = 1
        } else if (((String)o1).equals(o2)) {
            result = 0;
        } else {
            result = -1;
        }
        return result;
    }
}
```

Figure 8-9 Adapter design pattern example (Java). The static `sort()` method on `Arrays` takes two arguments, an arrays of `Objects` to be sorted and a `Comparator` defining the relative order of the elements. To sort an array of `MyStrings`, we need to define a comparator called `MyStringComparator` with the proper interface. `MyStringComparator` is an `Adapter`.

Inheritance and delegation in the Adapter pattern

The Adapter pattern uses specification inheritance between the `ClientInterface` and the `Adapter`. The `Adapter` in turn delegates to the `LegacyClass` implementor class to realize the operations declared in `ClientInterface`. On the one hand, this enables all client code that already uses the `ClientInterface` to work with instances of `Adapter` transparently and without modification of the client. On the other hand, the same `Adapter` can be used for subtypes of the `LegacyClass`.

Note that the Bridge and the Adapter patterns are similar in purpose and structure. Both decouple an interface from an implementation, and both use a specification inheritance relationship and a delegation relationship. They differ in the context in which they are used and in the order in which delegation and inheritance occur. The Adapter pattern uses inheritance first and then delegation, whereas the Bridge pattern uses delegation first and then inheritance. The Adapter pattern is applied when the interface (i.e., `ClientInterface`) and the implementation (i.e., `LegacyClass`) already exist and cannot be modified. When developing new code, the Bridge pattern is a better choice as it provides more extensibility.

8.4.3 Encapsulating Context with the Strategy Pattern

Consider a mobile application running on a wearable computer that uses different networks protocols depending on the location of the user: assume, for example, a car mechanic using the wearable computer to access repair manuals and maintenance records for the vehicle under repair. The wearable computer should operate in the shop with access to a local wireless network as well as on the roadside using a third-generation mobile phone network, such as UMTS. When updating or configuring the mobile application, a system administrator should be able to use the wearable computer with access to a wired network such as Ethernet. This means that the mobile application needs to deal with different types of networks as it switches between networks dynamically, based on factors such as location and network costs. Assume that during the system design of this application, we identify the dynamic switching between wired and wireless networks as a critical design goal. Furthermore we want to be able to deal with future network protocols without having to recompile the application.

To achieve both of these goals, we apply the **Strategy design pattern** (Appendix A.9, [Gamma et al., 1994]). The system model and implementation, respectively, are shown in Figures 8-10 and 8-11. The `Strategy` class is realized by `NetworkInterface`, which provides the common interface to all networks; the `Context` class is realized by a `NetworkConnection` object, which represents a point-to-point connection between the wearable and a remote host. The `Client` is the mobile application. The `Policy` is the `LocationManager`, which monitors the current location of the wearable and the availability of networks, and configures the `NetworkConnection` objects with the appropriate `NetworkInterfaces`. When the `LocationManager` object invokes the `setNetworkInterface()` method, the `NetworkConnection` object shuts down the current `NetworkInterface` and initializes the new `NetworkInterface` transparently from the rest of the application.

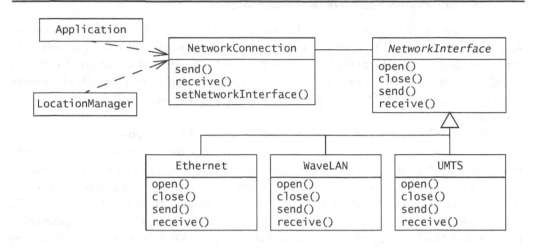

Figure 8-10 Applying the Strategy pattern for encapsulating multiple implementations of a `NetworkInterface` (UML class diagram). The `LocationManager` implementing a specific policy configures `NetworkConnection` with a concrete `NetworkInterface` (i.e., the mechanism) based on the current location. The `Application` uses the `NetworkConnection` independently of concrete `NetworkInterfaces`. See corresponding Java code in Figure 8-11.

Inheritance and delegation in the Strategy pattern

The class diagrams for the Bridge and the Strategy patterns (see Figures 8-7 and 8-10) are almost identical. The key difference is in the creator of the concrete implementation classes: In the Bridge pattern, the class `Abstraction` creates and initializes the `ConcreteImplementations`. In the Strategy pattern, however, the `Context` is not aware of the `ConcreteStrategies`. Instead, a client creates the `ConcreteStrategy` objects and configures the `Context`. Moreover, `ConcreteImplementations` in the Bridge pattern are usually created at initialization time, while `ConcreteStrategies` in the Strategy pattern are usually created and substituted several times during run time.

8.4.4   Encapsulating Platforms with the Abstract Factory Pattern

Consider an application for an intelligent house: the application receives events from sensors distributed throughout the house (e.g., light bulb on, light bulb off, window open, window closed, inside and outside temperature, weather forecasts), identifies predefined patterns, and issues commands for actuators (e.g., turn air-conditioning on, store statistics on energy consumption, close garage door, trigger theft alarm). Although several manufacturers provide the hardware to build such applications (e.g., EIB, Zumtobel's Luxmate), interoperability in this domain is currently poor, preventing the mix and match of devices from different manufacturers, and thus, making it difficult to develop a single software solution for all manufacturers.

```
/** The NetworkConnection object represents a single abstract connection
 *  used by the Client. This is the Context object in Strategy pattern. */
public class NetworkConnection {
    private String destination;
    private NetworkInterface intf;
    private StringBuffer queue;

    public NetworkConnect(String destination, NetworkInterface intf) {
        this.destination = destination;
        this.intf = intf;
        this.intf.open(destination);
        this.queue = new StringBuffer();
    }
    public void send(byte msg[]) {
        // queue the message to be send in case the network is not ready.
        queue.concat(msg);
        if (intf.isReady()) {
            intf.send(queue);
            queue.setLength(0);
        }
    }
    public byte [] receive() {
        return intf.receive();
    }
    public void setNetworkInterface(NetworkInterface newIntf) {
        intf.close();
        newIntf.open(destination);
        intf = newIntf;
    }
}
/** The LocationManager decides on which NetworkInterface to use based on
 *  availability and cost.   */
public class LocationManager {
    private NetworkInterface networkIntf;
    private NetworkConnection networkConn;
/* ... */

    // This method is invoked by the event handler when the location
    // may have changed
    public void doLocation() {
        if (isEthernetAvailable()) {
            networkIntf = new EthernetNetwork();
        } else if (isWaveLANAvailable()) {
            networkIntf = new WaveLANNetwork();
        } else if (isUMTSAvailable()) {
            networkIntf = new UMTSNetwork();
        } else {
            networkIntf = new QueueNetwork();
        }
        networkConn.setNetworkInterface(networkIntf);
    }
}
```

Figure 8-11 Applying the Strategy design pattern for encapsulating multiple implementation of a NetworkInterface (Java). This implementation is simplified and does not take into account exceptions. See corresponding UML class diagram in Figure 8-10.

We use the **Abstract Factory design pattern** (Appendix A.1) to solve this problem. In our intelligent house, each manufacturer provides temperature sensors, electric blinds that report if they are forced in, and intelligent light bulbs that report if they have burned out. As shown in Figure 8-12, these generic objects are called AbstractProducts (e.g., LightBulb, Blind), and their concrete realizations are called ConcreteProducts (e.g., EIBLightBulb, ZumtobelLightBulb, EIBBlind, ZumtobelBlind). One factory for each manufacturer (e.g., ZumtobelFactory, EIBFactory) provides methods for creating the ConcreteProducts (e.g., createLightBulb(), createBlind()). The Client classes (e.g., a TheftApplication) access only the interfaces provided by the AbstractFactory and the AbstractProducts, thereby shielding the Client classes completely from the manufacturer of the underlying products.

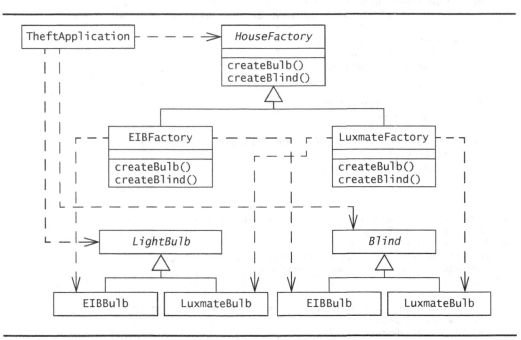

Figure 8-12   Applying the Abstract Factory design pattern to different intelligent house platforms (UML class diagram, dependencies represent «call» relationships).

Inheritance and delegation in the Abstract Factory pattern

The Abstract Factory pattern uses specification inheritance to decouple the interface of a product from its realization. However, since products of the same platform usually depend on each other and access the concrete product classes, products of different platforms cannot be substituted transparently. For example, EIBBulbs are incompatible with LuxmateBulbs and should not be mixed within the same intelligent house system. To ensure that a consistent set of products is created, the Client can only create products by using a ConcreteFactory, which delegates the creation operations to the respective products. By using specification inheritance to decouple ConcreteFactories from their interface, product families from different manufacturers can be substituted transparently from the client.

8.4.5 Encapsulating Control Flow with the Command Pattern

In interactive systems and in transaction systems, it is often desirable to execute, undo, or store user requests without knowing the content of the request. For example, consider the case of matches in the ARENA tournament management system. We want to record individual moves in matches so that these moves can be replayed by a spectator at a later date. However, we also want ARENA to support a broad spectrum of games, so we do not want the classes responsible for recording and replaying moves to depend on any specific game.

We can apply the **Command design pattern** (Appendix A.4, [Gamma et al., 1994]) to this effect. The key to decoupling game moves from their handling is to represent game moves as command objects that inherit from an abstract class called *Move* in Figure 8-13. The *Move* class declares operations for executing, undoing, and storing commands, whereas ConcreteCommands classes (i.e., TicTacToeMove and ChessMove in ARENA) implement specific commands. The classes responsible for recording and replaying games only access the *GameMove* abstract class interface, thus making the system extensible to new Games.

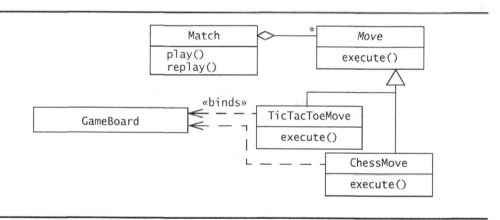

Figure 8-13 Applying the Command design pattern to Matches in ARENA (UML class diagram).

Inheritance and delegation in the Command pattern

The Command design pattern uses specification inheritance between the Command class and ConcreteCommands, enabling new commands to be added independently from the Invoker. Delegation is used between ConcreteCommands and Receivers, and between Invoker and Command, enabling ConcreteCommands to be dynamically created, executed, and stored. The Command pattern is often used in a Model/View/Controller software architecture, where Receivers are model objects, Invoker and Commands are controller objects, and Clients creating Commands are view objects.

8.4.6   Encapsulating Hierarchies with the Composite Design Pattern

User interface toolkits, such as Swing and Cocoa, provide the application developer with a range of classes as building blocks. Each class implements a specialized behavior, such as inputting text, selecting and deselecting a check box, pushing a button, or pulling down a menu. The user interface design can aggregate these components into Windows to build application-specific interfaces. For example, a preferences dialog may include a number of on-off check boxes for enabling different features in the application.

As windows become more complex and include many different user interface objects, their layout (i.e., moving and resizing each component so that the window forms a coherent whole) becomes increasingly unmanageable. Consequently, modern toolkits enable the developer to organize the user interface objects into hierarchies of aggregate nodes, called "panels," that can be manipulated the same way as the concrete user interface objects. For example, our preferences dialog can include a top panel for the title of the dialog and instructions for the user, a center panel containing the checkboxes and their labels, and a bottom panel for the 'ok' and 'cancel' button. Each panel is responsible for the layout of its subpanels, called "children," and the overall dialog only has to deal with the three panels (Figures 8-14 and 8-15).

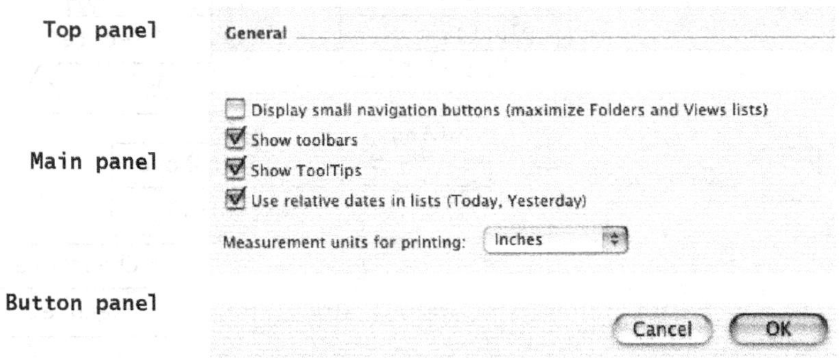

Figure 8-14   Anatomy of a preference dialog. Aggregates, called "panels," are used for grouping user interface objects that need to be resized and moved together.

Swing addresses this problem with the **Composite design pattern** (Appendix A.5, [Gamma et al., 1994]) as depicted in Figure 8-16. An abstract class called Component is the roof of all user interface objects, including Checkboxes, Buttons, and Labels. Composite, also a subclass of Component, is a special user interface object representing aggregates including the Panels we mentioned above. Note that Windows and Applets (the root of the instance hierarchy) are also Composite classes that have additional behavior for dealing with the window manager and the browser, respectively.

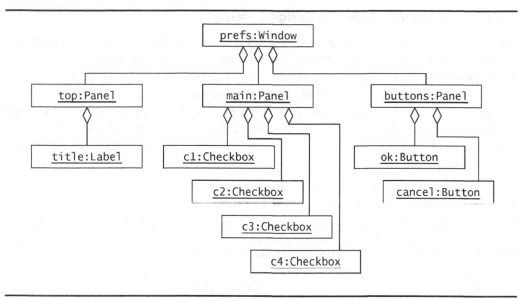

Figure 8-15   UML object diagram for the user interface objects of Figure 8-14.

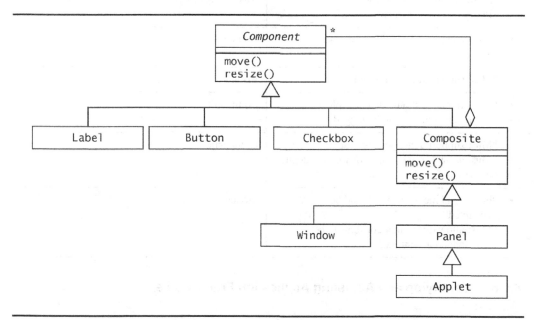

Figure 8-16   Applying the Composite design pattern to user interface widgets (UML class diagram). The Swing Component hierarchy is a Composite in which leaf widgets (e.g., Checkbox, Button, Label) specialize the Component interface, and aggregates (e.g., Panel, Window) specialize the Composite abstract class. Moving or resizing a Composite impacts all of its children.

8.4.7   Heuristics for Selecting Design Patterns

Identifying the correct design pattern for a given problem is difficult unless you already have some experience in using design patterns. Pattern catalogs are large and varied, and one cannot expect developers to read them completely. As design patterns address a specific design goal or a specific nonfunctional requirement, another technique is to use key phrases in the Requirements Analysis Document (RAD) and the System Design Document (SDD) to select candidate patterns. This is similar to the Abbott's natural language technique described in Chapter 5, *Analysis*. The heuristics box below provides example key phrases for the patterns covered in this chapter:

Natural language heuristics for selecting design patterns

Design patterns address specific design goals and nonfunctional requirements. Similar to Abbott's heuristics described in Chapter 5, *Analysis*, key phrases can be used to identify candidate design patterns. Below are examples for the patterns covered in this chapter.

Phrase	Design Pattern
• "Manufacturer independence" • "Platform independence"	Abstract Factory
• "Must comply with existing interface" • "Must reuse existing legacy component"	Adapter
• "Must support future protocols"	Bridge
• "All commands should be undoable" • "All transactions should be logged"	Command
• "Must support aggregate structures" • "Must allow for hierarchies of variable depth and width"	Composite
• "Policy and mechanisms should be decoupled". • "Must allow different algorithms to be interchanged at runtime."	Strategy

8.4.8   Identifying and Adjusting Application Frameworks

Application frameworks

An **application framework** is a reusable partial application that can be specialized to produce custom applications [Johnson & Foote, 1988]. In contrast to class libraries, **frameworks** are targeted to particular technologies, such as data processing or cellular communications, or to application domains, such as user interfaces or real-time avionics. The key benefits of application frameworks are reusability and extensibility. Framework reusability leverages the application domain knowledge and the prior effort of experienced developers to avoid recreation and revalidation of recurring solutions. An application framework enhances extensibility by providing **hook methods**, which are overwritten by the application to extend the application framework. Hook methods systematically decouple the interfaces and behaviors of an application domain from the variations required by an application in a particular context. Framework extensibility is essential to ensure timely customization of new application services and features.

Frameworks can be classified by their position in the software development process.

- **Infrastructure frameworks** aim to simplify the software development process. Examples include frameworks for operating systems [Campbell & Islam, 1993], debuggers [Bruegge et al., 1993], communication tasks [Schmidt, 1997], user interface design [Weinand et al., 1988], and Java Swing [JFC, 2009]. System infrastructure frameworks are used internally within a software project and are usually not delivered to a client.

- **Middleware frameworks** are used to integrate existing distributed applications and components. Common examples include Microsoft's MFC and DCOM, Java RMI, WebObjects [Wilson & Ostrem, 1999], WebSphere [IBM], WebLogic Enterprise Application [BEA], implementations of CORBA [OMG, 2008], and transactional databases.

- **Enterprise application frameworks** are application specific and focus on domains such as telecommunications, avionics, environmental modeling, manufacturing, financial engineering [Birrer, 1993], and enterprise business activities [JavaEE, 2009].

Infrastructure and middleware frameworks are essential to create rapidly high-quality software systems, but they are usually not requested by external customers. Enterprise frameworks, however, support the development of end-user applications. As a result, buying infrastructure and middleware frameworks is more cost effective than building them [Fayad & Hamu, 1997].

Frameworks can also be classified by the techniques used to extend them.

- **Whitebox frameworks** rely on inheritance and dynamic binding for extensibility. Existing functionality is extended by subclassing framework base classes and overriding predefined hook methods using patterns such as the template method pattern [Gamma et al., 1994].

- **Blackbox frameworks** support extensibility by defining interfaces for components that can be plugged into the framework. Existing functionality is reused by defining components that conform to a particular interface and integrating these components with the framework using delegation.

Whitebox frameworks require intimate knowledge of the framework's internal structure. Whitebox frameworks produce systems that are tightly coupled to the specific details of the framework's inheritance hierarchies, and thus changes in the framework can require the recompilation of the application. Blackbox frameworks are easier to use than whitebox frameworks because they rely on delegation instead of inheritance. However, blackbox frameworks are more difficult to develop because they require the definition of interfaces and hooks that anticipate a wide range of potential use cases. Moreover, it is easier to extend and reconfigure blackbox frameworks dynamically, as they emphasize dynamic object relationships rather than static class relationships. [Johnson & Foote, 1988].

Frameworks, class libraries, and design patterns

Frameworks are closely related to design patterns, class libraries, and components.

Design patterns versus frameworks.   The main difference between frameworks and patterns is that frameworks focus on reuse of concrete designs, algorithms, and implementations in a particular programming language. In contrast, patterns focus on reuse of abstract designs and small collections of cooperating classes. Frameworks focus on a particular application domain, whereas design patterns can be viewed more as building blocks of frameworks.

Class libraries versus frameworks.   Classes in a framework cooperate to provide a reusable architectural skeleton for a family of related applications. In contrast, class libraries are less domain specific and provide a smaller scope of reuse. For instance, class library components, such as classes for strings, complex numbers, arrays, and bitsets, can be used across many application domains. Class libraries are typically passive; that is, they do not implement or constrain the control flow. Frameworks, however, are active; that is, they control the flow of control within an application. In practice, developers often use frameworks and class libraries in the same system. For instance, frameworks use class libraries, such as foundation classes, internally to simplify the development of the framework. Similarly, application-specific code invoked by framework event handlers uses class libraries to perform basic tasks, such as string processing, file management, and numerical analysis.

Components versus frameworks.   Components are self-contained instances of classes that are plugged together to form complete applications. In terms of reuse, a component is a blackbox that defines a cohesive set of operations that can be used solely with knowledge of the syntax and semantics of its interface. Compared with frameworks, components are less tightly coupled and can even be reused on the binary code level. That is, applications can reuse components without having to subclass from existing base classes. The advantage is that applications do not always have to be recompiled when components change. The relationship between frameworks and components is not predetermined. On the one hand, frameworks can be used to develop components, where the component interface provides a facade pattern for the internal class structure of the framework. On the other hand, components can be plugged into blackbox frameworks. In general, frameworks are used to simplify the development of infrastructure and middleware software, whereas components are used to simplify the development of end-user application software.

A framework example

WebObjects is a set of frameworks for developing interactive Web applications by accessing existing data from relational databases. WebObjects consists of two infrastructure frameworks. The WebObjects framework handles the interaction between Web browsers and Web servers. The Enterprise Object Framework (EOF) handles the interaction between Web servers and relational databases. The EOF supports database adapters that allow applications to connect to database management systems from particular vendors. For example, the EOF provides database adapters for Informix, Oracle, and Sybase servers and ODBC-compliant adapters. In the following discussion, we concentrate on the WebObjects framework. More information on the EOF can be found in [Wilson & Ostrem, 1999].

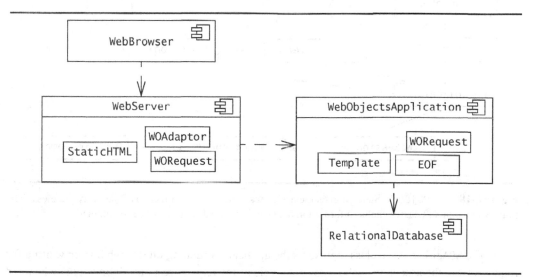

Figure 8-17   An example of dynamic site with WebObjects (UML component diagram).

Figure 8-17 shows an example of a dynamic publishing site built with WebObjects. The WebBrowser originates an HTTP request containing a URL, which is sent to the WebServer. If the WebServer detects that the request is to a static HTML page, it passes it on the StaticHTML object, which selects and sends the page back to the WebBrowser as a response. The WebBrowser then renders it for the user. If the WebServer detects that the request requires a dynamic HTML page, it passes the request to a WebObjects WOAdaptor. The WOAdaptor packages the incoming

HTML request and forwards it to the WebObjectsApplication object. Based on Templates defined by the developer and relevant data retrieved from the RelationalDatabase, the WebObjectsApplication then generates an HTML response page, which is passed back through the WOAdaptor to the WebServer. The WebServer then sends the page to the WebBrowser, which renders it for the user.

A key abstraction provided by the WebObjects framework is an extension of the HTTP protocol to manage state. HTTP is a stateless request-response protocol; that is, a response is formulated for each request, but no state is maintained between successive requests. In many Web-based applications, however, state must be kept between requests. For example in ARENA, Players should not identify themselves for each move they play. Moreover, Players must be able to continue playing in the same Match even if their WebBrowser is restarted. Several techniques have been proposed to keep track of state information in Web applications, including dynamically generated URLs, cookies, and hidden HTML fields. WebObjects provides the classes shown in Figure 8-18 to achieve the same purpose.

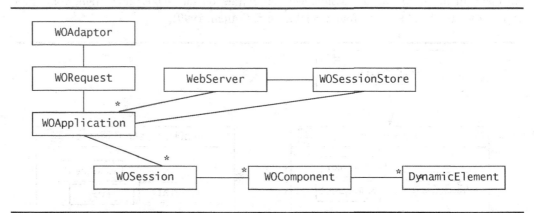

Figure 8-18   WebObject's State Management Classes. The HTTP protocol is inherently stateless. The State Management Classes enable information between individual requests to be maintained.

The WOApplication class represents the application running on the WebServer waiting for requests from the associated WebBrowser. A cycle of the request-response loop begins whenever the WOAdaptor receives an incoming HTTP request. The WOAdaptor packages this request in a WORequest object and forwards it to the application object of class WOApplication. Requests are always triggered by a URL submitted by the WebBrowser. The class WOSession encapsulates the state of an individual session, allowing it to track different users, even within a single application. A WOSession consists of one or more WOComponents, which represent a reusable Web page or portion of a Web page for display within an individual session. WOComponents may contain DynamicElements. When an application accesses the database, one or more of the DynamicElements of a component are filled with information retrieved from the database. The

`WOSessionStore` provides persistency for `WOSession` objects: it stores sessions in the server and restores them by the application upon request.

The essence of building a `WebObjects` application is to refine the classes `WOApplication`, `WOSession`, and `WOComponent` and to intercept the flow of requests sent and received between them. Inherited methods from these classes are overridden when the developer needs to extend the default behavior. The earliest control point for refining objects of type `WOApplication` is when they are constructed. The last point of control is when the application object terminates. By adding code to the application object constructor or overriding the `WOApplication` `terminate()` method, the developer can customize the behavior of the `WebObjects` application as desired.

8.5 Managing Reuse

Historically, software development started as a craft, in which each application was custom made according to the wishes and needs of a single customer. After all, software development represented only a fraction of the cost of hardware, and computing solutions were affordable only to few. With the price of hardware dropping and computing power increasing exponentially, the number of customers and the range of applications has broadened dramatically. Conversely, software costs increased as applications became more complex. This trend reached the point where software represented the largest cost in any computing solution, putting tremendous economic pressure on the project manager to reduce the cost of software. With no silver bullet in sight, systematic reuse of code, designs, and processes became an attractive solution. Reuse, whether design patterns, frameworks, or components, has many technical and managerial advantages:

- *Lower development effort.* When reusing a solution or a component, many standard errors are avoided. Moreover, in the case of design patterns, the resulting system is more easily extended and more resilient to typical changes. This results in less development effort and reduces the need for human resources, which can be redirected to testing the software to ensure better quality.

- *Lower risk.* When reusing repetitively the same design pattern or component, the typical problems that will be encountered are known and can be anticipated. Moreover, the time needed to adapt the design pattern or to glue the component is also known, resulting in a more predictable development process and fewer risks.

- *Widespread use of standard terms.* The reuse of a standard set of design patterns and components fosters the use of a standard vocabulary. For example, terms such as Adapter, Bridge, Command, or Facade denote precise concepts that all developers become familiar with. This reduces the number of different terms and solutions to common problems and reduces misunderstandings among developers.

- *Increased reliability.* Reuse by itself does not increase reliability or reduce the need for testing (see the Ariane 501 incident in Section 3.1 as an illustrative example).

Components and pattern solutions that worked in one context can exhibit unexpected failures in other contexts. However, a culture of reuse in a software organization can increase reliability for all of the above reasons: reduced development time can lead to an increased testing effort, repetitive use of components can lead to a knowledge base of typical problems to be anticipated, and use of standard terms reduces communication failures.

Unfortunately, reuse does not occur spontaneously within a development organization. The main challenges include

- *NIH (Not Invented Here) syndrome.* Since software engineering education (at least until recently) emphasizes mostly the design of new solutions, developers often distrust the reuse of existing solutions, especially when the customization of the solution under consideration is limited or constrained. In such situations, developers believe that they can develop a completely new solution that is better adapted to their specific problem (which is usually true) in less time than what they need to understand the reused solution (which is usually not true). Moreover, the advantages of reuse are visible only in the longer term, while the gratification of developing a new implementation is instantaneous.

- *Process support.* The processes associated with identifying, reusing, and customizing an existing solution are different than those involved in creating a brand new solution. The first set of activities requires painstakingly sifting through a large and evolving corpus of knowledge and carefully evaluating the findings. The second set of activities requires creativity and a good understanding of the problem. Most software engineering tools and methods are better adapted to creative activities than to reuse. For example, there are currently many catalogs of design patterns, but no systematic method for novice developers to identify quickly the appropriate pattern that should be used in a given situation.

- *Training.* Given the lack of knowledge support tools for reuse, training is the single most effective method in establishing a reuse culture. Consequently, the burden of educating developers to specific reusable solutions and components falls on the development organization.

In the following sections, we examine how we can document reuse and assign roles to address the above issues.

8.5.1 Documenting Reuse

Reuse activities involve two types of documentation: the documentation of the template solution being reused and the documentation of the system that is reusing the solution.

The documentation of a reusable solutions (e.g., the design pattern, a framework, or a component) includes not only a description of the solution, but also a description of the class of problems it addresses, the trade-offs faced by the developer, alternative implementations, and examples of use. This documentation is typically difficult to produce, as the author of the reusable solution may not be able to anticipate all the problems it can be used for. Moreover, such documentation is usually generic and abstract and must be illustrated by concrete examples for novice developers to fully understand the parameters of the solution. Consequently, documentation of a reusable solution is usually not ideal. However, developers can incrementally improve this documentation each time they reuse a solution by adding the following:

- *Reference to a system using the solution*. Minimally, the documentation of the reusable solution should include references to each use. If defects are discovered in the reused solution, these defects can be systematically corrected in all occurrences of reuse.

- *Example of use*. Examples are essential for developers to understand the strengths and limitation of the reused solution. Each occurrence of reuse constitutes an example. Developers should include a brief summary illustrating the problems being solved and the adopted solution.

- *Alternative solutions considered*. As we saw in this chapter, many design patterns are similar. However, selecting the wrong pattern can lead to more problems than developing a custom solution. In the documentation of the example, developers should indicate which other candidate solutions they discarded and why.

- *Encountered trade-offs*. Reuse, especially in the case of frameworks and components, often entails making a compromise and selecting a less than optimal solution for some criteria. For example, one component may offer an interface that is extensible, and another may deliver better response time.

The documentation of the system under construction should minimally include references to all the reused solutions. For example, design patterns are not immediately identifiable in the code, as the classes involved usually have names different from names used in the standard pattern. Many patterns draw their benefits from the decoupling of certain classes (e.g., the bridge client from the bridge implementations), so such classes should remain decoupled during future changes to the system. Similarly, explicitly documenting which classes use which components makes it easier to adapt the client classes to newer versions of the reused components. Consequently, developers can further increase of the benefits of reuse by documenting the links between reused solutions and their code, in addition to the standard object design documentation, which we discuss in Chapter 9, *Object Design: Specifying Interfaces*.

A contributing factor for the high cost of change late in the process is the loss of design context. Developers forget quickly the reasons behind designing complicated workarounds or complex data structures during early phases of the process. When changing code late in the process, the probability of introducing errors into the system is high. Hence, the reason for recording trade-offs, examples, alternatives, and other decision making information is also to reduce the cost of change. In Chapter 12, *Rationale Management*, we describe more techniques for systematically capturing such decision-making information.

8.5.2   Assigning Responsibilities

Individual developers assigned to subsystems will not spontaneously turn to design patterns and components unless they have experience with these topics. To foster a reuse culture, an organization needs to make the incentives of reuse as high as possible for the individual developer. This includes access to expert developers who can provide advice and information, and specific components or patterns, training, and emphasis on reuse during design reviews and code inspections. The availability of knowledge lowers the frustration experienced when experiencing the learning curve associated with a component. The explicit review of pattern usage (or lack thereof) increases the organizational incentive for investing time into looking for ready solutions.

Below are the main roles involved in reuse:

- **Component expert**. The component expert is familiar with using a specific component. The component expert is a developer and usually has received third-party training in the use of the component.

- **Pattern expert**. The pattern expert is the analog of the component expert for a family of design patterns. However, pattern experts are usually self-made and acquire their knowledge from experience.

- **Technical writer**. The technical writer must be aware of reuse and document dependencies between components, design patterns, and the system, as discussed in the previous section. This may require the technical writer to become familiar with the solutions typically reused by the organization and with their associated terms.

- **Configuration manager**. In addition to tracking configurations and versions of individual subsystems, the configuration manager must also be aware of the versions of the components that are used. While newer versions of the components may be used, their introduction requires tests to be repeated and changes related to the upgrade documented.

The technical means of achieving reuse (e.g., inheritance, delegation, design patterns, application frameworks) have been available to software engineers for nearly two decades. The success factors associated with reuse are actually not technical, but managerial. Only an organization that provides the tools for selecting and improving reusable solutions and the culture to encourage their use can reap the benefits of design and code reuse.

8.6 ARENA Case Study

In this section, we apply three design patterns to the object design of ARENA. As specified during requirements analysis, we anticipate ARENA to support many different types of games. Hence, in this section, we focus on the classes related to Games, Matches, and their respective boundary objects. In particular, we focus on the following design patterns:

- *Abstract Factory design pattern* (Section 8.6.1). We shield the Tournament and League objects from Game specifics by turning the Game abstract interface into an AbstractFactory. This way, only concrete Products need to be supplied for a new concrete Game.
- *Command design pattern* (Section 8.6.2). We shield the objects related to playing and replaying Matches by encapsulating concrete Moves for each Game.
- *Observer design pattern* (Section 8.6.3). We standardize the interactions between Match and Move entity objects with MatchView objects across all Games with a subscriber/publisher paradigm.

In this section, we only focus on Games that involve a sequence of Moves performed by Players who take turns. We do not consider Games that involve simultaneous or concurrent actions at this point.

8.6.1 Applying the Abstract Factory Design Pattern

Achieving game independence in ARENA is not as straightforward as it initially appears. In the analysis model (see Figure 8-19), we define an abstract Game interface to shield the Tournament and League objects from the specifics of each game. However, supporting a specific Game

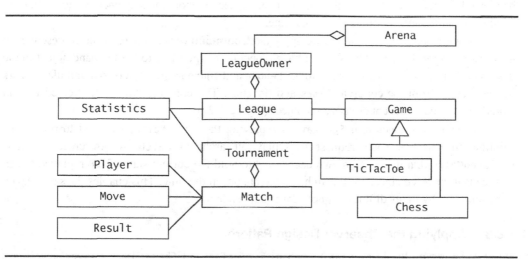

Figure 8-19 ARENA analysis objects related to Game independence (UML class diagram).

involves the tight collaboration of several objects representing the rules of Game, the state of a Match under progress, specific Moves played by the different contenders, and the Result of the Match. At the end of a Match, the Results are accumulated in Tournament and League-wide Statistics. We need to define a Game framework within ARENA that shields the Tournament and League objects from all the Game specifics, while supporting standard interactions among specialized Game, Match, Move, Result, and Statistics objects.

As several specialized objects need to collaborate, we first select the **Abstract Factory design pattern** to address the game independence design issue (see Figure 8-20). The abstract Game interface is an abstract factory that provides methods for creating Matches and Statistics. Each concrete Game (e.g., TicTacToe and Chess) realizes the abstract Game interface and provides implementations for the Match and Statistics objects. For example, the TicTacToe Game implementation returns TTTMatches and TTTStats objects when the createMatch() and the createStatistics() methods are invoked. The concrete Match objects (e.g., TTTMatch and ChessMatch) track the current state of the Match and enforce the Game rules. Each concrete Game also provides a concrete Statistics object for accumulating average statistics (e.g., average Match length, average number of Moves, number of wins and losses per player, as well as Game specific Statistics). The League and the Tournament objects each use a concrete Statistics object to accumulate statistics for the League and the Tournament scope, respectively. Because the League and Tournament objects only access the abstract Game, Match, Statistics interfaces, the League and Tournaments work transparently for all Games that comply with this framework.

8.6.2   Applying the Command Design Pattern

Although Spectators can watch Matches as they occur, we anticipate that many Matches will be viewed asynchronously, after the fact. Hence, we need to store the sequence of moves in each Match, so that it can be replayed at a later time.

As described in Section 8.4.5, we apply the **Command design pattern** and represent each move as a Command object. The abstract Move object (corresponding to the Command object in the design pattern) provides the interface to the League and Tournament objects to manipulate Moves independently from the concrete Games and Matches. The concrete Moves are created by and stored in a queue in the concrete Match object (Figure 8-21).

To deal with concurrent Spectators replaying the same Match, we need to refine this solution further. For each request to replay an archived Match, ARENA creates a new ReplayedMatch that includes its own GameBoard to hold the current state of the replayed Match and feeds it the Move objects of the archived Match, one at the time. This enables the same Match to be replayed by many different Spectators independently.

8.6.3   Applying the Observer Design Pattern

ARENA supports multi-player games, such as TicTacToe and Chess. Each Player accesses a Match in progress through a client application running on his local machine. Consequently,

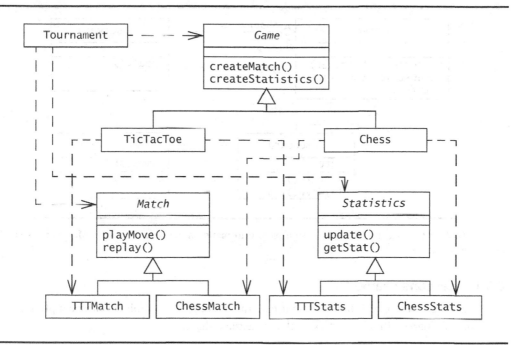

Figure 8-20   Applying the Abstract Factory design pattern to Games (UML class diagram).

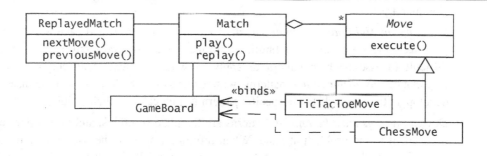

Figure 8-21   Applying the Command design pattern to `Match`es and `ReplayedMatch`es in ARENA (UML class diagram).

potentially many views of the same `Match` in progress must be kept consistent. To address this problem, we use a distributed version of the **Observer design pattern** (Figure 8-22), in which the `Observer`s are the boundary objects in each client, the `Subject`s are the `GameBoard` objects that maintain the current state of each `Match`. References between `Subject`s and `Observer`s are remote object references provided by Java RMI. In addition to maintaining consistency among different views of the same `Match`, this enables us to use the same pattern for `ReplayedMatch`es.

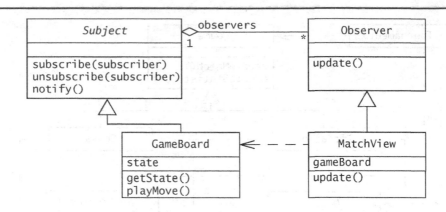

Figure 8-22   Applying the Observer design pattern to maintain consistency across MatchViews (UML class diagram).

8.6.4   Lessons Learned

In this section, we applied three different patterns to address the problem of decoupling ARENA from specific Games. In this short example, we learned that

- *Design patterns mesh and overlap.* For example, the Match class participates in two patterns. It is an AbstractProduct in the Abstract Factory and an Invoker in the Command pattern.

- *Selecting the right pattern is not trivial.* There are many published catalogs of design patterns. Unless a developer is familiar with them and has used them in the past, it is difficult to assess which pattern to apply in which context. This emphasizes the importance of documenting patterns with examples, which can then be used by developers to assess whether a specific pattern is applicable to their problem.

- *Design patterns must be refined.* Patterns are template solutions, and most often must be adapted to the problem at hand. When refining a pattern, the use of specification inheritance and delegation must be examined carefully so that the extensibility advantages provided by the pattern are not destroyed.

8.7 Further Readings

Inheritance has introduced a wide range of design challenges for the developer. Although it provides a powerful mechanism for designing reusable components and for existing classes, it also enables developers to create complex control structures that are difficult to understand and test, resulting in brittle systems. Ever since it was introduced in programming languages, researchers have attempted to provide ways of distinguishing "good" uses of inheritance from "bad" uses and come up with a generalized set of design principles.

Marvin Minsky is credited with inventing inheritance in Frames, a framework for representing knowledge in artificial intelligence [Minsky, 1975]. Inheritance was later refined and incorporated into early object-oriented programming languages such as Smalltalk [Goldberg & Kay, 1976]. Rumbaugh and his colleagues were the first to introduce inheritance into a modeling language called OMT [Rumbaugh et al., 1991], which has greatly influenced UML.

The *Liskov Substitution Principle* [Liskov, 1988] introduced a formal definition of subtyping, essentially differentiating specification inheritance from implementation inheritance. Although simple to understand, it is difficult to apply as a design principle.

In *Object-Oriented Software Construction* [Meyer, 1997], initially published in 1989, Bertrand Meyer formulated the open-closed principle, stating that abstract classes should be open for extension but closed to modification. *Object-Oriented Analysis and Design* [Martin & Odell, 1992] further developed these design principles.

The publication of *Design Patterns* [Gamma et al., 1994], however, opened up a different approach to reuse, by offering template solutions to problems that occur in almost every design. By combining, meshing, and overlapping individual patterns, a developer could address many extensibility and reusability issues by applying robust solutions. The pattern concept for encoding knowledge for reuse became so successful and popular that other authors applied it to other development activities, such as software architecture [Buschmann et al., 1996] and analysis [Fowler, 1997].

8.8 Exercises

8-1 Consider the ARENA object design model. For each of the following objects, indicate if it is an application object or a solution object:

- League
- LeagueStore
- LeagueXMLStoreImplementor
- Match
- MatchView
- Move
- ChessMove

8-2 Indicate which occurrences of the following inheritance relationships are specification inheritance and which are implementation inheritance:

- A Rectangle class inherits from a Polygon class.
- A Set class inherits from a BinaryTree class.
- A Set class inherits from a Bag class (a Bag is defined as an unordered collection).
- A Player class inherits from a User class.
- A Window class inherits from a Polygon class.

8-3 Consider an existing game of bridge written in Java. We are interested in integrating this bridge game into ARENA. Which design pattern would you use? Draw a UML class diagram relating the ARENA objects with some of the classes you would expect to find in the bridge game.

8-4   Consider a workflow system supporting software developers. The system enables managers to model the process the developers should follow in terms of activities and work products. The manager can assign specific processes to each developer and set deadlines for the delivery of each work product. The system supports several types of work products, including formatted text, picture, and URLs. The manager, while editing the workflow, can dynamically set the type of each work product at run time. Assuming one of your design goals is to design the system so that more work product types can be added in the future, which design pattern would you use to represent work products?

8-5   Consider a system that includes a database client and two redundant database servers. Both database servers are identical: the first acts as a main server, the second acts as a hot back-up in case the main server fails. The database client accesses the servers through a single component called a "gateway," hence hiding from the client which server is currently being used. A separate policy object called a "watchdog" monitors the requests and responses of the main server and, depending on the responses, tells the gateway whether to switch over to the back-up server. What do you call this design pattern? Draw a UML class diagram to justify your choice.

8-6   In Section 8.4.1, we used a Bridge pattern to decouple the implementation of the ARENA LeagueStore subsystem from its interface, enabling us to provide different implementations for the purpose of testing. Ideally, we would apply the Bridge pattern to each subsystem in our system design to facilitate testing. Unfortunately, this is not always possible. Give an example of a subsystem where the Bridge pattern cannot be used.

8-7   Consider the following design goals. Indicate the candidate pattern(s) you would consider to satisfy each goal:

- Given a legacy banking application, encapsulate the existing business logic component.

- Given a chess program, enable future developers to substitute the planning algorithm that decides on the next move with a better one.

- Given a chess program, enable a monitoring component to switch planning algorithms at runtime, based on the opposing player's style and response time.

- Given a simulation of a mouse solving a maze, enable the path evaluation component to evaluate different paths independently of the types of moves considered by the mouse.

8-8   Consider an application that must select dynamically an encryption algorithm based on security requirements and computing time constraints. Which design pattern would you select? Draw a UML class diagram depicting the classes in the pattern and justify your choice.

References

[BEA]	BEA WebLogic Platform, http://www.bea.com/products/weblogic/platform.
[Birrer, 1993]	E. T. Birrer, "Frameworks in the financial engineering domain: An experience report," *ECOOP'93 Proceedings*, Lecture Notes in Computer Science, No. 707, 1993.
[Bruegge et al., 1993]	B. Bruegge, T. Gottschalk, & B. Luo, "A framework for dynamic program analyzers," *OOPSLA' 93, (Object-Oriented Programming Systems, Languages, and Applications)*, Washington, DC, pp. 65–82, September 1993.
[Buschmann et al., 1996]	F. Buschmann, R. Meunier, H. Rohnert, P. Sommerlad, & M. Stal, *Pattern-Oriented Software Architecture: A System of Patterns*, Wiley, Chichester, U.K., 1996.
[Campbell & Islam, 1993]	R. H. Campbell & N. Islam, "A technique for documenting the framework of an object-oriented system," *Computing Systems*, 6, pp. 363–389, 1993.
[Fayad & Hamu, 1997]	M. E. Fayad & D. S. Hamu, "Object-oriented enterprise frameworks: Make vs. buy decisions and guidelines for selection," *The Communications of ACM*, 1997.
[Fowler, 1997]	M. Fowler, *Analysis Patterns: Reusable Object Models*, Addison-Wesley, Reading, MA, 1997.
[Gamma et al., 1994]	E. Gamma, R. Helm, R. Johnson, & J. Vlissides, *Design Patterns: Elements of Reusable Object-Oriented Software*, Addison-Wesley, Reading, MA, 1994.
[Goldberg & Kay, 1976]	A. Goldberg & A. Kay, *Smalltalk-72 Instruction Manual*, Xerox Palo Alto, CA, 1976.
[IBM]	IBM, *WebSphere Software Platform for E-Business*, http://www.ibm.com/websphere/.
[JavaEE, 2009]	*Java Platform, Enterprise Edition*, Javasoft, 2009, http://java.sun.com/.
[JFC, 2009]	*Java Foundation Classes*, JDK Documentation. Javasoft, 2009.
[Johnson & Foote, 1988]	R. Johnson & B. Foote, "Designing reusable classes," *Journal of Object-Oriented Programming*, Vol. 1, No. 5, pp. 22–35, 1988.
[Liskov, 1988]	B. Liskov, "Data abstraction and hierarchy," *SIGPLAN Notices*, Vol. 23, No. 3, May, 1988.
[Martin & Odell, 1992]	J. Martin & J. J. Odell, *Object-Oriented Analysis and Design*, Prentice Hall, Englewood Cliffs, NJ, 1992.
[Meyer, 1997]	B. Meyer, *Object-Oriented Software Construction*, 2nd ed., Prentice Hall, Upper Saddle River, NJ, 1997.
[Minsky, 1975]	M. Minsky, "A framework for representing knowledge," in P. Winston (ed.), *The Psychology of Computer Vision*, McGraw-Hill, 1975.
[OMG, 2008]	Object Management Group, *Common Object Request Broker Architecture (CORBA) Specification: Version 3.1*, http://www.omg.org 2008.
[Rumbaugh et al., 1991]	J. Rumbaugh, M. Blaha, W. Premerlani, F. Eddy, & W. Lorensen. *Object-Oriented Modeling and Design*, Prentice Hall, Englewood Cliffs, NJ, 1991.
[Schmidt, 1997]	D. C. Schmidt, "Applying design patterns and frameworks to develop object-oriented communication software," in Peter Salus (ed.), *Handbook of Programming Languages*, Vol. 1, MacMillan Computer, 1997.
[Weinand et al., 1988]	A. Weinand, E. Gamma, & R. Marty, "ET++ – An object-oriented application framework in C++," in *Object-Oriented Programming Systems, Languages, and Applications Conference Proceedings*, San Diego, CA, September 1988.
[Wilson & Ostrem, 1999]	G. Wilson & J. Ostrem, *WebObjects Developer's Guide*, Apple, Cupertino, CA, 1998.

9

Object Design: Specifying Interfaces

If you have a procedure with 10 parameters, you probably missed some.
—Alan Perlis, *Epigrams in Programming*

During object design, we identify and refine solution objects to realize the subsystems defined during system design. During this activity, our understanding of each object deepens: we specify the type signatures and the visibility of each of the operations, and, finally, we describe the conditions under which an operation can be invoked and those under which the operation raises an exception. As the focus of system design was on identifying large chunks of work that could be assigned to individual teams or developers, the focus of object design is on specifying the boundaries between objects. At this stage in the project, a large number of developers concurrently refines and changes many objects and their interfaces. The pressure to deliver is increasing and the opportunity to introduce new, complex faults into the design is still there. The focus of interface specification is for developers to communicate clearly and precisely about increasingly lower-level details of the system.

The interface specification activities of object design include

- identifying missing attributes and operations
- specifying type signatures and visibility
- specifying invariants
- specifying preconditions and postconditions.

In this chapter, we provide an overview of the concepts of interface specification. We introduce OCL (Object Constraint Language) as a language for specifying invariants, preconditions, and postconditions. We discuss heuristics and stylistic guidelines for writing readable constraints. Finally, we examine the issues related to documenting and managing interface specifications.

9.1 Introduction: A Railroad Example

Stuttgart: Evolving a streetcar into a light rail system

Until 1976, the main public mass transportation system in Stuttgart was a streetcar system. The system was extensive and used by many passengers. However, streetcars could only hold a rather limited amount of passengers and shared streets with cars. With car traffic continually increasing, the city of Stuttgart opted to convert the streetcar system into a more efficient off-street light rail system. The larger gauge of light rail cars would allow larger cars with more capacity than streetcars. Moreover, the construction of dedicated rails would allow light rail cars to move at faster speeds. And because light rail speed is independent of the street traffic, schedules could be predictable even during rush hour.

The conversion was initiated in 1976. However, given the extensive reach of the streetcar network and the number of lines to convert, the city took an evolutionary approach. The streetcar lines were converted one at the time, operating both types of rolling stock during the transition period. This evolutionary approach faced many challenges that arose from incompatibilities between light rail cars and streetcars.

- *Gauge.* The light rail system used a standard gauge (1450 mm), and the streetcar system used a meter gauge (1000 mm). As several stations needed to accommodate several lines, the tracks had to be fitted with three rails instead of the usual two, so that both types of cars could use the same track. In addition to more rails, this resulted in more complex switches.

One meter gauge (streetcar) 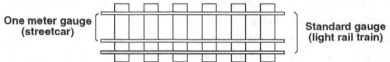 **Standard gauge (light rail train)**

- *Station platforms.* Streetcars were designed for passengers who entered the cars from the street level. Light rail cars were designed for passengers who enter from a raised platform. For stations that accommodated both types of rolling stock, platforms were raised on one end and low on the other end. Because each part of the platform must be at least as long as its respective trains, all platforms became much longer.

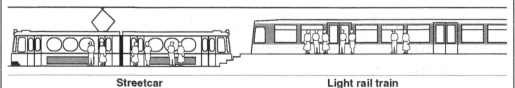

Streetcar   **Light rail train**

- *Signaling.* Streetcars observed signals that were similar to traffic lights observed by cars: traffic lights open and close on a periodic basis, mostly independent of the current traffic situation. Light rail signaling, however, is similar to freight train signaling, in which trains are dispatched from a central location and track circuits monitor the location of each train. Consequently, the signaling for the light rail had to be compatible with street car rolling stock.

Given the length of the transition period, addressing the challenges introduced by the dual gauge system enabled the city to avoid interruptions in the transport system and meet the rising passenger demand. The project was successfully completed in December 2007 when the last street car line was retired.

This example illustrates the concept of interface: a streetcar, like a software object, provides services to clients and makes certain assumptions about its environment. For rail tracks, the interface of the streetcar is the wheels. If the distance between the wheels of the street car is increased, the rails must be adjusted accordingly. For passengers, the interface to the streetcar is the door. If the door of the street car is higher, the passengers need a higher platform to enter the street car. For the signaling system, the interface is the driver who monitors the traffic signals. If a new signaling system is introduced, the driver needs to be retrained. If any attribute of these interfaces changes (e.g., distance between the wheels, height of the door, signaling equipment), the street car cannot provide its services until the interfacing system is adapted. The same applies to software development: objects interact with other objects through interfaces that include a set of operations, each accepting a set of parameters and producing a result, and a set of assumptions about the behavior of each operation. If the operations or the assumptions change, the object cannot accomplish its work and provide the advertised services. In this chapter, we discuss the object design activities related to interface specification.

Section 9.2 provides an overview of interface specification. Section 9.3 defines the main interface specification concepts, including type signatures, constraints, and contracts, and provide an introduction into UML's Object Constraint Language. Section 9.4 describes in more detail the activities of interface specification using the ARENA system as an example. Section 9.5 discusses management issues related to interface specification, and object design in general, including documenting object interfaces and assigning responsibilities.

9.2 An Overview of Interface Specification

At this point in system development, we have made many decisions about the system and produced a wealth of models:

- The *analysis object model* describes the entity, boundary, and control objects that are visible to the user. The analysis object model includes attributes and operations for each object.

- *Subsystem decomposition* describes how these objects are partitioned into cohesive pieces that are realized by different teams of developers. Each subsystem includes high-level service descriptions that indicate which functionality it provides to the others.

- *Hardware/software mapping* identifies the components that make up the virtual machine on which we build solution objects. This may include classes and APIs defined by existing components.

- *Boundary use cases* describe, from the user's point of view, administrative and exceptional cases that the system handles.

- *Design patterns* selected during object design reuse describe partial object design models addressing specific design issues.

All these models, however, reflect only a partial view of the system. Many puzzle pieces are still missing and many others are yet to be refined. The goal of object design is to produce an object design model that integrates all of the above information into a coherent and precise whole. The goal of interface specification, the focus of this chapter, is to describe the interface of each object precisely enough so that objects realized by individual developers fit together with minimal integration issues. To this end, interface specification includes the following activities:

- *Identify missing attributes and operations.* During this activity, we examine each subsystem service and each analysis object. We identify missing operations and attributes that are needed to realize the subsystem service. We refine the current object design model and augment it with these operations.

- *Specify visibility and signatures.* During this activity, we decide which operations are available to other objects and subsystems, and which are used only within a subsystem. We also specify the return type of each operation as well as the number and type of its parameters. This goal of this activity is to reduce coupling among subsystems and provide a small and simple interface that can be understood easily by a single developer.

- *Specify contracts.* During this activity, we describe in terms of constraints the behavior of the operations provided by each object. In particular, for each operation, we describe the conditions that must be met before the operation is invoked and a specification of the result after the operation returns.

The large number of objects and developers, the high rate of change, and the concurrent number of decisions made during object design make object design much more complex than analysis or system design. This represents a management challenge, as many important decisions tend to be resolved independently and are not communicated to the rest of the project. Object design requires much information to be made available among the developers so that decisions can be made consistent with decisions made by other developers and consistent with design goals. The Object Design Document, a live document describing the specification of each class, supports this information exchange.

9.3 Interface Specification Concepts

In this section, we present the principal concepts of interface specification:

- Class Implementor, Class Extender, and Class User (Section 9.3.1)
- Types, Signatures, and Visibility (Section 9.3.2)
- Contracts: Invariants, Preconditions, and Postconditions (Section 9.3.3)
- Object Constraint Language (Section 9.3.4)
- OCL Collections: Sets, Bags, and Sequences (Section 9.3.5)
- OCL Qualifiers: forAll and exists (Section 9.3.6).

9.3.1 Class Implementor, Class Extender, and Class User

So far, we have treated all developers as equal. Now that we are delving into the details of object design and implementation, we need to differentiate developers based on their point of view. While all use the interface specification to communicate about the class of interest, they view the specifications from radically different point of views (see also Figure 9-1):

- The **class implementor** is responsible for realizing the class under consideration. Class implementors design the internal data structures and implement the code for each public operation. For them, the interface specification is a work assignment.

- The **class user** invokes the operations provided by the class under consideration during the realization of another class, called the **client class**. For class users, the interface specification discloses the boundary of the class in terms of the services it provides and the assumptions it makes about the client class.

- The **class extender** develops specializations of the class under consideration. Like class implementors, class extenders may invoke operations provided by the class of interest, the class extenders focus on specialized versions of the same services. For them, the interface specification both a specifies the current behavior of the class and any constraints on the services provided by the specialized class.

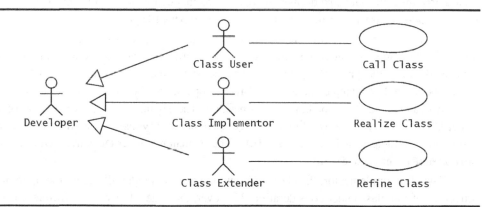

Figure 9-1 The Class Implementor, the Class Extender, and the Class User role (UML use case diagram).

For example, consider the ARENA Game abstract class (Figure 9-2). The developer responsible for realizing the Game class, including operations that apply to all Games, is a class implementor. The League and Tournament classes invoke operations provided by the Game interface to organize and start Matches. Developers responsible for League and Tournament are class users of Game. The TicTacToe and Chess classes are concrete Games that provide specialized extensions to the Game class. Developers responsible for those classes are class extenders of Game.

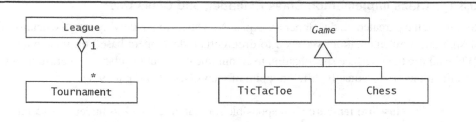

Figure 9-2   ARENA *Game* abstract class with user classes and extender classes.

9.3.2   Types, Signatures, and Visibility

During analysis, we identified attributes and operations without necessarily specifying their types or their parameters. During object design, we refine the analysis and system design models by completing type and visibility information. The **type** of an attribute specifies the range of values the attribute can take and the operations that can be applied to the attribute. For example, consider the attribute maxNumPlayers of the Tournament class in ARENA (Figure 9-3). maxNumPlayers represent the maximum number of Players who can be accepted in a given Tournament. Its type is int, denoting that it is an integer number. The type of the maxNumPlayers attribute also defines the operations that can be applied to this attribute: we can compare, add, subtract, or multiply other integers to maxNumPlayers.

Operation parameters and return values are typed in the same way as attributes are. The type constrains the range of values the parameter or the return value can take. Given an operation, the tuple made out of the types of its parameters and the type of the return value is called the **signature** of the operation. For example, the acceptPlayer() operation of Tournament takes one parameter of type Player and does not have a return value. The signature for acceptPlayer() is then acceptPlayer(Player):void. Similarly, the getMaxNumPlayers() operation of Tournament takes no parameters and returns an int. The signature of getMaxNumPlayers() is then getMaxNumPlayers(void):int.

The class implementor, the class user, and the class extender all access the operations and attributes of the class under consideration. However, these developers have different needs and are usually not allowed to access all operations of the class. For example, a class implementor accesses the internal data structures of the class that the class user cannot see. The class extender accesses only selected internal structures of superclasses. The **visibility** of an attribute or an operation is a mechanism for specifying whether the attribute or operation can be used by other classes or not. UML defines four levels of visibility:

- A *private attribute* can be accessed only by the class in which it is defined. Similarly, a *private operation* can be invoked only by the class in which it is defined. Private attributes and operations cannot be accessed by subclasses or calling classes. Private operations and attributes are intended for the class implementor only.

- A *protected attribute or operation* can be accessed by the class in which it is defined and by any descendant of that class. Protected operations and attributes cannot be accessed by any other class. Protected operations and attributes are intended for the class extender.

- A *public attribute or operation* can be accessed by any class. The set of public operations and attributes constitute the public interface of the class and is intended for the class user.

- An attribute or an operation with visibility *package* can be accessed by any class in the nearest enclosing package. This visibility enables a set of related classes (for example, forming a subsystem) to share a set of attributes or operations without having to make them public to the entire system.

Visibility is denoted in UML by prefixing the name of the attribute or the operation with a character symbol: – for private, # for protected, + for public, or ~ for package. For example, in Figure 9-3, we specify that the maxNumPlayers attribute of Tournament is private, whereas all the class operations are public.

```
                    ┌─────────────────────────────────────────┐
                    │              Tournament                   │
                    ├─────────────────────────────────────────┤
                    │ -maxNumPlayers:int                        │
                    ├─────────────────────────────────────────┤
                    │ +getMaxNumPlayers():int                   │
                    │ +getPlayers():List                        │
                    │ +acceptPlayer(p:Player)                   │
                    │ +removePlayer(p:Player)                   │
                    │ +isPlayerAccepted(p:Player):boolean       │
                    └─────────────────────────────────────────┘
```

```java
public class Tournament {
    private int maxNumPlayers;
    /* Other fields omitted */

    public Tournament(League l, int maxNumPlayers)
    public int getMaxNumPlayers() {…};
    public List getPlayers() {…};
    public void acceptPlayer(Player p) {…};
    public void removePlayer(Player p) {…};
    public boolean isPlayerAccepted(Player p) {…};

    /* Other methods omitted */
}
```

Figure 9-3   Declaration for the Tournament class (UML class model and Java excerpts).

Type information alone is often not sufficient to specify the range of legitimate values of an attribute. In the Tournament example, the int type allows maxNumPlayers to take negative values, which does not make sense in the application domain. We address this issue with contracts.

9.3.3   Contracts: Invariants, Preconditions, and Postconditions

Contracts are constraints on a class that enable class users, implementors, and extenders to share the same assumptions about the class [Meyer, 1997]. A contract specifies constraints that the class user must meet before using the class as well as constraints that are ensured by the class implementor and the class extender when used. Contracts include three types of constraints:

- An **invariant** is a predicate that is always true for all instances of a class. Invariants are constraints associated with classes or interfaces. Invariants are used to specify consistency constraints among class attributes.

- A **precondition** is a predicate that must be true before an operation is invoked. Preconditions are associated with a specific operation. Preconditions are used to specify constraints that a class user must meet before calling the operation.

- A **postcondition** is a predicate that must be true after an operation is invoked. Postconditions are associated with a specific operation. Postconditions are used to specify constraints that the class implementor and the class extender must ensure after the invocation of the operation.

For example, consider the Java interface for the Tournament from Figure 9-3. This class provides an acceptPlayer() method to add a Player in the Tournament, a removePlayer() method to withdraw a Player from the Tournament (e.g., because the player cancelled his application), and a getMaxNumPlayers() method to get the maximum number of Players who can participate in this Tournament.

An example of an invariant for the Tournament class is that the maximum number of Players in the Tournament should be positive. If a Tournament is created with a maxNumPlayers that is zero, the acceptPlayer() method will always violate its contract and the Tournament will never start. Using a boolean expression, in which t is a Tournament, we can express this invariant as

```
t.getMaxNumPlayers() > 0
```

An example of a precondition for the acceptPlayer() method is that the Player to be added has not yet already been accepted in the Tournament and that the Tournament has not yet reached its maximum number of Players. Using a boolean expression, in which t is a Tournament and p is a Player, we express this invariant as

```
!t.isPlayerAccepted(p) and t.getNumPlayers() < t.getMaxNumPlayers()
```

An example of a postcondition for the acceptPlayer() method is that the current number of Players must be exactly one more than the number of Players before the invocation of acceptPlayer(). We can express this postcondition as

```
t.getNumPlayers_afterAccept = t.getNumPlayers_beforeAccept + 1
```

where numPlayers_afterAccept and numPlayers_afterAccept are the current and number of Players before and after acceptPlayer(), respectively.

We use invariants, preconditions, and postconditions to specify special or exceptional cases unambiguously. It is also possible to use constraints to completely specify the behavior of an operation. Such a use of constraints, called "constraint-based specification," however, is difficult and can be more complicated than implementing the operation itself. In this book, we do not describe pure constraint-based specifications. Instead, we focus on specifying operations using both constraints and natural language and emphasizing boundary cases for the purpose of better communication among developers.

9.3.4   Object Constraint Language

A constraint can be expressed in natural language or in a formal language such as **Object Constraint Language (OCL)** [OMG, 2006]. OCL is a language that allows constraints to be formally specified on single model elements (e.g., attributes, operations, classes) or groups of model elements (e.g., associations and participating classes). In the next two sections, we introduce the basic syntax of OCL. For a complete tutorial on OCL, we refer to [Warmer & Kleppe, 2003].

A constraint is expressed as a boolean expression returning the value True or False. A constraint can be depicted as a note attached to the constrained UML element by a dependency relationship. Figure 9-4 depicts a class diagram of Tournament example of the previous section using UML and OCL.

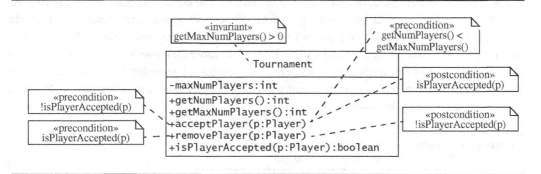

Figure 9-4   Examples of invariants, preconditions, and postconditions in OCL attached as notes to the UML model (UML class diagram).

Attaching OCL expressions to diagrams can lead to clutter. For this reason, OCL expressions can be alternatively expressed in a textual form. For example, the invariant for the Tournament class requiring the attribute maxNumPlayers to be positive is written as follows:

```
context Tournament inv:
    self.getMaxNumPlayers() > 0
```

The context keyword indicates the entity to which the expression applies. This is followed by one of the keywords inv, pre, and post, which correspond to the UML stereotypes «invariant», «precondition», and «postcondition», respectively. Then follows the actual OCL expression. OCL's syntax is similar to object-oriented languages such as C++ or Java. However, OCL is not a procedural language and thus cannot be used to denote control flow. Operations can be used in OCL expressions only if they do not have any side effects.

For invariants, the context for the expression is the class associated with the invariant. The keyword self (e.g., self.numElements) denotes all instances of the class.[1] Attributes and operations are accessed using the dot notation (e.g., self.maxNumPlayers accesses maxNumPlayers in the current context). The self keyword can be omitted if there is no ambiguity.

For preconditions and postconditions, the context of the OCL expression is an operation. The parameters passed to the operation can be used as variables in the expression. For example, consider the following precondition on the acceptPlayer() operation in Tournament:

```
context Tournament::acceptPlayer(p:Player) pre:
    !isPlayerAccepted(p)
```

The variable p in the constraint !isPlayerAccepted(p) refers to the parameter p passed to the acceptPlayer(p) operation. As this is a precondition, the constraint must be True before the execution of the acceptPlayer(p) operation. Hence, the constraint reads in English: "acceptPlayer(p) assumes that p has not yet been accepted in the Tournament". We can write several preconditions for the same operation. If there are more than one precondition for a given operation, all preconditions must be True before the operation can be invoked. For example, we can also state that the Tournament must not yet have reached the maximum number of Players before invoking acceptPlayer():

```
context Tournament::acceptPlayer(p:Player) pre:
    getNumPlayers() < getMaxNumPlayers()
```

---

1. Note that OCL uses the keyword self to represent the same concept as the Java and C++ keyword this.

Post conditions are written in the same way as preconditions, except for the keyword post indicating that the constraint is evaluated after the operation returns. For example, the following postcondition on acceptPlayer(p) states that the Player p should be known to the Tournament after acceptPlayer() returns:

```
context Tournament::acceptPlayer(p:Player) post:
    isPlayerAccepted(p)
```

For postconditions, we often need to refer to the value of an attribute before and after the execution of the operation. For this purpose, the suffix @pre denotes the value of self or an attribute before the execution of the operation. For example, if we want to state that the number of Players in the Tournament increases by one with the invocation of acceptPlayer(), we need to refer to the value of getNumPlayers() before and after the invocation of acceptPlayer(). We can write the following postcondition:

```
context Tournament::acceptPlayer(p:Player) post:
    getNumPlayers() = self@pre.getNumPlayers() + 1
```

@pre.getNumPlayers() denotes the value returned by getNumPlayers() before invoking acceptPlayer(), and getNumPlayers() denotes the value returned by the same operation after invoking acceptPlayer(). Similar to preconditions, if there is more than one postcondition for a given operation, all postconditions must be satisfied after the operation completes.

We can therefore write the contract for the removePlayer() operation with the same approach:

```
context Tournament::removePlayer(p:Player) pre:
    isPlayerAccepted(p)

context Tournament::removePlayer(p:Player) post:
    !isPlayerAccepted(p)

context Tournament::removePlayer(p:Player) post:
    getNumPlayers() = self@pre.getNumPlayers() - 1
```

The creators and users of OCL constraints are developers during object design and during implementation. In Java programs, tools such as iContract [Kramer, 1998] enable developers to document constraints in the source code using Javadoc style tags, so that constraints are more readily accessed and updated. Figure 9-5 depicts the Java code corresponding to the constraints introduced so far.

```java
/** A Tournament is a series of Matches among a set of Players
 * which ends with a single winner. The Game and TournamentStyle of a
 * Tournament is determined by the League in which the Tournament is
 * played.
 */
public class Tournament {

    /** The maximum number of players is positive at all times.
     * @invariant maxNumPlayers > 0
     */
    private int maxNumPlayers;

    /** The players List contains references to Players who are
     *  are registered with the Tournament.
     */
    private List players;

    /* Constructors omitted */

    /** Returns the current number of players in the tournament.
     */
    public int getNumPlayers() {…}

    /** Returns the maximum number of players in the tournament.
     */
    public int getMaxNumPlayers() {…}

    /** The acceptPlayer() operation assumes that the specified player
     * has not been accepted in the Tournament yet.
     * @pre !isPlayerAccepted(p)
     * @pre getNumPlayers() < maxNumPlayers
     * @post isPlayerAccepted(p)
     * @post getNumPlayers() = self@pre.getNumPlayers() + 1
     */
    public void acceptPlayer (Player p) {…}

    /** The removePlayer() operation assumes that the specified player
     * is currently in the Tournament.
     * @pre isPlayerAccepted(p)
     * @post !isPlayerAccepted(p)
     * @post getNumPlayers() = self@pre.getNumPlayers() - 1
     */
    public void removePlayer(Player p) {…}

    /* Other methods omitted */
}
```

Figure 9-5   Method declarations for the Tournament class annotated with preconditions, postconditions, and invariants (Java, constraints using Javadoc style tags).

9.3.5   OCL Collections: Sets, Bags, and Sequences

In general, constraints involve an arbitrary number of classes and attributes. Consider the class model of Figure 9-6 representing the associations among the League, Tournament, and Player classes. Let's assume we want to refine the model with the following constraints:

1. A Tournament's planned duration must be under one week.
2. Players can be accepted in a Tournament only if they are already registered with the corresponding League.
3. The number of active Players in a League are those that have taken part in at least one Tournament of the League.

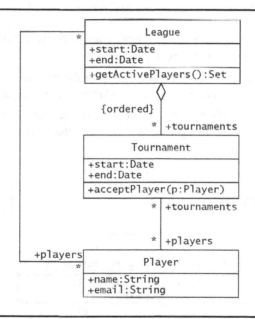

Figure 9-6   Associations among League, Tournament, and Player classes in ARENA.

To better understand these constraints, let's examine them for a specific group of instances (see Figure 9-7). The tttExpert:League includes four Players, alice, bob, marc, and joe, and two Tournaments, a winter:Tournament and a xmas:Tournament. alice and bob are competing in the winter:Tournament while bob, marc, and joe are competing in the xmas:Tournament. The chessNovice:League currently only includes one Player, zoe, and no Tournaments. Now, let's review the above constraints in terms of the instances of Figure 9-7:

1. The winter:Tournament lasts two days, the xmas:Tournament three days, both under a week.

2. All Players of the winter:Tournament and the xmas:Tournament are associated with tttExpert:League. The Player zoe, however, is not part of the tttExpert:League and does not take part in either Tournament.

3. tttExpert:League has four active Players, whereas the chessNovice:League has none, because zoe does not take part in any Tournament.

At first sight, these constraints vary quite a bit: for example, the first constraint involves attributes of a single class (Tournament.start and Tournament.end); the second one involves three classes (i.e., Player, Tournament, League) and their associations; the third involves a set of Matches within a single Tournament. In all cases, we start with the class of interest and navigate to one or more classes in the model.

In general, we distinguish three cases of navigation (Figure 9-8):

• *Local attribute.* The constraint involves an attribute that is *local* to the class of interest (e.g., duration of a Tournament in constraint 1),

• *Directly related class.* The expression involves the navigation of a single association to a directly related class (e.g., Players of a Tournament, League of a Tournament).

• *Indirectly related class.* The constraint involves the navigation of a series of associations to an indirectly related class (e.g., the Players of all Tournaments of a League).

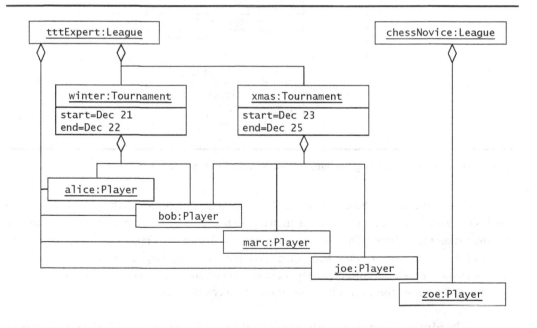

Figure 9-7   Example with two Leagues, two Tournaments, and five Players (UML object diagram).

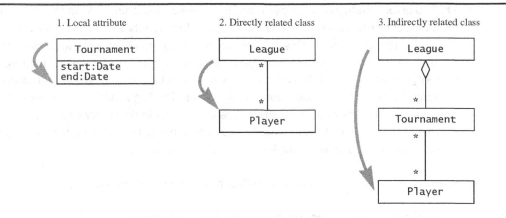

Figure 9-8   There are only three basic types of navigation. Any OCL constraint can be built using a combination of these three types.

All constraints can be built using a combination of these three basic cases of navigation. Once we know how to deal with these three cases of navigation, we can build any constraint. We already know how to deal with the first type of constraint with the dot notation, as we saw in the previous section. For example, we can write constraint 1 as follows:

```
context Tournament inv:
    self.end - self.start <= 7
```

In the second constraint, however, the expression `league.players` can actually refer to many objects, since the `players` association is a many-to-many association. To deal with this situation, OCL provides additional data types called **collections**. There are three types of collections:

- **OCL sets** are used when navigating a single association. For example, navigating the `players` association of the `winter:Tournament` yields the set {`alice`, `bob`}. Navigating the `players` association from the `tttExpert:League` yields the set {`alice`, `bob`, `marc`, `joe`}. Note, however, that navigating an association of multiplicity 1 yields directly an object, not a set. For example, navigating the `league` association from `winter:Tournament` yields `tttExpert:League` (as opposed to {`tttExpert:League`}).

- **OCL sequences** are used when navigating a single ordered association. For example, the association between `League` and `Tournament` is ordered. Hence, navigating the `tournaments` association from `tttExpert:League` yields [`winter:Tournament`, `xmas:Tournament`] with the index of `winter:Tournament` and `xmas:Tournament` being 1 and 2, respectively.

- **OCL bags** are multisets: they can contain the same object multiple times. Bags are used to accumulate the objects when accessing indirectly related objects. For example, when determining which `Players` are active in the `tttExpert:League`, we first navigate the `tournaments` association of `tttExpert`, then the `players` association from `winter:Tournament`, and finally the `players` association from `xmas:Tournament`, yielding the bag `{alice, bob, bob, marc, joe}`. The bag resulting from navigating the same associations from `chessNovice:League` results in the empty bag, as there are no `Tournaments` in the `chessLeague`. In cases where the number of occurrences of each object in the bag is undesired, the bag can be converted to a set.

OCL provides many operations for accessing collections. The most often used are

- `size`, which returns the number of elements in the collection
- `includes(object)`, which returns `True` if `object` is in the collection
- `select(expression)`, which returns a collection that contains only the elements of the original collection for which expression is `True`
- `union(collection)`, which returns a collection containing elements from both the original collection and the collection specified as parameter
- `intersection(collection)`, which returns a collection that contains only the elements that are part of both the original collection and the collection specified as parameter
- `asSet(collection)`, which returns a set containing each element of the collection.

To distinguish between attributes in classes from collections, OCL uses the dot notation for accessing attributes and the -> operator for accessing collections. For example, constraint 2 (on page 361) can be expressed with an `includes` operation as follows:

```
context Tournament::acceptPlayer(p:Player) pre:
    league.players->includes(p)
```

The context is the operation `acceptPlayer()` in the `Tournament` class. To get to the `Players` class, we need to navigate first via the association between `Tournament` and `League`, and then via the association between `League` and `Player`. We refer to the `league` class by using the role name attached to the association, or if no name is available, we use the name of the related class with the first letter in lowercase. The next association we navigate is the `players` association on the `League`, which results in a set because of the "many" multiplicity of the association. We use the OCL `includes()` operation on this set to test if the `Player` p is known to the `League`.

Navigating a series of at least two associations with one-to-many or many-to-many multiplicity results in a bag. For example, in the context of a `League`, the expression `tournaments.players` contains the concatenation of all `players` of the `Tournaments` related to the current League. As a result of this concatenation, elements can appear several times. To remove the duplicates in this bag, for example, when counting the number of Players in a League that have taken part in a Tournament, we can convert the bag into a set using the OCL asSet operation. Consequently, we can write constraint 3 (on page 361) as follows:

```
context League::getActivePlayers:Set post:
    result = tournaments.players->asSet()
```

9.3.6   OCL Quantifiers: forAll and exists

So far, we presented examples of constraints using common OCL collection operations such as includes, union, or asSet. Two additional operations on collections enable us to iterate over collections and test expressions on each element:

- forAll(variable|expression) is True if expression is True for all elements in the collection.
- exists(variable|expression) is True if there exists at least one element in the collection for which expression is True.

For example, to ensure that all Matches in a Tournament occur within the Tournament's time frame, we can repetitively test the start dates of all matches against the Tournament using forAll(). Consequently, we write this constraint as follows:

```
context Tournament inv:
    matches->forAll(m:Match | m.start.after(start) and m.end.before(end))
```

The OCL exists() operation is similar to forAll(), except that the expressions evaluated on each element are ORed, that is, only one element needs to satisfy the expression for the exists() operation to return True. For example, to ensure that each Tournament conducts at least one Match on the first day of the Tournament, we can write:

```
context Tournament inv:
    matches->exists(m:Match | m.start.equals(start))
```

9.4   Interface Specification Activities

Interface specification includes the following activities:

- Identifying Missing Attributes and Operations (Section 9.4.1)
- Specifying Type Signatures and Visibility (Section 9.4.2)
- Specifying Preconditions and Postconditions (Section 9.4.3)
- Specifying Invariants (Section 9.4.4)

- Inheriting Contracts (Section 9.4.5).

To illustrate these activities, we use the ARENA object design model resulting from the AnnounceTournament use case (Section 5.6). During analysis, we identified several boundary, control, and entity classes: The TournamentForm class is responsible for generating and processing all user interface forms, and the TournamentControl class is responsible for coordinating all transactions between the TournamentForm and the entity classes Tournament, Player, and Match. Figure 9-9 depicts the attributes, operations, and associations among these classes that have been identified during analysis. First, we resolve any remaining requirements issues and identify missing attributes and operations.

9.4.1 Identifying Missing Attributes and Operations

During this step, we examine the service description of the subsystem and identify missing attributes and operations. During analysis, we may have missed many attributes because we

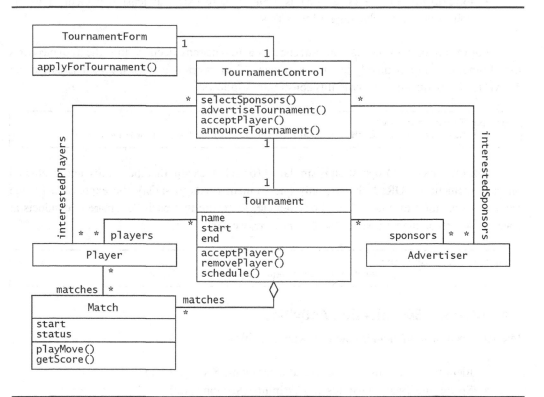

Figure 9-9 Analysis objects of ARENA identified during the analysis of AnnounceTournament use case (UML class diagram). Only selected information is shown for brevity.

focused on the functionality of the system: we described the functionality of the system primarily with the use case model (as opposed to operations in the object model). We focused on the application domain when constructing the object model and therefore ignored details related to the system that are independent of the application domain.

During the object design of ARENA, we soon realize that the number of concurrent tournaments and matches is the main consumer of server resources and constitutes a bottleneck. Consequently, we focus on possible misuse of the system in which players attempt to play several matches concurrently. When reviewing these issues with the client, we agree that such player behavior does not improve advertising income (i.e., advertisement banners sent simultaneously to the same client machine do not increase advertisement fees) nor match playing quality (i.e., a player involved in concurrent matches is distracted and makes mistakes). Hence, we decide to add checks during the ApplyForTournament use case to prevent such situations. However, we do not want to penalize players who play many tournaments sequentially, as we anticipate that such return players improve both match playing quality and advertisement revenue.

To prevent a player from applying to two different tournaments that will be conducted at the same time, we draw a sequence diagram representing the control and data flow needed (Figure 9-10). Drawing this diagram leads us to the identification of an additional operation, isPlayerOverbooked(), that checks if the start and end dates of the Tournament of interest overlap with those of other Tournaments into which the Player has already been accepted.

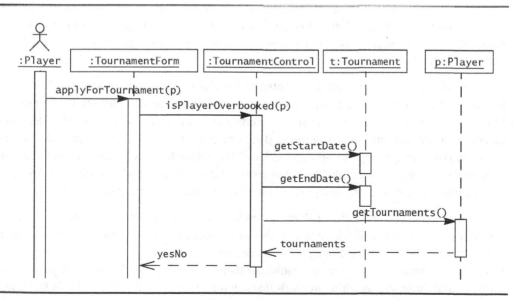

Figure 9-10 A sequence diagram for the applyForTournament() operation (UML sequence diagram). This sequence diagram leads to the identification of a new operation, isPlayerOverbooked() to ensure that players are not assigned to Tournaments that take place simultaneously.

Since isPlayerOverbooked() enforces a policy that we recently identified with the organizing of Tournaments, we attach this operation with the TournamentControl class, as opposed to the Player class or the Tournament class. This results in an entity object model that is simpler and modifiable. For example, other definitions of player commitments (e.g., a player can only play one tournament per week) or policies involving other objects (e.g., matches involving young players must occur before a certain time of the day) can be added or substituted in the TournamentControl class without changes to the entity classes.

At this point, we have identified an additional operation related to the ApplyForTournament use case. Note that the object design model will still be subject to change, as we review other subsystems and use cases. Next, we specify the interface of each of the classes using types, signatures, visibility, and contracts.

9.4.2   Specifying Types, Signatures, and Visibility

During this step, we specify the types of the attributes, the signatures of the operations, and the visibility of attributes and operations. Specifying types refines the object design model in two ways. First, we add detail to the model by specifying the range of each attribute. For example, by determining the type of the start and end date of a Tournament, we make decisions about the granularity of the time tracked by the application. By selecting a representation of time including days, hours, minutes, and seconds, we enable LeagueOwners to conduct several Tournaments per day. Second, we map classes and attributes of the object model to built-in types provided by the development environment. For example, by selecting String to represent the name attributes of Leagues and Tournaments, we can use all the operations provided by the String class to manipulate name values.

We also consider the relationship between the classes we identified and the classes from existing components. For example, a number of classes implementing collections are provided in the java.util package. The List interface provides a way to access an ordered collection of objects independent from the underlying data structure. The Map interface provides a table mapping from unique keys to arbitrary entries. We select the List interface for returning collections of objects, such as the Tournaments to which a Player has been accepted. We select the Map interface for returning mappings of objects, for example, Player to Scores.

Finally, we determine the visibility of each attribute and operation during this step. By doing so, we determine which attributes should be accessible only indirectly via the class's operations, and which attributes are public and can be modified by any other class. Similarly, the visibility of operations allows us to distinguish between operations that are part of the class interface and those that are utility methods that can only be accessed by the class. In the case of abstract classes and classes that are intended to be refined, we also define protected attributes and methods for the use of subclasses only. Figure 9-11 depicts the refinement of the object model depicted in Figure 9-9 after types, signatures, and visibility have been assigned.

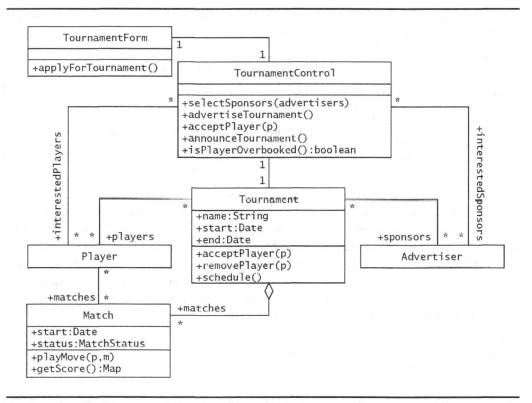

Figure 9-11 Adding type information to the object model of ARENA (UML class diagram). Only selected information is shown for brevity.

Once we have specified the types of each attribute, the signature of each operation, and its visibility, we focus on specifying the behavior and boundary cases of each class by using contracts.

9.4.3 Specifying Pre- and Postconditions

During this step, we define contracts for each public operation of each class. We already said that a contract is an agreement between the class user and the class implementor. The preconditions of an operation describe the part of the contract that the class user must respect. The postconditions describe what the class implementor guarantees in the event the class user fulfilled her part of the contract. When refining a class, class extenders inherit the contract from the original class implementor.

For example, in Section 9.4.1, we identified the operation isPlayerOverbooked() on the TournamentControl class, which checks if a Player's existing commitments would prevent him from taking part in the current Tournament. As a class implementor, we want to make sure that the class user checks Players that have not yet been accepted into the Tournament. If this is the case, we only need to check if the current Tournament overlaps any that the Player is already taking part in. We express this with the following contract:

```
/* isPlayerOverbooked assumes that the Player is not yet part of the
 * Tournament of interest. */
context TournamentControl::isPlayerOverbooked(p) pre:
    not p.tournaments->includes(self.tournament)

/* A player cannot take part in two tournaments whose dates overlap. */
context TournamentControl::isPlayerOverbooked(p) post:
    result = p.tournaments->exists(t| t.overlaps(self.tournament))
```

Preconditions and postconditions can also be used to specify dependencies among operations in the same class. Consider, for example, the operations on the TournamentControl class. Given a new Tournament, these operations must be invoked in a specific order. We cannot resolve the sponsorship of a Tournament without knowing which sponsors are interested. Also, we cannot advertise the Tournament before we resolve the sponsorship issue. For TournamentControl, we can simply write preconditions and postconditions that examine the state of the associations of the Tournament class. To state that sponsors cannot be selected before there are interested advertisers, we write the following:

```
context TournamentControl::selectSponsors(advertisers) pre:
    interestedSponsors->notEmpty()
```

To ensure that TournamentControl.selectSponsors() is invoked only once, we add the following precondition:

```
context TournamentControl::selectSponsors(advertisers) pre:
    tournament.sponsors->isEmpty()
```

Finally, to specify how TournamentControl.selectSponsors() sets the advertisers association, we add the following postcondition:

```
context TournamentControl::selectSponsors(advertisers) post:
    tournament.sponsors.equals(advertisers)
```

Below is the complete set of OCL constraints specifying the order of selectSponsors(), advertiseTournament(), and acceptPlayer().

```
                    ┌─────────────────────────────────────┐
                    │         TournamentControl           │
                    ├─────────────────────────────────────┤
                    ├─────────────────────────────────────┤
                    │ +selectSponsors(advertisers)        │
                    │ +advertiseTournament()              │
                    │ +acceptPlayer(p)                    │
                    │ +announceTournament()               │
                    │ +isPlayerOverbooked():boolean       │
                    └─────────────────────────────────────┘

/* Pre-and postconditions for ordering operations on TournamentControl */
context TournamentControl::selectSponsors(advertisers) pre:
    interestedSponsors->notEmpty() and
        tournament.sponsors->isEmpty()
context TournamentControl::selectSponsors(advertisers) post:
    tournament.sponsors.equals(advertisers)

context TournamentControl::advertiseTournament() pre:
    tournament.sponsors->isEmpty() and
        not tournament.advertised
context TournamentControl::advertiseTournament() post:
    tournament.advertised

context TournamentControl::acceptPlayer(p) pre:
    tournament.advertised and
        interestedPlayers->includes(p) and
            not isPlayerOverbooked(p)
context TournamentControl::acceptPlayer(p) post:
    tournament.players->includes(p)
```

9.4.4 Specifying Invariants

Once you master the syntax and the concepts behind a constraint language such as OCL, writing contracts for individual operations is relatively simple. The concept of a contract between the class user and the class implementor is intuitive (e.g., "this is what I can do if you ensure these conditions") and focuses on a relatively short increment in time (i.e., the execution of a single operation). However, grasping the essence of a class from operation-specific contracts is difficult; much information is distributed throughout many constraints in many operations, so identifying general properties of the class is difficult. Hence, the need for invariants.

Invariants are much more difficult to write than preconditions and postconditions, but they provide an overview of the essential properties of the class. Invariants constitute a permanent contract that extends and overwrites the operation-specific contracts. The activity of identifying invariants is similar to that of finding abstract classes during analysis (Section 5.4.10). A few are obvious and can be written from the start. Others can be identified by extracting common properties from operation-specific contracts.

An example of an obvious invariant is that all `Matches` of a `Tournament` must occur within the time frame of the `Tournament`:

```
context Tournament inv:
    matches->forAll(m|
        m.start.after(start) and m.start.before(end))
```

An example of an invariant that is not so obvious, but can be identified by examining the contracts of the `TournamentControl` class, is that no `Player` can take part in two or more Tournaments that overlap. Although this property can be inferred by examining `TournamentControl.isPlayerOverbooked()` operation, we can write this concisely as an invariant. Since it is a policy decision, we attach this invariant to the `TournamentControl` class, as opposed to the `Player` or the `Tournament` class.

```
context TournamentControl inv:
    tournament.players->forAll(p|
        p.tournaments->forAll(t|
            t <> tournament implies not t.overlap(tournament)))
```

When specified on several associations, constraints usually become complex and difficult to understand, especially when nested `forAll` statements are used. For example, consider an invariant stating that all `Matches` in a `Tournament` must involve only `Players` that are accepted in the Tournament:

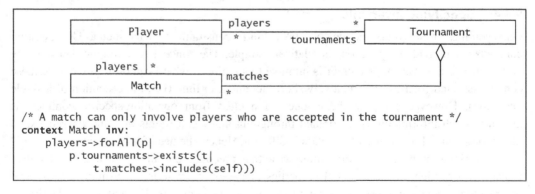

```
/* A match can only involve players who are accepted in the tournament */
context Match inv:
    players->forAll(p|
        p.tournaments->exists(t|
            t.matches->includes(self)))
```

This constraint involves three collections: `players`, `p.tournaments`, and `t.matches`. We can simplify this expression by using a bag created while navigating a series of associations:

```
context Match inv:
    players.tournaments.matches.includes(self)
```

In general, reducing the number of operations and nesting levels in a constraint makes it much more understandable.

As illustrated by these examples, it is relatively easy to generate a large number of constraints for each class. This does not guarantee readability. In fact, writing readable and correct constraints is difficult. Remember that the reason for writing invariants is to clarify the assumptions made by the class implementor to the class user. Consequently, when writing constraints, the class implementor should focus on simple, short constraints that describe boundary cases that may not otherwise be obvious. Figure 9-12 lists several heuristics to make constraints more readable.

Heuristics for writing readable constraints

Focus on the lifetime of a class. Constraints that are specific to operations or that hold only when the object is in certain states are better expressed as pre- and postconditions. For example:

- "Different players have different E-mail addresses" is an invariant.
- "A player can apply to only one tournament at a time" is a precondition of the
  `TournamentForm.applyForTournament()` operation.

Identify special values for each attribute. Zero and null values, attributes that have unique values within a certain scope, and attributes that depend on other attributes are often sources of misunderstandings and errors. For example:

- Matches involve at least one player.
- Completed matches have exactly one winner.

Identify special cases for associations. Identify, in particular, any special case that cannot be specified with multiplicity alone. For example:

- `tournament.players` is a subset of `tournament.league.players`

Identify ordering among operations. For example, see `TournamentControl` in Section 9.4.3.

Use helper methods to compute complex conditions. This yields shorter and more understandable constraints and code that can be more easily tested. For example:

- `Tournament.overlaps(t:Tournament)` to check if two tournament overlap in time.

Avoid constraints that involve many association traversals. This often increases the coupling among sets of unrelated classes, which is not desirable. For example:

- When specifying that the duration of a match should be under a maximum limit set by the game, we could be tempted to write `match.tournament.league.game.maxMatchDuration`. Instead, consider adding a `Match.getGame()` method, which would simplify the expression to `match.getGame().maxMatchDuration`.

Figure 9-12 Heuristics for writing readable constraints.

Invariants, preconditions, and postconditions specify the semantics of each operation by making explicit what must be true before and after an operation is executed. Hence, contracts provide clear documentation to the user. As we see in the next section, contracts are also useful for the class extender.

9.4.5   Inheriting Contracts

In a polymorphic language, a class can be substituted by any of its descendents. That is, a class user invoking operations on a class could be invoking instead a subclass. Hence, the class user expects that a contract that holds for the superclass still holds for the subclass. We call this **contract inheritance**.

For example, in ARENA, consider the inheritance hierarchy between User, LeagueOwner, Player, Spectator, and Advertiser (Figure 9-13). The User class has an invariant stating that the email address should be not null so that each user can be notified. If at some point in our design, we decide that Spectators do not really need an E-mail address, then this contract will be broken and classes invoking the User.notify() method may break. Consequently, either Spectators should be taken out of the User hierarchy (i.e., Spectator does not fulfill the User contract) or the invariant should be revised (i.e., the terms of the contract should be reformulated).

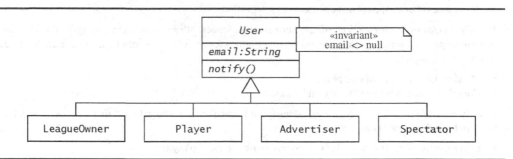

Figure 9-13   A simple example of contract inheritance: An invariant specified in a superclass must hold for all of its subclasses (UML class diagram with OCL constraint).

Contracts are inherited in the following manner:

- *Preconditions*. A method of subclass is allowed to weaken the preconditions of the method it overrides. In other words, an overwritten method can handle more cases than its superclass. For example, consider a concrete *TournamentStyle* class, SimpleKnockOutStyle, that can deal with any number of Players that is a power of 2. We can express this with a precondition on the planMatches() operation that restricts the number of Players to a power of 2. A ComplexKnockOutStyle class refining the SimpleKnockOutStyle could weaken this precondition by planning Tournaments for any number of Players.

- *Postconditions*. Methods must ensure the same postconditions as their ancestors or stricter ones. Assume you are implementing a Set by inheriting from a List (this is a case of implementation inheritance and questionable practice, as we discussed in Section 8.3.2). The postcondition of List.add() is that the size of the List increases by one. The Set.add() method, in this case, could not comply with this invariant, since adding an element to a set does not necessarily increase the size of the set. Hence, Set should not be implemented as a subclass of List.

- *Invariants*. A subclass must respect all invariants of its superclasses. However, a subclass can strengthen the inherited invariants. For example, List inherits from Collection. Collection has an invariant specifying that its size cannot be negative. Consequently, List must respect this invariant and cannot have a negative size. However, List adds a new invariant that stipulates that its elements are ordered.

Contract inheritance is particularly useful when specifying abstract classes or interfaces that are meant to be refined by class extenders. By precisely documenting the boundary between the client class and an interface, it is possible for class extenders to implement new refined extender classes without being familiar with the invoking source code. Contract inheritance is also a consequence of Liskov's Substitution Principle (Section 8.3.4), since extender classes must be able to substitute transparently for an ancestor.

9.5 Managing Object Design

In this section, we discuss management issues related to object design. There are two primary management challenges during object design:

- *Increased communication complexity*. The number of participants involved during this phase of development increases dramatically. The object design models and code are the result of the collaboration of many people. Management needs to ensure that decisions among these developers are made consistently with project goals.

- *Consistency with prior decisions and documents*. Developers often do not appreciate completely the consequences of analysis and system design decisions before object design. When detailing and refining the object design model, developers may question some of these decisions and reevaluate them. The management challenge is to maintain a record of these revised decisions and to make sure all documents reflect the current state of development.

We discuss these challenges in Section 9.5.1, where we focus on the Object Design Document, its development and maintenance, and its relationship with other documents, and in Section 9.5.2, where we describe the roles and responsibilities associated with object design.

9.5.1 Documenting Object Design

Object design is documented in the **Object Design Document (ODD)**. It describes object design trade-offs made by developers, guidelines they followed for subsystem interfaces, the decomposition of subsystems into packages and classes, and the class interfaces. The ODD is used to exchange interface information among teams and as a reference during testing. The audience for the ODD includes system architects (i.e., the developers who participate in the system design), developers who implement each subsystem, and testers.

There are three main approaches to documenting object design:

- *Self-contained ODD generated from model.* The first approach is to document the object design model the same way we documented the analysis model or the system design model: we write and maintain a UML model and generate the document automatically. This document would duplicate any application objects identified during analysis. The disadvantages of this solution include redundancy with the Requirements Analysis Document (RAD) and a high level of effort for maintaining consistency with the RAD. Moreover, the ODD duplicates information in the source code and requires a high level of effort whenever the code changes. This often leads to an RAD and an ODD that are inaccurate or out of date.

- *ODD as extension of the RAD.* The second approach is to treat the object design model as an extension of the analysis model. In other terms, the object design is considered as the set of application objects augmented with solution objects. The advantage of this solution is that maintaining consistency between the RAD and the ODD becomes much easier as a result of the reduction in redundancy. The disadvantages of this solution include polluting the RAD with information that is irrelevant to the client and the user. Moreover, object design is rarely as simple as identifying additional solution objects. Often, application objects are changed or transformed to accommodate design goals or efficiency concerns.

- *ODD embedded into source code.* The third approach is to embed the ODD into the source code. As in the first approach, we represent the ODD using a modeling tool (see Figure 9-14). Once the ODD becomes stable, we use the modeling tool to generate class stubs. We describe each class interface using tagged comments that distinguish source code comments from object design descriptions. We can then generate the ODD using a tool that parses the source code and extracts the relevant information (e.g., Javadoc [Javadoc, 2009a]). Once the object design model is documented in the code, we abandon the initial object design model. The advantage of this approach is that the consistency between the object design model and the source code is much easier to maintain: when changes are made to the source code, the tagged comments are updated and the ODD regenerated. In this section, we focus only on this approach.

The fundamental issue is one of maintaining consistency among two models and the source code. Ideally, we want to maintain the analysis model, the object design model, and the source code using a single tool. Objects would then be described once, and consistency among documentation, stubs, and code would be maintained automatically.

Presently, however, UML modeling tools provide facilities for generating a document from a model or class stubs from a model. For example, the glossary of the RAD can be generated from the analysis model by collating the description fields attached to each class. (Figure 9-14). The class stub generation facility, called **forward engineering**, can be used in the self-contained ODD approach to generate the class interfaces and stubs for each method.

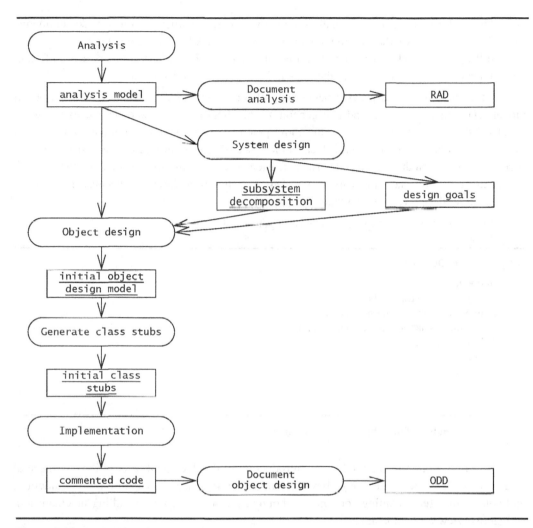

Figure 9-14 Embedded ODD approach. Class stubs are generated from the object design model. The object design model is then documented as tagged comments in the source code. The initial object design model is abandoned and the ODD is generated from the source code instead using a tool such as Javadoc (UML activity diagram).

Some modeling tools provide facilities for **reverse engineering**, that is, recreating a UML model from source code. Such facilities are useful for creating object models from legacy code. They require substantial hand processing, however, because the tool cannot recreate bidirectional associations based on reference attributes only.

Tool support currently falls short when maintaining two-way dependencies, in particular between the analysis model and the source code. Some tools, such as Rationale Rose [Rational, 2002] and Together Control Center [TogetherSoft, 2002], realize this functionality by embedding information about associations and other UML constructs in source code comments. Even though this allows the tool to recover syntactic changes from the source code, developers must still update model descriptions to reflect the changes. Because developers need different tools to change the source code and the model, the model often falls behind.

Until modeling tools provide better support for maintaining consistency between object models and source code, we find that generating the ODD from source code and focusing the RAD on the application domain is the most practical. It reduces the amount of redundant information to be maintained, and it locates the object design information where it is the most accessible, that is, in the source code. The consistency between the source code and the analysis model must still be maintained manually. This task is easier, however, because fewer code changes affect the analysis model than affect the object design model.

Figure 9-15 is an example template for a generated ODD.

Object Design Document

1. Introduction
    1.1 Object design trade-offs
    1.2 Interface documentation guidelines
    1.3 Definitions, acronyms, and abbreviations
    1.4 References
2. Packages
3. Class interfaces
    Glossary

Figure 9-15   Outline of the Object Design Document.

The first section of the ODD is an introduction to the document. It describes the general trade-offs made by developers (e.g., buy vs. build, memory space vs. response time), guidelines and conventions (e.g., naming conventions, boundary cases, exception handling mechanisms), and an overview of the document.

Interface documentation guidelines and coding conventions are the single most important factor that can improve communication between developers during object design. These include a list of rules that developers should use when designing and naming interfaces. These are examples of such conventions:

- Classes are named with singular nouns.
- Methods are named with verb phrases, fields, and parameters with noun phrases.
- Error status is returned via an exception, not a return value.
- Collections and containers have an `iterator()` method returning an `Iterator`.
- `Iterators` returned by `iterator()` methods are robust to element removals.

Such conventions help developers design interfaces consistently, even if many developers contribute to the interface specification. Moreover, making these conventions explicit before object design makes it easier for developers to follow them. In general, these conventions should not evolve during the project. An example of coding convention for Java are the Sun Java Coding Conventions [Sun, 2009].

The second section of the ODD, *Packages,* describes the decomposition of subsystems into packages and the file organization of the code. This includes an overview of each package, its dependencies with other packages, and its expected usage.

The third section, *Class interfaces*, describes the classes and their public interfaces. This includes an overview of each class, its dependencies with other classes and packages, its public attributes, operations, and the exceptions they can raise.

The initial version of the ODD can be written soon after the subsystem decomposition is stable. The ODD is updated every time new interfaces become available or existing ones are revised. Even if the subsystem is not yet functional, having a source code interface enables developers to more easily code dependent subsystems and communicate unambiguously. At this stage, developers usually discover missing parameters and new boundary cases. The development of the ODD is different from other documents, as more participants are involved and as the document is revised more frequently. To accommodate a high rate of change and many developers, the latter two sections can be generated by a tool from source code comments.

In Java, this can be done with Javadoc, a tool that generates Web pages from source code comments. Developers annotate interfaces and class declarations with tagged comments. For example, Figure 9-16 depicts the interface specification for the Tournament class of the ARENA example. The header comment in the file describes the purpose of the Tournament class, its authors, its current version, and cross references to related classes. The @see tags are used by Javadoc to create cross references between classes. Following the header comment is the class and the method declarations. Each method comment contains a brief description of the purpose of the method, its parameters, and its return result. When using constraints, we also include preconditions and postconditions in the method header. The first sentence of the comment and the tagged comments are extracted and formatted by Javadoc. Keeping material for the ODD with the source code enables the developers to maintain consistency more easily and rapidly.

For any system of useful size, the ODD represents a large amount of information that can translate to several hundreds or thousands of pages of documentation. Moreover, the ODD evolves rapidly during object design and integration, as developers understand better other subsystem's needs and find faults with their specifications. For these reasons, all versions of the ODD should be made available electronically, for example, as a set of Web pages. Moreover, different components of the ODD should be put under configuration management and synchronized with their corresponding source code files. We describe configuration management issues in more detail in Chapter 13, *Configuration Management.*

Note that generating an ODD from source code is not a substitute for object design. Although experienced developers may be able to hold an object design in their head and

```
/** A Tournament is a series of Matches among a set of Players
 * which ends with a single winner. The Game and TournamentStyle of a
 * TournamentStyle is determined by the League in which the Tournament is
 * played.
 *
 * The Tournament starts empty, a number of Players are accepted in
 * the Tournament, the Tournament is planned, and finally,
 * the Matches are played.
 *
 * Invariants:
 * The maximum number of players is positive at all times.
 *     @invariant getMaxNumPlayers > 0
 * The number of players is always less or equal than the max number.
 *     @invariant getPlayers().size() < getMaxNumPlayers()
 * The initial attributes of the Tournament are not null.
 *     @invariant getLeague() != null and getName() != null
 */
public class Tournament {

    /* Fields omitted */

    /** Public constructor. A Tournament starts with a league, a name,
     * and a maximum number of players. These attributes cannot be changed.
     */
    public Tournament(League league, String name, int maxNumPlayers) {…}

    /** Returns a list of the current Players
     */
    public List getPlayers() {…}

    /** This operation accepts a new Player in the Tournament.
     * @pre !isPlayerAccepted(p)
     * @pre getPlayers().size() < getMaxNumPlayers()
     * @post isPlayerAccepted(p)
     * @post getPlayers().size() = self@pre.getPlayers().size() + 1
     */
    public void acceptPlayer (Player p) {…}

    /** The removePlayer() operation assumes that the specified player
     * is currently in the Tournament.
     * @pre isPlayerAccepted(p)
     * @post !isPlayerAccepted(p)
     * @post getPlayers().size() = self@pre.getPlayers().size() - 1
     */
    public void removePlayer(Player p) {…}
```

Figure 9-16   Javadoc comments associated with the Tournament class (Java, constraints using Javadoc style tags).

document it solely using source code or Javadoc comments, this approach is not advisable in general. The object design and specification activities should precede coding and focus on the class interfaces. Once the interfaces are stable, developers generate stubs (possibly with a CASE tool) and realize the implementation of the specification. As the specification is carried over to the source code, it can be corrected there when changes are made by developers. However, writing a specification after the implementation is complete is bound to result in complex designs and incomplete specifications.

9.5.2 Assigning Responsibilities

Object design is characterized by a large number of participants accessing and modifying a large amount of information. To ensure that changes to interfaces are documented and communicated in an orderly manner, several roles collaborate to control, communicate, and implement changes. These include the members of the architecture team who are responsible for system design and subsystem interfaces, liaisons who are responsible for interteam communication, and configuration managers who are responsible for tracking change.

Below is an example of how roles can be assigned during object design. As in other activities, the same participant can be assigned more than one role.

- The **core architect** develops coding guidelines and conventions before object design starts. As for many conventions, the actual set of conventions is not as important as the commitment of all architects and developers to use the conventions. The core architect is also responsible for ensuring consistency with prior decisions documented in the System Design Document (SDD) and Requirements Analysis Document (RAD).

- The **architecture liaisons** document the public subsystem interfaces for which they are responsible. This leads to a first draft of the ODD, which is used by developers. Architecture liaisons also negotiate changes to public interfaces. Often, the issue is not of consensus, but of communication: developers depending on the interface may welcome the change if they are notified first. The architecture liaisons and the core architect form the architecture team.

- The **object designers** refine and detail the interface specification of the class or subsystem they implement.

- The **configuration manager** of a subsystem releases changes to the interfaces and the ODD once they become available. The configuration manager also keeps track of the relationship between source code and ODD revisions.

- **Technical writers** from the documentation team clean up the final version of the ODD. They ensure that the document is consistent from a structural and content point of view. They also check for compliance with the guidelines.

As in system design, the architecture team is the integrating force of object design. The architecture team ensures that changes are consistent with project goals. The documentation team, including the technical writers, ensures that the changes are consistent with guidelines and conventions.

9.5.3   Using Contracts During Requirements Analysis

Some requirements analysis approaches advocate the use of constraints much earlier, for example, during the definition of the entity objects. In principle, OCL can be used in requirements analysis as well as in object design. In general, developers consider specific project needs before deciding on a specific approach or level of formalism to be used when documenting operations. Examine the following trade-offs before deciding if and when to use constraints for which purpose:

- *Communication among stakeholders.* During software development, models support communication among stakeholders. Different models are used for different types of stakeholders. On the one hand, a use case or a user interface mock-up is much easier for a client to understand than an OCL constraint. On the other hand, an OCL constraint is much more precise statement for the class user.

- *Level of detail and rate of change.* Attaching constraints to an analysis model requires a much deeper understanding of the requirements. When this information is available, either from the user, the client, or general domain knowledge, this results in a more complete analysis model. When this information is not available, however, clients and developers may be forced to make decisions too early in the process, increasing the rate of change (and consequently, development cost) later in the development.

- *Level of detail and elicitation effort.* Similarly, eliciting detailed information from a user during analysis may require much more effort than eliciting this information later in the process, when early versions of the user interface are available and specific issues can be demonstrated. However, this approach assumes that modifying the components under consideration is relatively cheap and does not have a serious impact on the rest of the system. This is the case for user interface layout issues and dialog considerations.

- *Testing requirements.* During testing, we compare the actual behavior of the system or a class with the specified behavior. For automated tests or for stringent testing requirements (found, for example, in application domains such as traffic control, medicine, or pharmaceuticals), this requires a precise specification to test against. In this case, constraints help a lot if they are specified as early as possible. We discuss testing in detail in Chapter 11, *Testing*.

9.6   ARENA Case Study

In this section, we apply the concepts and methods described in this chapter to a more extensive example from the ARENA system. We focus on the classes surrounding *TournamentStyle*, which is responsible for creating a set of Matches, assigning Players from the Tournaments, and deciding on start and end dates for each Match. Specifying contracts for these classes is particularly critical, as *TournamentStyle* provides an open interface for other developers to create new *TournamentStyles*. Hence, the boundary between *TournamentStyle* and the rest of

ARENA should be sufficiently clear so that developers can write new *TournamentStyles* without having to understand the ARENA source code.

First, we identify any missing operations or classes. Next, we specify contracts for the abstract classes related to *TournamentStyle*. Finally, we show how these contracts can be strengthened when writing a new *TournamentStyle* (e.g., KnockOutStyle).

9.6.1   Identifying Missing Operations in *TournamentStyle* and *Round*

From the ARENA analysis model, we know that the responsibility of the *TournamentStyle* class is to map a list of Players participating in a Tournament onto a series of Matches. Examples of concrete *TournamentStyles* are the KnockOutStyle, in which only winners can move to the next Match, and the RoundRobinStyle, in which each Player competes against all of the other Players exactly once.

During this activity, we focus on the Application Programmer Interface (API) of *TournamentStyle* that a Tournament invokes to generate the series of Matches. First, we observe that *TournamentStyles* generate series of Matches that can be played in parallel (e.g., the first round of a championship) and series of Matches that have precedence constraints (e.g., both semifinals of a knock-out tournament must be completed before the final can start). We also observe that not all Matches will be assigned with Players from the start. In the KnockOutStyle, for example, it is only as Matches are won that subsequent Matches are assigned. This leads us to the following set of requirements:

- *Schedule representation.* We need to represent the graph of Matches to be played in the Tournament in such a way that all *TournamentStyles* can be represented.
- *Incremental planning.* We need to define a set of methods on *TournamentStyle* that enables Matches to be incrementally planned as the Tournament progresses.
- *Game independence.* The graph of Matches and the planning needs to be independent from the *Game*. In particular, the Match class that is part of the *Game* abstract factory should not be constrained by the above requirements.

This leads us to represent the graph of Matches with a new class, *Round* (Figure 9-17). A *Round* corresponds to a set of Matches that can be held concurrently. Hence, a schedule for a Tournament is simply a list of *Rounds*. Next, we define a *TournamentStyle.planRounds()* operation, returning a list of *Rounds*, that is responsible for creating all the Matches in the Tournament and organizing them into a sequence of *Rounds*. *TournamentStyle.planRounds()* also assigns Players to Matches of the first *Round* (and possibly to other *Rounds* as well). Then, we define a *Round.plan()* operation class that is responsible for incrementally assigning Players to Matches of the next *Round*, if necessary. To enable class extenders to define new styles, *TournamentStyle* and *Round* are abstract classes that are refined for each style. For example, the KnockOutStyle class extends *TournamentStyle*, while KnockOutRound extends *Round*. The Tournament class only accesses the abstract classes, hence decoupling it from the concrete style that was selected for the League.

We now specify the contracts of the *TournamentStyle* and *Round* abstract classes.

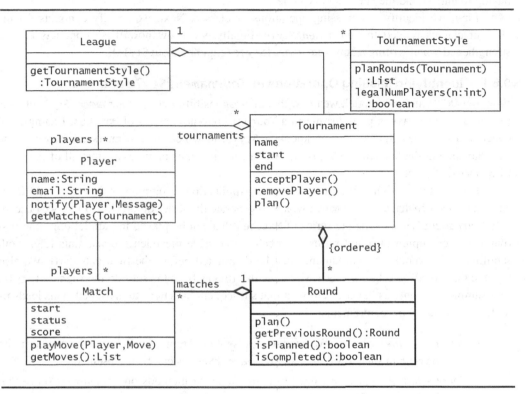

Figure 9-17 New *Round* class and changes in the *TournamentStyle*, Tournament, and *Round* APIs (UML class diagram). Thick lines indicate changes.

9.6.2   Specifying the *TournamentStyle* and *Round* Contracts

The *TournamentStyle* abstract class creates a list of *Rounds* for a given Tournament, and the Tournament stores the *Rounds*. Hence, the *TournamentStyle* does not have any state and, consequently, *TournamentStyle* does not have any invariants.

The *TournamentStyle.planRounds()* operation has one parameter, the Tournament being planned. A general precondition is that Tournaments can only be planned once. Hence, *TournamentStyle.planRounds()* only accepts Tournaments that do not include any *Rounds* yet. A more specific precondition is that concrete *TournamentStyles* may require a specific number of Players. For example, the KnockOutStyle requires a number of Players that is a power of 2. Since the number of Players required by different *TournamentStyles* can vary, we address this issue by adding an operation to the *TournamentStyle* class that returns the set of legal numbers of Players. Note that this set will be bounded by the maximum number of Players per Tournament allowed in the Arena.

```
/* Only tournaments without rounds and with the right number of players
 * can be planned.*/
context TournamentStyle::planRounds(t:Tournament) pre:
    t <> null and t.rounds = null and legalNumPlayers(t.players->size)
```

Another approach would be to express the number of Players expected by *TournamentStyles* as a precondition in the subclasses. KnockOutStyle.planRounds(), for example, can have a precondition stating that the number of Players should be a power of 2. While associating such specific preconditions with concrete classes is a good idea, we also need to ensure that the preconditions associated with the superclass are at least as strict as those associated with the subclasses, as explained in Section 9.4.5. Otherwise, we would violate the Liskov Substitution Principle. In concrete terms, it would mean that a class extender writing a subclass of *TournamentStyle* could introduce constraints that the Arena system would violate, and consequently crash the system, while respecting all existing contracts.

There are relatively few post conditions on the *TournamentStyle.planRounds()* operation, since, by design, we do not want to restrict the possible concrete *TournamentStyles*. First, we ensure that each Player is assigned to at least one Match after the initial invocation of planRounds(). Second, we ensure that Matches in different *Rounds* do not overlap, as it is possible for the same Player to take part in more than one *Round*. To express this second constraint, we add the getStartDate() and getEndDate() operations to the *Round* class that compute the start of the earliest Match in the *Round* and the latest end of a Match, respectively.

```
/* All players are assigned to at least one match */
context TournamentStyle::planRounds(t:Tournament) post:
t.getPlayers()->forAll(p|
    p.getMatches(tournament)->notEmpty()

context TournamentStyle::planRounds(t:Tournament) post:
result->forAll(r1,r2| r1<>r2 implies
    r1.getEndDate().before(r2.getStartDate()) or
        r1.getStartDate().after(r2.getEndDate())
```

To make it easier to write the above constraint, we added a helper operation, Player.getMatches(t:Tournament), to retrieve all the Matches in which a Player takes part within the scope of one Tournament. As the *Round* class is part of the *TournamentStyle* API, we also need to specify the contract of the *Round* class. A *Round* is essentially a list of Matches that can occur concurrently. Consequently, a given Player can take part in at most one Match per *Round*. We specify this with an invariant:

```
/* A player cannot be assigned to more than one match per round */
context Round inv:
matches->forAll(m1:Match|
    m1.players->forAll(p:Player|
        p.matches->forAll(m2:Match| m1 <> m2 implies m1.round <> m2.round)))
```

Note that the above invariant is still valid if no Players have been assigned to a Match yet.

Next, we focus on the planning status of the *Round*. A *Round* can have one of three states:

- Initially, a *Round* is not planned. It only contains Matches that may or may not have Players assigned.

- Its status becomes planned if the plan() operation manages to assign Players to all Matches.

- Its status becomes completed when all of its Matches have been played and have winners.

This leads to adding two methods, *Round.isPlanned()* and *Round.isCompleted()*, to make it easier for a *Round* to decide when to assign Players to Matches and for Tournaments to decide when a *Round* can be started. We represent the above as three OCL constraints (Figure 9-18) relating the status of the *Round* with the status of its Matches.

```
/* Invoking plan() on a Round whose previous Round is completed results
 * in a planned Round. */
context Round.plan() post:
    @pre.getPreviousRound().isCompleted() implies isPlanned()

/* A round is planned if all matches have players assigned to them. */
context Round.isPlanned() post:
    result implies
        matches->forAll(m|
            m.players->size = tournament.league.game.numPlayersPerMatch)

/* A round is completed if all of its matches are completed. */
context Round.isCompleted() post:
    result implies
        matches->forAll(m| m.winner <> null)
```

Figure 9-18   Contracts of the *Round* class.

As we see in the next section, some *TournamentStyles* require that the *Round* be planned only when the previous *Round* is completed.

9.6.3   Specifying the KnockOutStyle and KnockOutRound Contracts

Subclasses inherit the contracts of their ancestors (Section 9.4.5). The KnockOutStyle and the KnockOutRound concrete classes inherit the contracts of *TournamentStyle* and *Round*, respectively. However, subclasses can strengthen the invariants and postconditions of the inherited contract and weaken its preconditions. This enables us to specify the refinement of the subclass more precisely and to document in detail how its behavior from other refinements differs from other subclasses (e.g., RoundRobinStyle).

First, we define the return value of the operation KnockOutStyle.legalNumPlayers()
with a postcondition (Figure 9-19). The number of Players can be any power of 2 between 1
and the maximum number of Players in the Tournament. Next, we define the number of
Matches in each *Round:* the final *Round* has exactly one Match, and all other *Rounds* have exactly
twice as many Matches as the next *Round.* Next, we add a constraint stating that Players can be
part of a *Round* only if it is the first *Round* or if they won all other Matches in previous *Rounds.*
Finally, we strengthen the post condition of KnockOut.plan() by requiring that the previous
Round be completed before the current *Round* can be planned.

```
/* The number of players should be a power of 2. */
context KnockOutStyle::legalNumPlayers(n:int) post:
    result = (floor(log(n)/log(2)) = (log(n)/log(2)))

/* The number of matches in a round is 1 for the last round. Otherwise,
 * the number of matches in a round is exactly twice the number of matches
 * in the subsequent round.
 */
context KnockOutStyle::planRounds(t:Tournament) post:
    result->forAll(index:Integer|
        if (index = result->size) then
            result->at(index).matches->size = 1
        else
            result->at(index).matches->size =
                (2*result->at(index+1).matches->size))
        endif)

/* A player can play in a round only if it is the first round or if it is the
 * winner of a previous round.
 */
context KnockOutRound inv:
    previousRound = null or
        matches.players->forAll(p|
            round.previousRound.matches->exists(m| m.winner = p))

/* If the previous round is not completed, this round cannot be planned. */
context KnockOutRound::plan() post:
    not self@pre.getPreviousRound().isCompleted() implies not isPlanned()
```

Figure 9-19   Refining contracts of the *Round* class.

9.6.4   Lessons Learned

In the previous sections, we wrote contracts for the *TournamentStyle,* *Round,* KnockOutStyle,
and KnockOutRound classes. In doing so, we learned that

- *Identifying missing operations and writing contracts are overlapping activities.*
  Writing contracts forces us to look carefully at each object, and might result in finding
  new behaviors and boundary cases. In our example, we identified a new class, *Round,*

for modeling the relationship between Matches in a Tournament. While this concept is from the application domain, refining the definition of TournamentStyle leads to its identification.

- *Writing contracts leads to additional helper operations for inspecting objects.* Although the relevant object state is accessible by examining attributes and navigating relevant associations, writing simple contracts encourages us to add helper methods for examining state. This results in simpler constraints and classes that are more easily testable (see Chapter 11, *Testing*).

- *Writing contracts leads to better abstractions.* When inheriting contracts, only preconditions can be weakened. Postconditions and invariants can only be strengthened. Consequently, when writing contracts for abstract classes, we add abstract operations for describing properties of the concrete classes. For example, the TournamentStyle.legalNumPlayers() operation enables us to get around the problem that some of the concrete TournamentStyles may have constraints on the number of Players. In the end, adding such methods results in a better defined meta-model of the concrete classes.

Writing contracts leads to a specification of the legal parameter values. The next step is to define the behavior of the operation when the caller does not respect the contract. We examine the role of exceptions in Chapter 10, *Mapping Models to Code*.

9.7 Further Readings

Historically, the first languages that combined constraints with object orientation were ThingLab [Borning, 1981], Kaleidoscope [Freeman-Benson, 1990], and Eiffel [Meyer, 1997].

The term *Design by Contract* is credited to Bertrand Meyer, who, in *Object-Oriented Software Construction*, provides detailed methodological guidance for writing contracts and language constructs in the Eiffel language to specify contracts and handle contract violations [Meyer, 1997]. The programming language CLU also examined the use of constraints for specifying interfaces in abstract data types [Liskov & Guttag, 1986]. The notion of assertion came from the work on program correctness by Floyd [Floyd, 1967], Hoare [Hoare, 1969], and Dijkstra [Dijkstra, 1976].

The iContract tool [Kramer, 1998] introduced design by contract to the Java community by providing simple Javadoc comments for specifying constraints that are then checked during run-time. Recently, the design by contract for Java community has grown including many open source projects, such as Contract4J [Contract4J] and jContractor [jContractor].

9.8 Exercises

9-1 Consider the List interface in the java.util package for ordered collections of objects. Write preconditions and post conditions in OCL for the following operations:

- int size() returns the number of elements in the list.
- void add(Object e) adds an object at the end of the list.
- void remove(Object e) removes an object from the end of the list.
- boolean contains(Object e) returns true if the object is contained in the list.
- Object get(int idx) returns the object located at index idx, 0 being the index of the first object in the list.

9-2 Consider the Set interface in the java.util package. Write preconditions and post conditions in OCL for the following operations:

- int size() returns the number of elements in the set.
- void add(Object e) adds an object to the set. If the object is already in the set, does nothing.
- void remove(Object e) removes an object from the set
- boolean contains(Object e) returns true if the object is contained in the set.

9-3 Consider the Collection interface in the java.util package, which is the ancestor of both List and Set. Write preconditions and postconditions for the operations below and modify the constraints you wrote in exercises 9-1 and 9-2, knowing that contracts are inherited. Make sure you comply with the Liskov Substitution Principle.

- int size() returns the number of elements in the collection.
- void add(Object e) adds an object to the collection.
- void remove(Object e) removes an object from the collection.
- boolean contains(Object e) returns true if the object is in the collection.

9-4 Consider a Rectangle class and a Square class that inherits from the Rectangle class:

- Write post conditions for the Rectangle.setWidth(w:int) and the Rectangle.setHeight(h:int) operations in terms of the Rectangle.getWidth():int and the Rectangle.getHeight():int operations.
- Write an invariant for the Square class stating that the width and height of a Square should always be the same.
- Consider the rules for inheriting contracts described in Section 9.4.5 in the context of the Square.setWidth() and Square.setHeight() operations of the Square class. Are all rules met? Why not? What should change in the model?

9-5 Consider a sorted list. Write an invariant in OCL denoting that the elements of the list are sorted.

9-6 Consider a sorted binary tree data structure for storing integers. Write invariants in OCL denoting that

- All nodes in the left subtree of any node contain integers that are less than or equal to the current node, or the subtree is empty.
- All nodes in the right subtree of any node contain integers that are greater than the current tree, or the subtree is empty.
- The tree is balanced.

9-7   Consider a simple intersection with two crossing roads and four traffic lights. Assume a simple algorithm for switching lights, so that the traffic on one road can proceed while the traffic on the other road is stopped. Model each traffic light as an instance of a TrafficLight class with a state attribute that can be either red, yellow, or green. Write invariants in OCL on the state attribute of the TrafficLight class that guarantee that the traffic cannot proceed on both roads simultaneously. Add associations to the model to navigate the system, if necessary. Note that OCL constraints are written on classes (as opposed to instances).

9-8   After reading Sections 9.6.2 and 9.6.3, write constraints for a RoundRobinStyle class and a RoundRobinRound class, implementing the *TournamentStyle* and the *Round* interfaces, respectively. Assume that RoundRobinStyle plans a series of *Rounds* so that each Player is paired with the other Players exactly once in the Tournament. Note that the number of *Rounds* depends on whether the number of Players in the Tournament is odd or even, and that a given Player cannot play more than once in a given *Round*.

References

[Borning, 1981]   A. Borning, "The programming language aspects of ThingLab, a constraint-oriented simulation laboratory," in *ACM TOPLAS* 3 (4), October 1981.

[Contract4J]   http://www.contract4j.org/

[Dijkstra, 1976]   E.W. Dijkstra, *A Discipline of Programming*, Prentice Hall, Englewood Cliffs, NJ, 1976.

[Floyd, 1967]   R. W. Floyd, "Assigning meanings to programs," in *Proceedings of the American Mathematics Society Symposium in Applied Mathematics*, Vol. 19, pp. 19–31, 1967.

[Freeman-Benson, 1990]   B. Freeman-Benson, "Kaleidoscope: Mixing objects, constraints, and imperative programming," in *OOPSLA/SIGPLAN Notices* 25 (10): 77:88, October 1990.

[Hoare, 1969]   C.A.R. Hoare, "An axiomatic basis for computer programming," *Communications of the ACM*, Vol. 20, No. 6, pp. 576–580, October 1969.

[Horn, 1992]   B. Horn, "Constraint patterns as a basis for object-oriented programming," *Proceedings of the OOPSLA'92*, Vancouver, Canada, 1992.

[Javadoc, 2009a]   Sun Microsystems, Javadoc homepage, http://java.sun.com/j2se/javadoc/.

[Javadoc, 2009b]   Sun Microsystems, "How to write doc comments for Javadoc," http://java.sun.com/j2se/javadoc/writingdoccomments/.

[jContractor]   http://jcontractor.sourceforge.net/

[Johnson & Foote, 1988]   R. Johnson & B. Foote, "Designing reusable classes," *Journal of Object-Oriented Programming*, Vol. 1, No. 5, pp. 22–35, 1988.

[Kramer, 1998]   R. Kramer, "iContract–The Java Design by Contract Tool," *Technology of Object-Oriented Languages and Systems*, IEEE Computer Society Press, 1998, p.295.

[Liskov & Guttag, 1986]   B. Liskov & J. Guttag, *Abstraction and Specification in Program Development*. McGraw-Hill, New York, 1986.

[Meyer, 1997]   B. Meyer, *Object-Oriented Software Construction*, 2nd ed., Prentice Hall, Upper Saddle River, NJ, 1997.

[OMG, 2006]   Object Management Group, *Object Constraint Language OMG Available Specification Version 2.0*. http://www.omg.org 2006.

[Rational, 2002]   Rational Corp. Rational Rose. Cupertino, CA, 2002. http://www.rational.com.

[Rumbaugh et al., 1991]   J. Rumbaugh, M. Blaha, W. Premerlani, F. Eddy, & W. Lorensen, *Object-Oriented Modeling and Design*, Prentice Hall, Englewood Cliffs, NJ, 1991.

[Sun, 2009]   Sun Microsystems *Code Conventions for the Java Programming Language*. http://www.java.sun.com/docs/codeconv/ 2009.

[TogetherSoft, 2002]   TogetherSoft, *Together Control Center*, Raleigh, NC. . http://www.togethersoft.com 2002.

[Warmer & Kleppe, 2003]   J. Warmer & A. Kleppe, *The Object Constraint Language: Getting Your Modes Ready for MDA*, 2nd ed., Addison-Wesley, Reading, MA, 2003.

10

Mapping Models to Code

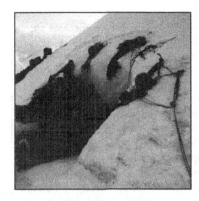

The major difference between a thing that might go wrong and a thing that cannot possibly go wrong is that when a thing that cannot possibly go wrong goes wrong it usually turns out to be impossible to get at or repair.

—Douglas Adams, in *Mostly Harmless*

If the design pattern selection and the specification of class interfaces were done carefully, most design issues should now be resolved. We could implement a system that realizes the use cases specified during requirements elicitation and system design. However, as developers start putting together the individual subsystems developed in this way, they are confronted with many integration problems. Different developers have probably handled contract violations differently. Undocumented parameters may have been added to the API to address a requirement change. Additional attributes have possibly been added to the object model, but are not handled by the persistent management system, possibly because of a miscommunication. As the delivery pressure increases, addressing these problems results in additional improvised code changes and workarounds that eventually yield to the degradation of the system. The resulting code would have little resemblance to our original design and would be difficult to understand.

In this chapter, we describe a selection of transformations to illustrate a disciplined approach to implementation to avoid such a system degradation. These include

- optimizing the class model
- mapping associations to collections
- mapping operation contracts to exceptions
- mapping the class model to a storage schema.

We use Java and Java-based technologies in this chapter. The techniques we describe, however, are also applicable to other object-oriented programming languages.

10.1 Introduction: A Book Example

The Lord of the Rings by J.R.R. Tolkien was first published in the U.K. in 1954 and in the U.S. in 1955.[a] Tolkien, a professor of English and a distinguished linguist, invented several languages and carefully constructed many imaginary names of places and characters for the universe of *The Lord of the Rings*. However, when the book was first published, it contained many typesetting and printing errors and well-intended corrections. For example, to Tolkien's horror, occurrences of *dwarves* and *elven* were systematically replaced by *dwarfs* and *elfin*. Then, in 1965, Ace Books published an unauthorized edition, believing that the copyright on the book did not apply in the United States. Tolkien started to work on a revision of the text so that a new authorized edition would compete against the Ace Books edition. Ballantine Books published the revised manuscript as a paperback in the U.S. in October 1965. Tolkien produced a first set of corrections that were implemented in the second printing of the paperback. Soon after, he produced a second set of corrections, which were implemented in the third and fourth printing of the paperback. These corrections were not always inserted correctly, resulting in more errors in the text.

In the U.K., Allen & Unwin published the revised manuscript as a hardcover edition in October 1966. However, the revised manuscript for the appendix of *The Lord of the Rings*, which Ballantine Books used to set the paperback edition, was lost and could not be used by Allen & Unwin. Instead, Allen & Unwin used an early copy of the Ballantine edition to set the appendix. Unfortunately, the copy did not include the second set of corrections, and, worse, many more errors were introduced during typesetting.

During the summer of 1966, Tolkien further revised the text. In June 1966, he was informed that this latest set of revisions was too late to be included into the Allen & Unwin edition. Consequently, by the end of 1966, there existed several widely different and inconsistent versions of *The Lord of the Rings*, none of which completely reflected Tolkien's intention.

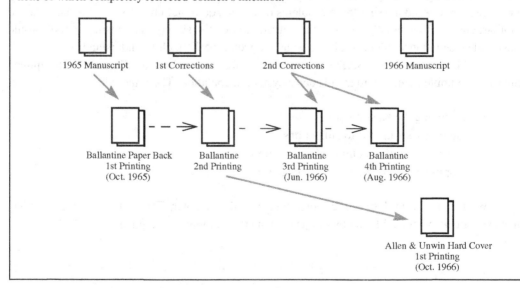

a. Source: "Note on The Text" by Douglas A. Anderson, in [Tolkien, 1995].

The publication of a book, such as *The Lord of the Rings*, requires a number of transformation steps from manuscript to the final printed book. The author first produces a typed manuscript and sends it to a publisher. The manuscript is then revised and copy edited before being finally typeset. The typesetting process requires the retyping of the manuscript, resulting in mistakes, such as misspellings and well-intended corrections. Finally, during the printing process, other mistakes occur, such as wrong ordering or orientation of printed pages.

Although many steps of the publishing process are now automated, mistakes still creep in, introduced by the author, the publisher, or the printer, resulting in a series of corrections that can introduce new errors. Although the processes involved are relatively simple (retyping a manuscript is intellectually not very challenging), the sheer volume and repetitiveness of the work makes it difficult to accomplish without errors (the six books of *The Lord of the Rings* total more than one thousand pages).

Working on an object design model similarly involves many transformations that are error prone. For example, developers perform local transformations to the object model to improve its modularity and performance. Developers transform the associations of the object model into collections of object references, because programming languages do not support the concept of association. Many programming languages also do not support contracts, so developers need to transform the contract specification of operations into code for detecting and handling contract violations. Developers revise the interface specification of an object to accommodate new requirements from the client. These transformations are not as intellectually challenging as other activities in the development process, such as analysis or system design, but they have a repetitive and mechanical aspect and are made difficult by the scale of the work involved. Moreover, they are accomplished mostly manually, as they require some amount of human judgement.

In each of these transformations, small errors usually creep in, resulting in bugs and test failures. We now focus on a set of techniques and example transformations to reduce the number of such errors.

10.2 An Overview of Mapping

A **transformation** aims at improving one aspect of the model (e.g., its modularity) while preserving all of its other properties (e.g., its functionality). Hence, a transformation is usually localized, affects a small number of classes, attributes, and operations, and is executed in a series of small steps. These transformations occur during numerous object design and implementation activities. We focus in detail on the following activities:

- *Optimization* (Section 10.4.1). This activity addresses the performance requirements of the system model. This includes reducing the multiplicities of associations to speed up queries, adding redundant associations for efficiency, and adding derived attributes to improve the access time to objects.

- *Realizing associations* (Section 10.4.2). During this activity, we map associations to source code constructs, such as references and collections of references.

- *Mapping contracts to exceptions* (Section 10.4.3). During this activity, we describe the behavior of operations when contracts are broken. This includes raising exceptions when violations are detected and handling exceptions in higher level layers of the system.

- *Mapping class models to a storage schema* (Section 10.4.4). During system design, we selected a persistent storage strategy, such as a database management system, a set of flat files, or a combination of both. During this activity, we map the class model to a storage schema, such as a relational database schema.

10.3 Mapping Concepts

We distinguish four types of transformations (Figure 10-1):

- *Model transformations* operate on object models (Section 10.3.1). An example is the conversion of a simple attribute (e.g., an address represented as a string) to a class (e.g., a class with street address, zip code, city, state, and country attributes).

- *Refactorings* are transformations that operate on source code (Section 10.3.2). They are similar to object model transformations in that they improve a single aspect of the system without changing its functionality. They differ in that they manipulate the source code.

- *Forward engineering* produces a source code template that corresponds to an object model (Section 10.3.3). Many modeling constructs, such as attribute and association specifications, can be mechanically mapped to source code constructs supported by the selected programming language (e.g., class and field declarations in Java), while the bodies and additional private methods are added by developers.

- *Reverse engineering* produces a model that corresponds to source code (Section 10.3.4). This transformation is used when the design of the system has been lost and must be recovered from the source code. Although several CASE tools support

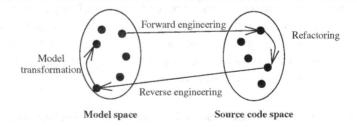

Figure 10-1 The four types of transformations described in this chapter: model transformations, refactorings, forward engineering, and reverse engineering.

reverse engineering, much human interaction is involved for recreating an accurate model, as the code does not include all information needed to recover the model unambiguously.

10.3.1 Model Transformation

A **model transformation** is applied to an object model and results in another object model [Blaha & Premerlani, 1998]. The purpose of object model transformation is to simplify or optimize the original model, bringing it into closer compliance with all requirements in the specification. A transformation may add, remove, or rename classes, operations, associations, or attributes. A transformation can also add information to the model or remove information from it.

In Chapter 5, *Analysis,* we used transformations to organize objects into inheritance hierarchies and eliminate redundancy from the analysis model. For example, the transformation in Figure 10-2 takes a class model with a number of classes that contain the same attribute and removes the redundancy. The Player, Advertiser, and LeagueOwner in ARENA all have an email address attribute. We create a superclass User and move the email attribute to the superclass.

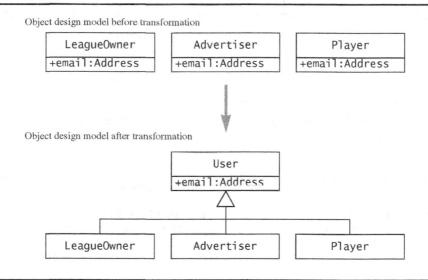

Figure 10-2   An example of an object model transformation. A redundant attribute can be eliminated by creating a superclass.

In principle, the development process can be thought as a series of model transformations, starting with the analysis model and ending with the object design model, adding solution domain details along the way. Although applying a model transformation is a fairly mechanical activity, identifying which transformation to apply to which set of classes requires judgement and experience.

10.3.2 Refactoring

A **refactoring** is a transformation of the source code that improves its readability or modifiability without changing the behavior of the system [Fowler, 2000]. Refactoring aims at improving the design of a working system by focusing on a specific field or method of a class. To ensure that the refactoring does not change the behavior of the system, the refactoring is done in small incremental steps that are interleaved with tests. The existence of a test driver for each class allows developers to confidently change the code and encourages them to change the interface of the class as little as possible during the refactoring.

For example, the object model transformation of Figure 10-2 corresponds to a sequence of three refactorings. The first one, Pull Up Field, moves the email field from the subclasses to the superclass User. The second one, Pull Up Constructor Body, moves the initialization code from the subclasses to the superclass. The third and final one, Pull Up Method, moves the methods manipulating the email field from the subclasses to the superclass. Let's examine these three refactorings in detail.

Pull Up Field relocates the email field using the following steps (Figure 10-3):

1. Inspect Player, LeagueOwner, and Advertiser to ensure that the email field is equivalent. Rename equivalent fields to email if necessary.

2. Create public class User.

3. Set parent of Player, LeagueOwner, and Advertiser to User.

4. Add a protected field email to class User.

5. Remove fields email from Player, LeagueOwner, and Advertiser.

6. Compile and test.

Before refactoring	After refactoring
| ```
public class Player {
    private String email;
    //...
}
public class LeagueOwner {
    private String eMail;
    //...
}
public class Advertiser {
    private String email_address;
    //...
}
``` | ```
public class User {
    protected String email;
}
public class Player extends User {
    //...
}
public class LeagueOwner extends User
{
    //...
}
public class Advertiser extends User {
    //...
}
``` |

Figure 10-3   Applying the *Pull Up Field* refactoring.

Then, we apply the *Pull Up Constructor Body* refactoring to move the initialization code for email using the following steps (Figure 10-4):

1. Add the constructor User(Address email) to class User.
2. Assign the field email in the constructor with the value passed in the parameter.
3. Add the call super(email) to the Player class constructor.
4. Compile and test.
5. Repeat steps 1–4 for the classes LeagueOwner and Advertiser.

Before refactoring	After refactoring
| ```
public class User {
    private String email;
}
``` | ```
public class User {
    public User(String email) {
        this.email = email;
    }
}
``` |
| ```
public class Player extends User {
    public Player(String email) {
        this.email = email;
        //...
    }
}
``` | ```
public class Player extends User {
    public Player(String email) {
        super(email);
        //...
    }
}
``` |
| ```
public class LeagueOwner extends User
{
    public LeagueOwner(String email) {
        this.email = email;
        //...
    }
}
``` | ```
public class LeagueOwner extends User
{
    public LeagueOwner(String email) {
        super(email);
        //...
    }
}
``` |
| ```
public class Advertiser extends User {
    public Advertiser(String email) {
        this.email = email;
    //...
    }
}
``` | ```
public class Advertiser extends User {
    public Advertiser(String email) {
        super(email);
    //...
    }
}
``` |

Figure 10-4 Applying the *Pull Up Constructor Body* refactoring.

At this point, the field email and its corresponding initialization code are in the User class. Now, we examine if methods using the email field can be moved from the subclasses to the User class. To achieve this, we apply the *Pull Up Method* refactoring:

1. Examine the methods of Player that use the email field. Note that Player.notify() uses email and that it does not use any fields or operations that are specific to Player.
2. Copy the Player.notify() method to the User class and recompile.
3. Remove the Player.notify() method.

4. Compile and test.

5. Repeat for LeagueOwner and Advertiser.

Applying these three refactorings effectively transforms the ARENA source code in the same way the object model transformation of Figure 10-2 transformed the ARENA object design model. Note that the refactorings include many more steps than its corresponding object model transformation and interleave testing with changes. This is because the source code includes many more details, so it provides many more opportunities for introducing errors. In the next section, we discuss general principles for avoiding transformation errors.

10.3.3 Forward Engineering

Forward engineering is applied to a set of model elements and results in a set of corresponding source code statements, such as a class declaration, a Java expression, or a database schema. The purpose of forward engineering is to maintain a strong correspondence between the object design model and the code, and to reduce the number of errors introduced during implementation, thereby decreasing implementation effort.

For example, Figure 10-5 depicts a particular forward engineering transformation applied to the classes User and LeagueOwner. First, each UML class is mapped to a Java class. Next, the

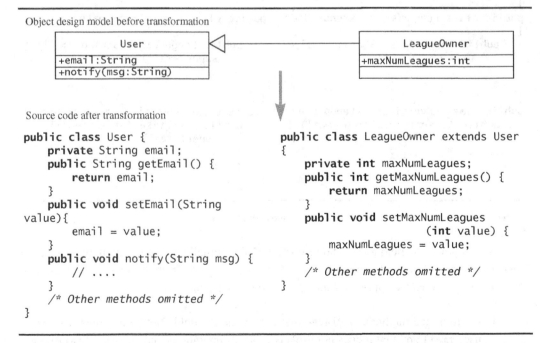

Figure 10-5 Realization of the User and LeagueOwner classes (UML class diagram and Java excerpts). In this transformation, the public visibility of email and maxNumLeagues denotes that the methods for getting and setting their values are public. The actual fields representing these attributes are private.

UML generalization relationship is mapped to an `extends` statement in the `LeagueOwner` class. Finally, each attribute in the UML model is mapped to a private field in the Java classes and to two public methods for setting and getting the value of the field. Developers can then refine the result of the transformation with additional behavior, for example, to check that the new value of `maxNumLeagues` is a positive integer.

Note that, except for the names of the attributes and methods, the code resulting from this transformation is always the same. This makes it easier for developers to recognize transformations in the source code, which encourages them to comply with naming conventions. Moreover, since developers use one consistent approach for realizing classes, they introduce fewer errors.

10.3.4 Reverse Engineering

Reverse engineering is applied to a set of source code elements and results in a set of model elements. The purpose of this type of transformation is to recreate the model for an existing system, either because the model was lost or never created, or because it became out of sync with the source code. Reverse engineering is essentially an inverse transformation of forward engineering. Reverse engineering creates a UML class for each class declaration statement, adds an attribute for each field, and adds an operation for each method. However, because forward engineering can lose information (e.g., associations are turned into collections of references), reverse engineering does not necessarily recreate the same model. Although many CASE tools support reverse engineering, CASE tools provide, at best, an approximation that the developer can use to rediscover the original model.

10.3.5 Transformation Principles

A transformation aims at improving the design of the system with respect to some criterion. We discussed four types of transformations so far: model transformations, refactorings, forward engineering, and reverse engineering. A model transformation improves the compliance of the object design model with a design goal. A refactoring improves the readability or the modifiability of the source code. Forward engineering improves the consistency of the source code with respect to the object design model. Reverse engineering tries to discover the design behind the source code.

However, by trying to improve one aspect of the system, the developer runs the risk of introducing errors that will be difficult to detect and repair. To avoid introducing new errors, all transformations should follow these principles:

- *Each transformation must address a single criteria.* A transformation should improve the system with respect to only one design goal. One transformation can aim to improve response time. Another transformation can aim to improve coherence. However, a transformation should not optimize multiple criteria. If you find yourself trying to deal with several criteria at once, you most likely introduce errors by making the source code too complex.

- *Each transformation must be local.* A transformation should change only a few methods or a few classes at once. Transformations often target the implementation of a method, in which case the callers are not affected. If a transformation changes an interface (e.g., adding a parameter to a method), then the client classes should be changed one at the time (e.g., the older method should be kept around for background compatibility testing). If you find yourself changing many subsystems at once, you are performing an architectural change, not an object model transformation.

- *Each transformation must be applied in isolation to other changes.* To further localize changes, transformations should be applied one at the time. If you are improving the performance of a method, you should not add new functionality. If you are adding new functionality, you should not optimize existing code. This enables you to focus on a limited set of issues and reduces the opportunities for errors.

- *Each transformation must be followed by a validation step.* Even though transformations have a mechanical aspect, they are applied by humans. After completing a transformation and before initiating the next one, validate the changes. If you applied an object model transformation, update the sequence diagrams in which the classes under consideration are involved. Review the use cases related to the sequence diagrams to ensure that the correct functionality is provided. If you applied a refactoring, run the test cases relevant to the classes under consideration. If you added new control statements or dealt with new boundary cases, write new tests to exercise the new source code. It is always easier to find and repair a bug shortly after it was introduced than later.

10.4 Mapping Activities

In this section, we present transformations that occur frequently to illustrate the principles we described in the previous section. We focus on transformations during the following activities:

- Optimizing the Object Design Model (Section 10.4.1)
- Mapping Associations to Collections (Section 10.4.2)
- Mapping Contracts to Exceptions (Section 10.4.3)
- Mapping Object Models to a Persistent Storage Schema (Section 10.4.4).

10.4.1 Optimizing the Object Design Model

The direct translation of an analysis model into source code is often inefficient. The analysis model focuses on the functionality of the system and does not take into account system design decisions. During object design, we transform the object model to meet the design goals identified during system design, such as minimization of response time, execution time, or memory resources. For example, in the case of a Web browser, it might be clearer to represent

HTML documents as aggregates of text and images. However, if we decided during system design to display documents as they are retrieved, we may introduce a proxy object to represent placeholders for images that have not yet been retrieved.

In this section, we describe four simple but common optimizations: adding associations to optimize access paths, collapsing objects into attributes, delaying expensive computations, and caching the results of expensive computations.

When applying optimizations, developers must strike a balance between efficiency and clarity. Optimizations increase the efficiency of the system but also the complexity of the models, making it more difficult to understand the system.

Optimizing access paths

Common sources of inefficiency are the repeated traversal of multiple associations, the traversal of associations with "many" multiplicity, and the misplacement of attributes [Rumbaugh et al., 1991].

Repeated association traversals. To identify inefficient access paths, you should identify operations that are invoked often and examine, with the help of a sequence diagram, the subset of these operations that requires multiple association traversal. Frequent operations should not require many traversals, but should have a direct connection between the querying object and the queried object. If that direct connection is missing, you should add an association between these two objects. In interface and reengineering projects, estimates for the frequency of access paths can be derived from the legacy system. In greenfield engineering projects, the frequency of access paths is more difficult to estimate. In this case, redundant associations should not be added before a dynamic analysis of the full system—for example, during system testing—has determined which associations participate in performance bottlenecks.

"Many" associations. For associations with "many" multiplicity, you should try to decrease the search time by reducing the "many" to "one." This can be done with a qualified association (Section 2.4.2). If it is not possible to reduce the multiplicity of the association, you should consider ordering or indexing the objects on the "many" side to decrease access time.

Misplaced attributes. Another source of inefficient system performance is excessive modeling. During analysis many classes are identified that turn out to have no interesting behavior. If most attributes are only involved in set() and get() operations, you should reconsider folding these attributes into the calling class. After folding several attributes, some classes may not be needed anymore and can simply removed from the model.

The systematic examination of the object model using the above questions should lead to a model with selected redundant associations, with fewer inefficient many-to-many associations, and with fewer classes.

Collapsing objects: Turning objects into attributes

After the object model is restructured and optimized a couple of times, some of its classes may have few attributes or behaviors left. Such classes, when associated only with one other class, can be collapsed into an attribute, thus reducing the overall complexity of the model.

Consider, for example, a model that includes Persons identified by a SocialSecurity object. During analysis, two classes may have been identified. Each Person is associated with a SocialSecurity class, which stores a unique social security number identifying the Person. Now, assume that the use cases do not require any behavior for the SocialSecurity object and that no other classes have associations with the SocialSecurity class. In this case, the SocialSecurity class should be collapsed into an attribute of Person (see Figure 10-6).

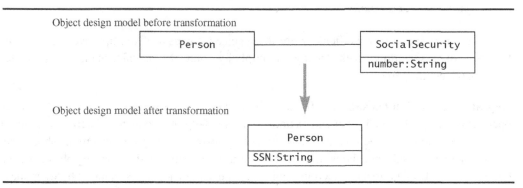

Figure 10-6   Collapsing an object without interesting behavior into an attribute (UML class diagram).

The decision of collapsing classes is not always obvious. In the case of a social security system, the SocialSecurity class may have much more behavior, such as specialized routines for generating new numbers based on birth dates and the location of the original application. In general, developers should delay collapsing decisions until the beginning of the implementation, when responsibilities for each class are clear. Often, this occurs after substantial coding has occurred, in which case it may be necessary to refactor the code.

The refactoring equivalent to the model transformation of Figure 10-6 is *Inline Class* refactoring [Fowler, 2000]:

1. Declare the public fields and methods of the source class (e.g., SocialSecurity) in the absorbing class (e.g., Person).
2. Change all references to the source class to the absorbing class.
3. Change the name of the source class to another name, so that the compiler catches any dangling references.
4. Compile and test.
5. Delete the source class.

Delaying expensive computations

Often, specific objects are expensive to create. However, their creation can often be delayed until their actual content is needed. For example, consider an object representing an image stored as a file (e.g., an ARENA AdvertisementBanner). Loading all the pixels that constitute the image from the file is expensive. However, the image data need not be loaded until the image is displayed. We can realize such an optimization using a **Proxy design pattern** [Gamma et al., 1994]. An ImageProxy object takes the place of the Image and provides the same interface as the Image object (Figure 10-7). Simple operations such as width() and height() are handled by ImageProxy. When Image needs to be drawn, however, ImageProxy loads the data from disk and creates a RealImage object. If the client does not invokes the paint() operation, the RealImage object is not created, thus saving substantial computation time. The calling classes only access the ImageProxy and the RealImage through the Image interface.

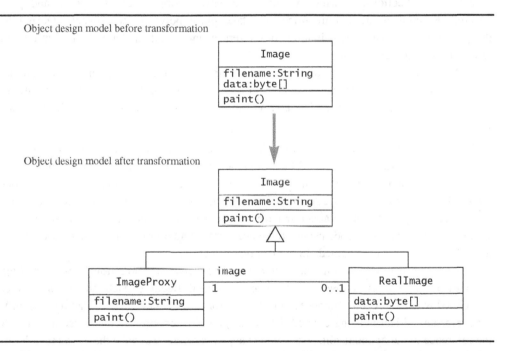

Figure 10-7   Delaying expensive computations to transform the object design model using a Proxy design pattern (UML class diagram).

Caching the result of expensive computations

Some methods are called many times, but their results are based on values that do not change or change only infrequently. Reducing the number of computations required by these methods substantially improve overall response time. In such cases, the result of the computation should be cached as a private attribute. Consider, for example, the

`LeagueBoundary.getStatistics()` operation, which displays the statistics relevant to all `Players` and `Tournaments` in a `League`. These statistics change only when a `Match` is completed, so it is not necessary to recompute the statistics every time a `User` wishes to see them. Instead, the statistics for a `League` can be cached in a temporary data structure, which is invalidated the next time a `Match` is completed. Note that this approach includes a time-space trade-off: we improve the average response time for the `getStatistics()` operation, but we consume memory space by storing redundant information.

10.4.2 Mapping Associations to Collections

Associations are UML concepts that denote collections of bidirectional links between two or more objects. Object-oriented programming languages, however, do not provide the concept of association. Instead, they provide references, in which one object stores a handle to another object, and collections, in which references to several objects can be stored and possibly ordered. References are unidirectional and take place between two objects. During object design, we realize associations in terms of references, taking into account the multiplicity of the associations and their direction.

Note that many UML modeling tools accomplish the transformation of associations into references mechanically. However, even with a tool that accomplishes this transformation, it is nevertheless critical that you understand its rationale, as you have to deal with the generated code.

Unidirectional one-to-one associations.   The simplest association is a unidirectional one-to-one association. For example (Figure 10-8), in ARENA, an `Advertiser` has a one-to-one association with an `Account` object that tracks all the charges accrued from displaying `AdvertisementBanners`. This association is unidirectional, as the `Advertiser` calls the operations of the `Account` object, but the `Account` never invokes operations of the `Advertiser`. In this case, we map this association to code using a reference from the `Advertiser` to the `Account`. That is, we add a field to `Advertiser` named `account` of type `Account`.

Creating the association between `Advertiser` and `Account` translates to setting the account field to refer to the correct `Account` object. Because each `Advertiser` object is associated with exactly one `Account`, a `null` value for the `account` attribute can only occur when a `Advertiser` object is being created. Otherwise, a `null` account is considered an error. Since the reference to the `Account` object does not change over time, we make the `account` field private and add a public `Advertiser.getAccount()` method. This prevents callers from accidentally modifying the `account` field.

Bidirectional one-to-one associations.   The direction of an association often changes during the development of the system. Unidirectional associations are simple to realize. Bidirectional associations are more complex and introduce mutual dependencies among classes. Assume that we modify the `Account` class so that the display name of the `Account` is computed from the name of the `Advertiser`. In this case, an `Account` needs to access its corresponding `Advertiser` object. Consequently, the association between these two objects must be bidirectional

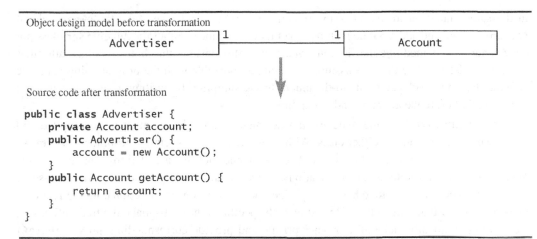

Figure 10-8   Realization of a unidirectional, one-to-one association (UML class diagram and Java).

(Figure 10-9). We add an owner attribute to Account in the Java source code, but this is not sufficient: by adding a second attribute to realize the association, we introduce redundancy into the model. We need to ensure that if a given Account has a reference to a specific Advertiser, the Advertiser has a reference to that same Account. In this case, as the Account object is created by the Advertiser constructor, we add a parameter to the Account constructor to initialize the owner field to the correct value. Thus, the initial values for both fields are specified

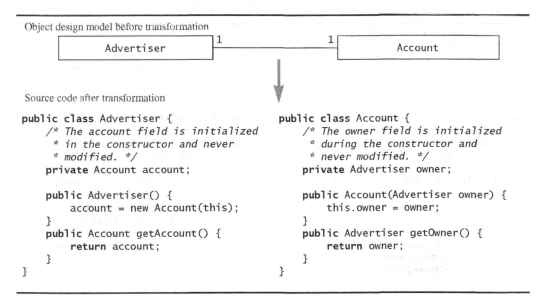

Figure 10-9   Realization of a bidirectional one-to-one association (UML class diagram and Java excerpts).

in the same statement in the Advertiser constructor. Moreover, we make the owner field of Account private and add a public method to get its value. Since neither the Advertiser class nor the Account class modifies the field anywhere else, this ensures that both reference attributes remain consistent. Note that this assumption is not enforceable with the programming language constraints. The developer needs to document this assumption by writing a one-line comment immediately before the account and owner fields.

In Figure 10-9, both the Account and the Advertiser classes must be recompiled and tested whenever we change either class. With a unidirectional association from the Advertiser class to the Account class, the Account class would not be affected by changes to the Advertiser class. Bidirectional associations, however, are usually necessary in the case of classes that need to work together closely. The choice between unidirectional or bidirectional associations is a trade-off to be evaluated in each specific context. To make the trade-off easier, we can systematically make all attributes private and provide corresponding getAttribute() and setAttribute() operations to access the reference. This minimizes changes to APIs when changing a unidirectional association to bidirectional or vice versa.

One-to-many associations.   One-to-many associations cannot be realized using a single reference or a pair of references. Instead, we realize the "many" part using a collection of references. For example, assume that an Advertiser can have several Accounts to track the expenses accrued by AdvertisementBanners for different products. In this case, the Advertiser object has a one-to-many association with the Account class (Figure 10-10). Because Accounts have no specific order and because an Account can be part of an Advertiser at most once, we

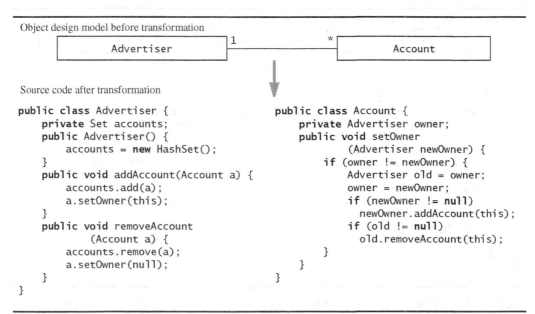

Figure 10-10   Realization of a bidirectional, one-to-many association (UML class diagram and Java).

use a set of references, called accounts, to model the "many" part of the association. Moreover, we decide to realize this association as a bidirectional association, and so add the addAccount(), removeAccount(), and setOwner() methods to the Advertiser and Account classes to update the accounts and owner fields.

As in the one-to-one example, the association must be initialized when Advertiser and Account objects are created. However, since an Advertiser can have a varying number of Accounts, the Advertiser object does not invoke the Account constructor. Instead, a control object for creating and archiving Accounts is responsible for invoking the constructor.

Note that the collection on the "many" side of the association depends on the constraints on the association. For example, if the Accounts of an Advertiser must be ordered, we need to use a List instead of a Set. To minimize changes to the interface when association constraints change, we can set the return type of the getAccounts() method to Collection, a common superclass of List and Set.

Many-to-many associations.   In this case, both end classes have fields that are collections of references and operations to keep these collections consistent. For example, the Tournament class of ARENA has an ordered many-to-many association with the Player class. This association is realized by using a List attribute in each class, which is modified by the operations addPlayer(), removePlayer(), addTournament(), and removeTournament() (Figure 10-11). We already identified acceptPlayer() and removePlayer() operations in the object design model (see Figure 9-11). We rename acceptPlayer() to addPlayer() to maintain consistency with the code generated for other associations.

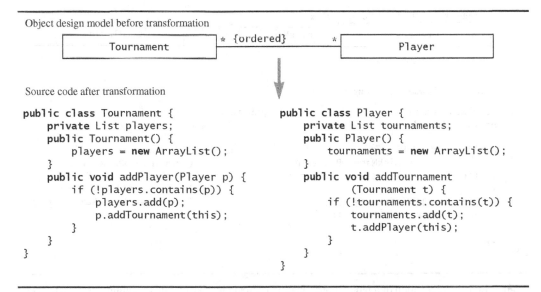

Figure 10-11   Realization of a bidirectional, many-to-many association (UML class diagram and Java).

As in the previous example, these operations ensure that both Lists are consistent. In the event the association between Tournament and Player should be unidirectional, we could then remove the tournaments attribute and its related methods, in which case a unidirectional many-to-many association or a unidirectional one-to-many association are very similar and difficult to distinguish at the object interface level.

Qualified associations.   As we saw in Chapter 2, *Modeling with UML*, qualified associations are used to reduce the multiplicity of one "many" side in a one-to-many or a many-to-many association. The qualifier of the association is an attribute of the class on the "many" side of the association, such as a name that is unique within the context of the association, but not necessarily globally unique. For example, consider the association between League and Player (Figure 10-12). It is originally a many-to-many association (a League involves many Players, a Player can take part in many Leagues). To make it easier to identify Players within a League, Players can choose a short nickname that must be unique within the League. However, the Player can choose different nicknames in different Leagues, and the nicknames do not need to be unique globally within an Arena.

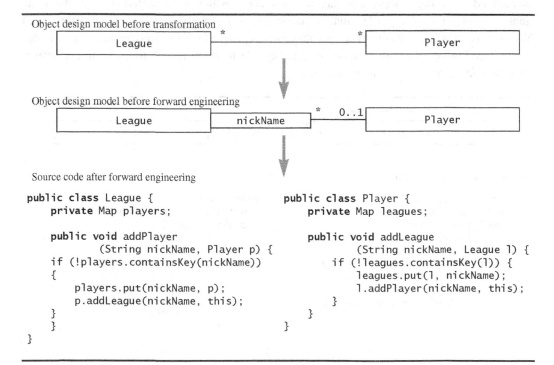

Figure 10-12   Realization of a bidirectional qualified association (UML class diagram; arrow denotes the successive transformations).

Qualified associations are realized differently from the way one-to-many and many-to-many associations are realized. The main difference is that we use a Map object to represent the qualified end, as opposed to a List or a Set, and we pass the qualifier as a parameter in the operations to access the other end of the association. To continue our example, consider the association between League and Player. We realize this qualified association by creating a private players attribute in League and a leagues attribute in Player. The players attribute is a Map indexed by the nickname of the Player within the League. Because the nickname is stored in the Map, a specific Player can have different nicknames across Leagues. The players attribute is modified with the operations addPlayer() and removePlayer(). A specific Player is accessed with the getPlayer() with a specific nickName, which reduces the need for iterating through the Map to find a specific Player. The other end of the association is realized with a Set, as before.

Associations classes. In UML, we use an association class to hold the attributes and operations of an association. For example, we can represent the Statistics for a Player within a Tournament as an association class, which holds statistics counters for each Player/Tournament combination (Figure 10-13). To realize such an association, we first transform the association class into a separate object and a number of binary associations. Then we can use the techniques discussed earlier to convert each binary association to a set of reference attributes. In

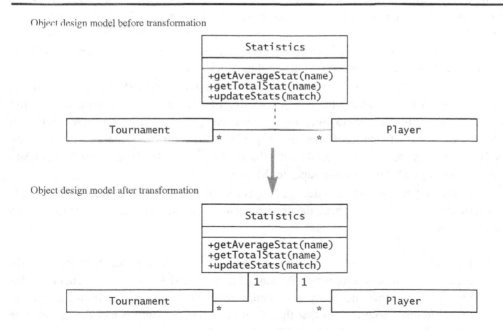

Figure 10-13 Transformation of an association class into an object and two binary associations (UML class diagram).

Section 10.6, we revisit this case and describe additional mappings for realizing association classes.

Once associations have been mapped to fields and methods, the public interface of classes is relatively complete and should change only as a result of new requirements, discovered bugs, or refactoring.

10.4.3 Mapping Contracts to Exceptions

Object-oriented languages that include constraints, such as Eiffel, can automatically check contracts and raise exceptions when a contract is violated. This enables a class user to detect bugs associated with incorrect assumptions about the used class. In particular, this is useful when developers reuse a set of classes to discover boundary cases. Raising exceptions when postconditions are violated enables class implementors to catch bugs early, to identify precisely the operation in which the violation occurred, and to correct the offending code.

Unfortunately, many object-oriented languages, including Java, do not provide built-in support for contracts. However, we can use their exception mechanisms as building blocks for signaling and handling contract violations. In Java, we raise an exception with the **throw** keyword followed by an exception object. The exception object provides a place holder for storing information about the exception, usually an error message and a backtrace representing the call stack of the throw. The effect of throwing an exception interrupts the control flow and unwinds the call stack until a matching **catch** statement is found. The catch statement is followed by a parameter, which is bound to the exception object, and an exception handling block. If the exception object is of the same type of the parameter (or a subclass thereof), the catch statement matches and the exception handling block is executed.

For example, in Figure 10-14, let us assume that the acceptPlayer() operation of TournamentControl is invoked with a player who is already part of the Tournament. In this case, TournamentControl.addPlayer() throws an exception of type KnownPlayer, which is caught by the caller, TournamentForm.addPlayer(), which forwards the exception to the ErrorConsole class, and then proceeds with the next Player. The ErrorConsole boundary object then displays a list of error messages to the user.

A simple mapping would be to treat each operation in the contract individually and to add code within the method body to check the preconditions, postconditions, and invariants relevant to the operation:

- *Checking preconditions.* Preconditions should be checked at the beginning of the method, before any processing is done. There should be a test that checks if the precondition is true and raises an exception otherwise. Each precondition corresponds to a different exception, so that the client class can not only detect that a violation occurred, but also identify which parameter is at fault.

- *Checking postconditions.* Postconditions should be checked at the end of the method, after all the work has been accomplished and the state changes are finalized. Each postcondition corresponds to a Boolean expression in an if statement that raises an exception if the contract is violated. If more than one postcondition is not satisfied, only the first detection is reported.

- *Checking invariants.* When treating each operation contract individually, invariants are checked at the same time as postconditions.

- *Dealing with inheritance.* The checking code for preconditions and postconditions should be encapsulated into separate methods that can be called from subclasses.

```java
public class TournamentControl {
    private Tournament tournament;
    public void addPlayer(Player p) throws KnownPlayerException {
        if (tournament.isPlayerAccepted(p)) {
            throw new KnownPlayerException(p);
        }
        //... Normal addPlayer behavior
    }
}
public class TournamentForm {
    private TournamentControl control;
    private List players;
    public void processPlayerApplications() {
        // Go through all the players who applied for this tournament
        for (Iterator i = players.iterator(); i.hasNext();) {
            try {
                // Delegate to the control object.
                control.acceptPlayer((Player)i.next());
            } catch (KnownPlayerException e) {
                // If an exception was caught, log it to the console, and
                // proceed to the next player.
                ErrorConsole.log(e.getMessage());
            }
        }
    }
}
```

Figure 10-14 Example of exception handling in Java. TournamentForm catches exceptions raised by Tournament and TournamentControl and logs them into an error console for display to the user.

A systematic application of the above rules to the Tournament.addPlayer() contract yields the code in Figure 10-15.

If we mapped every contract following the above steps, we would ensure that all preconditions, postconditions, and invariants are checked for every method invocation, and that violations are detected within one method invocation. While this approach results in a robust system (assuming the checking code is correct), it is not realistic:

```
public class Tournament {
//...
    private List players;

    public void addPlayer(Player p)
        throws KnownPlayer, TooManyPlayers, UnknownPlayer,
            IllegalNumPlayers, IllegalMaxNumPlayers
    {
        // check precondition!isPlayerAccepted(p)
        if (isPlayerAccepted(p)) {
            throw new KnownPlayer(p);
        }
        // check precondition getNumPlayers() < maxNumPlayers
        if (getNumPlayers() == getMaxNumPlayers()) {
            throw new TooManyPlayers(getNumPlayers());
        }
        // save values for postconditions
        int pre_getNumPlayers = getNumPlayers();

        // accomplish the real work
        players.add(p);
        p.addTournament(this);

        // check post condition isPlayerAccepted(p)
        if (!isPlayerAccepted(p)) {
            throw new UnknownPlayer(p);
        }
        // check post condition getNumPlayers() = @pre.getNumPlayers() + 1
        if (getNumPlayers() != pre_getNumPlayers + 1) {
            throw new IllegalNumPlayers(getNumPlayers());
        }
        // check invariant maxNumPlayers > 0
        if (getMaxNumPlayers() <= 0) {
            throw new IllegalMaxNumPlayers(getMaxNumPlayers());
        }
    }
    //...
}
```

Figure 10-15   A complete implementation of the `Tournament.addPlayer()` contract.

- *Coding effort.* In many cases, the code required for checking preconditions and postconditions is longer and more complex than the code accomplishing the real work. This results in increased effort that could be better spent in testing or code clean-up.

- *Increased opportunities for defects.* Checking code can also include errors, increasing testing effort. Worse, if the same developer writes the method and the checking code, it is highly probable that bugs in the checking code mask bugs in the actual method, thereby reducing the value of the checking code.

- *Obfuscated code.* Checking code is usually more complex than its corresponding constraint and difficult to modify when constraints change. This leads to the insertion of many more bugs during changes, defeating the original purpose of the contract.

- *Performances drawback.* Checking systematically all contracts can significantly slow down the code, sometimes by an order of magnitude. Although correctness is always a design goal, response time and throughput design goals would not be met.

Hence, unless we have a tool for generating checking code automatically, such as iContract [Kramer, 1998], we need to adopt a pragmatic approach and evaluate the above trade-offs in the project context. Remember that contracts support communication among developers, consequently, exception handling of contract violations should focus on interfaces between developers. Below are heuristics to evaluate these trade-offs:

Heuristics for mapping contracts to exceptions

- *Omit checking code for postconditions and invariants.* Checking code is usually redundant with the code accomplishing the functionality of the class, and is written by the developer of the method. It is not likely to detect many bugs unless it is written by a separate tester.
- *Focus on subsystem interfaces* and omit the checking code associated with private and protected methods. System boundaries do not change as often as internal interfaces and represent a boundary between different developers.
- *Focus on contracts for components with the longest life,* that is, on code most likely to be reused and to survive successive releases. Entity objects usually fulfill these criteria, whereas boundary objects associated with the user interface do not.
- *Reuse constraint checking code.* Many operations have similar preconditions. Encapsulate constraint checking code into methods so that they can be easily invoked and so that they share the same exception classes.

In all cases, the checking code should be documented with comments describing the constraints checked, both in English and in OCL. In addition to making the code more readable, this makes it easier to modify the checking code correctly when a constraint changes.

10.4.4 Mapping Object Models to a Persistent Storage Schema

So far, we have treated persistent objects like all other objects. However, object-oriented programming languages do not usually provide an efficient way to store persistent objects. In this case, we need to map persistent objects to a data structure that can be stored by the persistent data management system decided during system design, in most cases, either a database or a set of files. For object-oriented databases, no transformations need be done, since there is a one-to-one mapping between classes in the object model and classes in the object-oriented database. However, for relational databases and flat files, we need to map the object model to a storage schema and provide an infrastructure for converting from and to persistent storage. In this section, we look at the steps involved in mapping an object model to a relational database using Java and database schemas.

A **schema** is a description of the data, that is, a meta-model for data [Date, 2004]. In UML, class diagrams are used to describe the set of valid instances that can be created by the source code. Similarly, in relational databases, the database schema describes the valid set of data records that can be stored in the database. Relational databases store both the schema and the data. Relational databases store persistent data in the form of tables (also called *relations* in the database literature). A table is structured in columns, each of which represents an **attribute**. For example, in Figure 10-16, the User table has three columns, firstName, login, and email. The rows of the table represent data records, with each cell in the table representing the value of the attribute for the data record in that row. In Figure 10-16, the User table contains three data records each representing the attributes of specific users Alice, John, and Bob.

A **primary key** of a table is a set of attributes whose values uniquely identify the data records in a table. The primary key is used to refer unambiguously to a specific data record when inserting, updating, or removing it. For example, in Figure 10-16, the login attribute represents a unique user name within an Arena. Hence, the login attribute can be used as a primary key. Note, however, the email attribute is also unique across all users in the table. Hence, the email attribute could also be used as a primary key. Sets of attributes that could be used as a primary

firstName	login	email
"alice"	"am384"	"am384@mail.org"
"john"	"js289"	"john@mail.de"
"bob"	"bd"	"bobd@mail.ch"

User table — Primary key (login); Candidate key, Candidate key

Figure 10-16 An example of a relational table, with three attributes and three data records.

League table

name	login
"tictactoeNovice"	"am384"
"tictactoeExpert"	"am384"
"chessNovice"	"js289"

Foreign key referencing User table

Figure 10-17 An example of a foreign key. The owner attribute in the League table refers to the primary key of the User table in Figure 10-16.

key are called **candidate keys**. Only the actual candidate key that is used in the application to identify data records is the primary key.

A **foreign key** is an attribute (or a set of attributes) that references the primary key of another table. A foreign key links a data record in one table with one or more data records in another table. In Figure 10-17, the table League includes the foreign key owner that references the login attribute in the User table in Figure 10-16. Alice is the owner of the tictactoeNovice and tictactoeExpert leagues and John is the owner of the chessNovice league.

Mapping classes and attributes

When mapping the persistent objects to relational schemata, we focus first on the classes and their attributes. We map each class to a table with the same name. For each attribute, we add a column in the table with the name of the attribute in the class. Each data record in the table corresponds to an instance of the class. By keeping the names in the object model and the relational schema consistent, we provide traceability between both representations and make future changes easier.

When mapping attributes, we need to select a data type for the database column. For primitive types, the correspondence between the programming language type and the database type is usually trivial (e.g., the Java Date type maps to the datetime type in SQL). However, for other types, such as String, the mapping is more complex. The type text in SQL requires a specified maximum size. For example, when mapping the ARENA User class, we could arbitrarily limit the length of first names to 25 characters, enabling us to use a column of type text[25]. Note that we have to ensure that users' first names comply with this new constraint by adding preconditions and checking code in the entity and boundary objects.

Next, we focus on the primary key. There are two options when selecting a primary key for the table. The first option is to identify a set of class attributes that uniquely identifies the object. The second option is to add a unique identifier attribute that we generate.

For example, in Figure 10-16, we use the login name of the user as a primary key. Although this approach is intuitive, it has several drawbacks. If the value of the login attribute changes, we need to update all tables in which the user login name occurs as a foreign key. Also, selecting attributes from the application domain can make it difficult to change the database schema when the application domain changes. For example, in the future, we could use a single table to store users from different Arenas. As login names are unique only within a single Arena, we would need to add the name of the Arena in the primary key.

The second option is to use an arbitrarily unique identifier (id) attribute as a primary key. We generate the id attribute for each object and can guarantee that it is unique and will not change. Some database management systems provide features for automatically generating ids. This results in a more robust schema and primary and foreign keys that consist of one column.

For example, let us focus on the User class in ARENA (Figure 10-18). We map it to a User table with four columns: id, firstName, login, and email. The type of the id column is a long integer that we increment every time we create a new object.

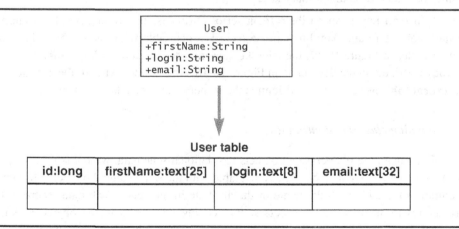

Figure 10-18   Forward engineering of the User class to a database table.

Mapping associations

After having mapped the classes to relational tables, we now turn to the mapping of associations. The mapping of associations to a database schema depends on the multiplicity of the association. One-to-one and one-to-many associations are implemented as a so-called **buried association** [Blaha & Premerlani, 1998], using a foreign key. Many-to-many associations are implemented as a separate table.

Buried associations.   Associations with multiplicity one can be implemented using a foreign key. For one-to-many associations, we add a foreign key to the table representing the class on the "many" end. For all other associations, we can select either class at the end of the association. For example (Figure 10-19), consider the one-to-many association between LeagueOwner and

League. We map this association by adding a owner column to the League table referring to the primary key of the LeagueOwner table. The value of the owner column is the value of the id (i.e., the primary key) of the corresponding league. If there are multiple Leagues owned by the same LeagueOwner, multiple data records of the League table have the id of the owner as value for this column. For associations with a multiplicity of zero or one, a null value indicates that there are no associations for the data record of interest.

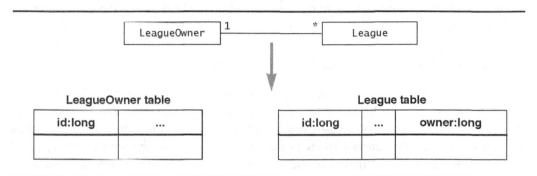

Figure 10-19   Mapping of the LeagueOwner/League association as a buried association.

Separate table.   Many-to-many associations are implemented using a separate two-column table with foreign keys for both classes of the association. We call this the *association table*. Each row in the association table corresponds to a link between two instances. For example, we map the many-to-many Tournament/Player association to an association table with two columns: one for the id of the Tournaments, the other for the id of the Players. If a player is part of multiple tournaments, each player/tournament association will have a separate data record. Similarly, if a tournament includes multiple players, each player will have a separate data record. The association table in Figure 10-20 contains two links representing the membership of "alice" and "john" in the "novice" Tournament.

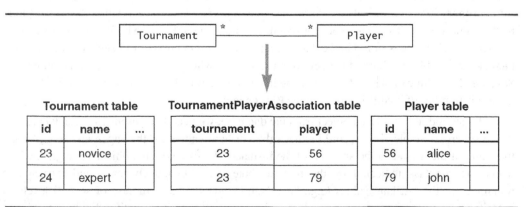

Figure 10-20   Mapping of the Tournament/Player association as a separate table.

Note that a one-to-one and one-to-many association could be realized with an association table instead of a buried association. Using a separate table to realize all associations results in a database schema that is modifiable. For example, if we change the multiplicity of a one-to-many association to a many-to-many association, we do not need to change the database schema. Of course, this increases the overall number of tables in the schema and the time to traverse the association. In general, we need to evaluate this trade-off in the context of the application, examining whether the multiplicity of the association is likely to change or if response time is a critical design goal.

Mapping inheritance relationships

Relational databases do not directly support inheritance, but there are two main options for mapping an inheritance relationship to a database schema. In the first option, called *vertical mapping*, similar to a one-to-one association, each class is represented by a table and uses a foreign key to link the subclass tables to the superclass table. In the second option, called *horizontal mapping*, the attributes of the superclass are pushed down into the subclasses, essentially duplicating columns in the tables corresponding to subclasses.

Vertical mapping.   Given an inheritance relationship, we map the superclass and subclasses to individual tables. The superclass table includes a column for each attribute defined in the superclass. The superclass includes an additional column denoting the subclass that corresponds to the data record. The subclass tables include a column for each attribute defined in the superclass. All tables share the same primary key, that is, the identifier of the object. Data records in the superclass and subclass tables with the same primary key value refer to the same object.

For example, in Figure 10-21, the classes User, LeagueOwner, and Player are each mapped to a table with columns for the attributes of the classes. The User table includes an additional column, role, which denotes the class of the data record. The three tables share the same primary key, that is, if data records have the same id value in each table, they correspond to the same object. The User Zoe, for example, is a LeagueOwner, who can lead at most 12 Leagues. Zoe's name is stored in the User table; the maximum number of leagues is stored in the LeagueOwner table. Similarly, the User John is a Player who has 126 credits (i.e., the number of Matches that John can play before renewing his membership). John's name is stored in the User table; his number of credits is stored in the Player table.

In general, to retrieve an object from the database, we need to examine first the data record in the superclass table. This record includes the attribute values for the superclass (e.g., "zoe", the name of the user) and the subclass of the instance. We use the same object id (e.g., "56") to query the subclass indicated by the role attribute (i.e., "LeagueOwner"), and retrieve the remainder of the attribute values (e.g., "maxNumLeagues = 12"). In case of several levels of inheritance, we repeat the same procedure and reconstruct the object with individual queries to each table.

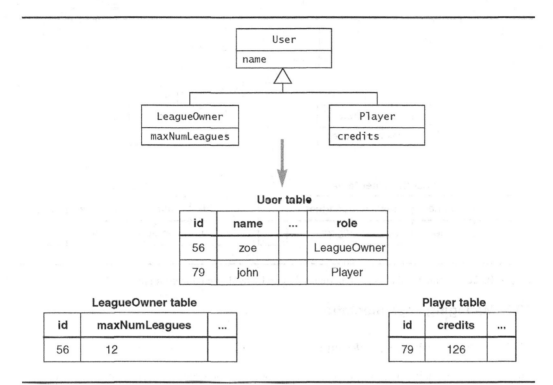

Figure 10-21   Realizing the User inheritance hierarchy with a separate table.

Horizontal mapping.   Another way to realize inheritance is to push the attributes of the superclass down into the subclasses, effectively removing the need for a superclass table. In this case, each subclass table duplicates the columns of the superclass.

For example, in the case of the User inheritance hierarchy, we create a table for LeagueOwners and a table for Players (Figure 10-22). Each table includes a column for its own attributes and for the attributes of the User class. In this case, we need a single query to retrieve all attribute values for a single object.

The trade-off between using a separate table for superclasses and duplicating columns in the subclass tables is between modifiability and response time. If we use a separate table, we can add attributes to the superclass simply by adding a column to the superclass table. When adding a subclass, we add a table for the subclass with a column for each attribute in the subclass. If we duplicate columns, modifying the database schema is more complex and error prone. The advantage of duplicating columns is that individual objects are not fragmented across a number of tables, which results in faster queries. For deep inheritance hierarchies, this can represent a significant performance difference.

In general, we need to examine the likelihood of changes against the performance requirements in the specific context of the application.

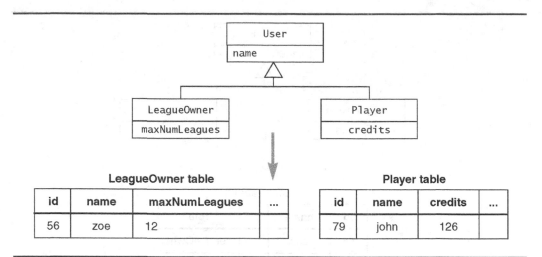

Figure 10-22   Realizing the User inheritance hierarchy by duplicating columns.

10.5 Managing Implementation

10.5.1 Documenting Transformations

Transformations enable us to improve specific aspects of the object design model and to convert it into source code. By providing systematic recipes for recurring situations, transformations enable us to reduce the amount of effort and the overall number of errors in the source code. However, to retain this benefit throughout the lifetime of the system, we need to document the application of transformations so that they can be consistently reapplied in the event of changes to the object design model or the source code.

Reverse engineering attempts to alleviate this problem by allowing us to reconstruct the object design model from the source code. If we could maintain a one-to-one mapping between the source code and the object design mode, we would not need any documentation: the tools at hand would automatically apply selected transformations and mirror changes in the source code and the object design model. However, most useful transformations, including those described in this chapter, are not one-to-one mappings. As a result, information is lost in the process of applying the transformation. For example:

- *Association multiplicity and collections.* Unidirectional one-to-many associations and many-to-many associations map to the same source code. A CASE tool that reverse-engineers the corresponding source code usually selects the least restrictive case (i.e., a many-to-many association). In general, information about association multiplicity is distributed in several places in the source code, including checking code in the boundary objects.

- *Association multiplicity and buried associations.* One-to-many associations and one-to-one associations implemented as a buried association in a database schema suffer from the same problem. Worse, when all associations are realized as separate tables, all information about association multiplicity is lost.

- *Postconditions and invariants.* When mapping contracts to exception-handling code (Section 10.4.3), we generate checking code only for preconditions. Postconditions and invariants are not mapped to source code. The object specification and the system become quickly inconsistent when postconditions or invariants are changed, but not documented.

These challenges boil down to finding conventions and mechanisms to keep the object design model, the source code, and the documentation consistent with each other. There is no single answer, but the following principles reduce consistency problems when applied systematically:

- *For a given transformation, use the same tool.* If you are using a modeling tool to map associations to code, use the same tool when you change association multiplicities. Modern modeling tools generate markers as source code comments to enable the repetitive generation of code from the same model. However, this mapping can easily break when developers use interchangeably a text editor or the modeling tool to change associations. Similarly, if you generate constraint-checking code with a tool, regenerate the checking code when the constraint is changed.

- *Keep the contracts in the source code, not in the object design model.* Contracts describe the behavior of methods and restrictions on parameters and attributes. Developers change the behavior of an object by modifying the body of a method, not by modifying the object design model. By keeping the constraint specifications as source code comments, they are more likely to be updated when the code changes.

- *Use the same names for the same objects.* When mapping an association to source code or a class to a database schema, use the same names on both sides of the transformation. If the name is changed in the model, change it in the source code. By using the same names, you provide traceability among the models and make it easier for developers to identify both ends of the transformation. This also emphasizes the importance of identifying the right names for classes during analysis, before any transformations are applied, to minimize the effort associated with renaming.

- *Make transformations explicit.* When transformations are applied by hand, it is critical that the transformation is made explicit in some form so that all developers can apply the transformation the same way. For example, transformations for mapping associations to collections should be documented in a coding conventions guide so that, when two developers apply the same transformation, they produce the same code. This also makes it easier for developers to identify transformations in the source code. As usual, the commitment of developers to use standard conventions is more important than the actual conventions.

10.5.2 Assigning Responsibilities

Several roles collaborate to select, apply, and document transformations and the conversion of the object design model into source code:

- The **core architect** selects the transformations to be systematically applied. For example, if it is critical that the database schema is modifiable, the core architect decides that all associations should be implemented as separate tables.

- The **architecture liaison** is responsible for documenting the contracts associated with subsystem interfaces. When such contracts change, the architecture liaison is responsible for notifying all class users.

- The **developer** is responsible for following the conventions set by the core architect and actually applying the transformations and converting the object design model into source code. Developers are responsible for maintaining up-to-date the source code comments with the rest of the models.

Identifying and applying transformations the first time is relatively trivial. The key challenge is in reapplying transformations after a change occurs. Hence, when assigning responsibilities, each role should understand who should be notified in the event of changes.

10.6 ARENA Case Study

We now apply the concepts and methods described in this chapter to a more extensive example from the ARENA system. We focus on the classes surrounding Statistics, which is responsible for tracking general and game-specific statistics for each *Game*, Player, Tournament, and League. The challenge in designing and realizing the associations among these classes is to find a reusable solution for many types of statistics, present and future, so that as little code as possible must be written when new *Games* or *TournamentStyles* are introduced.

First, we describe in detail the Statistics class. Next, we map the associations between the Statistics object and the other objects to collections. Next, we map the contracts of the Statistics class to exceptions. Finally, we design a database schema for these classes and associations.

10.6.1 ARENA Statistics

A Statistics instance is responsible for tracking a number of running counters within the context of a *Game* and for a number of scopes. For example, a Spectator should be able to view the Statistics associated with a specific Player within the scope of a single Tournament (e.g., the average number of moves per Match by player John in the winter Tic Tac Toe tournament) or within the more general scope of a League (e.g., the average number of moves per match by player John in the Tic Tac Toe novice league). Similarly, a Spectator should also be able to view average statistics over all Players in a League. The scope of a statistic are, from most general to most specific:

- All Matches in a *Game*
- All Matches in a League
- All Matches in a League played by a specific Player
- All Matches in a Tournament
- All Matches in a Tournament played by a specific Player.

Earlier (see Section 8.6.1), we addressed the issue of *Game* independence by defining Statistics as a product in an Abstract Factory pattern. For each new *Game* added to ARENA, developers are asked to refine the Statistics interface. For *Games* that do not need specialized Statistics, we provide a default implementation of the Statistics interface called DefaultStatistics. ARENA does not access the concrete *Game* and Statistics classes, thereby ensuring *Game* independence (Figure 10-23).

Our design goal is to keep the Statistics interface simple so that it can be easily specialized for different *Games*. In other words, the concrete Statistics class for a specific *Game* should only have to define the formulae for computing the *Game*-specific Statistics. Scopes

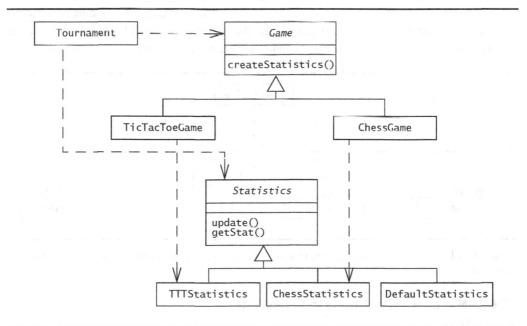

Figure 10-23 Statistics as a product in the *Game* Abstract Factory (UML class diagram).

should be handled by ARENA. Moreover, response time in ARENA has a higher priority than memory consumption.

This leads us, during object design, to the decision of computing all Statistics incrementally as each Match completes. We organize the individual counters we compute into Statistics objects, each representing a scope. Hence, there is a Statistics object for each *Game*, League, Tournament, and for each combination of Player/*Game*, Player/League, and Player/Tournament.

For example, let us assume that Player John takes part in the two Tournaments, t1 and t2, in the Tic Tac Toe novice League. He then moves on to the expert Tic Tac Toe League and takes part in one more Tournament, t3. Let us further assume that the Tic Tac Toe Statistics object tracks his win ratio, the ratio of the number of the *Games* he has won over all the *Games* he has played. Under these circumstances, six Statistics objects track John's win ratio:

- Three Statistics objects track John's win ratio for the Tournaments t1, t2, and t3.
- Two Statistics objects tracks John's win ratio over all his Tournaments within the novice and the expert Leagues, respectively.
- One for the Tic Tac Toe *Game*, tracking John's lifetime win ratio.

In UML, we can represent compactly this complex set of interactions with an N-ary association Statistics class relating the Player, the *Game*, the League, and the Tournament classes (Figure 10-24). For any given Statistics association, only one of *Game*, League, or Tournament is involved in the association, denoting whether the Statistics is value for all Leagues in a specific *Game*, for a single League, or for a single Tournament, respectively.

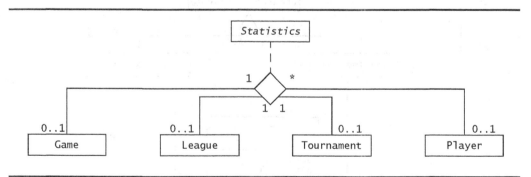

Figure 10-24   N-ary association class Statistics relating League, Tournament, and Player (UML class diagram).

10.6.2 Mapping Associations to Collections

We map the N-ary Statistics association to a Statistics Java class, whose sole purpose is to hold the values of the counters, and a singleton StatisticsVault, responsible for tracking the links between the Statistics objects and the relevant *Game*, League, Tournament, and Player instances (Figure 10-25). We add operations to StatisticsVault for retrieving a specific Statistics given a scope. If the Statistics object of interest does not exist, the StatisticsVault creates it using the corresponding *Game.createStatistics()* method. Internally, the StatisticsVault uses a private HashMap to store the relationship between the combination of Player, *Game*, League, and Tournament and the corresponding Statistics object.

SimpleStatisticsVault depicted in Figure 10-25 is a direct mapping of the N-ary association of Figure 10-24. SimpleStatisticsVault does not accomplish any other task beyond maintaining the state of the association. TournamentControl invokes methods of SimpleStatisticsVault to retrieve the needed Statistics objects, and then invokes the Statistics.update() method as Matches complete. StatisticsView (a boundary object displaying statistics to the user) retrieves the needed Statistics based on the user selection and invokes the Statistics.getStat() method to retrieve the individual values of the counters. In both cases, two steps are needed, one to retrieve the correct Statistics object, the other to invoke the method that does the actual work.

Ideally, we would like to avoid this situation and design an interface that enables TournamentControl and StatisticsView to invoke only one method. This would simplify the method calls related to Statistics in both objects. It would also centralize the scope look-up logic into a single object, making future changes easier. To accomplish this, we refine the SimpleStatisticsVault into a Facade design pattern (see Figure 6-30). We merge the getStatisticsObject() methods with the methods offered by the Statistics object; that is, we provide an update() method for TournamentControl and a set of getStat() methods for

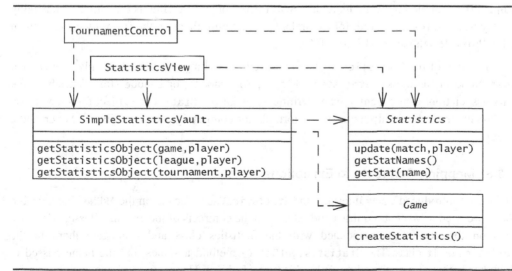

Figure 10-25 SimpleStatisticsVault object realizing the N-ary association of Figure 10-24.

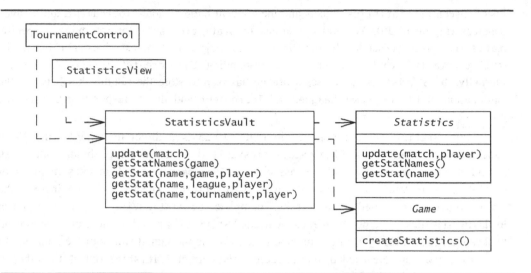

Figure 10-26 StatisticsVault as a Facade shielding the control and boundary objects from the Statistics storage and computation (UML class diagram).

StatisticsView. This results in a slightly more complex interface (Figure 10-26). However, the interface is still within 7 ± 2 methods, and all handling of Statistics objects is now centralized.

If we decide to add different scopes (e.g., match statistics), we will only need to add a method to StatisticsVault. Moreover, TournamentControl and StatisticsView are now completely decoupled from the individual Statistics objects, giving us the option of changing the way Statistics are stored, for example, by computing them on the fly or by caching them with a Proxy design pattern (Figure 10-7).

The role of the Statistics object is reduced to tracking counters (basically, name/value pairs). None of the classes Statistics, Player, Tournament, or League store data about the N-ary association. Consequently, when writing a specialized Statistics object for a new *Game*, the class extender need only focus on the formula for computing a statistic given a Match and a Player.

10.6.3 Mapping Contracts to Exceptions

Because we introduced a new interface, the StatisticsVault facade, in the ARENA object design model, we need to write its contract and relate it to the contracts of the existing classes. First, we focus on the constraints associated with the Statistics class and propagate them to the StatisticsVault class. The Statistcs.getStat() method assumes that the name passed in parameter is that of a statistic known by this type of object. Hence, we add one such constraint for each getStat() method in the StatisticsVault:

```
context StatisticsVault::getStat(name,game,player) pre:
    getStatNames()->includes(name)
context StatisticsVault::getStat(name,league,player) pre:
    getStatNames()->includes(name)
context StatisticsVault::getStat(name,tournament,player) pre:
    getStatNames()->includes(name)
```

Similarly, we add constraints to the StatisticsVault.update() method to reflect the constraint on the Statistics.update() method. In this case, we only need to ensure that the match is not null and has been completed.

```
context StatisticsVault::update(match) pre:
    match <> null and match.isCompleted()
```

Next, we need to examine the remaining parameters of the StatisticsVault methods and document any additional preconditions. We stipulate that the player parameter can be null (denoting the Statistics object for all players), but parameters specifying a game, league, and tournament cannot be null, because a null value, in this case, does not correspond to an application domain concept (e.g., no statistics are valid across all Games). In addition, if a player is specified, she must be related to the scope object (e.g., a player does not have statistics for a tournament in which she did not play).

```
context StatisticsVault::getStat(name,game,player) pre:
    game <> null and
        player <> null implies player.leagues.game->includes(game)
context StatisticsVault::getStat(name,league,player) pre:
    league <> null and
        player <> null implies league.players->includes(player)
context StatisticsVault::getStat(name,tournament,player) pre:
    tournament <> null and
        player <> null implies tournament.players->includes(player)
```

Finally, we map the above constraints to exceptions and checking code. For constraints that we propagated from the Statistics object, we simply forward the exceptions we receive from Statistics and omit the checking code. The UnknownStatistic is raised by Statistics.getStat() and forwarded by StatisticsVault.getStat() methods. The InvalidMatch and MatchNotCompleted exceptions are raised by Statistics.update() and forwarded by StatisticsVault.update() method. For the other constraints, we define a new exception, InvalidScope, for the cases where the game, league, or tournament parameters are null or are not related to the specified player. Finally, we add checking code at the beginning of the StatisticsVault.getStat() methods to check for null references and raise the InvalidScope exception, if needed. Figure 10-27 depicts the public interface of the StatisticsVault class.

```
public class StatisticsVault {
    public void update(Match m)
        throws InvalidMatch, MatchNotCompleted {...}

    public List getStatNames() {...}

    public double getStat(String name, Game g, Player p)
        throws UnknownStatistic, InvalidScope {...}

    public double getStat(String name, League l, Player p)
        throws UnknownStatistic, InvalidScope {...}

    public double getStat(String name, Tournament t, Player p)
        throws UnknownStatistic, InvalidScope {...}
}
```

Figure 10-27   Public interface of the StatisticsVault class (Java).

Note that, with the InvalidScope exception, we decided to cover three preconditions with one exception. This results in similar method declarations for all three getStat() methods, thereby making it easier for the calling class to handle violations of all three preconditions with the same handling code. In general, a set of overloaded methods should have similar interfaces since they implement the same operation for the different types of parameters.

10.6.4 Mapping the Object Model to a Database Schema

In the past two subsections, we transformed the N-ary Statistics association class (Figure 10-24) into a set of Java classes and operations. In this section, we start with the same object model and map it into a set of tables. As Statistics is an N-ary association class, we cannot use buried keys. We first map the association to a separate table, containing a foreign key for each of the association ends (*Game*, League, Tournament, Player). We then note that any given Statistic includes only one link to either a *Game*, a League, or a Tournament. Consequently, we can collapse the columns for *Game*, League, and Tournament into a single column denoting the id of the scope object and a column denoting the type of object (scopetype, Figure 10-28). We decide to encode the type of scope as a long value to save on storage space and on retrieval speed. The mapping between the long values and the actual class is done in the storage subsystem. This decision is a local optimization and does not affect the interface of the StatisticsVault. The id of the Statistics object is the primary key of the table.

As each Statistic has a variable number of name/value pairs, we use a separate table for the counter values, including one column for the name of the counter, one for the value, and a foreign key into the Statistics table (i.e., the Statistics id). The primary key for the StatisticsCounter table is the Statistics id and the counter name.

Statistics table

id:long	scope:long	scopetype:long	player:long

StatisticCounters table

id:long	name:text[25]	value:double

Game table

id:long	...

League table

id:long	...

Tournament table

id:long	...

Figure 10-28   Database schema for the Statistics N-ary association of Figure 10-24.

Note that when designing the database schema for the Statistics association, we started with the object design model, not the Java classes that we generated in the previous section. There are several reasons for starting with the object design model:

- The object design model represents a view of the application domain and is less likely to change than the source code.

- When starting from the object design model, the database schema uses names that come from the application domain (e.g., Statistics) instead of names that denote solution objects (e.g., StatisticsVault). This provides better and more direct traceability to the requirements.

- The transformation of the N-ary association into Java classes focused only on runtime concerns, not on data storage concerns.

10.6.5 Lessons Learned

In the previous section, we mapped the Statistics N-ary association class to source code and to a database schema. In doing so, we learned that

- *Applying one transformation leads to new opportunities for other transformations.* By converting the N-ary Statistics association into a separate object, we defined a facade shielding control and boundary objects from the details of the Statistics representation.

- *Introducing new interfaces results in forwarding existing exceptions.* When introducing a new interface, we need to make sure exceptions are not masked. When we introduced a facade in this example, we simply forwarded the lower-level exceptions (UnknownStatistic) to the Client class.

- *Database schema is based on the object design model, not on the source code.* In general, we need to ensure that the analysis concepts are visible in the implementation, providing traceability back to the requirements. Naming classes, attributes, methods, and tables in terms of names used during analysis is critical in maintaining conceptual integrity.

10.7 Further Readings

The history of refactoring can be traced back to program transformation. Many program transformation systems have focused on improving the performance of programs or on generating programs from formal specifications. *Specification and Transformation of Programs* [Partsch, 1990] provides a comprehensive treatment of this topic.

Although program transformation systems are becoming mature and reaching the marketplace, few tools exist for supporting the transformation of object models. *Object-Oriented Modeling and Design* [Rumbaugh et al., 1991] first introduced the concept of object model transformations. Later, *Object-Oriented Modeling and Design for Database Applications* [Blaha & Premerlani, 1998] introduced the concept of transformations of object models to relational database schemas.

Refactoring, made popular by Martin Fowler in *Refactoring: Improving The Design Of Existing Code* [Fowler, 2000] is essentially a variation of program transformation applied to object-oriented programs. Refactorings are applied manually and interleaved with unit tests. Refactoring is one of the cornerstones of Extreme Programming [Beck & Andres, 2005].

10.8 Exercises

10-1 In Web pages, tables consist of rows, which in turn consist of cells. The actual width and height of each cell is computed based in part on its content (e.g., the amount of text in the cell, the size of an image in the cell), and the height of a row is the maximum of the heights of all cells in the row. Consequently, the final layout of a table in a Web page can only be computed once the content of each cell has been retrieved from the Internet. Using the proxy pattern described in Figure 10-7, describe an object model and an algorithm that would enable a Web browser to start displaying a table before the size of all cells is known, possibly redrawing the table as the content of each cell is downloaded.

10-2 Apply the appropriate transformations described in Section 10.4.2 to the associations of Figure 10-29. Assume that all associations are bidirectional and that they can change during the lifetime of each object. Write the source code needed to manage the associations, including class, field, and method declarations, method bodies, and visibility.

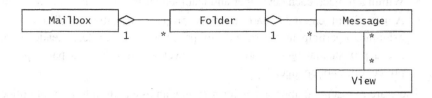

Figure 10-29 Associations among Messages, Folders, Mailboxes, and Views in a hypothetical E-mail client (UML class diagram).

10-3 Apply the appropriate transformations described in Section 10.4.2 to the associations of Figure 10-30. Assume that all associations are bidirectional, but that the aggregation associations do not change after each object has been created. In other words, the creator of each class must be modified so that aggregations are initialized during the creation of each object. Write the source code needed to manage the associations, including class, field, and method declarations, method bodies, and visibility.

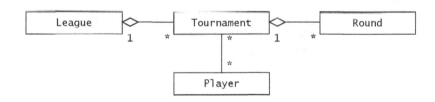

Figure 10-30 Associations among League, Tournament, *Round*, and Player (UML class diagram).

10-4 Figure 10-15 depicts the checking code for the addPlayer() method of Tournament. Write the checking code for the other constraints associated with Tournament depicted in Figure 9-16.

10-5 Write checking code for the contracts of *TournamentStyle* and *Round* described in Section 9.6.2. Write checking code for preconditions, postconditions, and invariants.

10-6 Design a relational database schema for the object model of Figure 10-30. Assume Leagues, Tournaments, Players, and *Rounds* have a name attribute and a unique identifier. Additionally, Tournaments and *Rounds* have start and end date attributes. When different transformations are available, explain the trade-off involved.

10-7 Draw a class diagram representing the application domain facts below, and map it to a relational schema.

- A project involves a number of participants.
- Participants can take part in a project either as project manager, team leader, or developer.

- Within a project, each developer and team leader is part of at least one team.
- A participant can take part in many projects, possibly in different roles. For example, a participant can be a developer in project A, a team leader in project B, and a project manager in project C. However, the role of a participant within a project does not change.

10-8   There are two general approaches for mapping an association to a set of collections. In Section 10.6.2, we map the N-ary association Statistics to two classes, a simple Statistics class to store the attributes of the association, and a StatisticsVault class to store the state of the links among the association links. In Section 10.4.2, we described an alternative approach where the association links are stored in one or both classes at the ends of the association. In the event associations were stored in both classes, we added mutually recursive methods to ensure that both data structures remained consistent. Use this second approach to map the N-ary Statistics association to Collections. Discuss the trade-offs you encounter and the relative advantages of each approach.

References

[Beck & Andres, 2005]   K. Beck & C. Andres, *Extreme Programming Explained: Embrace Change*, 2nd ed., Addison-Wesley, Reading, MA, 2005.

[Blaha & Premerlani, 1998]   M. Blaha & W. Premerlani, *Object-Oriented Modeling and Design for Database Applications*, Prentice Hall, Upper Saddle River, NJ, 1998.

[Date, 2004]   C. J. Date, *An Introduction to Database Systems*, 8th ed., Addison-Wesley, Reading, MA, 2004.

[Fowler, 2000]   M. Fowler, *Refactoring: Improving The Design of Existing Code*, Addison-Wesley, Reading, MA, 2000.

[Gamma et al., 1994]   E. Gamma, R. Helm, R. Johnson, & J. Vlissides, *Design Patterns: Elements of Reusable Object-Oriented Software*, Addison-Wesley, Reading, MA, 1994.

[Kramer, 1998]   R. Kramer, "iContract—The Java design by contract tool," *Technology of Object-Oriented Languages and Systems*, IEEE Computer Society Press, p.295, 1998.

[Partsch, 1990]   H. Partsch, *Specification and Transformation of Programs*, Springer-Verlag, 1990.

[Rumbaugh et al., 1991]   J. Rumbaugh, M. Blaha, W. Premerlani, F. Eddy, & W. Lorensen, *Object-Oriented Modeling and Design*, Prentice Hall, Englewood Cliffs, NJ, 1991.

[Tolkien, 1995]   J.R.R. Tolkien, *The Lord of The Rings*, Harper Collins, 1995.

11

Testing

The software is done.
We are just trying to get it to work.
—Statement made in a Joint STARS E-8A FSD
Executive Program Review

Testing is the process of finding differences between the expected behavior specified by system models and the observed behavior of the implemented system. Unit testing finds differences between a specification of an object and its realization as a component. Structural testing finds differences between the system design model and a subset of integrated subsystems. Functional testing finds differences between the use case model and the system. Finally, performance testing finds differences between nonfunctional requirements and actual system performance. When differences are found, developers identify the defect causing the observed failure and modify the system to correct it. In other cases, the system model is identified as the cause of the difference, and the system model is updated to reflect the system.

From a modeling point of view, testing is the attempt to show that the implementation of the system is inconsistent with the system models. The goal of testing is to design tests that exercise defects in the system and to reveal problems. This activity is contrary to all other activities we described in previous chapters: analysis, design, implementation, communication, and negotiation are constructive activities. Testing, however, is aimed at breaking the system. Consequently, testing is usually accomplished by developers that were not involved with the construction of the system.

In this chapter, we first emphasize the importance of testing. We provide a bird's-eye view of the testing activities, we describe in more detail the concepts of fault, erroneous state, failure, and test, and then we describe the testing activities that result in the plan, design, and execution of tests. We introduce UML profiles as an extension mechanism to describe model-based testing. We conclude this chapter by discussing management issues related to testing.

11.1 Introduction: Testing The Space Shuttle

Testing is the process of analyzing a system or system component to detect the differences between specified (required) and observed (existing) behavior. Unfortunately, it is impossible to completely test a nontrivial system. First, testing is not decidable. Second, testing must be performed under time and budget constraints. As a result, systems are often deployed without being completely tested, leading to faults discovered by end users.

The first launch of the Space Shuttle Columbia in 1981, for example, was canceled because of a problem that was not detected during development. The problem was traced to a change made by a programmer two years earlier, who erroneously reset a delay factor from 50 to 80 milliseconds. This added a probability of 1/67 that any space shuttle launch would fail. Unfortunately, in spite of thousands of hours of testing after the change was made, the fault was not discovered during the testing phase. During the actual launch, the fault caused a synchronization problem with the shuttle's five on-board computers that led to the decision to abort the launch. The following is an excerpt of an article by Richard Feynman that describes the challenges of testing the Space Shuttle.

In a total of about 250,000 seconds of operation, the engines have failed seriously perhaps 16 times. Engineering pays close attention to these failings and tries to remedy them as quickly as possible. It does this by test studies on special rigs experimentally designed for the flaws in question, by careful inspection of the engine for suggestive clues (like cracks), and by considerable study and analysis. . . .

The usual way that such engines are tested (for military or civilian aircraft) may be called the component system, or bottom-up test. First it is necessary to thoroughly understand the properties and limitations of the materials to be used (for turbine blades, for example), and tests are begun in experimental rigs to determine those. With this knowledge larger component parts (such as bearings) are designed and tested individually. As deficiencies and design errors are noted they are corrected and verified with further testing. Since one tests only one component at a time, these tests and modifications are not overly expensive. Finally one works up to the final design of the entire engine, to the necessary specifications. There is a good chance, by this time that the engine will generally succeed, or that any failures are easily isolated and analyzed because the failure modes, limitations of materials, etc., are so well understood. There is a very good chance that the modifications to the engine to get around the final difficulties are not very hard to make, for most of the serious problems have already been discovered and dealt with in the earlier, less expensive, stages of the process.

The Space Shuttle Main Engine was handled in a different manner, top down, we might say. The engine was designed and put together all at once with relatively little detailed preliminary study of the material and components. Then when troubles are found in the bearings, turbine blades, coolant pipes, etc., it is more expensive and difficult to discover the causes and make changes. For example, cracks have been found in the turbine blades of the high-pressure oxygen turbopump. Are they caused by flaws in the material, the effect of the oxygen atmosphere on the properties of the material, the thermal stresses of start-up or shutdown, the vibration and stresses of steady running, or mainly at some resonance at certain speeds, etc.? How long can we run from crack initiation to crack failure, and how does this depend on power level? Using the completed engine as a test bed to resolve such questions is extremely expensive. One does not wish to lose an entire engine in order to find out where and how failure occurs.

Yet, an accurate knowledge of this information is essential to acquire a confidence in the engine reliability in use. Without detailed understanding, confidence can not be attained. A further disadvantage of the top-down method is that, if an understanding of a fault is obtained, a simple fix, such as a new shape for the turbine housing, may be impossible to implement without a redesign of the entire engine.

The Space Shuttle Main Engine is a very remarkable machine. It has a greater ratio of thrust to weight than any previous engine. It is built at the edge of, or outside of, previous engineering experience. Therefore, as expected, many different kinds of flaws and difficulties have turned up. Because, unfortunately, it was built in the top-down manner, they are difficult to find and fix. The design aim of a lifetime of 55 missions' equivalent firings (27,000 seconds of operation, either in a mission of 500 seconds, or on a test stand) has not been obtained. The engine now requires very frequent maintenance and replacement of important parts, such as turbopumps, bearings, sheet metal housings, etc. The high-pressure fuel turbopump had to be replaced every three or four mission equivalents (although that may have been fixed, now) and the high-pressure oxygen turbopump every five or six. This is at most ten percent of the original specification.

Feynman's article[1] gives us an idea of the problems associated with testing complex systems. Even though the space shuttle is an extremely complex hardware and software system, the testing challenges are the same for any complex system.

Testing is often viewed as a job that can be done by beginners. Managers would assign the new members to the testing team, because the experienced people detested testing or are needed for the more important jobs of analysis and design. Unfortunately, such an attitude leads to many problems. To test a system effectively, a tester must have a detailed understanding of the whole system, ranging from the requirements to system design decisions and implementation issues. A tester must also be knowledgeable of testing techniques and apply these techniques effectively and efficiently to meet time, budget, and quality constraints.

Section 11.2 takes a bird's-eye view of testing. Section 11.3 defines in more detail the model elements related to testing, including faults, their manifestation, and their relationship to testing. Section 11.4 describes the testing activities found in the development process, including unit testing, which focuses on finding faults in a single component, and integration and system testing, which focus on finding faults in combination of components and in the complete system, respectively. We also discuss testing activities that focus on nonfunctional requirements, such as usability, performance, and stress tests. Section 11.4 concludes with the activities of field testing and installation testing. Section 11.5 discusses management issues related to testing.

---

1. Feynman [Feynman, 1988] wrote this article while he was a member of the Presidential Commission investigating the explosion of the Space Shuttle Challenger in January 1985. The cause of the accident was traced to an erosion of the O-rings in the solid rocket boosters. In addition to the testing problems of the main shuttle engine and the solid rocket boosters, the article mentions the phenomenon of gradually changing critical testing acceptance criteria and problems resulting from miscommunication between management and developers typically found in hierarchical organizations.

11.2 An Overview of Testing

Reliability is a measure of success with which the observed behavior of a system conforms to the specification of its behavior. **Software reliability** is the probability that a software system will not cause system failure for a specified time under specified conditions [IEEE Std. 982.2-1988]. **Failure** is any deviation of the observed behavior from the specified behavior. An **erroneous state** (also called an *error*) means the system is in a state such that further processing by the system will lead to a failure, which then causes the system to deviate from its intended behavior. A **fault**, also called "defect" or "bug," is the mechanical or algorithmic cause of an erroneous state. The goal of testing is to maximize the number of discovered faults, which then allows developers to correct them and increase the reliability of the system.

We define **testing** as the systematic attempt to *find faults in a planned way* in the implemented software. Contrast this definition with another common one: "testing is the process of demonstrating that *faults are not present*." The distinction between these two definitions is important. Our definition does not mean that we simply demonstrate that the program does what it is intended to do. The explicit goal of testing is to demonstrate the presence of faults and non-optimal behavior. Our definition implies that the developers are willing to dismantle things. Moreover, for the most part, demonstrating that faults are not present is not possible in systems of any realistic size.

Most activities of the development process are constructive: during analysis, design, and implementation, objects and relationships are identified, refined, and mapped onto a computer environment. Testing requires a different thinking, in that developers try to detect faults in the system, that is, differences between the reality of the system and the requirements. Many developers find this difficult to do. One reason is the way we use the word "success" during testing. Many project managers call a test case "successful" if it does not find a fault; that is, they use the second definition of testing during development. However, because "successful" denotes an achievement, and "unsuccessful" means something undesirable, these words should not be used in this fashion during testing.

In this chapter, we treat testing as an activity based on the falsification of system models, which is based on Popper's falsification of scientific theories [Popper, 1992]. According to Popper, when testing a scientific hypothesis, the goal is to design experiments that falsify the underlying theory. If the experiments are unable to break the theory, our confidence in the theory is strengthened and the theory is adopted (until it is eventually falsified). Similarly, in software testing, the goal is to identify faults in the software system (to falsify the theory). If none of the tests have been able to falsify software system behavior with respect to the requirements, it is ready for delivery. In other words, a software system is released when the falsification attempts (tests) show a certain level of confidence that the software system does what it is supposed to do.

There are many techniques for increasing the reliability of a software system:

* **Fault avoidance** techniques try to detect faults statically, that is, without relying on the execution of any of the system models, in particular the code model. Fault avoidance tries to prevent the insertion of faults into the system before it is released. Fault

avoidance includes development methodologies, configuration management, and verification.

- **Fault detection** techniques, such as debugging and testing, are uncontrolled and controlled experiments, respectively, used during the development process to identify erroneous states and find the underlying faults before releasing the system. Fault detection techniques assist in finding faults in systems, but do not try to recover from the failures caused by them. In general, fault detection techniques are applied during development, but in some cases they are also used after the release of the system. The blackboxes in an airplane to log the last few minutes of a flight is an example of a fault detection technique.

- **Fault tolerance** techniques assume that a system can be released with faults and that system failures can be dealt with by recovering from them at runtime. For example, modular redundant systems assign more than one component with the same task, then compare the results from the redundant components. The space shuttle has five onboard computers running two different pieces of software to accomplish the same task.

In this chapter, we focus on fault detection techniques, including reviews and testing. A **review** is the manual inspection of parts or all aspects of the system without actually executing the system. There are two types of reviews: walkthrough and inspection. In a code **walkthrough**, the developer informally presents the API (Application Programmer Interface), the code, and associated documentation of the component to the review team. The review team makes comments on the mapping of the analysis and object design to the code using use cases and scenarios from the analysis phase. An **inspection** is similar to a walkthrough, but the presentation of the component is formal. In fact, in a code inspection, the developer is not allowed to present the artifacts (models, code, and documentation). This is done by the review team, which is responsible for checking the interface and code of the component against the requirements. It also checks the algorithms for efficiency with respect to the nonfunctional requirements. Finally, it checks comments about the code and compares them with the code itself to find inaccurate and incomplete comments. The developer is only present in case the review needs clarifications about the definition and use of data structures or algorithms. Code reviews have proven to be effective at detecting faults. In some experiments, up to 85 percent of all identified faults were found in code reviews [Fagan, 1976], [Jones, 1977], [Porter et al., 1997].

Debugging assumes that faults can be found by starting from an unplanned failure. The developer moves the system through a succession of states, ultimately arriving at and identifying the erroneous state. Once this state has been identified, the algorithmic or mechanical fault causing this state must be determined. There are two types of debugging: The goal of correctness debugging is to find any deviation between observed and specified functional requirements. Performance debugging addresses the deviation between observed and specified nonfunctional requirements, such as response time.

Testing is a fault detection technique that tries to create failures or erroneous states in a planned way. This allows the developer to detect failures in the system before it is released to the customer. Note that this definition of testing implies that a successful test is a test that identifies faults. We will use this definition throughout the development phases. Another often-used definition of testing is that "it demonstrates that faults are not present." We will use this definition only after the development of the system when we try to demonstrate that the delivered system fulfills the functional and nonfunctional requirements.

If we used this second definition all the time, we would tend to select test data that have a low probability of causing the program to fail. If, on the other hand, the goal is to demonstrate that a program has faults, we tend to look for test data with a higher probability of finding faults. The characteristic of a good test model is that it contains test cases that identify faults. Tests should include a broad range of input values, including invalid inputs and boundary cases, otherwise, faults may not be detected. Unfortunately, such an approach requires extremely lengthy testing times for even small systems.

Figure 11-1 depicts an overview of testing activities:

- **Test planning** allocates resources and schedules the testing. This activity should occur early in the development phase so that sufficient time and skill is dedicated to testing. For example, developers can design test cases as soon as the models they validate become stable.

- **Usability testing** tries to find faults in the user interface design of the system. Often, systems fail to accomplish their intended purpose simply because their users are confused by the user interface and unwillingly introduce erroneous data.

- **Unit testing** tries to find faults in participating objects and/or subsystems with respect to the use cases from the use case model.

- **Integration testing** is the activity of finding faults by testing individual components in combination. **Structural testing** is the culmination of integration testing involving all components of the system. Integration tests and structural tests exploit knowledge from the SDD (System Design Document) using an integration strategy described in the Test Plan (TP).

- **System testing** tests all the components together, seen as a single system to identify faults with respect to the scenarios from the problem statement and the requirements and design goals identified in the analysis and system design, respectively:

  - **Functional testing** tests the requirements from the RAD and the user manual.

  - **Performance testing** checks the nonfunctional requirements and additional design goals from the SDD. Functional and performance testing are done by developers.

  - **Acceptance testing** and **installation testing** check the system against the project agreement and is done by the client, if necessary, with help by the developers.

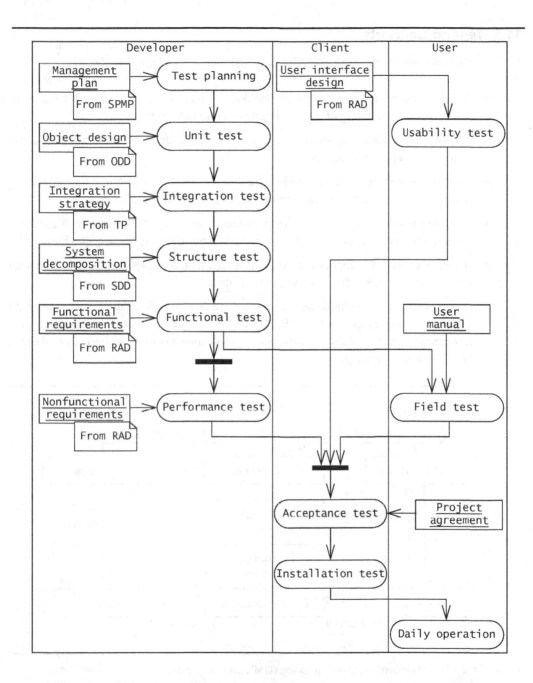

Figure 11-1 Testing activities and their related work products (UML activity diagram). Swimlanes indicate who executes the test.

11.3 Testing Concepts

In this section, we present the model elements used during testing (Figure 11-2):

- A **test component** is a part of the system that can be isolated for testing. A component can be an object, a group of objects, or one or more subsystems.

- A **fault**, also called *bug* or *defect*, is a design or coding mistake that may cause abnormal component behavior.

- An **erroneous state** is a manifestation of a fault during the execution of the system. An erroneous state is caused by one or more faults and can lead to a failure.

- A **failure** is a deviation between the specification and the actual behavior. A failure is triggered by one or more erroneous states. Not all erroneous states trigger a failure.[2]

- A **test case** is a set of inputs and expected results that exercises a test component with the purpose of causing failures and detecting faults.

- A **test stub** is a partial implementation of components on which the tested component depends. A **test driver** is a partial implementation of a component that depends on the test component. Test stubs and drivers enable components to be isolated from the rest of the system for testing.

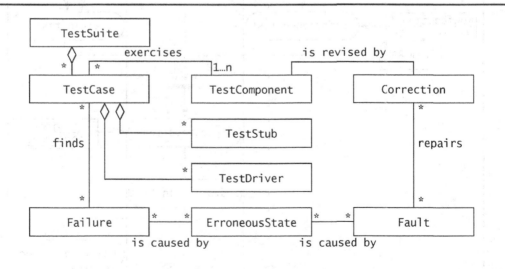

Figure 11-2   Model elements used during testing (UML class diagram).

2. Note that, outside the testing community, developers often do not distinguish between faults, failures, and erroneous states, and instead, refer to all three concepts as "errors."

- A **correction** is a change to a component. The purpose of a correction is to repair a fault. Note that a correction can introduce new faults.

11.3.1 Faults, Erroneous States, and Failures

With the initial understanding of the terms from the definitions in Section 11.3, let's take a look at Figure 11-3. What do you see? Figure 11-3 shows a pair of tracks that are not aligned with each other. If we envision a train running over the tracks, it would crash (fail). However, the figure actually does not present a failure, nor an erroneous state, nor a fault. It does not show a failure, because the expected behavior has not been specified, nor is there any observed behavior. Figure 11-3 also does not show an erroneous state, because that would mean that the system is in a state that further processing will lead to a failure. We only see tracks here; no moving train is shown. To speak about erroneous state, failure, or fault, we need to compare the desired behavior (described in the use case in the RAD) with the observed behavior (described by the test case). Assume that we have a use case with a train moving from the upper left track to the lower right track (Figure 11-4).

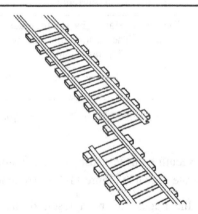

Figure 11-3   An example of a fault. The desired behavior is that the train remain on the tracks.

Use case name	DriveTrain
Participating actor	TrainOperator
Entry condition	TrainOperator pushes the "StartTrain" button at the control panel.
Flow of events	1. The train starts moving on track 1. 2. The train transitions to track 2.
Exit condition	The train is running on track 2.

Figure 11-4   Use case DriveTrain specifying the expected behavior of the train.

We can then proceed to derive a test case that moves the train from the state described in the entry condition of the use case to a state where it will crash, namely when it is leaving the upper track (Figure 11-5).

Test-case identifier	DriveTrain
Test location	http://www12.in.tum.de/TrainSystem/test-cases/test1
Feature to be tested	Continuous operation of engine for 5 seconds
Feature Pass/Fail Criteria	The test passes if the train drives for 5 seconds and covers the length of at least two tracks.
Means of control	1. The StartTrain() method is called via a test driver StartTrain (contained in the same directory as the DriveTrain test).
Data	2. Direction of trip and duration are read from a input file http://www12.in.tum.de/TrainSystem/test-cases/input. 3. If debug is set to TRUE, then the test case will output the system messages "Enter Track n, Exit Track n" for each n, where n is the number of the current track.
Test Procedure	The test is started by double-clicking the test case at the specified location. The test will run without further intervention until completion. The test should take no more than 7 seconds.
Special requirements	The test stub Engine is needed for the test execution.

Figure 11-5   Test case DriveTrain for the use case described in Figure 11-4.

In other words, when executing this test case, we can demonstrate that the system contains a fault. Note that the current state shown in Figure 11-6 is erroneous, but does not show a failure.

The misalignment of the tracks can be a result of bad communication between the development teams (each track had to be positioned by one team) or because of a wrong implementation of the specification by one of the teams (Figure 11-7). Both of these are examples of algorithmic faults. You are probably already familiar with many other algorithmic faults that are introduced during the implementation phase. For example, "Exiting a loop too soon," "exiting a loop too late," "testing for the wrong condition," "forgetting to initialize a variable" are all implementation-specific algorithmic faults. Algorithmic faults can also occur during analysis and system design. Stress and overload problems, for example, are object design specific algorithmic faults that lead to failure when data structures are filled beyond their specified capacity. Throughput and performance failures are possible when a system does not perform at the speed specified by the nonfunctional requirements.   •

Figure 11-6   An example of an erroneous state.

Figure 11-7   A fault can have an algorithmic cause.

Even if the tracks are implemented according to the specification in the RAD, they could still end up misaligned during daily operation, for example, if an earthquake happens that moves the underlying soil (Figure 11-8).

Figure 11-8   A fault can have a mechanical cause, such as an earthquake.

A fault in the virtual machine of a software system is another example of a mechanical fault: even if the developers have implemented correctly, that is, they have mapped the object model correctly onto the code, the observed behavior can still deviate from the specified behavior. In concurrent engineering projects, for example, where hardware is developed in parallel with software, we cannot always make the assumption that the virtual machine executes as specified. Other examples of mechanical faults are power failures. Note the relativity of the terms "fault" and "failure" with respect to a particular system component: the failure in one system component (the power system) is the mechanical fault that can lead to failure in another system component (the software system).

11.3.2 Test Cases

A **test case** is a set of input data and expected results that exercises a component with the purpose of causing failures and detecting faults. A test case has five attributes: name, location, input, oracle, and log (Table 11-1). The name of the test case allows the tester to distinguish between different test cases. A heuristic for naming test cases is to derive the name from the requirement it is testing or from the component being tested. For example, if you are testing a use case Deposit(), you might want to call the test case Test_Deposit. If a test case involves two components A and B, a good name would be Test_AB. The location attribute describes where the test case can be found. It should be either the path name or the URL to the executable of the test program and its inputs.

Table 11-1   Attributes of the class `TestCase`.

Attributes	Description
name	Name of test case
location	Full path name of executable
input	Input data or commands
oracle	Expected test results against which the output of the test is compared
log	Output produced by the test

Input describes the set of input data or commands to be entered by the actor of the test case (which can be the tester or a test driver). The expected behavior of the test case is the sequence of output data or commands that a correct execution of the test should yield. The expected behavior is described by the `oracle` attribute. The `log` is a set of time-stamped correlations of the observed behavior with the expected behavior for various test runs.

Once test cases are identified and described, relationships among test cases are identified. Aggregation and the `precede` associations are used to describe the relationships between the test cases. Aggregation is used when a test case can be decomposed into a set of subtests. Two test cases are related via the `precede` association when one test case must precede another test case.

Figure 11-9 shows a test model where `TestA` must precede `TestB` and `TestC`. For example, `TestA` consists of `TestA1` and `TestA2`, meaning that once `TestA1` and `TestA2` are tested, `TestA` is tested; there is no separate test for `TestA`. A good test model has as few associations as possible, because tests that are not associated with each other can be executed independently from each other. This allows a tester to speed up testing, if the necessary testing resources are available. In Figure 11-9, `TestB` and `TestC` can be tested in parallel, because there is no relation between them.

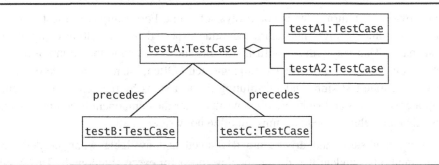

Figure 11-9   Test model with test cases. `TestA` consists of two tests, `TestA1` and `TestA2`. `TestB` and `TestC` can be tested independently, but only after `TestA` has been performed.

Test cases are classified into blackbox tests and whitebox tests, depending on which aspect of the system model is tested. **Blackbox tests** focus on the input/output behavior of the component. Blackbox tests do not deal with the internal aspects of the component, nor with the behavior or the structure of the components. **Whitebox tests** focus on the internal structure of the component. A whitebox test makes sure that, independently from the particular input/output behavior, every state in the dynamic model of the object and every interaction among the objects is tested. As a result, whitebox testing goes beyond blackbox testing. In fact, most of the whitebox tests require input data that could not be derived from a description of the functional requirements alone. Unit testing combines both testing techniques: blackbox testing to test the functionality of the component, and whitebox testing to test structural and dynamic aspects of the component.

11.3.3 Test Stubs and Drivers

Executing test cases on single components or combinations of components requires the tested component to be isolated from the rest of the system. Test drivers and test stubs are used to substitute for missing parts of the system. A **test driver** simulates the part of the system that calls the component under test. A test driver passes the test inputs identified in the test case analysis to the component and displays the results.

A **test stub** simulates a component that is called by the tested component. The test stub must provide the same API as the method of the simulated component and must return a value compliant with the return result type of the method's type signature. Note that the interface of all components must be baselined. If the interface of a component changes, the corresponding test drivers and stubs must change as well.

The implementation of test stubs is a nontrivial task. It is not sufficient to write a test stub that simply prints a message stating that the test stub was called. In most situations, when component A calls component B, A is expecting B to perform some work, which is then returned as a set of result parameters. If the test stub does not simulate this behavior, A will fail, not because of a fault in A, but because the test stub does not simulate B correctly.

Even providing a return value is not always sufficient. For example, if a test stub always returns the same value, it might not return the value expected by the calling component in a particular scenario. This can produce confusing results and even lead to the failure of the calling component, even though it is correctly implemented. Often, there is a trade-off between implementing accurate test stubs and substituting the test stubs by the actual component. For many components, drivers and stubs are often written after the component is completed, and for components that are behind schedule, stubs are often not written at all.

To ensure that stubs and drivers are developed and available when needed, several development methods stipulate that drivers be developed for every component. This results in lower effort because it provides developers the opportunity to find problems with the interface specification of the component under test before it is completely implemented.

11.3.4 Corrections

Once tests have been executed and failures have been detected, developers change the component to eliminate the suspected faults. A **correction** is a change to a component whose purpose is to repair a fault. Corrections can range from a simple modification to a single component, to a complete redesign of a data structure or a subsystem. In all cases, the likelihood that the developer introduces new faults into the revised component is high. Several techniques can be used to minimize the occurrence of such faults:

- *Problem tracking* includes the documentation of each failure, erroneous state, and fault detected, its correction, and the revisions of the components involved in the change. Together with configuration management, problem tracking enables developers to narrow the search for new faults. We describe problem tracking in more detail in Chapter 13, *Configuration Management*.

- *Regression testing* includes the reexecution of all prior tests after a change. This ensures that functionality which worked before the correction has not been affected. Regression testing is important in object-oriented methods, which call for an iterative development process. This requires testing to be initiated earlier and for test suites to be maintained after each iteration. Regression testing unfortunately is costly, especially when part of the tests is not automated. We describe regression testing in more detail in Section 11.4.4.

- *Rationale maintenance* includes the documentation of the rationale for the change and its relationship with the rationale of the revised component. Rationale maintenance enables developers to avoid introducing new faults by inspecting the assumptions that were used to build the component. We describe rationale maintenance in Chapter 12, *Rationale Management*.

Next, let us describe in more detail the testing activities that lead to the creation of test cases, their execution, and the development of corrections.

11.4 Testing Activities

In this section, we describe the technical activities of testing. These include

- **Component inspection**, which finds faults in an individual component through the manual inspection of its source code (Section 11.4.1)
- **Usability testing**, which finds differences between what the system does and the users' expectation of what it should do (Section 11.4.2)
- **Unit testing**, which finds faults by isolating an individual component using test stubs and drivers and by exercising the component using test cases (Section 11.4.3)
- **Integration testing**, which finds faults by integrating several components together (Section 11.4.4)

- **System testing**, which focuses on the complete system, its functional and nonfunctional requirements, and its target environment (Section 11.4.5).

11.4.1 Component Inspection

Inspections find faults in a component by reviewing its source code in a formal meeting. Inspections can be conducted before or after the unit test. The first structured inspection process was Michael Fagan's inspection method [Fagan, 1976]. The inspection is conducted by a team of developers, including the author of the component, a moderator who facilitates the process, and one or more reviewers who find faults in the component. Fagan's inspection method consists of five steps:

- *Overview.* The author of the component briefly presents the purpose and scope of the component and the goals of the inspection.
- *Preparation.* The reviewers become familiar with the implementation of the component.
- *Inspection meeting.* A reader paraphrases the source code of the component, and the inspection team raises issues with the component. A moderator keeps the meeting on track.
- *Rework.* The author revises the component.
- *Follow-up.* The moderator checks the quality of the rework and may determine the component that needs to be reinspected.

The critical steps in this process are the preparation phase and the inspection meeting. During the preparation phase, the reviewers become familiar with the source code; they do not yet focus on finding faults. During the inspection meeting, the reader paraphrases the source code, that is, he reads each source code statement and explains what the statement should do. The reviewers then raise issues if they think there is a fault. Most of the time is spent debating whether or not a fault is present, but solutions to repair the fault are not explored at this point. During the overview phase of the inspection, the author states the objectives of the inspection. In addition to finding faults, reviewers may also be asked to look for deviations from coding standards or for inefficiencies.

Fagan's inspections are usually perceived as time-consuming because of the length of the preparation and inspection meeting phase. The effectiveness of a review also depends on the preparation of the reviewers. David Parnas proposed a revised inspection process, the active design review, which eliminates the inspection meeting of all inspection team members [Parnas & Weiss, 1985]. Instead, reviewers are asked to find faults during the preparation phase. At the end of the preparation phase, each reviewer fills out a questionnaire testing his or her understanding of the component. The author then meets individually with each reviewer to collect feedback on the component.

Both Fagan's inspections and the active design reviews have been shown to be usually more effective than testing in uncovering faults. Both testing and inspections are used in safety-critical projects, as they tend to find different types of faults.

11.4.2 Usability Testing

Usability testing tests the user's understanding of the system. Usability testing does not compare the system against a specification. Instead, it focuses on finding differences between the system and the users' expectation of what it should do. As it is difficult to define a formal model of the user against which to test, usability testing takes an empirical approach: participants representative of the user population find problems by manipulating the user interface or a simulation thereof. Usability tests are also concerned with user interface details, such as the look and feel of the user interface, the geometrical layout of the screens, sequence of interactions, and the hardware. For example, in case of a wearable computer, a usability test would test the ability of the user to issue commands to the system while lying in an awkward position, as in the case of a mechanic looking at a screen under a car while checking a muffler.

The technique for conducting usability tests is based on the classical approach for conducting a controlled experiment. Developers first formulate a set of test objectives, describing what they hope to learn in the test. These can include, for example, evaluating specific dimensions or geometrical layout of the user interface, evaluating the impact of response time on user efficiency, or evaluating whether the online help documentation is sufficient for novice users. The test objectives are then evaluated in a series of experiments in which participants are trained to accomplish predefined tasks (e.g., exercising the user interface feature under investigation). Developers observe the participants and collect data measuring user performance (e.g., time to accomplish a task, error rate) and preferences (e.g, opinions and thought processes) to identify specific problems with the system or collect ideas for improving it [Rubin, 1994].

There are two important differences between controlled experiments and usability tests. Whereas the classical experimental method is designed to refute a hypothesis, the goal of usability tests is to obtain qualitative information on how to fix usability problems and how to improve the system. The other difference is the rigor with which the experiments are performed. It has been shown that even a series of quick focused tests starting as early as requirements elicitation is extremely helpful. Nielsen uses the term *discount usability engineering* to refer to simplified usability tests that can be accomplished at a fraction of the time and cost of a full-blown study, noting that a few usability tests are better than none at all [Nielsen & Mack, 1994]. Examples of discount usability tests include using paper scenario mock-ups (as opposed to a videotaped scenario), relying on handwritten notes as opposed to analyzing audio tape transcripts, or using fewer subjects to elicit suggestions and uncover major defects (as opposed to achieving statistical significance and using quantitative measures).

There are three types of usability tests:

- **Scenario test**. During this test, one or more users are presented with a visionary scenario of the system. Developers identify how quickly users are able to understand the scenario, how accurately it represents their model of work, and how positively they react to the description of the new system. The selected scenarios should be as realistic and detailed as possible. A scenario test allows rapid and frequent feedback from the user. Scenario tests can be realized as paper mock-ups[3] or with a simple prototyping environment, which is often easier to learn than the programming environment used for development. The advantage of scenario tests is that they are cheap to realize and to repeat. The disadvantages are that the user cannot interact directly with the system and that the data are fixed.

- **Prototype test**. During this type of test, the end users are presented with a piece of software that implements key aspects of the system. A **vertical prototype** completely implements a use case through the system. Vertical prototypes are used to evaluate core requirements, for example, response time of the system or user behavior under stress. A **horizontal prototype** implements a single layer in the system; an example is a **user interface prototype**, which presents an interface for most use cases (without providing much or any functionality). User interface prototypes are used to evaluate issues such as alternative user interface concepts or window layouts. A **Wizard of Oz prototype** is a user interface prototype in which a human operator behind the scenes pulls the levers [Kelly, 1984]. Wizard of Oz prototypes are used for testing natural language applications, when the speech recognition or the natural language parsing subsystems are incomplete. A human operator intercepts user queries and rephrases them in terms that the system understands, without the test user being aware of the operator. The advantages of prototype tests are that they provide a realistic view of the system to the user and that prototypes can be instrumented to collect detailed data. However, prototypes require more effort to build than test scenarios.

- **Product test**. This test is similar to the prototype test except that a functional version of the system is used in place of the prototype. A product test can only be conducted after most of the system is developed. It also requires that the system be easily modifiable such that the results of the usability test can be taken into account.

In all three types of tests, the basic elements of usability testing include [Rubin, 1994]

- development of test objectives

---

3. Using storyboards, a technique from the feature animation industry, consists of sketching a sequence of pictures of the screen at different points in the scenario. The pictures of each scenario are then lined up chronologically against a wall on a board (hence the term "storyboard"). Developers and users walk around the room when reviewing and discussing the scenarios. Given a reasonably sized room, participants can deal with several hundreds of sketches.

- a representative sample of end users
- the actual or simulated work environment
- controlled, extensive interrogation, and probing of the users by the person performing the usability test
- collection and analysis of quantitative and qualitative results
- recommendations on how to improve the system.

Typical test objectives in a usability test address the comparison of two user interaction styles, the identification of the best and the worst features in a scenario or a prototype, the main stumbling blocks, the identification of useful features for novice and expert users, when help is needed, and what type of training information is required.

11.4.3 Unit Testing

Unit testing focuses on the building blocks of the software system, that is, objects and subsystems. There are three motivations behind focusing on these building blocks. First, unit testing reduces the complexity of overall test activities, allowing us to focus on smaller units of the system. Second, unit testing makes it easier to pinpoint and correct faults, given that few components are involved in the test. Third, unit testing allows parallelism in the testing activities; that is, each component can be tested independently of the others.

The specific candidates for unit testing are chosen from the object model and the system decomposition. In principle, all the objects developed during the development process should be tested, which is often not feasible because of time and budget constraints. The minimal set of objects to be tested should be the participating objects in use cases. Subsystems should be tested as components only after each of the classes within that subsystem have been tested individually.

Existing subsystems, which were reused or purchased, should be treated as components with unknown internal structure. This applies in particular to commercially available subsystems, where the internal structure is not known or available to the developer.

Many unit testing techniques have been devised. Below, we describe the most important ones: equivalence testing, boundary testing, path testing, and state-based testing.

Equivalence testing

This blackbox testing technique minimizes the number of test cases. The possible inputs are partitioned into equivalence classes, and a test case is selected for each class. The assumption of equivalence testing is that systems usually behave in similar ways for all members of a class. To test the behavior associated with an equivalence class, we only need to test one member of the class. Equivalence testing consists of two steps: identification of the equivalence classes and selection of the test inputs. The following criteria are used in determining the equivalence classes.

- *Coverage*. Every possible input belongs to one of the equivalence classes.

- *Disjointedness.* No input belongs to more than one equivalence class.

- *Representation.* If the execution demonstrates an erroneous state when a particular member of a equivalence class is used as input, then the same erroneous state can be detected by using any other member of the class as input.

For each equivalence class, at least two pieces of data are selected: a typical input, which exercises the common case, and an invalid input, which exercises the exception handling capabilities of the component. After all equivalence classes have been identified, a test input for each class has to be identified that covers the equivalence class. If there is a possibility that not all the elements of the equivalence class are covered by the test input, the equivalence class must be split into smaller equivalence classes, and test inputs must be identified for each of the new classes.

For example, consider a method that returns the number of days in a month, given the month and year (see Figure 11-10). The month and year are specified as integers. By convention, 1 represents the month of January, 2 the month of February, and so on. The range of valid inputs for the year is 0 to maxInt.

```
class MyGregorianCalendar {
    ...
    public static int getNumDaysInMonth(int month, int year) {…}
    ...
}
```

Figure 11-10   Interface for a method computing the number of days in a given month (in Java). The getNumDaysInMonth() method takes two parameters, a month and a year, both specified as integers.

We find three equivalence classes for the month parameter: months with 31 days (i.e., 1, 3, 5, 7, 8, 10, 12), months with 30 days (i.e., 4, 6, 9, 11), and February, which can have 28 or 29 days. Nonpositive integers and integers larger than 12 are invalid values for the month parameter. Similarly, we find two equivalence classes for the year: leap years and non–leap years. By specification, negative integers are invalid values for the year. First we select one valid value for each equivalence class (e.g., February, June, July, 1901, and 1904). Given that the return value of the getNumDaysInMonth() method depends on both parameters, we combine these values to test for interaction, resulting in the six equivalence classes displayed in Table 11-2.

Boundary testing

This special case of equivalence testing focuses on the conditions at the boundary of the equivalence classes. Rather than selecting any element in the equivalence class, boundary testing requires that the elements be selected from the "edges" of the equivalence class. The assumption

Table 11-2   Equivalence classes and selected valid inputs for testing the getNumDaysInMonth() method.

Equivalence class	Value for month input	Value for year input
Months with 31 days, non–leap years	7 (July)	1901
Months with 31 days, leap years	7 (July)	1904
Months with 30 days, non–leap years	6 (June)	1901
Month with 30 days, leap year	6 (June)	1904
Month with 28 or 29 days, non–leap year	2 (February)	1901
Month with 28 or 29 days, leap year	2 (February)	1904

behind boundary testing is that developers often overlook special cases at the boundary of the equivalence classes (e.g., 0, empty strings, year 2000).

In our example, the month of February presents several boundary cases. In general, years that are multiples of 4 are leap years. Years that are multiples of 100, however, are not leap years, unless they are also multiple of 400. For example, 2000 was a leap year, whereas 1900 was not. Both year 1900 and 2000 are good boundary cases we should test. Other boundary cases include the months 0 and 13, which are at the boundaries of the invalid equivalence class. Table 11-3 displays the additional boundary cases we selected for the getNumDaysInMonth() method.

A disadvantage of equivalence and boundary testing is that these techniques do not explore combinations of test input data. In many cases, a program fails because a combination of certain values causes the erroneous fault. Cause-effect testing addresses this problem by establishing logical relationships between input and outputs or inputs and transformations. The inputs are called causes, the outputs or transformations are effects. The technique is based on the premise that the input/output behavior can be transformed into a Boolean function. For details on this technique and another technique called "error guessing," we refer you to the literature on testing (for example [Myers, 1979]).

Table 11-3   Additional boundary cases selected for the getNumDaysInMonth() method.

Equivalence class	Value for month input	Value for year input
Leap years divisible by 400	2 (February)	2000
Non–leap years divisible by 100	2 (February)	1900
Nonpositive invalid months	0	1291
Positive invalid months	13	1315

Path testing

This whitebox testing technique identifies faults in the implementation of the component. The assumption behind path testing is that, by exercising all possible paths through the code at least once, most faults will trigger failures. The identification of paths requires knowledge of the source code and data structures. The starting point for path testing is the flow graph. A flow graph consists of nodes representing executable blocks and edges representing flow of control. A flow graph is constructed from the code of a component by mapping decision statements (e.g., if statements, while loops) to nodes. Statements between each decision (e.g., then block, else block) are mapped to other nodes. Associations between each node represent the precedence relationships. Figure 11-11 depicts an example of a *faulty* implementation of the getNumDaysInMonth() method. Figure 11-12 depicts the equivalent flow graph as a UML

```java
public class MonthOutOfBounds extends Exception {…};
public class YearOutOfBounds extends Exception {…};

class MyGregorianCalendar {
    public static boolean isLeapYear(int year) {
        boolean leap;
        if ((year%4) == 0){
            leap = true;
        } else {
            leap = false;
        }
        return leap;
    }
    public static int getNumDaysInMonth(int month, int year)
            throws MonthOutOfBounds, YearOutOfBounds {
        int numDays;
        if (year < 1) {
            throw new YearOutOfBounds(year);
        }
        if (month == 1 || month == 3 || month == 5 || month == 7 ||
                month == 10 || month == 12) {
            numDays = 32;
        } else if (month == 4 || month == 6 || month == 9 || month == 11) {
            numDays = 30;
        } else if (month == 2) {
            if (isLeapYear(year)) {
                numDays = 29;
            } else {
                numDays = 28;
            }
        } else {
            throw new MonthOutOfBounds(month);
        }
        return numDays;
    }
}
```

Figure 11-11   An example of a (faulty) implementation of the getNumDaysInMonth() method (Java).

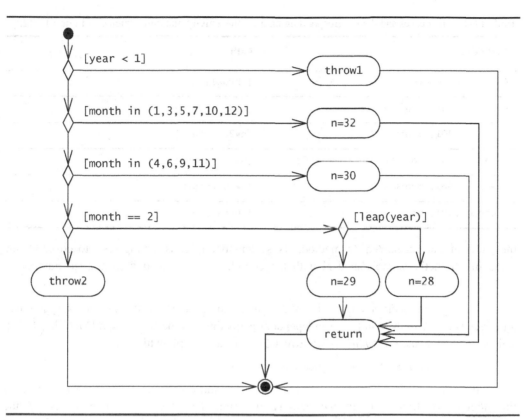

Figure 11-12 Equivalent flow graph for the (faulty) implementation of the getNumDaysInMonth() method of Figure 11-11 (UML activity diagram).

activity diagram. In this example, we model decisions with UML branches, blocks with UML actions, and control flow with UML transitions.

Complete path testing consists of designing test cases such that each edge in the activity diagram is traversed at least once. This is done by examining the condition associated with each branch point and selecting an input for the true branch and another input for the false branch. For example, examining the first branch point in Figure 11-12, we select two inputs: year=0 (such that year < 1 is true) and year=1901 (such that year < 1 is false). We then repeat the process for the second branch and select the inputs month=1 and month=2. The input (year=0, month=1) produces the path {throw1}. The input (year=1901, month=1) produces a second path {n=32 return}, which uncovers one of the faults in the getNumDaysInMonth() method. By repeating this process for each node, we generate the test cases depicted in Table 11-4.

We can similarly construct the activity diagram for the method isLeapYear() and derive test cases to exercise the single branch point of this method (Figure 11-13). Note that the test case (year = 1901, month = 2) of the getNumDaysInMonth() method already exercises one of

Table 11-4   Test cases and their corresponding path for the activity diagram depicted in Figure 11-12.

Test case	Path
(year = 0, month = 1)	{throw1}
(year = 1901, month = 1)	{n=32 return}
(year = 1901, month = 2)	{n=28 return}
(year = 1904, month = 2)	{n=29 return}
(year = 1901, month = 4)	{n=30 return}
(year = 1901, month = 0)	{throw2}

the paths of the isLeapYear() method. By systematically constructing tests to cover all the paths of all methods, we can deal with the complexity associated with a large number of methods.

Using graph theory, it can be shown that the minimum number of tests necessary to cover all edges is equal to the number of independent paths through the flow graph [McCabe, 1976]. This is defined as the *cyclomatic complexity* CC of the flow graph, which is

CC = number of edges - number of nodes + 2

where the number of nodes is the number of branches and actions, and the number of edges is the number of transitions in the activity diagram. The cyclomatic complexity of the getNumDaysInMonth() method is 6, which is also the number of test cases we found in Table 11-4. Similarly, the cyclomatic complexity of the isLeapYear() method and the number of derived test cases is 2.

By comparing the test cases we derived from the equivalence classes (Table 11-2) and boundary cases (Table 11-3) with the test cases we derived from the flow graph (Table 11-4 and Figure 11-13), several differences can be noted. In both cases, we test the method extensively for computations involving the month of February. However, because the implementation of isLeapYear() does not take into account years divisible by 100, path testing did not generate any test case for this equivalence class.

In general, path testing and whitebox methods can detect only faults resulting from exercising a path in the program, such as the faulty numDays=32 statement. Whitebox testing methods cannot detect omissions, such as the failure to handle the non–leap year 1900. Path testing is also heavily based on the control structure of the program; faults associated with violating invariants of data structures, such as accessing an array out of bounds, are not explicitly addressed. However, no testing method short of exhaustive testing can guarantee the discovery of all faults. In our example, neither equivalence testing or path testing uncovered the fault associated with the month of August.

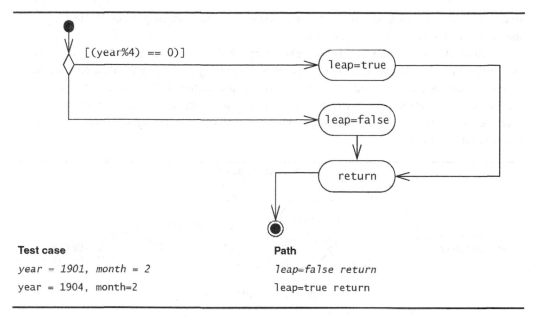

Test case	Path
year = 1901, month = 2	*leap=false return*
year = 1904, month=2	leap=true return

Figure 11-13 Equivalent flow graph for the (faulty) isLeapYear() method implementation of Figure 11-11 (UML activity diagram) and derived tests. The test in *italic* is redundant with a test we derived for the getNumDaysInMonth() method.

State-based testing

This testing technique was recently developed for object-oriented systems [Turner & Robson, 1993]. Most testing techniques focus on selecting a number of test inputs for a given state of the system, exercising a component or a system, and comparing the observed outputs with an oracle. State-based testing, however, compares the resulting state of the system with the expected state. In the context of a class, state-based testing consists of deriving test cases from the UML state machine diagram for the class. For each state, a representative set of stimuli is derived for each transition (similar to equivalence testing). The attributes of the class are then instrumented and tested after each stimuli has been applied to ensure that the class has reached the specified state.

For example, Figure 11-14 depicts a state machine diagram and its associated tests for the 2Bwatch we described in Chapter 2, *Modeling with UML*. It specifies which stimuli change the watch from the high-level state MeasureTime to the high-level state SetTime. It does not show the low-level states of the watch when the date and time change, either because of actions of the user or because of time passing. The test inputs in Figure 11-14 were generated such that each transition is traversed at least once. After each input, instrumentation code checks if the watch is in the predicted state and reports a failure otherwise. Note that some transitions (e.g., transition 3) are traversed several times, as it is necessary to put the watch back into the SetTime state (e.g., to test transitions 4, 5, and 6). Only the first eight stimuli are displayed. The test inputs for the DeadBattery state were not generated.

Currently, state-based testing presents several difficulties. Because the state of a class is encapsulated, test cases must include sequences for putting classes in the desired state before given transitions can be tested. State-based testing also requires the instrumentation of class attributes. Although state-based testing is currently not part of the state of the practice, it promises to become an effective testing technique for object-oriented systems as soon as proper automation is provided.

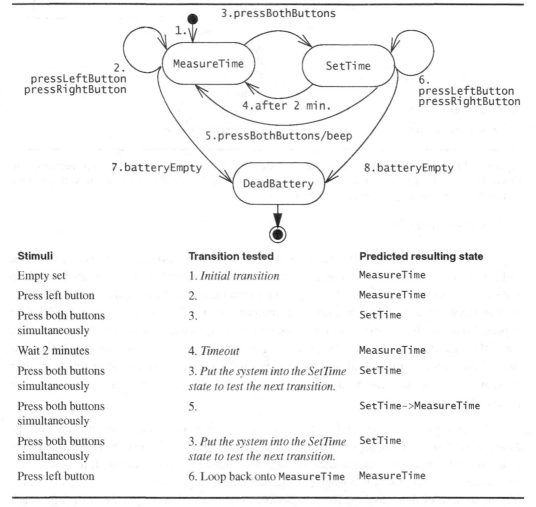

Stimuli	Transition tested	Predicted resulting state
Empty set	1. *Initial transition*	MeasureTime
Press left button	2.	MeasureTime
Press both buttons simultaneously	3.	SetTime
Wait 2 minutes	4. *Timeout*	MeasureTime
Press both buttons simultaneously	3. *Put the system into the SetTime state to test the next transition.*	SetTime
Press both buttons simultaneously	5.	SetTime->MeasureTime
Press both buttons simultaneously	3. *Put the system into the SetTime state to test the next transition.*	SetTime
Press left button	6. Loop back onto MeasureTime	MeasureTime

Figure 11-14 UML state machine diagram and resulting tests for 2Bwatch SetTime use case. Only the first eight stimuli are shown.

Polymorphism testing

Polymorphism introduces a new challenge in testing because it enables messages to be bound to different methods based on the class of the target. Although this enables developers to reuse code across a larger number of classes, it also introduces more cases to test. All possible bindings should be identified and tested [Binder, 2000].

Consider the `NetworkInterface` Strategy design pattern that we introduced in Chapter 8, *Object Design: Reusing Pattern Solutions* (see Figure 11-15). The Strategy design pattern uses polymorphism to shield the context (i.e., the `NetworkConnection` class) from the concrete strategy (i.e., the `Ethernet`, `WaveLAN`, and `UMTS` classes). For example, the `NetworkConnection.send()` method calls the `NetworkInterface.send()` method to send bytes across the current `NetworkInterface`, regardless of the actual concrete strategy. This means that, at run time, the `NetworkInterface.send()` method invocation can be bound to one of three methods, `Ethernet.send()`, `WaveLAN.send()`, `UMTS.send()`.

When applying the path testing technique to an operation that uses polymorphism, we need to consider all dynamic bindings, one for each message that could be sent. In `NetworkConnect.send()` in the left column of Figure 11-16, we invoke the `NetworkInterface.send()` operation, which can be bound to either `Ethernet.send()`, `WaveLAN.send()`, or the `UMTS.send()` methods, depending on the class of the `nif` object. To deal with this situation explicitly, we expand the original source code by replacing each invocation of `NetworkInterface.send()` with a nested `if` `else` statement that tests for all subclasses of `NetworkInterface` (right column of Figure 11-16). Depending on the class, `nif` is cast into the appropriate concrete class, and the associated method is invoked.

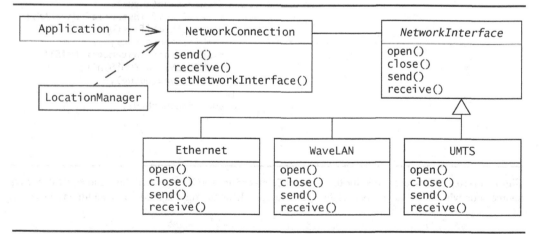

Figure 11-15 A Strategy design pattern for encapsulating multiple implementations of a `NetworkInterface` (UML class diagram).

Note that in some situations, the number of paths can be reduced by eliminating redundancy. For the sake of this example, we simply adopt a mechanical approach.

Once the source code is expanded, we extract the flow graph (Figure 11-17) and generate test cases covering all paths. This results in test cases that exercise the send() method of all three concrete network interfaces.

When many interfaces and abstract classes are involved, generating the flow graph for a method of medium complexity can result in an explosion of paths. This illustrates, on the one hand, how object-oriented code using polymorphism can result in compact and extensible components, and on the other hand, how the number of test cases increases when trying to achieve any acceptable path coverage.

```java
public class NetworkConnection {
//...
private NetworkInterface nif;
void send(byte msg[]) {
    queue.concat(msg);
    if (nif.isReady()) {
        nif.send(queue);
        queue.setLength(0);
    }
}
}
```

```java
public class NetworkConnection {
//...
private NetworkInterface nif;
void send(byte msg[]) {
    queue.concat(msg);
    boolean ready = false;
    if (nif instanceof Ethernet) {
        Ethernet eNif = (Ethernet)nif;
        ready = eNif.isReady();
    } else if (nif instanceof WaveLAN) {
        WaveLAN wNif = (WaveLAN)nif;
        ready = wNif.isReady();
    } else if (nif instanceof UMTS) {
        UMTS uNif = (UMTS)nif;
        ready = uNif.isReady();
    }
    if (ready) {
        if (nif instanceof Ethernet) {
            Ethernet eNif = (Ethernet)nif;
            eNif.send(queue);
        } else if (nif instanceof WaveLAN){
            WaveLAN wNif = (WaveLAN)nif;
            wNif.send(queue);
        } else if (nif instanceof UMTS){
            UMTS uNif = (UMTS)nif;
            uNif.send(queue);
        }
        queue.setLength(0);
    }
}
}
```

Figure 11-16 Java source code for the NetworkConnection.send() message (left) and equivalent Java source code without polymorphism (right). The source code on the right is used for generating test cases.

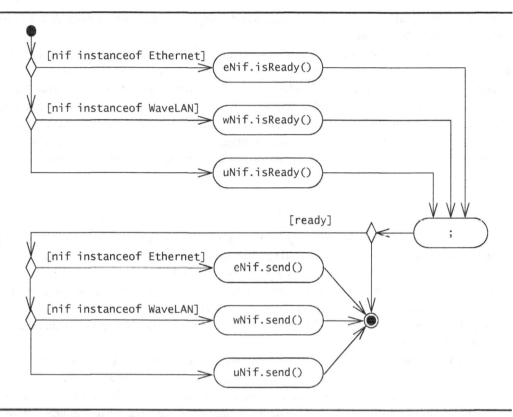

Figure 11-17   Equivalent flow graph for the expanded source code of the NetworkConnection.send() method of Figure 11-16 (UML activity diagram).

11.4.4 Integration Testing

Unit testing focuses on individual components. The developer discovers faults using equivalence testing, boundary testing, path testing, and other methods. Once faults in each component have been removed and the test cases do not reveal any new fault, components are ready to be integrated into larger subsystems. At this point, components are still likely to contain faults, as test stubs and drivers used during unit testing are only approximations of the components they simulate. Moreover, unit testing does not reveal faults associated with the component interfaces resulting from invalid assumptions when calling these interfaces.

Integration testing detects faults that have not been detected during unit testing by focusing on small groups of components. Two or more components are integrated and tested, and when no new faults are revealed, additional components are added to the group. If two components are tested together, we call this a *double test*. Testing three components together is a *triple test*, and a test with four components is called a *quadruple test*. This procedure allows the testing of increasingly more complex parts of the system while keeping the location of potential faults relatively small (i.e., the most recently added component is usually the one that triggers the most recently discovered faults).

Developing test stubs and drivers for a systematic integration test is time consuming. For that reason, Extreme Programming, for example, stipulates that drivers be written before components are developed [Beck & Andres, 2005]. The order in which components are tested, however, can influence the total effort required by the integration test. A careful ordering of components can reduce the resources needed for the overall integration test. In the next sections, we discuss **horizontal integration testing strategies**, in which components are integrated according to layers, and **vertical integration testing strategies**, in which components are integrated according to functions.

Horizontal integration testing strategies

Several approaches have been devised to implement a horizontal integration testing strategy: big bang testing, bottom-up testing, top-down testing, and sandwich testing. Each of these strategies was originally devised by assuming that the system decomposition is hierarchical and that each of the components belong to hierarchical layers ordered with respect to the "Call" association. These strategies, however, can be easily adapted to nonhierarchical system decompositions. Figure 11-18 shows a hierarchical system decomposition that we use for discussing these strategies.

The **big bang testing** strategy assumes that all components are first tested individually and then tested together as a single system. The advantage is that no additional test stubs or drivers are needed. Although this strategy sounds simple, big bang testing is expensive: if a test uncovers a failure, it is impossible to distinguish failures in the interface from failures within a component. Moreover, it is difficult to pinpoint the specific component (or combination of components) responsible for the failure, as all components in the system are potentially exercised. This results in integration strategies that integrate only a few components at the time.

The **bottom-up testing** strategy first tests each component of the bottom layer individually, and then integrates them with components of the next layer up. This is repeated until all components from all layers are combined. Test drivers are used to simulate the components of higher layers that have not yet been integrated. Note that no test stubs are necessary during bottom-up testing.

The **top-down testing** strategy unit tests the components of the top layer first, and then integrates the components of the next layer down. When all components of the new layer have been tested together, the next layer is selected. Again, the tests incrementally add one component at a time. This is repeated until all layers are combined and involved in the test. Test stubs are used to simulate the components of lower layers that have not yet been integrated. Note that test drivers are not needed during top-down testing.

The advantage of bottom-up testing is that interface faults can be more easily found: when the developers substitute a test driver for a higher-level component, they have a clear model of how the lower-level component works and of the assumptions embedded in its interface. If the

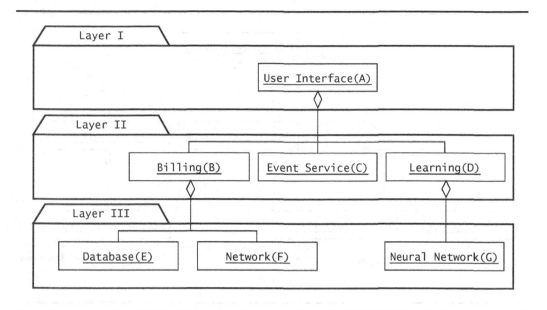

Figure 11-18 Example of a hierarchal system decomposition with three layers (UML class diagram, layers represented by packages).

higher-level component violates assumptions made in the lower-level component, developers are more likely to find them quickly. The disadvantage of bottom-up testing is that it tests the most important subsystems, namely the components of the user interface, last. Faults found in the top layer may often lead to changes in the subsystem decomposition or in the subsystem interfaces of lower layers, invalidating previous tests.

The advantage of top-down testing is that it starts with user interface components. The same set of tests, derived from the requirements, can be used in testing the increasingly more complex set of subsystems. The disadvantage of top-down testing is that the development of test stubs is time-consuming and prone to error. A large number of stubs is usually required for testing nontrivial systems, especially when the lowest level of the system decomposition implements many methods.

Figures 11-19 and 11-20 illustrate the possible combinations of subsystems that can be used during integration testing. Using a bottom-up strategy, subsystems E, F, and G are united tested first, then the triple test B-E-F and the double test D-G are executed, and so on. Using a top-down strategy, subsystem A is unit tested, then double tests A-B, A-C, and A-D are executed, then the quad test A-B-C-D is executed, and so on. Both strategies cover the same number of subsystem dependencies, but exercise them in different order.

The **sandwich testing** strategy combines the top-down and bottom-up strategies, attempting to make use of the best of both. During sandwich testing, the tester must be able to reformulate or map the subsystem decomposition into three layers, a target layer ("the meat"), a

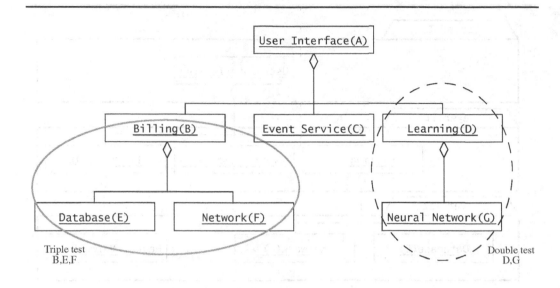

Figure 11-19 Bottom-up test strategy. After unit testing subsystems E, F, and G, the bottom up integration test proceeds with the triple test B-E-F and the double test D-G.

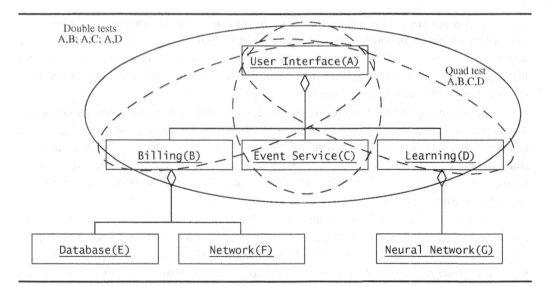

Figure 11-20 Top-down test strategy. After unit testing subsystem A, the integration test proceeds with the double tests A-B, A-C, and A-D, followed by the quad test A-B-C-D.

layer above the target layer ("the top slice of bread"), and a layer below the target layer ("the bottom slice of bread"). Using the target layer as the focus of attention, top-down testing and bottom-up testing can now be done in parallel. Top-down integration testing is done by testing the top layer incrementally with the components of the target layer, and bottom-up testing is used for testing the bottom layer incremental with the components of the target layer. As a result, test stubs and drivers need not be written for the top and bottom layers, because they use the actual components from the target layer.

Note that this also allows early testing of the user interface components. There is one problem with sandwich testing: it does not thoroughly test the individual components of the target layer before integration. For example, the sandwich test shown in Figure 11-21 does not unit test component C of the target layer.

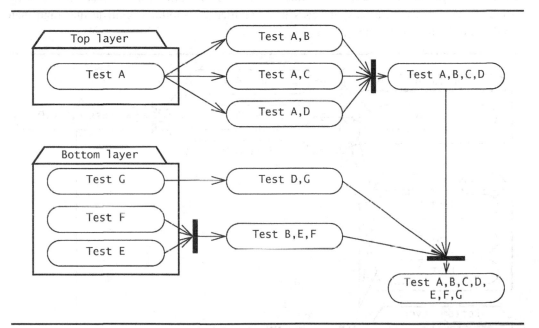

Figure 11-21   Sandwich testing strategy (UML activity diagram). None of the components in the target layer (i.e., B, C, D) are unit tested.

The **modified sandwich testing** strategy tests the three layers individually before combining them in incremental tests with one another. The individual layer tests consists of a group of three tests:

- a top layer test with stubs for the target layer
- a target layer test with drivers and stubs replacing the top and bottom layers
- a bottom layer test with a driver for the target layer.

The combined layer tests consist of two tests:

- The top layer accesses the target layer. This test can reuse the target layer tests from the individual layer tests, replacing the drivers with components from the top layer.

- The bottom layer is accessed by the target layer. This test can reuse the target layer tests from the individual layer tests, replacing the stub with components from the bottom layer.

The advantage of modified sandwich testing is that many testing activities can be performed in parallel, as indicated by the activity diagrams of Figures 11-21 and 11-22. The disadvantage of modified sandwich testing is the need for additional test stubs and drivers. Overall, modified sandwich testing leads to a significantly shorter overall testing time than top-down or bottom-up testing.

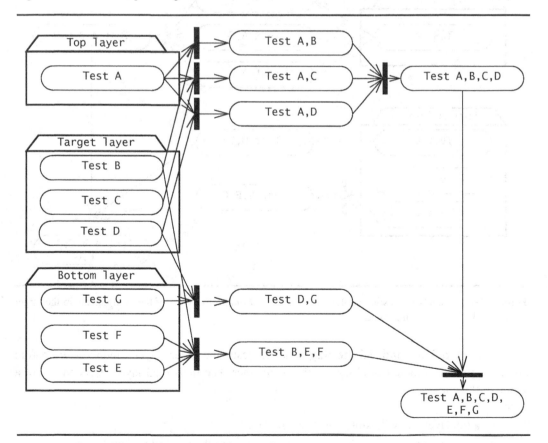

Figure 11-22 An example of modified sandwich testing strategy (UML activity diagrams). The components of the target layer are unit tested before they are integrated with the top and bottom layers.

Vertical integration testing strategies

In the previous section, we discussed horizontal integration testing strategies, in which components are integrated into layers, following the subsystem decomposition. As development responsibilities also follow the subsystem decomposition, horizontal integration is straightforward to manage, as tests verify the interfaces that have been negotiated between teams. The main drawback, however, is that an operational system that can be a release candidate, is only available very late during development.

Vertical integration testing strategies, in contrast, focus on early integration. For a given use case, the needed parts of each component, such the user interface, business logic, middleware, and storage, are identified and developed in parallel and integration tested. Note that this is different than the vertical prototypes for usability testing discussed in Section 11.4.2, as vertical prototypes are not release candidates. A system build with a vertical integration strategy produces release candidates.

For example, Extreme Programming [Beck & Andres, 2005], uses a vertical integration strategy in terms of a user stories. A user story is a single functional requirement formulated by the customer that is realized and integration tested during an iteration. At the end of an iteration, a release candidate is produced and demonstrated to the customer. The drawback of vertical integration testing, however, is that the system design is evolved incrementally, often resulting in reopening major system design decisions.

We discuss solutions to the early integration challenges when introducing continuous integration in Chapter 13, *Configuration Management*.

11.4.5 System Testing

Unit and integration testing focus on finding faults in individual components and the interfaces between the components. Once components have been integrated, **system testing** ensures that the complete system complies with the functional and nonfunctional requirements. Note that vertical integration testing is a special case of system testing: the former focuses only on a new slice of functionality, whereas the system testing focuses on the complete system.

During system testing, several activities are performed:

- **Functional testing**. Test of functional requirements (from RAD)
- **Performance testing**. Test of nonfunctional requirements (from SDD)
- **Pilot testing**. Tests of common functionality among a selected group of end users in the target environment
- **Acceptance testing.** Usability, functional, and performance tests performed by the customer in the development environment against acceptance criteria (from Project Agreement)
- **Installation testing**. Usability, functional, and performance tests performed by the customer in the target environment. If the system is only installed at a small selected set of customers it is called a *beta test*.

Functional testing

Functional testing, also called **requirements testing**, finds differences between the functional requirements and the system. Functional testing is a blackbox technique: test cases are derived from the use case model. In systems with complex functional requirements, it is usually not possible to test all use cases for all valid and invalid inputs. The goal of the tester is to select those tests that are relevant to the user and have a high probability of uncovering a failure. Note that functional testing is different from usability testing (described in Chapter 4, *Requirements Elicitation*), which also focuses on the use case model. Functional testing finds differences between the use case model and the observed system behavior, whereas usability testing finds differences between the use case model and the user's expectation of the system.

To identify functional tests, we inspect the use case model and identify use case instances that are likely to cause failures. This is done using blackbox techniques similar to equivalence testing and boundary testing (see Section 11.4.3). Test cases should exercise both common and exceptional use cases. For example, consider the use case model for a subway ticket distributor (see Figure 11-23). The common case functionality is modeled by the PurchaseTicket use case, describing the steps necessary for a Passenger to successfully purchase a ticket. The TimeOut, Cancel, OutOfOrder, and NoChange use cases describe various exceptional conditions resulting from the state of the distributor or actions by the Passenger.

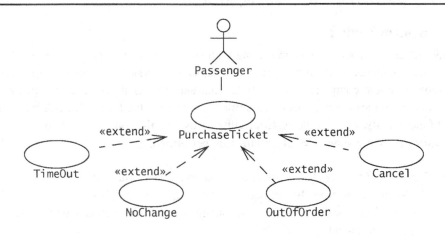

Figure 11-23 An example of use case model for a subway ticket distributor (UML use case diagram).

Figure 11-24 depicts the PurchaseTicket use case describing the normal interaction between the Passenger actor and the Distributor. We notice that three features of the Distributor are likely to fail and should be tested:

1. The Passenger may press multiple zone buttons before inserting money, in which case the Distributor should display the amount of the last zone.

2. The Passenger may select another zone button after beginning to insert money, in which case the Distributor should return all money inserted by the Passenger.

3. The Passenger may insert more money than needed, in which case the Distributor should return the correct change.

Use case name	PurchaseTicket
Entry condition	The Passenger is standing in front of ticket Distributor.
	The Passenger has sufficient money to purchase ticket.
Flow of events	1. The Passenger selects the number of zones to be traveled. If the Passenger presses multiple zone buttons, only the last button pressed is considered by the Distributor.
	2. The Distributor displays the amount due.
	3. The Passenger inserts money.
	4. If the Passenger selects a new zone before inserting sufficient money, the Distributor returns all the coins and bills inserted by the Passenger.
	5. If the Passenger inserted more money than the amount due, the Distributor returns excess change.
	6. The Distributor issues ticket.
	7. The Passenger picks up the change and the ticket.
Exit condition	The Passenger has the selected ticket.

Figure 11-24 An example of use case from the ticket distributor use case model PurchaseTicket.

Figure 11-25 depicts the test case PurchaseTicket_CommonCase, which exercises these three features. Note that the flow of events describes both the inputs to the system (stimuli that the Passenger sends to the Distributor) and desired outputs (correct responses from the Distributor). Similar test cases can also be derived for the exceptional use cases NoChange, OutOfOrder, TimeOut, and Cancel.

Test cases, such as PurchaseTicket_CommonCase, are derived for all use cases, including use cases representing exceptional behavior. Test cases are associated with the use cases from which they are derived, making it easier to update the test cases when use cases are modified.

Performance testing

Performance testing finds differences between the design goals selected during system design and the system. Because the design goals are derived from the nonfunctional requirements, the test cases can be derived from the SDD or from the RAD. The following tests are performed during performance testing:

Test case name	PurchaseTicket_CommonCase
Entry condition	The Passenger standing in front of ticket Distributor.
	The Passenger has two $5 bills and three dimes.
Flow of events	1. The Passenger presses in succession the zone buttons 2, 4, 1, and 2.
	2. The Distributor should display in succession $1.25, $2.25, $0.75, and $1.25.
	3. The Passenger inserts a $5 bill.
	4. The Distributor returns three $1 bills and three quarters and issues a 2-zone ticket.
	5. The Passenger repeats steps 1–4 using his second $5 bill.
	6. The Passenger repeats steps 1–3 using four quarters and three dimes. The Distributor issues a 2-zone ticket and returns a nickel.
	7. The Passenger selects zone 1 and inserts a dollar bill. The Distributor issues a 1-zone ticket and returns a quarter.
	8. The Passenger selects zone 4 and inserts two $1 bills and a quarter. The Distributor issues a 4-zone ticket.
	9. The Passenger selects zone 4. The Distributor displays $2.25. The Passenger inserts a $1 bill and a nickel, and selects zone 2. The Distributor returns the $1 bill and the nickel and displays $1.25.
Exit condition	The Passenger has three 2-zone tickets, one 1-zone ticket, and one 4-zone ticket.

Figure 11-25   An example of test case derived from the PurchaseTicket use case.

- *Stress testing* checks if the system can respond to many simultaneous requests. For example, if an information system for car dealers is required to interface with 6000 dealers, the stress test evaluates how the system performs with more than 6000 simultaneous users.

- *Volume testing* attempts to find faults associated with large amounts of data, such as static limits imposed by the data structure, or high-complexity algorithms, or high disk fragmentation.

- *Security testing* attempts to find security faults in the system. There are few systematic methods for finding security faults. Usually this test is accomplished by "tiger teams" who attempt to break into the system, using their experience and knowledge of typical security flaws.

- *Timing testing* attempts to find behaviors that violate timing constraints described by the nonfunctional requirements.

- *Recovery tests* evaluates the ability of the system to recover from erroneous states, such as the unavailability of resources, a hardware failure, or a network failure.

After all the functional and performance tests have been performed, and no failures have been detected during these tests, the system is said to be validated.

Pilot testing

During the **pilot test**, also called the **field test**, the system is installed and used by a selected set of users. Users exercise the system as if it had been permanently installed. No explicit guidelines or test scenarios are given to the users. Pilot tests are useful when a system is built without a specific set of requirements or without a specific customer in mind. In this case, a group of people is invited to use the system for a limited time and to give their feedback to the developers.

An *alpha test* is a pilot test with users exercising the system in the development environment. In a *beta test*, the pilot test is performed by a limited number of end users in the target environment; that is, the difference between usability tests and alpha or beta tests is that the behavior of the end user is not observed and recorded. As a result, beta tests do not test usability requirements as thoroughly as usability tests do. For interactive systems where ease of use is a requirement, the usability test therefore cannot be replaced with a beta test.

The Internet has made the distribution of software very easy. As a result, beta tests are more and more common. In fact, some companies now use it as the main method for system testing their software. Because the downloading process is the responsibility of the end user, not the developers, the cost of distributing the experimental software has decreased sharply. Consequently, a restricted number of beta testers is also a matter of the past. The new beta test paradigm offers the software to anybody who is interested in testing it. In fact, some companies charge their users for beta testing their software!

Acceptance testing

There are three ways the client evaluates a system during **acceptance testing**. In a *benchmark test*, the client prepares a set of test cases that represent typical conditions under which the system should operate. Benchmark tests can be performed with actual users or by a special test team exercising the system functions, but it is important that the testers be familiar with the functional and nonfunctional requirements so they can evaluate the system.

Another kind of system acceptance testing is used in reengineering projects, when the new system replaces an existing system. In *competitor testing*, the new system is tested against an existing system or competitor product. In *shadow testing*, a form of comparison testing, the new and the legacy systems are run in parallel and their outputs are compared.

After acceptance testing, the client reports to the project manager which requirements are not satisfied. Acceptance testing also gives the opportunity for a dialog between the developers and client about conditions that have changed and which requirements must be added, modified, or deleted because of the changes. If requirements must be changed, the changes should be reported in the minutes to the client acceptance review and should form the basis for another iteration of the software life-cycle process. If the customer is satisfied, the system is accepted, possibly contingent on a list of changes recorded in the minutes of the acceptance test.

Installation testing

After the system is accepted, it is installed in the target environment. A good system testing plan allows the easy reconfiguration of the system from the development environment to the target environment. The desired outcome of the **installation test** is that the installed system correctly addresses all requirements.

In most cases, the installation test repeats the test cases executed during function and performance testing in the target environment. Some requirements cannot be executed in the development environment because they require target-specific resources. To test these requirements, additional test cases have to be designed and performed as part of the installation test. Once the customer is satisfied with the results of the installation test, system testing is complete, and the system is formally delivered and ready for operation.

11.5 Managing Testing

In previous sections, we showed how different testing techniques are used to maximize the number of faults discovered. In this section, we describe how to manage testing activities to minimize the resources needed. Many testing activities occur near the end of the project, when resources are running low and delivery pressure increases. Often, trade-offs lie between the faults to be repaired before delivery and those that can be repaired in a subsequent revision of the system. In the end, however, developers should detect and repair a sufficient number of faults such that the system meets functional and nonfunctional requirements to an extent acceptable to the client.

First, we describe the planning of test activities (Section 11.5.1). Next, we describe the test plan, which documents the activities of testing (Section 11.5.2). Next, we describe the roles assigned during testing (Section 11.5.3). Next, we discuss the topics of regression testing(Section 11.5.4), automated testing (Section 11.5.5), and model-based testing (Section 11.5.6).

11.5.1 Planning Testing

Developers can reduce the cost of testing and the elapsed time necessary for its completion through careful planning. Two key elements are to start the selection of test cases early and to parallelize tests.

Developers responsible for testing can design test cases as soon as the models they validate become stable. Functional tests can be developed when the use cases are completed. Unit tests of subsystems can be developed when their interfaces is defined. Similarly, test stubs and drivers can be developed when component interfaces are stable. Developing tests early enables the execution of tests to start as soon as components become available. Moreover, given that developing tests requires a close examination of the models under validation, developers can find faults in the models even before the system is constructed. Note, however, that developing tests early on introduces a maintenance problem: test cases, drivers, and stubs need to be updated whenever the system models change.

The second key element in shortening testing time is to parallelize testing activities. All component tests can be conducted in parallel; double tests for components in which no faults were discovered can be initiated while other components are repaired. For example, the quad test A-B-C-D in Figure 11-26 can be performed as soon as double tests A-B, A-C, and A-D have not resulted in any failures. These double tests, in turn, can be performed as soon as unit test A is completed. The quad test A-B-C-D can be performed in parallel with the double test D-G and the triple test B-E-F, even if tests E, F, or G uncover failures and delay the rest of the tests.

Testing represents a substantial part of the overall project resources. A typical guideline for projects following a Unified Process life cycle is to allocate 25 percent of project resources to testing (see Section 15.4.2; [Royce, 1998]). However, this number can go up depending on safety and reliability requirements on the system. Hence, it is critical that test planning start early, as early as the use case model is stable.

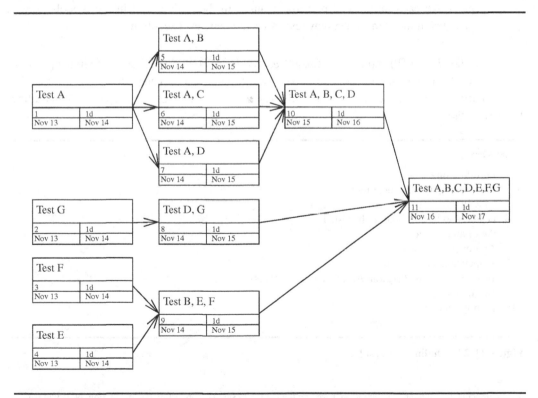

Figure 11-26   Example of a PERT chart for a schedule of the sandwich tests shown in Figure 11-21. The PERT chart notation is defined in Section 3.3.4.

11.5.2 Documenting Testing

Testing activities are documented in four types of documents, the *Test Plan*, the *Test Case Specifications*, the *Test Incident Reports*, and the *Test Summary Report:*[4]

- The *Test Plan* focuses on the managerial aspects of testing. It documents the scope, approach, resources, and schedule of testing activities. The requirements and the components to be tested are identified in this document.

- Each test is documented by a *Test Case Specification*. This document contains the inputs, drivers, stubs, and expected outputs of the tests, as well as the tasks to be performed.

- Each execution of each test is documented by a *Test Incident Report*. The actual results of the tests and differences from the expected output are recorded.

- The *Test Report Summary* document lists all the failures discovered during the tests that need to be investigated. From the *Test Report Summary*, the developers analyze and prioritize each failure and plan for changes in the system and in the models. These changes in turn can trigger new test cases and new test executions.

The *Test Plan* (TP) and the *Test Case Specifications* (TCS) are written early in the process, as soon as the test planning and each test case are completed. These documents are under configuration management and updated as the system models change. Figure 11-27 is an outline for a *Test Plan*.

Test Plan

1. Introduction
2. Relationship to other documents
3. System overview
4. Features to be tested/not to be tested
5. Pass/Fail criteria
6. Approach
7. Suspension and resumption
8. Testing materials (hardware/software requirements)
9. Test cases
10. Testing schedule

Figure 11-27   Outline of a Test Plan.

---

4. Documents described in this section are based on the IEEE 829 standard on testing documentation. Note that we omitted certain sections and documents (e.g., the Test Item Transmittal Report) for the sake of simplicity. Refer to the standard for a complete description of these documents [IEEE Std. 829-2008].

Section 1 of the test plan describes the objectives and extent of the tests. The goal is to provide a framework that can be used by managers and testers to plan and execute the necessary tests in a timely and cost-effective manner.

Section 2 explains the relationship of the test plan to the other documents produced during the development effort such as the RAD, SDD, and ODD (Object Design Document). It explains how all the tests are related to the functional and nonfunctional requirements, as well as to the system design stated in the respective documents. If necessary, this section introduces a naming scheme to establish the correspondence between requirements and tests.

Section 3, focusing on the structural aspects of testing, provides an overview of the system in terms of the components that are tested during the unit test. The granularity of components and their dependencies are defined in this section.

Section 4, focusing on the functional aspects of testing, identifies all features and combinations of features to be tested. It also describes all those features that are not to be tested and the reasons for not testing them.

Section 5 specifies generic pass/fail criteria for the tests covered in this plan. They are supplemented by pass/fail criteria in the test design specification. Note that "fail" in the IEEE standard terminology means "successful test" in our terminology.

Section 6 describes the general approach to the testing process. It discusses the reasons for the selected integration testing strategy. Different strategies are often needed to test different parts of the system. A UML class diagram can be used to illustrate the dependencies between the individual tests and their involvement in the integration tests.

Section 7 specifies the criteria for suspending the testing on the test items associated with the plan. It also specifies the test activities that must be repeated when testing is resumed.

Section 8 identifies the resources that are needed for testing. This should include the physical characteristics of the facilities, including the hardware, software, special test tools, and other resources needed (office space, etc.) to support the tests.

Section 9, the core of the test plan, lists the test cases that are used during testing. Each test case is described in detail in a separate *Test Case Specification* document. Each execution of these tests will be documented in a *Test Incident Report* document. We describe these documents in more details later in this section.

Section 10 of the test plan covers responsibilities, staffing and training needs, risks and contingencies, and the test schedule.

Figure 11-28 is an outline of a *Test Case Specification*.

The Test Case Specification identifier is the name of the test case, used to distinguish it from other test cases. Conventions such as naming the test cases from the features or the component being tested allow developers to more easily refer to test cases. Section 2 of the TCS lists the components under test and the features being exercised. Section 3 lists the inputs required for the test cases. Section 4 lists the expected output. This output is computed manually or with a competing system (such as a legacy system being replaced). Section 5 lists the hardware and software platform needed to execute the test, including any test drivers or stubs.

Test Case Specification

1. Test case specification identifier
2. Test items
3. Input specifications
4. Output specifications
5. Environmental needs
6. Special procedural requirements
7. Intercase dependencies

Figure 11-28   Outline of a Test Specification.

Section 6 lists any constraints needed to execute the test such as timing, load, or operator intervention. Section 7 lists the dependencies with other test cases.

The *Test Incident Report* lists the actual test results and the failures that were experienced. The description of the results must include which features were demonstrated and whether the features have been met. If a failure has been experienced, the test incident report should contain sufficient information to allow the failure to be reproduced. Failures from all *Test Incident Reports* are collected and listed in the *Test Summary Report* and then further analyzed and prioritized by the developers.

Note that the IEEE standard [IEEE Std. 829-2008] for software test documentation uses a slightly different outline that is more appropriate for large organizations and systems. Section 10, for example, is covered by several sections in the standard (responsibilities, staffing and training needs, schedule, risks, and contingencies).

11.5.3 Assigning Responsibilities

Testing requires developers to find faults in components of the system. This is best done when the testing is performed by a developer who was not involved in the development of the component under test, one who is less reticent to break the component being tested and who is more likely to find ambiguities in the component specification.

For stringent quality requirements, a separate team dedicated to quality control is solely responsible for testing. The testing team is provided with the system models, the source code, and the system for developing and executing test cases. *Test Incident Reports* and *Test Report Summaries* are then sent back to the subsystem teams for analysis and possible revision of the system. The revised system is then retested by the testing team, not only to check if the original failures have been addressed, but also to ensure that no new faults have been inserted in the system.

For systems that do not have stringent quality requirements, subsystem teams can double as a testing team for components developed by other subsystem teams. The architecture team can define standards for test procedures, drivers, and stubs, and can perform as the integration test team. The same test documents can be used for communication among subsystem teams.

One of the main problems of usability tests is with enrolling participants. Several obstacles are faced by project managers in selecting real end users [Grudin, 1990]:

- The project manager is usually afraid that users will bypass established technical support organizations and call the developers directly, once they know how to get to them. Once this line of communication is established, developers might be sidetracked too often from doing their assigned jobs.

- Sales personnel do not want developers to talk to "their" clients. Sales people are afraid that developers may offend the client or create dissatisfaction with the current generation of products (which still must be sold).

- The end users do not have time.

- The end users dislike being studied. For example, an automotive mechanic might think that an augmented reality system will put him out of work.

Debriefing the participants is the key to coming to understanding how to improve the usability of the system being tested. Even though the usability test uncovers and exposes problems, it is often the debriefing session that illustrates why these problems have occurred in the first place. It is important to write recommendations on how to improve the tested components as fast as possible after the usability test is finished, so they can be used by the developers to implement any necessary changes in the system models of the tested component.

11.5.4 Regression Testing

Object-oriented development is an iterative process. Developers modify, integrate, and retest components often, as new features are implemented or improved. When modifying a component, developers design new unit tests exercising the new feature under consideration. They may also retest the component by updating and rerunning previous unit tests. Once the modified component passes the unit tests, developers can be reasonably confident about the changes within the component. However, they should not assume that the rest of the system will work with the modified component, even if the system has previously been tested. The modification can introduce side effects or reveal previously hidden faults in other components. The changes can exercise different assumptions about the unchanged components, leading to erroneous states. Integration tests that are rerun on the system to produce such failures are called **regression tests**.

The most robust and straightforward technique for regression testing is to accumulate all integration tests and rerun them whenever new components are integrated into the system. This requires developers to keep all tests up-to-date, to evolve them as the subsystem interfaces change, and to add new integration tests as new services or new subsystems are added. As regression testing can become time consuming, different techniques have been developed for selecting specific regression tests. Such techniques include [Binder, 2000]:

- *Retest dependent components.* Components that depend on the modified component are the most likely to fail in a regression test. Selecting these tests will maximize the likelihood of finding faults when rerunning all tests is not feasible.

- *Retest risky use cases.* Often, ensuring that the most catastrophic faults are identified is more critical than identifying the largest number of faults. By focusing first on use cases that present the highest risk, developers can minimize the likelihood of catastrophic failures.

- *Retest frequent use cases.* When users are exposed to successive releases of the same system, they expect that features that worked before continue to work in the new release. To maximize the likelihood of this perception, developers focus on the use cases that are most often used by the users.

In all cases, regression testing leads to running many tests many times. Hence, regression testing is feasible only when an automated testing infrastructure is in place, enabling developers to automatically set up, initialize, and execute tests and compare their results with a predefined oracle. We discuss automated testing in the next section.

11.5.5 Automating Testing

Manual testing involves a tester to feed predefined inputs into the system using the user interface, a command line console, or a debugger. The tester then compares the outputs generated by the system with the expected oracle. Manual testing can be costly and error prone when many tests are involved or when the system generates a large volume of outputs. When requirements change and the system evolves rapidly, testing should be repeatable. This makes these drawbacks worse, as it is difficult to guarantee that the same test is executed under the same conditions every time.

The repeatability of test execution can be achieved with automation. Although all aspects of testing can be automated (including test case and oracle generation), the main focus of test automation has been on execution. For system tests, test cases are specified in terms of the sequence and timing of inputs and an expected output trace. The test harness can then execute a number of test cases and compare the system output with the expected output trace. For unit and integration tests, developers specify a test as a test driver that exercises one or more methods of the classes under tests.

The benefit of automating test execution is that tests are repeatable. Once a fault is corrected as a result of a failure, the test that uncovered the failure can be repeated to ensure that the failure does not occur anymore. Moreover, other tests can be run to ensure (to a limited extent) that no new faults have been introduced. Moreover, when tests are repeated many times, for example, in the case of refactoring (see Section 10.3.2), the cost of testing is decreased substantially. However, note that developing a test harness and test cases is an investment. If tests are run only once or twice, manual testing may be a better alternative.

An example of an automated test infrastructure is JUnit, a framework for writing and automating the execution of unit tests for Java classes [JUnit, 2009]. The JUnit test framework is made out of a small number of tightly integrated classes (Figure 11-29). Developers write new test cases by subclassing the TestCase class. The setUp() and tearDown() methods of the concrete test case initialize and clean up the testing environment, respectively. The runTest() method includes the actual test code that exercises the class under test and compares the results with an expected condition. The test success or failure is then recorded in an instance of TestResult. TestCases can be organized into TestSuites, which will invoke sequentially each of its tests. TestSuites can also be included in other TestSuites, thereby enabling developers to group unit tests into increasingly larger test suites.

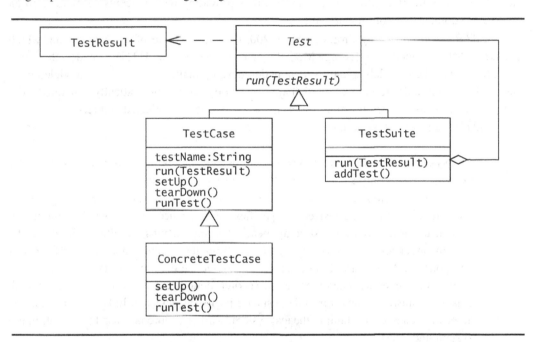

Figure 11-29 JUnit test framework (UML class diagram).

Typically, when using JUnit, each TestCase instance exercises one method of the class under test. To minimize the proliferation of TestCase classes, all test methods exercising the same class (and requiring the same test environment initialized by the setUp() method) are grouped in the same ConcreteTestCase class. The actual method that is invoked by runTest() can then be configured when creating instances of TestCases. This enables developers to organize and selectively invoke large number of tests.

11.5.6 Model-Based Testing

Testing (manual or automated) requires an infrastructure for executing tests, instrumenting the system under test, and collecting and assessing test results. This infrastructure is called the **test harness** or **test system**. The test system is made of software and hardware components that interact with various actors, which can then be modeled using UML. In Chapters 2-10, we have shown how the system under development and the development organization can be modeled in UML. Similarly, we can model the test system in UML. To be able to do this, we need to extend UML with new entity objects for modeling the test system.

UML profiles provide a way for extending UML. A **UML profile** is a collection of new stereotypes, new interfaces, or new constraints, thus providing new concepts specialized to an application domain or a solution domain.

U2TP (UML 2 Testing Profile, [OMG, 2005]) is an example of a UML profile, which extends UML for modeling testing. Modeling the test system in U2TP provides the same advantages as when modeling the system under development: test cases are modeled in a standard notation understood by all participants, test cases can be automatically generated from test models, test cases execution and results can be automatically collected and recorded.

U2TP extends UML with the following concepts:

- The **system under test** (stereotype «sut»), which may be the complete system under development, or only a part of it, such as a subsystem or a single class.
- A **test case** (stereotype «testCase») is a specification of behavior realizing one or more test objectives. A test cases specifies the sequence of interactions among the system under test and the test components. The interactions are either stimuli on the system under test or observations gathered from the system under test or from test components. A test case is represented as a sequence diagram or state machine. Test cases return an enumerated type called **verdict**, denoting if the test run passed, failed, was inconclusive, or an error in the test case itself was detected. In U2TP terminology, an error is caused by a fault in the test system, while a failure is caused by a fault in the system under test.
- A **test objective** (stereotype «testObjective») describes in English the goal of one or several test cases. A test objective is typically a requirement or a part of a requirement that is being verified. For example, the test objective of the displayTicketPrices test case is to verify that the correct price is displayed after selected a zone button on the ticket distributor.
- **Test components** (stereotype «testComponent»), such as test stubs and utilities needed for executing a test case. Examples of test components include simulated hardware, simulated user behavior, or components that inject faults.
- **Test contexts** (stereotype «testContext»), which include the set of test cases, the configuration of test components and system under test needed for every test case, and a test control for sequencing the test cases.

- An **arbiter** (interface Arbiter), which collects the local test results into an aggregated result.
- A **scheduler** (interface Scheduler), which creates and coordinate the execution of the test cases among test components and system under test.

Figure 11-30 depicts an example of a test system in U2TP for the TicketDistributor of Figures 11-23–11-25. The test context PurchaseTicketSuite groups all the test cases for the PurchaseTicket use case. The system under test is the TicketDistributor software. To make it easier to control and instrument the system to assess the success or failure of tests, we simulate the ticket distributor display with a DisplaySimulator test component.

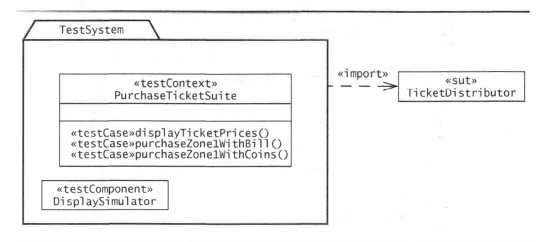

Figure 11-30 Example of a test system for the TicketDistributor (U2TP).

For example, Figure 11-31 depicts the expected interactions of the displayTicketPrices() test case resulting to a pass verdict. selectZone1(), selectZone2(), and selectZone4() are stimuli on the system under test. getDisplay() are observations to assess if individual test steps were successful. Note that only the expected interactions are displayed. Any unexpected interactions, missing interactions, or observations that do not match the oracles, lead to a failed verdict. U2TP also provides mechanisms, not discussed here, to explicitly model interactions that lead to an inconclusive or a failed verdict.

The displayTicketPrices() test case of Figure 11-31 explicitly models the mapping between zones and ticket prices. In a realistic system, this approach would not be sustainable, as many test cases are repeated for boundary values and with samples of different equivalence classes. To address this challenge, U2TP provides the concepts of DataPool, DataPartition, and DataSelector, to represent test data samples, equivalence classes, and data selection strategies, respectively. These allow to parameterize test cases with different sets of values, keeping the specification of test cases concise and reusable.

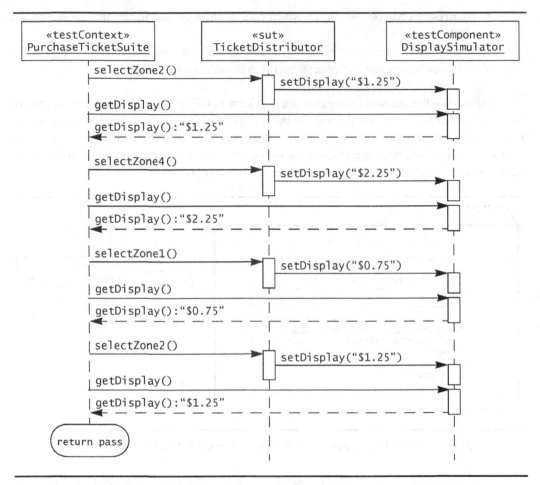

Figure 11-31   Example of test behavior for the test case displayTicketPrices() (U2TP). Only expected interactions leading to a pass verdict are represented.

11.6 Further Readings

Historically, the term "bug" was first used to denote a fault by Grace Hopper when a moth interfered with a computer relay, causing the program to stop [Hopper, 1981]. The term has been used since to denote design and coding faults caused by developers.

Fagan showed that code inspections can be more effective than testing for finding faults in a given amount of time [Fagan, 1976]. Many replicated experiments confirmed Fagan's finding. For that reason, inspections and peer reviews are stipulated by several standards, including ISO 9000. However, with the exception of critical systems, code inspections are not widely used because they are often perceived, ironically, as too time consuming.

Many books have been written about testing. However, progress in this discipline is slow and few new ideas have yielded results comparable to code inspections. *The Art of Software Testing*, although several decades old, remains a classic in the testing literature and relevant for today's systems [Myers, 1979].

The introduction of object-oriented programming techniques opened the door for increased modularity and reuse. However, polymorphism also increased drastically the number of paths to be tested. *Testing Object-Oriented Systems* contains the most comprehensive treatment of testing issues and techniques for object-oriented systems [Binder, 2000].

A common misconception is that usability testing requires large budgets and sophisticated know-how. *Handbook of Usability Testing* [Rubin, 1994] and *Usability Inspection Methods* [Nielsen & Mack, 1994] provide practical guidance and show how even limited usability tests can dramatically improve a system. *Usability Engineering Lifecycle* [Mayhew, 1999] integrates usability testing into object-oriented software engineering life cycle.

Developing reliable systems goes beyond testing. As discussed in the introduction of this chapter, alternative techniques, such as fault avoidance and fault tolerance, can complement testing to produce a highly reliable system. An excellent coverage of the topic is provided in [Siewiorek & Swarz, 1992].

U2TP is a response by a consortium to a request for proposals from OMG to develop a UML profile for testing. U2TP has been finalized and is now an official OMG standard [OMG, 2005]. Baker provides a practical introduction on model-based testing using U2TP [Baker et al., 2008].

11.7 Exercises

11-1   Correct the faults in the `isLeapYear()` and `getNumDaysInMonth()` methods of
       Figure 11-11 and generate test cases using the path testing method. Are the test cases
       you found different than those of Table 11-4 and Figure 11-13? Why? Would the test
       cases you found uncover the faults you corrected?

11-2   Generate equivalent Java code for the state machine diagram for the `SetTime` use case
       of `2Bwatch` (Figure 11-14). Use equivalence testing, boundary testing, and path testing
       to create test cases for the code you have just generated. How do these test cases
       compare with those generated using state-based testing?

11-3   Build the state machine diagram corresponding to the `PurchaseTicket` use case of
       Figure 11-24. Generate test cases based on the state machine diagram using the state-
       based testing technique. Discuss the number of test cases and differences with the test
       case of Figure 11-25.

11-4   Given the subsystem decomposition

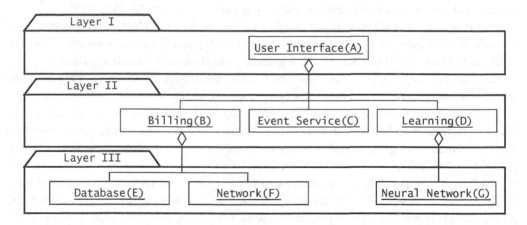

       comment on the testing plan used by the project manager:

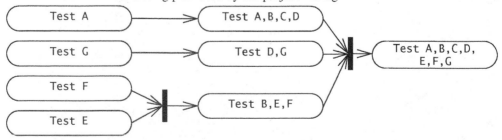

       What decisions were made? What are the advantages and disadvantages of this test
       plan?

11-5 You are responsible for the integration testing of a system that encrypts network traffic. This system includes a key generator subsystem that uses random numbers. During integration testing, you use a stub implementation of the key generator that produces a predictable result. However, for the release version of the system, you want to substitute the stub implementation with the random implementation, so that the generated keys are not predictable to an outsider. Implement a test infrastructure using one of the design patterns described in Chapter 8, *Object Design: Reusing Pattern Solutions* to enable the exchange of these two key generator implementations at run time. Justify your choice.

11-6 Use path testing to generate test cases for all the methods of the `NetworkConnection` class depicted in Figure 11-15 and in Figure 8-11. Expand first the source code to remove any polymorphism. How many test cases did you generate using path testing? How many test cases would you generate if the source code is not expanded?

11-7 Apply the software engineering and testing terminology from this chapter to the following terms used in Feynman's article mentioned in the introduction:
- What is a "crack"?
- What is "crack initiation"?
- What is "high engine reliability"?
- What is a "design aim"?
- What is a "mission equivalent"?
- What does "10 percent of the original specification" mean?
- How is Feynman using the term "verification," when he says that "As deficiencies and design errors are noted they are corrected and verified with further testing"?

References

[Beck & Andres, 2005]   K. Beck & C. Andres, *Extreme Programming Explained: Embrace Change*, 2nd ed., Addison-Wesley, Reading, MA, 2005.

[Baker et al., 2008]   P. Baker, Z. R. Dai, & R. Grabowski, *Model-Driven Testing: Using the UML Testing Profile*, Springer, Berlin, 2008.

[Binder, 2000]   R. V. Binder, *Testing Object-Oriented Systems: Models, Patterns, and Tools*, Addison-Wesley, Reading, MA, 2000.

[Fagan, 1976]   M. E. Fagan, "Design and code inspections to reduce errors in program development," *IBM Systems Journal*, Vol. 15, No. 3, 1976.

[Feynman, 1988]   R. P. Feynman, "Personal observations on the reliability of the Shuttle," Rogers Commission, *The Presidential Commission on the Space Shuttle Challenger Accident Report*, Washington, DC, June 1986.

[Grudin, 1990]   J. Grudin, "Obstacles to user involvement in interface design in large product development organizations," *Proceedings of IFIP INTERACT'90 Third International Conference on Human-Computer Interaction*, Cambridge, U.K., August 1990.

[Hopper, 1981]   G. M. Hopper, "The First Bug," *Annals of the History of Computing* 3, pp. 285–6, 1981.

[IEEE Std. 829-2008]   *IEEE Standard for Software Test Documentation*, IEEE Standards Board, July 2008.

[IEEE Std. 982.2-1988]   *IEEE Guide for the Use of IEEE Standard Dictionary of Measures to Produce Reliable Software*, IEEE Standards Board, June 1988.

[Jones, 1977]   T. C. Jones, "Programmer quality and programmer productivity," IBM TR-02.764, 1977.

[JUnit, 2009]   JUnit, http://www.junit.org/.

[Kelly, 1984]   J. F. Kelly, "An iterative design methodology for user-friendly natural language office information applications," *ACM Transactions on Information Systems*, Vol. 2, No. 1, January 1984.

[Mayhew, 1999]   D. J. Mayhew, *The Usability Engineering Lifecycle: A Practitioner's Handbook for User Interface Design*, Morgan Kaufmann, 1999.

[McCabe, 1976]   T. McCabe, "A software complexity measure," *IEEE Transactions on Software Engineering*, Vol. 2, No. 12, December 1976.

[Myers, 1979]   G. J. Myers, *The Art of Software Testing*, Wiley, New York, 1979.

[Nielsen & Mack, 1994]   J. Nielsen & R. L. Mack (eds.), *Usability Inspection Methods*, Wiley, New York, 1994.

[OMG, 2005]   Object Management Group *UML Testing Profile Version 1.0*. http://www.omg.org/ 2005.

[Parnas & Weiss, 1985]   D. L. Parnas & D. M. Weiss, "Active design reviews: principles and practice," *Proceedings of the Eighth International Conference on Software Engineering*, London, U.K., pp 132–136, August 1985.

[Popper, 1992]   K. Popper, *Objective Knowledge: An Evolutionary Approach*, Clarendon, Oxford, 1992.

[Porter et al., 1997]   A. A. Porter, H. Siy, C.A. Toman, & L.G. Votta, "An experiment to assess the cost-benefits of code inspections in large scale software development," *IEEE Transactions on Software Engineering*, Vol. 23, No. 6, pp. 329–346, June 1997.

[Royce, 1998]   W. Royce, *Software Project Management: A Unified Framework*, Addison-Wesley, Reading, MA, 1998.

[Rubin, 1994]   J. Rubin, *Handbook of Usability Testing*, Wiley, New York, 1994.

[Siewiorek & Swarz, 1992]   D. P. Siewiorek & R. S. Swarz, *Reliable Computer Systems: Design and Evaluation*, 2nd ed., Digital, Burlington, MA, 1992.

[Turner & Robson, 1993]   C. D. Turner & D. J. Robson, "The state-based testing of object-oriented programs," *Conference on Software Maintenance*, pp. 302–310, September 1993.

PART III
Managing Change

Rationale Management

The [motorcycle] description would cover the "what" of the motorcycle in terms of components, the "how" of the engine in terms of functions. It would badly need a "where" analysis in the form of an illustration and also a "why" analysis in the form of engineering principles that led to this particular conformation of parts.
—Robert Pirsig, in *Zen and the Art of Motorcycle Maintenance*

Rationale is the justification of decisions. The models we have described until now represent the system. Rationale models represent the reasoning that leads to the system, including its functionality and its implementation. Rationale is critical in two areas: it supports the decision making, and it supports the capture of knowledge. Rationale includes

- the issues that were addressed
- the alternatives that were considered
- the decisions that were made to resolve the issues
- the criteria that were used to guide decisions
- the debate developers went through to reach a decision.

In the context of decision making, the rationale improves the quality of decisions by making decision elements—such as criteria, priorities, and arguments—explicit. In the context of knowledge capture, the rationale is the most important information in the development process when changing the system. For example, when functionality is added to the system, the rationale enables developers to track which decisions should be revisited and which alternatives have already been evaluated. When new staff is assigned to the project, new developers can become familiar with past decisions by accessing the rationale of the system.

Unfortunately, rationale is also the most complex information that developers generate, and thus, is the most difficult to maintain and update. Moreover, capturing rationale represents an up-front investment with long-term returns. In this chapter, we describe issue-modeling, a representation for modeling rationale. We then describe the activities of creating, maintaining, and accessing rationale models. We conclude this chapter by describing management issues related to rationale management, such as decision support and negotiation.

12.1 Introduction: Slicing Ham

System models are abstractions of what the system does. The requirements analysis model, including the use case model, the class model, and the sequence diagrams (see Chapter 4, *Requirements Elicitation*, and Chapter 5, *Analysis*) represents the behavior of the system from the user's point of view. The system design model (see Chapter 6, *System Design: Decomposing the System*) represents the system through its subsystems, design goals, hardware nodes, data stores, access control, and so on. The rationale model represents why a given system is structured and behaves the way it does.[1] Why should we capture the *why*? Consider the following example:[2]

> Mary asks John, her husband, why he always cuts off both ends of the ham before putting it in the oven. John responds that he is following his mother's recipe and that he had always seen her cut the ends off the ham. He never really questioned the practice and thought it was part of the recipe. Mary, intrigued by this answer, calls her mother-in-law to find out more about this ham recipe.
>
> Ann, John's mother, provides more details on the ham cutting, but no culinary justification. She says that she has always trimmed about an inch off each end of the ham as her mother did, assuming it had something to do with improving the taste.
>
> Mary continues her investigation and calls John's maternal grandmother, Zoe. At first, Zoe is very surprised. She does not cut the ends of the ham and she cannot imagine how such practice could possibly improve the taste. After much discussion, Zoe eventually remembers that, when Ann was a little girl, she used to cook on a much narrower stove that could not accommodate standard-sized meat loaves. To work around this problem, she used to cut off about an inch from each end of the ham. She stopped this practice once she got a wider stove.

Developers and cooks are good at disseminating new practices and techniques. The rationale behind these techniques, however, is usually lost, making it difficult to improve them as their application context changes. The Y2K bug is such an example: in the 1960s and 1970s, memory costs drove developers to represent information as compactly as possible. For this reason, the year was often represented with two characters instead of four (e.g., "1998" was represented as "98"). The assumption of the developers was that the software would only be used for a few years. Arithmetic operations on years represented with two digits assumes that all dates are within the same century. Unfortunately, this shortcut breaks down at the turn of the century for software performing arithmetic on two-digit years. For example, when computing the age of a person, a person born in 1949 will be considered $01 - 49 = -48$ years old in 2001. The practice of encoding years with two digits became standard, even after memory prices dropped significantly and the year 2000 loomed. Moreover, new systems had to be backward-

1. Historically, much research about rationale focuses on design, hence, the term *design rationale* is most often used in the literature. Instead, we use the term *rationale* to avoid confusion and to emphasize that rationale models can be used during all phases of development.
2. Far-fetched example adapted for this chapter, original author unknown.

compatible with older ones. For these reasons, many systems delivered as late as the 1990s still have Y2K bugs.

Rationale models enable developers and cooks to deal with *change*, such as larger stoves or cheaper memory prices. Capturing the justification of decisions effectively models the dependencies between starting assumptions and decisions. When assumptions change, decisions can be revisited. In this chapter, we describe techniques for capturing, maintaining, and accessing rationale models. In this chapter, we have included

- a bird's-eye view of the activities related with rationale models (Section 12.2)
- issue modeling, the technique we use for representing rationale (Section 12.3)
- the activities necessary for creating and accessing rationale models (Section 12.4)
- management issues related with maintaining rationale models (Section 12.5).

First, let us define the concept of rationale model.

12.2 An Overview of Rationale

A **rationale** is the motivation behind a decision. More specifically, it includes

- **Issue**. To each decision corresponds an issue to be solved so that development can proceed. An important part of the rationale is a description of the specific issue that is being solved. Issues are usually phrased as questions: How should a ham be cooked? How should years be represented?
- **Alternatives**. Alternatives are possible solutions that could address the issue under consideration. These include alternatives that were explored but discarded because they did not satisfy one or more criteria. For example, buying a wide stove costs too much. Representing years with a binary 16-bit number requires too much processing.
- **Criteria**. Criteria are desirable qualities that the selected solution should satisfy. For example: a recipe for ham should be realizable on standard kitchen equipment. Developers in the 1960s minimized memory foot prints. During requirements analysis, criteria are nonfunctional requirements and constraints (e.g., usability, number of input errors per day). During system design, criteria are design goals (e.g., reliability, response time). During project management, criteria are management goals and trade-offs (e.g., timely delivery versus quality).
- **Argumentation**. Cooking and software development decisions are not algorithmic. Cooks and developers discover issues, try solutions, and argue their relative benefits. It is only after much discussion that a consensus is reached or a decision imposed. This argumentation occurs during all aspects of the decision process, including criteria, justifications, explored alternatives, and trade-offs.
- **Decisions**. A decision is the resolution of an issue representing the selected alternative according to the criteria that were used for evaluation and the justification of the

selection. Cutting an inch off each end of a ham and representing years with two digits are decisions. Decisions are already captured in the system models we develop during requirements analysis and system design. Moreover, many decisions are made without exploring alternatives or examining the corresponding issues.

We make decisions throughout the development process, and we can use rationale models during any development activity:

- During *requirements elicitation* and *requirements analysis*, we make decisions about the functionality of the system, most often together with the client. Decisions are motivated by user or organizational needs. The justification of these decisions is useful for creating test cases during system integration and user acceptance.

- During *system design*, we select design goals and design the subsystem decomposition. When identifying design goals, for example, we often base our decision on nonfunctional requirements. Capturing the rationale of these decisions enables us to trace dependencies between design goals and nonfunctional requirements. This allows us to revise the design goals when requirements change.

- During *project management*, we make assumptions about the relative risks present in the development process. We are more likely to start development tasks related to a recently released component as opposed to a mature one. Capturing the justifications behind the risks and the fallback plans facilitates mitigation if these risks become problems.

- During *integration and testing*, we discover interface mismatches between subsystems. Accessing the rationale for the subsystems, we can often determine which change or assumption introduced the mismatch and correct the situation with minimal impact on the rest of the system.

Maintaining rationale is an investment of resources for dealing with change: we capture information *now* to make it easier to revise decisions *later*, when changes occur. The amount of resources we are willing to invest depends on the type of project.

If we are building a complex system for a single customer, we will most likely revise and upgrade the system several times over a long period. In this case, the client may even require that rationale be recorded. If we are building a conceptual prototype for a new product, we will most likely throw out the prototype once product development is approved and underway. If we divert development resources to record rationale, we risk delaying the demonstration of the prototype and face project cancellation altogether. In this case, we do not record rationale, because the return on such an investment would be minimal.

More generally, we distinguish four levels of rationale capture:

- *No explicit rationale capture.* Resources are spent only on development. The documentation focuses on the system models only. Rationale information is present only in the developers' memories and in communication records such as E-mail messages, memos, and faxes.

- *Rationale reconstruction*. Resources are spent in recovering design rationale during the documentation effort. The design criteria and the motivation behind major architectural decisions is integrated with the corresponding system models. Discarded alternatives and argumentation are not captured explicitly.

- *Rationale capture*. Major effort is spent in capturing rationale as decisions are made. Rationale information is documented as a separate model and cross-referenced with other models. For example, issue models represent rationale with a graph of nodes, each representing an issue, an alternative, or an evaluation criteria. The rationale behind the requirements model can then be captured by attaching issue models to use cases.

- *Rationale integration*. The rationale model becomes the central model developers use. Rationale produced during different phases are integrated into a live and searchable information base. Changes to the system occur first in the information base as a discussion followed by one or more decisions. The system models represent the sum of the decisions captured in the information base.

In the first two levels of rationale capture, *No explicit rationale capture* and *Rationale reconstruction*, we rely on developers' memory to capture and store rationale. In the last two levels, *Rationale capture* and *Rationale integration*, we invest resources in constructing corporate memory that is independent of developers. The trade-off between these two extremes is the investment of resources during the early phases of development. In this chapter, we focus on the last two levels of rationale capture.

In addition to long-term benefits, maintaining rationale can also have short-term positive effects: making explicit the rationale of a decision enables us to understand better the criteria others follow. It also encourages us to make rational decisions instead of emotional ones. If nothing else, it helps us distinguish which decisions were carefully evaluated and which were made under pressure and rushed.

Rationale models represent a body of information that is larger and changing faster than the system models. This introduces issues related to complexity and change, and we have modeling techniques for dealing with those. Next, we describe how we represent rationale with issue models.

12.3 Rationale Concepts

In this section, we describe issue models, the representation we use for rationale. Issue modeling is based on the assumption that design occurs as a dialectic activity during which developers solve a problem by arguing the pros and cons of different alternatives. We can then capture rationale by modeling the argument that lead to the development decisions. We represent

- a question or a design problem as an issue node (Section 12.3.2)

- alternative solutions to the problem as proposal nodes (Section 12.3.3)
- pros and cons of different alternatives using argument nodes (Section 12.3.4)
- decisions we make to resolve an issue as a resolution node (Section 12.3.5)
- implementation of these resolutions as action items (Section 12.3.6).

In Section 12.3.7, we survey several issue representations of historical significance. But first, let us talk about centralized traffic control, the domain for the examples in this chapter.

12.3.1 Centralized Traffic Control

Centralized traffic control (CTC) systems enable train dispatchers to monitor and route trains remotely. Train tracks are divided into contiguous track circuits that represent the smallest unit a dispatcher can monitor. Signals and other devices ensure that at most one train can occupy a track circuit at any time. When a train enters a track circuit, a sensor detects its presence and the train identification appears on the dispatcher's monitor. The dispatcher operates switches to route trains. The system enables a dispatcher to plan a complete route by aligning a sequence of switches in the corresponding position. The set of track circuits controlled by a single dispatcher is called a "track section."

Figure 12-1 is a simplified display of a CTC user interface. Track circuits are represented by lines. Switches are represented by the intersection of three lines. Signals are represented with icons indicating whether a signal is open (i.e., allowing a train to pass) or closed (i.e., forbidding a train to pass). Switches, trains, and signals are numbered for reference in commands issued by the dispatcher. In Figure 12-1, signals are numbered S1–S4, switches are numbered SW1 and SW2, and trains are numbered T1291 and T1515. Computers near the tracks, called "wayside stations," ensure that the state of a group of switches and signals do not present any safety hazard. For example, a wayside station controlling the devices of Figure 12-1 ensures that opposing signals, such as S1 and S2, cannot be open simultaneously. Wayside stations are designed such that the state of the device they control is safe even in the case of failure. Such equipment is called "fail-safe." CTC systems communicate with wayside stations to modify the state of the tracks when

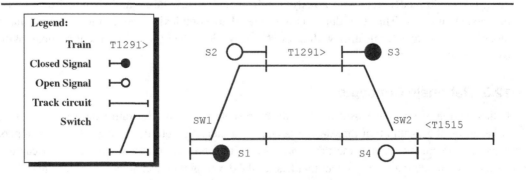

Figure 12-1   A simplified example of a CTC track section display.

dispatching trains. CTC systems are typically highly available but need not be fail-safe, given that the safety of trains is guaranteed by the wayside stations.

In the 1960s, CTC systems had a custom display board containing light bulbs to display the status of the track circuits. Switches and signals were controlled via an input board with many push buttons and toggle switches. In the 1970s, CRTs replaced the custom boards and provided dispatchers more detailed information with less real estate. More recently, workstation-based traffic control systems have been introduced, offering the possibility of a more sophisticated user interface to dispatchers and the ability to distribute processing among multiple computers.

Centralized traffic control systems need to be highly available. Although traffic control systems are not life-critical (safety is ensured by wayside stations), a failure of the system can lead to major traffic disruption in the controlled tracks, thus resulting in substantial economic loss. Consequently, the transition to a new technology, such as moving from a mainframe to a workstation environment or moving from a textual interface to a graphical user interface, should be carefully evaluated and accomplished much more gradually than for other systems. Traffic control is a domain in which capturing rationale is critical and thus serves as the basis for the examples of this chapter.

Let us discuss next how issue models are used to represent rationale.

12.3.2 Defining the Problem: Issues

An **issue** represents a concrete problem, such as a requirement, a design, or a management problem. *How soon should a dispatcher be notified of a train delay? How should persistent data be stored? Which technology presents the most risk?* Issues most often represent problems that do not have a single correct solution and that cannot be resolved algorithmically. Issues are typically resolved through discussion and negotiation.

We represent issues in UML with instances of class `Issue`. `Issue`s have a `subject` attribute, summarizing the issue, a `description` attribute, describing the issue in more detail and referring to supporting material, and a `status` attribute, indicating whether the issue has been resolved or not. The `status` of an issue is **open** if it has not yet been resolved and **closed** otherwise. A closed issue can be reopened. By convention, we give a short name to each issue, such as `train delay?:Issue`, for reference. For example, Figure 12-2 depicts the three issues we gave as examples in the previous paragraph.

Issues raised during development are often related. For example, issues can be decomposed into smaller **subissues**. *What are the response time requirements of the traffic control system?* includes *How soon should a dispatcher be notified of a train delay?* The complete system development can be phrased as a single issue—*Which traffic control system should we build?*—that can then be decomposed into numerous subissues. Issues can also be raised by decisions made on other issues. For example, the decision to cache data on a local node raises the issue of maintaining consistency between the central and cached copies of the data. Such issues are called **consequent issues**.

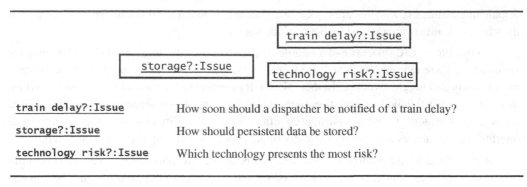

train delay?:Issue	How soon should a dispatcher be notified of a train delay?
storage?:Issue	How should persistent data be stored?
technology risk?:Issue	Which technology presents the most risk?

Figure 12-2   An example of issues (UML object diagram).

Consider the centralized traffic control system we previously described. Assume we are currently examining the transition from a mainframe system to a desktop system. In the future system, each dispatcher will have an individual desktop machine that communicates with a server, which manages the communication with field devices. During design discussions, two interface issues are raised: *How should commands be input to the system?* and *How should track circuits be displayed to the dispatcher?* Figure 12-3 depicts two issues represented with a UML object diagram.

An issue should focus only on the problem, not on possible alternatives to address it. A convention that encourages this is to phrase issues as questions. To reinforce this concept, we also include a question mark at the end of the issue name. Information about the possible alternatives addressing an issue are captured by proposals, which we discuss next.

12.3.3 Exploring the Solution Space: Proposals

A **proposal** represents a candidate answer to an issue. *A dispatcher need not be notified* is a proposal to the issue *How soon should a dispatcher be notified of a train delay?* A proposal need not be a good or valid answer to the issue it addresses. Proposals enable developers to explore the solution space thoroughly. Often when brainstorming, proposing a flawed solution triggers new ideas and solutions that would not have been thought of otherwise. Different proposals addressing the same issue can overlap. For example, proposals to the issue *How to store persistent data?* could include *Use a relational database* and *Use a relational database for*

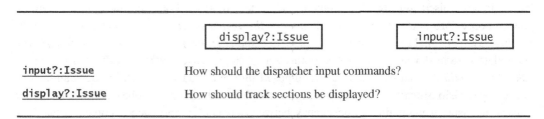

input?:Issue	How should the dispatcher input commands?
display?:Issue	How should track sections be displayed?

Figure 12-3   CTC interface issues (UML object diagram).

structured data and flat files for images. Proposals are used to represent the solution to the problem as well as to the discarded alternatives.

A proposal can address one or more issues. For example, *Use Model/View/Dispatcher architecture* can address *How to separate interface objects from entity objects?* and *How to maintain consistency across multiple views?* Proposals can also trigger new issues. For example, in response to the issue *How to minimize memory leaks?*, the proposal *Use garbage collection* may trigger the consequent issue *How to minimize response time degradation due to memory management?* When we address an issue, we need to ensure that all consequent issues associated with the selected proposals are addressed, as well.

We represent proposals in UML as instances of the class `Proposal`. Proposals, like `Issues`, have `subject` and `description` attributes. By convention, we give proposals a short name and phrase them as a statement starting with a verb. `Proposals` are related to the `Issues` they address with an `addressed by` association. `Issues` are related to the `Proposals` that triggered them with a `raises` association.

While discussing the interface issues of our centralized traffic control system, we consider two proposals: a `point&click` interface, which allows track circuits to be represented graphically, and a `text-based` interface, in which track sections are represented with special characters. The `text-based` proposal raises a consequent issue about which terminal emulation to use. Figure 12-4 depicts the addition of the two proposals and the consequent issue.

A proposal should only contain information related to the solution, not its value, advantages, and disadvantages. Criteria and arguments are used for this purpose. We describe these next.

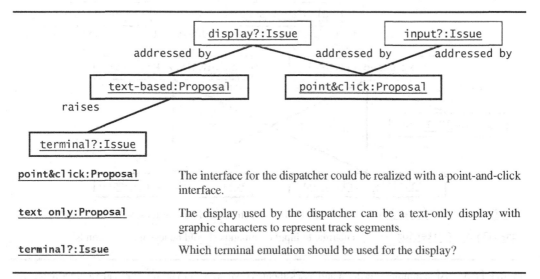

`point&click:Proposal`	The interface for the dispatcher could be realized with a point-and-click interface.
`text only:Proposal`	The display used by the dispatcher can be a text-only display with graphic characters to represent track segments.
`terminal?:Issue`	Which terminal emulation should be used for the display?

Figure 12-4   An example of proposals and consequent issue (UML object diagram). `Proposals` and consequent `Issue` are emphasized in bold.

12.3.4 Evaluating the Solution Space: Criteria and Arguments

A **criterion** is a desirable quality that proposals addressing a specific issue should have. Design goals, such as response time or reliability, are criteria used for addressing design issues. Management goals, such as minimum cost or minimum risk, are criteria used for addressing management issues. A set of criteria indicates the dimensions against which each proposal is assessed. A proposal that meets a criterion is said to be *assessed positively* against that criterion. Similarly, a proposal that fails to meet a criterion is said to be *assessed negatively* against that criterion. Criteria may be shared among several issues.

We represent criteria in UML as instances of the `Criterion` class. A `Criterion`, like `Issues` and `Proposals`, has `subject` and `description` attributes. The `subject` attribute is always phrased positively; that is, it should state the quality that proposals should maximize. *Fast*, *responsive*, and *cheap* are good `subject` attributes. *Cost* and *time* are not. A `Criterion` is associated to `Proposals` with `assessment` associations. `Assessment` associations have a `value` attribute, indicating whether it is positive or negative, and a `weight` attribute, indicating the strength of the proposal with respect to the criterion. By convention, we append a "$" sign to the end of a criterion name, emphasizing that criteria are **goodness measures** and should not be confused with arguments or issues.

While evaluating the interface of our centralized traffic control system, we identify two criteria: `availability`, which represents the nonfunctional requirement to maximize the up time of the system, and `usability`, which represents (in this case) the nonfunctional requirement to minimize the time to input valid commands (see Figure 12-5). These criteria are taken from the

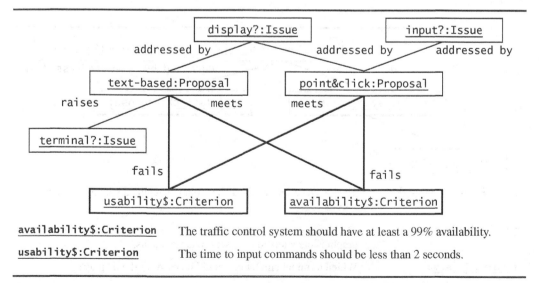

`availability$:Criterion`	The traffic control system should have at least a 99% availability.
`usability$:Criterion`	The time to input commands should be less than 2 seconds.

Figure 12-5   An example of criteria and assessments (UML object diagram). `Criteria` are emphasized in bold. A negative assessment is indicated by an association labeled `fails`, whereas positive assessments are indicated with an association labeled `meets`.

nonfunctional requirements of the system. We assess both proposals against those criteria: we decide that the point-and-click interface is negatively assessed against the availability criteria, being more complex than the text interface and thus presenting a higher likelihood of bugs. We decide, however, that the point-and-click interface is more usable than the textual interface, due to an easier selection of commands and input of data. Note that the set of associations linking the proposals and the criteria in Figure 12-5 represent a trade-off: each proposal maximizes one of the two criteria; the issue is to decide which criteria has a higher priority.

An **argument** is an opinion expressed by a person, agreeing or disagreeing with a proposal, a criterion, or an assessment. Arguments capture the debate that drives the exploration of the solution space, defines the goodness measures, and eventually leads to a decision. We represent arguments in UML with instances of the class Argument, including subject and description attributes. Arguments are related to the entity they discuss with an is supported by or an is opposed by association.

While discussing the relative priority of the availability and usability criteria, we decide that any benefit on the usability aspect would be offset by a reduced availability of the system. We capture this by creating an argument that supports the availability criterion (see Figure 12-6). Note that an argument can simultaneously support a node while opposing another.

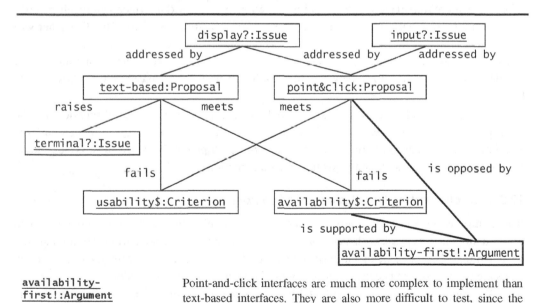

availability-
first!:Argument

Point-and-click interfaces are much more complex to implement than text-based interfaces. They are also more difficult to test, since the number of actions available to the dispatcher is much larger. The point-and-click interface risks introducing fatal errors in the system that would offset any usability benefit the interface would provide.

Figure 12-6   An example of an argument (UML object diagram). Argument is emphasized in bold.

When selecting criteria, assessing proposals, and arguing about them, we evaluate the design space. The next step is to use this evaluation to come to closure and resolve the issue.

12.3.5 Collapsing the Solution Space: Resolutions

A **resolution** represents the alternative selected to close an issue. A resolution represents a decision and has an impact on one of the system models or on the task model. A resolution can be based on several proposals and summarizes the justification that leads to the decision. We represent resolutions with an instance of class Resolution, including subject, description, justification, and status attributes. A Resolution is related to Proposals with based-on associations. A Resolution has exactly one resolves association to the Issue it resolves.

The status attribute of a Resolution indicates whether or not the Resolution is still relevant. When the Resolution is linked with its corresponding issue, its status is set to active and the status of the corresponding Issue is changed to closed. If the Issue is reopened, the status of the Issue is changed to open and the status of the Resolution is changed to obsolete. A closed Issue has exactly one active Resolution and any number of obsolete Resolutions.

Finalizing the traffic control interface issue, we select a text-based display and a keyboard interface as a basis for the user interface. This decision is motivated by treating the availability criterion as more important than the usability criterion: a text-based interface will result in much simpler and more reliable user interface code at the cost of some usability. The dispatcher will not be able to see as much data at one time and will not be able to issue commands as fast as using a point-and-click interface. We create a resolution node that contains the justification of the decision and create links between the resolution and the two issues it addresses (see Figure 12-7).

Adding a resolution to an issue model effectively concludes the discussion of the corresponding issue. As development is iterative, it is sometimes necessary to reopen an issue and reevaluate competing alternatives. At the end of development, however, most issues should be closed or listed as known problems in the documentation.

12.3.6 Implementing Resolutions: Action Items

A resolution is implemented in terms of one or more **action items**. A person is assigned to an action item, which is a task with a completion date. Action items are not part of the rationale per se, but rather they are part of the task model (see Chapter 11, *Project Management*). Action items are described here because they are tightly integrated into the issue model.

We represent an action item in UML with an instance of the ActionItem class. The ActionItem class has subject, description, owner, deadline, and status attributes. The owner is the person responsible for completing the ActionItem. The status of an ActionItem can be todo, notDoable, inProgress, or done. A Resolution is associated with the ActionItems with an is implemented by link. Figure 12-8 represents the ActionItems generated after the resolution of Figure 12-7.

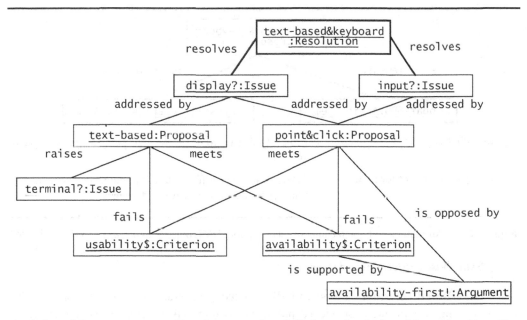

text-based &
keyboard:Resolution

We select a text-based display and a keyboard input for the traffic control user interface. The terminal emulation should provide line characters that allow track circuits to be drawn in text mode.

This decision is motivated by the relative simplicity and reliability of text-based interfaces compared with point-and-click interfaces. We are aware that this decision costs some usability, as fewer data can be presented to the dispatcher and issuing commands by the dispatcher will be slower and more prone to errors.

Figure 12-7   An example of closed issue (UML object diagram). Resolution emphasized in bold.

The issue notation we described and its integration with the task model is the modeling notation we use for representing rationale. Next, we survey other issue models that have been proposed in the literature.

12.3.7 Examples of Issue-Based Models and Systems

The capture of rationale as an issue model was originally proposed by Kunz and Rittel. Since then, many different models have been proposed and evaluated for software engineering and other disciplines. Here, we compare four: IBIS (Issue-Based Information System, [Kunz & Rittel, 1970]), DRL (Decision Representation Language, [Lee, 1990]), QOC (Questions, Options, and Criteria, [MacLean et al., 1991]), and the NFR Framework [Chung et al., 1999].

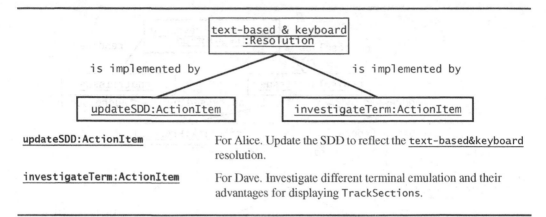

updateSDD:ActionItem   For Alice. Update the SDD to reflect the text-based&keyboard
                                    resolution.

investigateTerm:ActionItem   For Dave. Investigate different terminal emulation and their
                                    advantages for displaying TrackSections.

Figure 12-8   An example of implementation of a resolution (UML object diagram). ActionItems in bold.

Issue-Based Information System

Issue-Based Information System (IBIS) includes an issue model and a design method
for addressing ill-structured, or wicked problems (as opposed to tame problems). A *wicked*
problem is defined as a problem that cannot be solved algorithmically but, rather, has to be
resolved through discussion and debate.

The IBIS issue model (Figure 12-9) has three nodes (Issues, Positions, and Arguments)
related by seven kinds of links (supports, objects-to, replaces, responds-to, generalizes,
questions, and suggests). Each Issue describes a design problem under consideration.
Developers propose solutions to the problem by creating Position nodes (similar to the
Proposal nodes we described in Section 12.3.3). While alternatives are being generated,
developers argue about their value with Argument nodes. Arguments can either support a
Position or object-to a Position. Note that the same node can apply to multiple positions.
The IBIS model did not originally include Criterion and Resolution.

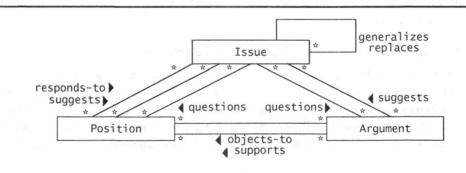

Figure 12-9   The IBIS model (UML class diagram).

IBIS is supported by a hypertext tool (gIBIS, [Conklin & Burgess-Yakemovic, 1991]) and is used for capturing rationale during face-to-face meetings. It provided the basis for most of the subsequent issue models, including DRL and QOC, which we discuss next.

Decision Representation Language

Decision Representation Language (DRL) aims at capturing the **decision rationale** of a design [Lee, 1990]. A decision rationale is defined by Lee as the representation of the qualitative elements of decision making, including the alternatives being considered, their evaluation, the arguments that led to these evaluations, and the criteria used in these evaluations. DRL is supported by SYBIL, a tool that enables the user to track dependencies among elements of the rationale when revising evaluations. DRL elaborates on the original IBIS model by adding nodes to capture Design Goals and Procedures. DRL views the construction of the rationale as a task comparable to the design of the artifact itself. DRL is summarized in Figure 12-10. The main drawbacks of DRL are its complexity (7 types of nodes and 15 types of links) and the effort spent in structuring the captured rationale.

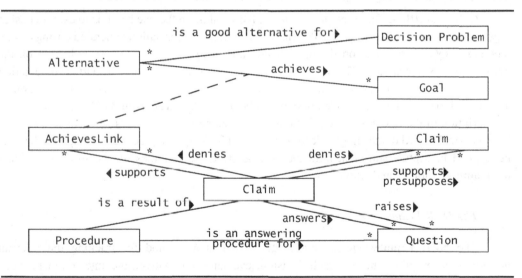

Figure 12-10   Decision Representation Language (UML class diagram).

Questions, Options, and Criteria

Questions, Options, and Criteria (QOC) is another elaboration of IBIS. Questions represent design problems to be solved (Issues in the issue model we presented). Options are possible answers to Questions (Proposals in our model). Options can trigger other Consequent Questions. Options are assessed negatively and positively against Criteria, which are relative measures of goodness defined by the developers. Also, Arguments can support

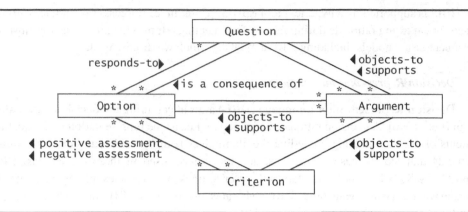

Figure 12-11   Questions, Options, and Criteria model (UML class diagram).

or challenge any Question, Option, Criterion, or relationship between those. Arguments may also support and challenge Arguments. Figure 12-11 depicts the QOC model.

QOC and IBIS differ at the process level. IBIS's aim, on the one hand, is to capture design argumentation as it occurs (e.g., gIBIS is used for capturing information generated during design meetings). QOC structures, on the other hand, are constructed as an act of reflection on the current state of the design. This conceptual separation of the construction and argumentation phases of the design process emphasizes the systematic elaboration and structuring of rationale as opposed to capturing it as a side effect of deliberation. Rationale, from QOC's perspective, is a description of the design space explored by the developers. From IBIS's perspective, rationale is a historical record of the analysis leading to a specific design. In practice, both approaches can be applied to capture sufficient rationale. We describe the activities related to capturing and maintaining rationale in Section 12.4.

The NFR Framework

The **NFR Framework** [Chung et al., 1999] is a method for tracking the relevant nonfunctional requirements for each decision, evaluated alternative, and interaction between nonfunctional requirements. Unlike the previous three issue models, the NFR Framework is specific to requirements engineering. Nonfunctional requirements are treated as *goals* to be met. To address the difficulty that nonfunctional requirements are usually high-level and subjective, goals are refined and clarified by decomposing them into subgoals. Goals and subgoals are represented as nodes in a goal graph. Decomposition relationships are represented as directed arcs. The NFR Framework provides two types of decompositions:

- *AND decomposition.* A goal can be decomposed into subgoals, all of which need to be met to help the parent goal.

- *OR decomposition*. A goal can be decomposed into alternative subgoals, any one of which needs to be satisfied to help the parent goal.

The top-level goals (specified by the client and the users) are hence refined into lower-level and more concrete goals. Note that a single subgoal can be related to more than one parent goal. Moreover, the NFR Framework provides additional types of links to capture other relationships. For example, correlation links between two goals indicate how one goal in the graph can support or hinder the other goal. Since nonfunctional requirements are rarely qualities that are either met or not, links in a goal graph represent how much a goal contributes to or hinders another goal. A goal is *satisficed* (as opposed to *satisfied*) when the selected alternative meets the goal within acceptable limits. Otherwise, the goal is said to be *denied*. Five weights can be associated with a link: *makes*, *helps*, *neutral*, *hurts*, and *breaks*. Root nodes represent high-level goals specified by the client. As these goals are successively refined into more concrete ones, the refinement activity moves towards system features. Goals that represent system features (as opposed to nonfunctional requirements) are called *operationalizing goals*.

Figure 12-12 depicts a partial goal graph indicating alternatives for an ATM authentication mechanism. In this goal graph, Flexibility, Low cost, and Security are high-level goals. Security is then decomposed using an AND relationship into Authentication, Confidentiality, and Integrity, denoting that for an account to be secure, the system must allow only authorized users to operate on the account, that all transactions must be held confidential, and that all transactions yield a valid result (i.e., no money can be created or destroyed by abusing the system). The Authentication subgoal is further refined, using an OR relationship, into Account+PIN, SmartCard+PIN, and FingerPrint reader. These last three goals, since they represent different features of the system, are operationalizing goals, and therefore,

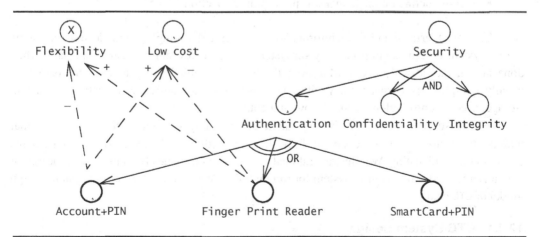

Figure 12-12   An example of goal refinement using the NFR Framework for the ATM authentication mechanism (NFR goal graph).

are represented using thicker circles. We use two correlation links to indicate (for example) that the Account+PIN goal helps the low cost goal but hurts the Flexibility goal.

Once an initial goal graph has been refined and several operationalizing goals have been developed, different subsets of operationalizing goals can be evaluated and selected. By following the decomposition and correlation links, the developers can check whether the high-level goals are met (at least to a sufficiently reasonable extent). In Figure 12-12, we evaluate the Account+PIN goal as a solution and observe that the Authentication and Low cost goals are satisficed, that the Security goal will be satisficed once the Confidentiality and the Integrity goals are satisficed, but that the Flexibility goal is not satisficed. For realistic problems, the goal graph becomes substantially larger, at which point tool support would be necessary for evaluating and comparing different alternatives. Other aspects of the NFR Framework not covered here include the reuse of goal decompositions from one system to another. This enables the developer to pick groups of solutions that were previously explored and evaluate them against new criteria.

12.4 Rationale Activities: From Issues to Decisions

Maintaining rationale helps developers deal with change. By capturing the justification of decisions, they can more easily revisit important decisions when user requirements or the target environment changes. For rationale models to be useful, however, they must be captured, structured, and easily accessible. In this section, we describe these activities, including

- capturing rationale during design meetings (Section 12.4.2)
- revising rationale models with subsequent clarifications (Section 12.4.3)
- capturing additional rationale during revisions (Section 12.4.4)
- reconstructing rationale that was not captured (Section 12.4.5).

The most critical rationale information is generated during system design: decisions during system design can impact every subsystem, and their revision is costly, especially when done late in the design process. Moreover, the rationale behind subsystem decomposition is usually complex, as it spans many different issues, such as hardware allocation, persistent storage, access control, global control flow, and boundary conditions.

For these reasons, we focus on system design in this chapter. Note, however, that maintaining rationale can be done similarly throughout the development, from requirements elicitation to field testing. We illustrate rationale activities with issues from the system design of CTC, a centralized traffic control system for freight trains. We describe the current system design model of CTC next.

12.4.1 CTC System Design

Consider the CTC system we described in Section 12.3.1. We are in the process of reengineering a legacy system, replacing a mainframe computer with a network of workstations. We are also enhancing the system, such as adding access control and increasing focus on security and usability. We are in the middle of system design. So far, we identified from the nonfunctional requirements several design goals (ordered by descending priority):

- **Availability**. The system should crash less than once per month and recover completely from a crash within 10 minutes.
- **Security**. No entity outside the control room should be able to access the state of the controlled tracks or manipulate any of their devices.
- **Usability**. Once trained, a dispatcher should input no more than two erroneous commands per day.

We allocate a client node per dispatcher. Two redundant server nodes maintain the global state of the system (see Figure 12-13). The servers are also responsible for persistent storage. Data are stored in flat files that can be copied off-line and imported into a database for off-line processing. Communication with devices on the tracks is done via modems managed by a dedicated machine. Middleware supports two types of communication among subsystems: method invocation for handling requests and notification of state changes for informing subsystems of state changes. Each subsystem subscribes to the events it is interested in. Presently, we must address access control issues and define the mechanisms that prevent dispatchers from manipulating the tracks of other dispatchers. We describe in the following sections how the access control issue is debated and resolved while capturing its rationale.

12.4.2 Capturing Rationale in Meetings

Meetings enable developers to present, negotiate, and resolve issues face to face. The physical presence of the respective developers involved in the discussion is important, adding the benefits of nonverbal communication: it allows people to assess the relative positions of each other and the trade-offs they are willing to make. Conversely, negotiating and making decisions via E-mail, for example, is difficult, as misunderstandings can easily occur. Face-to-face meetings are instead a more natural starting point for capturing rationale.

We described procedures for organizing and capturing meetings with minutes and agendas in Chapter 3, *Project Organization and Communication*. An agenda, posted in advance of the meeting, describes the status and points to be discussed. The meeting is recorded in minutes that are made available shortly after the meeting. Using the issue modeling concepts we described in Section 12.3, we write an agenda in terms of **issues** that we need to discuss and resolve. We state the objective of the meeting as coming to a resolution on these issues and any related subissues that are raised in the discussion. We structure the meeting minutes in terms of **proposals** that we explore during the meeting, **criteria** that we agree on, and **arguments** we use to support or oppose proposals. We capture decisions as **resolutions** and **action items** that implement resolutions. During the meeting we review status in terms of the action items that we produced in the previous meetings.

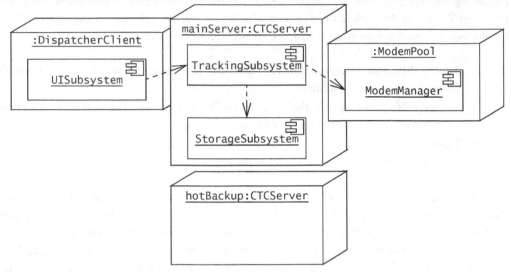

| DispatcherClient | Each dispatcher is assigned a DispatcherClient node running the user interface to the system. |

| CTCServer | A CTCServer is responsible for maintaining the state of the system. It transmits dispatcher commands to the field devices and receives state information from the field via the ModemPool node. A CTCServer is also responsible for storing persistent state (e.g., device addresses, device names, dispatcher assignments, train schedules). Two CTCServers, a main server and a hot back-up, are used to increase availability. |

| ModemPool | The ModemPool manages the modems used to communicate with the field devices. |

| ModemManager | The ModemManager is responsible for connecting to field devices and transmitting field commands. |

| StorageSubsystem | The StorageSubsystem is responsible for maintaining persistent state. |

| TrackingSubsystem | The TrackingSubsystem is responsible for maintaining track state, as notices of state changes are received from the field, and for issuing device commands via the ModemManager, based on user-level commands received from the UISubsystem. |

| UISubsystem | The UISubsystem is responsible for receiving commands and displaying track state to the dispatcher. The UISubsystem controls the validity of the dispatcher's commands before forwarding them to the CTCServer. |

Figure 12-13 Subsystem decomposition for CTC (UML deployment diagram). The state of the system is maintained by a mainServer. A hotBackup of the mainServer stands by in case the mainServer fails. The mainServer sends commands and receives state transitions from the tracks via the ModemPool.

For example, consider the access control issue of the CTC system. We need to organize a meeting of the architecture team, including the developers responsible for the UISubsystem, the TrackingSubsystem, and the NotificationService. Alice, the facilitator for the architecture team, posts the agenda depicted in Figure 12-14.

During the meeting, we review the action item generated in the previous architecture meeting—AI[1]: *Investigate access control model by middleware.* The middleware provides basic blocks for authentication and encryption but does not introduce any other constraints on the access model. Issues I[1] and I[2] are resolved quickly with domain knowledge: a dispatcher can see all TrackSections, but can only manipulate the devices of her TrackSection. Issue I[3], however, (*How should access control be integrated with* TrackSections *and* NotificationService?) is more difficult and sparks a debate.

AGENDA: Integration of access control and notification

When and Where	Role
Date: 9/13	**Primary Facilitator**: Alice
Start: 4:30 P.M.	**Timekeeper**: Dave
End: 5:30 P.M.	**Minute Taker**: Ed
Building: Train Hall	**Room**: 3420

1. Purpose

The first revisions of the hardware/software mapping and the persistent storage design have been completed. The access control model needs to be defined and its integration with the current subsystems, such as NotificationService and TrackingSubsystem, needs to be defined.

2. Desired outcome

Resolve issues about the integration of access control with notification.

3. Information sharing [Allocated time: 15 minutes]

AI[1]: Dave: Investigate the access control model provided by the middleware.

4. Discussion [Allocated time: 35 minutes]

I[1]: Can a dispatcher see other dispatchers' TrackSections?

I[2]: Can a dispatcher modify another dispatchers' TrackSections?

I[3]: How should access control be integrated with TrackSections and NotificationService?

5. Wrap up [Allocated time: 5 minutes]

Review and assign new action items.
Meeting critique.

Figure 12-14 Agenda for the access control discussion of CTC.

Dave, the developer responsible for the NotificationService, proposes to integrate the access control with the TrackSection (see Figure 12-15). The TrackSection would maintain an access list of the Dispatchers who can examine or modify any given TrackSection. Events would also be organized by TrackSections. To be notified about events in a TrackSection, a subsystem would need to subscribe to a TrackSection via the NotificationService. The NotificationService would then check with the given TrackSection if the current dispatcher had at least read access.

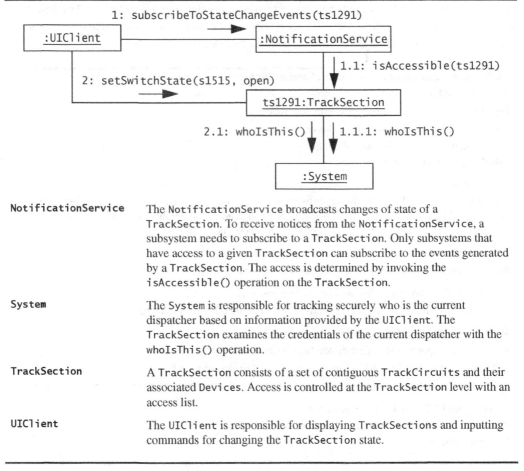

NotificationService	The NotificationService broadcasts changes of state of a TrackSection. To receive notices from the NotificationService, a subsystem needs to subscribe to a TrackSection. Only subsystems that have access to a given TrackSection can subscribe to the events generated by a TrackSection. The access is determined by invoking the isAccessible() operation on the TrackSection.
System	The System is responsible for tracking securely who is the current dispatcher based on information provided by the UIClient. The TrackSection examines the credentials of the current dispatcher with the whoIsThis() operation.
TrackSection	A TrackSection consists of a set of contiguous TrackCircuits and their associated Devices. Access is controlled at the TrackSection level with an access list.
UIClient	The UIClient is responsible for displaying TrackSections and inputting commands for changing the TrackSection state.

Figure 12-15 Proposal P[1]: The access is controlled by the TrackSection object with an access list. The NotificationService queries the TrackSection to determine whether a subsystem can receive notices about a given TrackSection (UML communication diagram.)

Alice, the developer responsible for the TrackSubsystem that includes the TrackSection class, proposes to reverse the dependency between the TrackSection and the Notification-Service (see Figure 12-16). In this proposal, the UIClient would interact only with the TrackSection class, including when subscribing to events. The UIClient would invoke the subscribeToEvents() method on the TrackSection, which would perform the access control checks and then invoke the subscribeToStateChangeEvents() on the NotificationService. The UIClient would then not have direct access to the NotificationService. This has the advantage of centralizing all the protected operations in one class and centralizing the access control checks. Moreover, the TrackSection would then also be able to unsubscribe UIClients when the access list is modified.

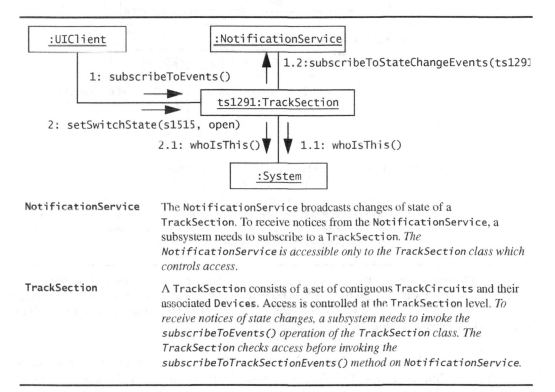

NotificationService	The NotificationService broadcasts changes of state of a TrackSection. To receive notices from the NotificationService, a subsystem needs to subscribe to a TrackSection. *The NotificationService is accessible only to the TrackSection class which controls access.*
TrackSection	A TrackSection consists of a set of contiguous TrackCircuits and their associated Devices. Access is controlled at the TrackSection level. *To receive notices of state changes, a subsystem needs to invoke the subscribeToEvents() operation of the TrackSection class. The TrackSection checks access before invoking the subscribeToTrackSectionEvents() method on NotificationService.*

Figure 12-16 Proposal P[2]: The UIClient subscribes to track section events via the subscribeToEvents() operation on the TrackSection. The TrackSection checks access and then invokes the subscribeToTrackSectionEvents() operation on the NotificationService. The NotificationService is not accessible to the UIClient class. (UML communication diagram, differences from Figure 12-15 highlighted in *italics*.)

Ed notes that every dispatcher is allowed to see other dispatcher's TrackSections, so only modification of state needs to be controlled. Assuming that all modifications are done via method invocation, and that the NotificationService is used only for broadcasting changes, the NotificationService need not be integrated with access control. In this case, a refinement of Dave's initial proposal could be used (see Figure 12-17).

The architecture team decides to use Ed's proposal based on its simplicity. Ed produces the chronological meeting minutes depicted in Figure 12-18.

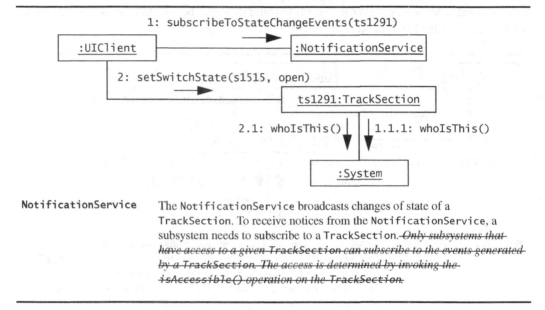

NotificationService   The NotificationService broadcasts changes of state of a
                       TrackSection. To receive notices from the NotificationService, a
                       subsystem needs to subscribe to a TrackSection. *Only subsystems that*
                       have access to a given TrackSection can subscribe to the events generated
                       by a TrackSection. The access is determined by invoking the
                       isAccessible() operation on the TrackSection.

Figure 12-17   Proposal P[3]: The access to operations that modify TrackSections is controlled by the TrackSection object with an access list. The NotificationService need not be part of the access control, because every dispatcher can see changes of state. (UML communication diagram, subtractions from Figure 12-15 highlighted in *strikeout italics*.)

Ed produces the minutes of Figure 12-18 by inserting in the agenda the discussion that is relevant to the different issues. The discussion, however, is recorded as a chronological list of statements made by the participants. Most of these statements mix the presentation of an alternative with the argumentation against another alternative. To clarify the minutes, Ed restructures them after the meeting with issue models (Figure 12-19).

The important results of the access control meeting are

• Dispatchers can see all TrackSections, but modify only the ones they are assigned to.

• An access list associated with TrackSections is used for access control.

• NotificationService is not integrated with access control, because state changes can be seen by all Dispatchers.

CHRONOLOGICAL MINUTES: Integration of access control and notification

When and Where	**Roles**
Date: 9/13, 4:30–6 P.M.	**Primary Facilitator**: Alice
Building: Train Hall, 3420	**Timekeeper**: Dave, **Minute Taker**: Ed

1. Purpose

The first revisions of the hardware/software mapping and the persistent storage design have been completed. The access control model needs to be defined and its integration with the current subsystems, in particular, NotificationService and TrackingSubsystem, needs to be defined.

2. Desired outcome

Resolve issues about the integration of access control with notification

3. Information sharing

AI[1]:Dave: Investigate the access control model provided by the middleware.

    Status: The middleware supports strong authentication and encryption. It does not introduce any constraints on the access model. Any access policy can be implemented on the server.

4. Discussion

I[1]: Can a dispatcher see other dispatchers' TrackSections?

    Ed: Yes, in CTC specification.

I[2]: Can a dispatcher modify another dispatcher's TrackSections?

    Zoe: No. Only the dispatcher assigned to the TrackSection can manipulate the devices of the section. Note that the dispatcher can be reassigned dynamically.

    Ed: Also in CTC specification.

I[3]: How should access control be integrated with TrackSections and NotificationService?

    Dave: The TrackSection maintains an access list. The notification service asks the TrackSection about which subsystems have access.

    Alice: We should probably reverse the dependency between TrackSection and NotificationService. Instead, the UIClient requests subscriptions from the TrackSection, which checks for access and then calls the NotificationService. This way, all protected methods are in one place.

    Dave: This way, the TrackSection can also more easily unsubscribe dispatchers when their access is revoked.

    Ed: Hey, no need for access control in NotificationService: Dispatchers can see all TrackSections. As long as the NotificationService is not used for changing the TrackSection state, there is no need to restrict subscriptions.

    Alice: But thinking about the access control on notification would be more general.

    Ed: But more complex. Let's just separate access control and notification at this point and revisit the issue if the requirements change.

    Alice: Ok. I'll take care of revising the TrackingSubsystem API.

5. Wrap up

AI[2]: Alice: Design access control for the TrackingSubsystem based on authentication and encryption provided by the middleware.

Figure 12-18   Chronological minutes for the access control discussion of CTC.

STRUCTURED MINUTES: Integration of access control and notification

When and Where	Roles
Date: 9/13, 4:30–6 P.M.	**Primary Facilitator**: Alice
Building: Train Hall, 3420	**Timekeeper**: Dave, **Minute Taker**: Ed

1. Purpose

The first revisions of the hardware/software mapping and the persistent storage design have been completed. The access control model needs to be defined and its integration with the current subsystems, in particular, NotificationService and TrackingSubsystem, needs to be defined.

2. Desired outcome

Resolve issues about the integration of access control with notification.

3. Information sharing

AI[1]:Dave: Investigate the access control model provided by the middleware.

Status: The middleware supports strong authentication and encryption. It does not introduce any constraints on the access model. Any access policy can be implemented on the server.

4. Discussion

I[1]: Can a dispatcher see other dispatchers' TrackSections?

R[1]: Yes (from CTC specification and confirmed by Zoe, a test user).

I[2]: Can a dispatcher modify another dispatcher's TrackSections?

R[2]: No. Only the dispatcher assigned to the TrackSection can manipulate the devices of the section. Note that the dispatcher can be reassigned dynamically (from CTC specification and confirmed by Zoe).

I[3]: How should access control be integrated with TrackSections and NotificationService?

P[3.1]:TrackSections maintain an access list of which subsystems can examine or modify the state of the TrackSection. To subscribe to events, a subsystem sends a request to the NotificationService, which in turns sends a request to the corresponding TrackSection to check access.

P[3.2]:TrackSections host all protected operations. The UIClient requests subscription to TrackSection events by sending a request to the TrackSection, which checks access and sends a request to the NotificationService.

A[3.1] for P[3.2]: Access control and protected operations are centralized into a single class.

P[3.3]: There is no need to restrict the access to the event subscription. The UIClient requests subscriptions directly from the NotificationService. The NotificationService need not check access.

A[3.2] for P[3.3] Dispatchers can see the state of any TrackSections (see R[1]).

A[3.3] for P[3.3]: Simplicity.

R[3]: P[3.3]. See action item AI[2].

5. Wrap up

AI[2]:Alice: Design access control for the TrackingSubsystem based on authentication and encryption provided by the middleware and on resolution R[3] discussed in these minutes.

Figure 12-19 Structured minutes for the access control discussion of CTC.

By focusing on the issue model, we have also captured the fact that

- Integrating the NotificationService with access control was investigated.
- Centralizing all protected methods into the TrackSection class was an accepted principle.

The last two pieces of information are rationale information and would usually be considered unimportant. However, this is the type of information that is captured by the minute taker and structured to facilitate future changes.

12.4.3 Capturing Rationale Asynchronously

Meeting discussions rely on context information. When the meeting starts, most participants already have a substantial amount of information about the system, its intended purpose, and its design. The facilitator of the meeting usually focuses on a small set of issues to be resolved. For example, in the meeting we presented in the previous section, all participants knew the purpose and functionality of the CTC system, its design goals, and current subsystem decomposition. The minutes of this meeting record only the issues under discussion and, therefore, do not contain much or any background information. Unfortunately, this information is lost over time, and meeting minutes become obsolete quickly.

We can use issue modeling to address this problem. In Chapter 3, *Project Organization and Communication*, we described the use of groupware for supporting asynchronous communication. By integrating the preparation and recording of the meeting with the asynchronous communication, we can capture additional contextual information.

In the CTC example, assume that Mary, the developer responsible for the UISubsystem, was not able to attend the access control meeting. She reads the agenda and the meeting minutes, which were posted on the newsgroup dedicated to the architecture team. Although she understands the outcome of the meeting, the discussion about the NotificationService requires clarification: Argument A[3.3] for proposal P[3.3] claims that, because Dispatchers can see every TrackSection, all events can be visible, so there is no need to control the access to the events. This implies that the NotificationService is used only for notifying other subsystems of state changes. In other words, the TrackSection does not change its state as a consequence of events generated by other subsystems. Mary wants to confirm that this assumption is correct; consequently, she posts an issue on the newsgroup (Figure 12-20). She also proposes to disallow the TrackingService from subscribing to any events in order to ensure proper access control.

Follow-up on meeting minutes enables developers to capture more of the context surrounding the design. As a consequence, more rationale and clearer information are captured. Using the same issue model for both meetings and online discussions allows us to integrate all rationale information. Although this can be done with minimal technology, such as newsgroups, the representation of the issue model, the meeting agendas and minutes, and related messages can be integrated into a groupware tool, such as a custom Lotus Notes database or a multi-user

---

Newsgroup: ctc.architecture.discuss
Subject: **Date:**
I[1]: Can a dispatcher see other dispatcher's TrackSections?   9/14
I[2]: Can a dispatcher modify another dispatcher's TrackSections?   9/14
I[3]: How should access control be implemented?   9/14
       P[3.1]: TrackSection has access list   9/14
       P[3.2]: TrackSection has subscription operations   9/14
              +A[3.1]: Extensibility.   9/14
              +A[3.2]: Centralize all protected operations.   9/14
       P[3.3]: NotificationService is not part of access   9/14
              +A[3.3]: Dispatchers can see all TrackSections   9/14
              +A[3.4]: Simplicity.   9/14

From: Mary
Newsgroups: ctc.architecture.discuss
Subject: Consequent Issue: Should notification not be used for requests?
Date: Thu, 15 Sep 13:12:48 -0400

I[4] responding to A[3.3]: for access lists against capabilities
> Dispatchers can see all TrackSections and, thus, should be able
> to see all events.
This assumes that the TrackSection does not rely on events to change its state
and that events are used only for informing other subsystems of state changes.
For the purpose of robustness, should we disallow the TrackingService to
subscribe to any events?

Figure 12-20   Example of a consequent issue posted asynchronously (newsgroup post). Mary, a developer who did not attend the meeting, requests clarification. This leads to the post of an additional issue and the capture of more rationale.

issue base hosted on a Web site (see example in Figure 12-21). Once we institute procedures for organizing and recording rationale in meetings and expanding it with groupware, we are able to capture a great deal of rationale. The next challenge is to keep this information up to date as changes occur.

12.4.4 Capturing Rationale when Discussing Change

Rationale models help us deal with change. Unfortunately, rationale is itself subject to change when we revise decisions. When we design a solution in response to a requirements change, for example, we look at past rationale to assess which decisions should be revised and design the change. Not only do we need to capture the rationale for the change and its solution, but we also need to relate it with past rationale.

For example, in the CTC system, assume the requirements on the access control changed. Before, Dispatchers were allowed to see all TrackSections. The client informed us that, unlike previously specified, Dispatchers should be able to see only the neighboring TrackSections. In response to this change, we need to modify the design of the access control and organize a meeting with the architecture team. In particular, we need to search past rationale associated with access control. Alice, the primary facilitator of the architecture team, posts the agenda depicted in Figure 12-22.

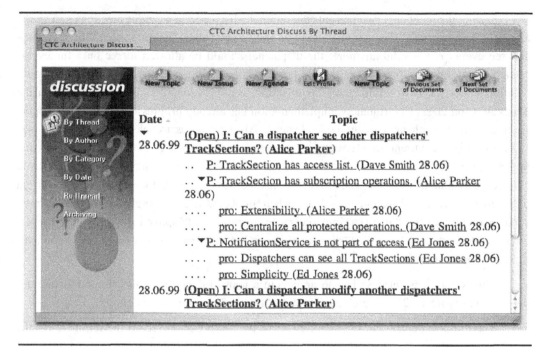

Figure 12-21   An example of an issue database (LN IBIS database template in Domino Lotus Notes). Developers can access and post issues, proposals, arguments, and resolutions with Web forms.

AGENDA: Revision of access control, dispatchers can access only neighboring tracks.

When and Where	Role
Date: 10/13, 4:30–5:30 P.M.	**Primary Facilitator**: Alice
Location: Signal Hall 2300	**Timekeeper**: Dave, **Minute Taker**: Ed

1. Purpose

The client requested that dispatchers be able to access only neighboring TrackSections.

2. Desired outcome

Resolve access control issues related to this change of requirement.

3. Information sharing [Allocated time: 15 minutes]

AI[1]: Dave: Recover rationale for access control.

4. Discussion [Allocated time: 35 minutes]

I[1]: How should access control be revised based on the neighboring track requirement?

5. Wrap up [Allocated Time: 5 minutes]

Review and assign new action items.
Meeting critique.

Figure 12-22   Agenda for the access control revision of CTC.

During the meeting, Dave presents the rationale discussed in previous meetings and on the architecture newsgroup. The architecture team notices that the assumption that all subsystems can see events is not valid anymore: the dispatcher should be allowed to see only the events related to neighboring TrackSections. Proposal P[2] (see Figure 12-16) seems to be the better solution under the new requirements, as all protected operations could be centralized in the TrackSection class. Unfortunately, implementation has already progressed, and the developers want to minimize changes to the code. Instead, Alice proposes to select proposal P[1] (see Figure 12-15): the current UIClient stays unchanged, as the interfaces to the TrackSection and NotificationService classes need not change. Only the NotificationService needs to change such that it sends requests to the TrackSection to check the access of the current dispatcher. To revoke dispatcher privileges when an access list is changed, the TrackSection sends a request to the NotificationService to unsubscribe Dispatchers. This introduces a circular dependency between TrackSection and NotificationService, but minimizes modifications to existing code.

This solution is selected by the architecture team. Ed produces the structured minutes depicted in Figure 12-23 (chronological minutes not displayed for brevity).

The minutes depicted in Figure 12-23 serve two purposes: to record the rationale for the new change and to relate it to past rationale. This is done by quoting the past rationale that was used to revisit the access control decision. Furthermore, these new minutes are posted on the architecture newsgroup and discussed by other developers who could not attend the meeting, thus completing the cycle of recording and clarifying rationale information. When groupware is used, new rationale can be related to past rationale with a hyperlink, making it easier for developers to navigate to the related information.

STRUCTURED MINUTES: Revision of access control, dispatchers access only neighboring tracks.

When and Where	Role
Date: 10/13, 4:30–5:30 P.M.	**Primary Facilitator**: Alice
Location: Signal Hall 2300	**Timekeeper**: Dave, **Minute Taker**: Ed

1. Purpose

The client requested that dispatchers be able to access only neighboring TrackSections.

2. Desired outcome

Resolve access control issues related to this change of requirement.

3. Information sharing

AI[1]: Dave: Recover rationale for access control.

      Result: Issues I[1] (from 9/13) and I[2] (from 9/15) recovered:

Figure 12-23 Structured minutes for the access control revision of CTC. *Italics* denote the rationale that was recovered for the purpose of the meeting. *(Continued on next page)*.

I[1]: How should access control be integrated with TrackSections and NotificationService? (Minutes from 9/14)

    P[3.1]:   *TrackSections maintain an access list of who can examine or modify the state of the TrackSection. To subscribe to events, a subsystem sends a request to the NotificationService, which in turns sends a request to the corresponding TrackSection to check access.*

    P[3.2]:   *TrackSections host all protected operations. The UIClient requests subscription to TrackSection events by sending a request to the TrackSection, which checks access and sends a request to the NotificationService.*

              A[3.1] for P[3.2]: Extensibility.

              A[3.2] for P[3.2]: Access control and protected operations are centralized into one class.

    P[3.3]:   *There is no need to restrict the access to the event subscription. The UIClient requests subscriptions directly from the NotificationService. The NotificationService need not check access.*

              A[3.3] for P[3.3] Dispatchers can examine the state of any TrackSections (see R[1]).

              A[3.4] for P[3.3]: Simplicity.

              R[3]: P[3.3]. See action item AI[2].

I[2]: Should notification not be used for requests? (from Mary's news post 9/15)

    R[2]:   *Notification should be used only for informing of state changes. TrackSections and, more generally, TrackingSubsystem should not change their state based on events.*

4. Discussion

I[1]: How should access control be revised based on the neighboring track requirement?

    P[1.1]:   Protected operations, including subscription, centralized in TrackSection, as in P[3.2] (from 9/13).

            A[1.1] against P[1.1]: This requires all subsystems subscribing to notification events to be modified, since the subscription operation is moved from the NotificationService to the TrackSection.

    P[1.2]:   NotificationService sends requests to TrackSections to check access. TrackSection sends request to NotificationService to unsubscribe dispatchers whose access has been revoked. P[3.1] (from 9/13)

            A[1.2] for P[1.2]: Minimal change to existing implementation.

            A[1.3] against P[1.2]: Circular dependencies.

    R[1]:   P[1.2], see AI[2] and AI[3].

5. Wrap up

    AI[2]:   Alice: Change the TrackSection to unsubscribe dispatchers when their rights are revoked.

    AI[3]:   Dave: Modify NotificationService to check access with TrackSection when subscribing to a new subsystem.

Figure 12-23   *Continued.*

Note that even when an issue base is used to maintain and track open issues, this information base can grow quickly into a large unstructured chaos. Moreover, some issues are not recorded, as not all issues are discussed in meetings. Many issues are discussed and resolved informally in hallway conversations. It is necessary, therefore, to reconstruct the missing rationale of the system and integrate it with past rationale. We discuss this in the next section.

12.4.5 Reconstructing Rationale

Reconstructing rationale is a different method for capturing the rationale of the system. Instead of capturing decisions and their justifications as they occur, rationale is systematically reconstructed from the system model, the communication record, and developers' memories. With this method, rationale is captured and structured more systematically. Fewer resources are invested during the early phases of the process, thus enabling developers to come to a solution faster. Also, separating the design activity from the rationale capture enables developers to step back and critique their design more objectively. Reconstructing rationale, however, focuses mostly on the selected solution. Capturing discarded alternatives is much more difficult as developers forget. For example, assume that we did not capture the rationale of the access control in CTC and that the only information we had was the system design model (Figure 12-24).

We want to recover the rationale of the system design for review and documentation. We decide to organize each issue as a table with two columns, the left column for the proposals and the right column for their corresponding arguments. In Figure 12-25, we recover the rationale for the integration of access control with notification. We identify two possible solutions: P[1],

---

4. Access control

Access in CTC is controlled at the level of TrackSections: the Dispatcher who is assigned to a TrackSection can modify its state, that is, open and close signals and switches and modify other devices. Moreover, the Dispatcher can examine the state of neighboring TrackSections without modifying their state. This is necessary for the Dispatcher to observe the Trains that are about to enter the controlled TrackSection.

Access control is implemented with an access list maintained by the TrackSection. The access list contains the identity of the Dispatcher, who can modify the TrackSection (i.e., writers), and the identify of the Dispatcher, who can see the state of the track section (i.e., readers). For the sake of generality, the access list is implemented such that it can include multiple readers and multiple writers. The TrackSection checks the access list for every operation that modifies or queries the state of the TrackSection.

When subsystems subscribe to events, the NotificationService sends a request to the TrackSection to check access. The TrackSection sends a request to the NotificationService to unsubscribe dispatchers whose access is revoked.

The communication diagram of Figure 12-15 depicts this solution.

Figure 12-24   Excerpt from system design document, access control section.

I[1]: **How should access control of TrackSections be integrated with notification?**

Access in CTC is controlled at the level of TrackSections: the Dispatcher who is assigned to a TrackSection can modify its state, that is, open and close signals and switches and modify other devices. Moreover, the Dispatcher can examine the state of neighboring TrackSections without modifying their state. This is necessary for the Dispatcher to observe the Trains that are about to enter the controlled TrackSection.

P[1]: **TrackSection class controls all state modification and notification subscription access.** Access control is implemented as an access list in TrackSection. The TrackSection class checks access of the caller for every operation that examines or modifies state. In particular, the caller subscribes to notification events by invoking methods on TrackSection, which in turn forwards the request to the NotificationService if access is granted. This solution is illustrated in Figure 12-16.	For: • Central solution: all protected methods related to the TrackSection are in one place.
P[2]: **TrackSection class controls state modification; NotificationService controls subscription.** Like P[1], except that the caller requests subscriptions to events directly from the NotificationService, which checks access with the TrackSection before granting the subscription. This solution is illustrated in Figure 12-15.	For: • Access-independent interface: the interfaces of NotificationService and TrackSection are the same as if there were no access control (legacy argument). Against: • Circular dependency between NotificationService and TrackSection: the TrackSection invokes operations on the NotificationService to generate events; the NotificationService subscription methods invoke operations on the TrackSection to check access.

R[1]:
P[2]. P[1] would have been a better solution; however, access control did not apply to notification. To minimize code and design rework, P[2] was selected.

Figure 12-25 Reconstructed rationale for the notification access control issue of CTC.

in which the TrackSection class exports all operations whose access is controlled, including subscription to notifications, and P[2], in which the NotificationService delegates the access control check to the TrackSection. We then enumerate the advantages and disadvantages of each solution in the right column and summarize the justification of the decision as a resolution at the bottom of the table.

A reconstructed rationale, such as the one in Figure 12-25, costs less to capture than the activities we described previously. It is more difficult, however, to capture the discarded alternatives and the reasons for such choices, especially when decisions are revised over time. In Figure 12-25, the resolution states that we did not select the better proposal, and we were able to remember the reasons for this nonoptimal decision (i.e., that substantial code had been completed prior to this decision, and we wanted to minimize code rework). Alternatively, reconstructing rationale is an effective tool for review and for identifying decisions that are inconsistent with the design goals of the project. Moreover, even if the reviewed decisions cannot be revised at a late stage in the project, this knowledge can benefit new developers assigned to the project or developers revising the system in later iterations.

The balance between rationale capture, maintenance, and reconstruction differs for each project and must be carefully managed. It is relatively frequent to see rationale capture efforts accumulate enormous amounts of information that is either useless or not easily accessible to developers who should benefit from it. We focus on management issues next.

12.5 Managing Rationale

In this section, we describe issues related to managing rationale activities. Recording justifications for design decisions is often seen as an intrusion from management into the work of developers, and thus rationale techniques encounter resistance from developers and often degenerate into a bureaucratic process. Rationale techniques need to be carefully managed to be useful. In this section, we describe how to

- document rationale (Section 12.5.1)
- assign responsibilities for capturing and maintaining rationale models (Section 12.5.2)
- communicate about rationale models (Section 12.5.3)
- use issues to negotiate (Section 12.5.4)
- resolve conflicts (Section 12.5.5).

As before, we continue focusing on the system design activity. Note, however, that these techniques can be applied uniformly throughout system development.

12.5.1 Documenting Rationale

Rationale models (e.g., issue models) are different in structure than system models (e.g., use case models, class models, source code). While system models for realistic systems are large and complex, developers can organize them into layers or hierarchies, cross-reference them by use cases, and attach object design documentation to the source code. Rationale models are much more voluminous (many alternatives and arguments are generated for every decision) and continuously evolving (decisions are revisited and reopened). Hence, thinking of a rationale as a document usually defeats the purpose of capturing it: the rationale document is always out of date and inconsistent with system documents, which are kept up to date more often.

Instead, most approaches store rationale in a repository that is continuously updated and augmented with new issues and decisions. The key challenges for these repositories are that they must be kept up to date and that they can be easily accessed when needed. In recent work, this led to integrating the rationale repository tightly with the development tools and processes. For example, REQuest is a tool for rationale-based use case specification [Dutoit & Paech, 2002]. Figure 12-26 depicts a view of REQuest. The left column is used to access the requirements, written in terms of use cases and nonfunctional requirements. The right column is used to access the rationale represented as an augmented QOC model. Buttons at the top of the left column enable developers to ask different types of questions (about clarity, completeness, consistency, well-formedness, correctness, and justification) and attach them to the current element. Green, yellow, and red rationale indicators in the left column indicate questions associated with a specific element and whether or not the questions have been resolved. Clicking a rationale indicator displays the corresponding issues in the right column.

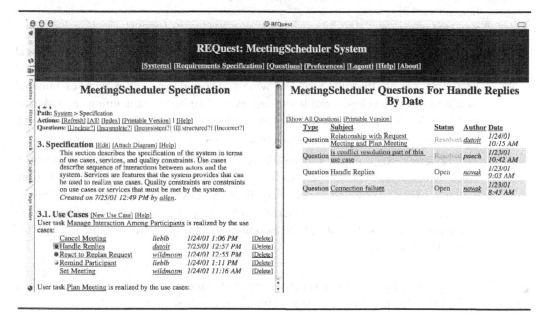

Figure 12-26   An example of rationale repository for requirements engineering: REQuest enables issue models to be attached to different requirements elements [Dutoit & Paech, 2002]. The left column depicts the requirements model in terms of use cases and nonfunctional requirements, and the right column depicts the issue model.

By integrating the specification and the rationale views, the rationale repository is more likely to include useful and up-to-date rationale, because developers can access it easily. For long-term use, a rationale editor consolidates and maintains the rationale model as needed. Next, we describe further the roles associated with rationale management.

12.5.2 Assigning Responsibilities

Assigning responsibilities for capturing and maintaining rationale is the most critical management decision in making rationale models useful. Maintaining rationale can easily be perceived as an intrusive bureaucratic process through which developers need to justify all decisions. Instead, rationale models should be maintained by a small number of people who have access to all developers' information, such as drafts of design documents and developer newsgroups. This small group of people, historians of the system design, becomes useful to the other developers when providing rationale information, and thus creates an incentive for developers to provide their members with information. Below are the main roles in rationale model maintenance:

- The **minute taker** records rationale in meetings. This includes recording chronological statements during the meeting and restructuring them with issues after the meeting (see Section 12.4.2).

- The **rationale editor** collects and organizes information related to rationale. This includes obtaining the meeting minutes from the minute taker, prototype and technology evaluations reports from developers, and drafts of all system models and design documents from the technical writers. The rationale editor imposes minimal overhead on the developers and the writers by performing the structuring and indexing role. The developers need not provide information structured as issue models; however, the rationale editor constructs an index of all issues.

- The **reviewer** examines the rationale captured by the rationale editor and identifies holes to be reconstructed. The reviewer then collects the relevant information from communication records and, if necessary, from the developers. This role should not be a management role or a quality assurance role: the reviewer must directly benefit the developers to be able to collect valid information. This role can be combined with the rationale editor role.

The size of the project determines the number of minute takers, rationale editors, and reviewers. The following heuristics can be used for assigning these roles:

- *One minute taker per team.* Meetings are usually organized by subsystem team or by cross-functional team. A developer of each team can function as a minute taker, thus distributing this time-consuming role across the project.

- *One rationale editor per project.* The role of rationale editor for a project is a full-time role. Unlike the role of minute taker, which can be rotated, the role of rationale editor requires consistency and should be assigned to a single person. In small projects, this role can be assigned to the system architect (see Chapter 6, *System Design: Decomposing the System*).

- *Increase the number of reviewers after delivery.* When the system is delivered and the number of developers directly needed for the project decreases, some developers should be assigned the reviewer role for salvaging and organizing as much information as possible. Rationale information is still recoverable from developers' memories, but disappears quickly as developers move to other projects.

12.5.3 Heuristics for Communicating about Rationale

A large part of communication *is* rationale information, given that argumentation is, by definition, rationale (see Section 12.2). Developers argue about design goals, whether a given issue is relevant or not, the benefit of several solutions, and their evaluation. Rationale constitutes a large and complex body of information, usually larger than the system itself. Communication, moreover, occurs most often in small forums; for example, in a team meeting or a conversation at the coffee machine. The challenge of communicating about rationale is to make this information accessible to all concerned parties without causing an information overload. In this chapter, we focused on techniques for capturing and structuring rationale, such as using issue models in minutes, follow-up conversations, and storing rationale in a repository. In addition, the following heuristics can be used to increase the structure of rationale and facilitate its navigation:

- *Name issues consistently.* Issues should be consistently and uniquely named across minutes, newsgroups, E-mail messages, and documents. Issues can have a number (e.g., 1291) and a short name (e.g., "the access/notification issue") for ease of reference.

- *Centralize issues.* Although issues will be discussed in a variety of contexts, encourage one context (e.g., a newsgroup or an issue base) to be a central repository of issues. This issue base should be maintained by the rationale editor, but could be used and extended by any developer. This enables developers to search for information quickly.

- *Cross-reference issues and system elements.* Most issues apply to a specific element in the system model (e.g., a use case, an object, a subsystem). Finding which model element a specific issue applies to is straightforward. However, finding which issues apply to a specific model element is a much more difficult problem. To facilitate this type of query, issues should be attached to the applicable model element when they are raised.

- *Manage change.* Rationale evolves as system models do. Thus, configuration management should be applied as consistently to rationale and documents as it is to system models.

Capturing and structuring rationale not only improves communication about rationale, but also facilitates communication about the system models. Integrating both rationale and system information enables developers to better maintain both types of information.

12.5.4 Issue Modeling and Negotiation

Most important decisions in development are the result of negotiation. Different parties representing different, and often conflicting, interests come to a consensus on some aspect of the system. Requirements analysis includes the negotiation of functionality with a client. System design includes the negotiation of subsystem interfaces among developers. Integration includes the resolution of conflicts between developers. We use issue modeling to represent the information exchanged during these negotiations to help capture rationale. We can also use issue modeling to facilitate negotiations.

Traditional negotiation, which consists of bargaining over positions, is often time consuming and inefficient, especially when the negotiating parties hold incompatible positions. Effort is spent in defending one's position, citing all its advantages, and denigrating the other's position, citing all its disadvantages. The negotiation either progresses in small steps toward a consensus or is ended by an arbitrary solution. These difficulties can occur even when negotiating parties have compatible interests: when defending positions, people have greater trouble evolving or changing their position without losing credibility. The Harvard method of negotiation [Fisher et al., 1991] addresses these points by taking the focus away from positions. We rephrase several important points of the Harvard method in terms of issue modeling:

- *Separate developers from proposals.* Developers can spend a lot of resources developing a specific proposal (i.e., a position), to the point that a criticism of the proposal is taken as a personal criticism of the developer. Developers and proposals should be separated to make it easier to evolve or discard a proposal. This can be done by having multiple developers work on the same proposal or by having all concerned parties participate in the development of all proposals. Separating design and implementation work can further facilitate this distinction. By ensuring that negotiation comes before implementation and before substantial resources are committed, developers are able to negotiate proposals that all can live with.

- *Focus on criteria, not on proposals.* When developers make proposals and argue about them, they have some criteria in mind. The proposal they make usually satisfies the criteria that are important to them, but not necessarily other developers' criteria. By making these criteria explicit, developers can more easily identify the root of conflicts and negotiate a compromise. Once an accepted set of criteria is in place, evaluating and selecting proposals is far less controversial. Furthermore, criteria are much less subject to change than other factors in the project.

- *Take into account all criteria instead of maximizing a single one.* Different criteria reflect interests of different parties. Performance criteria are usually motivated by usability concerns. Modifiability criteria are motivated by maintenance concerns. Even if some criteria are considered higher priority than others, optimizing only these high-priority criteria risks leaving one or more parties out of the negotiation.

Viewing development as a negotiation acknowledges its social aspects. Developers are people who, in addition to technical opinions, can have an emotional perspective on different solutions. This can influence (and sometimes interfere) with their relationships with other developers as conflicts arise. Using issue modeling to capture rationale and drive decisions can integrate and improve both the technical and social aspects of development.

An example of such an approach is WinWin, a requirements elicitation tool and technique for negotiating different viewpoints among stakeholders [Boehm et al., 1998]. WinWin resulted from the observation that satisfying all key stakeholders is a necessary condition for project success. Often, the issue of dealing with conflicting success criteria is not only to reconcile conflicting views, but also to identify the key stakeholders of the system and to clarify their success criteria. Once these criteria are known to all, it is much easier to identify conflicts and to resolve them by negotiating compromise alternatives.

The WinWin tool uses an issue model similar to the QOC model (Figure 12-27). A significant difference is that each node in the issue model is attached to a taxonomy category that represents the application domain under consideration. The Criteria node is named Win Condition and represents a stakeholder success criterion. The WinWin process starts by identifying key stakeholders and their Win Conditions. Conflicting Win Conditions are detected and discussed using the issue model. Once an Agreement is achieved, it is entered in the tool and linked back to the conflicting Win Conditions. This ensures that consensus is found and documented.

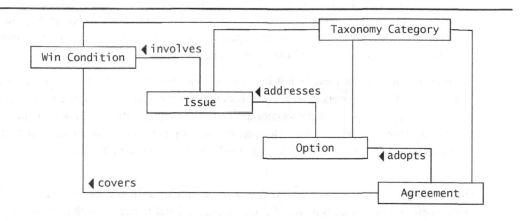

Figure 12-27 WinWin issue model (UML class diagram).

12.5.5 Conflict Resolution Strategies

Occasionally, project participants fail to come to a consensus through negotiation. In such cases, it is critical that conflict resolution strategies already be in place to deal with the situation. The worst design decisions are those that are not taken because of the lack of consensus or the absence of conflict resolution strategies. This delays critical decisions until late in development, resulting in high redesign and recording costs.

Many different conflict resolution strategies are possible; these are five examples:

- **Majority wins**. In case of conflict, a majority vote could remove the deadlock and resolve the decision. Several collaboration tools enable users to attach weights to different arguments in the issue model, and thus to compute which proposal should be selected with an arithmetic formula [Purvis et al., 1996]. This assumes that the opinion of each participant matters equally and that, statistically, the group usually makes the right decisions.

- **Owner has last word**. In this strategy, the owner of an issue (the person who raised it) is responsible for deciding the outcome. This assumes that the owner has the largest stake in the issue.

- **Management is always right**. An alternative strategy is to fall back on the organizational hierarchy. If a group is unable to reach consensus, the manager of the group imposes a decision based on the argument. This assumes that the manager is capable of understanding the argument and making the right trade-offs.

- **Expert is always right**. In this strategy, an external expert, foreign to the debate, assesses the situation and advises the best course of action. For example, during requirements analysis, a test user can be interviewed to evaluate the different proposals on an issue. Unfortunately, such an expert has limited knowledge of other system decisions or, more generally, of the design context.

- **Time decides**. As an issue is left unresolved, time becomes a pressure and forces a decision. Also, controversial issues may become easier to resolve as other decisions are made and other aspects of the system defined. The danger with this strategy is that it leads to decisions that optimize short-term criteria (such as ease of implementation) and disregard long-term criteria (such as modifiability and maintainability).

The *majority wins* and the *owner has last word* strategies do not work well. They both result in inconsistent results (multiplicity of decision makers) and in decisions that are not well supported by the rest of the participants. The *management is always right* and *expert is always right* strategies lead to better technical decisions and better consensus when the manager and the Expert are sufficiently knowledgeable. The *time decides* strategy is a fallback, albeit one that may result in costly rework.

In practice, we first attempt to reach consensus, and, in case of lack of consensus, fall back on an expert or management strategy. If the expert or manager strategy fails, we let time decide or take a binding majority vote.

12.6 Further Readings

Most of the issue-based work in rationale research finds its roots in the work of Rittel [Kunz & Rittel, 1970]. Rittel, however, proposed the IBIS issue model as a solution for negotiating complex problems in political science. Conklin introduced IBIS to software engineering in the late 1980s and contributed the gIBIS tool [Conklin & Burgess-Yakemovic, 1991], which was used for an extensive case study in industry. gIBIS has led to a commercial tool called *QuestMap*, which has been used effectively in the context of capturing and structuring rationale during meetings.

In the early 1990s, QOC was proposed as an alternative model to IBIS, focusing on the systematic evaluation of options against criteria (as opposed to the opportunistic posting of arguments) [MacLean et al., 1991]. Since then, it has generally been accepted that IBIS is a more appropriate representation for capturing rationale on the fly, whereas QOC is a more appropriate representation for structuring rationale for long-term use.

Applications of rationale to software engineering are few [Moran & Carroll, 1996] [Dutoit et al., 2006]. Major challenges include the technical issues (e.g., rationale models are large and difficult to search) and non-technical issues, in particular, the perception that rationale is an overhead that benefits only other participants [Dutoit & Paech, 2001]. However, there have been successful cases that have illustrated the importance of tightly integrating the capture and use of rationale within a specific process. In this chapter, we mentioned three examples from the requirements engineering domain: *WinWin* [Boehm et al., 1998], the *NFR Framework* [Chung et al., 1999], and *REQuest* [Dutoit & Paech, 2002].

12.7 Exercises

12-1 In Section 12.3, we examined an issue related to access control and notification in the CTC system. Select a similar issue that could occur in the development of CTC, populate it with relevant proposals, criteria, and arguments, and justify a resolution. Examples of such issues include

- How can consistency between mainServer and hotBackup be maintained?
- How should failure of the mainServer be detected and the subsequent switch to the hotBackup be implemented?

12-2 You are developing a UML modeling tool. You are considering the integration of rationale into the tool. Describe how a developer could attach issues to different model elements. Draw a class diagram of the issue model and its association with model elements.

12-3 Below is an excerpt from a system design document for an accident management system. It is a natural language description of the rationale for a relational database for permanent storage. Model this rationale with issues, proposals, arguments, criteria, and resolutions, as defined in Section 12.3.

One fundamental issue in database design was database engine realization. The initial nonfunctional requirements on the database subsystem insisted on the use of an object-oriented database for the underlying engine. Other possible options included using a relational database, a file system, or a combination of the other options. An object-oriented database has the advantages of being able to handle complex data relationships and is fully buzzword compliant. On the other hand, OO databases may be too sluggish for large volumes of data or high-frequency accesses. Furthermore, existing products do not integrate well with CORBA, because that protocol does not support specific programming language features such as Java associations. Using a relational database offers a more robust engine with higher performance characteristics and a large pool of experience and tools to draw on. Furthermore, the relational data model integrates nicely with CORBA. On the downside, this model does not easily support complex data relationships. The third option was proposed to handle specific types of data that are written once and read infrequently. This type of data (including sensor readings and control outputs) has few relationships with little complexity and must be archived for extended periods of time. Files offer an easy archival solution and can handle large amounts of data. Conversely, any code would need to be written from scratch, including serialization of access. We decided to use only a relational database, based on the requirement to use CORBA and in light of the relative simplicity of the relationships between the system's persistent data.

12-4   Consider the NFR Framework described in Section 12.3.7. Draw a QOC model that is equivalent to the goal graph depicted in Figure 12-12. Discuss the respective advantage and disadvantages of QOC and the NFR Framework for representing rationale during requirements.

12-5   You are integrating a bug reporting system with a configuration management tool to track bug reports, bug fixes, feature requests, and enhancements. You are considering an issue model for integrating these tools. Draw a class diagram of the issue model, the corresponding discussion, configuration management, and bug-reporting elements.

References

[Boehm et al., 1998] B. Boehm, A. Egyed, J. Kwan, D. Port, A. Shah, & R. Madachy. "Using the WinWin spiral model: A case study," *IEEE Computer* 31(7): 33–44, 1998.

[Chung et al., 1999] L. Chung, B. A. Nixon, E. Yu, & J. Mylopoulos, *Non-Functional Requirements in Software Engineering*, Kluwer Academic, Boston, 1999.

[Conklin & Burgess-Yakemovic, 1991] J. Conklin & K. C. Burgess-Yakemovic, "A process-oriented approach to design rationale," *Human-Computer Interaction*, Vol. 6, pp. 357–391, 1991.

[Dutoit & Paech, 2001] A. H. Dutoit & B. Paech, "Rationale management in software engineering," in S.K. Chang (ed.), *Handbook of Software Engineering and Knowledge Engineering,* Vol. 1, World Scientific Publishing, 2001.

[Dutoit & Paech, 2002] A. H. Dutoit & B. Paech, "Rationale-based use case specification," *Requirements Engineering Journal*, 7(1): 3–19, 2002.

[Dutoit et al., 2006] A. H. Dutoit, R. McCall, I. Mistrik, B. Paech (eds.) *Rationale Management in Software Engineering*, Springer, Heidelberg, 2006.

[Fisher et al., 1991] R. Fisher, W. Ury, & B. Patton, *Getting to Yes: Negotiating Agreement Without Giving In*, 2nd ed., Penguin Books, New York, 1991.

[Kunz & Rittel, 1970] W. Kunz & H. Rittel, "Issues as elements of information systems," *Working Paper No. 131*, Institut für Grundlagen der Plannung, Universität Stuttgart, Germany, 1970.

[Lee, 1990] J. Lee, "A qualitative decision management system," in P. H. Winston & S. Shellard (eds.), *Artificial Intelligence at MIT: Expanding Frontiers*, Vol. 1, pp. 104–133, MIT Press, Cambridge, MA, 1990.

[MacLean et al., 1991] A. MacLean, R. M. Young, V. Bellotti, & T. Moran, "Questions, options, and criteria: Elements of design space analysis," *Human-Computer Interaction*, Vol. 6, pp. 201–250, 1991.

[Moran & Carroll, 1996] T. P. Moran & J. M. Carroll (eds.), *Design Rationale: Concepts, Techniques, and Use*, Lawrence Erlbaum Associates, Mahwah, NJ, 1996.

[Purvis et al., 1996] M. Purvis, M. Purvis, & P. Jones, "A group collaboration tool for software engineering projects," *Conference proceedings of Software Engineering: Education and Practice (SEEP '96)*, Dunedin, NZ, January 1996.

Configuration
Management

*Those who would repeat the past must control
the teaching of history.*
—Frank Herbert, in *Chapterhouse: Dune*

Change pervades the development process: requirements change when developers improve their understanding of the application domain, the system design changes with new technology and design goals, the object design changes with the identification of solution objects, and the implementation changes as faults are discovered and repaired. These changes can affect every work product, from the system models to the source code and the documentation. *Configuration management* is the process of controlling and monitoring change to work products. Once a baseline is defined, configuration management minimizes the risks associated with changes by defining a formal approval and tracking process for changes.

In this chapter, we describe the following activities:

- *Configuration item identification* is the modeling of the system as a set of evolving components.
- *Promotion management* is the creation of versions for other developers.
- *Release management* is the creation of versions for the client and the users.
- *Branch management* is the management of concurrent development.
- *Variant management* is the management of versions intended to coexist.
- *Change management* is the handling, approval, and tracking of change requests.

We conclude this chapter by discussing project management issues related to configuration management. In particular, we discuss continuous integration, in which the creation of promotions and the execution of regression tests are automated, to ensure the early detection of integration problems.

13.1 Introduction: An Aircraft Example

Passenger aircraft are one of the most complex engineering feats to be attempted by a private corporation. They must be safe and reliable, and they must be economical. Unlike trains or cars, the aircraft systems cannot simply be shut down in the event of a failure. Unlike NASA, airlines need to post a profit and pay dividends to their stockholders. These requirements result in very complex designs that include many redundancies and diagnostic systems. A Boeing 747, for example, is composed of more than 6 million parts. To develop and maintain such complex systems, while remaining economically competitive, aircraft manufacturers extend the life of a model by incrementally improving on the same design. The Boeing 747, for example, was first released in 1967 and is still in production at the time of this writing. It has gone through four major revisions, the latest, the 747-400, released in 1988. Another approach to dealing with the high complexity of aircraft is the reuse of as many parts and subsystems across aircraft models as possible. Consider the following example.

Airbus A320

In 1988, Airbus Industries, a consortium of European aircraft industries, released the A320, the first fly-by-wire passenger aircraft. The pilots control the plane like an F16 fighter jet by using a small joystick located on their side. Digital impulses are then transmitted to a computer, which interprets and relays them to the wings and tail controls. Unlike hydraulic systems, computerized control allows for envelope protection, which prevents the pilot from exceeding certain parameters, such as maximum and minimum speed, maximum angle of attack, and maximum G-values. The A320 has 150 seats and is targeted for short- to medium-haul routes.

A321 and A319

The commercial success of the A320 allowed Airbus to work on two derivative airplanes, the A319, a shorter, 124-seat version, and the A321, a longer, 185-seat version. Changing the length of a basic design to obtain a new aircraft has been a standard practice in the industry. This allows the manufacturer to save on cost and time by leveraging an existing design. It also saves operating costs for airlines, who then need only maintain one stock of spare parts. In this case, however, Airbus pushed the concept even further, ensuring that all three aircraft have the same cockpit controls and the same handling characteristics. The A321, for example, has slotted flaps and slightly modified wing controls to make the plane feel like the A320, even though the A321 is longer. Consequently, any pilot certified for one of the aircraft can fly the other two. This results in cost savings for airline operators who need to train pilots only once, share flight simulators, spare parts, and maintenance crews for all three versions.

A330 and A340

Pursuing this philosophy even further, Airbus paid great care to the handling characteristics of the A330 and A340. These two aircraft, built for the long-haul and ultra-long-haul markets, can carry twice as many passengers as the A320 and up to three times as far. They have the same cockpit layout and fly-by-wire system. Pilots trained on the A320 family can fly the A330 or the A340 with minimal retraining, further reducing the operating costs of the airline. Comparatively, the handling characteristics of a 737 (comparable to the A319) are very different from a 747 (comparable to the larger version of the A340).

Incremental refinement and subsystem reuse are not without problems. Each change that is made to one model must be carefully evaluated in the context of the other two. For example, if we decide to install a new, more efficient powerplant on the A320, we would need to evaluate if the same powerplant could also be used on the A319 and the A321, to retain the advantage of sharing parts across all three models. Then, we need to evaluate whether the handling of each aircraft changes significantly, in which case we may need to modify the computerized control software to account for this. Otherwise, all pilots flying the A320 would need to be retrained and recertified, not to mention the loss of a common platform and training program for all three aircraft. Then, the modified aircraft would have to be recertified by the governing authority (e.g., the Federal Aviation Agency in the United States, the Joint Aviation Authorities in the European Community), which would decide on the safety of the aircraft and whether new maintenance or pilot training procedures are necessary. Finally, the state of each individual aircraft must be carefully documented so that the correct parts can be replaced. In summary, any change that would threaten the safety of the aircraft, its efficiency, or the portability of pilots across aircraft models must be identified and rejected. These issues require aircraft manufacturers and operators to follow sophisticated version and change control procedures.

Although usually not quite as complex as a passenger aircraft, software system development nevertheless suffers from similar problems. Software systems have a long life cycle to allow the recouping of initial investment: for example, many Unix systems still contain code dating as far back as the 1970s. Software systems can exist in many different variants: for example, some flavors of Unix operating systems can run on mainframes as well as home PCs and Macintosh computers. Maintenance changes to existing and running software systems must be controlled and evaluated carefully to ensure a certain level of reliability: For example, the introduction of the Euro currency, a simple change in scale, has had a very visible and substantial impact on many financial and business software systems around the globe. Finally, software systems evolve much more rapidly than aircraft, requiring developers to track change and its impact.

Configuration management enables developers and aircraft manufacturers to deal with change. The first function of configuration management is the identification of configuration items. Which subsystems are likely to change? Which subsystem interfaces should not change? Each subsystem likely to change is modeled as a configuration item and its state labeled with a version number. The fly-by-wire software of the A320 is a configuration item. The device driver for a serial port in a Unix operating system is a configuration item.

The second function of configuration management is to manage change through a formal process. A change request is first logged, then analyzed, then accepted if consistent with the goals of the project. A change request for an aircraft is a thick report listing all the subsystems and contractors involved in the change. A change request for a simple software system can be merely an E-mail requesting a new feature. The change is then approved or rejected, depending on the foreseen impact of the change on the overall system.

Finally, the third function of configuration management is to record sufficient status information on each version of each configuration item and its dependencies. By looking at the maintenance book of an A320 and the version numbers of its subsystems, a maintenance engineer is able to tell which subsystems need to be replaced or upgraded. Looking at the latest release of a serial port device driver, its improvements and the changes since the last release, we are able to determine whether or not we should upgrade to the new driver.

Configuration management has been traditionally treated as a maintenance topic. The distinction between development and maintenance has become blurred, however, and often configuration management is introduced quite early in the process. In this chapter, we focus primarily on the early phases of configuration management and briefly address its use during maintenance. But first, we define more formally the concept of configuration management.

13.2 An Overview of Configuration Management

Configuration management is the discipline of managing and controlling change in the evolution of software systems [IEEE Std. 1042-1987]. Configuration management systems automate the identification of versions, their storage and retrieval, and supports status accounting. Configuration management includes the following activities:

- **Identification of configuration items**. Components of the system and its work products and their versions are identified and labeled uniquely. Developers identify configuration items after the *Project Agreement* (Section 14.3.6), once the principal deliverables and components of the system are agreed on. Developers create versions and additional configuration items as the system evolves.

- **Change control**. Changes to the system and releases to the users are controlled to ensure consistency with project goals. Change control can be done by the developers, by management, or by a control board, depending on the level of quality required and the rate of change.

- **Status accounting**. The status of individual components, work products, and change requests are recorded. This allows developers to distinguish versions more easily and track issues related to changes. This also allows management to track project status.

- **Auditing**. Versions selected for releases are validated to ensure the completeness, consistency, and quality of the product. Auditing is accomplished by the quality control team.

In addition, the following activities are often considered part of configuration management [Dart, 1991]:

- **Build management**. Most configuration management systems enable the automatic building of the system as developers create new versions of the components. The configuration management system has sufficient knowledge of the system to minimize the amount of recompilation. It may also be able to combine different versions of components to build different variants of the system (e.g., for different operating system and hardware platforms).

- **Process management**. In addition to change control, projects may have policies about the creation and documentation of versions. One such policy can be that only syntactically correct code can be part of a version. Another policy can be that builds are attempted (and should succeed) every week. Finally, the configuration management process includes policies for notifying relevant developers when new versions are created or when a build fails. Some configuration management systems enable developers to automate such work flows.

Traditionally, configuration management is seen as a management discipline, helping project managers with change control, status accounting, and auditing activities ([Bersoff et al., 1980] and [IEEE Std. 1042-1987]). More recently, however, configuration management has also been seen as a development support discipline, helping developers deal with the complexity associated with large numbers of changes, components, and variants [Babich, 1986]. In this chapter, we focus in more detail on the latter view and only briefly address the activities of change control and status accounting.

In our view, configuration management pervades the software life cycle. It begins with the identification of configuration items after the deliverables and principal components of the system have been defined. It continues throughout development as developers create versions of work products during analysis, system design, object design, and implementation. With rationale management (see Chapter 12, *Rationale Management*), configuration management is the principal tool available to developers for dealing with change.

Next, let us focus in more detail on the concepts of configuration management.

13.3 Configuration Management Concepts

In this section, we present the main concepts of configuration management (Figure 13-1). As often as possible, we use the same terminology as the IEEE guidelines on configuration management [IEEE Std. 1042-1987]:

- A **configuration item** is a work product or a piece of software that is treated as a single entity for the purpose of configuration management. A composite of configuration items is defined as a **configuration management aggregate** (CM aggregate). The fly-by-wire software of the A320 is a configuration item; the A320 is a CM aggregate. The serial port device driver is a configuration item; the Linux operating system is a CM aggregate.

- A **change request** is a formal report issued by a user or a developer to request a modification in a configuration item. For example, the *Engineering Change Proposal*

[MIL Std. 480], the standard change request form in the United States government, is seven pages long. An informal change request can be a one-line E-mail message.

- A **version** identifies the state of a configuration item or a configuration aggregate at a well-defined point in time. Given a CM aggregate, a consistent set of versions of its configuration items is defined as a **configuration**. A configuration can be thought as a version of a CM aggregate.

- Versions that are intended to coexist are called **variants**.

- A **promotion** is a version that has been made available to other developers in the project. A **release** is a version that has been made available to the client or the users.

- A **software library** stores versions and provides facilities to track the status of changes. A **repository** is a library of releases. A **master directory** is a library of promotions.

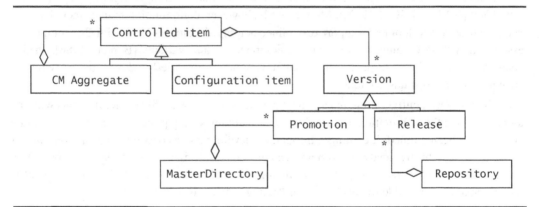

Figure 13-1   Configuration management concepts (UML class diagram).

13.3.1 Configuration Items and CM Aggregates

A **configuration item** is a work product or a component of a work product that is under configuration management and treated as a single entity for such purposes. For example, the fly-by-wire software of the A320 is a configuration item (Figure 13-2). During an upgrade, the complete software is replaced. The fly-by-wire software cannot be broken down into smaller components that can be installed independently. Similarly, the device driver for the serial port in any operating system is a configuration item. This component is simple enough that it cannot be further broken down for installation.

A **CM aggregate** is a composition of configuration items. The 747 is a CM aggregate of six million parts. The Linux[1] operating system is a CM aggregate that includes a process

---

1. Linux is a freely available POSIX [POSIX, 1990] operating system created by Linus Torvalds. For more information check http://www.linux.org/.

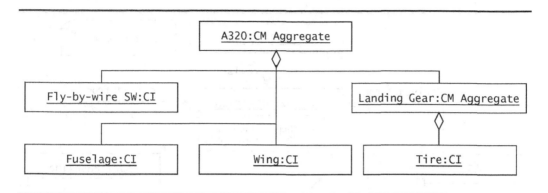

Figure 13-2   An example of CM aggregates and configuration items (UML object diagram).

scheduler, a memory manager, many device drivers, network daemons, file systems, and many other subsystems.

13.3.2 Versions and Configurations

A **version** identifies the state of a configuration item at a well-defined point in time. Successive versions of a work product differ by one or more changes, such as the correction of a fault, the addition of new functionality, or the removal of unnecessary or obsolete functionality. A **configuration** identifies the state of a CM aggregate.

A **baseline** is a version of a configuration item that has been formally reviewed and agreed on, by management or the client, and which can be changed only through a change request. For example, each aircraft must undergo a rigorous certification process by the governing agency (i.e., the FAA or the JAA) before it can be operated by an airline. Any change to the aircraft after certification requires a formal change process and recertification. This ensures that changes are made consistently with project goals (e.g., safety and reliability) and regulations, and that they are communicated to relevant developers and users (e.g., the airline passengers and the airline operator).

Versions that are intended to coexist are called **variants**. For example, the A319, the A320, and the A321 are variants of the same basic aircraft (Figure 13-3). The principal difference is their length, that is, the number of passenger and freight that they can carry. The A320-200, however, is a version of the A320 that replaced the initial version. In other words, an airline can buy both the A319 and the A320-200, but it cannot buy the older A320-100. In the case of a software system, the system can have a Macintosh variant, a Windows variant, and a Linux variant, each providing identical functionality. A system may also have a standard variant and a professional or deluxe variant, supporting a different range of functionality. Variants share a large amount of code that implements the core functionality, and differences are confined to a small number of lower level subsystems.

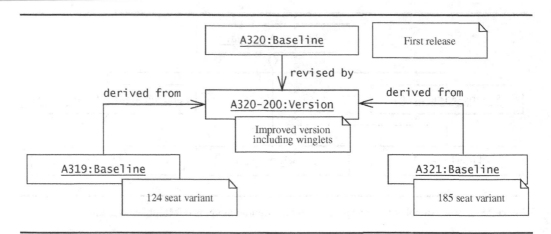

Figure 13-3   Examples of baselines, versions, and variants (UML object diagram). The A319, A320, and the A321 are all based on the same design. They vary mostly by the length of their fuselage.

13.3.3 Change Requests

A **change request** is a formal step initiating the change process. A user, client, or developer discovers a fault in a work product or wants a new feature. The author of the change request specifies the configuration item to which the requests applies, its version, the problem to be solved, and a proposed solution. In the case of a formal change process, the costs and benefits of the change are then assessed before the change is approved or rejected. In both cases, the rationale of the decision is recorded with the change request.

For example, shortly after the A320 was certified in February 1988, a revised version, the A320-200, was recertified. The new version included a few modifications that yielded a longer range and greater take-off weight. One of these changes was the addition of winglets at the end of the wings that significantly reduced drag and thereby reduced fuel consumption. Fuel consumption is a major cost for the airline operator and, thus, a strong selling argument for the airline manufacturer. During the A320 design, a change request was issued, describing the winglet change, its performance evaluation, and its estimated cost. The change was approved, implemented, and the A320-200 passed certification in November 1988. A change request for the Linux operating system kernel is an E-mail message to Linus Torwalds.

13.3.4 Promotions and Releases

A **promotion** is a version that is made available to other developers. A promotion denotes a configuration item that has reached a relatively stable state and can be used or reviewed by other developers. For example, subsystems are promoted for other teams using that subsystem. Subsystems are then promoted for the quality control team to assess their quality. Later, as faults are discovered and repaired, revisions of the subsystem are promoted for reevaluation.

A **release** is a version that is made available to users. A release denotes that a configuration item has met the quality criteria set by the quality control team and can be used or reviewed by the users. For example, the system is released to beta testers for finding additional faults and assessing the perceived quality of the system. As faults are discovered and repaired, revisions of the subsystem are promoted for reevaluation by the quality control team and, when the quality criteria are met, released again to the users.

13.3.5 Repositories and Workspaces

A **software library**, as defined in [IEEE Std. 1042-1987], provides facilities to store, label, and identify versions of the configuration items (i.e., documentation, models, and code). A software library also provides functionality to track the status of changes to the configuration items. We distinguish between three types of libraries:

1. The developer's **workspace**, also known as the *dynamic library*, is used for everyday development by the developers. Change is not restricted and is controlled by the individual developer only.

2. The **master directory**, also known as the *controlled library*, tracks promotions. Change needs to be approved and versions need to meet certain project criteria (e.g., "Only code that can be compiled without errors may be checked in") before they are made available to the rest of the project.

3. The software **repository**, also known as the *static library*, tracks releases. Promotions need to meet certain quality control criteria (e.g., "All faults detected by regression tests must be repaired") before a promotion becomes a release.

Note that, in present configuration management systems, the term *repository* usually denotes the library in which both promotions and releases are tracked. Developers create new promotions by checking in changes from their workspace to the repository. Releases are then distinguished from promotions using a naming convention or a version identification scheme.

13.3.6 Version Identification Schemes

Versions are uniquely identified by developers and systems using a **version identifier**, also called a *version number*. Some exotic examples include

- The Ada specification went through five successive major versions, named Strawman, Woodenman, Tinman, Ironman, and Steelman [Steelman, 1978].
- The version identification scheme for T$_{\mathrm{E}}$X, a typesetting program for technical texts [Knuth, 1986], is based on decimals of the number π: Each time a bug is found (which is rare) and repaired the version number of T$_{\mathrm{E}}$X is incremented to add another digit. The current version number is 3.1415926.

In general, however, version numbers of a given configuration item can be quite large. In this case, developers and configuration management systems use version identification schemes that support automation more easily, such as sequential numbers with two or three decimals. For example, consider a UML editor called MUE (for My UML Editor), which is built and released incrementally. We can use a three-digit scheme to distinguish between functional changes, small improvements, and bug fixes (Figure 13-4). The leftmost digit denotes a major version (e.g., overhaul of functionality or of the user interface), the second digit, the minor version (e.g., addition of limited functionality), and the third digit denotes revisions (e.g., corrections). By convention, versions before 1.0.0 denote versions released for alpha or beta testing.

Such a simple sequential scheme, however, only works with a sequential series of versions. A **branch** identifies a concurrent development path requiring independent configuration management. Releases are seen by the user as an incremental and sequential development process. The development of different features, however, can be done by different teams concurrently and later merged into a single version. The sequence of versions created by each team is a branch, which is independent from the versions created by the other teams. When versions of different branches need to be reconciled, the versions are merged; that is, a new version is created containing selected elements from both ancestor versions.

For releases, the sequential identification scheme is usually sufficient, because the concept of branch is not visible to the users. For developers and configuration management systems, however, this is not sufficient, because branches are often used for supporting concurrent development. The version identification scheme used by CVS [Berliner, 1990], for example,

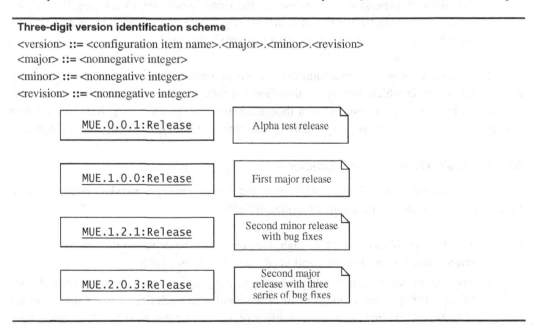

Three-digit version identification scheme

<version> ::= <configuration item name>.<major>.<minor>.<revision>
<major> ::= <nonnegative integer>
<minor> ::= <nonnegative integer>
<revision> ::= <nonnegative integer>

MUE.0.0.1:Release	Alpha test release
MUE.1.0.0:Release	First major release
MUE.1.2.1:Release	Second minor release with bug fixes
MUE.2.0.3:Release	Second major release with three series of bug fixes

Figure 13-4   Three-digit version identification scheme (Backus-Naur Form and UML object diagram).

explicitly represents branches and versions. Version numbers include a branch identifier followed by a revision number. The branch identifier includes the version number from which the branch was started, followed by a unique number identifying the branch. This enables developers to identify to which branch a version belongs and in which order versions of one branch were produced.

In Figure 13-5, two branches are depicted: the main trunk (left package) and the branch 1.2.1 derived from version 1.2 (right package). In the MUE example, the branch may have been derived for the purpose of evaluating competing implementations of the same feature (e.g., support for UML interaction diagrams in MUE). Note that this identification scheme does not identify how versions are merged back onto the main trunk. In Figure 13-5, version 1.2.1.2 is merged with version 1.3 onto the main trunk to produce version 2.0.

CVS version identification scheme

<version> ::= <configuration item name>.<version identifier>

<version identifier> ::= <branch>.<revision>

<branch> ::= <version identifier>.<branch number> | <branch number>

<branch number> ::= <nonnegative integer>

<revision> ::= <nonnegative integer>

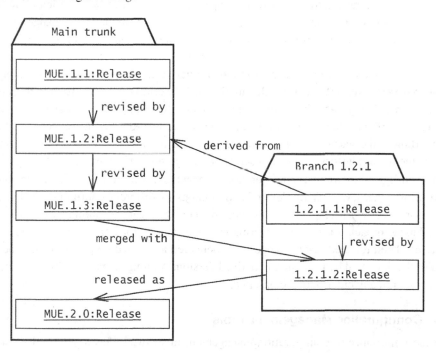

Figure 13-5 CVS version identification scheme (Backus-Naur Form and UML object diagram). Branches are identified with the version they were derived from followed by a unique number.

13.3.7 Changes and Change Sets

The evolution of a configuration item can be modeled in two ways:

- *State-based view.* As a series of versions, that is, as a series of states of the configuration item. Each state is identified by a version number (e.g., the A320-200, MUE.1.0). This is the view most often encountered in practice.

- *Changed-based view.* As a baseline followed by a series of *changes* called **deltas**. A change represents the difference between two successive versions, in terms of lines or paragraphs that have been added or removed from the configuration item. Often, repairing a fault or adding functionality to a system requires changes to several configuration items. All the changes to configuration items associated with a single revision of a configuration are grouped into a **change set**. If two change sets do not overlap (i.e., if they apply to different and unrelated sets of configuration items), they can be applied to the same baseline in arbitrary order, thus providing more flexibility to the developer when selecting configurations.

Continuing the MUE example, assume that we revised the first baseline twice: MUE.1.1 was released to fix a bug related to classes with no operations, and MUE.1.2 was released to fix a bug related to drawing dashed lines. Each of these revisions corresponded to changes in a single subsystem. The change sets corresponding to each of these revisions is thus independent, and could be applied to the baseline in any order. For example, when the emptyClassFix: ChangeSet is applied to the MUE.1.0:Release, we derive the MUE.1.1:Release. Applying the dashedLineFix:ChangeSet next results in the MUE.1.2:Release. If instead, we apply the dashedLineFix:ChangeSet first, we would obtain the MUE.1.1a:Release. Applying the emptyClassFix:ChangeSet next, however, also results in the MUE.1.2:Release. The change set corresponding to the second baseline, however, depends on both of these revisions. Figure 13-6 illustrates the release history of MUE as a series of change sets and their dependencies.

The change-based view of configuration management is more general than the state-based view. It allows the developer to view related versions of different configuration items as one action. Moreover, when change sets do not overlap, they can be applied to more than one version. This approach is used for delivering bug fixes and minor improvements after a piece of software has been released; each change set is delivered as a separate patch that can be directly applied to the delivered baseline or any derived version. As long as patches do not overlap, they can be applied in any order onto the baseline.

13.3.8 Configuration Management Tools

Due to the importance of configuration management in software development, there are many configuration management and version management tools available to developers. In this section, we briefly describe four of them, RCS [Tichy, 1985], CVS [Berliner, 1990], Perforce [Perforce], and ClearCase [Leblang, 1994].

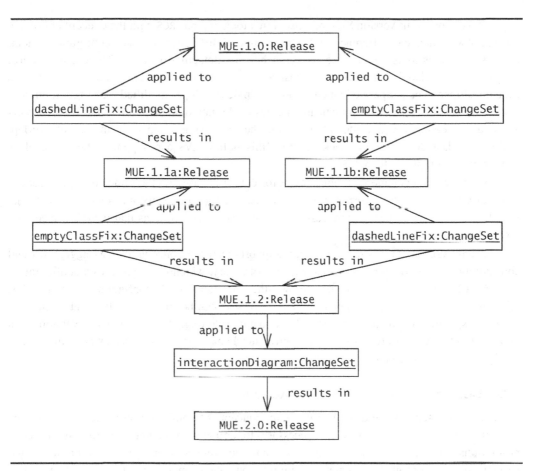

Figure 13-6 Change set representation of the MUE release history (UML object diagram). dashedLineFix:ChangeSet and emptyClassFix:ChangeSet can be applied to the MUE.1.0:Release in arbitrary order because they do not overlap.

RCS (Revision Control System), a free tool, controls a repository storing all versions of the configuration items. To obtain a specific version, developers check out a version into their workspace by specifying a version number or a date. To change a configuration item, the developer needs to lock the item first, preventing all other developers from changing the item. When the change is completed, the developer checks the modified item back into the repository, simultaneously creating a new version and releasing the lock. To optimize storage, RCS only stores the latest version of each configuration item and the differences between each version. The concept of configuration can be realized by attaching a developer-specified label to all versions that belong to the configuration. Developers can then check out a consistent set of versions by using the label. Note that this approach does not allow version control of the configuration itself. RCS does not support the concept of branch.

CVS (Concurrent Version System), also a free tool, extends RCS with the concept of branch. Instead of a sequence of differences, CVS stores a tree of differences for each configuration item. CVS also provides tools for merging two branches and detecting overlaps. The change control policy of CVS is also different from RCS. Instead of locking a configuration item, CVS considers each developer to be a separate branch. If only a single developer modified a configuration item between two check-ins, CVS automatically merges the branch onto the main trunk. If CVS detects a concurrent change, it first attempts to merge the two changes and then, in case of overlap, notifies the last developer to check in. With this policy, CVS can support a higher level of concurrent development than RCS.

Perforce is a commercial replacement for CVS. It is based on the same concept of central repository as CVS and RCS. Perforce, however, also supports the concept of change and change set, allowing the developer to more easily track the configuration items that were involved on a given change.

ClearCase, another commercial tool, supports also the concepts of CM aggregates and configurations. A CM aggregate is realized as a directory, which is managed as a configuration item by ClearCase. ClearCase also allows the specification of configurations with rules, selecting versions of each configuration item. A version can be specified with a static rule (i.e., refer to a specific version number) or with a dynamic rule (e.g., refer to the latest version of an item). ClearCase also provides access control mechanisms to define the ownership of each configuration item and configuration.

13.4 Configuration Management Activities

In the previous section, we described the main concepts of configuration management. In this section, we focus on the activities necessary to define and manage configuration items, promotions, and releases. We also describe activities related with the use of branches and variants for concurrent development. Configuration management activities described in this section include

- Configuration Item and CM Aggregate Identification (Section 13.4.1)
- Promotion Management (Section 13.4.2)
- Release Management (Section 13.4.3)
- Branch Management (Section 13.4.4)
- Variant Management (Section 13.4.5)
- Change Management (Section 13.4.6).

For the basis of the examples in this section, we use a distributed car parts catalog called myCarParts. MyCarParts allows car dealers and car owners alike to browse and order parts from their computer. MyCarParts has a client/server architecture, with two types of clients: the EClient for expert users, such as car mechanics and part dealers, and the Nclient for novice users, including car owners who repair their own cars. The system requires users to authenticate, which allows it to determine the list price of the parts given the particular user. A user who orders many parts is eligible for volume discounts, whereas an occasional client pays the full list price. The system also tracks the interests of each user, using this information to better optimize the network usage. The user is also sent customized notices about new products or new discount prices. Figure 13-7 displays the subsystem decomposition of myCarParts.

The development and evolution of the myCarParts system requires the coordinated release of several components.

- The protocol used by the clients and the server to exchange information is occasionally upgraded to support new client functionality and to improve response time and

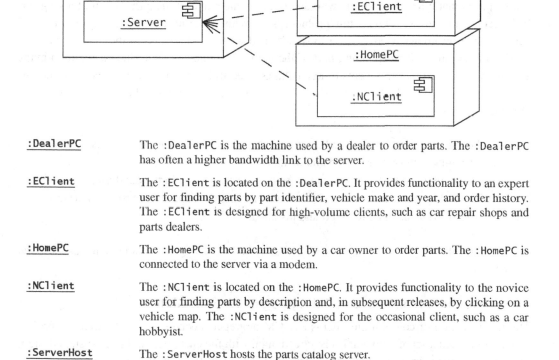

:DealerPC	The :DealerPC is the machine used by a dealer to order parts. The :DealerPC has often a higher bandwidth link to the server.
:EClient	The :EClient is located on the :DealerPC. It provides functionality to an expert user for finding parts by part identifier, vehicle make and year, and order history. The :EClient is designed for high-volume clients, such as car repair shops and parts dealers.
:HomePC	The :HomePC is the machine used by a car owner to order parts. The :HomePC is connected to the server via a modem.
:NClient	The :NClient is located on the :HomePC. It provides functionality to the novice user for finding parts by description and, in subsequent releases, by clicking on a vehicle map. The :NClient is designed for the occasional client, such as a car hobbyist.
:ServerHost	The :ServerHost hosts the parts catalog server.
:Server	The :Server enables client to retrieve lists of parts by criteria and part entries, to order parts, and to track client activity.

Figure 13-7   MyCarParts hardware allocation (UML deployment diagram).

throughput. Because there is no guarantee that all users have the same version of the client, it is necessary for the server to maintain backward compatibility with older clients. Every new revision must be tested with older clients to validate this property.

- New client versions may implement functionality that is supported only in new versions of the server. Therefore, the server must be upgraded first, before the new client versions can be made available.

- When a new version of either client is available, the user can download a patch. The corresponding hardcopy manual, however, is sent via standard mail. In the event that several versions are released in a short time, a user should be able to identify which manual corresponds to which version.

For example, assume that the initial release of myCarParts allows users to browse the catalog using textual information only. Parts have a part identifier, a name, a description, the list of vehicles and years for which this part is manufactured, and cross references to other parts with which it can be assembled. The user can search the database using any of these fields. This can be problematic for novice users who do not know the name of the part they are looking for. In a second release, we address this problem by providing the user with a navigation map of parts. If the user knows what the part looks like and where it is located in the vehicle, he only needs to click on the corresponding part of the map. The change to introduce navigation maps and the releases of the components of myCarParts need to be carefully sequenced, considering the constraints we described before. Adding the navigation map requires the following sequence of steps:

1. The Server must be modified to support the storage and retrieval of subassembly maps.
2. The Server must be released and installed.
3. One map per vehicle and year must be created and stored in the database.
4. The NClient must be modified to use the navigation maps as a possible interface.
5. The NClient must be released and installed.

In the following sections, we use myCarParts and the navigation map change as the basis for the examples.

13.4.1 Configuration Item and CM Aggregate Identification

The identification of configuration items and CM aggregates occurs primarily after the project agreement, when a set of deliverables is agreed upon with the customer, and after system design, when most of the subsystems have been identified. The identification of configuration items and CM aggregates, however, continues throughout the development as the set of deliverables is redefined and as subsystems are added and removed from the subsystem decomposition.

Identifying configuration items and CM aggregates is similar to identifying objects during analysis. It is not algorithmic because some configuration items are trivial to identify (e.g., the

RAD, the SDD), while others are more subtle (e.g., a client server protocol definition). Configuration items are self-contained documents or pieces of code whose evolution must be tracked and controlled. These include deliverable documents, work products, subsystems, off-the-shelf components that can evolve during the life cycle of the system, and interface descriptions.

In the myCarParts example, we identify each of the deliverable documents as a configuration item. In the myCarParts *Project Agreement*, the following were defined as deliverables:

- user level documents, including the RAD and the User Manual (UM)
- system documents, including the SDD and the ODD
- the source code of the system, including its subsystems (depicted in Figure 13-7) and various installation programs.

We identify, moreover, the interfaces between subsystems entities whose evolution should be carefully controlled, as changes to these can introduce major problems. We identify two components of the SDD, the *Client Server Protocol Specification* and the *Data Schema Description*, as configuration items.

Figure 13-8 depicts the configuration items and the CM aggregates we identified for myCarParts. Because myCarParts subsystems can be released independently, we identify one CM aggregate for each subsystem that includes the configuration items relevant to the subsystem. For example, if we modify the NClient subsystem to include the navigation map functionality, we need to revise the RAD to specify the new use cases, change the NClient UM:CI to explain how this functionality is used, modify the NClient ODD:CI to include new classes for the map, and implement and test the changes in the source code.[2] The NClient:CM Aggregate is then revised to include the most recent versions of the configuration items related to the NClient, before it is released to the users. Note that this change can be done without modifying the EClient:CM Aggregate, so configuration items related to the EClient and the NClient subsystems are modeled as separate configuration items and CM aggregates.

The three subsystems constituting the myCarParts system, however, are not completely independent. Before we can add navigation maps to the NClient subsystem, we need first to provide functionality for storing and retrieving these tables in the Server subsystem. Although this functionality is realized and released separately, we still need to make sure that the releases of clients are coordinated with server releases (in the sense that servers should be upgraded before clients). For this purpose, we also identify system-level CM aggregates for each of the deliverables. The RAD:CM Aggregate, the SDD:CM Aggregate, and the ODD:CM Aggregate represent consistent versions of the deliverables. For example, the versions of the

---

2. For brevity, the source code, test, and test manual are not depicted in Figure 13-8.

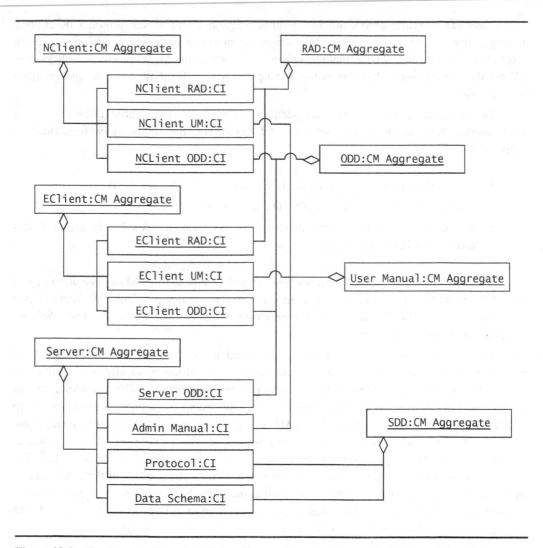

Figure 13-8   Configuration items and CM aggregates for myCarParts (UML object diagram).

ODD:CM Aggregate with the NClient ODD:CI describing the navigation map classes also contain the Server ODD:CI describing how to store and retrieve these maps.

13.4.2 Promotion Management

Creating a new promotion for a configuration item occurs when a developer wants to share the configuration item with others. Developers create promotions to make the configuration item available for review or for the purpose of debugging another configuration item. Once the promotion is created and stored in the repository, developers interested in the promotion check it out of the repository. Developers not interested in the promotion continue to work with earlier versions. Once a promotion is created, it cannot be modified. The developer who created the promotion can continue modifying the configuration item without interfering with the developers using the promotion. To distribute new changes, the developer needs to create a new promotion.

For example, consider the navigation map change in myCarParts (Figure 13-9). First, developers modify the analysis model to specify the navigation map use cases and its interaction with the existing use cases, resulting in the NClient RAD.2.0:Promotion. The system design model is then modified to accommodate the storage and downloading of maps, resulting in the Protocol.2.0:Promotion and Data Schema.2.0:Promotion. Then, a first implementation of the server side of the protocol is realized in the Server.2.0:Promotion, which is made available to the novice client team to test their implementation of the navigation map (NClient 2.0:Promotion and above). Several bugs are found in the server while testing the NClient. The server team identifies and addresses these bugs, resulting in the Server.2.1:Promotion and Server.2.2:Promotion. In the meantime, the documentation team revises the NClient UM2.0:Promotion based on the NClient RAD.2.0:Promotion. Note that during this time, the expert client team may be repairing bugs in the EClient.1.5, independently of the navigation map change. To test the EClient, the expert client team continues to use the former release of the server (i.e., Server.1.4). Figure 13-9 illustrates the above scenario by depicting a snapshot of each team's workspace. Even though teams are working toward a consistent system, they may all be working on different promotions of the same components until all components stabilize.

Promotions represent the state of a configuration item at the time it is made available for other developers. A project may usually require that code promotions do not contain compiler errors, but it makes few other constraints to encourage the exchange of work products among teams. Once the quality of configuration items is improved and assessed by the quality control team, the promotion may become eligible for a release.

13.4.3 Release Management

The creation of a new release for a configuration item or an CM aggregate is a management decision, usually based on marketing and quality control. A release is made available to offer additional (or revised) functionality or to address critical bugs.

Although creating a release seems similar to creating a promotion, it is a much more complicated and expensive process. Developers deal with change as part of their work. If the new version of a component introduces more problems than it addresses, they can simply roll back to an earlier promotion. A user manual that is not up to date does not interfere with their work, given that they know the product. Users, on the other hand, are not in the business of testing software. Discovering inconsistencies in the system and its documentation interferes with their work and can lead them to switch products or contractors. Releases, therefore, are created in a much more controlled process than promotions, attempting to ensure consistency and

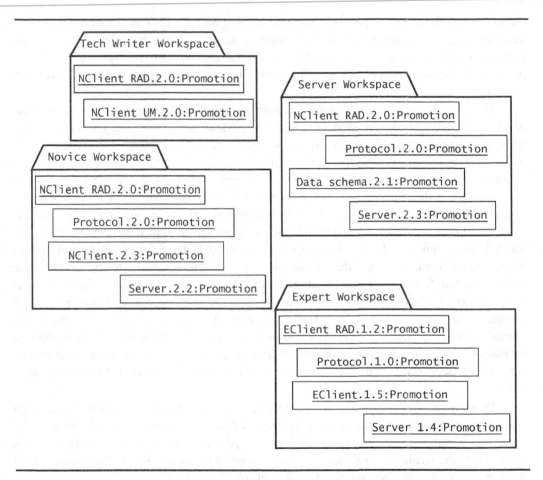

Figure 13-9 Snapshot of the workspaces used by myCarParts developers (UML object diagram). The Novice Workspace, the Tech Writer Workspace, and the Server Workspace contain promotions related to the navigation map functionality. The Expert Workspace, however, contains older and more stable versions. For all configuration items, version numbers of the form 1.x refer to the promotions without navigation maps functionality, whereas version numbers of the form 2.x refer to the promotions containing partial or complete implementations of the navigation maps.

quality. The quality control team assesses the quality of the individual components of a release and coordinates revisions to defective components. This auditing process allows the quality control team to ensure the consistency of the release with minimal interference with the developer's work.

For example, consider the release of the navigation map functionality for myCarParts (Figure 13-10). We first create a stable promotion of the NClient.2.4 and the Server.2.3 that implements the new functionality. The quality control team tests the NClient.2.4 promotions against the latest version of the RAD (i.e., NClient RAD.2.0). Quality control finds a bug, which is fixed in a subsequent promotion of the NClient.2.5. When testing the new functionality, quality control also tests the current version of the EClient (i.e., EClient.1.5, not shown in Figure 13-10) with Server.2.3. Satisfied with the state of the software, quality control decides to include NClient.2.5, EClient.1.5, and Server.2.3 in the next major release of myCarParts. Quality control then checks the user manual (NClient UM.2.0) for consistency against NClient.2.5. A few additional problems are found and addressed in the promotion NClient UM.2.1, which is then included in the release under construction. The release is then system tested with a selected set of users. Two more problems with the NClient.2.5 and Server.2.3 are discovered by a system tester and are addressed in NClient.2.6 and Server.2.4. The software is retested and released to the users as myCarParts.2.0.

The administrator of the myCarParts site first upgrades the Server and its database schema and observes, during a system test, if any user discovers unforeseen compatibility problems with the older clients. After the system test, the administrator then makes available the NClient.2.6 to the users who would like to use the navigation map functionality. Once the stability of the new release is validated in the field, all users are encouraged to upgrade. Older versions of the server and the clients are discontinued. Any change to the documentation or subsystems of myCarParts will be delivered as a patch or as a third release.

The focus of the release process in the myCarParts example is on quality and consistency. The quality control team acts as a gatekeeper between the users and the developers. The assumption behind this process is that users are not interested in debugging the systems they use. They expect that these systems support their work. This assumption does not hold when the users are software developers. In this case, a substantial number of tools used by this group of users are also developed and maintained by them. These can range from simple scripts that make it more convenient to accomplish a repetitive task, to full-fledged programming languages, syntax editors, or configuration management systems. With the popularity of the Internet among software developers, an increasing number of these ad hoc tools are shared and distributed, especially those that address common problems. This leads to the availability of numerous freely available programs, ranging from simple scripts to operating systems (e.g., Linux). In this situation, users (who are software developers) are willing to test, debug, and send contributed code to the program author in exchange for early access to the piece of software. In this software development model, known as the *bazaar model* [Raymond, 1998], releases and promotions become much more similar than in the context of the controlled process we described above.

13.4.4 Branch Management

Until now, we have examined the management of promotions and releases in the context of a single change. Various configuration items are revised until the change is completed and assessed by quality control. During this process, we have dealt with the complexity caused by the difficulty in maintaining consistency among related promotions and in minimizing the introduction of new faults. We have focused, however, on only a single thread of development.

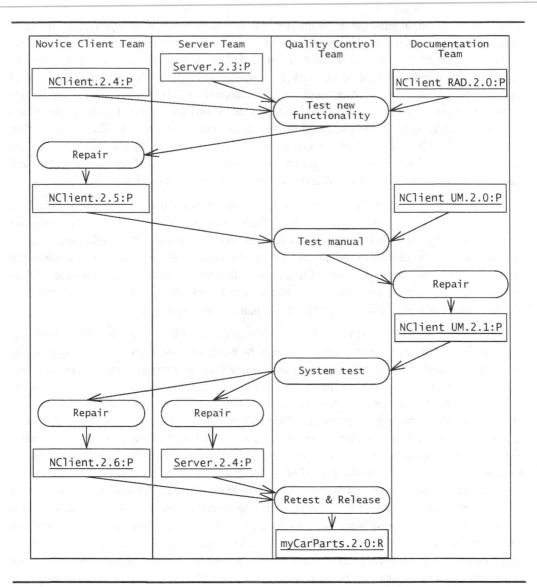

Figure 13-10   Release process for the navigation map functionality of myCarParts.2.0 (UML activity diagram). :P denotes a promotion, :R denotes a release.

Usually, developers work on multiple improvements concurrently. For example, while some developers implement the navigation map functionality in the NClient and the Server, other developers may be improving the Server response time, and yet another group of developers may be extending the EClient to store the history of queries issued by the user. When threads of development focus on different subsystems of myCarParts (e.g., navigation maps in the NClient and the Server, query history in EClient), teams can be isolated by working on different configurations of the same group of subsystems. For example, the navigation map effort works with the most recent versions of the NClient and the Server, while the query history effort works with the most recent version of the EClient and an older, stable version of the Server. This approach works only if changes affect nonoverlapping sets of components and if subsystems interfaces remain backward compatible. However, when two changes require modifications to the same component, a different approach is required. Concurrent branches and subsequent merging can be used to coordinate changes.

For example, let us focus on two concurrent and overlapping changes: while one team of developers implement the navigation map functionality (described in Section 13.4.2 and in Section 13.4.3), we assign another team the task of improving the response time of the Server. Both teams may change the Server, the NClient, and their interfaces to accomplish their respective goals.

These changes are assigned to different teams because of the difference in their associated risks. The navigation map improvement extends the functionality of myCarParts and is well defined. The response time improvement, however, requires experimental work and is open ended: The developers first need to identify performance bottlenecks and design heuristics to speed up common requests. The resulting improvement then must be measured and assessed against any loss of reliability and decrease in maintainability. Finally, separating both changes provides us with more flexibility during delivery: if the response time improvement is completed early, we can merge it with the functional improvement and release it at the same time, otherwise, we can deliver it later as a patch.

To support both changes concurrently while keeping teams independent, we set up a branch, starting from the latest promotions of the subsystems at the time the changes are approved (see Figure 13-11).

The teams working on functional improvements continue working on the main trunk (starting at Server.1.5 and NClient.1.6). The team responsible for the response time improvement works on the branch (starting at Server.1.5.1.1).[3] The performance improvement team restricts its changes to the Server subsystem and decides to avoid modifying the Server interface. Both teams then work independently until they complete their improvements. The navigation map improvement is completed first and made part of the second release of myCarParts, as we saw in Figure 13-10 (as Server.2.4). Soon after, the response time improvement is completed (Server.1.5.1.7, in Figure 13-11). The response time improvement is considered successful, yielding a fourfold decrease in response time for common requests, while marginally extending the client server protocol. At this point, we need to integrate this improvement with the main trunk, hoping to produce a version of myCarParts which has both the navigation map functionality and the fourfold improvement in response time.

---

3. We use the CVS identification scheme for identifying versions and branches [Berliner, 1990].

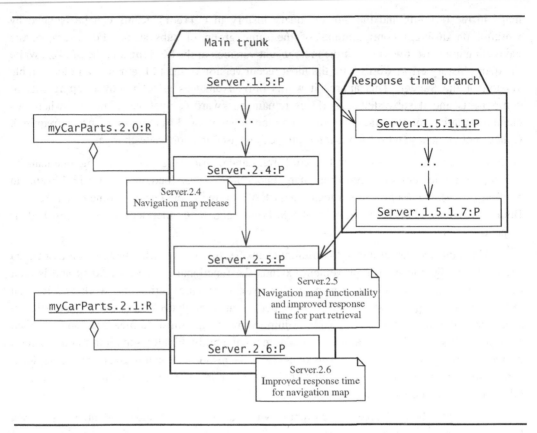

Figure 13-11   An example of branch (UML object diagram, some promotions were omitted for brevity, : P denotes a promotion, :R denotes a release). On the main trunk, developers add the navigation map functionality to myCarParts. On a concurrent branch, developers improve the response time of the server by integrating a cache between the server and the database. The response time improvement is completed after the release of the navigation map functionality and made available as a patch.

Merges can usually be done with the help of the configuration management tool, which attempts to merge the most recent parts of the versions. When conflicts are detected, that is, when both versions contain modifications to the same classes or methods, the configuration management tool reports the problem back to the developer. The developer then resolves the conflict manually. In our example, the tool reports a conflict in the DBInterface class, which was modified by both teams (Figure 13-12).

The navigation map team added a method, processMapRequest(), to retrieve maps from the database. The response time improvement team modified the processPartRequest(), which retrieves parts from the database given a part id. We construct a merged version of the DBInterface class by selecting the processMapRequest() from the main trunk and the processPartRequest() from the branch. We then test the revised DBInterface class to make

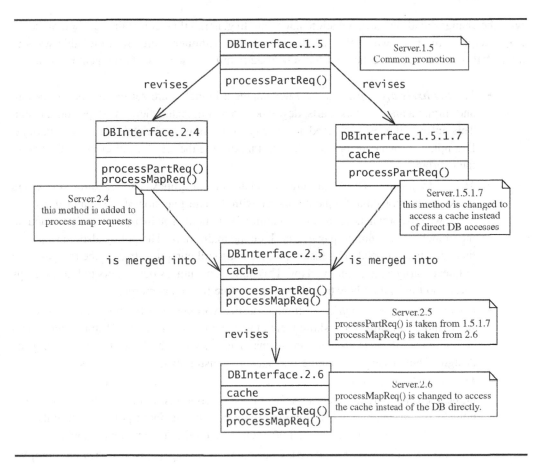

Figure 13-12 An example of merge for the DBInterface class of the myCarParts system (UML class diagram).

sure we have dealt with all the conflicts, which results in the Server.2.5:Promotion. Later, we realize that the same caching mechanism can be used for the processMapRequest(), which can result in further response time improvements. We modify the processMapRequest() method, retest the server, and create the Server.2.6:Promotion.

Heuristics for branch management

As we saw in this example, merging two branches is a nontrivial operation. It usually needs to be supported by a configuration management tool and requires substantial intervention and testing by developers. In the myCarParts example, illustrating a very simple case, the response time improvement team was careful not to change the Server interface and limited their changes to the Server subsystem. These constraints minimized the likelihood of an overlap with the changes made by the navigation map team. In general, if no constraints are set, branches can diverge to the point where they cannot be merged. Although there are no reliable ways to address this problem, several heuristics can be used to mitigate the risk of divergent branches:

- *Identify likely overlaps.* Once the development branches are set up, but before design and implementation work starts, developers can anticipate where overlaps could occur. This information is then used to specify constraints for containing these overlaps. Examples of such constraints include not modifying the interface of classes involved in the overlap.

- *Merge frequently.* The configuration management policy can require developers working on a branch to frequently merge with the latest version of the main trunk (e.g., daily, weekly, or whenever a new promotion is created). The merges are only created on the branch and are not propagated back on the main trunk. The policy also may specify that such merges need only ensure that the code still compiles; that is, the merges need not necessarily address all overlaps. This policy encourages developers to find overlaps early and think about how to address them before the actual merge.

- *Communicate likely conflicts.* Although teams working on different branches need to work independently, they should anticipate conflicts during the future merge and communicate them to the relevant teams. This also has the benefit of improving the design of both changes by taking into account constraints from both teams.

- *Minimize changes on the main trunk.* Minimizing the number of changes to one of the branches to be merged reduces the likelihood of conflicts. Although this constraint is not always acceptable, it is a good configuration management policy to do only bug fixes on the main branch and do all other changes on the development branch.

- *Minimize the number of branches.* Configuration management branches are complex mechanisms that should not be abused. Merge work caused by reckless branching may result in substantially more effort than if a single branch had been used. Changes that may result in overlaps and conflicts usually depend on each other and can be addressed sequentially. Branches should be used only when concurrent development is required and when conflicts can be reconciled.

In all cases, creating a branch is a significant event in the development. It should require management approval and should be carefully planned.

13.4.5 Variant Management

Variants are versions that are intended to coexist. A system has multiple variants when it is supported on different operating systems and different hardware platforms. A system also has multiple variants when it is delivered with different levels of functionality (e.g., novice version vs. expert version, standard version vs. deluxe version). Two fundamental approaches are possible when dealing with variants (Figure 13-13):

- *Redundant teams.* A team is assigned to each variant. Each team is given the same requirements and is responsible for the complete design, implementation, and testing of the variant. A small number of configuration items are shared across variants, such as the user manual and the RAD.

- *Single project.* Design a subsystem decomposition that maximizes the amount of code shared across variants. For multiple platforms, confine variant-specific code in low-level subsystems. For multiple levels of functionality, confine increments of functionality in individual and mostly independent subsystems.

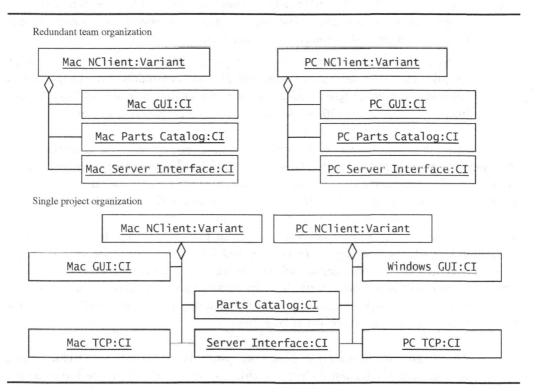

Figure 13-13 Examples of redundant variants and variants sharing configuration items (UML object diagram). In the redundant team organization, the myCarParts NClients for the Macintosh and the PC are realized independently. In the single project organization, the myCarParts NClients for the Macintosh and the PC differ in their UI.

The redundant team option leads to multiple smaller projects that share a requirements specification. The single project option leads to a larger, single project with most teams sharing core subsystems. At first glance, the redundant team option leads to redundancies in the project as the core functionality of the system will be designed and implemented multiple times. The single project option seems more efficient, given that a potentially large amount of code can be reused across variants, given a good system design. Surprisingly, the redundant team option is often chosen in commercial developments to avoid organizational complexity [Kemerer, 1997].

Issues introduced by code sharing include

- *Single supplier/multiple consumers.* Core subsystems are used by teams working on different variants, and, thus, with possibly diverging requirements. The core subsystem teams need to satisfy their requirements uniformly.

- *Long change request turnaround.* When one variant-specific team issues a change request for a core subsystem, the approval and implementation of the change can take longer than for other changes. The longer turnaround is needed to ensure the change does not interfere with the other variant-specific teams.

- *Cross platform inconsistencies.* Core subsystems introduce constraints on variant specific subsystems that can interfere with platform constraints. For example, a core subsystem can be designed with a threaded control flow in mind, whereas the user interface toolkit of a specific variant assumes an event-driven flow of control.

Each of these issues can be perceived by variant-specific teams as a motivation to implement their own core subsystems. These issues can be addressed, however, by anticipating variant-specific issues during system design and through effective configuration management. A good system design is resilient to platform and variant-specific issues. This results in a subsystem decomposition that is identical for all variants, where each system variant differs by substituting one or more subsystems. For example in Figure 13-13, the Macintosh and PC variants of the NClient share the Parts Catalog and the Server Interface subsystem. The user interface and the network interface subsystems are different, but have the same interface. This results in a subsystem decomposition in which each subsystem is either variant independent (i.e., supporting all variants) or variant specific (i.e., supporting a small number of variants). The issues we raised before can then be addressed as follows:

- The *single supplier/multiple consumers* issue is addressed by careful change management: If a requested change is variant specific, it should not be addressed in a core subsystem. If the requested change benefits all variants, then it should be addressed only in the core subsystems.

- *Long change request turnaround* is shortened by involving the team that issued the change request during validation. The suggested change is implemented in a new promotion of the core subsystem and released to the team who requested the change. The team evaluates the solution and tests its implementation, whereas other teams continue using the former promotion. Once the change is validated, other variant teams may start using the revised subsystem. We described such a scenario with the Server side changes required by the navigation map (see Section 13.4.4): the novice client team validated the new version of the server, and the EClient team continued working with a former (and more stable) release. Note that when variant teams require concurrent changes to the core subsystem, core developers can use branches to isolate the impact of each change until they reach a stable state.

- *Cross-platform inconsistencies* are avoided as much as possible during system design by focusing on a variant-independent subsystem decomposition. Lower-level, cross-platform inconsistencies are addressed in variant-specific subsystems, at the cost of some glue objects or redundancy between core and variant-specific subsystems. If all else fails, independent development paths should be considered when the supported variants are substantially different.

Managing multiple variants with shared subsystems is complex, as we indicated earlier. After an up-front investment during system design, however, the shared code approach yields numerous advantages, such as increased quality and stability of the shared code and greater consistency in quality across variants. Finally, when the number of variants is large, considering variant-specific issues early and designing configuration management mechanisms to meet them lead to substantial savings in time and cost.

13.4.6 Change Management

The creation of new promotions and releases is driven by change requests. A team repairs a fault and creates a promotion for quality control to evaluate. Clients define new requirements or developers take advantage of a new implementation technology, causing a new release of the system. Change requests can range from correcting a typo in a menu label to reimplementing a major subsystem to address performance issues. Change requests also vary in their timing: a request for additional functionality during the requirements review can lead to modifying the draft RAD, whereas the same request made during testing can additionally lead to major subsystem surgery. Change requests must be handled differently depending on their scope and their timing. The handling of change requests, called *change management*, is part of configuration management.

Change management processes vary in their formality and complexity with the project goals. In the case of a complex system with high reliability requirements, for example, the change request form has several pages (e.g., [MIL Std. 480]), requires the approval of several managers, and takes several weeks to be processed. In the case of a simple tool written by one developer, informal communication is sufficient. In both cases, the change process includes the following steps (Figure 13-14):

1. The change, identifying a fault or a new feature, is requested. This can be done by anyone, including a user or a developer.
2. The request is assessed against project goals. In large projects, this is done by a control board. In smaller projects, this is done by the project manager. This may include a cost–benefit analysis and an evaluation of the impact of the change on the rest of the system.

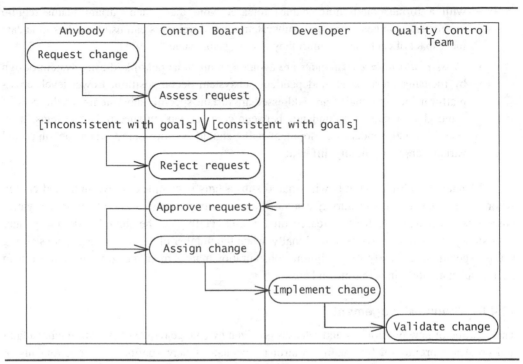

Figure 13-14   An example of change management process (UML activity diagram).

3. Following the assessment, the request is either accepted or rejected.

4. If it is accepted, the change is planned, prioritized, and assigned to a developer and implemented.

5. The implemented change is audited. This is done by the quality control team or whoever is responsible for managing releases.

13.5 Managing Configuration Management

In this section, we address management issues related to configuration management. These include

- Documenting Configuration Management (Section 13.5.1)

- Assigning Configuration Management Responsibilities (Section 13.5.2)

- Planning Configuration Management Activities (Section 13.5.3)

- Continuous Integration: Integration Testing and Promotion Management (Section 13.5.4).

13.5.1 Documenting Configuration Management

[IEEE Std. 828-2005] is a standard for writing **Software Configuration Management Plans (SCMP)**. Such a plan documents all the relevant information to the configuration management activities of a specific project. The plan is generated during the planning phase, put under configuration management, and revised as necessary. The scope and the length of the plan may vary according to the needs of the project. A mission-critical project with a formal change control process may require a 30-page document. A project developing a conceptual prototype may only require a 5-page document.

Software Configuration Management Plan

1. Introduction
    1.1 Purpose
    1.2 Scope
    1.3 Key terms
    1.4 References
2. Management
    2.1 Organization
    2.2 Responsibilities
3. Activities
4. Schedule
5. Resources
6. Plan Maintenance

Figure 13-15 An example of a template for the Software Configuration Management Plan.

An SCMP contains six types of information: introduction, management, activities, schedules, resources, and plan maintenance (see Figure 13-15).

The *Introduction* describes the scope and audience of the document, key terms, and references.

The *Management* section describes the organization of the project (which can be a reference to the corresponding section in the *Software Project Management Plan*; see Chapter 14, *Project Management*) and how the configuration management responsibilities are assigned within this organization.

The *Activities* section describes in detail the identification of configuration items, the change control process, the process for creating releases and for auditing, and the process for status accounting. Responsibilities for each of these activities are assigned to a role defined in the management section.

The *Schedule* denotes when configuration management activities take place and how they are coordinated. In particular, it defines at which point changes can be requested and approved through the formal change process.

The *Resources* section identifies the tools, techniques, equipment, personnel, and training necessary for accomplishing the configuration activities.

Finally, *Plan Maintenance* defines how the SCMP, itself under configuration management, is maintained and revised. In particular, this section details the person responsible for its maintenance, the frequency of updates, and the change process for updating the plan.

The [IEEE Std. 828-2005] standard is defined such that the above outline can be applied to any project, from a reliable systems design to a freeware product.

13.5.2 Assigning Configuration Management Responsibilities

Configuration management is a project function that involves many different tasks and participants in the project. As in the case of system design, tasks that require consistency should be performed by a small number of people. During system design, a small team of architects makes decisions about subsystem decomposition. Similarly, a small team of configuration managers identifies the configuration items and CM aggregates to be controlled. As in the case of testing, quality control tasks such as release management should be performed by different participants than development tasks such as object design and implementation.

Configuration management includes the following roles:

- **Configuration manager**. This role is responsible for identifying configuration items and CM aggregates, and may also be responsible for defining the procedures for creating promotions and releases. This role is often combined with the role of architect.

- **Change control board**. This role is responsible for approving or rejecting change requests based on project goals. Depending on the complexity of the change process, this role can also be involved in assessing the change and in planning accepted changes. This role is often combined with the role of team or project manager.

- **Developer**. This role creates promotions triggered by change requests or the normal activities of development. The main configuration management activity of developers is to check in changes and resolve merge conflicts.

- **Auditor**. This role is responsible for selecting and evaluating promotions for release. The auditor is also responsible for ensuring the consistency and completeness of the release. This role is often accomplished by the quality control team.

The roles for configuration management are defined during project planning and assigned early to ensure consistency. Reassigning configuration management roles too often can severely limit the benefits of configuration management and fail to control change.

13.5.3 Planning Configuration Management Activities

Project managers should plan configuration management activities during the project start phase. Most of the configuration management procedures can be defined before the project starts since they do not depend on the system itself, but rather on project goals and nonfunctional requirements such as safety and reliability.

The key elements in planning configuration management are

- defining the configuration management processes
- defining and assigning roles
- defining change criteria; that is, what attributes of the work products can be changed and how late in the process can changes occur
- defining release criteria; that is, which criteria should be evaluated when auditing promotions for a release

Moreover, configuration management procedures and tools should be in place before changes begin to occur, so that they can be recorded, approved, and tracked.

13.5.4 Continuous Integration: Testing and Promotion Management

Object-oriented development is an iterative process, characterized by the incremental addition of features and improvements to an existing product. In configuration management terms, each developer works on their own branch, testing the new feature locally, and then merging their changes onto the main trunk. Each merge is the integration of a revised subsystem, requiring the execution of integration and regression tests. As the number of features that are concurrently developed grows, merging changes back onto the main trunk becomes a bottleneck, with each developer having to wait until the previous change is integrated. Conflicts between changes from different developers are detected late, further blocking the work of other developers.

Continuous integration [Duval et al., 2007] is a method combining promotion management (Section 13.4.2) and integration testing (Section 11.4.4) that aims at detecting integration problems early, thus reducing integration bottlenecks. Continuous integration is characterized by the following points:

- *Single public branch.* Developers make changes and test them locally in their own private branch. However, promotions are created on a single main trunk shared by all developers. There are no concurrent development branches that will require a costly merge down the road.
- *Automated build and regression test.* Committing changes to the main trunk (i.e., creating a new promotion) triggers an automated build and the necessary regression tests. If the build fails, the developer committing the change is notified immediately, so that either the problem is solved quickly or the change is backed out of the main trunk. When the build is broken, no other developer can commit to the main trunk. If a regression test fails and it is shown that the failure is localized, other developers may continue merging their changes, while the offending change is repaired. However, the

goal of continuous integration is to keep the head version on the main trunk stable so that all developers have a solid base to develop on.

- *Frequent promotions.* Developers design and implement their changes so that they can commit frequently, typically once a day. High risk changes and refactoring that impact the software architecture are merged first, details local to the new feature are added last. This ensures that overlaps between changes are detected and resolved before the new features have been completely implemented based on a flawed design.

- *Transparent build status.* The status of the build is visible to all developers. On the one hand, it increases the pressure to repair broken builds quickly. On the other hand, it encourages developers to check in their code only after they are reasonably confident that it will not break the build.

For example, Figure 13-16 shows a dashboard in CruiseControl [CruiseControl]. Each box represents a subsystem with its accompanying tests. Successful builds are depicted by check marks, failed builds are depicted by exclamation marks. The dashboard further distinguishes builds that were newly broken and those that were recently repaired. Clicking on the box enables the user to examine more details about the build, for example, which tests or compilation activity failed, what changes were recently made that could have caused the build failure. An overview picture such as Figure 13-16 provides a quick impression about the relative maturity of the different subsystems.

The main benefit of continuous integration is that new integration problems are detected early. Consequently, it is critical to keep the build and test duration short, even as the size and complexity of the product increases. **Staged builds** address this problem by separating build and test actions into several phases. During the first phase, a new executable is built and a minimal set of regression tests (also called smoke tests) detect the most serious problems. After the first phase succeeds, other developers can integrate their changes. During the second phase, longer running tests, such as performance tests or end-to-end tests using realistic data, ensure that the maturity of the main trunk. Assigning a test to the first phase or the second phase is a trade-off between detecting as many new problems early and keeping the build time short.

Continuous integration leverages off the techniques presented in this chapter and in Chapter 11, *Testing*, but differs in its emphasis and time scale. During continuous integration, many small changes and integration occurs frequently. In a top-down or a bottom-up integration approach, large changes are integrated at the subsystem level once over a substantial period of time. Continuous integration works best for projects with an evolving architecture and an integrated team of developers. Subsystem level integration works best for projects where the architecture is well-defined and subsystems are contributed by different (and often competing) suppliers.

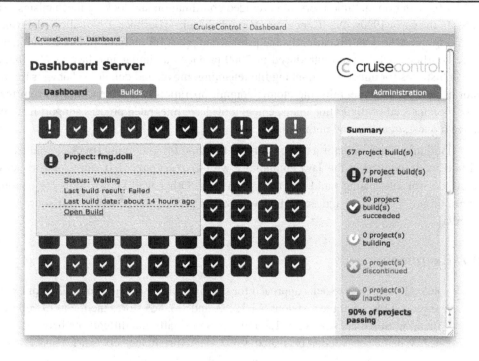

Figure 13-16 An example of continuous integration build status (CruiseControl). Each square represents a project. The darkest squares correspond to builds that were successful for more than 24 hours.

13.6 Further Readings

Historically, configuration management emerged as a discipline around the same time as the "software crisis" was identified. Much of the early work on configuration management was motivated by large contract development projects in which requirements changes and successive releases needed to be managed carefully. The Capability Maturity Model of the SEI rates organizations that do not have configuration management at the bottom maturity level (see Section 15.3). Although configuration management is increasingly relevant in current projects with many variants or many development sites, the discipline is still underdeveloped. *Software Configuration Management* [Babich, 1986] is still a relatively standard textbook.

The first version control tools appeared in the early 1970s, as magnetic storage media, such as hard disks and tape drives, became widespread. Often, version control and build management would be part of the operating system: VAX VMS, for example, created a new file whenever a change was made and let the user remove the versions that were not needed. In the Unix world, SCCS (Source Code Control System), distributed as part of the operating system, enabled a developer to store successive versions and branches of the same file as a series of increments [Rochkind, 1975]. In the mid 1980s, RCS (Revision Control System) improved on

SCCS by focusing on multiple users and provided coordination and locking mechanisms [Tichy, 1985]. In the early 1990s, CVS (Concurrent Version System) [Berliner, 1990] allowed developers modifying the same files concurrently and provided support for merging branches and handling merge conflicts. Subversion introduced in 2000 provides a similar interface as CVS, but adds version histories for directories, tracking file renaming, move, and deletions. Subversion tracks histories using a database, allowing atomic commit operations on the repository. From the late 1990s, commercial configuration management tools have integrated process support features for change request, tracking, and notification.

Continuous integration is a corner stone of Extreme Programming [Beck & Andres, 2005] and was made popular in the Java community with CruiseControl [CruiseControl], an open source tool for automating build and regression tests. Other well-known tools for continuous integration are Tinderbox and Bonsai, developed as part of the Mozilla open source project [Mozilla].

13.7 Exercises

13-1   RCS adopts a reverse delta approach for storing multiple versions of a file. For example, assume a file has three revisions—1.1, 1.2, and 1.3. RCS stores the file as of version 1.3, then the differences between 1.2 and 1.3, and finally the differences between 1.1 and 1.2. When a new version is created, say 1.4, the difference between 1.3 and 1.4 is computed and stored, and the 1.3 version is deleted and replaced by 1.4. Explain why RCS does not simply store the initial version (in this case 1.1) and the differences between each successive version.

13-2   CVS uses a simple text-based rule to identify overlaps during a merge: there is an overlap if the same line was changed in both versions that are being merged. If no such line exists, then CVS decides there is no conflict and the versions are merged automatically. For example, assume a file contains a class with three methods—a(), b(), and c(). Two developers work independently on the file. If they both modify the same lines of code, say the first line of method a(), then CVS decides there is a conflict. Explain why this approach will fail to detect certain types of conflicts. Provide an example in your answer.

13-3   Configuration management systems such as RCS, CVS, and Perforce use file names and their paths to identify configuration items. Explain why this feature prevents the configuration management of CM aggregates, even in the presence of labels.

13-4   Explain how configuration management can be beneficial to developers, even in the absence of a change control or auditing process. List two scenarios illustrating your explanation.

13-5   In Chapter 12, *Rationale Management*, we described how rationale information can be represented using an issue model. Draw a UML class diagram for a problem tracking system that uses an issue model for the description and discussion of changes and their relationship with versions. Focus only on the domain objects of the system.

13-6   In Chapter 11, *Testing*, we described how the quality control team find faults in promotions created by subsystem teams. Draw a UML activity diagram including the change process activities and testing activities of a multi-team project.

References

[Babich, 1986]	W. A. Babich, *Software Configuration Management*, Addison-Wesley, Reading, MA, 1986.
[Beck & Andres, 2005]	K. Beck & C. Andres, *Extreme Programming Explained: Embrace Change*, 2nd ed., Addison-Wesley, Reading, MA, 2005.
[Berliner, 1990]	B. Berliner, "CVS II: Parallelizing software development," *Proceedings of the 1990 USENIX Conference*, Washington, DC, pp. 22–26, January 1990.
[Bersoff et al., 1980]	E. H. Bersoff, V. D. Henderson, & S.G. Siegel, *Software Configuration Management: An Investment in Product Integrity*, Prentice Hall, Englewood Cliffs, NJ, 1980.
[CruiseControl]	http://cruisecontrol.sourceforge.net/.
[Dart, 1991]	S. Dart, "Concepts in configuration management systems," *Third International Software Configuration Management Workshop*, ACM, June 1991.
[Duval et al., 2007]	P. Duval, S. Matyas, & A. Glover, *Continuous Integration: Improving Software Quality and Reducing Risk*, Addison-Wesley, Reading, MA, 2007.
[IEEE Std. 828-2005]	*IEEE Standard for Software Configuration Management Plans*, IEEE Standards Board, August 2005.
[IEEE Std. 1042-1987]	*IEEE Guide to Software Configuration Management*, IEEE Standards Board, September 1987.
[Kemerer, 1997]	C. F. Kemerer, "Case 7: Microsoft Corporation: Office Business Unit," *Software Project Management: Readings and Cases*, Irwin/McGraw-Hill, Boston, MA, 1997.
[Knuth, 1986]	D. E. Knuth, *The TeXbook*, Addison-Wesley, Reading, MA, 1986.
[Leblang, 1994]	D. Leblang, "The CM challenge: Configuration management that works," in W. F. Tichy (ed.), *Configuration Management*, Vol. 2 of *Trends in Software*, Wiley, New York, 1994.
[MIL Std. 480]	MIL Std. 480, U.S. Department of Defense, Washington, DC.
[Mozilla]	http://www.mozilla.org/
[Perforce]	http://www.perforce.com/
[POSIX, 1990]	*Portable Operating System Interface for Computing Environments*, in IEEE Std. 1003.1, 1990.
[Raymond, 1998]	E. Raymond, "The cathedral and the bazaar," Available at http://www.tuxedo.org/~esr/writings/cathedral-bazaar/cathedral-bazaar.html, 1998.
[Rochkind, 1975]	M.J. Rochkind, "The Source Code Control System," *IEEE Transactions on Software Engineering*, SE-1(4), p. 255–265., 1975.
[Steelman, 1978]	*Requirements for high order computer programming languages: Steelman*, U.S. Department of Defense, Washington, DC, 1978.
[Tichy, 1985]	W. Tichy, "RCS—A system for version control," *Software Practice and Experience*, Vol. 15, No. 7, 1985.

Project Management

Take off your engineering hat and put on your management hat.
—Statement made during the 51-L launch discussion

Managers do not generate a useful product on their own. Instead, they provide and coordinate resources so that others can generate useful products. Managing a software project requires a combination of managerial and social skills to foresee potentially damaging problems and to implement the appropriate response. Because of the lack of visible product and the reliance on nontechnical skills, management is usually the target of jokes by developers and others. Management, however, is a critical function for bringing a project to a successful end, given the complexity of current systems and the high rate of change during development.

Managers do not make technical decisions and often do not have the background to make such decisions. Instead, they are responsible for coordinating and administering the project and ensuring that a high-quality system is delivered on time and within budget. The main tools of management are planning, monitoring, controlling, risk management, and contingency handling.

In this chapter, we describe project management activities from a project manager's point of view. We assume a two-level project management hierarchy, typical for today's software industry. We describe topics associated with classical project management, such as work breakdown structures, task plans, role assignments, risk management, and software project management plans. We discuss both classical methods to management, which aim to deliver a product to address a fixed set of requirements and milestones, and agile methods, which aim at delivering a product incrementally, while renegotiating requirements as the project progresses.

In the next chapter, Chapter 15, *Software Life Cycle*, we focus on models, called "software life cycles," for reusing and improving project management knowledge across projects. In both this chapter and the next chapter, we take an optimistic view of project management and focus on academic concepts. In Chapter 16, *Methodologies: Putting It All Together*, we examine what happens outside of textbook situations. We provide methodologies and heuristics for adapting the building blocks presented in this chapter to specific situations.

14.1 Introduction: The STS-51L Launch Decision

Consider the following example:

Example: The STS-51L launch decision[a]

On January 28, 1986, the Space Shuttle Challenger flying mission STS-51L exploded 73 seconds into flight, killing all seven crew members aboard. The Rogers Presidential Commission, formed to investigate the accident, determined that combustion gases leaking through a joint in the right solid rocket booster caused the ignition of hydrogen fuel from the external fuel tank. The Rogers Commission also determined that there were serious flaws in the decision-making process at NASA.

The main components of the Space Shuttle are the orbiter, the solid rocket boosters, and the external tank. The orbiter is the vehicle that transports cargo and astronauts. The solid rocket boosters provide most of the thrust necessary to put the orbiter into orbit. When they consume all their fuel, they are detached and fall back into the ocean. The external tank, providing fuel to the orbiter's engine, is also detached before reaching orbit. The solid booster rockets were built by a private contractor, Morton Thiokol. They were constructed in sections for easy transport, then assembled at the launch site. Each section is connected by a joint. A design flaw of this joint was responsible for the combustion gas leak that caused the accident.

The Rogers Commission determined that the engineers at Thiokol were aware of possible failure of the solid booster rocket joints. Solid booster rockets recovered from previous shuttle flights indicated that rubber gaskets, called "O-rings," in the field joints had been eroded by combustion gases. This erosion seemed particularly severe on flights that launched in cold temperatures. This erosion concerned engineers because the O-rings had not been designed to come in contact with the combustion gases. Managers treated the joint problem as an acceptable risk, given that erosion had occurred in previous missions without causing an incident. Engineers at Thiokol had repeatedly and unsuccessfully attempted to communicate the severity of the problem to their management. In the days preceding the STS-51L launch, engineers were alarmed by the low temperatures at the launch site and attempted to convince their management to recommend against a launch. Thiokol initially recommended against the launch and then later reversed its position, at the urging of NASA.

Both NASA and Thiokol have hierarchical reporting structures, typical of public administration organizations, and the information flow through the organization follows the reporting structure. Engineers report to their group manager who then reports to the project manager, and so on. Each level can choose to modify, distort, or suppress any information before sending it upward, based on its own objectives. The STS-51L mission had been delayed repeatedly and was already several months late. Management at both NASA and Thiokol wanted to meet the deadline. This situation resulted in improper information dissemination and inadequate risk evaluation at both NASA and Thiokol.

The Rogers Commission determined that the primary cause of the Challenger accident was a design flaw in the solid rocket booster joint. The Rogers Commission, however, also determined that the decision-making process and the communication structure at Thiokol and NASA were flawed and failed to assess the risks of launching the flawed vehicle.

---

a.   The Challenger accident has been summarized here as an example of project management failure. Both the mechanical and administrative failures that caused the Challenger accident are much more complex than this summary suggests. For a complete report of the investigation, refer to the Rogers Commission report [Rogers et al., 1986] and related books on the subject [Vaughan, 1996].

Project management ensures the delivery of a quality system on time and within budget; the essential components of this definition are quality, time, and money. Ensuring delivery within budget requires a manager to estimate and assign the resources required by the project in terms of participants, training, and tools. Ensuring on-time delivery requires a manager to plan work effort and to monitor the status of the project in terms of tasks and work products. Finally, ensuring quality requires a manager to provide problem-reporting mechanisms and monitor the status of the product in terms of defects and risks. All three aspects of the project—quality, budget, and time—are essential for success.

In this chapter, we describe the role of management in software projects. However, the material presented here is far from sufficient for learning to act as a project manager on the Shuttle program or elsewhere. This chapter is oriented toward project leaders in innovative projects in industry, instructors of team-based project courses, and developers who are about to become team leaders. We assume a two-level management hierarchy, with the project manager at the top, the team leaders at the middle, and developers at the bottom. This is large enough for experiencing the effects of complexity on management and to be typical of today's software industry.

In Section 14.2, we provide a bird's-eye view of management and its relationship to other development activities. In Section 14.3, we describe the models used for management, such as roles, work products, tasks, and schedules. These models are documented in the software project management plan. In Section 14.4, we describe the management activities for classical team-based projects. In Section 14.5, we describe the management activities for agile projects.

14.2 An Overview of Project Management

We provided a model of a project in Chapter 3, *Project Organization and Communication*, from the developer's point of view. The goal was to provide enough information for a developer to *understand* project management artifacts and activities. Work to be done was not structured beyond the task level. Project management artifacts were already created and could only be read and commented on. The focus in this chapter is on the project manager who has to *create* project management artifacts. A project consists of the following components:

- *Outcome*. This is a work product or a group of **work products**. Work products produced for the customer are also called **deliverables**.

- *Work*. This is the work to be performed to achieve the outcome. The work is broken down into units of work, which can be **tasks** or **activities**. A task is the smallest amount of work that can be managed. Tasks and activities can also be recursively grouped into higher-level activities. Work is described in **work packages**.

- *Schedule*. A **schedule** maps on a timeline the units of work performed to achieve the outcome. Units of work can depend on each other. A schedule has a start, a duration, and an end.

- *Resource*. The people (called **participants**), funds, equipment, and facilities required to perform the work are the project's resources. People assume one or more roles in the project. Each **role** is responsible for one or more **work packages**.

Projects are subject to the same barriers as software systems: complexity and change. Complex products require a large number of participants with diverse skills and backgrounds. Competitive markets and evolving requirements introduce change in the development, triggering frequent resource reallocation and making it difficult to track the status of the project.

Dealing with change in a project is further complicated because the project components `Outcome`, `Schedule`, `Work`, and `Resources` are interdependent. A change in one component usually has an impact on the others. For example, adding a new feature to a deliverable usually increases development time and resources. Shortening the duration of a project usually implies that some features cannot be delivered.

Project managers can deal with project complexity and change the same way developers deal with system complexity: through modeling, communication, rationale, and configuration management. Communication, rationale, and configuration aspects of project management have already been dealt with in previous chapters (Chapters 3, 11, and 12, respectively). In this chapter we use a variety of object, dynamic, and functional models to describe project management. To distinguish these models from the system models we call them "management models."

Management models allow us to represent project components, the constraints these components are subjected to, and the relationship among components. The **work breakdown structure** is a decomposition of the work into manageable tasks. The **task model** or *network diagram* considers temporal dependencies between tasks. The **organization** chart shows the project participants and their roles in the project.

The main task of a project manager is to construct, realize, and validate these models throughout the duration of a project. Using these models, the project manager communicates with customers and developers about the status of the project and responsibilities.

From a functional point of view, **project management** can be defined as the process of guiding a project from the beginning through its complete duration to its end using a set of management models. Project management includes four basic activities:

- *Planning*. This activity is concerned with specifying the results to be achieved and the activities and tasks to produce these results, determining a schedule and estimating the required resources such as people and funds.
- *Organizing*. This activity defines the organization of the project and the identification of roles and responsibilities. The roles are mapped to the work identified during the planning activity.
- *Controlling*. This activity is concerned with making sure to identify when actual activities deviate from the planned ones. This involves reconfirming people's expected

performance, monitoring actions taken and results achieved, addressing problems encountered, and sharing information with people interested in the project. If a substantial deviation occurs between the planned work and the actual work, the project manager needs to reallocate resources, change the schedule, or renegotiate the outcome.

- *Terminating.* This activity is concerned with finishing the project. It involves delivering the system to the client according to the acceptance criteria defined in the project agreement, installing the accepted system at the customer site, reviewing the project history to extract lessons learned from the project, and modifying of project templates for the next iteration of the project or for a new project.

From a dynamic point of view, a project can be in one of several phases, which we have already mentioned in Chapter 3. We refine this model by adding another state, Conception (see Figure 14-1).

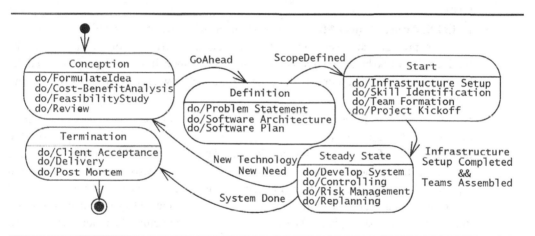

Figure 14-1 Phases of a Software Project (UML state machine diagram).

Project conception. During this phase, also called *concept phase*, the idea for the project is born. In a software project this is usually a new requirement triggered by the need of an existing a market or a new technology. The concept phase is handled in many different ways. For a small project it may consist of an informal discussion between interested people and a go-ahead decision based on a verbal agreement.

In a larger project, the idea is investigated thoroughly, usually with a cost–benefit analysis and a technical feasibility study. The cost–benefit analysis is a comparative assessment of all costs that will be incurred to perform the project and of all benefits anticipated from the project's outcome. Some benefits can be reduced operating costs or increased revenue. Other benefits might include improved morale, reduced turnover, increased productivity, or fewer absences.

The technical feasibility study investigates if the outcome is technically feasible. A typical issue to be addressed is whether the required innovation can be made available in time during the duration of the project. Proceeding to the next phase usually requires a formal review and a formal go-ahead decision.

Project definition.   During this phase, the project manager, a client, and the software architect are involved. The project manager can be one of the interested people from the concept phase or, as it is quite common, brought in from the outside at the beginning of this phase. The project definition phase includes the following activities:

- **Problem definition.** During this activity, the client and the project manager define the scope of the system in terms of functionality, constraints, and deliverables. The client and the project manager also agree on acceptance criteria and target dates. The resulting document, called the **problem statement**, serves as the starting point of the Requirements Analysis Document (RAD), which is developed during the steady state phase.

- **Initial Software Project Management Plan (SPMP).** During this activity, the project manager provides an overview of the project, a description of the results to be produced, a work breakdown structure, roles and responsibilities, a project schedule, budgets for required resources, and a description of how risks will be identified and managed.

- **Initial software architecture**. This activity is performed in parallel to the development of the SPMP. The focus is on the software architecture, in particular on the decomposition of the system into subsystems. The software architecture is crucial for managing the project, because it also serves as the basis for the initial team organization. It therefore requires a close interaction between the software architect and the project manager. The software architect revises the subsystem decomposition during the steady state phase. The initial software architecture document will expand into the System Design Document (SDD).

- **Project Agreement definition**. The client and the project manager formally agree on the scope of the system and the delivery date as baselined in the *Project Agreement* document.

Project start.   During this phase, the project manager sets up the project infrastructure, hires participants, organizes them in teams, and kicks off the project. Project start includes the following activities:

- **Infrastructure set-up.** In project-based organizations, it cannot be assumed that the infrastructure exists. The project manager must therefore define the requirements for the infrastructure of the project. These requirements address the communication channels for project participants like bulletin boards, web sites, and meeting management procedures, tools for configuration management, building and testing environments and workflows for the authoring and reviews of documents. The project manager can then give this infrastructure specification to an infrastructure team, which will set up this infrastructure and maintain it throughout the project.[1]

- **Skill identification**. During this activity, the project manager identifies the skills and interests of the developers and records them in a skills matrix.
- **Team assembly**. The project manager uses the skill matrix to assign the participants to teams for each subsystem defined in the initial software architecture document, defines cross-functional teams, and selects team leaders. The project manager and the team leaders together then assign roles and responsibilities to participants. When skills and roles do not match, the project manager identifies additional training needs and tutorials for the team members during this phase. Finally, the project manager assigns work packages to the teams.
- **Project kick-off.** The project manager, the team leaders, and the client officially start the project in a kick-off meeting with all developers being present. The purpose of the kick-off meeting is to share with all the project participants the scope of the project, the communication infrastructure, and the responsibilities of each team. After project kick-off, the project enters steady state.

Project steady state.   During project definition and project start, most decisions are made by the project manager. During the steady state, team leaders are taking over some management functions. In particular, they are responsible for tracking the status of their team and identifying problems in team meetings. Team leaders report the status of their team to the project manager, who then evaluates the status of the complete project. Team leaders respond to deviations from the plan by reallocating tasks to developers or obtaining additional resources from the project manager. The project manager is responsible for the interaction with the client, obtaining formal agreements and renegotiating resources and deadlines. Steady state project management includes the following activities:

- **Project scope definition**. Once the analysis model is stable, the client and the project manager formally agree on the functional and nonfunctional requirements of the system, which might lead to an update in the *Project Agreement* document.
- **Controlling**. Throughout the remaining project phases, team leaders and the project manager monitor status in a weekly meeting and compare it with the planned schedule from the SPMP. The team leaders are responsible for collecting status information through meetings, reviews, problem reports, and work product completion. They are also responsible to report status to the project manager.

---

1. Depending on the size and complexity of the project, financial and personal management systems are set up as well. These systems are not covered in this book.

- **Risk management**. During this activity, project participants identify additional potential problems that could cause delays in the schedule and budget overruns. The project manager and the team leaders identify, analyze, and prioritize risks, and prepare contingency plans.

- **Project replanning**. Whenever the project deviates from the schedule or when a contingency plan is activated, the project manager needs to revise the schedule and reallocates resources to meet the delivery deadline. The project manager can hire new staff, create new teams, or merge existing teams. Project replanning can also be triggered when the client changes the requirements.

Project termination. During this phase, the project outcome is delivered to the customer and the project history is collected. Most of the developers' involvement with the project ends just before this phase when they clean up models and code and complete the documentation. A handful of key developers, the technical writers, and the team leaders are involved with wrapping up the system for installation and acceptance and collecting the project history for future use.

- **Delivery**. This activity consists of two subactivities, the client acceptance test and installation, usually in that order.

  - **Client acceptance test**. The software system is evaluated with the client according to the acceptance criteria set forth in the Project Agreement. Functional and nonfunctional requirements are demonstrated and tested using scenarios defined in the Project Agreement. The client formally accepts the product at this stage.

  - **Installation**. The system is deployed in the target environment and documents are delivered. The installation may include user training and a roll-out phase, during which data is migrated from the previous system to the new system.

- **Postmortem**. The project manager and the team leaders collect the history of the project to allow the organization to learn from it. By capturing the history of major and minor failures and by analyzing their causes, an organization can avoid repeating mistakes and improve its practice.

Each of the states allows significant parallelism of the project management activities. This is modeled in the activity diagram in Figure 14-2. In the following we describe these activities in more detail. In the next section we describe project management models used for the various project phases, in particular for the work to be performed, schedules, and team-based organizations. We also describe how to document these models in a software project management plan.

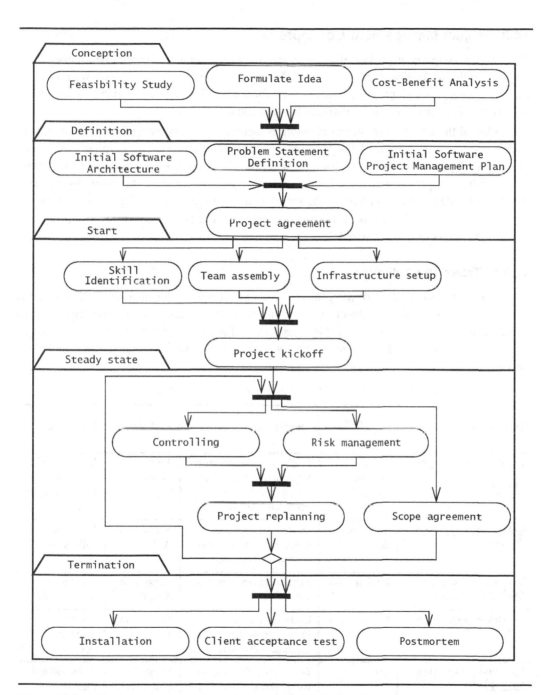

Figure 14-2 Management activities in a software project (UML activity diagram).

14.3 Project Management Concepts

The basic assumption of project planning is that the project outcome cannot be produced in a single monolithic activity. If this could be done, we would not need a project, we would just do the work instead of planning it. Because we cannot do this, we use a divide-and-conquer approach to decompose the work into smaller, more doable pieces.

One of the key tasks in project planning is therefore the decomposition of the total work package into smaller tasks. This involves two things: identifying appropriate tasks and identifying dependencies between tasks. We will first talk about tasks and how to identify them. A hierarchical representation of all the tasks in a project is called the **work breakdown structure (WBS)**. We then talk about the representation of the temporal dependencies between tasks, which is called the **task model** or network diagram. The task model is then mapped onto a time line which is the project **schedule**.

14.3.1 Tasks and Activities

A **task** is a well-defined work assignment for a project participant or a team. A task is the smallest unit of work that is subject to project management. A task includes a description and a duration, and is assigned to a role filled by a participant. Tasks consume resources and produce one or more a work products. They often consume work products produced by other tasks. Table 14-1 provides simple examples of tasks.

Table 14-1   Examples of tasks for the realization of the database subsystem.

Task name	Assigned role	Description	Task input	Task output
Database subsystem requirements elicitation	System designer	Elicit requirements from subsystem teams about storage needs, identify persistent objects	Team liaisons	Database API, persistent object analysis model
Database subsystem design	Subsystem design	Design the database subsystem, recommend commercial product	Subsystem API	Database subsystem design
Database subsystem implementation	Implementor	Implements the database subsystem	Subsystem design	Database sub-system code
Database subsystem inspection	Implementor	Conducts a code inspection of the database subsystem	Subsystem source code	List of discovered defects
Database subsystem test plan	Tester	Develops a test suite for the database subsystem	Subsystem source code	Tests and test plan
Database subsystem test	Tester	Executes the test suite for the database subsystem	Subsystem test plan	Test results, list of defects

Related tasks are grouped into activities. **Activities** are larger units of work. Their duration is often the same as a development phase, such as requirements analysis or system design. When activities span the whole duration of a project, they are called *project functions*. Examples of project functions are configuration management and project management itself (Figure 14-3).

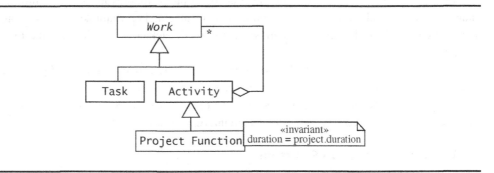

Figure 14-3 Tasks, Activities, and Project Functions (UML class diagram).

14.3.2 Work Products, Work Packages, and Roles

A manager assigns tasks, activities, and project functions to participants or a team, who carry it out, while the manager monitors the progress and completion of the work. In a small project this can be done informally, often with a shake of hands. In larger projects, this must be spelled out more explicitly in form of a **work package** (Figure 14-4). A work package describes the **work products** to be produced, the resources needed to perform the work, the expected duration, dependencies on inputs, which are work products produced by other tasks as well as dependencies on other tasks. It also specifies the acceptance criteria and the name of the responsible individual or organizational unit.

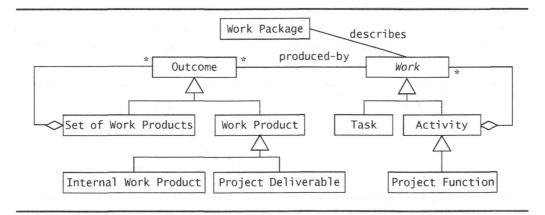

Figure 14-4 Relationship between Outcome, Work, and Work Packages (UML class diagram).

Work packages are important management artifacts, because we assign them to participants to do the work. We can specify a work package right after the tasks have been identified. An example of a small work package is an **action item**, which contains only the name of the participant, the description of the task to be performed, and the time by which it must be completed. Examples of larger work packages are descriptions for creating an object model, a class diagram, source code, a document section, or a document. For example, each section of the requirements analysis document can correspond to a work package specifying who has to write the section and by when.

Any work product to be delivered to the customer is called a **deliverable**. The software system and the accompanying documentation, such as the user manual, are deliverables. All other types of work products consumed only by other project participants are called **internal work products**. For example, action items are internal work products.

14.3.3 Work Breakdown Structure

The hierarchical representation of all the tasks in a project is called the **work breakdown structure (WBS)**. The work breakdown structure is a very simple model of the work to be performed, because it uses only aggregation to model all the identified tasks (see Figure 14-5).

Figure 14-6 depicts a partial work breakdown structure for building a house. The activities on the right can be assigned to different companies. The cost of an aggregate activity (e.g., Build Structure) is computed by aggregating the cost of its children (e.g., Build Foundation, Build Walls, Build Roof). The node at the root of the hierarchy (e.g., Build House) represents all the work that is required to complete the project. Note that a work breakdown structure does not denote the sequencing of activities. For example, in Figure 14-6, Install Sewer Pipes and Build House are accomplished in parallel, even though they are part of different branches of the hierarchy. Temporal dependencies are captured in the task model, which we describe next.

14.3.4 Task Model

Tasks are related by temporal dependencies. An example of a temporal dependency is that the Build Roof task cannot start before the Build Walls task is completed. The set of tasks and their dependencies is called the **task model** or network diagram. Figure 14-7 depicts in UML the task model corresponding to Figure 14-6.

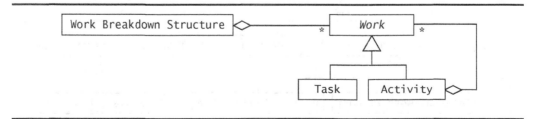

Figure 14-5 The Work Breakdown Structure is the aggregation of all the work to be performed in a project (UML class diagram).

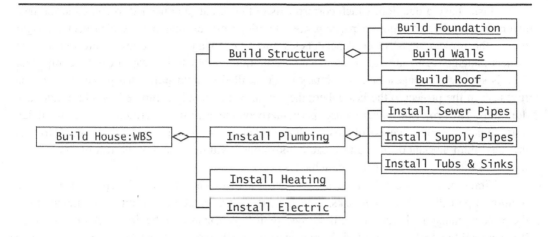

Figure 14-6 Partial work breakdown structure for a house (UML instance diagram).

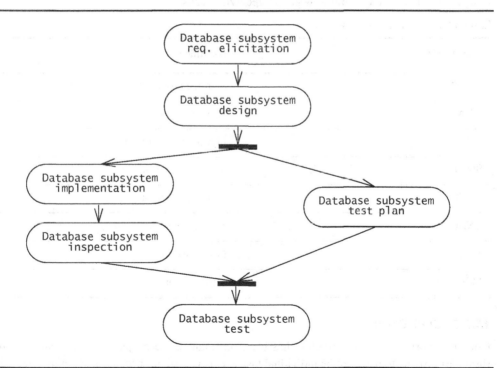

Figure 14-7 An example of a task model with temporal dependencies for the database subsystem example of Table 14-1 (UML activity diagram).

Tasks have a duration, which corresponds to the actual time needed to complete the task given the number of required participants. Durations are estimated by the project manager before the project starts. Once dependencies among tasks and task durations are known, the project manager can compute the shortest possible time in which the project can be completed. This is simply the longest path in the task model, called **critical path**, that proceeds from the first task in the project to the last, where the length of the path is computed by adding the task durations. The project manager focuses particularly on the tasks on the critical path, as any delay in these tasks results in delays of the overall project and missed deadlines. A task's **slack time** is the maximum amount of time a task can be postponed without delaying the rest of the project. By definition, tasks on the critical path have a zero slack time.

Time constraints can be used to specify the start or end of a task independent from the relationship of the task to other tasks. Time constraints are usually the result of an interaction of the project manager with the client. If the system must be finished in the first week of December, it has an MFO constraint. If a task T must start on a Monday, it has an MSO (see Table 14-2) constraint. ASAP is the most commonly used constraint by people ordering tasks; ALAP is the most commonly used constraint by people receiving tasks.

Table 14-2   Time constraints.

Constraint	Definition
ASAP	Start the task as soon as possible
ALAP	As late as possible
FNET	Finish no earlier than
SNET	Start no earlier than
FNLT	Finish no later than
SNLT	Start no later than
MFO	Must finish on
MSO	Must start on

14.3.5 Skill Matrix

Once the work breakdown structure has been formulated, the project manager has to find the right participants to perform the individual tasks. This is difficult because project managers must work with people they may not know well.

Making a special effort to identify skills, knowledge, and interests helps the manager to make more appropriate use of any special talents and improves the morale and productivity of the project team.

A skills matrix is a convenient form of relating the skills, knowledge, and interests of people to the tasks to be performed in the project. The rows of a skill matrix (see Table 14-3) denote the units of work—tasks, activities, and project functions—from the work breakdown structure. The columns denote project participants. An entry in the matrix identifies the skill and knowledge level of the particular participant for the task. We distinguish three types of entries: primary skill, a secondary skill, and an interest. A primary skill or knowledge qualifies a person to lead a unit of work. A secondary skill or knowledge qualifies a person to participate in a task. Interest means the person is interested but has no skill in a task.

Table 14-3   Example of a skill matrix with 4 tasks and 4 participants.

● primary skill   ○ secondary skill   △ interest

Tasks\ Participant	Bill	Mary	Sue	Ed
Control Design			▲	△
Database Design	△	△		●
User Interface Design			○	▲
Configuration Management	○			△

14.3.6 The Software Project Management Plan

The management models described so far are summarized in Figure 14-8. This is a refinement of the model we defined in Chapter 3. We added three composite patterns to generalize the classes WorkProduct, Task, and Participant. We also added the Work Breakdown Structure and the Organization classes, which are usually not visible to the developers.

The project management models are summarized in the Software Project Management Plan (SPMP) [IEEE Std. 1058-1998]. In waterfall projects, this document is created before the project kick-off by the project manager. In architecture-centric projects, it is created after the software architecture is defined. In agile projects, this document is updated after each iteration. Figure 14-9 depicts an example outline for the SPMP.

The audience of the SPMP includes the management and the developers. The SPMP documents all issues related to client requirements (such as deliverables and acceptance criteria), the project goals, the project organization, the division of labor into tasks, and the allocation of resources and responsibilities. The first three sections of the SPMP provide background information for the rest for the document. It briefly describes the project, the client deliverables, the project milestones, and expected document changes. This section contains the hard constraints from the *Project Agreement* that are relevant to the developers.

The fourth section of the SPMP describes the *Project organization*. The section describes the organizational structure of subsystem teams and cross-functional teams. The boundaries of

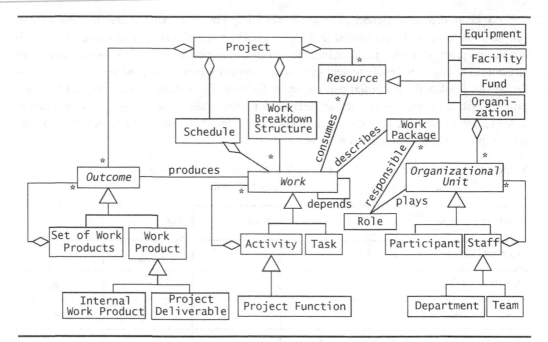

Figure 14-8 Model of a `Project` from a project manager's point of view. This is a refinement of the model used in Chapter 3: we have added three composite patterns to generalize the classes `WorkProduct`, `Task` and `Participant` (UML class diagram).

each team and of the management are defined and responsibilities assigned. Communication roles, such as liaisons, are also described in this section. By reading this section, developers are able to identify the participants in other teams they need to communicate with.

The fifth section of the SPMP, *Managerial process plans*, describes how management deals with project initiation, steady state, and termination, and how it addresses unforeseen problems. Anticipated risks and contingency plans are made public.

The sixth section of the SPMP, *Technical process plans*, describes the technical standards that all teams are required to adopt. These cover the process model, development methodology, the coding guidelines, infrastructure, and the product acceptance plan.

The seventh section of the SPMP, *Supporting process plans,* includes provisions for each of the supporting processes, such as configuration management, verification and validation, documentation, quality assurance, reviews and audits, problem reporting, subcontractor management, and process improvement.

An initial version of the SPMP should be written by the project manager during the project definition phase, and it should be coordinated with its companion document, the initial software architecture document.

We call the software project management plan and the software architecture *initial,* because the documents should not be finalized until the beginning of the project steady state

Software Project Management Plan (SPMP)

1. Overview
    1.1 Project summary
    1.2 Evolution of the plan
2. References
3. Definitions
4. Project organization
    4.1 External interfaces
    4.2 Internal structure
    4.3 Roles and responsibilities
5. Managerial process plans
    5.1 Start-up plan
    5.2 Work plan
    5.3 Control plan
    5.4 Risk management plan
    5.5 Closeout plan
6. Technical process plans
    6.1 Process model
    6.2 Methods, tools, and techniques
    6.3 Infrastructure plan
    6.4 Product acceptance plan
7. Supporting process plans
    7.1 Configuration management plan
    7.2 Verification and validation plan
    7.3 Documentation plan
    7.4 Quality assurance plan
    7.5 Reviews and audits
    7.6 Problem resolution plan
    7.7 Subcontractor management plan
    7.8 Process improvement plan
8. Additional plans

Figure 14-9 An example of a template for the SPMP.

phase. In fact, we recommend a baseline of these documents only after the requirements analysis phase. Only then will all the project participants be able to understand the impact of the requirements on the work.

The completed SPMP document should be reviewed both by management and by developers to ensure that the plans are feasible and realized in the project.

The evolution section of the SPMP provides a history of changes, including the author responsible for the change, date of change, and a brief description of the change. The SPMP should be updated whenever decisions that effect the outcome are made or problems are discovered. In very large-scale projects this project function continues during the duration of the project. In this case updating all aspects of the SPMP is assigned to a separate person employed as a planner.

In smaller projects, the role of the planner is usually played by the project manager. Keeping the SPMP constantly up-to-date might become impossible because of the high workload. In this case, we recommend that the project manager create three versions of the SPMP: an initial version as the basis for project planning, the baselined version after the project agreement is signed, and a final version at the end of the project termination as the basis for the postmortem session.

14.4 Classical Project Management Activities

In this section, we describe the activities of a project manager managing a team-based software project. Omitting the concept phase activities, our focus begins with the project definition phase.

The main activities of the project manager during project definition are to define the organization structure, and to identify work products, tasks, schedule, and roles. Team leaders join the project at the end of the project definition phase and their main effort is spent in monitoring and managing teams during steady state. Team leaders should be aware, however, of the project activities preceding their involvement and of the interaction with the client. We discuss the following management activities:

- *Planning the Project* (Section 14.4.1): defining the problem, identifying the initial task model and organization structure, estimating needed resources such as personnel and funds.

- *Organizing the Project* (Section 14.4.2): hiring participants, skill identification, mapping roles and responsibilities to participants, and organizing tutorials and the project kick-off meeting.

- *Controlling the Project* (Section 14.4.3): project monitoring, risk management, and the project agreement.

- *Terminating the Project* (Section 14.4.4): the client acceptance test, installation, and project postmortem.

In this section, we focus on classical projects, in which the scope of the product is relatively well defined at the beginning of the project and the goal of the project is to deliver within a specific deadline and budget. In Section 14.5, we revisit these activities for an agile project, in which the scope and requirements of the product are defined as the project progresses, and the product is delivered in increments.

14.4.1 Planning the Project

Project planning focuses on the definition phase—the definition of the problem, planning a solution, and estimating resources— and results in the following work products (Figure 14-10):

- The **problem statement** is a short document describing the problem the system should address, the target environment, client deliverables, and acceptance criteria. The problem statement is an initial description and is the seed for the *Project Agreement*, formalizing the common understanding of the project by the client and management, and for the *Requirements Analysis Document* (RAD), a precise description of the system under development.

- The **top-level design** represents the initial decomposition of the system into subsystems. It is used to assign subsystems to individual teams. The top-level design will be the seed for the *System Design Document* (SDD), a precise description of the software architecture.

- The **Software Project Management Plan (SPMP)** describes all the managerial aspects of the project, in particular the work breakdown structure, the schedule, organization, work packages, and budget.

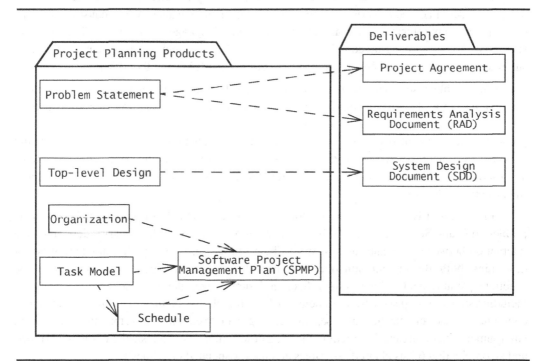

Figure 14-10   Work products generated during project planning and their relationship with typical project deliverables (UML class diagram).

Moving the design of the software architecture to the beginning is called *architecture-centric* project management. Designing the top-level design and the SPMP in parallel is highly desirable. However, pushing the design of the subsystem decomposition into the project organization phase is a deviation from long-standard software project management practices. In university environments and in small company projects, the software project manager and software architect roles are often assumed by the same person. Because the work load is high, this requires a technically competent and highly motivated manager. In large projects the roles should be assumed by different people. The software architect and project manager should work closely together as a decision-making team, dividing responsibilities between management and technical decisions [Paulish, 2001].

Developing the problem statement

The *Problem Statement* is developed by the project manager and the client as a mutual understanding of the problem to be addressed by the system. The problem statement describes the current situation, the functionality it should support, and environment in which the system will be deployed. It also defines the deliverables expected by the client, together with delivery dates and a set of acceptance criteria. The problem statement may also specify constraints on the development environment, such as the programming language to be used. The problem statement is not a precise or complete specification of the system. Instead, it is a high-level summary of two project documents yet to be developed, the RAD and the SPMP.

The problem statement is developed iteratively by the project manager and the client. Developing the problem statement is both a negotiation activity and an information-gathering activity during which each party learns the expectations and constraints of the other. The problem statement contains a high-level description of the functionality of the system. It should also provide concrete examples to ensure that both parties are sharing the same vision. Scenarios are used for describing both the current situation and the future situation (see Chapter 4, *Requirements Elicitation*).

Figure 14-11 is an example outline for a problem statement. The first section describes the problem domain. Section 2 of the problem statement provides example scenarios describing the interaction between users and the system for the essential functionality. Scenarios are used for describing both the current situation and the future situation. Section 3 summarizes the functional requirements of the system. Section 4 summarizes the nonfunctional requirements including constraints placed by the client, such as the choice of the programming language, component reuse, or selection of a separate testing team. Section 5 describes the deployment environment, including platform requirements, a description of the physical environment, users, and so on. Section 6 lists client deliverables and their associated deadlines.

Defining the top-level design

The top-level design describes the software architecture of the system. The top-level design should be done by the software architect. A project manager assuming the role of the software architect must have enough technical expertise to accomplish this.

PROBLEM STATEMENT

1. Problem domain
2. Scenarios
3. Functional requirements
4. Nonfunctional requirements
5. Target environment
6. Deliverables & deadlines

Figure 14-11   Outline of problem statement document. Note that the sections 2, 3, and 4 are not a complete or precise specification of the system. They provide the basis for requirements elicitation. Section 6, however, describes contractual deliverables and their associated due dates.

The subsystem decomposition should be high level, focusing on functionality. It should be kept constant until the analysis phase produces a stable system model. The subsystem decomposition can and should be revisited during subsystem design, and new subsystems are usually created during the system design phase. In this case the organization might have to be changed to reflect the new design. The software architect identifies the major subsystems and their services, but does not yet define their interfaces at this point. The subsystem decomposition is refined and modified later during system design (see Chapter 6, *System Design: Decomposing the System*).

Later, during the project start phase, the subsystem decomposition serves as the basis of the organizational units. Each subsystem is assigned to a team that is responsible for its definition and realization. Teams who work on dependent subsystems will negotiate individual services and their interfaces as these become necessary.

Identifying the work breakdown structure

There are several different approaches to developing the work breakdown structure (WBS) for a project. The most commonly used approach is functional decomposition based on the software process. For example, the work breakdown structure in Table 14-4 is based on a functional breakdown of the work to be performed.

A functional decomposition based on the functions of the product itself can also be used to define the tasks. This is often used in a high-risk projects where the system functionality is released incrementally in a set of prototypes. For example, if a software system provides three main functions, a system function–oriented work breakdown structure could consist of tasks that build and deliver these system functions in a series of three prototypes.

An object-oriented work breakdown structure is also possible. For example, if a product consists of five components, an object-oriented WBS would include five tasks associated with the construction of each of these components. Specifying the development of these subsystems of the software architecture as tasks comes quite naturally in object-oriented software projects.

Table 14-4 Example of functional work breakdown structure for a simple ATM.

Use case	Work breakdown structure

Authenticate	1. Realize authentication use case
	    1.1. Develop user interface forms (Login, change PIN)
	    1.2. Realize authentication protocol with server
	    1.3. Develop initial account creation

Withdraw Money	2. Develop money withdrawal use case
	    2.1. Develop user interface forms (Select Account,
	          Specify Amount)
	    2.2. Realize communication with server
	    2.3. Develop business logic for approving withdrawal
	    2.4. Develop interface with cash distributor

Deposit Check	3. Develop deposit check use case
	    3.1. Develop user interface forms (Specify Check, Insert Check)
	    3.2. Realize communication with server
	    3.3. Develop business logic for recording the deposit
	    3.4. Develop interface with label printer

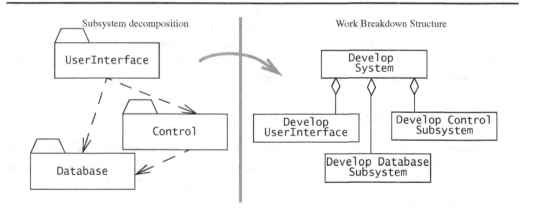

Figure 14-12 An example of an object-oriented work breakdown structure where the subsystem decomposition is used to identify high-level activities and tasks (UML object diagram).

Figure 14-12 shows such a work breakdown structure for a system consisting of three subsystems.

Another decomposition is based on geographical areas. If the project has developer teams in different geographical regions, the tasks might be identified for each of these regions. Another

WBS is based on organizational units. These can be the organizational units of the company (marketing, operations, and sales) or they can be based on the people in the project.

No matter what approach is used, the ultimate goal is to decompose the total work into tasks that are small enough to be doable, whose duration can easily be estimated, and that can be assigned to a single person.[2]

When creating a work breakdown structure, the following heuristics are quite useful for the project manager:

- *Reuse an existing WBS.* Consult people who have worked on similar projects. Incorporate the information into the work breakdown structure.

- *Involve key developers.* Developers with knowledge about the solution domain should participate in the development of the work breakdown structure. If they join the project after the work breakdown structure is developed, they should be able to review and critique it before they begin to work on their assigned tasks.

- *Identify work gaps.* All work to be performed in the project must be mapped onto tasks. Work that is associated with an activity must eventually be addressed by at least one task. If new work appears, an activity should be found or newly defined that includes this task.

- *Identify work overlaps.* The same task should not be included in more than one activity. For example, the project manager should not let the developers do subsystem testing, if all subsystems tests are performed by a separate testing team.

Creating the initial schedule

After the temporal dependencies are established in the task model, we can create a schedule. This requires the estimation of durations for each of the tasks. Estimating task durations is quite difficult. Estimated times can of course be based on prior experience of the manager or the estimator, but they often do not give the needed precision. It is impossible to come up with a precise model for the complete project. One solution is to start with an initial schedule representing deadlines mutually agreed by the client and the project manager. These dates are generous enough that, even in the event of change, they can still be met.

Initially, the project manager should create a schedule that is detailed enough for the first weeks of the project, showing events for the project kick-off meetings, the initial team meetings, and tutorials. The rest of the project schedule should not be more detailed than the schedule in the problem statement. The initial version of the SPMP should be viewed as a proposed version

---

2. There are things you have to do in a project such as coming to work, eating food, etc., which are usually not considered tasks. That is, the project participant is not responsible to report the status of these things to the project manager or team leader. Managers who try to turn these things into tasks as well are often called "micro-managers" because they get too involved and manage low-level details.

to be reviewed by the software architecture and subsystem teams before it can be considered binding for all project participants.

The individual teams should start working on a revision of the initial version of the subsystem decomposition right after the initial team meeting, focusing on their subsystem and work breakdown structure for the development of the subsystem.

This planning activity has to be done by the team in parallel with ongoing requirements analysis and system design activities. The newly found tasks should be presented during a formal planning review scheduled during or near the end of the analysis phase. The result of the planning review should be a revised work breakdown structure and software architecture. This revision, in turn, is the basis for the second version of the SPMP, which should be baselined and used as the basis for the project agreement with the client.

Scheduling requires a continuing trade-off between resources, time, and implemented functionality and should be done regularly by the project manager. However, creating and updating schedules are complicated activities, especially when people have to juggle between commitments on more than one project. Resolving overloaded resources is a topic that is beyond the scope of this book.

14.4.2 Organizing the Project

During project start, project management assembles the teams according to the top-level design described in the software architecture, sets up the communication infrastructure, and then kicks off the project by organizing the first two meetings. Once all participants are assigned tasks and status reporting mechanisms are in place, the project is considered to be in steady state.

Project start activities are crucial for project-based organizations and are usually performed under time pressure. The main problem is that the project members don't yet know each other. They have not yet had time to discover their different personalities and different working styles. Getting to know the diversity of the responsibilities within the project is another issue that needs to be addressed by the project manager.

Setting up the communication infrastructure

Clear and accurate communication is critical for the success of a development project. Moreover, communication becomes crucial when the number of project participants increases. Consequently, setting up the communication infrastructure for a project must occur as early as possible. The project manager needs to address the following modes of communication:

- *Scheduled modes of communication.* These include planned milestones, such as client and project reviews, team status meetings, inspections, and so on. Scheduled modes of communication are the formal means through which project participants gather and share information. These are best supported by synchronous or face-to-face communication, such as meetings, formal presentations, video conferences, and telephone conference calls. The manager schedules dates and designates facilitators for each of these interactions.

- *Event-based modes of communication.* These include problem reports, change requests, issue discussion, and resolution. Event-based modes usually arise from unforeseen problems and crises. Asynchronous mechanisms such as E-mail, groupware, and problem databases need to be set up early, and participants need to be trained to use them. When the number of participants is large, centralized infrastructures, such as Web sites and bulletin boards, are preferable as they make information visible to more people than E-mail or bilateral conversations.

Identifying skills

Once the initial work breakdown structure and task models have been created, the project manager knows the type of skills required for each task. For example, tasks related to requirements elicitation require application domain knowledge. Tasks that involve discussions with the client require effective communication skills. Tasks related to testing require attention to detail and quality-oriented thinking. In general, a software engineering development project requires a variety of skills:

- *Application domain skills.* These include knowledge of the application domain, such as banking terms and procedures and credit rating formulae in the context of banking applications.
- *Communication skills.* These include the ability to communicate with stakeholders who are not familiar with software development or with the application domain, the ability to summarize and present complex ideas, and the ability to negotiate and achieve consensus.
- *Technical skills.* These include knowledge of specific technology used in the project, such as programming skills or knowledge of a specific component, the ability to assess risks and bottlenecks in a software design, and the ability to find workarounds to unexpected problems.
- *Quality skills.* These include attention to detail, the ability to identify boundary cases and generate the corresponding test cases, and the ability follow procedures.
- *Management skills.* These include the ability to assess personal skills, motivate, provide feedback, and assess project-level risks.

The task of the project manager, when organizing the project, is to identify individuals with the right combination of skills for each task using a skill matrix (see Section 14.3.5). The rows of the skill matrix come from the required skills for each tasks. The columns come from the pool of available staff. In project-based organizations, the skills of each individual are recorded in a profile, as the individual gains experience through projects and attends specific courses. For resources hired from outside the organization (e.g., freelancers), a profile can be reconstituted from a combination of self-assessment (e.g., the individual's resume) and from the organization's own assessment (e.g., interviews, tests). The set of profiles available to an organization represents the competence of the organization.

Assigning management roles

Management roles are assigned to individual participants. A role such as team leader cannot be filled effectively if is shared. First, a team leader fills a communication function by acting as a liaison between higher-level management and developers and thus must be able to communicate a consistent picture of status back and forth. Second, although a team leader usually seeks the consensus of developers, he or she occasionally has to impose time-critical decisions. Other management roles, such as liaisons between teams, also require the same degree of consistency and thus are assigned to a single individual.

A good project manager seeks three skills in a participant when assigning management roles: the ability to communicate, the ability to recognize risks early, and the discipline to separate management decisions from technical ones. Such skills often come from experience in previous projects. Having experience with teams is an important prerequisite for a team leader.

Assigning technical roles

In projects with small resources, the role of the software architect is often assumed by the project manager. The advantage is a tight coordination of managerial and high-level technical activities. The disadvantage is the additional time required by the project manager, which often leads to task overload. The two roles should be assigned to different people.

Technical roles can be assigned to a team of participants. Complex software projects, for example, can have a separate testing team composed of only testers. Once the project manager has defined the responsibilities of the teams, it is the task of the team leader to assign individual tasks to each team member based on availability or skill. Technical roles do not require the same level of consistency as management roles do, given that their tasks are better defined and that they rely on management and liaisons for coordination.

Dealing with skill shortages

In general, there are rarely sufficient skills for a given project (that is, not all rows in the matrix can be assigned to a column), in part because of the rapid evolution of technology. The project manager generates a training plan when skills are missing. This can include in-house training, courses by vendors, and on-the-job training. Formal training can become expensive for an organization, so in practice, much training happens on the job. The project manager should distribute new or inexperienced staff across the project such that each team has at least one experienced developer. Experienced developers provide technical leadership and can often serve as mentors for the unexperienced developers who then gain experience more quickly. For example, peer-programming techniques in which two developers share a computer and collaborate on a single development task are advocated in the extreme programming life cycle process (see Chapter 15, *Software Life Cycle*) as a means to disseminate skills through the organization with minimal formal training.

Formal training and learning by practice is a trade-off the project manager evaluates within the given project time constraints. Formal training enables developers to become more productive earlier; however, it is expensive and constitutes a longer-term investment benefiting future projects.

Selecting team sizes

Although technical roles can be assigned to teams, the size of a single team is constrained by management and communication overhead. When there are more participants on a team, then the communication overhead is higher and team effectiveness is lower. The observations below are adapted from [Kayser, 1990], who originally applied these heuristics to the formation of subgroups during meetings. Given that team meetings are a significant tool for collecting status, negotiation, and decision making, constraints on the number of participants in meetings are the upper limits on the team size:

- *Three members.* During meetings, every member has a chance to speak. Issues are discussed thoroughly and resolved easily. A possible problem with this team size is that one member can dominate the other two. Also, small teams suffer from the cumulation of multiple roles for each participant ("too many hats" syndrome).

- *Four members.* Starting with teams of this size allows the team to continue to function even if a participant drops out. Reaching consensus with a team of even numbers can be problematic since there can be a tie when voting. As a result, resolving issues can take a relatively long time.

- *Five and six members.* This is the ideal size for a software development team. Members can still meet face to face. Diverse perspectives, supported by a mix of ideas, opinions, and attitudes, promotes creative thinking. Single roles can be assigned to each member, creating a mini-organization in which each member complements the others.

- *Seven members.* This is still a relatively effective team size, but team meetings tend to become long. Reviewing the status requires more than half an hour. If teams of seven are necessary, it is advisable to form subteams during the formal team meetings, each having the task to discuss and resolve a subset of the open issues from the agenda.

- *Eight and more members.* Teams of this size become difficult to manage. The internal structure often starts to break down into subteams. Coalitions and side conversations often occur during formal meetings. Members have more opportunities to compete than to cooperate. Although results are usually satisfactory, the time to reach these results is longer than with a team of smaller size.

Assembling the teams

The next step in the project organization phase is to assemble the teams who will produce the deliverables. The project manager selects the team leaders before the teams are formed. In addition to being capable of understanding the team status, the team leader needs to be able to communicate effectively, recognize pending crises (technical or social), and make trade-offs taking into account project level concerns.

The project start phase is an ideal time for training team leaders and familiarizing them with project procedures and ground rules. The team leader role is distinct from the role of technical leader. The technical leader, usually the liaison to the architecture team, interacts with the chief architect and the architecture liaisons from the other teams and has final say on the technical decisions within the team. The role of architecture liaison requires excellent technical skill and development experience.

In a training context, such as a university project course or an industrial pilot project exploring a new software method, the team leader can be split into two roles. A coach trains, explains, advises the team and acts as a liaison to the project manager. A team leader trainee fills all other responsibilities of the team leader, including facilitating status meetings and assigning tasks. In a university project course, this role can be filled by the instructor or an experienced teaching assistant, whereas the architecture liaison can be filled by a student. In a development project at a company, the team leader is filled by a developer who has experience and knowledge with the organization's management procedures, whereas the architecture liaison is filled by a developer who has strong technical skills.

Developers who will work for the project can be assigned to the project all at once (**flat staffing**), or the project can be gradually ramped up by hiring people as needed (**gradual staffing**). On the one hand, gradual staffing is motivated by saving resources in the early part of the project. Requirements elicitation and analysis do not require as many people as coding and testing. Moreover, analyst and implementor are roles requiring different skills and thus should be assigned to different people. On the other hand, flat staffing has the advantage of establishing teams early and the social environment necessary for spontaneous communication. Some of the developers can be assigned to the analysis activities with the analysts, and the others may already start other activities such as setting up the configuration management environment, technology survey and evaluation, and training. With shorter projects and market deadlines, flat staffing is becoming the preferred staffing scheme. The dilemma between gradual staffing and flat staffing has been discussed in length by Brooks [Brooks, 1995].

Kick-off meeting

The project manager, the team leaders, and the client officially start the project in a kick-off meeting with all developers present. The purpose of kick-off meetings is to share information with all the project participants about the scope of the project, the communication infrastructure, and the responsibilities of each team. The presentation should be split between client and project manager. The client presents the requirements and the scope of the project. The project manager presents the project infrastructure, top-level design and team responsibilities.

Agreeing on project scope

This document formally defines the scope, duration, cost, and deliverables for the project. The *Project Agreement* can be in the form of a contract, a statement of work, a business plan, or a project charter. The *Project Agreement* is typically finalized after the analysis model is stabilized and the planning of the rest of the project is underway.

A *Project Agreement* should contain at least the following:

- list of deliverable documents
- criteria for demonstrations of functional requirements
- criteria for demonstrations of nonfunctional requirements, including accuracy, reliability, response time, and security
- criteria for acceptance.

The *Project Agreement* represents the baseline of the client acceptance test. Any change in the functionality to be delivered, the nonfunctional requirements, the deadlines, or the budget of the project requires the renegotiation of the *Project Agreement*.

After the completion of the project kick-off and agreement in the project scope, the project enters steady state.

14.4.3 Controlling the Project

To make effective decisions in the steady state phase of the project, the project manager needs accurate status information. Unfortunately, collecting accurate status information is difficult. While a complex system is difficult to understand in itself, the status of its components and its impact on future deliveries are even more difficult to understand. Developers will not report to their team leader any problem they believe they can address in time. However, small departures from the schedule, not worth reporting independently, aggregate and degenerate into large departures much later in the schedule. By the time team leaders discover and report a major problem to the project manager, it has already caused a substantial delay in the project.

Several tools are available to collect status information. Because none of them are accurate or reliable alone, team leaders and project managers need to use a combination of these. Below we review their advantages and disadvantages.

Meetings

- *Periodic status meetings*. Status meetings conducted at the team level have the best potential for reporting status and information required for corrective decisions. Status meetings, however, can also provide inaccurate status information if team members do not cooperate. Participants are naturally reluctant to report problems or mistakes. They cooperate only if they can trust a manager not to step into problems that they can resolve themselves. Managers need to make problem reporting beneficial to developers by intervening only when necessary.

- *Sharp milestones.* Progress can be measured by determining if developers deliver work products on time. Managers can increase the accuracy of this method by defining sharp milestones such that they can be accurately monitored. For example, the "coding completed" milestone is not a sharp milestone, because it does not take into account the quality of the code delivered. The code could contain few or many defects and the milestone would be considered completed in either case. Conversely, defining a milestone as the completion of the test, demonstration, documentation, and integration of a specific feature yields better status information. When defining and monitoring sharp milestones, managers do not need the cooperation of developers.

- *Project reviews.* A project review is a means for all participants to exchange status and plan information about all the teams with formal presentation. Project reviews suffer from similar problems as status meetings. If participants are already reluctant to admit problems in front of their team leader, they definitively will not admit problems in a public forum.

- *Code inspections.* Formal peer review of code is an effective method for discovering defects early. When performed frequently, results can also be used as an indication of progress.

- *Prototype demonstrations.* Prototype demonstrations are partial implementations of the system for evaluating technology or functionality. They usually do not illustrate how borderline cases are dealt with or how robust the implementation is. They are good for measuring initial progress, but are not sharp measures of completion.

Metrics

It is difficult to manage the evolution of a product without objective measures. Although meetings and inspections help assess the status of a project, they rely on the perception of selected participants and their willingness to communicate what they know. The optimism of a single participant can lead to the belief that the project has progressed much further than it has. Software metrics are quantitative measures of selected aspects of the process or the system. Instrumenting the process and the evolving system with automated metrics attempts to provide a tool for measuring progress objectively.

Many software metrics have been proposed, such as the number of lines of source code, the number of branching points [McCabe, 1976], the number of variables and operators [Halstead, 1977], and the number of functional requirements [Albrecht & Gaffney, 1983]. Using software metrics as a management tool has been difficult, as many work products are not software items, and the values and trends observed require much interpretation from the manager. Many project or product parameters have a potential impact on the metric being measured. For example, if the size of a subsystem in lines of source code increases rapidly, maybe the developers assigned to the subsystem are productive, or they maybe are duplicating code. With iterative and architecture-centric approaches, however, software components to test and measure become available much earlier. Moreover, metrics can also measure attributes of the process, such as deviations with the schedule, resources expended, and number of participants leaving prematurely.

- *Measuring financial status*. Comparing planned costs against actual costs in the context of actual progress enables a manager to assess the financial health of the project. Software development projects are labor intensive; consequently, most of the cost associated with the project is staffing. The planned staffing profile of the project over time provides a cost baseline against which to compare actual costs. In addition, the task model and the schedule provides us with the estimated effort and the deadline for each task. An earned value assessment enables us to assess both the cost and schedule situation of a project using one chart. For example, in Figure 14-13, the thin line depicts the planned costs of the project over time. A project that is on budget and on schedule would follow the same line very closely. The thick line represents the actual costs of the project over time. In the example of Figure 14-13, we actually spent less than planned. However, if we only looked at these two curves, we would not be able to assess whether or not the project is in a good financial state. The project could be under cost because we accomplished the planned work for less money, or because we did not accomplish as much as planned. Consequently, we plot a third curve, the earned value, which represents the value of the work we completed so far. The earned value is measured by adding the planned costs of the tasks that have been completed. In this example, the earned value is between the actual cost and the planned cost, indicating that the project is under budget and late. If the earned value had been above the planned costs, the project would have been under budget and early.

- *Measuring technical progress*. While measuring financial status is well understood in software engineering and in project management in general, software development projects introduce a special challenge when determining what tasks have actually been accomplished. Measuring technical progress requires size metrics for each team. For the development team, this can include the number of lines of source code under baseline or the number of closed change requests. For the testing team, this can include the number of defects found or the number of open change requests. For the architecture team, it might be the number of critical use cases that have been demonstrated. Size metrics, however, must be viewed in combination with quality metrics to ensure that participants are not locally optimizing their numbers. For example, change requests should be considered closed only after all regression tests related to the change do not discover new defects.

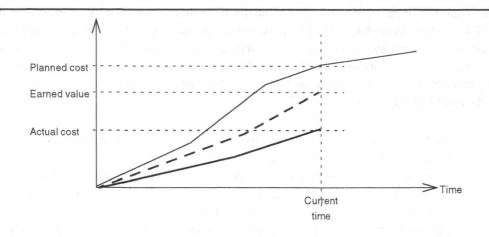

Figure 14-13 Assessing the financial status of a project using earned value. An earned value above actual costs indicates that more work was accomplished for the same a mount of money (i.e., the project is under budget). An earned value below planned costs indicates that not as much work was completed as planned (i.e., the project is late).

- *Measuring stability.* Once an initial version of the system is baselined, change requests are issued to control and track changes to the baseline. Measuring the rate of new change requests corresponding to defects in the system indicates how stable the system becomes over time. Measuring the rate of change requests to the requirements similarly indicates how stable the requirements have become in the view of the client. If work completion indicates that the project is almost finished but the rate of change requests is still high, the project may not be achieving its target quality goals.

- *Measuring modularity.* Breakage is a measure of the impact of a change on the baseline (which can be measured in terms of lines of code, number of files, function points, or any size metric that is appropriate in the context of the project). It is expected that early changes affect more source code than later ones, as the architecture should become more modular over the project time. Measuring breakage can encourage this trend and make visible early any architectural issues (e.g., identifying specific types of changes that yield high breakage). Increasing breakage indicates a degrading modularity over the lifetime of the project, probably resulting from an inadequate architecture or specific nonfunctional requirements that are difficult to meet.

- *Measuring maturity.* Mean time between failures measures the time between discovered defects during testing. As the project nears delivery, the number of discovered defects should decrease, indicating an increasing maturity of the product. A decreasing maturity can indicate that developers are under pressure to address open change requests and do not pay sufficient attention to quality. Decreasing maturity can also result from a lack of stability (see *measuring stability*, above).

Finally, independently of the methods used for determining status, the project manager, the team leaders, and the developers need to communicate status information in understandable terms. Next, we describe risk management as a method for controlling projects, communicating potential problems, and planning contingencies.

Managing risk

The focus of risk management is to identify possible problems in the project and address them before they can significantly affect the delivery date or the budget. The key element of risk management is to set up the appropriate information flows such that risks and problems are accurately reported in a timely manner. Many projects fail either because simple problems were reported too late or because the wrong problem was addressed. In this section, we focus on the activities of risk management for identifying, analyzing, and addressing risks. For more details on risk management in software engineering, we refer the reader to the specialized literature (e.g., [Boehm, 1991] and [Charette, 1989]).

The first step of risk management is to identify risks. Risks are potential problems that result from an area of uncertainty. Risks can be managerial or technical. Managerial risks include any uncertainty related to the organization, work products, roles, or task plan. Technical risks include any uncertainty related to the system models, including changes of the functionality of the system, the nonfunctional requirements, the architecture, or the implementation of the system. In particular, technical risks include defects discovered late in the development. Table 14-5 depicts examples of risks in a software project.

Table 14-5   Examples of risks identified in the OWL project.

Risk	Risk type
Behavior of a commercial off-the-shelf (COTS) component does not comply with published standard.	Technical
COTS components delivery date is later than planned.	Managerial
Users are not willing to use chosen user interface to interact with system.	Technical
Selected middleware is too slow to meet performance requirement for data logging.	Technical
Development of subsystems takes more time than scheduled.	Managerial

Developers are often aware of the risks applicable to their tasks. The challenge is to encourage developers to report risks so they can be managed. This entails rewarding developers for reporting risks and problems and making the risk management activities directly beneficial to developers. Spontaneous risk reporting is usually not sufficient. Project participants, including the client, the developers, and the managers, are usually reluctant to communicate potential failures or shortcomings and are too optimistic about their outcome. A more systematic approach to risk identification is to interview the project participants using a structured questionnaire. Participants are asked in group sessions to list the risks they anticipate with respect to specific tasks. Figure 14-14 depicts example questions from the Taxonomy-Based Risk Identification process [Carr et al., 1993]. In this example, the interviewer attempts to determine if there are any risks related to nonfunctional requirements. Depending on the answer to the first question, the interviewer can ask follow-up questions to make sure no other related risks are present. The rationale behind this questionnaire is to cover all the areas of development in which risks are typically found.

---

1. Requirements

    . . .

    d. Performance

    . . .

        [23] Has a performance analysis been done?
            (Yes) (23.a) What is your level of confidence in the performance analysis?
            (Yes) (23.b) Do you have a model to track performance through design and implementation?

Figure 14-14 Questions for eliciting performance risks in the Taxonomy-Based Risk Identification process. If the question to question 23 is positive, questions 23.a and 23.b are asked of the developers [Carr et al., 1993].

Systematic risk identification produces a large number of managerial and technical risks, some of them critical, others unimportant. Prioritizing risks allows managers to focus on the critical risks. Risks are characterized by the likelihood they can become problems and by their potential impact to the project when they become problems. By using these two attributes, risks can be assigned to one of four categories:

- likely, high potential impact
- unlikely, high potential impact
- likely, low potential impact
- unlikely, low potential impact.

Managers should worry about the risks of the first category: likely, high potential impact. For these risks, developers and managers should draw contingency plans and monitor the risk carefully. If the likelihood of the risk increases, managers can activate the contingency plan and address the problem in time. Moreover, managers should monitor the risks of the second category: unlikely, high potential impact. Contingency plans do not need to be drawn for them unless their likelihood increases. Finally, the risks in the third and fourth categories can be ignored unless sufficient resources are available for monitoring them. Table 14-6 orders the risks presented in Table 14-5.

Table 14-6 Prioritized risks for a project.

Risk	Likelihood	Potential impact
Behavior of a COTS component does not comply with published standard.	Not likely	High
New COTS component delivery date is later than planned.	Likely	High
Users are not willing to use user interface.	Likely for users spending less than 2 hours per day in front of a computer	High
Selected middleware is too slow to meet performance requirement for data logging.	Not likely, low sampling frequency	High
Development of components takes more time than scheduled.	Likely, first occurrence	High

Once risks have been identified and prioritized, mitigation strategies should be designed for the critical risks. Mitigation strategies can include lowering the likelihood of the risk or decreasing its potential impact. Risks are usually caused by an area of uncertainty, such as missing information or lack of confidence in some information. Developers decrease the likelihood of a risk by further investigating the causes of the risk, by changing suppliers or components, or by selecting a redundant supplier or component. Similarly, developers reduce the impact of the risk on the project by developing an alternate or redundant solution. In most cases, however, mitigating a risk incurs additional resources and cost. Table 14-7 describes mitigation strategies for the risks presented in Table 14-5.

Once risks are identified, prioritized, and mitigated, the risk management plan should be communicated to all concerned. Risk management relies on timely communication. Spontaneous and timely reporting of potential problems should be encouraged. Risk management plans and technical documents are communicated using the same channels. Developers and other project participants review risks at the same time they review the technical content of the project. As mentioned earlier, communication is the most significant barrier when dealing with uncertainty.

14.4.4 Terminating the Project

In the project termination phase the project manager prepares for the client acceptance test, manages the system integration, testing, and installation at the client's site. Finally the project manager oversees the project postmortem.

Table 14-7   Mitigation strategies for a project.

Risk	Mitigation strategy
Behavior of a COTS component does not comply with published standard.	• Run benchmarks to identify nonconformance. • Investigate if nonconforming functions can be avoided.
COTS component delivery date later than planned.	• Monitor risk by asking manufacturer for intermediate status reports.
Users are not willing to use user interface.	• Perform usability studies using mock-ups. • Develop alternate interface.
Selected middleware is too slow to meet performance requirement for data logging.	• Monitor risk. Plan for a performance evaluation prototype.
Development of components takes more time than scheduled.	• Increase the priority of this task with respect to other implementation tasks. • Assign key developers to this task.

Accepting the system

The purpose of the client acceptance test is the presentation of the system and the approval of the client according to acceptance criteria set forth in the *Project Agreement*. The result is the formal acceptance (or rejection) of the system by the client. Installation of the system and field tests by the client may already have occurred. The client acceptance test constitutes the visible end of the project.

The client acceptance test is conducted as a series of presentations of functionality and novel features of the system. Important scenarios from the *Problem Statement* are exercised and demonstrated by the developers or by future users. Additional demonstrations focus on the nonfunctional requirements of the system such as accuracy, reliability, response time, or security. If installation and user evaluations occurred prior to the client acceptance test, their results are presented and summarized. Finally, the client acceptance test also serves as a discussion forum for subsequent activities such as maintenance, knowledge transfer, or system enhancement.

Installation

The installation phase of a project includes the field test of the system, the comparison of the system results with the legacy system, the rollout of the legacy system, and the training of users. The installation may be conducted by the supplier, by a contractor, or by the client, depending on the *Project Agreement*.

To minimize risks, installation and field testing are usually done incrementally, with noncritical sites used as a field test environment. When the client is convinced that the disruption to his business will be minimal, the delivered system enters full-scale operation. Replacement systems and upgrades are rarely introduced in a "big-bang" fashion because the largest number of problems are discovered during the first few days of operation.

Postmortem

Every project uncovers new problems, unforeseen events, and unexpected failures. Each project, therefore, constitutes an opportunity for learning and anticipating new risks. Many software companies conduct a postmortem study of each project after its completion. The postmortem includes collecting data about planned vs. actual delivery dates and number of defects discovered, qualitative information about technical and managerial problems encountered, and suggestions for future projects. Although this phase is the least visible in the life cycle, the company depends on it for learning and improving its efficiency.

14.5 Agile Project Management Activities

The project management method described in the previous section evolved out of the management of large complex projects, in which the goal of project management was to develop repeatable and predictable processes as a basis for planning and decision making. While such methods are appropriate for well-defined requirements and mature technology, they lead to organizations that are rigid and slow to respond to unexpected events or ill-defined requirements typical of new product developments.

Agile methods deal better with ill-defined requirements and emerging solution technologies, which are characterized by frequent change. Requirements change as new insights are gained by the client and the users, software architecture changes as new technologies are adopted or discarded, thus straining the classical approaches in which change is controlled or even discouraged. Agile methods attempt to deal with these challenges by focusing on small product increments that are developed in short time bursts. After each product increment, progress is reviewed, lessons are learned, the project organization or goals are adjusted accordingly.

In this section, we describe Scrum [Schwaber & Beedle, 2002], an example of agile project management method, and contrast it with the previous section. Note that many activities described in the previous section, such as skill management, risk management, system installation, are relevant in both approaches.

14.5.1 Planning the Project: Create Product and Sprint Backlogs

The Scrum approach is characterized by short iterations, called **sprints**, during which a release candidate is developed. In Scrum, this is called a **potentially deliverable product increment**. Consequently, Scrum is an example of vertical integration (see Section 11.4.4).

The project is started with a **project kick off meeting**, during which the product owner and the Scrum master brainstorm a first version of the requirements. At the end of the kick off, the requirements are prioritized into a list called the **product backlog**. The project backlog starts as a vision formulated in terms of business requirements, and is updated and refined in terms of system requirements as the team makes progress in realizing the product. The project backlog reflects the current understanding of the product between the client and the project, rather than a fixed contract specifying the final product.

A sprint starts with a **sprint planning meeting**, during which the stakeholders (the client, management, and the team) select which items of the product backlog should be considered for the next product increment. The team then determines a set of tasks, together with an effort estimate, for realizing the selected requirements. The list of tasks and their effort estimates constitute the **sprint backlog**. At the end of the sprint planning meeting, the team takes responsibility for the sprint backlog and commits to delivering the product increment at the end of the sprint. A sprint is timeboxed to typically 30 days. At the end of the sprint, the product increment is reviewed and the scope of the next sprint is defined. Any unfinished work is returned to the product backlog.

The items in the product backlog are grouped into releases with planned release dates. As sprints result into completed increments, the product owner has three options:

1. decide whether to turn the sprint result into a product increment
2. declare the project finished and deliver the final product
3. adjust the release planning by shifting items between releases or adjusting release dates, based on the team's progress

14.5.2 Organizing the Project

Scrum defines three roles:

- The **product owner** is responsible for the requirements. The product owner participates in the creation of the product backlog, and prioritizes the product backlog before each sprint. The product owner represents the client and users with a single voice. The product owner changes and re-prioritizes the product backlog before each sprint to reflect lessons learned. The product owner is solely responsible for the product backlog and has no influence on the team during the sprint.
- The **Scrum master** is a management role responsible for the process. The Scrum master sets up and enforces the rules and practices of the project. The Scrum master facilitates the daily Scrum meetings, monitors progress, and removes obstacles preventing the team to do its work. The Scrum master is the interface between the Scrum team and the product owner, ensures the team productivity, and shields the team from distractions.

- The **Scrum team** is responsible for developing the product increment. The team is cross functional including all the skills required to build the product increment. The team is self organizing in that each member commits to work based on their own skills and availability. There are no roles or job descriptions assigned to specific members, such as analysts, programmers, or testers. Members learn and adapt their skills based on the work to be done. The team participates in the sprint planning meeting and commits to the list of tasks defined in the sprint backlog.

14.5.3 Controlling the Project: Daily Scrums and Burn Down Charts

The Scrum master monitors the progress of the project with daily Scrum meetings and burn down charts.

The **daily Scrum meeting** takes place at the beginning of the work day, and lasts at most 15 minutes. During the daily Scrum meeting, each team member reports individually:

- status: work done since the last daily Scrum meeting
- new issues: obstacles that are preventing them to accomplish their work
- new action items: work promised for the rest of the day

Reporting on these three points allows the Scrum master to monitor the progress of each member and to identify corrective actions, such as:

- Planning new work that was not identified in the sprint planning meeting or in the previous daily Scrum meetings
- Reallocation of tasks between members due to mismatch of skills or lack of interest
- Removing obstacles

Compared to the meeting templates presented in Chapter 3, *Project Organization and Communication* (Section 3.4.3) and in Chapter 12, *Rationale Management* (Section 12.4.2), Scrum uses a meeting template reduced to the absolute minimum. For example, discussion and resolution of new issues is postponed to follow-up meetings scheduled later in the day in which only the relevant stakeholders participate. The Scrum approach thus minimizes the time developers spend in unnecessary meetings, by timeboxing status reporting and by sparing them from discussions that are not relevant to them. The daily occurrence of the Scrum meetings allows the team to identify unexpected issues early and make decisions quickly.

The daily Scrum meetings provide a short-term view of the sprint. To review progress and assess trends, the Scrum master uses a **burn down chart**, which depicts the estimated remaining effort as a function of time (see Figure 14-15). Each backlog item in the sprint log contains an informal estimate in hours necessary to complete the item. The team members update their estimates daily, based on the work they have accomplished so far and on the insights gained. Work completed decreases the remaining effort in the sprint backlog. New work or a revised estimate for a task that turned out to be more complex increases the remaining effort in the sprint. As the sprint burn down chart plots the cumulative estimated amount of work for the sprint backlog, the Scrum master can assess the general trend of the sprint and identify any need for corrective actions

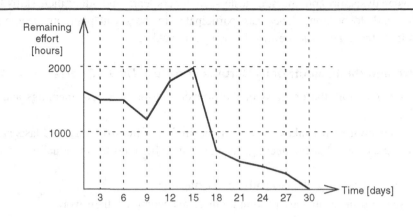

Figure 14-15   Assessing progress trend with a burn down chart. An increase corresponds to an upward revision of estimated work (new work, tasks initially underestimated). A decrease corresponds to a downward estimate of remaining work (work completed, obsolete tasks taken out of the plan).

Similarly, a release burn down chart, updated at the end of every sprint, shows the remaining effort in days for releases, based on estimates of product backlog items in days.

14.5.4 Terminating the Project: Sprint Reviews

While the daily progress of the team is highly visible (e.g., daily Scrum meetings, daily sprint backlog updates), the product owner cannot interfere with the team during the sprint. After the sprint planning meeting, the team assumes complete authority for the product increment and is left to its own devices while the Scrum master is responsible for removing obstacles raised by the team. At the end of the sprint, management may adjust team composition or the product owner may change requirements based on past team performance. If the goals of a sprint become obsolete or not reachable, the sprint may also be terminated abnormally by the team or by management. As sprints are normally short, abnormal termination occurs rarely.

With the end of each sprint, the product owner may renegotiate the product backlog with the client. Based on the latest product increment, the product owner may propose to revise specific requirements or assign new priorities. Based on the performance of the team, the product owner may propose a release schedule or change the allocation of requirements to releases.

Figure 14-16 shows an overview of the Scrum process.

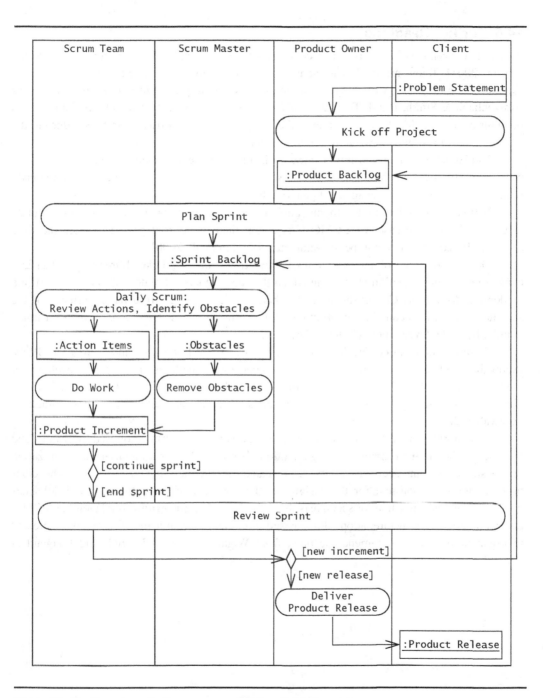

Figure 14-16   Overview of a Scrum process (UML activity diagram).

14.6 Further Readings

A good overview of generic project management concepts can be found in Portny [Portny, 2001]. Teams are the key to many project-based organizations. Katzenbach provides a categorization of different team types, ranging from working groups to high-performing teams [Katzenbach & Smith, 1994]. The IEEE-1058 described in this chapter is under revision and to be approved in 2009. Royce describes the early role of a software architect during the development of a software system using the Unified Process [Royce, 1998].

Paulish's book on architecture-centric project management contains a detailed description of the opportunities and challenges when the software architecture is formulated simultaneously with the software project management plan [Paulish, 2001].

Estimation of software development effort is difficult, and few approaches yield accurate results in the general case. COCOMO II is a statistical model that provides effort and time estimates based on a large number of parameters [Boehm et al., 2000].

On the other end of the spectrum of estimation, Planning Poker [Grenning, 2002] is a consensus-driven estimation method, in which the stakeholders estimate and discuss effort in a moderated discussion. Consensus-driven methods aim to leverage from the experience of the stakeholders while reconciling conflicting goals. Consensus-based methods have been made popular by agile development [Cohn, 2006].

Scrum, which was co-developed by Ken Schwaber and Jeff Sutherland in the early 1990s [Schwaber, 1995], is one of the earliest agile management methods. The Scrum development method is described in [Schwaber & Beedle, 2002]. Many books have followed on this topic, including adoption patterns for agile methods [Elssamadisy, 2009] and best practices [Schwaber, 2004].

Of historical interest are two software project organization forms proposed by Brooks and Weinberg. The **chief programmer organization** [Brooks, 1995] is a hierarchical organization that assigns all team decisions to the team leader, called the *chief programmer*. The chief programmer is responsible for the design and development of the subsystem and delegates programming tasks to a pool of specialists. In contrast, **egoless programming** [Weinberg, 1971] takes a democratic structure, adopted by the self organizing Scrum teams. For people interested in organizations, we recommend the book from Wigand, Picot, and Reichwald [Wigand et al., 1997].

14.7 Exercises

14-1 In Figure 14-1, we modeled the phases of a project with a state chart. Use the state pattern by making each of these phases a different class. Use the project management activities introduced in this chapter to make them public operations on these classes. Assume a team-based project organization.

14-2 What are the relative advantages of flat staffing versus gradual staffing?

14-3 What is the difference between reporting status and making decisions in a meeting? Should they always be kept separate in a meeting?

14-4 Why should the software architect and project leader be different people?

14-5 Draw a UML model of the team organization of the ARENA project for each the main phases (i.e., conception, definition, start, steady state, termination).

14-6 Draw a task model of the system design of the MyTrip system presented in Chapter 6, *System Design: Decomposing the System.*

14-7 Estimate the time to complete each task of the task model produced in Exercise 14-6 and determine the critical path.

14-8 Identify, prioritize, and plan for the top five risks related to the system design of MyTrip presented in Chapter 6, *System Design: Decomposing the System.*

14-9 Identify, prioritize, and plan for the top five risks related to the user interface subsystem of CTC presented in Chapter 12, *Rationale Management.*

14-10 Linux, developed using the bazaar model, is more reliable and more responsive than many operating systems running on Intel PCs. Make a case why the bazaar model should or should not be used for the Space Shuttle control software.

14-11 Organize the project participants into teams of four people. Each team has the following resources available: 2 eggs, 1 roll of TESA film, 1 roll of toilet paper, a cup with water, a bucket with two liters of sand, 20 foam balls (each about 1 cm diameter), 1 table whose surface is about 1 meter above the ground. Each team has 25 minutes time to build and test an artifact that allows an egg to be released 75 cm above the table such that the egg falls on the table without cracking. Each team has another 5 minutes to demonstrate the artifact to project management.

14-12 Organize the project into teams of four people. Each team has the following resources available: 2 buckets of DUPLO pieces, 2 tables separated by a distance of 1.50 meters. Each team has 25 minutes time to build and test a bridge solely out of the available DUPLO pieces that hangs free for at least one minute between the two table surfaces. Each team has another 5 minutes to demonstrate the artifact to project management.

14-13 Specify all management models for the icebreaker project described in Exercise 14-11.

14-14 Write an SPMP for the icebreaker project described in Exercise 14-11.

14-15 What does a flat section in a burn down chart mean (for example the section between days 3 and 6 in Figure 14-15)?

References

[Albrecht & Gaffney, 1983]   A. J. Albrecht & J. E. Gaffney, Jr., "Software function, source lines of code, and development effort prediction: A software science validation," *IEEE Transactions on Software Engineering*, Vol. SE-9, No. 6, November 1983.

[Boehm, 1991]   B. Boehm, "Software risk management: Principles and practices," *IEEE Software*, Vol. 1, pp. 32–41, 1991.

[Boehm et al., 2000]   B. Boehm, E. Horowitz, R. Madachy, D. Reifer, B. K. Clark, B. Steece, A. W. Brown, S. Chulani, & C. Abts, *Software Cost Estimation with COCOMO II*, Prentice Hall, Upper Saddle River, NJ, 2000.

[Brooks, 1995]   F. P. Brooks, *The Mythical Man Month, Anniversary Edition: Essays on Software Engineering*, Addison-Wesley, Reading, MA, 1995.

[Carr et al., 1993]   M. J. Carr, S. L. Konda, I. Monarch, F. C. Ulrich, & C. F. Walker, *Taxonomy-Based Risk Identification,* Technical Report CMU/SEI-93-TR-6, Software Engineering Institute, Carnegie Mellon University, Pittsburgh, PA, 1993.

[Charette, 1989]   R. N. Charette, *Software Engineering Risk Analysis and Management*, McGraw-Hill, New York, 1989.

[Cohn, 2006]   M. Cohn, *Agile Estimating and Planning*, Pearson, Upper Saddle River, NJ, 2006.

[Elssamadisy, 2009]   A. Elssamadisy, *Agile Adoption Patterns*, Addison-Wesley, Reading, MA, 2009.

[Grenning, 2002]   J. Grenning, Planning Poker, http://www.planningpoker.com/ 2002.

[Halstead, 1977]   M. H. Halstead, *Elements of Software Science,* Elsevier, New York, 1977.

[IEEE Std. 1058-1998]   *IEEE Standard for Software Project Management Plans*, IEEE Computer Society, New York, 1998.

[Katzenbach & Smith, 1994]   J. R. Katzenbach & D. K. Smith, *The Wisdom of Teams: Creating The High-Performance Organization*, Harper Business, 1994.

[Kayser, 1990]   T. A. Kayser, *Mining Group Gold*, Serif, El Segundo, CA, 1990.

[McCabe, 1976]   T. McCabe, "A software complexity measure," *IEEE Transactions on Software Engineering*, Vol. 2, No. 12, December 1976.

[Paulish, 2001]   D. J. Paulish, *Architecture-Centric Software Project Management: A Practical Guide*, SEI Series in Software Engineering, Addison-Wesley, Reading, MA, 2001.

[Portny, 2001]   S. E. Portny, *Project Management for Dummies*, John Wiley & Sons, 2000.

[Rogers et al., 1986]   *The Presidential Commission on the Space Shuttle Challenger Accident Report.* Washington, DC, June 6, 1986.

[Royce, 1998]   W. Royce, *Software Project Management: A Unified Framework*, Addison-Wesley, Reading, MA, 1998.

[Schwaber, 1995]   K, Schwaber, "Scrum Development Process," *Business Object Design and Implementation Workshop*, OOPSLA'95, Austin, TX, October 1995.

[Schwaber & Beedle, 2002]   K. Schwaber & M. Beedle, *Agile Software Development with Scrum*, Prentice Hall, Upper Saddle River, 2002.

[Schwaber, 2004]   K. Schwaber, *Agile Project Management With Scrum*, Microsoft, Redwood, 2004.

[Vaughan, 1996]   D. Vaughan, *The Challenger Launch Decision: Risky Technology, Culture, and Deviance at NASA*, The University of Chicago Press, Chicago, 1996.

[Weinberg, 1971]   G. M. Weinberg, *The Psychology of Computer Programming*, Van Nostrand, New York, 1971.

[Wigand et al., 1997]   R. T. Wigand, A. Picot, & R. Reichwald, *Information, Organization and Management: Expanding Markets and Corporate Boundaries*, John Wiley & Sons, London, 1997.

15

Software Life Cycle

There must always be a discrepancy between concepts and reality, because the former are static while the latter is dynamic and flowing.
—Robert Pirsig, in *Lila*

A software life cycle model represents all the activities and work products necessary to develop a software system. Life cycle models enable managers and developers to deal with the complexity of the process of developing software in the same way as an analysis model or a system design model enables developers to deal with the complexity of a software system. In the case of software systems, the reality being modeled includes phenomena such as watches, accidents, trains, sensors, and buildings. In the case of software development, the reality includes phenomena such as participants, teams, activities, and work products. Many life cycle models have been published in the literature in an attempt to better understand, measure, and control the development process. Life cycle models make the software development activities and their dependencies visible and manageable.

In this chapter, we revisit the activities described in previous chapters from the perspective of life cycle modeling. The modeling techniques we used for modeling software systems can also be used to represent life cycles. Whereas life cycle models are usually represented with ad hoc notations, we try to use UML diagrams whenever possible. First, we describe the typical activities and work products of a software life cycle as defined by the IEEE standard 1074 [IEEE Std. 1074-2006]. Next, we introduce the Capability Maturity Model, a framework for assessing the maturity of organizations and their life cycles. We then discuss different life cycle models that have been proposed for developing complex software systems; these include the waterfall model, the spiral model, the V-model, and the unified software process. We also discuss a life cycle model called the issue-based model, in which products and activities are modeled as a set of issues stored in a knowledge base. The issue-based model is an entity-centered view of the software life cycle that can accommodate frequent changes over the duration of a project.

15.1 Introduction: Polynesian Navigation

Polynesian navigation

Polynesia is a large set of islands roughly forming a triangle with Tahiti at the center, Hawaii at the north, Easter Island at the east, and New Zealand at the southwest. Polynesians came from southeast Asia, settling Pacific islands systematically from west to east. Polynesians had already completed their settlement several hundreds of years before Columbus arrived in the Caribbean. They reached Tahiti in 1400 B.C., Hawaii in 500 A.D., and New Zealand sometime between 500 A.D. and 1100 A.D.

Polynesian fishermen would discover a new island opportunistically, identify its location, and tell people back home. The settlement of the new island was deliberate, involving the transplantation of families, plants such as bananas, sugar cane, and yams, and domesticated animals such as dogs, pigs, and chickens.

What makes this feat even more remarkable was that Polynesians were technologically in the Stone Age. They built multi-hulled canoes with tools of bones and stones and without using any metal. Their canoes were designed to stay on a specific course and withstand storms, and could sail significantly faster than the European ships of the time. They transmitted knowledge of seafaring and the location of islands by word of mouth from one generation to the next.

Polynesians navigated without instruments, relying on the rising and setting of stars, the direction of the wind, and the swell of the ocean to maintain a course. The people of the island of Truk in Micronesia, east of Polynesia, have preserved these ancient navigation skills and enable us to speculate about how Polynesians managed to travel several thousands of kilometers by canoe. Near the equator, stars rise and set around a north–south axis. Altair, for example, rises in the east and sets in the west. Some stars rise and set further north: Vega rises in the northeast and sets in the northwest. Other stars rise and set further south: Antares rises in the southeast and sets in the southwest. When facing the rising point of Vega, the navigator would turn his back on the setting point of Antares. By memorizing the relative position of 16 stars, the Polynesian navigator could always find a visible star to adjust his course. During the day or overcast nights, the navigator would use the direction of the wind and the swell of the ocean, which he would have memorized in relationship with these stars.

Near landfall, the shape and sound of the waves would change. At that point, they looked for specific species of land-based birds that would fly out to sea in the morning to fish and return to land in the evening. When spotting these birds in the evening, they would follow their flight. When spotting them in the morning, they would sail toward their point of origin.

By contrast, the shipbuilders of the age of Columbus had mastered the use of metal for several thousands of years. Columbus's logs indicate that he was not a celestial navigator. Instead of following stars, he used dead reckoning: the helmsman held course by looking at a magnetic compass. Every hour, the speed of the boat was measured by throwing a piece of flotsam in the water and by measuring the time it took to clear the length of the ship. By knowing the direction and the speed of the ship at all times, Columbus could compute the distance he had sailed since leaving port. We know from records that he did not use a corrected compass, as his course towards America drifted to the south. On his way back, his course drifted by the same amount to the north, so he did not notice the limitations of the magnetic compass.

The example above illustrates how similar goals can be accomplished with very different processes. Polynesians evolved their craft of navigation and their knowledge of the stars during increasingly long ocean trips, as the distance between islands increased significantly as they moved toward the east. They invented and refined a process that could be repeated accurately every time a new island was discovered. At the time of Columbus, most navigators stayed close to the coast, as they sailed toward the East Indies around Africa using dead reckoning. Columbus applied an existing navigation process to cross the Atlantic. In both cases, the navigator had a goal (e.g., settling a specific island, finding a transatlantic route to the Indies) and a set of survival skills applied to local situations that eventually supported that goal (e.g., recognizing the proximity of islands, ability to set a course, ability to correct a course). If Columbus and the Polynesians had met and been able to communicate, each could have learned a range of new skills and modified their respective processes accordingly. This transfer of knowledge, however, assumes that Columbus and the Polynesians would have been able to share a common model of navigation.

In the previous chapters, we used UML as a modeling language for describing and communicating about systems. In this chapter, we focus on models of the software development process, called **software life cycle models**. Modeling the software life cycle is a difficult undertaking because it is a complex and changing system. Like software systems, software life cycles can be described by several different models. Most proposed life cycle models have focused on the activities of software development and represented them explicitly as class objects. This view of the software life cycle is called **activity centered**. Another view of the software life cycle is to focus on the work products created by these activities. This other view is called **entity centered**. The activity-centered view leads participants to focus on how work products are created. The entity-centered view leads participants to focus on the content and structure of the work products. Figure 15-1 depicts a simple life cycle for software development using three activities: Problem definition, System development, and System operation.

Figure 15-2 shows an activity-centered view of this simplistic life cycle model. The associations between the activities show a linear time dependency, which is implied by the use of the activity diagram notation: the problem statement precedes system development, which in turn precedes system operation. Other time dependencies are possible.

For example, in the software life cycle of Figure 15-3, the activities System development and Market creation can be done concurrently.

Figure 15-4 is an entity-centered view of the model depicted by Figure 15-2. Software development produces four entities: a Market survey document, a Requirements specification document, an Executable system, and a Lessons learned document.

The activity-centered and entity-centered views are complementary, as illustrated by Figure 15-5. Every product is generated by one or more activities. The Problem definition activity uses a Market survey document as input and generates a Requirements specification document. The System development activity takes the Requirements specification document as input and produces an Executable system. System operation

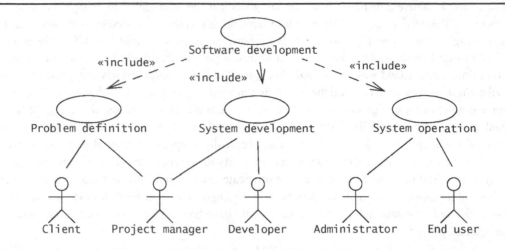

Figure 15-1   Simple life cycle for software development (UML use case diagram).

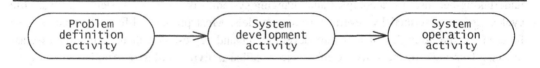

Figure 15-2   Simple life cycle for software development (UML activity diagram).

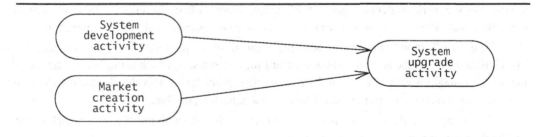

Figure 15-3   Another simple life cycle (UML activity diagram).

generates a Lessons learned document that could be used during the development of the next product. Alternatively, every activity generates one or more products.

In Section 15.2, we describe the life cycle activities defined by the IEEE 1074 standard [IEEE Std. 1074-2006]. This standard introduces precise definitions that enable project participants to understand and communicate effectively about the life cycle. In this section, we also describe the information flows between activities.

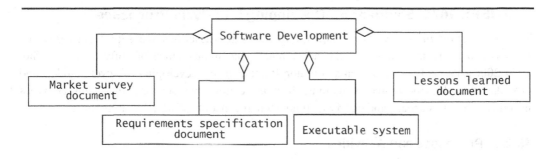

Figure 15-4   Entity-centered view of software development (UML class diagram).

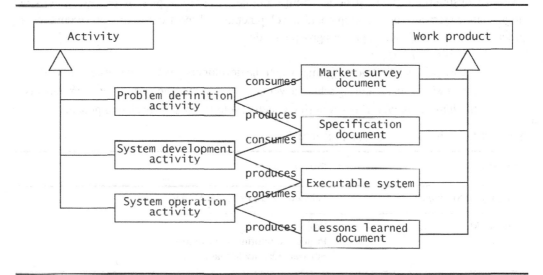

Figure 15-5   Activities and products of the simple life cycle of Figure 15-2 (UML class diagram).

In Section 15.3, we describe the Capability Maturity Model, a framework for assessing the maturity of organizations and their life cycles. This framework enables organizations and projects to be compared based on the activities of their life cycles.

In Section 15.4, we survey several activity-centered life cycle models that propose different orderings of activities. We discuss two sequential models, the waterfall model [Royce, 1970] and the V-model [Jensen & Tonies, 1979], and two iterative models, the spiral model [Boehm, 1987] and the Unified Software Process [Jacobson et al., 1999]. We also describe an entity-based life cycle model based on issues.

15.2 IEEE 1074: Standard for Developing Life Cycle Processes

The *IEEE Standard for Software Life Cycle Processes* describes the set of activities and processes that are mandatory for the development and maintenance of software [IEEE Std. 1074-2006]. Its goal is to establish a common framework for developing life cycle models and provide examples for typical situations. In this section, we describe the main activities introduced by the standard and clarify its fundamental concepts using UML diagrams.

15.2.1 Processes and Activities

A **process** is a set of activities that is performed toward a specific purpose (e.g., requirements, management, delivery). The IEEE standard lists a total of 17 processes, grouped into higher levels of abstractions called **process groups** (Table 15-1). Examples of process groups are project management, pre-development, development, and post-development. Examples of processes in the development process group include

- the *Requirements Process* during which the developers develop the system models
- the *Design Process* during which developers decompose the system into components
- the *Implementation Process* during which developers realize each component.

Table 15-1   Software processes in IEEE 1074.

Process group	Processes
Life Cycle Modeling	Selection of a Life Cycle Model
Project Management	Project Initiation Project Monitoring and Control Software Quality Management
Pre-Development	Concept Exploration System Allocation
Development	Requirements Design Implementation
Post-Development	Installation Operation and Support Maintenance Retirement
Integral	Verification and Validation Software Configuration Management Documentation Development Training

Each process is composed of activities. An **activity** is a task or group of subactivities that are assigned to a team or a project participant to achieve a specific purpose. The *Requirements Process*, for example, is composed of three activities:

- *Define and Develop Software Requirements* during which the functionality of the system is defined precisely
- *Define Interface Requirements* during which the interactions between the system and the user are defined precisely
- *Prioritize and Integrate Software Requirements* during which all requirements are integrated for consistency and prioritized by client preference.

Tasks consume resources (e.g., personnel, time, money) and produce a work product. During planning, activities are decomposed into project-specific tasks, are given a start and ending date, and are assigned to a team or a project participant (Figure 15-6). During the project, actual work is tracked against planned tasks, and resources are reallocated to respond to problems.

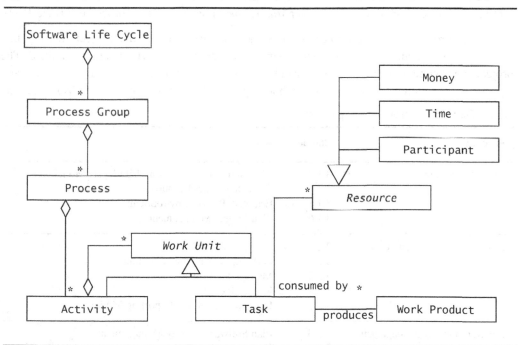

Figure 15-6 Model of the software life cycle (UML class diagram). A software life cycle consists of process groups, which in turn consist of processes. A process accomplishes a specific purpose (e.g., requirements, design, installation). A process consists of activities, which in turn consist of subactivities or tasks. Tasks represent the smallest piece of work that is relevant to management. Tasks consume resources and produce one or more work products. A project is an instance of a software life cycle.

The processes required by IEEE 1074 are listed in Table 15-1. From the developers' point of view, the first six processes (i.e., the *Life Cycle Modeling*, the *Project Management*, and the *Pre-Development Processes*) have often already been initiated before their involvement with the project.

15.2.2 Life Cycle Modeling

During *Life Cycle Modeling*, the project manager customizes the activities defined in IEEE 1074 for a specific project (i.e., for an instance of a life cycle model). Not all projects require the same activities and the same sequencing of activities. For example, projects that do not deal with a persistent storage do not need to execute the activity *Design Data Base*. The selected life cycle model serves as input to the *Project Initiation Process* described in the next section.

15.2.3 Project Management

During *Project Management*, the project manager initiates, monitors, and controls the project throughout the software life cycle. *Project Management* consists of three processes (Table 15-2).

The *Project Initiation Process* creates the infrastructure for the project. During this process, the task plan, schedule, budget, organization, and project environment are defined. The project environment includes project standards, communication infrastructure, meeting and reporting procedures, development methodology, and development tools. Most of the

Table 15-2   Project management processes.

Process	Clause[a]	Activities
Project Initiation	3.1.3	Map Activities to Software Life Cycle Model
	3.1.4	Allocate Project Resources
	3.1.5	Establish Project Environment
	3.1.6	Plan Project Management
Project Monitoring and Control	3.2.3	Analyze Risks
	3.2.4	Perform Contingency Planning
	3.2.5	Manage the Project
	3.2.6	Retain Records
	3.2.7	Implement Problem Reporting Model
Software Quality Management	3.3.3	Plan Software Quality Management
	3.3.4	Define Metrics
	3.3.5	Manage Software Quality
	3.3.6	Identify Quality Improvement Needs

a.   The Clause Column in this table and the other tables in this chapter refers to a clause number in IEEE 1074. This is a cross-reference to the standards document as published in [IEEE Std. 1074-2006].

information generated during this process is documented in the *Software Project Management Plan (SPMP)*. The *Project Initiation Process* is complete as soon as a stable environment for the project is established.

The *Project Monitoring and Control Process* ensures that the project is executed according to the task plan and budget. If the project manager observes any deviation from the schedule, she will take corrective action such as reallocating some of the resources, changing procedures, or replanning the schedule. The SPMP is updated to reflect any of these changes. The *Project Monitoring and Control Process* is active throughout the life cycle.

The *Software Quality Management Process* ensures that the system under construction meets the required quality standards (which were selected during *Project Initiation*). This process is executed by a separate quality management team to avoid conflicts of interest (i.e., the goal of the developers is to complete the system on time, and the goal of the quality management team is to ensure that the system is not considered complete until it meets the required quality standard). The *Software Quality Management Process* is active throughout most of the life cycle.

We described in Chapter 14, *Project Management*, the activities of *Project Initiation* and *Project Monitoring and Control* that are related to planning, organization, and tracking. The activity *Establish Project Environment* requires particular attention in the context of a team-based project. One of the critical parts of the project environment is the communication infrastructure that will support the dissemination of information among the participants. To be able to react rapidly to changes and report problems without introducing unreasonable overhead, all project participants need to be aware of the information flow through the project and the mechanisms for disseminating information. We described in Chapter 3, *Project Organization and Communication*, the activities related to defining and using the communication infrastructure. Note that to define the development team structure, and thereby the communication infrastructure, the initial system architecture (produced by the *System Allocation Process* described in the next section) must first be defined.

15.2.4 Pre-Development

During *Pre-Development*, management (or marketing) and a client identify an idea or a need. This can be addressed with a new development effort (greenfield engineering), or a change to the interface of an existing system (interface engineering), or software replacement of an existing business process (reengineering). The *System Allocation Process* establishes the initial system architecture and identifies hardware, software, and operational requirements. Note that the subsystem decomposition is the foundation of the communication infrastructure among the project members. The requirements, subsystem decomposition, and communication infrastructure are described in the *Problem Statement*,[1] which serves as input for the *Development* process. The *Pre-Development* processes are depicted in Table 15-3.

---

1. The *Statement of Need* mentioned in the IEEE 1074 standard is similar to the *Problem Statement*, but does not contain any project organization information.

Table 15-3   Pre-development processes.

Process	Clause	Activities
Concept Exploration	4.1.3	Identify Ideas or Needs
	4.1.4	Formulate Potential Approaches
	4.1.5	Conduct Feasibility Studies
	4.1.6	Plan System Transition (if Applicable)
	4.1.7	Refine and Finalize the Idea or Need
System Allocation	4.2.3	Analyze Functions
	4.2.4	Develop System Architecture
	4.2.5	Decompose System Requirements

15.2.5 Development

Development consists of the processes directed toward the construction of the system (Table 15-4).

The *Requirements Process* starts with the informal description of the requirements and defines the system requirements in terms of high-level functional requirements, producing a complete specification of the system and a prioritization of the requirements. We describe the *Requirements Process* in Chapter 4, *Requirements Elicitation*, and Chapter 5, *Analysis*.

The *Design Process* takes the architecture produced during the *System Allocation Process* and the specification from the *Requirements* and produces a coherent and well-organized representation of the system. The activities *Perform Architectural Design* and *Design Interfaces*

Table 15-4   Development processes.

Process	Clause	Activities
Requirements	5.1.3	Define and Develop Software Requirements
	5.1.4	Define Interface Requirements
	5.1.5	Prioritize and Integrate Software Requirements
Design	5.2.3	Perform Architectural Design
	5.2.4	Design Data Base (if Applicable)
	5.2.5	Design Interfaces
	5.2.6	Select or Develop Algorithms (if Applicable)
	5.2.7	Perform Detailed Design
Implementation	5.3.3	Create Test Data
	5.3.4	Create Source
	5.3.5	Generate Object Code
	5.3.6	Create Operating Documentation
	5.3.7	Plan Integration
	5.3.8	Perform Integration

refine the subsystem decomposition. This also includes the allocation of requirements to hardware and software systems, the description of boundary conditions, the selection of off-the-shelf components, and the definition of design goals. The detailed design of each subsystem is done during the *Perform Detailed Design* activity. The *Design Process* results in the definition of design objects, their attributes and operations, and their organization into packages. By the end of this activity, all methods and their type signatures are defined. New classes are introduced to take into account nonfunctional requirements and component-specific details. The *Design* process used in this book is described in Chapter 6, *System Design: Decomposing the System*, Chapter 8, *Object Design: Reusing Pattern Solutions*, and Chapter 9, *Object Design: Specifying Interfaces*.

The *Implementation Process* takes the design model and produces an equivalent executable representation. The *Implementation Process* includes integration planning and integration activities. Note that tests performed during this process are independent of those performed during quality control or *Verification and Validation*. We describe in Chapter 11, *Testing*, the testing and integration aspects of the *Implementation*.

15.2.6 Post-Development

Post-Development consists of the installation, maintenance, operation and support, and retirement processes (Table 15-5).

During *Installation*, the system software is distributed and installed at the client site. The installation culminates with the client acceptance test according to the criteria defined in the *Project Agreement*. *Operation and Support* is concerned with user training and operation of the system. *Maintenance* is concerned with the resolution of software errors, faults, and failures after the delivery of the system. *Maintenance* requires a ramping of the software life cycle

Table 15-5   Post-development processes.

Process	Clause	Activities
Installation	6.1.3	Plan Installation
	6.1.4	Distribution of Software
	6.1.5	Installation of Software
	6.1.7	Accept Software in Operational Environment
Operation and Support	6.2.3	Operate the System
	6.2.4	Provide Technical Assistance and Consulting
	6.2.5	Maintain Support Request Log
Maintenance	6.3.3	Reapply Software Life Cycle
Retirement	6.4.3	Notify Users
	6.4.4	Conduct Parallel Operations (If Applicable)
	6.4.5	Retire System

processes and activities into a new project. *Retirement* removes an existing system, terminating its operations or support; this occurs when the system is upgraded or replaced by a new system. To ensure a smooth transition between the two systems, both systems are often run in parallel until the users have gotten used to the new system. Except for client delivery and acceptance, we do not address the post-development processes in this book.

15.2.7 Integral Processes (Cross-Development)

Several processes take place during the complete duration of the project. These are called *Integral processes* (we also use the term *cross-development processes*) and include *Validation and Verification*, *Software Configuration Management*, *Documentation Development*, and *Training* (Table 15-6).

  Verification and Validation includes verification and validation tasks. Verification tasks focus on showing that the system models comply with the specification. Verification includes reviews, audits, and inspections. Validation tasks ensure that the system addresses the client's needs and includes system testing, beta testing, and client acceptance testing. *Verification and Validation* activities occur throughout the life cycle with the intent of detecting anomalies as early as possible. For example, each model could be reviewed against a checklist at the end of the process that generated it. The review of a model, say the design model, may result in the modification of a model generated in other processes, say the analysis model. The activity

Table 15-6   Integral processes (also called cross-development processes).

Process	Clause	Activities
Verification and Validation	7.1.3	Plan Verification and Validation
	7.1.4	Execute Verification and Validation Tasks
	7.1.5	Collect and Analyze Metric Data
	7.1.6	Plan Testing
	7.1.7	Develop Test Requirements
	7.1.8	Execute the Tests
Software Configuration Management	7.2.3	Plan Configuration Management
	7.2.4	Develop Configuration Identification
	7.2.5	Perform Configuration Control
	7.2.6	Perform Status Accounting
Documentation Development	7.3.3	Plan Documentation
	7.3.4	Implement Documentation
	7.3.5	Produce and Distribute Documentation
Training	7.4.3	Plan the Training Program
	7.4.4	Develop Training Materials
	7.4.5	Validate the Training Program
	7.4.6	Implement the Training Program

Collect and Analyze Metric Data generates project data that can also serve for future projects and contribute to the knowledge of the organization. The activities *Plan Testing* and *Develop Test Requirements* can be initiated as early as after the completion of the requirements. In large projects, these tasks are performed by different participants than the developers. We describe mechanisms for reviews, audits, and inspections in Chapter 3, *Project Organization and Communication*. We describe specific reviews associated with requirements elicitation, analysis, and system design in Chapters 4, 5, and 6, respectively. We describe testing activities in Chapter 11, *Testing*.

The *Configuration Management Process* focuses on the tracking and control of changes of work products. Items under configuration management include the source code for the system, all development models, the software project management plan, and all documents visible to the project participants. We describe configuration management in Chapter 13, *Configuration Management*.

The *Documentation Process* deals with the work products (excluding code), documenting the results produced by the other processes. Document templates are selected during this activity. The IEEE 1074 standard, however, does not prescribe any specific document or template. Development and cross-development specific documentation issues are discussed in chapters where documents are produced (e.g., Chapter 5, *Analysis*, discusses the *Requirements Analysis Document*; Chapter 13, *Configuration Management*, discusses the *Software Configuration Management Plan*).

15.3 Characterizing the Maturity of Software Life Cycle Models

In the previous section we introduced the activities and artifacts that constitute a software life cycle. Which of these activities and artifacts are chosen for a specific project is not defined by the standard. One of the goals of the **Capability Maturity Model (CMM)** is to provide guidelines for selecting life cycle activities. The CMM assumes that the development of software systems is made more predictable when an organization uses a well-structured life cycle process, visible to all project participants, and when the organization adapts to change. CMM uses the following five levels to characterize the maturity of an organization [Paulk et al., 1995]:

Level 1: Initial. An organization on the initial level applies ad hoc activities to develop software. Few of these activities are well defined. The success of a project on this maturity level usually depends on the heroic efforts and skills of key individuals. From the client's point of view, the software life cycle model, if it exists at all, is a black box: after providing the problem statement and negotiating the project agreement, the client must wait until the end of the project to inspect the deliverables of the project. During the duration of the project, the client has effectively no way to interact with project management.

Level 2: Repeatable. Each project has a well-defined software life cycle model. Models, however, differ among projects, reducing the opportunity for teamwork and reuse of know-how.

Basic project management processes are used to track cost and schedule. New projects are based on the experience of the organization with similar previous projects and success is predictable for projects in similar application domains. The client interacts with the organization at well-defined points in time, such as client reviews and the client acceptance test, allowing some corrections before delivery.

Level 3: Defined. This level uses a documented software life cycle model for all managerial and technical activities across the organization. A customized version of the model is produced at the beginning of each project during the *Life Cycle Modeling* activity. The client knows the standard model and the model selected for a specific project.

Level 4: Managed. This level defines metrics for activities and deliverables. Data are constantly collected during the duration of the project. As a result, the software life cycle model can be quantitatively understood and analyzed. The client is informed about risks before the project begins and knows the measures used by organization.

Level 5: Optimized. The measurement data are used in a feedback mechanism to improve the software life cycle model over the lifetime of the organization.The client, project managers, and developers communicate and work together during the development of the project.

To be able to measure the maturity of an organization, a set of **key process areas (KPA)** has been defined by the Software Engineering Institute (SEI). To achieve a specific level of maturity, the organization must demonstrate that it addresses all the key process areas defined for that level. Some of these key process areas go beyond activities defined in the IEEE 1074 standard. Table 15-7 shows a mapping between maturity level and key process areas.

Table 15-7   Mapping process maturity level and key process areas.

Maturity Level	Key Process Area
1. Initial	Not applicable
2. Repeatable	Focus: Establish basic project management controls. • *Requirements management:* Requirements are baselined in a project agreement and maintained during the project. • *Project planning and tracking:* A software project management plan is established at the beginning of the project and is tracked during the project. • *Subcontractor management:* The organization selects and effectively manages qualified software subcontractors. • *Quality assurance management:* All deliverables and process activities are reviewed and audited to verify that they comply with standards and guidelines adopted by the organization. • *Configuration management:* A set of configuration management items is defined and maintained throughout the entire project.

Table 15-7 *Continued.*

Maturity Level	Key Process Area
3. Defined	Focus: Establish an infrastructure that allows a single effective software life cycle model across all projects. • *Organization process focus:* The organization has a permanent team to constantly maintain and improve the software life cycle model. • *Organization process definition:* A standard software life cycle model is used for all projects in the organization. A database is used for software life cycle-related information and documentation. • *Training program:* The organization identifies the needs for training for specific projects and develops training programs. • *Integrated software management:* Each project team can its tailor its specific process from the standard process. • *Software product engineering:* The software is built in accordance with the defined software life cycle, methods, and tools. • *Intergroup coordination:* The project teams interact with each other to address requirements and issues. • *Peer reviews:* Developers examine each other's deliverables to identify potential defects and areas where changes are needed.
4. Managed	Focus: Quantitative understanding of the software life cycle process and deliverables. • *Quantitative process management:* Productivity and quality metrics are defined and constantly measured across the project. It is critical that these data are not immediately used during the project, in particular to assess the performance of developers, but are stored in a database to allow for comparison with other projects. • *Quality management:* The organization has defined a set of quality goals for software products. It monitors and adjusts the goals and products to deliver high-quality products to the user.
5. Optimized	Focus: Keep track of technology and process changes that may cause changes in the system model or deliverables, even during a project. • *Defect prevention:* Failures in past projects are analyzed, using data from the metrics database. If necessary, specific actions are taken to prevent those defects from occurring again. • *Technology change management:* Technology enablers and innovations are constantly investigated and shared throughout the organization. • *Process change management:* The software process is constantly refined and changed to deal with inefficiencies identified by the software process metrics. Constant change is the norm, not the exception.

15.4 Life Cycle Models

Figure 15-7 depicts the information flow among processes in the IEEE 1074 standard. The complexity of the standard is significant as can be seen in the many dependencies among the processes. Each association represents a work product that is generated by one process and consumed by another process. Each association also represents a formal communication channel between project participants supported by the exchange of documents, models, or code.

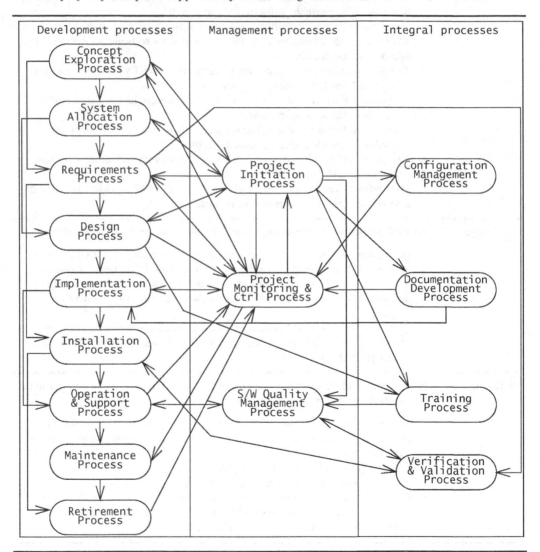

Figure 15-7 Process interrelationships in the IEEE 1074 standard (UML activity diagram, adapted from [IEEE Std. 1074-2006]). As suggested by this picture, dependencies among processes and activities are complex and seldom allow a sequential execution of processes.

In this section we review several life cycle models. Most of these models focus on the development processes exclusively.

15.4.1 Sequential Activity-Centered Models

We start with activity-centered life cycle models. The oldest software life cycle model is the waterfall model, which prescribes a sequential execution of the activities. The V-model is a variation of the waterfall model that introduces different levels of abstractions for the activities.

Waterfall model

The **waterfall model**, first described by Royce [Royce, 1970], is an activity-centered life cycle model that prescribes sequential executions of subsets of the development processes and management processes described in the previous section (Figure 15-8).

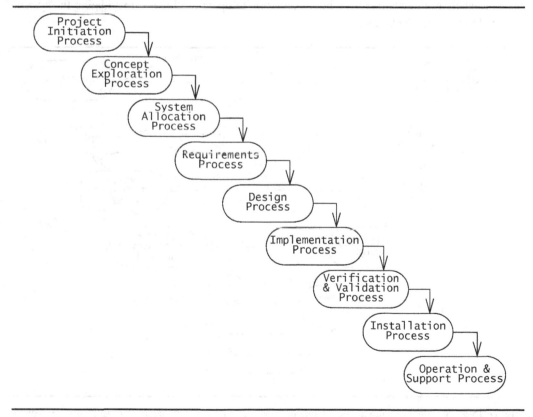

Figure 15-8   The waterfall model of software development is an activity-centered view of the software life cycle. Software development activities are performed in sequence (UML activity diagram adapted from [Royce, 1970] using IEEE 1074 names; project management and cross-development processes are omitted).

All requirements activities are completed before the system design activity starts. The goal is never to turn back once an activity is completed. The key feature of this model is the constant verification activity (called "verification step" by Royce) which ensures that each development activity does not introduce unwanted or delete mandatory requirements. This model provides a simple (or even simplistic) view of software development that measures progress by the number of tasks that have been completed. The model assumes that software development can be scheduled as a step-by-step process that transforms user needs into code.

V-Model

The **V-model** is a variation of the waterfall model that makes explicit the dependency between development activities and verification activities. The difference between the waterfall model and the V-model is that the latter depicts the level of abstraction. All activities from requirements to implementation focus on building an increasingly detailed representation of the system, whereas all activities from implementation to operation focus on validating the system. Figure 15-9 depicts the V-model.

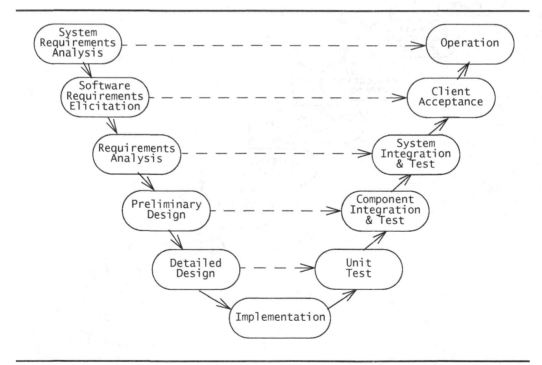

Figure 15-9   V-model of software development (UML activity diagram; adapted from [Jensen & Tonies, 1979]). The horizontal object flow denotes the information flow between activities at the same abstraction level. The V-shape layout of the activities was conserved to reflect the original drawing. However, the layout of the activities has no semantics in UML.

Higher levels of abstractions of the V-model deal with the requirements in terms of elicitation and operation. The middle level of the V-model focuses on mapping the problem into a software architecture. The lower level of the V-model focuses on details such as the assembly of software components and the coding of new ones. For example, the goal of the *Unit Test* activity is to validate units against their description in the detailed design. The *Component Integration and Test* activity validates functional components against the preliminary (or high-level) design. In many aspects, the waterfall model and its variants are simplistic abstractions of the software development process. The weakness of these models is that they assume that after an activity is finished and reviewed, the associated work product can be baselined. Such an idealized model is appropriate only if the specification of the requirements is highly reliable and stable. In practice, system development rarely conforms to this ideal model. Changes during an activity often require reworking a prior activity.

15.4.2 Iterative Activity-Centered Models

Boehm's spiral model and the more recent Unified Process model are based on the iterative execution of activities.

Spiral model

Boehm's **spiral model** [Boehm, 1987] is an activity-centered life cycle model that was devised to address the source of weaknesses in the waterfall model, in particular, to accommodate infrequent change during the software development. It is based on the same activities as the waterfall model; however, it adds several activities such as risk management, reuse, and prototyping to each activity. These extended activities are called *cycles* or *rounds*.

The spiral model focuses on addressing risks incrementally, in order of priority. Each round is composed of four phases (Figure 15-10). During the first phase (upper left quadrant), developers explore alternatives, define constraints, and identify objectives. During the second phase (upper right quadrant), developers manage risks associated with the solutions defined during the first phase. During the third phase (lower right quadrant), developers realize and validate a prototype or the part of the system associated with the risks addressed in this round. The fourth phase (lower left quadrant) focuses on planning the next round based on the results of the current round. The last phase of the round is usually conducted as a review involving the project participants, including developers, clients, and users. This review covers the products developed during the previous and current rounds and the plans for the next round. Boehm's spiral model distinguishes the following rounds: *Concept of Operation, Software Requirements, Software Product Design, Detailed Design, Code, Unit Test, Integration and Test, Acceptance Test,* and *Implementation.*[2]

---

2. Note that the figure illustrates only the first three activities (*Concept of Operation, Software Requirements,* and *Software Product Design*). The rounds for the remaining activities—*Detailed Design, Code, Unit Test, Integration and Test, Acceptance Test*—are not shown in detail, but only as blocks at the end of the last layer of the spiral.

Each round follows the waterfall model and includes the following activities:

1. Determine objectives
2. Specify constraints
3. Generate alternatives
4. Identify risks
5. Resolve risks
6. Develop and verify next-level product
7. Plan.

The first two activities define the problem addressed by the current cycle. The third activity, *Generate alternatives*, defines the solution space. The activities *Identify risks* and *Resolve risks* identify future problems that may result in high cost or cancellation of the project. The activity *Develop and verify next-level product* is the realization of the cycle. The activity *Plan* is a management activity to prepare for the next cycle. These rounds can be viewed in a

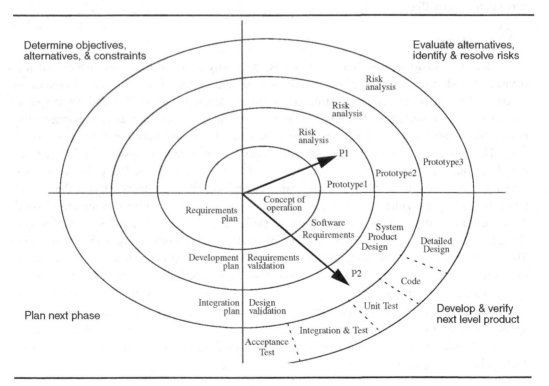

Figure 15-10 Boehm's spiral model (adapted from [Boehm, 1987]). The distance from the origin represents the cost accumulated by the project. The angle from the horizontal represents the type of activity. For example, the project P1 is currently in the risk analysis activity associated with software requirements. The project P2 is in the development of the system product design.

polar-coordinate system shown in Figure 15-10. The first round, *Concept of Operation*, starts in the upper left quadrant. Subsequent rounds are represented as additional layers on the spiral. The notation makes it easy to determine the status of the project at any time. The distance from the origin is the cost accumulated by the project. The angular coordinate indicates the progress accomplished within each phase.

Unified Software Development Process

The **Unified Software Development Process** (also called the **Unified Process**) is a life cycle model proposed by Booch, Jacobson, and Rumbaugh [Jacobson et al., 1999]. The unified process distinguishes important time ranges called *cycles* in the lifetime of a software system. Note that these are different from the cycles in the spiral model: they can be thought of as characterizing the stage of maturity of the software system during its lifetime. Cycles have no specific names. However, starting with the "birth" of the system, we can think of the system to be in the "childhood," "adulthood," or "retirement" cycle until it "dies." A cycle generally ends with a release of the system as a product to a customer. Each cycle can be in one of four states called *phases: Inception, Elaboration, Construction*, and *Transition* (see Figure 15-11). During the inception phase, the scope of the system is established, in particular what should be included and not included. This phase also identifies the use cases that will drive the trade-off decisions between conflicting design goals; these use cases are also called the *core use cases*. At least one candidate software architecture is identified, and the core use cases are demonstrated against this architecture. A first estimation and schedule for the entire project, including detailed estimates for the elaboration phase, are also established during this phase.

During the elaboration phase, the user's view of the requirements is captured in a repository. The software architecture is designed, and an initial set of build vs. buy decisions is made, so that cost, schedule, and resource estimates can be derived. During the construction phase, components are bought or built, and the release is compared with the acceptance criteria. The transition phase is entered when the baselined system is mature enough for deployment to the user community.

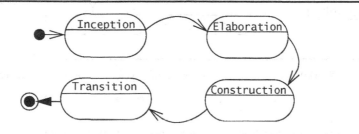

Figure 15-11   States of a software system called *phases* in the Unified Process. The Unified Process distinguishes four phases: inception, elaboration, construction, and transition (UML state machine diagram).

Each phase can consist of a number of iterations. Each iteration addresses a set of related use cases or mitigates some of the risks identified at the beginning of the iteration. An iteration in the Unified Process is generally associated with a project as we defined it in Chapter 14, *Project Management.*

For the duration of each iteration, several activities are performed in parallel. To emphasize the parallelism and the fact that they are active across the complete iteration, these activities are called **workflows** in the Unified Process.[3] Development-oriented workflows are called *engineering workflows*. The Unified Process distinguishes between *Requirements, Design, Implementation,* and *Test* as engineering workflows (Figure 15-12). These workflows have already been described in previous chapters of this book. The *Requirements* workflow involves analysis of the application domain and creation of requirements artifacts such as the analysis model (see Chapter 5). The *Design* workflow focuses on the creation of solution and design artifacts such as the system design model (see Chapter 6) or the object design model (see Chapter 8). The *Implementation* workflow realizes the solution in source code (see Chapter 10). The *Test* workflow is involved in the testing of the models and the maintenance of implementation and deployment artifacts (source code) (see Chapter 11).

The Unified Process distinguishes four cross-functional activities called *supporting workflows: Management, Environment, Assessment,* and *Deployment.* The *Management* workflow addresses all planning aspects for the software system as described in Chapter 14. The *Environment* workflow is concerned with the automation of the software process itself and

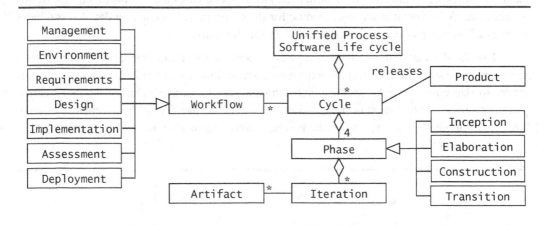

Figure 15-12   Workflows in the unified software life cycle used by Royce [Royce, 1998] (UML class diagram).

---

3. The Unified Process does not follow the naming conventions in the IEEE standard. *Workflows* can be considered as special *activities* spanning more than one iteration (project). *Engineering workflows* are project functions because their duration is the same as the duration of an iteration, i.e., the project. The term *supporting workflow* can be equated with *integral process.*

maintenance of the development environment, in particular the infrastructure for communication and configuration management. The *Assessment* workflow assesses processes and products needed for reviews, walkthroughs, and inspections. The *Deployment* workflow enables the transition of the software system to the end user.

The Unified Process emphasizes the staging of resources for each of the workflows during phases and iterations, thereby coupling project management issues very closely with software life cycle issues (see Figure 15-13). This is done by managing each iteration as a software project, as described in Chapter 14, *Project Management*. Because the duration of the workflows is the duration of the project, they can be seen as project functions with differing phase-specific needs. For example, during the *Elaboration* phase, the *Requirements* workflow needs most of the resources, while the *Implementation* workflow resource requirements are less. During the *Construction* phase, the resource needs for the *Requirements* workflow diminish, and the *Design* and *Implementation* workflows need increasingly more resources.

Figure 15-14 shows an entity-centered view of the Unified Process as a set of models. The requirements are captured in the *use case model*. The *analysis model* describes the system as a set of classes. The *design model* defines the structure of the system as a set of subsystems and interfaces, and the *deployment model* defines the distribution across. The *implementation model* maps the classes to components, and the *test model* verifies that the executable system provides the functionality described in the use case model.

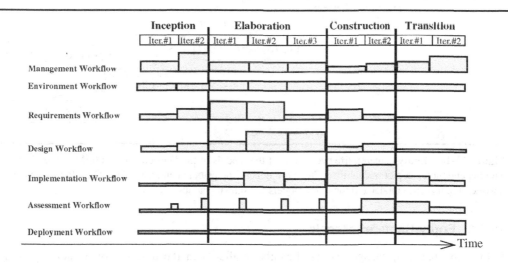

Figure 15-13 The seven workflows in the Unified Process–*Management, Environment, Requirements, Design, Implementation, Assessment,* and *Deployment*–are project functions performed during the entire lifetime of a system. Each of the workflows has different resource needs depending on the phase and iteration of the software system. The histograms for each workflow indicate the amount of work per iteration—the higher the block, the more resources are consumed by the workflow in that iteration (adapted from [Jacobson et al., 1999] and [Royce, 1998]).

All models are related to each other through traceability dependencies. A model element can be traced to at least one element in an associated model. For example, every use case has a traceable relationship with at least one class in the analysis model. Traceability allows us to understand the effect of change in one model on other models, in particular, it allows us to provide traceability in the requirements.

The dependencies between the models in Figure 15-14 can be maintained in different ways. During **forward engineering**, analysis and design models are established from the use case model, and the implementation model and test models are then generated from these models. During **reverse engineering**, the analysis and design models are extracted or updated from existing code. **Round-trip engineering** is a combination of reverse and forward engineering. It allows the developer to switch between these development modes at any time, depending on which model is undergoing the most amount of change.

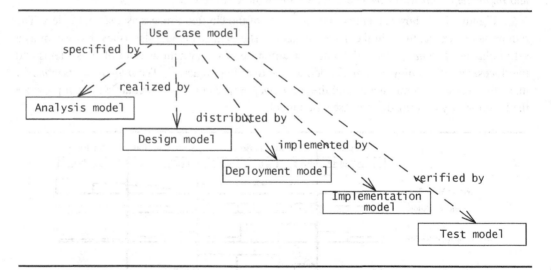

Figure 15-14 Entity-centered life cycle view of the models of the Unified Process (UML class diagram). The dependencies depict traceability. There are dependencies between all models. Only the dependencies between the use case model and the other models are shown [Jacobson et al., 1999].

15.4.3 Entity-Centered Models

If the time between changes is significantly smaller than the duration of an activity, and if changes can occur in the application domain as well as in the solution domain, both the waterfall model and the spiral model exhibit problems. For example, assume that the development team selects the hardware platform and that new platforms appear every three to four years. As long as the project time is significantly less than three years, the knowledge of the development team at the beginning of the project is usually sufficient to select a platform once during system design. However, if a new platform appears every three to four months and the duration of the project is also three or four months, the platform decision will probably have to be reconsidered during the project.

In this section, we describe an entity-centered life cycle model, called the **issue-based life cycle model**, that aims at dealing with frequent changes. This model is based on the rationale behind the system as an issue model (Chapter 12, *Rationale Management*). Each project starts with a set of issues. If the project starts from scratch, these issues are drawn from the project manager's experience or from a standard template. In a reengineering or interface project, issues may be available from the rationale of the previous project. If the project has a long history, the rationale should be well populated. Examples of issues are *What should be the initial teams? Should the mechanic have access to driver-specific information? What is the appropriate middleware? What software architecture should we use?* and *Which implementation language should we use?* All issues are stored in an issue base accessible to project participants.

The status of an issue can be closed or open. A **closed issue** is an issue that has been resolved. For example, a closed issue can be a decision about the platform on which the system should run (e.g., Solaris). Closed issues can be reopened, however, as changes occur in the application or solution domain. For example, if we need to support additional platforms (e.g., Linux and Windows NT), we reopen the issue, reevaluate the alternatives, and provide a new resolution. **Open issues** are resolved by discussion and negotiation among project participants (see Chapter 3, *Project Organization and Communication*). An issue i2 depends on another issue i1 if the resolution of i1 constrains the alternatives available for i2. Tracking the dependencies among issues enables developers to assess the impact of revisiting a given issue. The issue base also tracks dependencies among issues. Figure 15-15 shows a snapshot of the issue base of a project, depicting the issue status and dependencies.

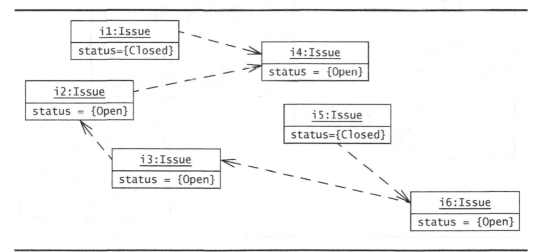

Figure 15-15 Snapshot of a project issue base (UML object diagram). Issues i1 and i5 have been resolved, whereas all other issues are still open. Dependencies among issues indicate that the resolution of an issue can constrain the alternatives for dependent issues.

Issues can be mapped to the activities of life cycle models described earlier. For example, assume the activities *Planning* and *System Design* are part of the selected life cycle model. *How do we set up the initial teams?* can be categorized as a planning issue, and *What software architecture shall we use?* can be categorized as a system design issue. The status of issues can then be used to track the status of each activity. If any system design issues are still open, the *System Design* activity has not yet been completed. The life cycle models we described earlier can then be seen as special cases of the issue-based model. In the Waterfall model, for example, developers completely resolve the issues associated with an activity before moving to the next activity. Figure 15-16 depicts the state of a project during *System Design*.

In Boehm's spiral model, risks correspond to issues that are evaluated and reopened at the beginning of each round. Issues are resolved in the order of their priority as defined during risk analysis. Note, however, that "issue" is a more general concept than "risk." For example, the issue *Which access control model should we use?* is a design problem, not a risk.

In the general case (Figure 15-17), all activities may still have associated open issues, which means that all activities must be managed concurrently. The goal of the project manager is to keep the number of open issues small and manageable without imposing time or activity-based constraints on the resolution of issues. Using issues and their dependencies for managing the life cycle activities allows all life cycle activities to proceed concurrently.

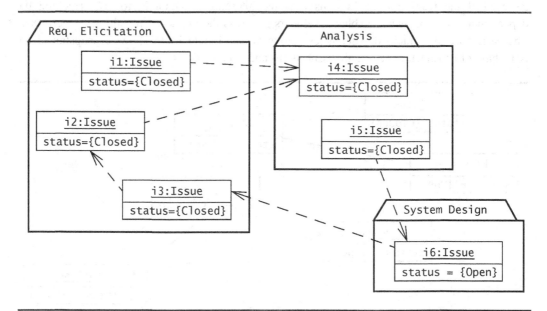

Figure 15-16 The waterfall model as a special case of the issue-based life cycle model (UML object diagram). All issues that belong to the same issue category are contained in the same UML package. In the project status shown in the figure, all the requirements elicitation and analysis issues have been closed; that is, the requirements elicitation and analysis activities have been completed.

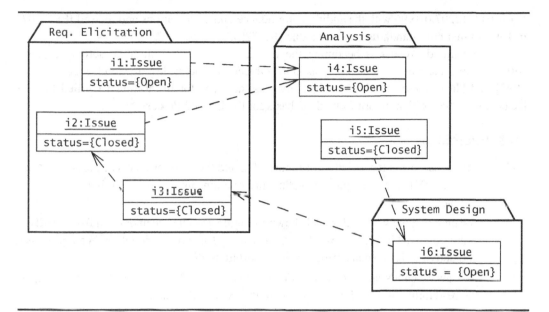

Figure 15-17   In a complex project state, all activities can still have some open issues, which means that all activities need to be managed concurrently.

15.5 Further Readings

Waterfall-based software life cycle models are still widely used. Into the 1990s, software companies contracted by the U.S. Department of Defense, for example, were required to use the 2167A standard [DoD-STD-2167A], which was based on the waterfall model. The sawtooth model [Rowen, 1990] was an attempt to improve the V-model by solving discrepancies between the user and software developer's perception of the system at different levels of abstractions over time.

ISO/IEC 12207: 1995 Standard for Information Technology–Software life cycle processes [ISO/IEC 12207, 1995] is a framework for software life cycle processes, with well-defined terminology, processes, activities, and tasks to be applied during the acquisition, supply, development, operation, and maintenance of software. This standard is occasionally (and erroneously) thought to be a replacement for IEEE 1074, the standard covered in this chapter [IEEE Std. 1074-2006]. ISO/IEC 12207 is a high-level description of the activities needed in a two-party relationship, one acquiring software, the other supplying software. It describes an architecture for software life cycles, but does not specify details about how particular activities should be implemented or performed. The IEEE 1074 standard is at a lower level of abstraction, as it is targeted for the user who needs to build a specific software life cycle for project or set of projects. For example, IEEE 1074 specifies dependencies and interfaces between the activities in terms of documents and work products. IEEE has subsequently adopted ISO/IEC 12207 as

IEEE/EIA 12207.0-1996 with the addition of guidance and clarifications and revised IEEE 1074 in 1997 so that both standards are compatible [IEEE/EIA, 1996].

The Unified Process is becoming the de facto standard for iterative activity-centered software life cycle models. It has its roots in the Objectory process described in [Jacobson et al., 1992] and [Jacobson et al., 1995]. Objectory was the basis for the Rational Unified Process [Kruchten, 1998], which in turn formed the basis for the Unified Process.

15.6 Exercises

15-1   Model as classes the activities of Figure 15-2 and the work products of Figure 15-4 and draw a UML class diagram depicting the relationships between activities and work products.

15-2   Assume that the waterfall model shown in Figure 15-8 has been derived from the IEEE standard model in Figure 15-7 during the activity Life Cycle Modeling. What processes and activities have been omitted in the waterfall model?

15-3   Redraw Boehm's spiral model in Figure 15-10 as a UML activity diagram. Compare the readability of the original figure with the activity diagram.

15-4   Draw a UML activity diagram describing the dependency between activities for a life cycle in which requirements, design, implementation, test, and maintenance occur concurrently. (This is called an evolutionary life cycle.)

15-5   Describe how testing activities can be initiated well before implementation activities. Explain why this is desirable.

15-6   In project management, a relationship between two tasks is usually interpreted as a precedence relationship; that is, one task must complete before the next one is initiated. In a software life cycle, a relationship between two activities is a dependency; that is, one activity uses a work product from another activity. Discuss this different. Provide an example in the context of the V-model.

15-7   Assume you are part of the IEEE committee that will revise the IEEE 1074 standard. You have been assigned the task of modeling communication as an explicit integral process. Make a case for the activities that would belong to this process.

References

[Boehm, 1987]
B. Boehm, "A spiral model of software development and enhancement," *Software Engineering Project Management*, pp. 128-142, 1987.

[DoD-STD-2167A]
DoD-STD-2167A, *Military Standard, Defense Systems Software Development*, US Department of Defense, Washington, DC, 1988.

[IEEE Std. 1074-2006]
IEEE Standard for Developing Software Life Cycle Processes, IEEE Computer Society, New York, 2006.

[IEEE/EIA, 1996]
IEEE/EIA 12207.0-1996. *Industry Implementation of International Standard ISO/IEC 12207: 1995 Standard for Information Technology–Software life cycle processes*, IEEE Computer Society & Electronic Industries Association, March 1998.

[ISO/IEC 12207, 1995]
ISO/IEC 12207, *Information technology–Software life cycle processes*, International Organization for Standardization & International Electrotechnical Commission, August 1995.

[Jacobson et al., 1992]
I. Jacobson, M. Christerson, P. Jonsson, & G. Overgaard, *Object-Oriented Software Engineering—A Use Case Driven Approach*, Addison-Wesley, Reading, MA, 1992.

[Jacobson et al., 1995]
I. Jacobson, M. Ericsson, & A. Jacobson, *The Object Advantage: Business Process Reengineering with Object Technology*, Addison-Wesley, Reading, MA, 1995

[Jacobson et al., 1999]
I. Jacobson, G. Booch, & J. Rumbaugh, *The Unified Software Development Process*, Addison-Wesley, Reading, MA, 1999.

[Jensen & Tonies, 1979]
R. W. Jensen & C. C. Tonies, *Software Engineering*, Prentice Hall, Englewood Cliffs, NJ, 1979.

[Kruchten, 1998]
P. Kruchten, *The Rational Unified Process: An Introduction*, Addison-Wesley, Reading, MA, 1998.

[Paulk et al., 1995]
M. C. Paulk, C. V. Weber, & B. Curtis (eds.), *The Capability Maturity Model: Guidelines for Improving the Software Process*, Addison-Wesley, Reading, MA, 1995.

[Rowen, 1990]
R. B. Rowen, "Software project management under incomplete and ambiguous specifications," *IEEE Transactions on Engineering Management*, Vol. 37, No. 1, 1990.

[Royce, 1970]
W. W. Royce, "Managing the development of large software systems," in *Tutorial: Software Engineering Project Management*, IEEE Computer Society, Washington, DC, pp. 118–127, 1970.

[Royce, 1998]
W. Royce, *Software Project Management: A Unified Framework*, Addison-Wesley, Reading, MA, 1998.

16

Methodologies: Putting It All Together

We should be careful to get out of an experience only the wisdom that is in it—and stop there; lest we be like the cat that sits down on a hot stove-lid. She will never sit down on a hot stove-lid again—and that is well; but also she will never sit down on a cold one anymore.

—Mark Twain, *Following the Equator: A Journey Around the World*

In the previous chapters, we described a range of development and management methods covering many different aspects of complex and changing software systems. For dealing with system and application domain complexity, we described methods such as use case modeling, object modeling, applying architectural styles, reusing design patterns, and mapping of models to source code. For communicating knowledge about the system, we discussed UML diagrams, issue models, informal communication mechanisms, and documents. For dealing with change, we examined a variety of organizations, processes, and life cycles.

By now, you have an overview of the current state of the art of methods in object-oriented software engineering, which you can view as a thick cookbook of recipes. In practice, however, a cookbook is rarely enough for the novice to cook a complete meal. Moreover, not all ingredients are always available, and the cook has to improvise to bridge the gaps.

In this chapter, we present methodologies as guidance for the manager to select and customize the recipe to the specific project environment. The discussion about the right methodology for software development is far from over. We present a design space ranging from light-weight approaches to heavy-weight approaches. The idea is to help you understand this space for yourself when organizing and running software projects. Although we cannot replace experience with a book, we provide actual project examples to illustrate how trade-offs are made when defining, setting up, and running a software project.

We also present case studies conducted as software engineering project courses that cover a wide range from a four-month, two-developer project collocated with the client to a distributed, one-year, 100-person project with a remote client. In each of these case studies we describe the selection of specific methods and techniques. All of our case studies involve actual clients and developers who are technically fluent with respect to programming, but new to software engineering concepts.

16.1 Introduction: The First Ascent of K2[1]

When Mount Everest (8,850 m) was successfully climbed with oxygen in 1953—after many unsuccessful attempts without oxygen—it was assumed that one had to use oxygen to reach a summit in such an extreme altitude. When the second highest peak K2 (8,611 m) was attempted by an Italian expedition in 1954, oxygen was included in the equipment list.

Unplanned bivouac on K2

On July 30, 1954, Walter Bonatti and high-altitude porter Mahdi started at Camp 8 with a crucial carry of oxygen to Camp 9. The oxygen load was for the lead climbers Achille Compagnoni and Lino Lacedelli, who had arrived at Camp 9 earlier. The expedition leader had selected them as candidates for the final summit push, and the oxygen was intended to help them climb in the extreme altitude. When Bonatti and Mahdi arrived at the location of the agreed Camp 9 spot, they could not find anybody. Constantly searching for Compagnoni and Lacedelli, they eventually established voice communication with the lead climbers, but they were not able to join them. Around 9:30 P.M. they were forced to bivouac.

An unplanned bivouac at an altitude of 8,100 m is a very serious affair. Bonatti and Mahdi endured a horrible night in a snow blizzard without any protection from the winds. Unbelievably, Bonatti came out of the ordeal unhurt, but Mahdi got severe frostbite and eventually had to undergo various amputations on his fingers and toes. The next day, Bonatti and Mahdi left their load at the bivouac site and stumbled down to Camp 8. Compagnoni and Lacedelli left their tent, went to the bivouac site to pick up the oxygen and started for the summit. In the official account of the climb, Compagnoni and Lacedelli ran out of oxygen about 200 m below the summit, which they reached at 6 P.M. Some of the summit pictures show the oxygen packs at their feet.

Discussion

The fact that Bonatti was unscathed from the bivouac led to many accusations, in particular that he had tried to climb K2 against the order of the expedition leader.

Compagnoni and Lacedelli claimed they ran out of oxygen early because Bonatti had used up part of the oxygen supply during the unplanned bivouac so he would stay strong enough for the summit attempt. Bonatti did not have a respirator mask with him, so he could have not possibly used oxygen. A detailed analysis of the summit pictures in 1993 demonstrated that Compagnoni and Lacedelli had worn their oxygen masks all the way up to the summit of K2 [Marshall, 2001]. Why did they lie? Marshall thinks that Compagnoni must have been horrified when going back to Camp 8 after the successful summit push to discover what happened the night before. He must have worried he would be blamed, particularly if he felt even partially responsible for the unplanned bivouac. He must have also felt threatened when he was questioned by the expedition leader about Mahdi's injuries.

Mahdi told his liaison officer, who in turn relayed it to the expedition leader, that Bonatti had intended to reach the summit. Bonatti cannot possibly have told his intentions to Mahdi, because he spoke only Italian and Mahdi spoke only Urdu. But how did Mahdi arrive at this conclusion?

---

1. This discussion leaves out many of the fascinating details of the problems that occurred during the first ascent of K2. To fully appreciate the complex interdependencies between equipment, motivations, reward structures, hidden agendas, expectations, novices and experts, and different view points, we refer the reader to the K2 chapters in Bonatti's book [Bonatti, 2001].

> Before the Second World War, all 8,000-m summit attempts were made with the help of experienced high-altitude Sherpas from Nepal. Even expeditions to K2 and Nanga Parbat, located in the Karakorum, hired Sherpas. After the war, Karakorum expeditions would get their climbing permit only if they hired local porters. The Hunzas in the north of Pakistan were the obvious choice. Hunzas are highly capable mountain people, but at that time they were still rather inexperienced in high-altitude expeditions.
>
> In 1953, the Hunza Mahdi was hired as a rookie porter during the first ascent of Nanga Parbat. The Nanga Parbat expedition started as a traditional fixed-rope expedition with a hierarchical organization, but the final summit push was made by Hermann Buhl in a heroic 40-hour solo climb. Buhl did this against the order of the expedition leader [Buhl, 1956].
>
> By observing Buhl's method, Mahdi must have concluded how successful climbing of 8,000-m peaks had to be done. He had reason to assume that Bonatti was attempting to copy Buhl's feat, instead of simply delivering oxygen bottles to the lead climbers so they could reach the summit.
>
> Mahdi's (false) allegation, that Bonatti had plotted to reach the summit first, must have produced quite an explosive reaction in Compagnoni because this was in violation of the expedition leader's orders. Compagnoni now thought he had a perfect excuse to lay the entire blame for Mahdi's injuries on Bonatti. To protect themselves further from being responsible for Mahdi's injuries, Compagnoni and Lacedelli most probably invented the story of the early loss of oxygen as well.

An expedition leader has to make several key decisions to create a successful expedition: which mountain should be climbed, what process should be used, what type of tools, and who should be part of the team. The answers to these questions lead to a variety of styles. The fixed-rope style focuses on the creation of a base camp followed by several high camps. These camps are then connected by fixed ropes that allow the climbers to move fast between these camps. In the Alpine style, climbers do not use fixed ropes at all. The climbers carry everything they need, setting up camp only when the night falls or when the weather stops them.

After the failures on Mount Everest and K2 in the 1920s and 1930s, it became an almost universal opinion that Mount Everest and K2 could not be climbed without oxygen. After Mount Everest was climbed with oxygen in 1953, oxygen was seen as fundamental to a successful climb. In 1978, Reinhold Messner and Peter Habeler climbed Mount Everest without oxygen.

Even the question whether an expedition leader is needed at all can be answered in different ways. From the early 1920s to the late 1960s, many expeditions were organized almost like the military. They used a hierarchical organization with an expedition leader, several lead climbers, a support team, many porters, and a liaison officer, whose task was to resolve difficult communication problems between the porters and the rest of the expedition members. The 1954 expedition to K2 involved more than 300 porters. In 1980, Reinhold Messner went to Mt. Everest with a support team of two people who accompanied him only to base camp. From there he went solo without oxygen all the way to the summit and back in one single push.

Like an expedition leader, the project manager of a software project must deal with key decisions about project goals, software life cycle, project organization, tools, methods, and team members. Although some of these decisions are made by other people or even imposed by the organization, the character of the project and the ability for the project manager to respond to unexpected events are strongly formed by these decisions. In Chapter 14, *Project Management*, we discussed project management decisions such as those related to time, schedule, cost, and project organization. In Chapter 15, *Software Life Cycle*, we discussed project-independent decisions, such as process model, dependencies among activities, process maturity, and process improvement. To deal with the complexity of the material, we discussed these issues separately in Chapters 14 and 15. During a project, however, the manager has to deal with these issues together, as they depend on the project context and are strongly interdependent. In this chapter, we discuss how to approach these decisions within a coherent framework. To facilitate this discussion, we distinguish between project goals, environment, methods, tools, and software engineering methodologies (Table 16-1).

The project **goals** include the criteria that are used to evaluate the success of a project. The project goal may be simply the on-time delivery of the specified system. In other cases, project goals can include broader strategic aspects, such as ensuring repeat business from the client or decreasing business costs.

Table 16-1   Examples of goals, environments, methods, and methodologies in mountain climbing and in software engineering.

	Mountain climbing	Software engineering
Goal	Mount Everest K2 Nanga Parbat	The delivery of an emergency information system within quality, budget, and schedule constraints.
Environment	Clear, cold weather Porters Climbing permit requirement	Local client Novice developers Project duration Project distribution Emergency response plan
Method	Free climbing Belaying & repelling Liaison officer	Use case modeling Design pattern reuse Project-based organization
Tool	Oxygen bottles Rope	CASE tool Version control tool
Methodology	Alpine style Fixed rope style	Extreme Programming Royce's methodology

The **environment** includes the elements present at the beginning of the project. In software development, the environment is defined by the client and by the current state of the development organization. The environment constrains the project manager. Examples includes the participants' background, the problem type, and the location of the project.

Methods are recipes that the project manager can freely select to bring the project to a successful end in the given environment. Examples include the methods we described so far in this book, such as use case requirements elicitation or design pattern reuse. Different methods work in different environments; an expedition using oxygen needs more porters.

Tools are devices or programs that support specific activities. Mountaineering tools include oxygen bottles, ropes, pitons, tents, and so on. Software engineering tools include modeling tools, compilers, debuggers, change tracking tools, and version control tools. Developers often rely on specific tools to automate steps stipulated by the methods they use.

A software engineering **methodology** is a collection of methods and tools for developing and managing a software system to achieve a specific goal in a given environment. It specifies when methods or tools should be used and what to do when unexpected events occur.

Section 16.2 describes typical elements of the environment that have a high impact on the project. Section 16.3 discusses typical issues that are addressed by methodologies considering a given environment and a set of available methods. Section 16.4 describes two general software engineering methodologies, Extreme Programming [Beck & Andres, 2005] and Royce's software engineering unified methodology [Royce, 1998], to illustrate the spectrum of methodologies available to a software project manager. Section 16.5 discusses the typical methodology issues in the context of three case studies.

16.2 Project Environment

During a software development project, many factors can influence the selection of methods. In this section, we consider the following aspects of the environment, which have a substantial impact on the initiation of the project: participants' expertise, client type, end users, technological climate, distribution, and project duration.

Participants' expertise.   The background of the client, project manager, and developers can constrain or open the field of methods that can be used during the project. Expertise includes the familiarity with the application domain, the solution domain, and with various development techniques and management practices.

Client type.   The client type affects the nature and amount of feedback during requirements elicitation and the speed of decisions when changes are requested. The client type includes two aspects: the ability to make decisions and knowledge of the application domain. Hence, we distinguish between four types of clients (Table 16-2):

- The **local king client** is a client who can answer developer questions and make decisions without having to ask anybody else. The local king has deep knowledge of the application domain and is usually collocated with the project. Local kings do not report to anybody else and can effectively collaborate with the developers and the project manager.

- The **proxy client** stands in for the real client. Proxy clients are sent by the real client, either because of lack of time or because of physical distance would make collaboration with an organization difficult. Proxy clients have sufficient knowledge of the application domain to answer clarification questions from the developers, but do not have sufficient power of representation to make major decisions.

- The **pseudo client** is a member of the development organization (e.g., the marketing department) who acts as a client, because the system is targeted at a new market segment, as opposed to a single individual or company. Pseudo clients can make decisions within a short time and can collaborate well with the development organization, but have a limited knowledge of the application domain. Often developers act as pseudo clients.

- **No client**. Many projects start without a client, for example, when a visionary product is developed before a market segment is opened. In most cases, however, the project selects a pseudo client, so that the stakes of the developers can be balanced against the stakes of the future user.

Table 16-2   Types of clients, decision power, and knowledge of the application domain.

Domain knowledge Decision power	High	Low
High	Local king client	Pseudo client
Low	Proxy client	No client

End user access.   Although clients may have deep domain knowledge, they have different stakes than the end user. Clients are usually interested in an early delivery date, with as much functionality as possible, and low cost. End users are interested in a system with a user interface that they are familiar with or is easy to learn and that supports their specific task well. When the stakes of the client and the end user are different, the project success may also depend on a usability test conducted by end users.

Technological climate.   Depending on the requirements expressed by the client, a project may be constrained in the technological components it has to use. A project improving a legacy system deals with well-known and mature technology. A project developing a first-of-a-kind prototype based on a technology enabler may have to deal with preliminary versions of components and immature technology.

Geographical distribution. Projects where all participants are located in a single room are the easiest to manage, as all participants can get to know each other and much of the important coordination can occur informally. However, there are many situations when single-room projects are not possible or not desirable. The organization may have resulted from the merger or acquisition of several individual companies with different skills. In other situations, the development organization is a consortium or a temporary alliance of several subcontractors, located in different geographical locations. In yet other situations, some part of the development organization may need to be collocated with the client. While geographical distribution increases the availability of skill, it also introduces new challenges, such as slower communication, lower awareness among teams, and loss of information between sites. In the first successful ascent of K2, the organization was highly distributed, which contributed to the information loss: the expedition leader remained in the base camp, the lead climbers were in Camp 9, and the support climbers bringing the last bottles of oxygen were in Camp 8.

Project duration vs. rate of change. The relationship between the project duration and the rate of requirements and technological change affects which life cycles can be selected for the project. A short project in which requirements do not change does not require extensive configuration management or rationale management. Conversely, a multi-year project with many requirement changes and staff turnover benefits from systematic configuration management and rationale management approaches.

16.3 Methodology Issues

Methodologies provide general principles and strategies for selecting methods. Such high-level guidance is also useful when dealing with new situations. In this section, we present selected issues for which methodologies typically provide guidance. These include

- How much planning should be done in advance? (Section 16.3.1)
- How much of the design should result from reusing past solutions? (Section 16.3.2)
- How much of the system should be modeled before it is coded? (Section 16.3.3)
- In how much detail should the process be defined? (Section 16.3.4)
- How often should the work be controlled and monitored? (Section 16.3.5)
- When should the project goals be redefined? (Section 16.3.6)

16.3.1 How Much Planning?

Software project management plans are one of the keys in running a successful project. However, plans have limitations. Thomas Gladwin has demonstrated this in an article in which he compared the methods by which the Polynesians and the Europeans navigate the open sea ([Gladwin, 1964] as cited by [Suchman, 2007]). The European navigator begins with a plan of the course. His effort throughout the voyage is directed to following the plan. If unexpected events occur, the plan is altered and corrective activities are introduced to still achieve the planned goal. This type of planning and controlling works well for assembly productions similar to those described by Taylor in the early 1920s [Taylor, 1911] for the production of many identical cars, but not for building systems that require creative problem solving and reactivity to change.

The Polynesian navigator begins with an objective instead of a plan. He sets off toward the objective and responds to conditions as they arise in an ad hoc fashion. He uses his skills and experience by observing the wind, the waves, the tides and currents, the fauna, the stars, the clouds, the sound of the water on the side of the boat, to figure out the direction of his objective or the proximity of land. If asked, he can point to his objective at any moment, but he cannot describe his course. This type of project management is the key element of agile methodologies and can be used with advantage in projects exploring new technology—projects whose purpose is break existing paradigms.

Another limitation of plans is described in [Suchman, 2007]: "In planning to run a series of rapids in a canoe, one is very likely to sit for a while above the falls and plan one's descent. The plan might go something like: 'I'll get as far over to the left as possible, try to make it between those large rocks, then backferry hard to the right to make it around that next bunch.' ... But, however detailed, the plan stops short of the actual business of getting your canoe through the falls. When it really comes down to the details of responding to currents and handling a canoe, you effectively abandon the plan and fall back on whatever embodied skills are available to you."

In general, software project management plans are especially useful to kick off a software project and to stay on course when no major changes are expected. They are limited in helping the project manager or developers control the project when unexpected change occurs. In this case a project manager generally cannot anticipate an alternative activity, or its consequence, until *some* course of action is already under way. "It is frequently only on acting in a present situation that its possibilities become clear, and we often do not know ahead of time, or at least not with any specificity, what future state we desire to bring about" [Suchman, 2007].

16.3.2 How Much Reuse?

Reusing architectures, design patterns, and off-the-shelf components can significantly reduce the development effort required to deliver a system (Chapters 6 through 8). This assumes, however, that finding the appropriate solution or component to reuse can be done efficiently and reliably, and that participants understand the reused elements sufficiently well to assess their impact on the rest of the system. Moreover, while reuse decreases development time, it does not decrease significantly the time needed to test the system and may increase the time to repair defects. For commercial components, reuse also introduces risks associated with the amount and length of support provided by the vendor.

In general, the project manager faces three different trade-offs:

- *Architecture reuse.* In this case, the project participants adopt a preexisting system design and adapt it to the system (Chapter 6). As no actual software is reused, assessing an existing architecture is not more difficult than assessing an ad hoc architecture built from scratch. Given an architecture that fits the needs of the system, selecting an existing architecture is always more advantageous than recreating one from scratch. The challenge in this approach, however, is to select an architecture that will enable participants to meet the nonfunctional requirements of the system.

- *Design pattern reuse.* Similar to architecture reuse, design pattern reuse does not involve existing software (Chapter 8). However, design patterns provide solutions to partial design problems. Hence, developers will reuse, adapt, and combine many different design patterns during object design. This can lead to an over-engineered system when design patterns are used only for the sake of using design patterns. In particular, the project manager and the chief architect should ensure that the nonfunctional requirements and design goals are not hurt by the introduction of specific patterns.

- *Framework and component reuse.* The reuse of a framework or a set of components constrains the system design and may force developers to use specific design patterns (Chapter 8). Moreover, components are usually black boxes provided by a vendor, and they cannot be modified. The project manager must carefully assess the risks associated with the reuse. In general, framework assessments are shared among several projects in the organization, enabling projects to reduce the overhead associated with selecting a framework.

In the end, the project environment is the determining factor for selecting a reuse strategy. For well-defined application domains and flexible client requirements, a component-based approach may be the most cost effective. For new systems, building from scratch may be the only solution.

16.3.3 How Much Modeling?

Modeling constructs an abstraction of the system focusing only on the relevant aspects and ignoring all other. Modeling enables developers to deal with complexity by reasoning with simpler concepts. As development goes on, models are often refined to include more and more details, and if one is not careful, the complexity of the models may become comparable to the complexity of the system being modeled. Modeling makes implicit knowledge about the system explicit and formalizes it so that a number of participants can share this knowledge without misunderstanding. **Models** can support three different types of activities:

- *Design.* Models provide a representation that enables developers to reason about the system. The models also form the basis for coding, as CASE tools are able to convert models into source code templates.
- *Communication.* Models provide a common vocabulary that enables developers to discuss specific design details, even though the corresponding system has not yet been

realized. Models can support a broad range of communication activities, from exchanging models on paper napkins during lunch to formal inspections in the meeting room.

- *Archive*. Models provide a compact representation for storing the design and its rationale for future reference. Successful systems have extended life cycles, requiring several generations of developers to become familiar with early decisions.

A project manager can use modeling to support one or more of the activities above. In general, modeling presents several challenges to the manager:

- *Formalizing knowledge is expensive*. It takes time and effort from developers, and requires validation and consensus so that every participant agrees on the same meanings.

- *Models introduce redundancy*. If changes are made to the system, the models must be updated as well. If several models depict the same aspects of the system, all must be updated. If one model becomes out of sync, it loses its value.

- *Models become complex*. As the model complexity becomes similar to the complexity of the system, the benefit of having a model is reduced significantly.

The project manager can choose to create activities dedicated to maintaining model consistency and correctness or to minimize the amount of modeling by redirecting effort towards coding and testing. In general, the trade-off depends on the project environment. On the one hand, in a single-site project with a local king client, writing a complete requirements model is not as critical, since the client is continuously involved in the project and available for questions. The client can be seen as a "walking" specification of the system instead of a written specification. On the other hand, a distributed project requires knowledge about requirements and system design to be made as explicit as possible, as participants may have different stakes in the project and have no opportunities to communicate this knowledge informally. Developing a detailed use case model annotated with scenarios enables participants to converge toward a single-system concept and to document the decisions and commitments they made (Chapter 4). Similarly, a long-running project can challenge participants' memories and suffer a high staff turnaround, in which case making knowledge explicit for long-term use is an investment. In such cases, methods such as rationale management (Chapter 12) and configuration management (Chapter 13) enable participants to capture the justifications behind decisions and the history of decisions, respectively.

Deciding whether or not to externalize knowledge can also depend on control factors. Participants can make themselves indispensable to the project by refusing to share their know-how with other participants. In the first ascent of the K2, the expedition leader actually kept Mahdi's account secret, because he was angry that a participant of the organization had worked against his order (or at least that is how it seemed). As a result, for many years Bonatti actually did not know why he was avoided by the fellow expedition members, who thought of him as a liar who would sell his grandmother to get to the summit.

16.3.4 How Much Process?

Modeling the software life cycle presents similar benefits and challenges as modeling the system. On the one hand, it enables participants to reason over a simplified representation of the process, devise and implement improvements, and, consequently, share this knowledge across projects with the rest of the organization. On the other hand, process knowledge is difficult to make explicit and to keep up to date.

The trade-off faced by the project manager ranges from no modeling to a detailed and continuously refined model, depending on how many resources can be expended in this activity. The project manager selects a specific solution based on the project environment. A well-known application or solution domain leads to repeatable processes [Paulk et al., 1995], increasing the benefit of modeling the process and attempting to share it across projects. In distributed organizations, sharing process knowledge enables a high degree of standardization and, hence, a lower level of miscommunication. For example, having a single well-defined configuration management and change control process (Chapter 13) enables a manager to easily track the status of individual changes and anticipate the rate of change for the near future. Rapid prototyping efforts and concept exploration usually exhibit a much more chaotic process that resembles brainstorming. There is less benefit in capturing or trying to control such a process as it is usually not repeated and of much shorter duration. In such situations, the project could follow either an entity-based life cycle or no explicit life cycle.

When modeling a software life cycle process and reusing it in a different project, the project manager should make sure that the correct knowledge is being generalized and reused. In the first ascent of the K2, Mahdi had experienced one climb (Nanga Parbat), which started as a hierarchical, fixed-rope expedition. At the end he saw one climber (Buhl) refusing to listen to the expedition leader and going solo for the summit (in Alpine style, so to speak). He concluded that this was the way such expeditions were conducted.

16.3.5 How Much Control and Monitoring?

A detailed software life cycle model can lead to a detailed plan that can then be checked against actual progress. On one end of the spectrum, a plan could be so detailed as to plan and monitor the progress of each participant on each day. At the other end of the spectrum, a plan could include a single milestone indicating the delivery, leaving participants to plan their own work accordingly. Although both approaches are unreasonable, the project manager must choose a point somewhere in between that fits the project environment.

In general, both planning and assessing the actual progress requires experience. Consequently, novice participants are poor judges of their progress. Similarly, the lack of precedents make it difficult to plan innovative systems. To deal with novices, a project manager can select a hierarchical reporting organization with more experienced participants in the middle levels. The project manager can also define milestones as demonstration and scenario-based reviews (as opposed to documents) to force participants to confront difficult issues early. To control an innovative development, a project manager can increase the frequency of milestones while leaving their exact content flexible to provide more opportunities for project goals to be refined and redirected. Conversely, a project manager could leverage the knowledge of experienced developers by enabling them to revise the project plan or the process model. For a project with a mixture of experienced and novice participants, the project manager can select peer-reviews, walkthroughs, and peer programming techniques to facilitate the transfer of knowledge from experts to novices and to create a web of informal communication channels.

In the first ascent of the K2, the hierarchical organization led to thin communication channels, which contributed to several miscommunications. For example, Mahdi talked with the liaison officer, who relayed his statements to the expedition leader. However, the expedition leader did not talk to Bonatti to confirm Mahdi's statements.

16.3.6 When to Redefine Project Goals?

Sometimes a project goal is too ambitious or the original goal is simply wrong. When this situation occurs, it is best to admit the failure and do a thorough analysis to understand what went wrong. It requires a certain psychological capability from the manager to admit that the goal cannot be achieved. After all, from the beginning of the project to the point of failure, the main job of the manager was to convince everybody that the project was doable. One way to deal with this is to declare the outcome of the project as a successful failure. Instead of focusing on the failure, the manager focuses on an analysis of the project and determines lessons learned. Many lessons cannot be learned in a successful project. The insights resulting from this analysis can often be used to improve the next project, or to recognize dangerous obstacles in the future that are suddenly now so clearly visible.

Although declaring a successful failure is a way to cancel a project and learn from one's mistakes, this option is not always available. Another possibility is to redefine the status at the end of the project as the original goal. Sometimes this redefinition allows the project manager and the developers to deal with unexpected outcomes and to reach an intermediate, less ambitious goal that should have been defined as the original goal. In other cases, the original goal becomes irrelevant, and the redefinition of the project goal is a way to recycle the work that has been achieved so far.

16.4 A Spectrum of Methodologies

A software engineering methodology is a coherent set of principles for addressing the issues we described in the previous section. In mountaineering, fixed-rope styles and Alpine styles are methodologies. Once an expedition leader selects one of these styles, the selection of many methods follows. For example, humans cannot sustain the lack of oxygen at high altitudes. As the fixed-rope style requires the incremental establishment of a large number of camps, complete with tents, sleeping bags, food supplies, and fuel, many climbers and porters will be exposed to high altitudes longer than sustainable without oxygen. Most fixed-rope style expeditions of 8,000-m summits will then count on supplying the highest camps with oxygen bottles. Conversely, an Alpine-style expedition can plan a quick enough attempt at the summit to avoid prolonged exposure at critical altitudes.

In the same way, different styles of software development consist of the combinations of different project organizations and software life cycles. Traditionally, software engineering methodologies have evolved out of large complex, one-time projects, leading to an extensive planning phase, detailed modeling (i.e., documentation), a hierarchical organization, and fine-grained planning. This requires high overhead that is not always justified for shorter or routine projects. As a reaction to these heavier methodologies, agile methodologies, such as Extreme Programming [Beck & Andres, 2005], Feature Driven Design [Palmer & Felsing, 2002], and Scrum [Schwaber & Beedle, 2002], have appeared in recent years. In these more agile methodologies, planning is accomplished incrementally, the source code is treated as the only model of interest, and loose teams of experienced programmers are given the freedom to plan and organize their own work. Another advantage of agile methodologies is that they can adapt to fundamental changes in requirements [Cockburn, 2001]. A well-accepted definition of agility is "the ability to both create and respond to change in order to profit in a turbulent business environment" [Highsmith, 2004].

As in mountaineering, the environment constrains the set of methods that can be selected. An Alpine-style expedition may be a way to conquer a mountain at high speed, but it is certainly not the best way to bring paying customers to the top of Mt. Everest. Similarly, agile methodologies can achieve spectacular results with the right set of skills, but may not be appropriate without a critical mass of experience among participants.

In Section 16.4.1, we describe Royce's methodology [Royce, 1998], the software engineering equivalent of the fixed-rope climbing. Royce follows the Unified Process and provides many project management heuristics for estimating, controlling, and monitoring projects. In Section 16.4.2, we describe Extreme Programming (XP) [Beck & Andres, 2005], an early agile methodology and the software engineering equivalent of Alpine climbing. XP minimizes the generation of models and documentation by focusing on methods for making the design of the system explicit in the source code and for disseminating knowledge among the organization through peers. In Section 16.4.3, we describe the evolution of agile methodologies starting with the Rugby approach from Takeuchi and Nonaka [Takeuchi & Nonaka, 1986], to modern agile methodologies with a main focus on Scrum [Schwaber & Beedle, 2002]. Rugby methodologies are the software engineering equivalent of expedition climbing to unknown summits.

16.4.1 Royce's Methodology

Royce's methodology is based on the **Unified Process** life cycle described in Chapter 15. It is iterative, focuses on risk management and change management, and departs significantly from the conventional waterfall approaches typical of large projects. Key principles of the methodology include

- *Architecture-first approach.* Focus on critical use cases, significant architecture decisions, and life cycle plans before committing resources for full-scale development. Address requirements, architecture, and plan together at the beginning of each iteration.

- *Iterative life cycle process that confronts risks early.* Focus on critical use cases, high architectural risks, and planning uncertainties as early as possible. Each iteration should focus on a specific risk and move the requirements, the architecture, and the planning in a balanced manner.

- *Component-based development.* Minimize number of human-generated lines of code. This includes the reuse of commercial components, the use of code-generating tools, and the use of high-level programming languages.

- *Change management environment.* Introduce controlled baselines and automated change processes to deal with changes introduced by the iterative life cycle process.

- *Round-trip engineering.* Use automation to more tightly couple models and source code, thereby decreasing the cost of change.

- *Objective quality control.* Use automated metrics and quality indicators to assess progress as an architecture evolves toward a finished product.

- *Visual modeling languages.* Use visual languages such as UML to support modeling, communication, and documentation.

- *Demonstration-based approach.* Identify and follow performance issues early and assess intermediate artifacts.

In the following, we describe how Royce's methodology addresses the issues of planning, modeling, reuse, process, and control.

How much planning?

In Royce's methodology a project plan is developed iteratively, similar to the software. Plans are detailed and refined as the stakeholders increase their knowledge of the application and solution domains. Planning errors are like software defects: the earlier they are resolved, the less impact they have on project success.

Royce's methodology organizes the work breakdown structure around software life cycle activities. The first-level elements in the work breakdown structure represent the life cycle workflows—management, requirements, design, implementation, assessment, and deployment. The second-level elements represent phases—inception, elaboration, construction, and transition. Finally, the third-level elements correspond to artifacts that are produced during the phase. Complex projects add levels to group sets of related artifacts within a phase. The organization of the work breakdown structure around the life cycle instead of the system shields it from changes to the system.

While recognizing that estimation of new projects is difficult, Royce suggests to compute the initial estimate with a model, such as COCOMO II [Boehm et al., 2000], and refine it with the project manager, developers, and testers. This enables multiple points of view to be factored into the estimate. Moreover, this enables the project participant to feel ownership of the estimate. After each iteration, the plan is revised to reflect the performance of the project and to repair any planning error.

How much reuse?

A key principle in Royce's methodology is to minimize the amount of human-generated source code, by reusing commercial components, using code generation tools, and using high-level visual programming languages. Royce treats reuse as a return-on-investment decision. Using any of these methods decreases development time. Mature components and tools also reduce time to repair defects; immature components and tools can increase quality problems so drastically that they offset any economic benefit. Hence, buy-versus-build decisions are treated as risks that should be confronted early in the life cycle (e.g., in the first iterations of the elaboration phase). When components are reused in more than one project, the return on investment can be further increased.

How much modeling?

Royce organizes artifacts based on the activities of the Unified Process (Section 15.4.2):

- The *management set* captures the artifacts associated with planning and monitoring activities. These artifacts use ad hoc notations to capture the "contracts" among project participants and other stakeholders. Specific artifacts included in this set are the problem statement, the software process management plan, the configuration management plan, and status descriptions.

- The *requirements set* consists of artifacts describing the visionary scenarios, prototypes for user interfaces, and the requirements analysis model.

- The *design set* consists of artifacts describing software architecture and interface specifications.

- The *implementation set* consists of source code, components, and executables needed for testing the components and the system.

- The *deployment set* includes all the deliverables negotiated between the project manager and the client: in general, the executable code, the user manual, and the administrator manual.

Test artifacts resulting from the assessment workflow are part of each of the above sets. The management set includes the test plan and procedures. Test specifications are part of the requirements set. Tests are simply viewed as an integral part of the system, and the same tools and techniques are used for developing tests.

The diagram of all artifact sets generated over the phases of a software system is called the **artifact road map**. Figure 16-1 shows an example of an artifact map for managing a large software project according to Royce's methodology.

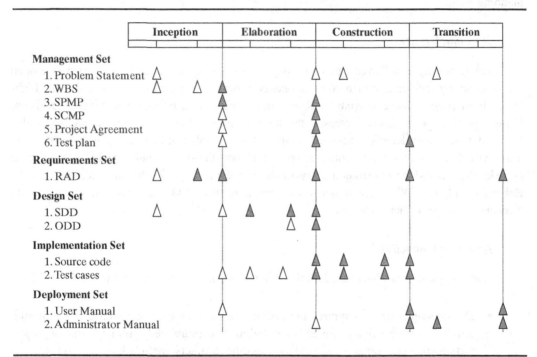

Figure 16-1   Example of an artifact road map of work products in a project using the Unified Process as a software life cycle model. The artifact names are the ones used in this book. Informal releases are shown as hollow triangles, baselined artifacts are shown as solid triangles, dotted lines represent the end of a phase (adapted from [Royce, 1998]).

How much process?

Royce's methodology includes heuristics and guidelines for tailoring the life cycle process based on the technical and managerial complexity of the project. Royce considers the following factors when tailoring the process:

- *Scale*. The number of participants in a project is the single most important factor in determining the process. Small projects (1 to 5 participants) require much less management overhead than larger projects (>100 participants). In smaller projects, performance is highly dependent on the technical skills of each participant and on the tools they use. In larger projects, the management skills of team leaders becomes a primary performance bottleneck. With small projects, management can be informal, with focus on the technical artifacts, few milestones, and no formal processes. Larger projects must be much more formal, with well-defined milestones and focus on change management artifacts, such as change requests and baselines.

- *Stakeholder cohesion.* A *cooperative* set of stakeholders allows a flexible plan and informal agreements. For example, projects with a few stakeholders who share a common goal (e.g., the development of an off-the-shelf product by a start-up company) often have cooperative stakeholders. This enables plans and requirements to be refined at the beginning of each iteration. Conversely, contention among stakeholders requires more formal agreements and well-defined processes to achieve consensus. For example, projects accomplished by a consortium of organizations often feature contentious sets of stakeholders with conflicting goals. A *contentious* set of stakeholders results in more emphasis on use case modeling and demonstration-based reviews. The assessment workflow becomes critical, and review and quality ensuring activities take precedence over other workflows to ensure stakeholder acceptance.

- *Process flexibility.* The rigor of the contract binding the client with the development organization determines the rigor of the process definition. A rigorous contract, typical in one-time, custom development contracts for the government, requires precise and detailed process definitions, whereas internal developments, such as experimental prototypes, enjoy much more flexibility.

- *Process maturity.* Organizations with mature processes are easier to manage than organizations with immature processes. Mature organizations have achieved a level of experience and process definition that enables precise planning and a high degree of process automation.

- *Architectural risk.* Ideally, the feasibility of the architecture should be demonstrated before full-scale commitment to develop the system. However, it is not always possible to eliminate all architectural risks before the start of the construction phase. For example, because the architecture is new and untested, higher architectural risk during construction results in higher levels of implementation and rework. Addressing this risk earlier results in more design effort during elaboration and more emphasis on demonstrations.

- *Domain experience.* An organization that includes participants with domain expertise shortens the earlier phases of the life cycle by increasing the reuse of experience and processes from previous projects. A team of participants that has developed similar systems in the past requires fewer elaboration iterations and fewer status assessments.

When initiating a project, a project manager assesses all of these factors when deciding the level of detailed process definition and the amount of effort to budget for each phase.

How much control?

A software development project is difficult to manage if its current status cannot be measured objectively. This is one of the reasons why conventional software projects are difficult to manage, as most intermediate artifacts are documents. An iterative life cycle addresses this problem in part, as many more technical artifacts than just documents are available early. The goals of software metrics are to provide an accurate picture to the development and management team of the progress to date and the current quality of evolving software products, so that budget and schedule accuracy can be improved over time.

At the beginning of each iteration, the plan, the requirements, and the architecture are updated. Moreover, each new iteration results in change requests for baselined work products to accommodate the resolution of new risks. Hence, change management is critical during an iterative process. The change process needs to track changes from request through approval and to assignment and implementation. The amount of code scraped or reworked, the size of the change, and other such metrics are critical to control the overall quality of the system. Royce's methodology focuses on three management metrics and four quality metrics:

- Management metrics:
  - *Work:* How many tasks have been completed compared to the plan?
  - *Costs:* How many resources have been consumed compared to the budget?
  - *Team dynamics:* How many participants leave the project prematurely, and how many new participants are added?
- Quality metrics:
  - *Change traffic:* How many change requests are issued over time?
  - *Breakage:* How much source code is reworked per change?
  - *Rework:* How much effort is needed to implement a change?
  - *Mean time between failures:* How many defects are discovered per hour of testing?

When metric collection is automated or otherwise accomplished with minimal human intervention, the project manager can rely on an increasingly accurate picture of the current status of the system and its quality. For example, the number of change requests over time can be computed when a change-tracking tool is used. Breakage and other code metrics can be computed when changes are completed and checked into a version control tool. Mean time between failures can be computed from data entered in a defect-tracking tool.

Summary

Table 16-3 below summarizes the methods used by Royce's methodology for each methodological issue.

Table 16-3   Methods in Royce's methodology categorized by methodological issues.

Issues	Methods
Planning	Evolutionary WBS Initial model-based estimation of cost and schedule (e.g., COCOMO II) Iteration planning, including all stakeholders
Modeling	Critical use cases and driving requirements first Architecture first UML Round-trip engineering
Reuse	Buy vs. build decisions during elaboration Focus on mature components for reducing amount of human-generated source code
Process	Scale Stakeholder cohesion Process flexibility Process maturity Architectural risk Domain experience
Control	Management indicators (work, cost, team dynamics) Quality indicators (change traffic, breakage, rework, MTBF)

16.4.2 Extreme Programming

Extreme Programming (XP) is a methodology targeted at small teams of developers who need to develop software quickly in a changing environment. It aims at making the design of the system as explicit as possible in the source code, hence reducing the need for documentation and the risk of inconsistencies among different documents. System design is approached in an incremental way. Only features that are needed for the requirement under consideration are implemented. The developers do not first design a general extensible architecture that could deal with future requirements. Instead, requirements are addressed one at a time: The existing code is first refactored to improve the system design in light of the current requirement. The refactored code is tested; tests for the current requirements are then written. Finally, the requirement is implemented. In short, system design is improved for extensibility only immediately before the system needs to be extended.

XP contains a collection of project management heuristics. For example, code is not owned by a specific developer, but rather owned by the team. Every line of code must actually be written by a pair of programmers who match themselves dynamically for a specific task. The *driver* has the control of the keyboard and mouse and the *partner* watches the driver over her shoulder. After the task is done, the pair disassembles. Afterward, anybody can change the code;

there is no "owner" with sole authority to make the necessary changes. This form of ownership is quite close to the egoless programming scheme originally proposed by Weinberg [Weinberg, 1971].

XP can be boiled down into five key principles:

- *Rapid feedback*. Confronting issues early results in more time for resolving issues. This applies both to client feedback and feedback from testing.

- *Simplicity*. The design should focus on the current requirements. As many changes will occur and few of them can be predicted, it is easier to deal with new requirements when they occur. A simple design is easier to understand and to change than a complex one with many layers of indirection for protecting against anticipated changes.

- *Incremental change*. It is easier to deal with changes one at the time instead of many concurrent changes. Changes should be integrated one by one with the current baseline.

- *Embracing change*. Change is inevitable and frequent in XP projects. It should be treated as a normal phenomenon and not as an exception to be avoided.

- *Quality work*. XP focuses on rapid projects where progress is demonstrated frequently. Nevertheless, each incremental change should be implemented carefully and completely. Investing time to do excellent work the first time will reduce scrap and rework later.

Next, we describe how XP addresses the issues of planning, reuse, modeling, process, and control.

How much planning?

In XP, planning is driven by requirements and their relative priorities. Requirements are elicited by writing stories with the client. Stories are high-level use cases that encompass a set of coherent features. Developers then decompose each story in terms of the development tasks needed to realize the features of the story. Developers estimate the duration of each task in terms of days; if a task is planned for more than a couple of weeks, it is further decomposed into smaller tasks. After estimating the effort needed for each story, the client and the developers meet to assign specific stories to releases, which correspond to versions of the system that will be deployed to the end user. The user stories are organized into stacks of related functionality. The client prioritizes the stacks so that essential requirements can be addressed early and optional requirements later. This leads to the release plan: it specifies which story will be implemented for which release and when it will be deployed to the end user. Releases are scheduled frequently (e.g., every one or two months) to ensure rapid feedback from the end users.

The effort needed to realize user stories is initially estimated in terms of ideal weeks. An **ideal week** is a week in which all work time is dedicated to this single purpose. When estimating the cost of a release, this number is then adjusted by a factor to reflect such overhead activities as meetings, holidays, and sick days. This factor also takes into account uncertainties associated with planning. For new teams with no previous experience in XP, authors recommend starting with a default factor of three—three actual weeks are needed to accomplish the work of a single ideal week. This factor can be lowered as time progresses. The inverse of this factor—how many ideal weeks can be accomplished during a fixed amount of time—is called the **project velocity**.

Every release is made up of a number of smaller iterations that typically last for two or three weeks. Each iteration produces a promotion of the system, which is submitted to the client for acceptance testing. By exposing the client to small increments of functionality, the client has the opportunity to introduce changes many times during development. Each iteration represents a small step toward a release, so changes are small and can easily be undone if necessary.

The beginning of an iteration starts with the so-called "planning game," in which the client selects the stories to be implemented. The ordering and priority of each user story scheduled for the current release is also decided with the client. The client then specifies acceptance tests for each story. An acceptance test is a scenario that exercises the system and is used to validate a specific story. Acceptance tests are also used for system regression testing before each release.

At the end of an iteration, the team computes the actual project velocity by adding the ideal weeks of the completed user stories (i.e., that passed the acceptance tests). During the next iteration, the client can only select a set of stories whose estimated effort does not exceed the number of ideal weeks accomplished during the previous iteration. This enables the client to trade off functionality for cost, and developers to transparently justify the cost of each feature. The planning for an iteration also includes time to address any acceptance tests that failed at the end of the previous iteration. If the project velocity deviates substantially from the original plan for more than two iterations, a new release planning meeting is called with the client to adjust the schedule.

From a project management point of view, stories can be thought of as work packages in a work breakdown structure. The difference with respect to traditional project management is that the task estimations come from the developers, not from the project manager.

How much reuse?

XP does not emphasize reuse as a key method for increasing productivity. And although XP does not rule out the use of design patterns, developers are encouraged to select the simplest solution that addresses the user story currently being implemented. Design patterns might be introduced as a result of refactoring, when changes are actually implemented. In this respect, XP differs from conventional methodologies in that it does not focus on the system architecture, which would allow such reuse to be planned at the onset. Instead, the system architecture is refined and discovered one story at the time, as the prototype evolves toward the complete system.

How much modeling?

XP minimizes documentation. The assumption is that fewer deliverables reduces the amount of work and duplication of issues. Instead, knowledge is communicated directly among participants—for example, the client is a walking specification, the design is discussed during CRC card sessions, all developers can modify any part of the code. The system design is made as explicit as possible in the source code by using explicit names and by decomposing methods into many simpler ones, each with a descriptive name. Refactoring is used to improve design incrementally. Coding standards further help developers communicate using only source code.

How much process?

XP follows a simple life cycle process consisting of four activities: planning, design, coding, and testing. Planning occurs at the beginning of each iteration. Design, coding, and testing occur incrementally in rapid succession. There are only a few constraints on these activities, which are summarized below:

- *Test first.* Unit tests are written by the developer and before units are written. This enables the developer to refine the API (Application Programmer Interface) to the class and ensures the existence of unit tests early.

- *Write tests for each new bug.* When defects are discovered, a unit test is created to reproduce the defect. Then the defect is repaired and all unit tests are run again.

- *Refactor before extending.* When new features are implemented, refactoring may be necessary to create a design that accommodates the change. The refactoring is done first, then the extension is implemented. This ensures that the design does not decay as new features are added. As ownership of the code is shared, refactoring may affect code that the developer did not initially write.

- *Production code is written in pairs.* Whereas individual developers may write prototypes for experiments or proof of concepts, production code (i.e., code that is part of a release) is written in pairs to ensure fewer defects, an improved design, and shared knowledge about the design.

- *Integrate often.* Source code from developers is integrated into the main branch, one contribution at the time. Unit tests for all integrated units are used for regression testing.

XP encourages developers to improve on this process when necessary. There are, however, no formal process instrumentation or process improvement activities; they are unnecessary given the small project sizes for which XP is suited.

How much control?

XP attempts to reduce the number of meetings developers need to attend so that they can spend more time writing tests, coding, and refactoring. Status is communicated in the team by means of a daily stand-up meeting. All project participants stand up in a circle and take turns briefly updating the team about the tasks they completed the previous day, the tasks they are currently working on, and the open issues they are facing. No discussions are allowed, to keep the meeting short. If any discussion is necessary, only the participants involved meet informally later that day.

The need for inspections and peer review is eliminated by using pair programming. Since all production code (including unit tests) are written in pairs, the review occurs during the code writing. As code is not owned by any specific pair, many programmers become familiar with any specific piece of code. Moreover, pairs are rotated often to enable a better distribution of knowledge throughout the project.

XP replaces the command and control structure of large projects, such as those found in Royce's methodology, by a self-organizing system [Highsmith & Orr, 2000]. A leader (as opposed to a manager) communicates a vision of system requirements and architecture, cultivates an environment where innovative ideas can be promoted and elaborated, and encourages risk taking. The leader must encourage an environment where participants can collaborate, share information, and develop mutual trust. The leader must still make the hard decisions to ensure that participants pull in the same direction, and get the product shipped. The leader must be able to decide when to build consensus and when to dictate. The leader is like the Polynesian navigator guiding his boat toward an objective, as opposed to managing his project according to a rigid step-by-step plan.

Summary

Table 16-4 summarizes the methods used by XP for each issue.

16.4.3   Rugby Methodologies

In 1986, Takeuchi and Nonaka published a methodology to address the specific problems that occur in new product development [Takeuchi & Nonaka, 1986]. They named it the Rugby approach, because the rugby game requires all team members to go the distance as a unit, passing the ball back and forth while moving simultaneously. This approach was in contrast to the methodologies that existed at that time, which Takeuchi and Nonaka compared with a relay race, where one runner moves at a time, passing the baton to the next runner. For many situations, these relay-based methodologies were seen as too slow, too heavy, and not able to react well to change.

In rugby, the normal flow of the game is stopped after an infringement occurs, for example after the ball is passed forward (which is not allowed in Rugby) or after the ball has been trapped. The game is then restarted with a formation called the scrum, which is quite a physical

Table 16-4   XP methods by methodological issues.

Issue	Methods
Planning	Write user stories with the client. Plan frequent small releases (every 1 to 2 months). Create schedule with release planning. Kick off an iteration with iteration planning.
Modeling	Select the simplest design that addresses the current story. Use a system metaphor to model difficult concepts. Use CRC cards for the initial object decomposition. Write code that adheres to standards. Refactor whenever possible.
Process	Code the unit test first. Code unit tests for all production code. Do not release before all unit tests pass. Write a new test for each uncovered bug. Do not add functionality early. Collocate the project with the client. Program all production code in pairs. Integrate code one pair at the time.
Control	Code is owned collectively. Adjust schedule. Rotate pairs. Start the day with a stand-up status meeting. Run acceptance tests often and publish the results.

event where injuries can occur. In software development, agile methodologists argue that developers should also stop and review the situation whenever change has occurred, such as changes in the requirements. To reduce the risk of overlooking unexpected changes, agile methodologists propose to meet as regularly as possible to identify these changes as early as possible. So while heavyweight methodologists tried to avoid unexpected change, agile methodologists regard unexpected change as the normal situation to be accepted at regular points during project-runtime.

XP described in the previous section was one of the first "light-weight" methodologies to address the slowness and bureaucracy of these methodologies [Beck & Andres, 2005]. Based on the Rugby approach, Ken Schwaber published the Scrum approach in 1995 [Schwaber, 1995]. Other light-weight methodologies with similar goals emerged during the same time such as Adaptive Software Development (ASD) [Highsmith & Orr, 2000], Crystal Clear [Cockburn, 2004]. In 2005, Martin Fowler published an overview of these methodologies [Fowler, 2005].

In 2000 a group of XP experts and other methodologists discussed the relationship of XP with other "light-weight" methodologies. During that meeting, the name agile methodology was chosen instead of light-weight methodology, because the term light-weight was considered to evoke the wrong idea of being "light-headed". The key points of an agile methodology were then published with four so-called value statements in the Agile Alliance Manifesto [AgileManifesto, 2001]:

- *Individuals and interactions over processes and tools.* The most important factor in a software project are the people and how they work together. Software development is better done by a social network of self-organizing people than an organizational hierarchy with strict lines of authority, processes with fixed roles and sophisticated tools.
- *Working software over comprehensive documentation.* The goal of software development is to create software, not documentation.
- *Customer collaboration over contract negotiation.* Having a contract with the customer is important, but it is not a substitute for communication. Successful developers work closely with their customers to discover what they need, and they educate their customers along the way.
- *Responding to change over following a plan.* A good software project should start with a plan, but that does not mean it must be followed literally, it must be changeable if the situation changes and change is a reality in software development. As work progresses, the understanding of the application and solution domain, the business environment and the underlying technology changes and developers should be able to respond to these changes.

In this section, we describe elements of Rugby methodologies not covered by XP, addressing the five methodological questions in this chapter.

How much planning?

Agile methodologies have had a poor reputation with respect to planning. Critics of agile methodologies often say that "agile teams don't plan" or "agile teams won't commit to dates and features." In fact, agile methodologies advocate a lot of planning, but not all of it at the beginning of a project. Agile planning is iterative and refines estimates as requirements stabilize and more experience is gained by the team. In a deterministic model of development, the SPMP is developed up front, in a nondeterministic model of development, the SPMP is developed incrementally and iteratively, and adapts to the current situation.

Iterative planning implies that the agile planner is always prepared to acknowledge that the plan itself is wrong instead of trying to get the project back to the planned course. This can happen as a response to change, for example, when requirements change or when promising new technology appears in the middle of the project. At the start of a project the plan may state that a product should fulfill a specific set of requirements, but in the middle of the project the client decides that a different set of requirements would increase the value of the product significantly.

This uncertainty is also reflected in the estimate models used for incremental planning. Cohn, for example, advocates three distinct estimates: The order of magnitude estimate, done at the beginning of the project, which can be off by as much as an order of magnitude from the eventual values. The next level estimate is the budgetary estimate with a precision of +25% to -10%. Late in the project follows the definite estimate, with a precision of +10% to -5% [Cohn, 2006].

Closely related to agile planning is agile estimation, such as Planning Poker [Grenning, 2002]. Planning Poker involves a moderator and the team members. It starts with a list of features of the system to be developed. These can be the functional or nonfunctional requirements, often presented in terms of user stories or scenarios. Each team member gets a deck of cards containing a set of different values, for example 1, 2, 3, 5, 8, 13, 20, 40, 100. For each feature on the list, the team members discuss their difficulty and privately choose a value card that they think represents the correct estimate. Then the moderator asks that all the cards are simultaneously revealed. In general, there will not be an immediate consensus about the estimates and the team members with the highest and lowest estimates are asked to justify their choices. This usually leads to another round of discussion and another estimation. This process is repeated until a consensus is reached. There are different ways to reach a consensus. For example, the developer who is responsible for the requirement may have more weight in the consensus vote, the moderator may also get more power to negotiate the consensus.

As agile estimation is iterative, planners improve their estimates as they gain a better understanding of the development team and the application domain.

How much reuse?

Rugby methodologies are used with advantage in new product development, in our terminology greenfield engineering, where the focus is not so much on the reuse of models or existing processes, but more on the reuse of knowledge.

Knowledge acquisition is encouraged on the individual level as well as on the team level. Team level learning takes place on the technical level in terms of tutorials and training programs as well as on the social level. Furthermore, the team members are encouraged to accumulate experience in areas other than their own. This allows team members to speak with people from other domains, an important aspect for the elicitation of requirements and the discovery of innovative designs.

Subsequently, knowledge is transferred between projects by reassigning key experts to different teams. While organizations learn by converting individual project successes to standard practice, institutionalization often creates a problem when the project environment changes significantly. In such a situation, standard practices established from previous projects are rarely applicable. In contrast, Takeuchi and Nonaka claim that learning from mistakes is more helpful than learning from success. Project managers as well as developers can usually learn more from mistakes than from successes [Petroski, 1992]. Allowing mistakes during a project is an important aspect of the Scrum methodology: the key is to find the mistakes early and having the time to correct them. This is made possible by the daily Scrum meetings.

How much modeling?

Throughout the book we have introduced the concept of modeling as a key to solve software engineering problems. UML has become one of the dominating languages to model applications and software systems. We use UML to specify requirements with functional models for the customer (use case models), we realize the dynamic behavior (workflows) with state chart and activity diagrams, and we use deployment diagrams to describe a software installation.

We have emphasized the need for keeping the models consistent which each other (Section 4.3.3). Ambler advocates to update models only "when it hurts" [Ambler, 2002], that is, developers should not try to make models consistent with each other after a change in one of the models. Agile Modeling also assumes that there are many ways to model the same concept. Ambler also proposes to create several models in parallel, drawing models with the simplest notations and using the simplest tools. For example, in Scrum tasks are written on slips of paper and organized on a white board.

One particularly simple modeling technique is paper prototyping, where end users are asked to perform realistic tasks by interacting with a paper version of the interface [Norman, 2002]. The user interface is executed by a person playing the computer, who doesn't explain how the user interface is going to be implemented. Paper prototyping can be used for usability testing of any type of human-computer interaction, but is mostly used for testing Web-browsers, and hand-held devices. Its purpose is to get quick feedback from users while the user interface design is still in the drawing stage. User interface paper prototypes can be hand-drawn drawings or screen shots, often changed with the help of drawing or photo-editing tools.

To encourage natural behavior, the developers often prefer to do these tests without the end user knowing that the system is not yet implemented. This can be done with the Wizard of Oz technique, where a human (the wizard, usually sitting in another room) simulates the behavior of the system by intercepting all communications between the end user and the system. That is, the end user does not know that a human generates the responses. The Wizard of Oz technique can provide valuable information on which to base future designs, by gathering information about the nature of the interaction, testing the interaction of a device before building a functional model and identifying problems users will have with the devices and interactions.

For example, the user types a search query, and the wizard provides the result as if it comes from a real search engine. This allows testing the user interface, in particular query formulation and filtering of results, before implementing it. The Wizard of Oz technique can also be used with advantage when designing natural language interfaces: The design and syntax of the command language of the eventual system is driven by the actual language and formulations used by the users during the tests [Kelly, 1984].

How much process?

A deterministic process model, also called "defined process control model" by Tunde [Tunde & Ray, 1994] assumes that, given a well-defined set of inputs, the same outputs can be generated every time. Deterministic models have their roots in the early 1900s, when Frederick Taylor formulated his ideas of scientific management [Taylor, 1911]. Taylor said that any process based upon tradition, heuristics and rules of thumb should be replaced by precise procedures. With the advancement of statistical methods, his approach was later called quality control and quality management. Total quality management (TQM) in the 1980s was another attempt to make production deterministic by reducing and, if possible, eliminating variations in the process so that greater consistency in the desired product could be obtained [Deming, 1982].

The waterfall software life cycle model can be seen as an attempt to treat software development as a deterministic process. However, trying to model software development as a deterministic process has led to many projects with incomplete products, loss of control, and clients receiving the wrong product in spite of frozen requirements. Software development is better modeled with a non-deterministic model, also called "empirical process control model" [Tunde & Ray, 1994]. The use of such a model in software development is justified by the fact that software processes exhibit too much complexity to be fully understood where changes with unpredictable impact can occur at any time. Project managers using a non-deterministic model accept these unexpected events and deals with them through frequent inspection. For example, in Scrum, the next "Sprint" is planned based on the experience of the last iteration. While planning this Sprint, a redirection of the project goals and requirements by the client is explicitly allowed. That is, Scrum empirically responds to any changes, that is, it is based on the empirical process control model.

How much control?

Control in agile methodologies is based on the concept called *subtle control* by Takeuchi and Nonaka. On the one hand, the team commits to challenging goals. On the other hand, the team is self-organizing. This tension, between challenge and freedom creates a built-in instability in which innovative solutions can by rapidly developed. Takeuchi and Nonaka call teams *self-organizing* if they are:

- *autonomous:* each team can make its own decisions, independent from its place in the organizational hierarchy.
- *self-transcendent:* the teams establish their own goals and pursue their own ideas independent from the current patterns and knowledge used in the application as well as solution domains. Teams are encouraged to think out of the box. Contradictory goals are allowed, even encouraged to overcome the current way of thinking and to prepare for the discovery of new ideas.
- *multi-disciplinary:* each of the team members is selected with respect to different skills needed for the project.

Scrum teams are self organizing. Although the teams are encouraged to work on their own, they are not uncontrolled. Management establishes enough checkpoints to prevent instability turning into chaos. But the control is not based on externally imposed rigid schemes and deadlines but on self-control. That is, the project monitoring is done by the teams themselves, for example through peer pressure. This can be done by controlling the group dynamics of the team, by selecting the team members based on their experience and their energy, or by adding more experienced team members to a team of beginners. Important is the ability of the project manager to tolerate and anticipate errors.

To be able react to upcoming problems, issues must be identified as early as possible. Scrum advocates the daily Scrum meeting, in which the team members regularly share their work progress and problems they have encountered. This allows the team to identify obstacles as early as they appear, and react to them.

Summary

Table 16-5 summarizes the methods used by Rugby for each issue.

Table 16-5 Rugby methods by methodological issues.

Issue	Methods
Planning	Plan project as a prioritized list of high-level requirement. Define consensus goals of the current iteration. Agree on a consensus effort estimate; a precise estimate is only done for the current iteration. Revise estimates daily, based on newly identified work and progress.
Modeling	Sketches Paper prototype Wizard of Oz
Reuse	Reuse knowledge, not models. Reassign key experts to other projects to disseminate knowledge within the organization.
Process	Overlap development activities. Integrate completed items into a potentially deliverable product increment. Return incomplete items to the global todo list.
Control	Conduct brief daily status meetings. Assess trends with burn down charts. Review iteration results with product owner and client. Readjust team for next iteration, if necessary.

16.5 Case Studies

Novice project managers tend to be strict about the decisions made at the beginning of a project, and are usually not willing to adjust to the challenges of new situations that occur in any real project, whether technical or managerial. This unwillingness often has its roots in the inexperience of the manager with the methods and techniques applied in the project. A project manager needs to view himself as a continual apprentice, exploring the possibilities of applying tools and methods in a project as an n-dimensional parameter space. In this space each project occupies a point or a subspace spanned by the particular choice of values for the project parameters.

To get experience, a novice project manager should start with simple project parameters; for example, a team of five people, focusing on a single project parameter, either an unknown requirement, a new technology, a new method, or a new methodology. It is not recommended to change more than one of these parameters. It is not advisable to start with a large project with unknown requirements, new experimental technologies and 50 team members. For example, we do not recommend experimenting with a new methodology when addressing a new requirement from the client. With more and more project experience, managers and developers can advance to larger and larger projects with more degrees of freedom.

In this section, we provide three case studies of projects from the point of view of a novice project manager. All three projects involved a set of senior software engineering students and a real client:

- ATRACT (Automated Test and RAtionale Capture Tool) is a six-month XP project focusing on the development of a test infrastructure for a middleware environment (Section 16.5.1). ATRACT featured one requirement iteration followed by three development iterations.

- FRIEND (First Responder Interactive Emergency Navigational Database) is a five-iteration project with a collocated king client focusing on an emergency response system (Section 16.5.2). We describe the first iteration as a single project, then how the combination of five iterations formed another project.

- JAMES (Java Architecture for Mobile Extended Services) is a distributed, two-iteration project focusing on the use of smart card applications for the car driver (Section 16.5.3).

Note that these projects are all student projects. Students are often concurrently pursuing other instructional courses during the period of the software development. This is similar to a matrix development organization in which each individual can be working on a number of projects. For each project, we examine the project goals, the project environment, the methods selected to address planning, reuse, modeling, process, and control, and the lessons learned.

16.5.1 XP Project: ATRACT

Project goal

The goal of ATRACT was to provide a framework for writing and executing tests for a middleware environment specialized for small wireless devices, such as cell phones and MP3 players. The framework had to provide services for moving files between devices. Devices, based on the type of file received, could either process, store, or ignore the files. As many new types of devices and files had to be supported, the vendor of the middleware environment had a need for a testing environment for specifying and automating tests. As the development and execution of tests could involve several developers, the tool also had to include features for discussing tests using an issue-based model.

The goal for the first release was to achieve a robust testing environment with at least the minimum amount of functionality and documentation needed for conducting actual tests. An additional goal for all participants was to learn about XP and evaluate its effectiveness for small projects conducted in pairs.

Project environment

Local king client. The client of this project was the middleware vendor. He was familiar with both the technology and the platform.

Novice participants. In addition to the client, two developers and a supervisor took part in the project. All participants had taken part in software development projects; however, all were new to XP. The developers relied on the advice of an external participant for the application and customization of XP.

Mature technology. Because the platform for the system was Java, developers were able to select relatively mature components for developing the test infrastructure.

End user access. The client of the project was also an end user.

Project located at the client site. The developers were collocated at the client site and had unrestricted access to the client. The client was able to make immediate decisions and did not have to refer questions to other members of the company.

Project duration. As the developers were familiar with use case modeling and the requirements tool that was used, the project was divided into two phases: In a first two-month phase that focused only on requirements, a set of vertical prototypes and a use case model of the visionary system were developed. The developers validated the mock-ups with the client and used the use case model for tracking requirements issues. The second phase, which lasted for four months, was dedicated to realizing the first release of the system according to an XP process. At the beginning of the second phase, the use case model was converted into user stories that were used by the developers and the client for requirements prioritization and estimation. This two-phase approach enabled us to minimize the risks associated with using a new methodology (XP) by restricting its use to the construction phase of the project.

How much planning?

The milestones of the project were fixed from the start, due to constraints on the developer and management side. Previous experience in such projects (six months, few developers, new client), suggested a requirements phase of about 6 to 8 weeks. The end of the requirements phase also coincided with the beginning of the year, which made it easier to schedule in the client's calendar. The release plan and the decomposition of the first release into three iterations was decided only after the requirements phase was completed. The developers chose a high-velocity schedule from the start, confident in their ability to produce (an ideal week was estimated to take only about 1.5 actual weeks). To the surprise of most participants, the velocity did not change during the project.

How much reuse?

Initially, the developers did not plan to reuse any software packages because of the short time constraints associated with the development phase. Much of the project time was already spent understanding the application domain, in particular the existing middleware and infrastructure. While implementing the user stories, however, the developers found themselves writing a custom interpreter for creating tests scripts, including setting variables, specifying loops, and manipulating files. As the custom language for the test script became more complex, the developers decided to discard their custom interpreter and reused, instead, an open-source implementation based on Javascript. This actually put the project back on schedule and resulted in additional functionality for the client and a lower learning curve for end users.

How much modeling?

The requirements were initially represented as use cases for the first phase. After the start of the second phase, only user stories and tasks were written down on index cards, which were also used to track actual effort. The use case model was not kept up to date after the switch to XP. Otherwise, no visual models were constructed. All system and object design knowledge was embedded into the code as source code comments and as method and class names. The lack of a model was not an issue given that only one pair of developers worked on the project and for a short period of time.

How much process?

During iteration 2, the XP process, including the activities iteration planning, refactoring, writing tests, realizing user stories, and test, was followed closely by the developers. The client, however, did not write user stories or acceptance tests directly, due to lack of time; instead, the developers would write the stories and the tests based on meetings with the client. As there were no schedule deviations or difficult issues, the manager turned into an observer and did not participate very much past the requirements phase.

How much control?

The developers met the manager shortly before the end of each iteration, before meeting with the client, to demonstrate the current status of the code and to assess any open issues. As the project followed the initial schedule closely and there were few open issues at the end of an iteration, the meetings were used mostly to bring the manager up to date on the application domain. The meeting was then followed a few days later by a meeting with the client for the iteration acceptance test.

Outcome

The project ended on time, delivering the required user documentation, installation scripts, source, and executable code. A brief post-development phase led to the update of the use case model to reflect the changes that had been made to the requirements. The client was satisfied with the result, and most importantly, his expectations were in line with the outcome because he had closely followed the complete development process.

Lessons learned

Training the client. Even though the project was collocated with the client organization, the client did not have enough resources to dedicate to writing user stories and acceptance tests. The organization was too small to spare that much time for an infrastructure project. Hence, the client did not learn as much about the process as originally planned. In this situation, the first two months of requirements paid off as developers were able to elicit and validate a stable set of requirements from a small number of meetings with the client, using scenarios, mock-ups, and use cases. For a longer running project, it is critical that the client understand the ground rules of XP when prioritizing user stories, estimating effort, and readjusting the schedule as a result of velocity changes. Put in Royce's terms, an XP project works for cohesive sets of stakeholders.

Training the developers about the process. XP requires a core of experienced developers. Experience enables developers to produce accurate estimates, to localize changes, and to make judgement calls about when to communicate issues with other participants. ATRACT was a small enough project where both developers knew all that needed to be known about the current status of the project. In a larger project, the rotation of pairs can be used to bring new developers, in particular beginners, up to date and introduce redundancy into the system. We anticipate, however, that running a larger project with only novice developers following XP would entail a severe learning curve before the project reached a steady state of changes.

16.5.2 Local King Client: FRIEND

Project goal

The FRIEND system is an emergency management system for coordinating field units working on an accident. When the FRIEND project started in 1992, accident management was accomplished mostly with paper-based processes. The appearance of technology enablers such as digital wireless technology and PDAs (personal digital assistants) led to the goal of replacing the paper process with an electronic process. FRIEND was designed for various types of accidents, from minor traffic accidents to such major incidents as fires and storms. The project was structured in five iterations demonstrating increasingly more complex prototypes. Many examples of Chapter 4 are taken from this project.

Each development iteration of the project was executed as a one-semester software engineering course with senior students as developers. The goal of the project was to develop a demonstration prototype of the FRIEND system. A second goal was to expose the students to state-of-the-art software engineering methods and tools. Although FRIEND did not follow closely Royce's methodology, it started with many of its elements, including a project-based organization, well-defined change processes, and similar artifact sets.

Project environment

Local king client. The client for FRIEND was the police chief of a local community. He initially did not have any background in software engineering or wireless technology. He had detailed knowledge about the application domain, and could make immediate decisions about the scope and the direction of the project.

Novice participants. The project included an average of 40 participants, mostly novice developers, with strong technical skills but little experience in projects of this scale. Management had conducted several projects of this scale. The application domain was new to all the participants.

End user accessible. The client was also an end user. Moreover, a selected set of other end users was available for usability testing.

State-of-the-art technology. FRIEND focused on wireless technology and PDAs as a platform for the prototype. Although the technology used was relatively stable, it was new and required additional training for the students before working code could be produced.

Single-site project. The project occurred in one location. All students had access to a single lab. The client was available on short notice.

Project duration. The project initially included two months of preparation, followed by a four-month development iteration. As the results of the first iteration were successful, the project led to four successor projects that further refined the concept and architecture of the system, and a spin-off company that realized a product. The overall project eventually lasted three years.

How much planning?

As FRIEND was a concept exploration project, the functionality and the platform of the prototypes were not specified in detail. The milestones, however, were fixed from the start. As the participants had little experience in large-scale development, the schedule of the project was based on the waterfall model. The requirements, system design, object design, and coding were each planned for approximately four weeks, with a formal review at the end of each development activity.

How much reuse?

Both the application domain (accident management) and the technology enablers (Apple Newtons, wireless Motorola modems) used for the project were new to the students. Little reuse was possible for the domain-specific parts of the system. Off-the-shelf packages were used for the graphical user interface and the networking subsystems. In general, the short duration of the project limited the complexity and the number of off-the-shelf packages that could be used.

How much modeling?

The project produced three artifact sets: a *client set*, a *management set* and a *system set*. The system set corresponds to the requirements, design, implementation, and deployment set in Royce's methodology. The client set included the documents under the client's responsibility and written in collaboration with project management. This included the *Problem Statement* and the *Initial Schedule* (Table 16-6).

Table 16-6   Client documents. The problem statement was handed out to the students at the beginning of the project.

Document	Purpose	Produced by
Problem Statement	Describes the needs, visionary scenarios, target environment, requirements and constraints	Concept Exploration
Initial Schedule	Describes major milestones	Project Initiation

Task models representing management information were constructed during project initiation by management and revised throughout the project. They were documented in the *Software Project Management Plan*, the *Software Configuration Management Plan*, and the *Top-Level Design* document that was used to set up the initial teams (Table 16-7).

System models represent the system at different levels of abstraction and from different perspectives. The use case model describes the system from the user's point of view. The analysis model describes entities modeling the accident management domain. The system and object design models represent the software architecture and the solution objects based on the

Table 16-7   Management documents.

Document	Purpose	Produced by
Top-Level Design	Describes the preliminary software architecture, in particular the subsystem decomposition.	Top-Level Design
Software Project Management Plan	The controlling document to manage the project	Project Initiation Project Monitor and Control
Software Configuration Management Plan	The controlling document describing the software configuration management activities	Software Configuration Management

chosen technology of PDA and wireless communication. The analysis models were documented in the *Requirements Analysis Document* (Table 16-8).

The system design was documented in the *System Design Document*. The object design model was documented in the *Object Design Document*. Models in the analysis and object design phase were written in OMT [Rumbaugh et al., 1991] and entered into a small CASE tool called OMTool. The OMT models were used both for generating the initial code fragments as well as figures in the design documents.

The purpose of models in FRIEND was primarily to support design and communication. As the goal of FRIEND was to demonstrate a prototype, we expected the system to evolve rapidly, making it costly and difficult to maintain consistency between models and the system. Hence, archiving was not a primary goal. Instead, we expected knowledge to be transmitted across iterations by way of the prototype and the implicit knowledge carried by the students who continued with the project.

How much process?

The life cycle model included three phases. During the pre-development phase, preliminary requirements and the initial software architecture were developed. Infrastructure choices were also made, in particular a single room was chosen and dedicated solely for the students working on the project. Only the client, project manager, and coaches were involved in this phase. At the beginning of the development phase, all students were assigned to a team to work toward the construction of the system. The goal of the development phase was to validate the architecture of the system and expose the participants to all aspects of an iterative software life cycle. The requirements, design, implementation, and test cases were developed incrementally. Core functionality was developed during the development phase. Some optional functionality was added during the post-development phase. The rationale for this approach was to deliver a system with required functionality on time, as opposed to delivering a complete

Table 16-8 System documents for FRIEND.

Document	Purpose	Produced by
Requirements Analysis Document (RAD)	Describes the functional and global requirements of the system as well as four models: use case, object, functional, and dynamic models.	Requirements
User Manual	Describes the use of the system (in the form of a tutorial).	Requirements
System Design Document (SDD)	Describes design goals, trade-offs made between design goals, high-level decomposition of the system, concurrency identification, hardware/software platform, data management, global resource handling, software control, and boundary conditions.	System Design
Object Design Document (ODD)	Describes the system in terms of refined object models, in particular the chosen data structures and algorithms, as well as full signatures for all public methods. This document results in the detailed specification of each class used by the programmers during the implementation phase.	Object Design
Test Manual	Describes testing strategy—the unit and system tests performed on the system along with expected and actual results.	Testing
Administrator Manual	Describes the administrative procedures to install, operate, and bring down the system. Also contains a list of error codes, and failure and termination conditions.	Install Software

system late. Table 16-9 describes the three phases in the terminology of the IEEE 1074 life cycle model.

Note that the life cycle did not include operation and support activities because the goal of the project was to develop only a demonstration prototype.

How much control?

Because of the large number of participants (42 students, 5 coaches) and their lack of experience in large-scale development, we adopted a hierarchical project organization and strict control. During pre-development, a preliminary top-level design of the system was created to serve as a basis for team decomposition. The project team was organized in five subsystem

Table 16-9   Software life cycle activities for FRIEND.

Phase	Purpose	Activities	IEEE 1074 activities	
Pre-development	Initiate project	Project Initiation Concept Exploration Top-Level Design	3.1 4.1 4.2	Project Initiation Concept Exploration System Allocation
Development	Validate architecture Train participants Demonstrate core requirements Demonstrate feasibility	Project Management Requirements Elicitation Analysis Analysis Review System Design System Design Review Object Design Object Design Review Implementation Unit Testing System Integration Testing System Testing (alpha test) Configuration Management Tutorials	3.2 5.1 5.2 5.2.7 5.3 7.1 7.2 7.4	Project Monitor & Control Requirements Design Perform Detailed Design Implementation Verification & Validation Software Configuration Management Training
Post-development	Demonstrate optional requirements Deliver prototype Client acceptance	Project Management Refinement Install Software Client Acceptance Test Field Testing (beta test) Configuration Management	3.2 6.3 6.1.5 6.1.6 7.1 7.2	Project Monitor & Control Maintenance Install Software Accept Software Verification & Validation Software Configuration Management

teams (*Campus*, *Communication*, *Database*, *EMOC*, and *UI*), each responsible for one subsystem (Figure 16-2). A cross-functional architecture team was composed of liaisons from each subsystem team. A tool team was responsible for providing the infrastructure to the other teams, including build scripts, configuration management, and test harness. For the initial assignment of students to teams, we used a skill matrix considering programming knowledge, knowledge of specific tools, wishes, and interests. The identification of the skills and interests was based on information provided by the students.

During the first week of the project, we trained the students to use a well-defined process for reporting status and conducting reviews. Each team met weekly to discuss status. The weekly team meeting was facilitated by a coach, who posted a meeting agenda prior to the meeting. A student would record the meeting content in meeting minutes and action items and post them shortly after the meeting. The coaches of the teams also met weekly with the project

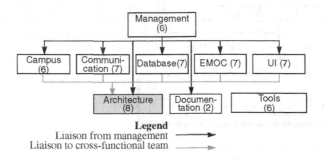

Figure 16-2   Team organization of FRIEND during iteration 1 (CMU Fall course 15-413, 1992). White rectangles indicate subsystem teams; gray rectangles, cross-functional teams. The numbers in parentheses indicate the number of team members.

manager. Progress was assessed in monthly project reviews. During the first month, the project manager and the coaches ensured that the status reporting and meeting process was followed rigorously. This resulted in the project status being visible for all students, thus allowing them to recognize the value of such information. Moreover, during the first two months, roles within teams were rotated, enabling each student to facilitate a status meeting, act as a liaison to the architecture team, and specialize in a tool role. The motivation for role rotation was pedagogical—each student had the opportunity to learn most roles; it also acted as a selection mechanism—students who performed well in a specific role often ended up serving in that role for the rest of the project.

After the system design review (i.e., the second project review), both process enforcement and role rotation were relaxed. Students were told to keep the tools and methods that worked, and discard those that got in the way. As a result, the status reporting process remained in place, but increasingly more decisions were made locally as coding progressed. Students who displayed communication skills usually ended up in the liaison roles. Students who excelled at technical tasks ended up carrying the technical tasks of the team. Conflicts and interface problems discovered during builds were resolved face to face in the lab. Only major integration issues resulted in ad hoc meetings.

In essence, the organization of the project evolved from hierarchical to a series of XP subprojects, one for each subsystem. Each subproject treated the other teams using the subsystem as collocated clients. This organization was only possible once a solid architectural concept was in place, defining the responsibilities of each team.

Outcome

The project produced a conceptual prototype that demonstrated how Geographical Information Systems could be used to organize and display incident information. The success of

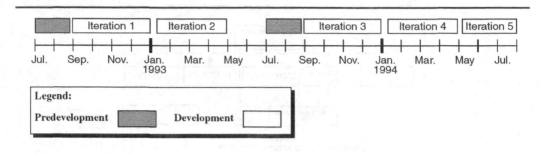

Figure 16-3   Iterations in the FRIEND project.

the first project led to four more iterations exploring a variety of technologies and functionality (Figure 16-3):

- *Iteration 2* focused on consolidating the feedback from the client into the prototype. It included a subset of the students who had worked on the first prototype, and followed an iterative software life cycle process focusing on the prototype. Each review focused on new functionality to be added to the working prototype.

- *Iteration 3* started from scratch with a new set of students and a more ambitious problem statement. The scope of the system was extended to include Emergency Operations Plan functionality for disasters that would need to be coordinated at the state level. This iteration reverted to a waterfall process, as there were many novice developers.

- *Iteration 4* consolidated the feedback from the client and investigated technological issues, such as the use of WaveLAN networks and cellular phone modems. A prototype of the system was demonstrated using Newton PDAs. Iteration 4 included a subset of students who took part in iteration 3 and followed an iterative software life cycle.

- *Iteration 5* investigated the use of NeXTStep's Distributed Objects as middleware technology for managing all communication among nodes.

A company was spun off after iteration 5 to turn FRIEND into a product.

Lessons learned

Training the client.   At the beginning of the project the client did not have any computer background. However, the client invested quite a bit of time in the project and learned how to communicate with the developers directly. By the fourth prototype, the client could understand and criticize high-level class diagrams. In general, developers should not expect this to happen, as clients usually do not plan time to learn about the project infrastructure. However, for a long-term project with a collocated client, it is worthwhile to identify ways to train them.

Training the developers about the application domain. The students were able to learn the main concepts of the application domain fairly quickly, as the client was available on short notice for clarifying ambiguities and misunderstandings. Projects without a collocated client have to find other ways to validate requirements and carefully track questions, ambiguities, and changes.

Setting up a dedicated lab. The project benefited from a dedicated lab for students to program, meet, prepare demonstrations, drink coffee, and conduct client presentations. A white board was used for tracking current issues, task assignments, and project status, and was often more up to date than the project web site. Having a single dedicated lab enabled informal communication to take place and many design and management issues to be uncovered early and resolved quickly.

Maintaining the infrastructure. The project organization chose to set up a tool team whose responsibility was to find new development tools and existing class libraries and thereby to support the infrastructure of the project. Because the participants of the tool team were novices—which is typical for a student project course—they had little understanding of the requirements of an infrastructure for supporting a large project. Moreover, as they did not participate in the main development effort, they did not have much credibility with the other students and were sidelined. We recommend instead to assign the responsibility of the infrastructure to an administrative group independent of the specific project. Even in project-based organizations, there is a need for project-independent support functions such as infrastructure maintenance. Having a permanent infrastructure group makes it easier to reuse the infrastructure across projects and increase the return on investment. The infrastructure group also gains credibility with the developers with the accumulated experience from multiple projects.

Using version control as an integration tool. The early set-up of a version control scheme and build infrastructure in pre-development provided the teams with a concrete mechanism for detecting and resolving conflicts early. Beginning with the pre-development phase of iteration 2 of this project, a "Hello World" prototype with corresponding build and test scripts was checked into the version control repository. This practice is also being followed by many software development companies, such as Microsoft [Cusumano & Selby, 1997].

16.5.3 Distributed Project: JAMES

Project goal

Smart card technology has opened up a vast range of applications. Some of the key applications include pay phones, mobile communications, electronic cash, parking, health care and network access. Another important application is the use of the smart card for the automotive industry as a value-added service.

The goals of the JAMES project were twofold: First, to investigate JavaCard technology and assess if it can be used to host multiple applications on the same card, the purpose being to reduce the number of cards each individual needs to carry around. Second, to define a system architecture that would enable users to select a combination of applications and dynamically store them on their cards. This allows the car manufacturer to offer new services and applications that could be added even after the purchase of the vehicle.

To accomplish these two goals, JAMES was to demonstrate a technology prototype that included three smart card applications: *Travel*, a system for planning and following routes on an onboard digital street map; *Bonus*, a reward system similar to a frequent flier mileage program; and *VIP*, a system for storing and customizing individual preferences, such as seat position, radio station, and audio volume settings.

Project environment

Proxy client.   A proxy client from DaimlerChrysler was available full time during the project. The proxy client presented the problem statement to the students during a kick-off meeting. After the kick-off meeting, all communication with the client was through the proxy client. A separate Lotus Notes database was set up exclusively for communication between the proxy client and the students.

Novice participants.   The developers of the JAMES project were drawn from the same pool of senior students as the FRIEND project. The client and the proxy client came from the information technology department of DaimlerChrysler and had knowledge of the application domain and the software engineering methods used in the project.

No end user access.   There was no access to the end user. Vehicle owners among the developers and the proxy client were used as semi-representative end users.

Immature technology.   The technology under evaluation (the Cyberflex kit developed by Schlumberger [Schlumberger]) was in beta release. The JavaCard API it implemented was also new, which resulted in a general lack of developer documentation and substantial time spent working around bugs.

Three-site project.   The project was distributed among three sites. One set of students was working in Carnegie Mellon University (CMU), Pittsburgh, PA. The other set was working in Technical University Munich (TUM), Germany. The client was located at Stuttgart, Germany, and the proxy client for iteration 1 was located in Pittsburgh, collocated with the first team of students. The proxy client returned to Stuttgart for the remaining iterations.

Project duration   The project included three iterations, each lasting approximately four months. The first was initiated at CMU; iteration 2 involved both the CMU and the TUM sites; iteration 3 involved only the CMU site (Figure 16-4). The overall project, including pre- and post-development, lasted 11 months.

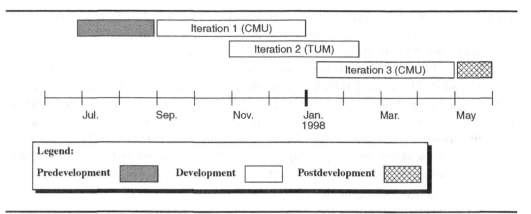

Figure 16-4   Iterations in the JAMES project.

How much planning?

The goal of the project was the demonstration of a conceptual prototype. Unlike FRIEND, the demonstration environment was known in advance and constrained the development kit used for programming the smart cards. This required more planning to take place earlier than in the FRIEND project, as the project often worked with pre-release versions of the development tools. Iteration 1 was planned as a waterfall iteration, similar to FRIEND. Fixed milestones delimited the requirements, system design, implementation, and coding activities. Iteration 2 featured an iterative prototyping approach, with prototypes of increasing functionality demonstrated every month. The TUM and the CMU sites worked on different subsystems, but shared the same architecture.

How much reuse?

The conceptual prototype was required to interact with an existing software system for accessing dealer data. The existence of this legacy system and the short iteration times reduced the opportunity to reuse components that were not already part of the existing infrastructure.

How much modeling?

Distributed software development can have several advantages. For example, a project can leverage specific combinations of skills without relocating participants within the organization.

In JAMES, a substantial amount of knowledge needed to be transferred between sites at the beginning of the second development phase. At CMU, most students participating in iteration 3 had participated in iteration 1. Hence, the knowledge transfer from iteration 1 to iteration 3 was not an issue at CMU. At TUM, however, none of the participants were familiar with the system, except for the instructor and one of the coaches. The participants at TUM were given access to all the deliverables of iteration 1 and could communicate with the CMU team via Lotus Notes and E-mail. To encourage further information exchange between both sites, two members from the TUM team traveled to Pittsburgh early in iteration 2, and one member of the CMU team traveled to Munich for the integration phase and the client acceptance test.

As in FRIEND, models in JAMES were used primarily as a basis for design and for communication. The archival value of the documents produced by iteration 1 was limited, as they were not consistent with the current version of the prototype. Students at the TUM site reverse-engineered the first prototype system to recover an up-to-date model of the system, correcting inconsistencies and omissions in the accompanying documentation. The result of this activity, which we called Inventory Analysis, was an *Inventory Analysis Document* describing the components of the first prototype and their implementation status (Table 16-10).

Table 16-10   Inventory documents.

Document	Purpose	Produced by
Inventory Analysis Document	Describes the models and components that have been realized, their status, and the problems associated with them	Inventory Analysis

How much process?

We refined the life cycle of the FRIEND project to include a second development iteration and added activities focused on transferring knowledge from one site to the other (Table 16-11). Both development iterations were structured in the same way, such that the same documents, methods, and procedures could be used. The second development iteration, however, was an improvement iteration that produced a refined version of the *Requirements Analysis Document*, the *System Design Document*, the *Object Design Document*, and the prototype system.

Since the project relied on the JavaCard technology, one team on the TUM site was responsible for developing focused technology prototypes showing how specific risks associated with the prerelease state of the technology could be addressed. The technology team interacted directly with the technology provider (Schlumberger's smart card division), reported on its current list of issues, and demonstrated its prototypes during the monthly reviews associated with each document. These prototypes were subsequently used by other teams as sample code for implementing their own subsystems.

In general, the process in iteration 2 evolved into an entity-based process—a process focusing on the prototype, open issues, and changes, as opposed to focusing on the activities (Section 15.4)—as issues associated with the JavaCard environment presented the highest risks.

How much control?

As in FRIEND, the JAMES project organization started as a strict hierarchical organization. During iteration 1, 41 participants were organized into five teams (see Figure 16-5) each responsible for a subsystem (*Logbook*, *Maintenance*, *Travel*, *VIP* and *Vehicle*). Two cross-

Table 16-11   Activities for JAMES. Differences from FRIEND highlighted in *italics*.

Phase	Purpose	Activities	IEEE 1074 activities	
Pre-development phase	Initiate project	Project Initiation Concept Exploration Top-level Design	3.1 4.1 4.2	Project Initiation Concept Exploration System Allocation
First development phase	Validate architecture Train participants of first site Demonstrate core requirements Demonstrate feasibility	Project Management Requirements Elicitation Analysis System Design Object Design Implementation Unit Testing System Integration Testing System Testing (alpha test) Configuration Management Lectures & Tutorials	3.2 5.1 5.2 5.2.7 5.3 7.1 7.2 7.4	Project Monitor & Control Requirements Design Perform Detailed Design Implementation Verification & Validation Software Configuration Management Training
Second development phase	*Improve architecture* *Train participants of second site* *Demonstrate extensibility* *Demonstrate desirable requirements*	*Inventory Analysis* Inventory Review *Project Management* *Requirements Elicitation* Analysis Requirements Review *System Design* System Design Review *Object Design* Object Design Review *Implementation* *Unit Testing* *System Integration Testing* *System Testing (alpha test)* *Configuration Management* Tutorials	 *3.2* *5.1* *5.2* *5.2.7* *5.3* *7.1* *7.2* 7.4	 *Project Monitor & Control* *Requirements* *Design* *Perform Detailed Design* *Implementation* *Verification & Validation* *Software Configuration Management* Training
Post-development phase	Demonstrate complete functionality Deliver prototype Client acceptance	Project Management Refinement Install Software Client Acceptance Test Field Testing (beta test) Configuration Management	3.2 6.3 6.1.5 6.1.6 7.1 7.2	Project Monitor & Control Maintenance Install Software Accept Software Verification & Validation Software Configuration Management

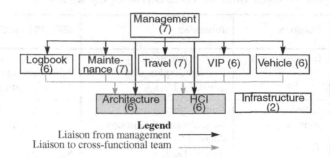

Figure 16-5 Team organization of the development teams in Pittsburgh during iteration 1 (CMU Fall course 15-413, 1997). White rectangles indicate subsystem teams; gray rectangles, cross-functional teams. The numbers in parentheses indicate the number of team members.

functional teams, *Architecture* and *HCI*, composed of liaisons from the subsystem teams, were responsible for coordinating issues related to system architecture and user interface, respectively. Each team met weekly to report status and resolve open issues. Coaches of the teams met with the project manager weekly.

During iteration 2, the two subsystem teams *Bonus* and *VIP* were located at TUM (23 participants), and the subsystem team *Travel* was at CMU (10 participants). The *HCI* and *Architecture* teams were located at TUM and made into subsystem teams (as opposed to being a cross-functional team). The team coaches reported to a site manager, who then reported to the project manager. The coaches met weekly with the site manager. The project manager traveled between sites every three weeks to coordinate and synchronize development at both sites.

As in FRIEND, the process was relaxed after two months into the iteration. During iterations 1 and 2, this lead to similar results, with students finding roles in which they performed best and a sustained meeting process that externalized status knowledge on the bulletin boards. In the third iteration, however, the CMU team was sufficiently small that all members could meet face to face in the same room. Consequently, it did not follow the meeting process and posted fewer and fewer information on the bulletin boards, making it difficult to communicate with the other site.

Outcome

The JAMES project ended in the successful demonstration of a prototype illustrating the potential of automotive applications using the JavaCard technology. The demonstrated prototype was not integrated, however: the final CMU and TUM demonstrations were based on different versions of the architecture. The CMU team had simply ignored the revisions performed by the TUM team and continued working on a branch dating back to the first development iteration.

This being our first experience with distributed projects, we encountered many difficult issues that would have been simple to resolve in a non-distributed setting. For example, the final client acceptance test was conducted on March 30, 1998, via a three-way video conference between Pittsburgh, Munich, and Stuttgart. It was originally scheduled for 9 A.M. Pittsburgh time and 3 P.M. German time. Unfortunately, Germany had switched to daylight saving time the previous weekend, but the United States was to switch the following weekend. An American student traveling to Munich caught the mistake (i.e., 3 P.M. CED was 8 A.M. EST), less than 48 hours before the meeting. Such miscalculations and misunderstandings cost the project quite a bit in resources and additional stress.

Lessons learned

Training the client.   Collaboration with the client turned out to be much more complicated than originally expected for two reasons:

- During iteration 1, the proxy client was physically present at the development site and always available. The proxy client quickly became familiar with the project process and infrastructure, but she often had to forward information to the client for decisions. The proxy client had the background and time to learn to use the infrastructure, but the modeling information put out by the students was not at the right level of abstraction for briefings at the client organization. Instead, all materials had to be translated and summarized by the proxy client, which led to delayed responses from the client. A scenario-based briefing approach, which we introduced at the end of the project, improved this situation.
- During iteration 2, the proxy client was not physically present at either site. Electronic communication and video conferencing during formal reviews were the only communication medium during most of the iteration. Although this made it difficult for the TUM team to come up to speed on the application domain, having the proxy client back in her organization made it easier for the project to promote its results.

Training the developers about the process.   In short iterations with students, quickly teaching the software life cycle process know-how is critical to setting up the organization. Starting with iteration 2, coaches were recruited from the best students of the previous iterations, which made such quick ramp-up possible. Coaches were also able to disseminate application domain knowledge and catch requirements problems early. Short iterations and high staff turnover limit the number of tools that could be introduced. In general, changing the tools used in the process and changes in the process itself are easier to accomplish between projects (as opposed to during the project). For long-running projects, infrastructure and process changes should occur only between releases.

Iteration overlap.   The amount of time overlap between iterations in distributed projects presents a critical project management trade-off. A small overlap prevents sufficient knowledge to be transferred: participants from the second site will have to learn most of the knowledge from work products only. A large overlap provides more opportunities for knowledge transfer in the form of targeted questions and answers. If the second development phase starts too early, however, participants of the second site interfere with the participants of the first site, who are still in the process of creating the knowledge to be transferred.

Transferring implicit knowledge.   Informal communication was not possible across sites, because participants from different sites did not know each other. This prevented the spontaneous information exchanges necessary for resolving issues and transferring implicit knowledge. The only mechanism that worked effectively was travelling to the other sites.

Version control as an integration tool.   In FRIEND, version control served as an integration mechanism for teams to communicate. Occasionally, when a hand-over was necessary before a change was fully integrated or debugged, incomplete versions were created for the sole purpose of transferring files from one team to another. This use of the version control system, and more generally, any informal use of a tool for communication, was not possible across sites.

16.5.4 Case Studies Summary

The projects we presented in this section spanned a broad spectrum in size, duration, and clients. ATRACT included four participants; JAMES, more than 80. ATRACT was completed within six months; FRIEND lasted two years. The types of clients each project interacted with also varied significantly, from a chief of police with little experience of software engineering to an information technology specialist with car manufacturing domain knowledge. Table 16-12 summarizes the variations in the project environment in all three projects.

Table 16-12   Summary of the project environment for the three case studies.

	Problem	Client	Duration	Distribution
ATRACT	Test environment for middleware	King	6 months	Local client
FRIEND	Emergency response system (Greenfield engineering & reengineering)	King	4 months (2 years, including follow-on projects)	Local client
JAMES	Smart card vehicle Applications	Proxy	11 months	Remote client, 2 developer sites

As a result, each project selected different methods with different results. In the following sections we discuss heuristics that we extracted from the three case studies in the areas of planning, modeling, process, and control. Table 16-13 summarizes the decisions made by each

Table 16-13   Summary of the methods selected in the three case studies.

	Planning	Modeling	Process	Control
ATRACT	XP-based planning after detailed requirements	Use cases User stories	Requirements phase followed by three XP development iterations	Client demonstrations at the end of each iteration
FRIEND	Royce-based iteration planning	Client, management, and system artifact sets OMT	Waterfall, followed by four unified process iterations	Weekly team meetings, monthly client reviews
JAMES	Royce-based iteration planning	Client, management, and system artifact sets UML	Waterfall, then unified process iterations	Weekly team meetings, monthly project reviews, monthly management travel, inventory analysis

project for these aspects. We do not discuss reuse since there was not a significant amount of reuse in any of the three projects.

How much planning?

The milestones to plan and the level of detail in describing them depends on the project goal. ATRACT produced a detailed functional specification within two months that enabled client and developers to prioritize requirements, because the goal of the ATRACT project was a tool that the client could use in a production environment. In iteration 1 of FRIEND, neither the client nor the developers knew enough of each other's domain to plan anything. Instead, demonstration and review dates were agreed upon that provided flexibility in milestone content. As the project made progress and the knowledge of both client and developers improved, more detailed plans were developed.

In general, detailed planning should not be done before client and developers agree on functionality and architecture. If the functionality or the architecture is still subject to substantial change, then detailed planning is possible only for the next iteration. In all cases, it is important to involve the client and the developers in the planning and ensure that likely planning changes are made visible.

How much modeling?

The amount of modeling depends on the amount of knowledge that must be made explicit and transferred among participants. In ATRACT, participants wrote use cases until they were relatively confident that they understood the client's requirements and that the client could picture the system to be developed. After that point, no modeling took place as all three participants shared the same location and could provided changes to the requirements informally.

In FRIEND, detailed object models of the application domain and the system were constructed; these were used to generate code. The application domain was much more foreign to the developers than in ATRACT, and there were many more participants to bring up to speed. The models were used primarily as a basis for design and for communication, but not for archiving, as the prototype evolved rapidly.

In the distributed JAMES project, transferring knowledge across sites required that more knowledge be made explicit. As in FRIEND, the models and the system were not kept consistent, as the prototype evolved rapidly. Instead, students recovered the design of iteration 1 with inventory analysis. Building detailed models would have been well worth the effort because of the need to share knowledge across continents. However, this was difficult, given the fast pace of changes and the scarce amount of resources. Moreover, detailed modeling was perceived as an overhead activity benefiting the other site, and as contention developed between the sites, it was not perceived as a critical activity. Sending developers across sites so they could meet in person was more effective in sharing knowledge and in reducing contention than keeping detailed models up to date.

In general, the cost of formalizing knowledge and keeping it up to date is high. It should be viewed as an investment for

- enabling the validation of requirements or architectural decisions
- enabling participants of a single site to converge on a single-system concept
- supporting participants traveling among multiple sites.

The return on the investment is lowest for short projects and few participants. In this situation, peer reviews seem to be a much more effective way to transfer knowledge.

How much process?

ATRACT followed an entity-based life cycle throughout development. FRIEND and JAMES started with a waterfall iteration and switched to an entity-based life cycle after the client reviewed the first prototype. At the beginning of the FRIEND and JAMES projects, iteration 1 was necessary to train novice developers. By the end of all three projects, however, developers were following a life cycle similar to XP with short iterations and daily builds. All three projects were small enough that they could maintain a small team atmosphere locally. Note that in the case of JAMES, the entity life cycle was not integrated across sites. Although JAMES met its goals and was considered successful, it failed to keep the system design at both sites in sync. An activity-based life cycle for managing cross-site issues would have been necessary in a project developing production code to enable sufficient control. Entity-based life cycles require close collaboration and informal communication to enable developers to resolve problems discovered in daily builds.

How much control?

The amount of control evolved and spanned the entire spectrum during the life cycle of each project. FRIEND and JAMES started with strict hierarchical organizations in the first two months of the iteration. This enabled the systematic rotation of roles in the project and a large amount of status and technical information made explicit on the bulletin board. Consequently, by the time coding was started (usually around Thanksgiving), students with leadership and communication skills naturally assumed team leader and liaisons roles, respectively. Moreover, the procedures that yielded benefits (e.g., writing meeting minutes) were deemed worth the overhead associated with them, so they were kept by the students. In our experience, this enabled us to relax the enforcement of procedures when students came back from Thanksgiving break, leading to an agile, entity-based process. Technical decisions were made locally within teams, and conflicts and issues could be dealt with faster than they could be communicated to management.

In other words, the first two months of the iteration were used to set up a consistent vision of the requirements and the architecture. Once these seeds were firmly planted, project management could be relaxed. The project then evolved as a living organism, using natural selection and self-organization. The team structure, the communication paths set up by the liaison, and the meeting procedures usually survived the transition. The increasing deadline pressure associated with the client acceptance test (which could not be rescheduled) ensured that the project remained focused and that all teams worked in the same direction. Although the level of experience and the number of participants prevented us from starting with a self-organizing project, we were able to evolve into one by planting the appropriate seeds early in the iteration. In FRIEND, this was possible because all developers had access to the client, who was able to provide a coherent picture of the application domain. In JAMES, the distribution of the project made a coherent evolution toward the client acceptance test much more difficult.

In general, an agile organization can function when all key participants share the same goal and the same architectural concept, either because they are provided with the same vision from the client or because the system concept is strong enough to herd them in a single direction. Hierarchical organizations become necessary when stakeholders put forward many conflicting criteria and contend for a limited amount of resources.

Methodological Heuristics

Be prepared to change the system. Changes to the software system will occur throughout the project. The changes come from the client side (unforeseen usability issues, new requirements) as well as from the development side (unforeseen technical issues, new architectural decisions). Trying to freeze the specification may be desirable to make a project predictable, but it usually leads to an inferior product that doesn't meet the end users' expectations. Instead, accept the concept that requirements and architecture change throughout the project and define change management processes.

Be prepared to change the organization. Hierarchical projects and self-organizing projects have different strengths. Hierarchical organizations are more predictable and more effective for getting a project off the ground. Self-organizing projects foster more innovation and can lead to superior products, with appropriate guidance. After developer expertise in the software life cycle increases and after a common vision for the system requirements and architecture emerges, one should consider delegating decision making to the individuals who have the knowledge to make the decision. This in turn requires increased ability to assess actual progress with quality indicators and management metrics.

Be prepared to change the process. Expertise and common vision also facilitates adapting the process. The software life cycle model can evolve from an activity-based process to an entity-based process in which work is assigned in terms of changes to the baseline. As the core requirements are completed, the project can be driven by time (e.g., release on a certain date) instead of by feature (e.g., release when specific features are completed).

Shorten client decision time. The client must often be involved when dealing with major changes in the project (new functionality, new release plan). Shortening the time needed for such critical decisions is key to preventing the project from moving in the wrong direction. This requires an effective communication mechanism for providing information to the client and resolving the issue with the right decision maker. Local king clients are ideal for this. For projects without local kings, responsive information and decision channels need to be put in place between the client and the project.

Build trust. Participants are reluctant to report bad news, especially if it stems from their own mistakes. Moreover, if they believe they might be punished for making or reporting mistakes, the issue will simply be covered up. Knowing about these mistakes early, however, is often the difference between a success and a failure. Conversely, providing the resources and control to participants to address the reported, unexpected problems helps keep the focus on a successful project outcome.

Learn the right lessons and nothing more. Delegating decision making can lead to perceived short-term successes, which can result in the wrong lessons being learned. A solo heroic effort can be the difference between meeting a milestone and missing it. However, the concentration of knowledge in a limited number of participants can hurt the project and may lead to more serious failures down the road. Moving from a command-and-control organization to a leadership-and-collaboration organization requires the manager to become a teacher. Often, mistakes have to be made to ensure that the right lessons are learned.

16.6 Further Readings

The word is still open to whether Scrum scales up to very large projects with multiple development teams. Proposals to solve this challenge include Scrums of Scrums which include representatives of each development team, starting the project with a single Scrum and seeding new teams with members of the first Scrum [Larman & Vodde, 2008].

Some researchers argue that software development is chaotic (in the sense of the mathematical chaos theory); that is, small variations can have a big influence on the outcome of a software project. Gleick has written a very readable introduction to chaos theory [Gleick, 1987]. Dee Hock introduced the notion of chaordic systems to describe organizations in which the chaos of competition and the order of cooperation coexist and thrive [Hock, 1999].

Petroski has described the critical role that failure plays in successful designs ([Petroski, 1994]). In particular, he argues that technological innovation is often a response to the failures of existing products. His books are written from the point of view of civil engineering, but many observations are applicable to software engineering as well.

16.7 Exercises

16-1 What is the difference between a software life cycle and a methodology?

16-2 You are improving a legacy system. You need to customize a software life cycle for your project. Which activities would you need? In which order?

16-3 Royce uses a management metric that counts the number of participants who leave the project or join the project. You are managing a multi-team project and notice that the staff turnover in one team is high. Hypothesize what causes could lead to such a symptom. For each cause, propose a remedy.

16-4 The heuristics we outlined in Section 16.5.4 indicate that the need for models is higher in distributed organizations. Open-source projects are highly distributed projects that follow an entity-based life cycle and typically do not have requirements or system design documents. Provide examples of how modeling knowledge is made explicit and transferred among participants in such cases.

16-5 Royce's methodology considers six project factors (scale, stakeholder cohesion, process flexibility, process maturity, architectural risk, and domain experience) when tailoring a process for a specific project (Section 16.4.1). Use these factors to describe which types of projects could use XP as an appropriate methodology. Justify your choice for each factor.

16-6 While working with Staphylococcus bacteria in 1928, Sir Alexander Fleming accidently dropped some bread crumbs on one of the dishes. After a week the bacteria on this dish did not grow as expected. Fleming noticed a bacteria-free circle around a mold that was contaminating the staphylococcus culture. Instead of throwing the dish away because the planned experiment had failed, he isolated the mold, grew it in a fluid medium, and discovered a substance that prevented growth of the bacteria even when it was diluted 800 times. Discuss the discovery of penicillin using the terminology and issues introduced in this chapter.

16-7   Based on the assumption that the earth was round, Columbus's goal was to find a shorter way to India by going west instead of east. He encountered America instead of India. Discuss the discovery of America by Columbus using the terminology and issues introduced in this chapter.

16-8   Select a project you have been involved with. Using the methodological categories defined in this chapter, describe the trade-offs that occurred in the project.

References

[AgileManifesto, 2001]   http://www.agilemanifesto.org.

[Aguanno, 2005]   K. Aguanno, *Managing Agile Projects, Multi-Media Publications,* Ontario, 2005.

[Ambler, 2002]   S. Ambler, *Agile Modeling: Effective Practices for Extreme Programming and the Unified Process*, John Wiley & Sons, 2002.

[Beck & Andres, 2005]   K. Beck & C. Andres, *Extreme Programming Explained: Embrace Change*, 2nd ed., Addison-Wesley, Reading, MA, 2005.

[Boehm et al., 2000]   B. Boehm, E. Horowitz, R. Madachy, D. Reifer, B. K. Clark, B. Steece, A. W. Brown, S. Chulani, & C. Abts, *Software Cost Estimation with COCOMO II*, Prentice Hall, Upper Saddle River, NJ, 2000.

[Bonatti, 2001]   W. Bonatti, *The Mountains of My Life*, Modern Library, Random House, New York, 2001.

[Buhl, 1956]   H. Buhl, *Nanga Parbat Pilgrimage*, Hodder & Stoughton, London, 1956.

[Cockburn, 2001]   A. Cockburn, *Agile Software Development*, Addison-Wesley, Reading, MA, 2001.

[Cohn, 2006]   M. Cohn, *Agile Estimating and Planning*, Pearson, Upper Saddle River, NJ, 2006.

[Cusumano & Selby, 1997]   M. A. Cusumano & R. W. Selby, "How Microsoft Builds Software," *Communications of the ACM*, Vol. 40, No. 6, pp. 53–61, 1997.

[Deming, 1982]   E. W. Deming, *Out of the Crisis,* MIT Press, Cambridge, MA, 1982. 2ed. published 2000.

[Fowler, 2005]   M. Fowler, *The new methodology*, http://www.martinfowler.com/articles/newMethodology.html. Revised 2005.

[Gleick, 1987]   J. Gleick, *Chaos - Making a New Science,* Penguin Books Ltd, Harmondsworth, Middlesex, 1987.

[Gladwin, 1964]   T. Gladwin, "Culture and logical process," in W. Goodenough (ed.), *Explorations in Cultural Anthropology: Essays Presented to George Peter Murdock*, McGraw-Hill, New York, 1964.

[Grenning, 2002]   J. Grenning, Planning Poker, http://www.planningpoker.com/ 2002.

[Highsmith & Orr, 2000]   J. Highsmith & K. Orr, *Adaptive Software Development: A Collaborative Approach to Managing Complex Systems*, Dorset House, 2000.

[Highsmith, 2004]   J. Highsmith, *Agile Project Management,* Pearson Education, Boston, 2004.

[Hock, 1999]   D. Hock, *Birth of the Chaordic Age,* Berrett-Koehler Publishers, San Francisco, 1999.

[Kelly, 1984]   J. F. Kelly, "An iterative design methodology for user-friendly natural language office information applications," *ACM Transactions on Information Systems*, Vol. 2, No. 1, January 1984.

[Larman & Vodde, 2008]	C. Larman & B. Vodde, *Scaling Lean & Agile Development: Thinking and Organizational Tools for Large-Scale Scrum,* Addison-Wesley, Reading, MA, 2008.
[Marshall, 2001]	R. Marshall, *What really happened at K2?* Chapter 24 in [Bonatti, 2001].
[Norman, 2002]	D. A. Norman, *The Design of Everyday Things*, Basic Books, New York, 2002.
[Palmer & Felsing, 2002]	S. Palmer & J. Felsing, *A Practical Guide to Feature-Driven Development,* Prentice Hall, Upper Saddle River, NJ, 2002.
[Paulk et al., 1995]	M. C. Paulk, C. V. Weber, B. Curtis (eds.), *The Capability Maturity Model: Guidelines for Improving the Software Process*, Addison-Wesley, Reading, MA, 1995.
[Petroski, 1992]	H. Petroski, *To Engineer is Human*, Vintage Books, Random House, New York, 1992.
[Petroski, 1994]	H. Petroski, *The Evolution of Useful Things*, Vintage Books, Random House, New York, 1994.
[Royce, 1998]	W. Royce, *Software Project Management: A Unified Framework*, Addison-Wesley, Reading, MA, 1998.
[Rumbaugh et al., 1991]	J. Rumbaugh, M. Blaha, W. Premerlani, F. Eddy, & W. Lorensen, *Object-Oriented Modeling and Design*, Prentice Hall, Englewood Cliffs, NJ, 1991.
[Schlumberger]	Schlumberger, http://www.cyberflex.com/.
[Schwaber, 1995]	K, Schwaber, "Scrum Development Process," *Business Object Design and Implementation Workshop*, OOPSLA'95, Austin, TX, October 1995.
[Schwaber & Beedle, 2002]	K. Schwaber & M. Beedle, *Agile Software Development with Scrum*, Prentice Hall, Upper Saddle River, NJ, 2002.
[Suchman, 2007]	L. A. Suchman, *Human-Machine Reconfiguration: Plans and Situated Actions,* 2nd ed. Cambridge University Press, 2007.
[Takeuchi & Nonaka, 1986]	H. Takeuchi & I. Nonaka. "The New New Product Development Game" Harward Business Review, 1986.
[Taylor, 1911]	F. W. Taylor, *The Principles of Scientific Management*, Harper Bros., New York, 1911.
[Tunde & Ray, 1994]	A. O. Babatunde & W. H. Ray, *Process Dynamics, Modeling and Control*, Oxford University Press, 1994.
[Weinberg, 1971]	G. M. Weinberg, *The Psychology of Computer Programming*, Van Nostrand, New York, 1971.

PART IV
Appendices

Design Patterns

Design patterns are partial solutions to common problems, such as separating an interface from a number of possible implementations, wrapping around a set of legacy classes, or protecting a caller from changes associated with specific platforms. A design pattern is composed of a small number of classes that, through delegation and inheritance, provide a robust and modifiable solution. These classes can be adapted and refined for the specific system under construction. In addition, design patterns provide examples of inheritance and delegation.

Since the publication of the first book on design patterns for software [Gamma et al., 1994], many additional patterns have been proposed for a broad variety of problems, including analysis [Fowler, 1997] [Larman, 2005], system design [Buschmann et al., 1996], middleware [Mowbray & Malveau, 1997], process modeling [Ambler, 1998], dependency management [Feiler & Tichy, 1998], configuration management [Brown et al., 1999], and methodology adoption [Elssamadisy, 2009]. The term itself has become a buzzword attributed to many different definitions. In this book, we focused only on the original catalog of design patterns, as it provides a concise set of elegant solutions to many common problems. This appendix summarizes the design patterns we use in the book and natural language heuristics for applying them. For each pattern, we provide pointers to the examples in the book. Our goal is to provide a quick reference. We assume from the reader a basic knowledge of design patterns, object-oriented concepts, and UML class diagrams.

A.1 Abstract Factory: Encapsulating Platforms

Name	Abstract Factory Design Pattern
Problem description	Shield the client from different platforms that provide different implementations for the same set of concepts.
Solution	A platform (e.g., a windowing system) is represented as a set of AbstractProducts, each representing a concept (e.g., a button) that is supported by all platforms. An AbstractFactory class declares the operations for creating each individual product. A specific platform is then realized by a ConcreteFactory and a set of ConcreteProducts (one for each AbstractProduct). A ConcreteFactory depends only on its related ConcreteProducts. The Client depends only on the AbstractProducts and the AbstractFactory classes, making it easy to substitute platforms.

Consequences	• Client is shielded from concrete product classes. • Substituting families at runtime is possible. • Adding new products is difficult since new realizations for each factory must be created.
Examples	• Statically encapsulating incompatible infrastructures for intelligent houses (Section 8.4.4) • Game independence in ARENA (Section 8.6.1)
Related concept	• Specification inheritance and implementation inheritance (Section 8.3.2).

Figure A-1   The Abstract Factory design pattern (adapted from [Gamma et al., 1994]).

A.2 Adapter: Wrapping Around Legacy Code

Name	Adapter Design Pattern
Problem description	Convert the interface of a legacy class into a different interface expected by the client, so that the client and the legacy class can work together without changes.
Solution	An `Adapter` class implements the `ClientInterface` expected by the client. The `Adapter` delegates requests from the client to the `LegacyClass` and performs any necessary conversion.

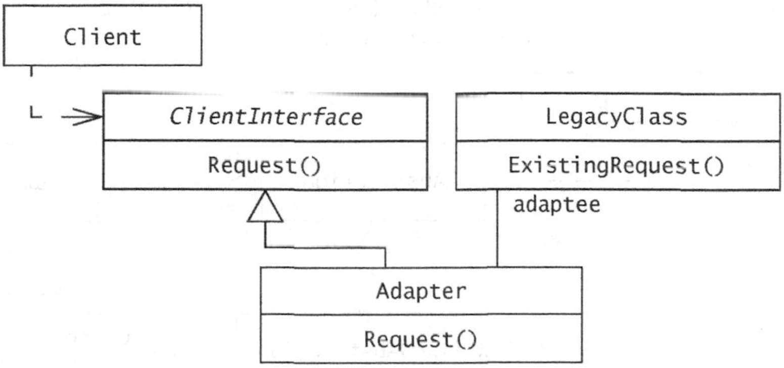

Consequences	• `Client` and `LegacyClass` work together without modification of either `Client` or `LegacyClass`. • `Adapter` works with `LegacyClass` and all of its subclasses. • A new `Adapter` needs to be written for each specialization (e.g., subclass) of `ClientInterface`.
Example	• Sorting instances of an existing `String` class with an existing `sort()` method (Section 8.4.2): `MyStringComparator` is an `Adaptor` for bridging the gap between the `String` class and the `Comparator` interface used by the `Array.sort()` method.
Related concept	• The `Bridge` (Section A.3) fills the gap between an interface and its implementations.

Figure A-2 The Adapter design pattern (adapted from [Gamma et al., 1994]).

A.3 Bridge: Allowing for Alternate Implementations

Name	Bridge Design Pattern
Problem description	Decouple an interface from an implementation so that implementations can be substituted, possibly at runtime.
Solution	The *Abstraction* class defines the interface visible to the client. The *Implementor* is an abstract class that defines the lower-level methods available to *Abstraction*. An *Abstraction* instance maintains a reference to its corresponding *Implementor* instance. *Abstraction* and *Implementor* can be refined independently.

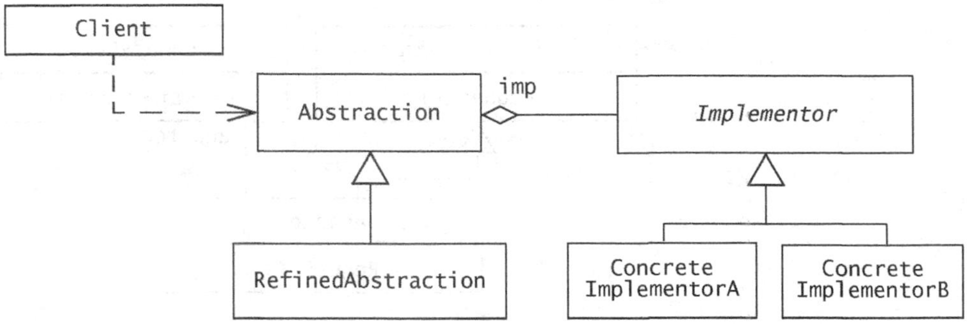

Consequences	• Client is shielded from abstract and concrete implementations. • Interfaces and implementations can be refined independently.
Example	• Testing different implementations of the same interface (Section 8.4.1).
Related concept	• The Adapter pattern (Section A.2) fills the gap between two interfaces.

Figure A-3   The Bridge design pattern (adapted from [Gamma et al., 1994]).

A.4 Command: Encapsulating Control Flow

Name	Command Design Pattern
Problem description	Encapsulate requests so that they can be executed, undone, or queued independently of the request.
Solution	A *Command* abstract class declares the interface supported by all ConcreteCommands. ConcreteCommands encapsulate a service to be applied to a Receiver. The Client creates ConcreteCommands and binds them to specific Receivers. The Invoker actually executes or undoes a command.

Consequences	<ul><li>The object of the command (Receiver) and the algorithm of the command (ConcreteCommand) are decoupled.</li><li>Invoker is shielded from specific commands.</li><li>ConcreteCommands are objects. They can be created and stored.</li><li>New ConcreteCommands can be added without changing existing code.</li></ul>
Examples	<ul><li>Providing an undo stack for user commands: All user-visible commands are refinements of the *Command* abstract class. Each command is required to implement the do(), undo(), and redo() methods. Once a command is executed, it is pushed onto an undo stack. If the user wishes to undo the last command, the *Command* object on the top of the stack is sent the message undo().</li><li>Decoupling interface objects from control objects (Section 8.4.5, see also Swing Actions, [JFC, 2009]): All user-visible commands are refinements of the *Command* abstract class. Interface objects, such as menu items and buttons, create and send messages to *Command* objects. Only *Command* objects modify entity objects. When the user interface is changed (e.g., a menu bar is replaced by a tool bar), only the interface objects are modified.</li><li>Decoupling Moves from Games in ARENA (Section 8.6.2)</li></ul>
Related concept	<ul><li>MVC architecture (Figure 6-15).</li></ul>

Figure A-4 The Command design pattern (adapted from [Gamma et al., 1994]).

A.5 Composite: Representing Recursive Hierarchies

Name	Composite Design Pattern
Problem description	Represent a hierarchy of variable width and depth so that leaves and composites can be treated uniformly through a common interface.
Solution	The *Component* interface specifies the services that are shared among Leaf and Composite (e.g., move(x,y) for a graphic element). A Composite has an aggregation association with *Components* and implements each service by iterating over each contained *Component* (e.g., the Composite.move(x,y) method iteratively invokes the Component.move(x,y)). The Leaf services do the actual work (e.g., Leaf.move(x,y) modifies the coordinates of the Leaf and redraws it).

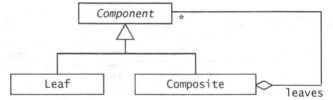

Consequences	• Client uses the same code for dealing with Leaves or Composites. • Leaf-specific behavior can be modified without changing the hierarchy. • New classes of Leaves can be added without changing the hierarchy.
Examples	• Groups of drawable elements: Drawable elements can be organized in groups that can be moved and scaled uniformly. Groups can also contain other groups. • Hierarchy of files and directories (Figure 2-28): Directories can contain files and other directories. The same operations are available for moving, renaming, and removing files as well as directories. • Describing subsystem decomposition (Figure 6-3): We use a Composite pattern to describe subsystem decomposition. A subsystem is composed of classes and other subsystems. Note that subsystems are not actually implemented as Composites to which classes are dynamically added. • Describing hierarchies of tasks (Figure 6-8): We use a Composite pattern to describe the organizations of Tasks (Composites) into Subtasks (*Components*) and ActionItems (Leaves).We use a similar model to describe Phases, Activities, and Tasks (Figure 15-6).
Related concept	• Facade pattern (Section A.6).

Figure A-5   The Composite design pattern (adapted from [Gamma et al., 1994]).

A.6 Facade: Encapsulating Subsystems

Name	Facade Design Pattern
Problem description	Reduce coupling between a set of related classes and the rest of the system.
Solution	A single Facade class implements a high-level interface for a subsystem by invoking the methods of lower-level classes. A Facade is opaque in the sense that a caller does not access the lower-level classes directly. The use of Facade patterns recursively yields a layered system.

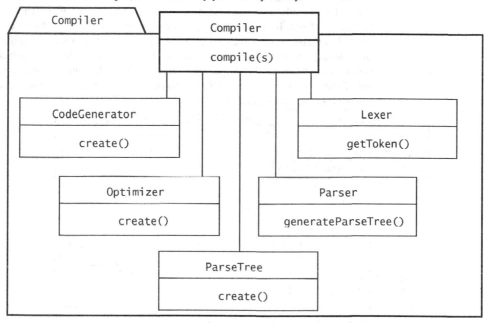

Consequences	• Shields a client from the low-level classes of a subsystem.
	• Simplifies the use of a subsystem by providing higher-level methods.
Example	• Subsystem encapsulation (Figure 6-30): A Compiler is composed of Lexer, Parser, ParseTree, a CodeGenerator, and an Optimizer. When compiling a string into executable code, however, a caller deals only with the Compiler class, which invokes the appropriate methods on the contained classes.
Related concept	• Coupling and cohesion (Section 6.3.3), layers and partitions (Section 6.3.4), Composite patterns (Section A.5).

Figure A-6 The Facade design pattern (adapted from [Gamma et al., 1994]).

A.7 Observer: Decoupling Entities from Views

Name	Observer Design Pattern
Problem description	Maintain consistency across the states of one Publisher and many Subscribers.
Solution	A *Publisher* (called a Subject in [Gamma et al., 1994]) is an object whose primary function is to maintain some state—for example, a matrix. One or more *Subscribers* (called *Observers* in [Gamma et al., 1994]) use the state maintained by a *Publisher*—for example, to display a matrix as a table or a graph. This introduces redundancies between the states of the *Publisher* and the *Subscribers*. To address this issue, *Subscribers* invoke the subscribe() method to register with a Publisher. Each ConcreteSubscriber also defines an update() method to synchronize the state between the *Publisher* and the ConcreteSusbcriber. Whenever the state of the *Publisher* changes, the *Publisher* invokes its notify() method, which iteratively invoke each Subscriber.update() method.

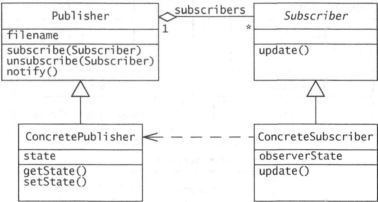

Consequences	• Decouples a *Publisher* from the *Subscribers*. • Can result in many spurious broadcasts when the state of a *Publisher* changes.
Examples	• The Observer interface and Observable class are used in Java to realize an Observer pattern ([JFC, 2009]). • The Observer pattern can be used for realizing subscription and notification in a Model/View/Controller architecture (Figure 6-15). • Decoupling Match state from MatchView in ARENA (Section 8.6.3).
Related concept	• Entity, interface, control objects (Section 5.3.2).

Figure A-7 The Observer design pattern (adapted from [Gamma et al., 1994]).

A.8 Proxy: Encapsulating Expensive Objects

Name	Proxy Design Pattern
Problem description	Improve the performance or the security of a system by delaying expensive computations, using memory only when needed, or checking access before loading an object into memory.
Solution	The ProxyObject class acts on behalf of a RealObject class. Both classes implement the same interface. The ProxyObject stores a subset of the attributes of the RealObject. The ProxyObject handles certain requests completely (e.g., determining the size of an image), whereas others are delegated to the RealObject. After delegation, the RealObject is created and loaded in memory.

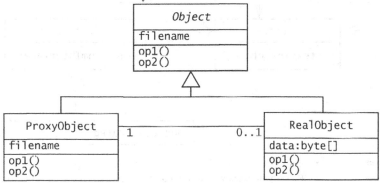

Consequences	• Adds a level of indirection between Client and RealObject.
	• The Client is shielded from any optimizations for creating RealObjects.
Examples	• Protection proxy (Figure 7-9): An Access association class contains a set of operations that a Broker can use to access a Portfolio. Every operation in the PortfolioProxy first checks with isAccessible() if the invoking Broker has legitimate access. Once access has been granted, PortfolioProxy delegates the operation to the actual Portfolio object. If access is denied, the actual Portfolio object is not loaded into memory.
	• Storage proxy (Figure 10-7): An ImageProxy object acts on behalf of an Image stored on disk. The ImageProxy contains the same information as the Image (e.g., width, height, position, resolution) except for the Image contents. The ImageProxy services all content-independent requests. Only when the Image contents must be accessed (e.g., when the Image is drawn on the screen) does the ImageProxy create the RealImage object and load its contents from disk.
Related concept	• Caching expensive computations (Section 10.4.1).

Figure A-8 The Proxy design pattern (adapted from [Gamma et al., 1994]).

A.9 Strategy: Encapsulating Algorithms

Name	Strategy Design Pattern
Problem description	Decouple a policy-deciding class from a set of mechanisms so that different mechanisms can be changed transparently from a client.
Solution	A Client accesses services provided by a Context. The Context services are realized using one of several mechanisms, as decided by a Policy object. The abstract Strategy class describes the interface that is common to all mechanisms that Context can use. The Policy class creates a Concrete-Strategy object and configures the Context to use it.

Consequences	• ConcreteStrategies can be substituted transparently from Context. • Policy decides which Strategy is best, given the current circumstances (e.g., speed vs. space trade-off). • New algorithms can be added without modifying Context or Client.
Example	• Network switching in mobile applications (Section 8.4.3): A mobile application needs to deal with a variety of network access protocols (phone, wireless, LAN), depending on the context of the user (location, communication costs, etc.). To decouple the policy from selecting a network from the network interface, we encapsulate the network access protocol implementations with a Strategy pattern.
Related concept	Adaptor pattern (Section A.2) and Bridge pattern (Section A.3).

Figure A-9   The Strategy design pattern (adapted from [Gamma et al., 1994]).

A.10 Heuristics for Selecting Design Patterns

Natural language heuristics for selecting design patterns

Design patterns address specific design goals and nonfunctional requirements. Similar to Abbott's heuristics described in Chapter 5, *Analysis*, key phrases can be used to identify candidate design patterns. Below are examples for the patterns covered in this chapter.

Phrase	Design Pattern
• "Manufacturer independence" • "Platform independence"	Abstract Factory
• "Must comply with existing interface" • "Must reuse existing legacy component"	Adapter
• "Must support future protocols"	Bridge
• "All commands should be undoable" • "All transactions should be logged"	Command
• "Must support aggregate structures" • "Must allow for hierarchies of variable depth and width"	Composite
• "Policy and mechanisms should be decoupled" • "Must allow different algorithms to be interchanged at runtime"	Strategy

References

[Ambler, 1998]	S. W. Ambler, *Process Patterns: Building Large-Scale Systems Using Object Technology*, Cambridge University Press, New York, 1998.
[Brown et al., 1999]	W. J. Brown, H. W. McCormick, & S. W. Thomas, *AntiPatterns and Patterns in Software Configuration Management*, Wiley, New York, 1999.
[Buschmann et al., 1996]	F. Buschmann, R. Meunier, H. Rohnert, P. Sommerlad, & M. Stal, *Pattern-Oriented Software Architecture: A System of Patterns*, Wiley, Chichester, U.K., 1996.
[Elssamadisy, 2009]	A. Elssamadisy, *Agile Adoption Patterns*, Addison-Wesley, Reading, MA, 2009.
[Feiler & Tichy, 1998]	P. Feiler & W. Tichy, "Propagator: A family of patterns," *Proceedings of TOOLS-23'97*, July 28–August 1 1997, Santa Barbara, CA.
[Fowler, 1997]	M. Fowler, *Analysis Patterns: Reusable Object Models*, Addison-Wesley, Reading, MA, 1997.
[Gamma et al., 1994]	E. Gamma, R. Helm, R. Johnson, & J. Vlissides, *Design Patterns: Elements of Reusable Object-Oriented Software*, Addison-Wesley, Reading, MA, 1994.
[JFC, 2009]	*Java Foundation Classes*, JDK Documentation, Javasoft, 2009.
[Larman, 2005]	C. Larman, *Applying UML and Patterns: An Introduction to Object-Oriented Analysis and Design*, 3rd ed., Prentice Hall, Upper Saddle River, NJ, 2005.
[Mowbray & Malveau, 1997]	T. J. Mowbray & R. C. Malveau, *CORBA Design Patterns*, Wiley, New York, 1997.

Glossary

abstract class   Superclass that is used only for specialization and never instantiated. Abstract class names are italicized.

abstract data type   A data type defined by an implementation-independent specification.

abstraction   The classification of phenomena into concepts. *See also* modeling.

acceptance testing   A system testing activity during which the client decides whether the system meets the acceptance criteria.

access control list   A representation of the access control matrix in which legitimate rights are represented as a list of (actor, operation) pairs attached to the class that is controlled.

access right   A cell in the access control matrix that represents which operations a specific actor may invoke on a specific class.

accuracy   A quantitative measure of the magnitude of error.

action   A fundamental unit of behavior. Actions can take a set of inputs, produce a set of outputs, and change the state of the system. Actions are fundamental in the sense that they are not decomposed further. Actions can be associated with specific points in a state machine, such as transitions, state entry, and state exit. Actions normally take a short amount of time to execute and cannot be interrupted.

action item   A task assigned to a participant with a completion date, usually as a result of an issue resolution.

activity   In a software life cycle, a set of tasks performed toward a specific purpose. Activities can include few or many tasks, depending on their goal. Examples of activities include requirements elicitation, object identification, and unit testing. *See also* process.

In a state machine diagram, a behavior executed as long as an object resides in some state. Whereas an action is short and non-interruptible, an activity can take a substantial amount of time and is interrupted when a transition exiting the state is fired. *Contrast with* action.

activity-centered software life cycle model   A software life cycle model that represents primarily the activities of development. *Contrast with* entity-centered software life cycle model.

activity diagram   UML notation representing the behavior of a system in terms of activities. An activity is a state that represents the execution of a set of operations. The completion of these operations then triggers a transition to another activity. Activity diagrams are used to illustrate combinations of control and data flow.

activity partition   *See* swimlane.

actor   External entity that needs to exchange information with the system. An actor can represent either a user role or another system.

adaptability   The ability to change the system to deal with additional application domain concepts.

aggregation   An association denoting a whole–part relationship between two classes. For example, a System is composed of Subsystems is an aggregation association.

alternative   *See* proposal.

ambiguity   Property of a model indicating whether a concept corresponds to two or more unrelated phenomena.

analysis   An activity during which developers ensure that the system requirements are correct, complete, consistent, and unambiguous. Analysis produces the analysis model.

analysis model   A model of the system that aims to be correct, complete, consistent, and unambiguous. The analysis model consists of the functional model, the analysis object model, and the dynamic model.

analysis object model   The object model produced during analysis. The analysis object model describes the application domain concepts that the system manipulates and the user-visible interfaces of the system.

analyst   The role of the developers who elicit application domain information from users and clients and construct a use case model of the system under development.

API   *See* Application Programmer Interface.

API engineer   A role concerned with defining the API of a subsystem. This role is often combined with the role of architecture liaison.

application domain   Represents all aspects of the user's problem. This includes the physical environment in which the system will run, the users, and their work processes. The application domain is represented by the analysis model during requirements and analysis activities. The application domain is also called the *problem domain. Contrast with* solution domain.

application domain specialist A consultant role responsible for providing application domain expertise to a project.

application framework A reusable partial application that can be specialized to produce custom applications. See also class libraries.

application object Object in the analysis model that represents an application domain concept. The application object is also called the *application domain object*.

Application Programmer Interface (API) Set of fully specified operations provided by a subsystem.

architect The role of the developers who make strategic system decisions and construct the system design model.

architectural pattern *See* architectural style.

architectural style A general system design model that can be used as a starting point for system design. Examples of architectural styles include client/server, peer to peer, pipe and filter, and model/view/controller.

architecture *See* system design model.

architecture liaison The role of the developers who represent a subsystem team in the architecture team. They convey information from their team, negotiate interface changes, and ensure the consistency of APIs across the system.

argument Value passed along with a message.

argumentation The debate among participants to resolve an issue.

as-is scenario Scenario that describes an existing system. As-is scenarios can be used to validate the developers' understanding of the system with users.

association A relationship between two or more classes denoting the possible links between instances of the classes. An association has a name and can have multiplicity and role information attached to each of its ends.

association class An association with attributes and operations.

attribute A named property of a class defining a range of the values an object can contain. For example, `time` is an attribute of the class `Watch`.

attribute type *See* type.

attribute visibility Specifies whether or not the attribute can be accessed by other classes.

auditing Validation of versions before a release to ensure consistent and complete delivery.

auditor The role responsible for selecting and evaluating promotions for release.

authentication The process of associating a person with access rights.

availability   The degree to which a system or component is operational and accessible when required for use.

base class   *See* superclass.

baseline   A version of a configuration item that has been formally reviewed and agreed on.

bazaar model   A project organization that includes a dynamic and distributed set of collaborating groups. *Contrast with* cathedral model.

big bang testing   An integration testing strategy in which all components are tested together as a whole after they have been unit tested.

blackbox framework   A framework that relies on well-defined interfaces for extensibility. *Contrast with* whitebox framework.

blackbox test   A test which focuses on the input/output behavior of a component without considering its implementation. *Contrast with* whitebox test.

bottom-up testing   An integration testing strategy in which components are incrementally integrated starting at the lowest level. Bottom-up testing does not require any test stubs. *Contrast with* top-down testing, sandwich testing.

boundary object   An object that represents the interactions between the user and the system.

boundary condition   A special condition the system must handle. Boundary conditions include start-up, shutdown, and exceptions.

boundary use case   A use case for dealing with a boundary condition.

brainstorming   A scheduled communication event during which participants generate a large number of alternatives.

branch   A concurrent development path under configuration management.

bug   *See* fault.

build management   Tool support for automatically rebuilding the system when new versions are added.

buried association   A foreign key used to represent a one-to-many or a many-to-many association when mapping an object model to a relational schema.

callback   An operation that is temporary and dynamically registered with a class, usually for the purpose of notification. For example, the subject object in the observer pattern invokes callbacks to notify subscribed observers.

candidate key   In a database management system, a set of attributes that could be used as a primary key.

capability   A representation of access control in which legitimate rights are represented as (class, operation) pairs attached to an actor. Examples of capabilities include a door key, a smart card, and a theater ticket.

Capability Maturity Model (CMM) Framework for assessing the maturity of organizations characterized by five levels of maturity.

cathedral model A project organization emphasizing planning, system architecture, and hierarchical control. The chief programmer team is an example of cathedral model. *Contrast with* bazaar model.

Centralized Traffic Control (CTC) Procedures and systems enabling dispatchers to monitor and control train traffic remotely from a central location.

change The adaptation of an aspect of the system, such as the addition or modification of a requirement, or the substitution of a component for another. *See also* delta.

change control A process of approving or rejecting a change request to ensure that system evolution is consistent with project goals.

change control board Team approving change requests in the context of a formal change process.

change request An unscheduled communication event during which a participant requests a modified or a new feature in a work product. In configuration management, a formal report requesting the modification of a configuration item.

change set A set of deltas indicating the differences between two configurations.

chief programmer organization A hierarchical project organization in which the team leader makes all the critical technical decisions.

clarity *See* ambiguity.

class An abstraction of a set of objects with the same attributes, operations, relationships, and semantics. Classes are different than abstract data types in that a class can be defined by specializing another class. For example, programming languages such as Modula and Ada provide mechanisms for defining abstract data types; object-oriented languages such as Java, C++, or Smalltalk provide mechanisms for defining classes.

class diagram UML notation representing the structure of the system in terms of objects, classes, attributes, operations, and associations. Class diagrams are used to represent object models during development.

class extender A developer that realizes specializations of the class under consideration. Although, like class implementors, class extenders may invoke operations provided by the class of interest, class extenders focus on specialized versions of the same services.

class implementor A developer that realizes the class under consideration. Class implementors are responsible for designing the internal data structures and implementing the code for each publication operation.

class user A developer that invokes the operations provided by the class under consideration during the realization of another class, called the *client class*.

client   A role representing the person or company paying for the development of the system.

client class   In a design pattern, a class that accesses the pattern interface.

client review   A scheduled communication event during which a client monitors the status of a project.

client/server architectural style   An architectural style in which user interactions are managed by simple client programs and functionality is delivered by a central server program.

closed architecture   A layered system in which a layer can depend only on layers immediately below it. *Contrast with* open architecture.

closed issue   An issue that has been resolved.

CM aggregate   *See* configuration management aggregate.

CMM   *See* Capability Maturity Model.

cohesion   The strength of dependencies within a subsystem or a class. High coherence is desirable as it keeps related classes together so they can be modified consistently.

communication   An activity during which developers exchange information, either synchronously or asynchronously, and either spontaneously or according to a schedule.

communication diagram   UML notation representing the behavior of the system as a series of interactions among a group of objects. Each object is depicted as a rectangle in an instance diagram. Interactions are depicted as lines between objects, annotated with the name of the message sent. The order of interactions is represented with numbers next to the message names. *See also* sequence diagram.

communication event   A type of information exchange that has a defined objective and scope. A communication event can be scheduled or event driven. Examples of communication events include client reviews, status reviews, and problem reports.

communication mechanism   A tool or a procedure that can be used to transmit and receive information. Communication mechanisms support one or more communication events. Examples of communication mechanisms include telephone, fax, E-mail, and groupware. Communication mechanisms can be either synchronous or asynchronous, depending whether or not the sender and receiver need to be available at the same time.

communication relationship   A type of relationship in a use case diagram denoting the flow of information between an actor and a use case.

completeness   The property of a model describing whether or not all relevant phenomena are modeled. A model is incomplete if one or more relevant phenomena do not have a corresponding concept in the model.

component   A physical and replaceable part of the system that complies to an interface. Examples of components include class libraries, frameworks, and binary programs.

component expert A role of the developers responsible for providing detailed knowledge about using a specific component.

component inspection A testing technique that finds faults in a component through the manual inspection of the source code.

composition aggregation An aggregation relationship in which the existence of the parts depends on the whole. *Contrast with* shared aggregation.

concept An abstraction of a set of phenomena with common properties. For example, this book, my black watch, and the Valley Fisherman's Club are phenomena. Textbooks on object-oriented software engineering, black watches, and fisherman's clubs are concepts. *Contrast with* phenomenon.

configuration A version of a configuration management aggregate.

configuration item A work product that is treated as a single entity for the purpose of configuration management and that needs to be baselined. *See also* configuration management aggregate.

configuration management An activity during which developers monitor and control changes to the system or its models. Goals of configuration management include saving enough information so that it is possible to restore the system to a prior version; preventing changes that are not consistent with project goals; and managing concurrent development paths aimed at evaluating competing solutions.

configuration management aggregate (CM aggregate) An aggregate of related configuration items.

configuration manager A role of the developers responsible for tracking, baselining, and archiving work products.

consistency The property of a model that indicates whether or not it contradicts itself. A model is inconsistent if it provides several incompatible views of the system.

constraint A rule attached to a UML element restricting its semantics. Constraints can be depicted by a note containing natural language text or an expression in a formal language (e.g., OCL).

consultant role Any role that is concerned with providing temporary and specialized support where project participants lack expertise. Consultant roles include the user, the client, the technical consultant, and the application domain specialist.

contract A set of constraints on a class or a component allowing the caller and the callee to share the same assumptions about the class or the component. *See also* invariant, precondition, and postcondition.

contract inheritance The propagation of the contract of the superclass to its subclasses.

control flow The sequence of execution of operations in the system. *Contrast with* data flow.

control node   In an activity diagram, nodes that coordinate the control flow in a diagram. *See* decision, fork node, join node.

control object   An object that represents a task performed by the user and supported by the system.

controller   In the Model/View/Controller architectural style, a type of subsystem or object that manages the sequence of interactions with the user.

correction   A change to a component for the purpose of repairing a fault.

correctness   The property of a model that indicates if it accurately represents the system that the client needs and that the developers intend to build.

cost criterion   A design goal related to the cost of developing, operating, or installing the system.

coupling   The strength of the dependencies between two subsystems or two classes. Low coupling results in subsystems that can be modified with minimal impact on other subsystems.

CRC card   An index card representing a class. The name of the *Class* is depicted on the top, its *Responsibilities* in the left column, and the names of the classes (called *Collaborators*) it needs to accomplish its responsibilities are depicted in the right column.

criterion   A measure of goodness used when evaluating alternatives for an issue.

critical path   The longest path in the task model. Delays on critical path tasks directly result in a delay in the overall schedule.

cross-development   A process group that includes processes that occur throughout the project and that ensure the completion and quality of project functions. Examples of cross-development processes include validation and verification, configuration management, documentation, and training. Also called *integral processes*.

cross-functional role   Any role concerned with coordinating the work of more than one team. Examples of cross-functional roles include the configuration manager, the architecture liaison, the tester, and the document editor.

cross-functional team   A team responsible for supporting a subsystem team during a cross-functional activity such as configuration management, integration, or testing. *Contrast with* subsystem team.

CTC   *See* centralized traffic control.

data flow   The sequence in which data is transferred, used, and transformed in the system. *Contrast with* control flow.

data type   An abstraction of a set of values in the context of a programming language. For example, `int` is the Java data type that abstracts all the integer values.

debugging A fault detection technique that attempts to find a fault from an unplanned failure by stepping through successive states of the system.

decision In the context of activity diagrams, a branch in the control flow of an activity diagram. A decision denotes alternative transitions based on a condition. In the context of issue modeling, an issue resolution.

Decision Representation Language (DRL) An issue model extending IBIS to represent the qualitative elements of decision making.

defect *See* fault.

delegation A mechanism for code reuse in which an operation merely resends (i.e., delegates) a message to another class to accomplish the desired behavior.

deliverable A work product destined for the client.

delta A set of differences between two successive versions. Also called *change*.

dependability The property of a computer system that describes how reliably it performs.

dependability criterion A design goal related to minimizing the number of system crashes and the consequences of a system crash. Examples of dependability criteria include robustness, reliability, availability, fault tolerance, security, and safety.

deployment diagram A UML diagram representing run-time components and their assignments to hardware nodes.

derived class *See* subclass.

design goal A quality that the system should optimize. Design goals are often inferred from nonfunctional requirements and are used to guide design decisions. Examples of design goals include usability, reliability, security, and safety.

design object *See* solution object.

design pattern A template solution that developers have refined over time to solve a range of recurring problems. A design pattern includes a name, a problem description, a solution, and a set of consequences. Specific design patterns are described in Appendix A.

designer *See* object designer.

developer Any role that is concerned with specifying, designing, and constructing subsystems. Examples of development roles include the analyst, the system architect, the object designer, and the implementor.

different time, different place groupware See groupware.

document editor A role of the person who integrates the documents.

domain object *See* application object.

DRL *See* Decision Representation Language.

dynamic access control   An access control policy that can be set at runtime. *Contrast with* static access control.

dynamic model   Describes the components of the system that have interesting behavior. In this book, we represent the dynamic model with state machine diagrams, sequence diagrams, and activity diagrams.

egoless programming   A project organization in which responsibilities are assigned to a team instead of individuals. Roles within a team are interchangeable.

encryption   A translation of a message, called *plaintext*, into an encrypted message, called ciphertext, such that it cannot be understood by unauthorized persons.

end user   A role of the people who will use the delivered system.

end user criterion   A design goal related to user-visible attributes of the system not yet covered under a dependability or performance criterion.

enterprise application framework   An application-specific framework used for enterprise business activities.

entity-centered software life cycle model   A software life cycle model that primarily represents the work products produced during development. *Contrast with* activity-centered software life cycle model.

entity object   An object that represents persistent or long-lived information tracked by the system.

entry condition   A condition that needs to be satisfied before a use case is initiated.

environment   The elements that are present at the beginning of a project.

erroneous state   State of the system such that further processing will lead to a failure.

error   *See* erroneous state.

evaluation scenario   Scenario that describes an instance of a user task against which the system is to be evaluated.

event   A relevant occurrence in the system. An event is an instance of an event class. Examples of events include a stimulus from an actor, a time-out, or the sending of a message between two objects.

event class   An abstraction representing a set of events for which the system has a common response.

event-driven control   A control flow paradigm in which a main loop waits for an event and dispatches it to the appropriate object.

exception   An unexpected event that occurs during the execution of the system.

exception handling   A mechanism by which a system treats an exception.

exit condition   A condition that are satisfied after the completion of a use case.

extend relationship A type of relationship in a use case diagram denoting that one use case extends the flow of events of another one. Extends relationships are typically used for modeling exceptional behavior, such as exception handling and help functionality.

extender class The class that specializes an implementor class to provide a different implementation or an extended behavior of the design pattern.

extensibility The quality of a system indicating how easily the system can be changed to accommodate new functionality.

external behavior The behavior of the system from the user's point of view. The use case model describes the external behavior of the system.

Extreme Programming (XP) A methodology targeted for small teams of developers who need to develop software quickly in a changing environment. Extreme Programming aims at making the design of the system as explicit as possible in the source code, hence reducing the need for documentation and the risk of inconsistencies among different documents.

facilitator A meeting management role responsible for organizing and executing a meeting. The primary facilitator writes the meeting agenda, notifies the meeting participants, and ensures during the meeting that the agenda is followed. A secondary facilitator supports the primary facilitator's role in keeping the meeting on track.

failure Deviation of the observed behavior from the specified behavior.

falsification The process of explicitly trying to demonstrate that a model has faults (e.g., the model omits relevant details or represents relevant details incorrectly). Prototype and testing are examples of falsification.

fault The mechanical or algorithmic cause of an error. Also called a *bug* or a *defect*.

fault avoidance A method aimed at preventing the insertion of faults while building the system. Examples of fault avoidance techniques include development methodologies, configuration management, verification, and reviews.

fault detection A method aimed at discovering faults in the running system. Examples of fault detection techniques include debugging and testing.

fault tolerance A method aimed at constructing systems that do not fail in the presence of faults. The ability to withstand faults without failing.

field testing *See* pilot testing.

firewall A packet filter that allows or denies network packets to go through based on their source and destination.

flow of events A sequence of events in a use case describing the interactions between the actor and the system.

foreign key In a database management system, an attribute (or a set of attributes) that references the primary key of another table.

fork node   In an activity diagram, a control node that represents the spilling of the control flow into multiple threads.

forward engineering   The process of applying a transformation to a set of model elements, resulting in a set of corresponding source code statements, such as a class declaration, a Java expression, or a database schema. *Contrast with* reverse engineering.

four-tier architectural style   An architectural style that organizes the system into four layers: presentation client, presentation server, application logic, and storage.

framework   A set of classes providing a general solution that can be refined to provide an application or a subsystem.

functional model   Describes the functionality of the system from the user's point of view. In this book, we represent the functional model with use cases.

functional requirement   An area of functionality the system must support. The functional requirements describe the interactions between the actors and the system independent of the realization of the system.

functional testing   A system testing activity during which developers find differences between the observed functionality and the use case model.

Gantt chart   A notation for representing the schedule of a software project along the time axis. A Gantt chart is a bar graph in which the horizontal axis represents time and the vertical axis represents the different tasks to be done. Tasks are represented as bars whose lengths correspond to the planned duration of the task.

generalization   A modeling activity that results in identifying abstract concepts from lower-level ones.

generalization-specialization relationship   *See* inheritance relationship.

global access table   A representation of access rights in which every legitimate right is represented as an (actor, class, operation) tuple.

goal   A high-level principle used to guide the project. Goals define the important attributes of the system: for example, safety in a transportation vehicle, low cost in shrinkwrapped software.

goodness measure   A qualitative or quantitative criterion used to assess a proposal. *See also* criterion.

greenfield engineering   A development project that starts from scratch. *See also* re-engineering, interface engineering.

groupware   Any software tool supporting the exchange of information among a set of participants. Same time, different place groupware supports synchronous exchanges. Different time, different place groupware supports asynchronous exchanges.

hallway conversation   A synchronous mechanism of communication during which participants meet face to face accidentally.

hierarchical decomposition   A subsystem decomposition that yields an ordered set of layers. *See also* layer.

hierarchical organization   An organization in which reporting and decision-making structures are hierarchical; that is, decisions are made at the root of the organization and communicated down to the team leaders and the team members. *See also* cathedral model.

hook method   A method provided by a framework class that is meant to be overwritten in a subclass to specialize the framework.

horizontal prototype   A prototype that partially implements a broad range of functionality, for example, only the interface objects for a number of use cases.

ideal week   In Extreme Programming, a week in which all work time is dedicated to the implementation of a user story. See also project velocity.

imperative language   *See* procedural language.

implementation   An activity during which developers translate the object model into code.

implementation decision   A design decision that does not affect the public interface of a class or a subsystem.

implementation domain   *See* solution domain.

implementation inheritance   Inheritance used solely as a mechanism for reuse, and violating Liskov's Substitution Principle.

implementation requirement   A constraint on the implementation of the system, including the use of specific tools, programming languages, or hardware platforms.

implementor   *See* class implementor.

implementor class   A class that provides the lower-level behavior of the pattern. In many patterns, a number of collaborating implementor classes are needed to realize the pattern behavior.

include relationship   A type of relationship in a use case diagram denoting that a use case invokes another use case. A use case inclusion is analogous to a method invocation.

infrastructure framework   A framework used to realize an infrastructure subsystem, such as a user interface or a storage subsystem.

inheritance   A reusability technique in which a child class inherits all the attributes and operations of a parent class. Inheritance is the mechanism used to realize an inheritance relationship.

inheritance relationship   The relationship between a general class and a more specialized class. The specialized class adds semantics and functionality to the general class. The specialized class is called the *subclass* and the general class is called the *superclass*.

inspection   A scheduled communication event during which developers formally peer review a work product with respect to a list of pre-defined criteria. *See also* walkthrough.

installation   An activity during which the system is installed and tested in its operating environment. Installation can also include the training of users.

installation testing   A system testing activity during which developers and the client test the system in the operational environment.

instance   Member of a specific data type. For example, 1291 is an instance of the data type int. 3.14 is an instance of the data type float.

integral processes   *See* cross-development.

integration testing   A testing activity during which developers find faults by combining a small number of subsystems or objects.

interaction diagram   UML notation for representing the system's behavior in terms of interactions among a set of objects. Interaction diagrams are used to identify objects in the application and implementation domains. Interaction diagrams is a general term for referring to communication diagrams and sequence diagrams.

interface engineering   A development project in which the interface of a system is redesigned and reimplemented, and the core functionality is left untouched. *See also* greenfield engineering, reengineering.

interface inheritance   *See* specification inheritance.

interface requirement   Constraint imposed by external systems, including legacy systems and interchange formats.

internal transition   A transition that does not leave the state. Internal transitions are triggered by events and can have associated actions. However, firing an internal transition does not result in executing any exit or entry actions. *See also* action, transition.

internal work product   A work product destined only for the internal consumption of the project.

invariant   A predicate that is always true for all instances of a class.

IBIS   *See* Issue-based information system.

issue   A critical problem that has no clear solution.

Issue-Based Information System (IBIS)   An issue model proposed by Kunz Rittel composed of three types of nodes: issue, position, and argument.

issue-based development   *See* issue-based life cycle model.

issue-based life cycle model   An entity-based software life cycle model in which an issue model is used to monitor and control progress in the project.

issue model   A model representing the rationale of one or more decisions as a graph. Nodes of an issue model typically includes issues, proposals, arguments, criteria, and resolutions.

issue resolution   An unscheduled communication event during which participants reach a consensus or a decision on an issue.

join node   In an activity diagram, a control node that denotes the synchronization of multiple threads of control into a single thread.

Joint Application Design (JAD)   A requirements elicitation technique involving the collaboration of clients, users, and developers in constructing a requirements specification through a week-long working meeting.

Key Process Area (KPA)   A set of activities that achieve a goal considered important for attaining a given level of process maturity. Examples of KPA include configuration management, requirements change management, and risk management.

kick-off meeting   A meeting including all project participants that marks the end of the project initiation phase and the beginning of steady state.

knowledge acquisition   The activity of collecting data, organizing it into information, and formalizing it into knowledge.

KPA   *See* key process area.

layer   A subsystem in a hierarchical decomposition. A layer can depend only on lower-level layers and has no knowledge of the layers above it.

legal requirement   Constraint concerned with licensing, regulation, and certification issues. An example of a legal requirement is that software developed for the U.S. federal government must comply with Section 508 of the Rehabilitation Act of 1973, which requires that government information systems be accessible to people with disabilities.

liaison   A communication role responsible for the information flow between two teams. For example, an architecture liaison represents a subsystem team at the architecture team.

life cycle   *See* software life cycle.

link   An instance of an association. A link connects two objects.

Liskov Substitution Principle   Formal definition for specification inheritance. It essentially states that, if a client code uses the methods provided by a superclass, then developers should be able to add new subclasses without having to change the client code.

local king client   A client who can answer developer questions and make decisions without having to ask anybody else. The local king has deep knowledge of the application domain and is usually collocated with the project.

maintainability   The ability to change the system to deal with new technology or to fix defects.

maintenance criterion   A design goal related to the difficulty of changing or upgrading the system after it has been delivered.

management role   Any role that is concerned with planning, monitoring, and controlling the project. Examples of management roles include project manager and team leader. See also *project management*.

many-to-many association   An association with 0..n or 1..n multiplicity on both ends.

mapping   A mathematical correspondence that assigns an element (or a set of elements) of one model to each element of another model.

master directory   A library of promotions.

meeting   A synchronous mechanism of communication during which participants present, discuss, negotiate, and resolve issues, either face-to-face or via telephone or videoconferencing.

meeting agenda   Document used to prepare and conduct a meeting. A meeting agenda usually consists of at least three sections: a header identifying the planned meeting location, time, and participants; a list of items participants will report on; and a list of issues to be discussed and resolved.

meeting minutes   A document used to record the content and decisions of a meeting. Meeting minutes usually consist of three sections that correspond to the sections of the agenda, as well as action items and decision items.

message   A mechanism by which a sending object requests the execution of an operation in the receiving object. A message is composed of a name and a number of arguments. The receiving object matches the name of the message to one or more operations and passes the arguments to the operation. The message send ends when the results of the operation are returned to the sending object.

method   In the context of development, a repeatable technique for solving a specific problem. For example, a recipe is a method for cooking a specific dish. In the context of a class or an object, the implementation of an operation. For example, SetTime(t) is a method of the class Watch.

methodology   A collection of methods for solving a class of problems. A seafood cookbook is a methodology for preparing seafood. This book describes a methodology for dealing with complex and changing systems.

middleware framework   A framework used to integrate distributed applications and components.

minute taker   A meeting role responsible for recording a meeting, in particular, the resolutions that participants have agreed on and their implementation in terms of action items.

model   An abstraction of a system aimed at simplifying the reasoning about the system by omitting irrelevant details. For example, if the system of interest is a ticket distributor for a train, blue prints for the ticket distributor, schematics of its electrical wiring, and object models of its software are models of the ticket distributor.

model object   See entity object model/view/controller architectural style.

model transformation   A transformation that is applied to an object model and results in another object model. The purpose of object model transformation is to simplify or optimize the original model, bringing it closer to a system that complies with all requirements in the specification.

Model/View/Controller (MVC) architectural style   A three-tier architectural style in which domain knowledge is maintained by model objects, displayed by view objects, and manipulated by control objects. In this book, model objects are called *entity objects* and view objects are called *boundary objects*.

modeling   An activity during which participants construct an abstraction of a system by focusing on interesting aspects and omitting irrelevant details. What is interesting or irrelevant depends on the task in which the model is used. *See also* abstraction.

modifiability   The quality of a system describing how easily existing models can be modified.

multiplicity   A set of integers attached to an association end indicating the number of links that can legitimately originate from an instance of the class at the association end. For example, an association denoting that a Car has four Wheels has a multiplicity of 1 on the Car end and 4 on the Wheel end.

MVC   *See* Model/View/Controller.

name   In a class, a mandatory string identifying the class within a subsystem. The class name is unique within the subsystem. In an association, an optional string describing the association between two classes. In an attribute, a mandatory string identifying the attribute within the class. The attribute name is unique within the class.

navigation   Direction in which an association can be followed.

nested state   A state within a nested state machine.

nested state machine   A state machine that models the behavior of a single state as a set of nested states, internal transitions, and actions.

NFR Framework   A method for tracking the relevant nonfunctional requirements for each decision, evaluated alternative, and interaction between nonfunctional requirements.

nonfunctional requirement   A user-visible constraint on the system. Nonfunctional requirements describe user-visible aspects of the system that are not directly related with the functionality of the system. *See also* design goal.

notation   A graphical or textual set of rules for representing a model. For example, the Roman alphabet is a notation for representing words; UML is a graphical notation for representing system models.

note   A comment attached to a UML diagram.

object   An instance of a class. An object has an identity and stores attribute values.

Object Constraint Language (OCL)   A formal language defined as part of the UML used for expressing constraints.

object design   An activity during which developers define custom objects to bridge the gap between the analysis model and the hardware/software platform. This includes specifying object and subsystem interfaces, selecting off-the-shelf components, restructuring the object model to attain design goals, and optimizing the object model for performance. Object design results in the object design model.

Object Design Document (ODD)   A document describing the object design model. The object design model is often generated from comments embedded in the source code.

object design model   A detailed object model representing the application and solution objects that make up the system. The object design model includes detailed class specifications, contracts, types, signatures, and visibilities for all public operations.

object designer   A role of developers who refine and specify the interface of classes during object design.

object diagram   A class diagram that includes only instances.

object model   Describes the structure of a system in terms of objects, attributes, associations, and operations. During requirements and analysis, the object model starts as the *analysis object model* and describes the application concepts relevant to the system. During system design, the object model is refined into the *system design object model* and includes descriptions of the subsystem interfaces. During object design, the object model is refined into the *object design model* and includes detailed descriptions of solution objects.

object-oriented analysis   An activity concerned with modeling the application domain with objects.

object-oriented design   An activity concerned with modeling the solution domain with objects.

OCL   *See* Object Constraint Language.

OCL bag   An OCL collection representing an unordered multi-set (i.e., a set that can contain the same element several times). OCL bags are used to represent the result of navigating a series of associations.

OCL collection   An OCL abstract type representing a group of objects.

OCL sequence   An OCL collection representing an ordered list. OCL sequences are used to represent the result of navigating a single ordered association.

OCL set   An OCL collection representing a mathematical set. OCL sets are used to represent the result of navigating a single association.

ODD *See* Object Design Document.

one-to-many association An association that has a multiplicity of 1 on one end and a 0..n or a 1..n multiplicity on the other end.

one-to-one association An association with multiplicity of 1 on each end.

open architecture A layered architecture in which a layer may make use of services in any layer below it (as opposed to only the layer immediately below it). *Contrast with* closed architecture.

open issue An issue that has not yet been resolved.

operation An atomic piece of behavior that is provided by a class. A calling object triggers the execution of an operation by sending a message to the object on which the operation should be executed

operations requirement Constraint on the administration and management of the system in the operational setting.

organization A set of teams, roles, communication paths, and reporting structure tailored to a specific project (project organization) or a class of projects (division or corporate organization).

package A UML grouping concept denoting that a set of objects or classes are related. Packages are used in use case and class diagrams to deal with the complexity associated with large numbers of use cases or classes.

packaging requirement Constraint on the actual delivery of the system (e.g., constraint on the installation media for setting up the software).

participant Any person involved with a software development project.

participating actor An actor interacting with a use case.

participating actor instance An actor instance interacting with a scenario.

participating object An analysis object that is involved in a given use case.

partition A subsystem in a peer-to-peer architectural style.

pattern expert A role of the developers responsible for providing detailed knowledge about specific patterns.

pattern interface That part of the design pattern visible to the client class. Often, the pattern interface is realized by an abstract class or an interface.

peer-based communication structure A communication structure in which developers from different teams communicate directly.

peer review A scheduled communication event during which team members identify defects and find solutions in preliminary work products. *See also* inspection, walkthrough.

peer-to-peer architectural style A generalization of the client/server architectural style in which subsystems can act either as clients or servers.

performance   Any quantifiable attribute of the system, such as response time, throughput, availability, and accuracy.

performance criterion   A design goal related to the speed or space attributes of a system. Examples of performance criteria include response time, throughput, and memory space.

performance testing   A system testing activity during which developers find differences between nonfunctional requirements and system performance.

persistent data   Data that outlive a single execution of the system.

PERT chart   A notation representing a schedule as an acyclic graph of tasks.

phase   Often used as a synonym for *activity* or *process*.

phenomenon   An object of a reality as perceived by the modeler. Modeling consists of selecting the phenomena of a reality that are of interest, identifying their common properties, and abstracting them into concepts. *Contrast with* concept.

pilot testing   A testing activity during which a selected set of users exercises the system in the deployment environment.

pipe and filter architectural style   An architectural style in which subsystems sequentially process data from a set of inputs and send their results to other subsystems via a set of outputs. Associations between subsystems are called pipes. Subsystems are called filters. Filters do not depend on each other and can thus be rearranged in different orders and configurations.

portability   The ease with which a system or component can be transferred from one hardware or software environment to another.

postmortem review   A scheduled communication event during which participants capture the lessons learned during the project.

postcondition   A predicate that must be true after an operation is invoked.

precondition   A predicate that must be true before an operation is invoked.

primary facilitator   *See* facilitator.

primary key   In a database management system, a set of attributes whose values uniquely identify the data records in a table.

problem definition   A scheduled communication event during which the client and manager define the scope of the system.

problem domain   *See* application domain.

problem inspection   A scheduled communication event during which developers gather information from the problem statement, the client, and the user about their needs and the application domain.

problem presentation   A scheduled communication event during which the client and the manager communicate the high-level requirements of the system to the project participants.

problem solving A search activity that includes the generation and evaluation of alternatives addressing a given problem, often by trial and error.

problem statement A document cooperatively written by the client and project management that briefly describes the scope of the system, including high-level requirements, target environment, deliverables, and acceptance criteria. *See also* Project Agreement.

procedural language A programming language in which the developer specifies an explicit sequence of steps to produce a result. Also known as an *imperative language*.

procedure-driven control A control flow paradigm in which operations wait for input. The sequencing of operations is otherwise done explicitly through sending messages.

process A set of activities that is performed toward a specific purpose. Examples of processes include requirements elicitation, analysis, project management, and testing. A process is synonymous with a high-level activity. *See also* activity.

process group A group of related processes. Examples of process groups include management, pre-development, development, and post-development.

process management In configuration management, a set of policies dictating how versions should be created and documented, including policies for notifying developers when new versions are created or when a build fails.

project agreement A document that formally defines the scope, duration, cost, and deliverables of a project. Requirements are often categorized into core requirements (which the system must meet when delivered), desirable requirements (which must be satisfied eventually), and optional requirements (which may or may not be required in the future). The Project Agreement subsumes the Problem Statement.

project-based organization A corporate organization in which work is divided according to projects; that is each participant works on exactly one project at any one time.

project conception phase The first phase of a project during which the idea for the project is born. In a software project this is usually a new requirement triggered by the need of an existing market or a new technology.

project definition phase The phase of a project, during which a possible client, the project manager, and the software architect are involved in agreeing on an initial problem statement, schedule, and software architecture.

project initiation In IEEE 1074, a project management activity during which the project scope and resources are defined. In this book, project initiation is called *project start phase*.

project management An activity during which managers plan, budget, monitor, and control the development process. Project management ensures that constraints and project goals are met.

project member *See* participant.

project review   A scheduled communication event during which a project manager monitors the status of a project.

project start phase   A project phase that occurs after the client and the project manager commit to the project. During the start phase, the project manager sets up the project infrastructure, hires participants, organizes them in teams, defines the major milestones, and kicks off the project.

project steady state   A management activity during which management monitors and controls the progress of the project.

project termination   A management activity during which the project is concluded: the system is delivered and accepted by the client.

project velocity   In Extreme Programming, a factor indicating how many ideal weeks can be accomplished during a fixed amount of time.

promotion   A version that has been made available internally to other developers in the project. *See also* release.

proposal   A possible resolution of an issue.

prototyping   A process of designing and realizing a simplified version of the system for evaluation with the user or the manager. For example, a usability prototype evaluates the usability of different interfaces. A performance prototype assesses the performance of different alternatives.

proxy client   A participant who stands in for the real client. Proxy clients have sufficient knowledge of the application domain to answer clarification questions from the developers, but do not have sufficient power to make major decisions.

pseudo client   A member of the development organization who acts as a client because the system is targeted at a new market segment, as opposed to a single individual or company. Pseudo clients can make decisions within a short time and can collaborate well with the development organization, but have a limited knowledge of the application domain.

pseudo requirement   A nonfunctional requirement that can be in the implementation, interface, operation, packaging, or legal domains.

QOC   *See* Questions, Options, and Criteria.

qualification   A technique for reducing the multiplicity of associations by replacing many-to-many or one-to-many associations with qualified associations.

qualified association   An association in which one end is indexed by an attribute. For example, the association between `Directory` and `File` is a qualified association indexed by a filename on the `Directory` end.

qualifier   Attribute used to index the qualified end of a qualified association.

questionnaire   A synchronous mechanism of communication during which information is elicited from a participant with a structured set of questions.

Questions, Options, and Criteria (QOC)   An issue model, proposed by McLean et al., extending IBIS to represent criterion and assessment information.

RAD   *See* Requirements Analysis Document.

rationale   The justification of decisions. For example, selecting myDBMS as a database management system is a system design decision. Stating that myDBMS is reliable and responsive enough to attain the project's goals is part of the rationale for this design decision. Also called *design rationale*.

rationale editor   A role responsible for collecting and organizing rationale information.

rationale management   An activity during which developers create, capture, update, and access rationale information.

rationale model   *See* issue model.

readability   The quality of a system describing how easy it can be understood from its source code.

realizability   The property of a model indicating whether the system it represents can be realized.

reengineering   A development project in which a system and its accompanying business processes are redesigned and reimplemented. *See also* greenfield engineering, interface engineering.

refactoring   Transformation of the source code that improves its readability or modifiability without changing the behavior of the system. Refactoring aims at improving the design of a working system by focusing on a specific field or method of a class.

refined class   *See* subclass.

regression testing   A testing activity during which integration tests are rerun to ensure that the system does not regress after a change; that is, the system passes all the integration tests it did before the change.

release   In communication, a scheduled communication event during which a developer makes available to the rest of the project a new version of a work product. *See also* promotion. In configuration management, a version that has been made available externally, that is, to the client or the users.

reliability   Ability of a system or component to perform its required functions under stated conditions for a specified period of time. Reliability requirements include, for example, an acceptable mean time to failure, the ability to detect specified faults, or to withstand specified security attacks. Reliability includes dependability, robustness, and safety.

reporting structure   The structure representing the chain of control and status reporting.

repository   In a repository architectural style, the central subsystem that manages persistent data. In configuration management, a library of releases.

repository architectural style   An architectural style in which persistent data is managed and stored by a single subsystem. Peripheral subsystems are relatively independent and interact only through the central subsystem.

request for change   *See* change request.

request for clarification   An unscheduled communication event during which a participant requests more information.

requirement   A function that the system must have (a functional requirement) or a user-visible constraint on the system (nonfunctional requirement).

Requirements Analysis Document (RAD)   The document describing the analysis model.

requirements elicitation   An activity during which project participants define the purpose of the system. Requirements elicitation produces the functional model.

requirements engineering   An activity that includes requirements elicitation and analysis.

requirements specification   A complete and precise description of the system from the user's point of view. A requirements specification, unlike the analysis model, is understandable to the user. In object-oriented software engineering, the requirements specification includes use cases and scenarios.

requirements testing   *See* functional testing.

response time   An attribute of the system denoting how quickly it can react to a user input.

resolution   The proposal selected by participants to close an issue.

resources   Assets that are used to accomplish work, including time, equipment, and labor.

reverse engineering   The process of applying a transformation to a set of source code elements, resulting in a set of model elements. The purpose of reverse engineering is to recreate the model for an existing system, either because the model was lost, never created, or because it became out of sync with the source code. *Contrast with* forward engineering.

reviewer   A role of people validating work products for quality criteria such as completeness, correctness, consistency, and clarity.

risk   An area of uncertainty that can lead to a deviation in the project plan (e.g., late delivery, requirements not met, cost above budget), including the failure of the project.

risk-based development   A software life cycle driven by the identification and resolution of risks. *See also* Spiral model.

risk management   A management method for identifying and addressing areas of uncertainty before they negatively affect the schedule of the project or the quality of the system.

robustness   The degree to which a system or component can function correctly in the presence of invalid inputs or stressful environment conditions.

role   In the context of an organization, a set of responsibilities in the project assigned to a person or a team. A person can fill one or more roles. Examples of roles include analyst, system architect, tester, developer, manager, reviewer. In the context of an association end, a string indicating the role of the class at the association end with respect to the association.

round-trip engineering   A model maintenance activity that combines forward and reverse engineering. Changes to the implementation model are propagated to the analysis and design models through reverse engineering. Changes to the analysis and design models are propagated to the implementation model through forward engineering.

Royce's methodology   An iterative risk-driven methodology proposed by Royce based on the Unified Process life cycle.

safety   A measure of the absence of catastrophic consequences to the environment.

same time, different place groupware   *See* groupware

sandwich testing   An integration testing strategy that combines top-down and bottom-up testing.

schedule   A map of a task model on a time line. A schedule represents work in terms of calendar time.

schema   In a database management system, a meta-model for the data.

scenario   Instance of a use case. A scenario represents a concrete sequence of interactions between one or more actors and the system.

SCMP   *See* Software Configuration Management Plan.

SDD   *See* System Design Document.

secondary facilitator   *See* facilitator.

security   Property of a system indicating its ability to protect the resources against unauthorized use, whether malicious or accidental.

sequence diagram   UML notation representing the behavior of the system as a series of interactions among a group of objects. Each object is depicted as a column in the diagram. Each interaction is depicted as an arrow between two columns. Sequence diagrams are used during analysis to identify missing objects, attributes, or relationships. Sequence diagrams are used during object design to refine the specification of classes. *See also* communication diagram.

service   A set of related operations offered by a subsystem.

shared aggregation   An aggregation relationship in which the whole and the part can exist independently. *Contrast with* composition aggregation.

signature   Given an operation, the tuple made up of the types of its parameters and the type of the return value. Operation signatures are specified during object design.

slack time   For a task, the maximum amount of time a task can be delayed without affecting the overall project schedule.

software architecture   *See* system design model.

Software Configuration Management Plan (SCMP)   A document defining the procedures and conventions associated with the configuration management of a project. These include identifying configuration items, accounting for their status, approving change requests, and auditing.

software library   A store of versions with facilities to track the status of changes.

software life cycle   All activities and work products necessary for the development of a software system.

software life cycle model   An abstraction representing the development of software for the purpose of understanding, monitoring, or controlling it. Examples of software life cycle models include the waterfall model, the V-model, Boehm's spiral model, the Unified Process, and the issue-based life cycle model.

Software Project Management Plan (SPMP)   The controlling document of a software project. The SPMP defines the activities, work products, milestones, and resources allocated to the project. Also defined in the SPMP are the management procedures and conventions applicable to the project such as status reporting, risk management, and contingency management.

software reliability   The property of a software system indicating the probability that the software will not cause a failure of the system for a specified duration.

solution domain   The space of all possible systems. The solution domain is the focus of the system design, object design, and implementation activities. *Contrast with* application domain.

solution domain specialist   A consultant role responsible for providing knowledge about solutions to implement the system. This can include the development method, the process, implementation technology, or the development environment.

solution object   An object in the system design or object design model that represents a solution domain concept. Also called *design object*.

specialization   A modeling activity that results in identifying more specific concepts from a high-level one.

specification inheritance   Inheritance used as a means of subtyping.

spiral model   An iterative and incremental software life cycle model centered around risk management.

SPMP   *See* Software Project Management Plan.

state   A condition that is satisfied by the attribute values of an object or a subsystem.

state machine diagram   UML notation representing the behavior of an individual object as a number of states and transitions between these states. A state represents a particular set of values for an object. Given a state, a transition represents a future state the object can move to and the conditions associated with the change of state. State machine diagrams are used during analysis to describe objects with state-dependent behavior.

static access control   An access control policy that can be set only at compile time. *Contrast with* dynamic access control.

status accounting   In configuration management, the tracking of change requests, change approval, and rationale for change.

status meeting   A scheduled communication event during which team leaders monitor the status of their team.

status review   *See* status meeting.

stereotype   An extension mechanism to classify model elements in UML. A stereotype is represented by a string enclosed by guillemets (e.g., «control») and attached to the model element to which it applies, such as a class or an association. Formally, attaching a stereotype to a model element is semantically equivalent to creating a new class in the UML meta-model (i.e., the model that represents the constructs of UML). For example, the stereotype «control» attached to an object denotes a control object.

stimulus   A message sent to an object or to the system by an actor or another object; it usually results in the invocation of an operation. Examples of stimuli include clicking on a user interface button, selecting a menu item, typing a command, or sending a network packet.

strict inheritance   An inheritance relationship that complies with the Liskov Substitution Principle.

structural testing   A testing activity that finds differences between the system and the system design model.

structured interview   An interview, following a questionnaire, whose purpose is to clarify incomplete or ambiguous answers.

subclass   The specialized class in a generalization relationship. *See also* generalization.

subsystem   In general, a smaller, simpler part of a larger system; in system design, a well-defined software component that provides a number of services to other subsystems. Examples of subsystems include storage subsystems (managing persistent data), user interface subsystems (managing the interaction with the user), networking subsystems (managing the communication with other subsystems over a network).

subsystem decomposition   The division of the system into subsystems. Each subsystem is described in terms of its services during system design and its API during object design. Subsystem decomposition is part of the system design model.

subsystem interface   The set of operations of a subsystem that is publicly available to other subsystems.

subsystem team   A team responsible for developing a subsystem. *Contrast with* cross-functional team.

superclass   The general class in a generalization relationship. *See also* generalization.

supportability   The ease of changing the system after deployment.

swimlane   A UML grouping concept denoting activities that are carried out by the same object or set of objects.

synchronicity   *See* communication mechanism, groupware.

system   An organized set of communicating parts designed for a specific purpose. For example, a car, composed of four wheels, a chassis, a body, and an engine, is designed to transport people. A watch, composed of a battery, a circuit, wheels, and hands, is designed to measure time.

system architect   *See* architect.

system design   An activity during which developers define the system design model, including the design goals of the project, and decompose the system into smaller subsystems that can be realized by individual teams. System design also leads to the selection of the hardware/software platform, persistent data management strategy, global control flow, access control policy, and boundary condition strategies.

System Design Document (SDD)   A document describing the system design model.

system design model   A high-level description of the system, including design goals, subsystem decomposition, hardware/software platform, persistent storage strategy, global control flow, access control policy, and boundary condition strategies. The system design model represents the strategic decisions made by the architecture team that allow subsystem teams to work concurrently and cooperate effectively.

system model   The set of all models built during development to reason about the system. The system model includes the analysis model, the system design model, the object design model, and the source code.

system testing   A testing activity during which developers test all the subsystems as a single system. System testing includes functional testing, performance testing, acceptance testing, and installation testing.

task   An atomic unit of work that can be managed. Tasks consume resources and produce one or more work products.

task model   A model of work for a project represented as tasks and their interdependencies.

team   A set of participants who work on a common problem in a project.

team-based organization   An organization in which project participants are assigned to teams that are responsible for specific subsystems or project functions. Participants in a team-based organization are allocated full-time to the project.

team leader   A management role responsible for planning, monitoring, and controlling a single team.

technical consultant   A consultant role that provides solution domain expertise to the project.

technical writer   *See* document editor.

test case   A set of inputs and expected results that exercises a component with the purpose of causing failures.

test driver   A partial implementation of a component that exercises the tested component. Test drivers are used during unit and integration testing.

Test Manual   A document describing the test cases used to test the system, along with their results.

test planning   An activity that allocates resources for tests and schedules testing activities.

test stub   A partial implementation of a component on which the tested component depends. Test stubs are used to isolate components during unit and integration testing and allow components to be tested even when their dependent components have not yet been implemented.

tester   A role concerned with the planning, design, execution, and analysis of tests.

testing   An activity during which developers find differences between the system and its models by executing the system (or parts of it) with sample input data sets. Testing includes unit testing, integration testing, system testing, and usability testing.

thread   A control flow paradigm in which the system creates an arbitrary number of threads to handle an arbitrary number of input channels.

three-tier architectural style   An architectural style that organizes the system into an interface layer, an application logic layer, and a storage layer.

throughput   An attribute of the system denoting how much work it can accomplish within a specified amount of time.

timekeeper   A meeting role responsible for tracking time so that the primary facilitator can accelerate the resolution of an issue (or table it) if necessary.

top-down testing   An integration testing strategy in which components are incrementally integrated together starting with the highest level components. Top down testing does not require any test drivers. *Contrast with* bottom-up testing, sandwich testing.

top-level design   Initial subsystem decomposition used for team organization and initial planning.

traceability   The property of a model describing whether a model element can be traced to the original requirement or rationale that motivated its existence.

training scenario   Tutorial scenario used for introducing new users to the system. These are step-by-step instructions designed to hand-hold the user through common tasks.

transformation   A mapping from one model to another that aims at improving one aspect of the transformed model (e.g., its modularity) while preserving all of its other properties (e.g., its functionality). A transformation is usually localized, affects a small number of classes, attributes, and operations, and is executed in a series of small steps.

transition   A possible change of state associated triggered by events, conditions, or time.

tuple   An ordered set of values. Common uses for the tuple are representing a set of value attributes in a relational database and representing an access right.

type   In an attribute or a variable: describes the legal values the attribute or variable can take.

UML state machine   *See* state machine diagram.

unambiguous requirement   *See* ambiguity.

Unified Modeling Language (UML)   A standard set of notations for representing models.

Unified Process   *See* Unified Software Development Process.

Unified Software Development Process   An iterative software life cycle model characterized by cycles of four phases, called *Inception*, *Elaboration*, *Construction*, and *Transition*.

unit testing   Testing individual components.

usability   Ease with which a user can learn to operate, prepare inputs for, and interpret outputs of a system or component.

usability testing   The validation of a system or a model through the use of prototypes and simulations by a user.

use case   A general sequence of interactions between one or more actors and the system. *See also* scenario.

use case diagram   UML notation used during requirements elicitation and analysis to represent the functionality of the system. A use case describes a function of the system in terms of a sequence of interactions between an actor and the system. A use case also includes entry conditions that must be true before executing the use case and the exit conditions that are true at the completion of the use case.

user   *See* end user.

User Manual   A document describing the user interface of the system such that a user unfamiliar with the system can use it.

V-model   A variation of the waterfall model that makes explicit the dependencies between development processes and verification processes.

validation   An activity that ensures that the system addresses the client's needs.

variant   Versions that are intended to coexist. For example, if a system can be executed on different platforms, the system has a variant for each platform (e.g., a Windows variant, a Macintosh variant, a Linux variant).

verifiability   The property of a model indicating whether or not it can be falsified.

verification   A set of formal methods that attempt to detect faults without executing the system.

version   A state of a configuration item or a CM aggregate at a well-defined point in time. The version of a CM aggregate is called a *configuration*.

version identifier   A number or a name that uniquely identifies a version.

vertical prototype   A prototype that completely implements a restricted functionality, for example, all the interface, control, and entity objects for one use case.

view   In modeling, a subset of a model. Views focus on selected model elements to make them more understandable. In the Model/View/Controller architectural style, a type of object or subsystem responsible for displaying to the user information from model objects or subsystems.

visibility   *See* attribute visibility.

visionary scenario   Scenario that describes a future system. Visionary scenarios are used both as a point in the modeling space by developers as they refine their ideas of the future system and as a communication medium to elicit requirements from users.

walkthrough   A scheduled communication event during which a developer presents a work product line by line and other developers ask questions and challenge the work product. *See also* inspection.

waterfall model   A software life cycle model in which all development processes occur sequentially.

WBS   *See* work breakdown structure.

whitebox framework   A framework that relies on inheritance and dynamic binding for extensibility. *Contrast with* blackbox framework.

whitebox test   A test that focuses on the internal structure of a component. *Contrast with* blackbox test.

Work Breakdown Structure (WBS)   A hierarchical decomposition of project work into tasks. Leaves represent tasks that are assigned to participants. Aggregates represent the work associated with a work product.

work package   A specification of work to be accomplished in completing a task or activity.

work product   An artifact produced during development. Examples of work products include the Requirements Analysis Document, the System Design Document, user interface prototypes, market surveys, as well as the delivered system.

workflow   In the Unified Process, a thread of cohesive and mostly sequential activities that produce the artifacts. Engineering workflows (*Requirements*, *Design*, *Implementation*, *Assessment*, *Deployment*) focus on development activities. Supporting workflows (*Management*, *Configuration and Change*, *Environment*) focus on overhead activities needed to coordinate the development activities.

workspace   In configuration management, a library of promotions.

XP   *See* Extreme Programming.

Bibliography

[Abbott, 1983]   R. Abbott, "Program design by informal English descriptions," *Communications of the ACM*, Vol. 26, No. 11, 1983.

[Adams, 2000]   D. N. Adams, *Mostly Harmless*, Ballantine Books, 2000.

[Aguanno, 2005]   K. Aguanno, Managing Agile Projects, Multi-Media Publications, Ontario, 2005.

[AgileManifesto, 2001]   http://www.agilemanifesto.org.

[Albrecht & Gaffney, 1983]   A. J. Albrecht & J. E. Gaffney Jr., "Software function, source lines of code, and development effort prediction: A software science validation," *IEEE Transactions on Software Engineering*, Vol. SE-9, No. 6, November 1983.

[Allen, 1985]   T. J. Allen, *Managing the Flow of Technology: Technology Transfer and the Dissemination of Technological Information within the R&D Organization*, 2nd ed., MIT Press, Cambridge, MA, 1995.

[Ambler, 1998]   S. W. Ambler, *Process Patterns: Building Large-Scale Systems Using Object Technology*, Cambridge University Press, New York, 1998.

[Ambler, 2002]   S. Ambler, *Agile Modeling: Effective Practices for Extreme Programming and the Unified Process*, John Wiley & Sons, 2002.

[Apache]   Apache, http://www.apache.org/.

[Babich, 1986]   W. A. Babich, *Software Configuration Management*, Addison-Wesley, Reading, MA, 1986.

[Baker et al., 2008]   P. Baker, Z. R. Dai, & R. Grabowski, *Model-Driven Testing: Using the UML Testing Profile*, Springer, Berlin, 2008.

[Barone & Switzer, 1995]   J.T.T. Barone & J. Switzer, *Interviewing: Art and Skill*, Allyn & Bacon, 1995.

[Bass et al., 2003]   L. Bass, P. Clements, & R. Kazman, *Software Architecture in Practice*, 2nd ed., Addison-Wesley, Reading, MA, 2003.

[BEA]   BEA WebLogic Platform, http://www.bea.com/products/weblogic/platform.

[Beck & Andres, 2005]   K. Beck & C. Andres, *Extreme Programming Explained: Embrace Change*, 2nd ed., Addison-Wesley, Reading, MA, 2005.

[Beck & Cunningham, 1989]   K. Beck & W. Cunningham, "A laboratory for teaching object-oriented thinking," *OOPSLA'89 Conference Proceedings*, New Orleans, LA, October 1–6, 1989.

[Berliner, 1990]   B. Berliner, "CVS II: Parallelizing software development," *Proceedings of the 1990 USENIX Conference*, Washington, DC, pp. 22–26, January 1990.

[Bersoff et al., 1980]   E. H. Bersoff, V. D. Henderson, & S. G. Siegel, *Software Configuration Management: An Investment in Product Integrity*, Prentice Hall, Englewood Cliffs, NJ, 1980.

[Bezier, 1990]   B. Bezier, *Software Testing Techniques*, 2nd ed., Van Nostrand, New York, 1990.

[Binder, 2000]   R. V. Binder, *Testing Object-Oriented Systems: Models, Patterns, and Tools*, Addison-Wesley, Reading, MA, 2000.

[Birrer, 1993]   E. T. Birrer, "Frameworks in the financial engineering domain: An experience report," *ECOOP'93 Proceedings*, Lecture Notes in Computer Science, No. 707, 1993.

[Blaha & Premerlani, 1998]   M. Blaha & W. Premerlani, *Object-Oriented Modeling and Design for Database Applications*, Prentice Hall, Upper Saddle River, NJ, 1998.

[Boehm, 1987]   B. Boehm, "A spiral model of software development and enhancement," *Software Engineering Project Management*, pp. 128–142, 1987.

[Boehm, 1991]   B. Boehm, "Software risk management: Principles and practices," *IEEE Software*, Vol. 1, pp. 32–41, 1991.

[Boehm et al., 1998]   B. Boehm, A. Egyed, J. Kwan, D. Port, A. Shah, & R. Madachy, "Using the WinWin spiral model: A case study," *IEEE Computer* 31(7): 33–44, 1998.

[Boehm et al., 2000]   B. Boehm, E. Horowitz, R. Madachy, D. Reifer, B. K. Clark, B. Steece, A. W. Brown, S. Chulani, C. Abts, *Software Cost Estimation with COCOMO II*, Prentice Hall, Upper Saddle River, NJ, 2000.

[Bonatti, 2001]   W. Bonatti, *The Mountains of My Life*, Modern Library, Random House, New York, 2001.

[Booch, 1994]   G. Booch, *Object-Oriented Analysis and Design with Applications*, 2nd ed., Benjamin/Cummings, Redwood City, CA, 1994.

[Booch et al., 2005]   G. Booch, J. Rumbaugh, & I. Jacobson, *The Unified Modeling Language User Guide*, Addison-Wesley, Reading, MA, 2005.

[Borghoff & Schlichter, 2000]   U. W. Borghoff & J. Schlichter, *Computer Supported Cooperative Work: An Introduction into Distributed Applications*, Springer-Verlag, 2000.

[Borning, 1981]   A. Borning. "The programming language aspects of ThingLab, a constraint-oriented simulation laboratory," in *ACM TOPLAS* 3(4), October 1981.

[Brooks, 1995]   F. P. Brooks, *The Mythical Man Month: Anniversary Edition: Essays on Software Engineering*, Addison-Wesley, Reading, MA, 1995.

[Brown et al., 1999]   W. J. Brown, H. W. McCormick, & S. W. Thomas, *AntiPatterns and Patterns in Software Configuration Management*, Wiley, New York, 1999.

[Bruegge, 1992]   B. Bruegge, "Teaching an industry-oriented software engineering course," *Software Enginering Education, SEI Conference*, Lecture Notes in Computer Sciences, Vol. 640, Springer-Verlag, San Diego, CA, pp. 65–87, October 1992.

[Bruegge, 1994]   B. Bruegge, "From toy systems to real system development," *Improvements in Software Engineering Education*, Workshop of the German Chapter of the ACM, B.G. Teubner Verlag, Stuttgart, pp. 62–72, February 1994.

[Bruegge & Coyne, 1993]   B. Bruegge & R. Coyne, "Model-based software engineering in larger scale project courses," *IFIP Transactions on Computer Science and Technology,* Vol. A-40, pp. 273–287, 1993.

[Bruegge & Coyne, 1994]   B. Bruegge & R. Coyne, "Teaching iterative object-oriented development: Lessons and directions," in Jorge L. Diaz-Herrera (ed.), *7th Conference on Software Engineering Education,* Lecture Notes in Computer Science, Vol. 750, Springer-Verlag, pp. 413–427, January 1994.

[Bruegge et al., 1992]   B. Bruegge, J. Blythe, J. Jackson, & J. Shufelt, "Object-oriented system modeling with OMT," *Conference Proceedings OOPSLA '92 (Object-Oriented Programming Systems, Languages, and Applications),* pp. 359–376, October 1992.

[Bruegge et al., 1993]   B. Bruegge, T. Gottschalk, & B. Luo, "A framework for dynamic program analyzers," *OOPSLA' 93 (Object-Oriented Programming Systems, Languages, and Applications),* Washington, DC, pp. 65–82, September 1993.

[Bruegge et al., 1994]   B. Bruegge, K. O'Toole, & D. Rothenberger, "Design considerations for an accident management system," in M. Brodie, M. Jarke, & M. Papazoglou (ed.), *Proceedings of the Second International Conference on Cooperative Information Systems,* University of Toronto Press, Toronto, pp. 90–100, May 1994.

[BSCW]   Basic Support for Cooperative Work, http://bscw.gmd.de.

[Buckingham Shum & Hammond, 1994]   S. Buckingham Shum & N. Hammond, "Argumentation-based design rationale: What use at what cost?" *International Journal of Human-Computer Studies,* Vol. 40, pp. 603–652, 1994.

[Buhl, 1956]   H. Buhl, *Nanga Parbat Pilgrimage,* Hodder & Stoughton, London, 1956.

[Buschmann et al., 1996]   F. Buschmann, R. Meunier, H. Rohnert, P. Sommerlad, & M. Stal, *Pattern-Oriented Software Architecture: A System of Patterns,* Wiley, Chichester, U.K., 1996.

[Campbell & Islam, 1993]   R. H. Campbell & N. Islam, "A technique for documenting the framework of an object-oriented system," *Computing Systems,* 6, pp. 363–389, 1993.

[Carr et al., 1993]   M. J. Carr, S. L. Konda, I. Monarch, F. C. Ulrich, & C. F. Walker, *Taxonomy-Based Risk Identification,* Technical Report CMU/SEI-93-TR-6, Software Engineering Institute, Carnegie Mellon University, Pittsburgh, PA, 1993.

[Carroll, 1995]   J. M. Carroll (ed.), *Scenario-Based Design: Envisioning Work and Technology in System Development,* Wiley, New York, 1995.

[Charette, 1989]   R. N. Charette, *Software Engineering Risk Analysis and Management,* McGraw-Hill, New York, 1989.

[Chung et al., 1999]   L. Chung, B. A. Nixon, E. Yu & J. Mylopoulos, *Non-Functional Requirements in Software Engineering,* Kluwer Academic, Boston, 1999.

[Clements et al., 2002]   P. Clements, R. Kazam, & M. Klein. *Evaluating Software Architectures: Methods and Case Studies,* SEI Series in Software Engineering, Addison-Wesley, Reading, MA, 2002.

[Coad et al., 1995]   P. Coad, D. North, & M. Mayfield, *Object Models: Strategies, Patterns, & Applications,* Prentice Hall, Englewood Cliffs, NJ, 1995.

[Cockburn, 2001a]   A. Cockburn, *Writing Effective Use Cases,* Addison-Wesley, Reading, MA, 2001.

[Cockburn, 2001b]   A. Cockburn, *Agile Software Development,* Addison-Wesley, Reading, MA, 2001.

[Cohn, 2006]   M. Cohn, *Agile Estimating and Planning*, Pearson, Upper Saddle River, NJ, 2006.

[Conklin & Burgess-Yakemovic, 1991] J. Conklin & K. C. Burgess-Yakemovic, "A process-oriented approach to design rationale," *Human-Computer Interaction*, Vol. 6, pp. 357–391, 1991.

[Conradi & Westfechtel, 1998]   R. Conradi & B. Westfechtel, "Version models for software configuration management," *ACM Computing Surveys*, Vol. 30, No. 2, June 1998.

[Constantine & Lockwood, 1999]   L. L. Constantine & L. A. D. Lockwood, *Software for Use*, Addison-Wesley, Reading, MA, 1999.

[Constantine & Lockwood, 2001]   L. L. Constantine & L. A. D. Lockwood, "Structure and style in use cases for user interface design," in M. van Harmelen (ed.), *Object-Oriented User Interface Design*, 2001.

[Contract4J]   http://www.contract4j.org/

[Coyne et al., 1995]   R. Coyne, B. Bruegge, A. Dutoit, & D. Rothenberger, "Teaching more comprehensive model-based software engineering: Experience with Objectory's use case approach," in Linda Ibraham (ed), *8th Conference on Software Engineering Education*, Lecture Notes in Computer Science, Springer-Verlag, Berlin, pp. 339–374, April 1995.

[CruiseControl]   http://cruisecontrol.sourceforge.net/.

[Curtis et al., 1988]   B. Curtis, H. Krasner, & N. Iscoe, "A field study of the software design process for large systems," *Communications of the ACM*, 31(11), pp. 1268–87, 1988.

[Cusumano & Selby, 1997]   M. A. Cusumano, R. W. Selby, "How Microsoft Builds Software," *Communications of the ACM*, Vol. 40, No. 6, pp. 53–61, 1997.

[Dart, 1991]   S. Dart, "Concepts in configuration management systems," *Third International Software Configuration Management Workshop*, ACM, June 1991.

[Date, 2004]   C. J. Date, *An Introduction to Database Systems*, 8th ed., Addison-Wesley, Reading, MA, 2004.

[Day & Zimmermann, 1983]   J. D. Day & H. Zimmermann, "The OSI Reference Model," *Proceedings of the IEEE*, Vol. 71, pp. 1334–1340, December 1983.

[De Marco, 1978]   T. De Marco, *Structured Analysis and System Specification*, Yourdon, New York, 1978.

[Dijkstra, 1968]   E. W. Dijkstra, "The Structure of the 'T.H.E' Multiprogramming System," *Communication of the ACM*, 18(8), pp. 453–457, 1968.

[Dijkstra, 1976]   E. W. Dijkstra, *A Discipline of Programming*, Prentice-Hall, Englewood Cliffs, NJ, 1976.

[DoD-STD-2167A]   DoD-STD-2167A, *Military Standard, Defense Systems Software Development*, US Department of Defense, Washington, DC, 1988.

[Douglass, 1999]   B.P. Douglass, *Doing Hard Time: Using Object Oriented Programming and Software Patterns in Real Time Applications*, Addison-Wesley, Reading, MA, 1999.

[Doyle & Straus, 1982]   M. Doyle, & D. Straus, *How to make meetings work*, The Berkeley Publishing Group, New York, NY, 1982.

[D'Souza & Wills, 1999]   D. F. D'Souza & A. C. Wills, *Objects, Components, and Frameworks with UML: The Catalysis Approach*, The Addison-Wesley Object Technology Series, Addison-Wesley, Reading, MA, 1999.

[Dumas & Redish, 1998]   Dumas & Redish, *A Practical Guide to Usability Testing*, Ablex, NJ, 1993.

[Dutoit & Bruegge, 1998]   A. H. Dutoit & B. Bruegge, "Communication metrics for software development," *IEEE Transactions on Software Engineering*, August 1998.

[Dutoit & Paech, 2001]   A. H. Dutoit & B. Paech. "Rationale management in software engineering," in S.K. Chang (ed.), *Handbook of Software Engineering and Knowledge Engineering*, Vol. 1, World Scientific Publishing, 2001.

[Dutoit & Paech, 2002]   A. H. Dutoit & B. Paech. "Rationale-based use case specification," *Requirements Engineering Journal*, 7(1), pp. 3–19, 2002.

[Dutoit et al., 1996]   A. H. Dutoit, B. Bruegge, & R. F. Coyne, "The use of an issue-based model in a team-based software engineering course," *Conference Proceedings of Software Engineering: Education and Practice (SEEP'96)*, Dunedin, NZ, January 1996.

[Dutoit et al., 2006]   A. H. Dutoit, R. McCall, I. Mistrik, B. Paech (eds.) *Rationale Management in Software Engineering*, Springer-Verlag, Heidelberg.

[Duval et al., 2007]   P. Duval, S. Matyas, & A. Glover, *Continuous Integration: Improving Software Quality and Reducing Risk*, Addison-Wesley, Reading, MA, 2007.

[Elssamadisy, 2009]   A. Elssamadisy, *Agile Adoption Patterns*, Addison-Wesley, Reading, MA, 2009.

[Erl, 2005]   T. Erl, *Service-Oriented Architectures:Concepts, Technology, and Design*, Prentice Hall, Upper Saddle River, NJ, 2005.

[Erman et al., 1980]   L. D. Erman, F. Hayes-Roth, et al., "The Hearsay-II Speech-Understanding System: Integrating knowledge to resolve uncertainty," *ACM Computing Surveys*, Vol. 12, No. 2, pp. 213–253, 1980.

[Fagan, 1976]   M. E. Fagan, "Design and code inspections to reduce errors in program development," *IBM System Journal*, Vol. 15, No. 3, pp. 182–211, 1976.

[Fayad & Hamu, 1997]   M. E. Fayad & D. S. Hamu, "Object-oriented enterprise frameworks: Make vs. buy decisions and guidelines for selection," *The Communications of ACM*, 1997.

[Feiler & Tichy, 1998]   P. Feiler & W. Tichy, "Propagator: A family of patterns," in *Proceedings of TOOLS-23'97*, Santa Barbara, CA, July 28–August 1 1997.

[Feynman, 1988]   R. P. Feynman, "Personal observations on the reliability of the Shuttle," in [Rogers et al., 1986]. This article is also available on the Web, e.g.,http://www.virtualschool.edu/mon/SocialConstruction/FeynmanChallengerRpt.html.

[Fisher et al., 1991]   R. Fisher, W. Ury, & B. Patton, *Getting to Yes: Negotiating Agreement Without Giving In*, 2nd ed., Penguin Books, 1991.

[Floyd, 1967]   R. W. Floyd, "Assigning Meanings to Programs," in *Proceedings of the American Mathematics Society Symposium in Applied Mathematics*, Vol. 19, pp. 19–31, 1967.

[Fowler, 1997]   M. Fowler, *Analysis Patterns: Reusable Object Models*, Addison-Wesley, Reading, MA, 1997.

[Fowler, 2000]   M. Fowler. *Refactoring: Improving The Design of Existing Code*, Addison-Wesley, Reading, MA, 2000.

[Fowler, 2003]   M. Fowler & K. Scott, *UML Distilled: A Brief Guide To The Standard Object Modeling Language*, 3rd ed., Addison-Wesley, Reading, MA, 2003.

[Fowler, 2005]   M. Fowler, *The new methodology*, http://www.martinfowler.com/articles/newMethodology.html. Revised 2005.

[Freeman-Benson, 1990]   B. Freeman-Benson. "Kaleidoscope: Mixing Objects, Constraints, and
                              Imperative Programming." In *OOPSLA/SIGPLAN Notices* 25 (10): 77:88,
                              October 1990.

[FRIEND, 1994]   *FRIEND Project Documentation*, School of Computer Science, Carnegie
                              Mellon University, Pittsburgh, PA, 1994.

[Gamma et al., 1994]   E. Gamma, R. Helm, R. Johnson, & J. Vlissides, *Design Patterns: Elements of
                              Reusable Object-Oriented Software*, Addison-Wesley, Reading, MA, 1994.

[Gantt, 1910]   H. L. Gantt, "Work, wages, and profits," *The Engineering Magazine*, New
                              York, 1910.

[Gleick, 1987]   J. Gleick, *Chaos - Making a New Science,* Penguin Books Ltd,
                              Harmondsworth, Middlesex, 1987.

[Gladwin, 1964]   T. Gladwin, "Culture and logical process," in W. Goodenough (ed.),
                              *Explorations in Cultural Anthropology: Essays Presented to George Peter
                              Murdock*, McGraw-Hill, New York, 1964.

[Goldberg & Kay, 1976]   A. Goldberg & A. Kay, *Smalltalk-72 Instruction Manual*, Xerox Palo
                              Alto,CA, 1976.

[Grady, 1992]   R. Grady, *Practical Software Metrics for Project Management and Process
                              Improvement*, Prentice Hall, Englewood Cliffs, NJ, 1992.

[Grenning, 2002]   J. Grenning, Planning Poker, http://www.planningpoker.com/ 2002.

[Grudin, 1988]   J. Grudin, "Why CSCW applications fail: Problems in design and evaluation
                              of organization interfaces," *Proceedings of CSCW'88*, Portland, OR, 1988.

[Grudin, 1990]   J. Grudin, "Obstacles to user involvement in interface design in large product
                              development organizations," *Proceedings of IFIP INTERACT'90 Third
                              International Conference on Human-Computer Interaction*, Cambridge, U.K.,
                              August 1990.

[Halstead, 1977]   M. H. Halstead, *Elements of Software Science,* Elsevier, New York, 1977.

[Hammer & Champy, 1993]   M. Hammer & J. Champy, *Reengineering The Corporation: A Manifesto for
                              Business Revolution*, Harper Business, New York, 1993.

[Harel, 1987]   D. Harel, "Statecharts: A visual formalism for complex systems," *Science of
                              Computer Programming*, pp. 231–274, 1987.

[Hartkopf et al., 1997]   V. Hartkopf, V. Loftness, A. Mahdavi, S. Lee, & J. Shankavarm, "An
                              integrated approach to design and engineering of intelligent buildings—The
                              Intelligent Workplace at Carnegie Mellon University, *Automation in
                              Construction*, Vol. 6, pp. 401–415, 1997.

[Herbert, 1985]   F. Herbert, *Chapterhouse: Dune*, Orion Publishing, 1985.

[Highsmith, 2004]   J. Highsmith, *Agile Project Management,* Pearson Education, Boston, 2004.

[Highsmith & Orr, 2000]   J. Highsmith, & K. Orr, *Adaptive Software Development: A Collaborative
                              Approach to Managing Complex Systems*, Dorset House, 2000.

[Hoare, 1969]   C. A. R. Hoare, "An axiomatic basis for computer programming,"
                              Communications of the ACM, Vol. 20, No. 6, pp. 576–580, October 1969.

[Hoare, 1980]   C. A. R. Hoare, "The emperor's old clothes," Turing Award Lecture, 1980.

[Hofmeister, 2000]   C. Hofmeister, R. Nord, & D. Soni, *Applied Software Architecture*, Object
                              Technology Series, Addison-Wesley, 2000.

[Hopper, 1981]   G. M. Hopper, "The First Bug," *Annals of the History of Computing*, 3, pp.
                              285–286, 1981.

[Horn, 1992]   B. Horn, "Constraint patterns as a basis for object-oriented programming," in *Proceedings of the OOPSLA'92*, Vancouver, Canada, 1992.

[Humphrey, 1989]   W. Humphrey, *Managing the Software Process*, Addison-Wesley, Reading, MA, 1989.

[IBM]   IBM, *WebSphere Software Platform for E-Business*, http://www.ibm.com/websphere/.

[IEEE Std. 610.12-1990]   Institute of Electrical and Electronics Engineers, *IEEE Standard Computer Dictionary: A Compilation of IEEE Standard Computer Glossaries*, New York, NY, 1990.

[IEEE Std. 828-2005]   *IEEE Standard for Software Configuration Management Plans*, IEEE Standards Board, August 2005.

[IEEE Std. 829-2008]   *IEEE Standard for Software Test Documentation*, IEEE Standards Board, July 2008.

[IEEE Std. 830-1998]   *IEEE Standard for Software Requirements Specification*, IEEE Standards Board, June 1998.

[IEEE Std. 982.2-1988]   *IEEE Guide for the Use of IEEE Standard Dictionary of Measures to Produce Reliable Software*, IEEE Standards Board, June 1988.

[IEEE Std. 1042-1987]   *IEEE Guide to Software Configuration Management*, IEEE Standards Board, September 1987.

[IEEE Std. 1058-1998]   *IEEE Standard for Software Project Management Plans*, IEEE Computer Society, New York, December 1998.

[IEEE Std. 1074-2006]   *IEEE Standard for Developing Software Life Cycle Processes*, IEEE Computer Society, New York, July 2006.

[IEEE/EIA, 1996]   IEEE/EIA 12207.0-1996, *Industry Implementation of International Standard ISO/IEC 12207: 1995 Standard for Information Technology–Software life cycle processes*, IEEE Computer Society & Electronic Industries Association, March 1998.

[ISO Std. 9126]   International Standards Organization. *Software engineering -- Product quality*. ISO/IEC-9126, Geneva, Switzerland, 2001.

[ISO/IEC 12207, 1995]   ISO/IEC 12207. *Information technology–Software life cycle processes*. International Organization for Standardization & International Electrotechnical Commission, August 1995.

[JavaEE, 2009]   *Java Platform, Enterprise Edition*, Javasoft, 2009, http://java.sun.com/.

[Jackson, 1995]   M. Jackson, *Software Requirements & Specifications: A Lexicon of Practice, Principles and Prejudices*, Addison-Wesley, Reading, MA, 1995.

[Jacobson et al., 1992]   I. Jacobson, M. Christerson, P. Jonsson, & G. Overgaard, *Object-Oriented Software Engineering—A Use Case Driven Approach*, Addison-Wesley, Reading, MA, 1992.

[Jacobson et al., 1995]   I. Jacobson, M. Ericsson, & A. Jacobson, *The Object Advantage: Business Process Reengineering with Object Technology*, Addison-Wesley, Reading, MA, 1995.

[Jacobson et al., 1999]   I. Jacobson, G. Booch, & J. Rumbaugh, *The Unified Software Development Process*, Addison-Wesley, Reading, MA, 1999.

[Jarke, 1998]   M. Jarke, "Requirements Tracing," *Communications of the ACM*, Vol. 41, No. 12, December 1998.

[Javadoc, 2009a]   Sun Microsystems, Javadoc homepage, http://java.sun.com/j2se/javadoc/.

[Javadoc, 2009b]   Sun Microsystems, "How to write doc comments for Javadoc," http://
                                    java.sun.com/j2se/writingdoccomments/.

[jContractor]   http://jcontractor.sourceforge.net/

[JDBC, 2009]   *JDBC*[TM]*—Connecting Java and Databases*, JDK Documentation, Javasoft,
                                    2009.

[Jensen & Tonies, 1979]   R. W. Jensen & C. C. Tonies, *Software Engineering*, Prentice Hall,
                                    Englewood Cliffs, NJ, 1979.

[JFC, 2009]   *Java Foundation Classes*, JDK Documentation, Javasoft, 2009.

[Johnson, 1992]   P. Johnson, *Human Computer Interaction: Psychology, Task Analysis and
                                    Software Engineering*, McGraw-Hill International, London, 1992.

[Johnson & Foote, 1988]   R. Johnson & B. Foote, "Designing reusable classes," *Journal of
                                    Object-Oriented Programming*, Vol. 1, No. 5, pp. 22–35, 1988.

[Jones, 1977]   T. C. Jones, "Programmer quality and programmer productivity," IBM
                                    Technical Report TR–02.764, 1977.

[JUnit, 2009]   JUnit, http://www.junit.org/.

[Katzenbach & Smith, 1994]   J. R. Katzenbach & D. K. Smith, *The Wisdom of Teams: Creating The High-
                                    Performance Organization*, Harper Business, 1994.

[Kayser, 1990]   T. A. Kayser, *Mining Group Gold*, Serif, El Segundo, CA, 1990.

[Kelly, 1984]   J. F. Kelly, "An iterative design methodology for user-friendly natural
                                    language office information applications," *ACM Transactions on Information
                                    Systems*, Vol. 2, No. 1, January 1984.

[Kemerer, 1997]   C. F. Kemerer, *Software Project Management: Readings and Cases*,
                                    Irwin/McGraw-Hill, Boston, MA 1997.

[Knuth, 1986]   D. E. Knuth, *The TeXbook*, Addison-Wesley, Reading, MA, 1986.

[Kotonya & Sommerville, 1996]   G. Kotonya & I. Sommerville, "Requirements Engineering with Viewpoints,"
                                    Software Engineering Journal 11(1), 1996.

[Kramer, 1998]   R. Kramer, "iContract—The Java Design by Contract Tool," *Technology of
                                    Object-Oriented Languages and Systems*, IEEE Computer Society Press,
                                    1998, p.295.

[Kraut & Streeter, 1995]   R. E. Kraut, & L. A. Streeter, "Coordination in software development,"
                                    Communications of the ACM, Vol. 38, No. 3, March 1995.

[Kruchten, 1998]   P. Kruchten, *The Rational Unified Process: An Introduction,* Reading, MA,
                                    Addison-Wesley 1998.

[Kunz & Rittel, 1970]   W. Kunz & H. Rittel, "Issues as elements of information systems," Working
                                    Paper No. 131, Institut für Grundlagen der Plannung, Universität Stuttgart,
                                    Germany, 1970.

[Larman, 2005]   C. Larman, *Applying UML and Patterns: An Introduction to Object-Oriented
                                    Analysis and Design*, 3rd ed., Prentice Hall, Upper Saddle River, NJ, 2005.

[Leblang, 1994]   D. Leblang, "The CM challenge: Configuration management that works," in
                                    W. F. Tichy (ed.), *Configuration Management*, Vol. 2, *Trends in Software*,
                                    Wiley, New York, 1994.

[Lee, 1990]   J. Lee, "A qualitative decision management system," in P. H. Winston &
                                    S. Shellard (eds.), *Artificial Intelligence at MIT: Expanding Frontiers*, MIT
                                    Press, Cambridge, MA, Vol. 1, pp. 104–33, 1990.

[Lee, 1997]   J. Lee, "Design rationale systems: Understanding the issues," *IEEE Expert*,
                                    May/June 1997.

[Leveson, 1995]	N. G. Leveson, *Safeware: System Safety And Computers*, Addison-Wesley, Reading, MA, 1995.
[Lions, 1996]	J.-L. Lions, *ARIANE 5 Flight 501 Failure: Report by the Inquiry Board,* http://ravel.esrin.esa.it/docs/esa-x-1819eng.pdf, 1996.
[Liskov, 1988]	B. Liskov, "Data abstraction and hierarchy," *SIGPLAN Notices*, Vol. 23, No. 3, May, 1988.
[Liskov & Guttag, 1986]	B. Liskov & J. Guttag, *Abstraction and Specification in Program Development*, MIT Press, McGraw-Hill, New York, 1986.
[Lotus]	Lotus, http://www.lotus.com/.
[Macaulay, 1996]	L. Macaulay, *Requirements Engineering*, Springer-Verlag, London, 1996.
[MacLean et al., 1991]	A. MacLean, R. M. Young, V. Bellotti, & T. Moran, "Questions, options, and criteria: Elements of design space analysis," *Human-Computer Interaction*, Vol. 6, pp. 201–250, 1996.
[Marshall, 2001]	R. Marshall, *What really happened at K2?* Chapter 24 in [Bonatti 2001].
[Martin & Odell, 1992]	J. Martin & J. J. Odell, *Object-Oriented Analysis and Design*, Prentice Hall, Englewood Cliffs, NJ, 1992.
[Mayhew, 1999]	D. J. Mayhew, *The Usability Engineering Lifecycle: A Practitioner's Handbook for User Interface Design*, Morgan Kaufmann, 1999.
[McCabe, 1976]	T. McCabe, "A software complexity measure," *IEEE Transactions on Software Engineering*, Vol. 2, No. 12, December 1976.
[Mellor & Shlaer, 1998]	S. Mellor & S. Shlaer, *Recursive Design Approach*, Prentice Hall, Upper Saddle River, NJ, 1998.
[Meyer, 1997]	B. Meyer, *Object-Oriented Software Construction*, 2nd ed., Prentice Hall, Upper Saddle River, NJ, 1997.
[Microsoft]	Microsoft, http://www.microsoft.com/.
[MIL Std. 480]	MIL Std. 480, U.S. Department of Defense, Washington, DC.
[Miller, 1956]	G. A. Miller, "The magical number seven, plus or minus two: Some limits on our capacity for processing information." *Psychological Review*, Vol. 63, pp. 81–97, 1956.
[Minsky, 1975]	M. Minsky, "A framework for representing knowledge," in P. Winston (ed.), *The Psychology of Computer Vision*, McGraw-Hill , 1975.
[Moran & Carroll, 1996]	T. P. Moran & J. M. Carroll (eds.), *Design Rationale: Concepts, Techniques, and Use*, Lawrence Erlbaum Associates, Mahwah, NJ, 1996.
[Mowbray & Malveau, 1997]	T. J. Mowbray & R. C. Malveau, *CORBA Design Patterns*, Wiley, New York, 1997.
[Mozilla]	Mozilla, http://www.mozilla.org/.
[Myers, 1979]	G. J. Myers, *The Art of Software Testing*, Wiley, New York, 1979.
[Neumann, 1995]	P. G. Neumann, *Computer-Related Risks*, Addison-Wesley, Reading, MA, 1995.
[Nielsen, 1993]	J. Nielsen, *Usability Engineering*, Academic, New York, 1993.
[Nielsen & Mack, 1994]	J. Nielsen & R. L. Mack (eds.), *Usability Inspection Methods*, Wiley, New York, 1994.
[Norman, 2002]	D. A. Norman, *The Design of Everyday Things*, Basic Books, New York, 2002.

[OMG, 2005]   Object Management Group *UML Testing Profile Version 1.0.* 05-07-07. http://www.omg.org/ 2005.

[OMG, 2006]   Object Management Group, *Object Constraint Language OMG Available Specification Version 2.0.* http://www.omg.org 2006.

[OMG, 2008]   Object Management Group, *Common Object Request Broker Architecture (CORBA) Specification: Version 3.1.* http://www.omg.org/ 2008.

[OMG, 2009]   Object Management Group, *OMG Unified Modeling Language Superstructure, Version 2.2.* http://www.omg.org/ 2009.

[OWL, 1996]   *OWL Project Documentation*, School of Computer Science, Carnegie Mellon Univ., Pittsburgh, PA, 1996.

[Palmer & Felsing, 2002] S. Palmer, & J. Felsing, *A Practical Guide to Feature-Driven Development,* Prentice Hall, Upper Saddle River, NJ, 2002.

[Parnas, 1972]   D. Parnas, "On the criteria to be used in decomposing systems into modules," *Communications of the ACM*, 15(12), pp. 1053–1058, 1972.

[Parnas & Weiss, 1985]   D. L. Parnas & D. M. Weiss, "Active design reviews: principles and practice," *Proceedings of the Eighth International Conference on Software Engineering*, London, England. pp 132–136, August 1985.

[Partsch, 1990]   H. Partsch, *Specification and Transformation of Programs*, Springer-Verlag, 1990.

[Paulish, 2001]   D. J. Paulish, *Architecture-Centric Software Project Management: A Practical Guide*, SEI Series in Software Engineering, Addison-Wesley, Reading, MA, 2001.

[Paulk et al., 1995]   M. C. Paulk, C. V. Weber, & B. Curtis (eds.), *The Capability Maturity Model: Guidelines for Improving the Software Process*, Addison-Wesley, Reading, MA, 1995.

[Perforce]   http://www.perforce.com/.

[Perlis, 1982]   A. Perlis, "Epigrams in Programming," *ACM, SIGPLAN*, 1982.

[Petroski, 1992]   H. Petroski, *To Engineer is Human*, Vintage Books, Random House, New York, 1992.

[Petroski, 1994]   H. Petroski, *The Evolution of Useful Things*, Vintage Books, Random House, New York, 1994.

[Pfleeger, 1991]   S. L. Pfleeger, *Software Engineering: The Production of Quality Software*, 2nd ed., Macmillan, 1991.

[Pirsig, 1984]   R. M. Pirsig, *Zen and the Art of Motorcycle Maintenance*, Bantam Books, 1984.

[Pirsig, 1991]   R. M. Pirsig, *Lila: An Inquiry into Morals*, Bantam Doubleday Dell, 1991.

[Popper, 1992]   K. Popper, *Objective Knowledge: An Evolutionary Approach*, Clarendon, Oxford, 1992.

[Porter et al., 1997]   A. A. Porter, H. Siy, C. A. Toman, & L. G. Votta, "An experiment to assess the cost-benefits of code inspections in large scale software development," *IEEE Transactions on Software Engineering*, Vol. 23, No. 6, pp. 329–346, June 1997.

[Portny, 2001]   S. E. Portny, *Project Management for Dummies*, John Wiley & Sons, 2000.

[POSIX, 1990]   *Portable Operating System Interface for Computing Environments*, IEEE Std. 1003.1, IEEE, 1990.

[Potts, 1996]	C. Potts, "Supporting software design: Integrating design methods and design rationale," in T. P. Moran & J. M. Carroll (eds.), *Design Rationale: Concepts, Techniques, and Use*, Lawrence Erlbaum Associates, Mahwah, NJ, 1996.
[Potts & Bruns, 1988]	C. Potts & G. Bruns, "Recording the Reasons for Design Decisions," in *Proceedings of the 10th International Conference on Software Engineering*, pp. 418–427, 1988.
[Potts et al., 1994]	C. Potts, K. Tkahashi, & A. I. Anton, "Inquiry-based requirements analysis," *IEEE Software*, Vol. 11, No. 2, pp. 21–32, 1994.
[Pressman, 2009]	R. S. Pressman, *Software Engineering: A Practitioner's Approach*, 7th ed., McGraw-Hill, 2009.
[Purvis et al., 1996]	M. Purvis, M. Purvis, & P. Jones, "A group collaboration tool for software engineering projects," *Conference Proceedings of Software Engineering: Education and Practice (SEEP'96)*, Dunedin, NZ., January 1996.
[Rational]	Rationale, http://www.rational.com.
[Rational, 2002]	*Rationale Rose*, Rational Software Corp., Cupertino, CA, 2002.
[Raymond, 1998]	E. Raymond, "The cathedral and the bazaar," http://www.tuxedo.org/~esr/writings/cathedral-bazaar/cathedral-bazaar.html, 1998.
[Ritchie & Thompson, 1974]	D. M. Ritchie & K. Thompson, "The Unix Time-sharing System," *Communications of the ACM*, Vol. 17, No. 7, pp. 365–37, July 1974.
[RMI, 2009]	*Java Remote Method Invocation*, JDK Documentation, Javasoft, 2009.
[Rochkind, 1975]	M.J. Rochkind, "The Source Code Control System," *IEEE Transactions on Software Engineering*, SE-1(4), p. 255–265., 1975.
[Rogers et al., 1986]	*The Presidential Commission on the Space Shuttle Challenger Accident Report*, Washington, DC, June 1986.
[Rowen, 1990]	R. B. Rowen, "Software project management under incomplete and ambiguous specifications," *IEEE Transactions on Engineering Management*, Vol. 37, No. 1, 1990.
[Royce, 1970]	W. W. Royce, "Managing the development of large software systems," in *Tutorial: Software Engineering Project Management*, IEEE Computer Society, Washington, DC, pp. 118–127, 1970.
[Royce, 1998]	W. Royce, *Software Project Management: A Unified Framework*, Addison-Wesley, Reading, MA, 1998.
[Rubin, 1994]	J. Rubin, *Handbook of Usability Testing*, Wiley, New York, 1994.
[Rumbaugh et al., 1991]	J. Rumbaugh, M. Blaha, W. Premerlani, F. Eddy, & W. Lorensen, *Object-Oriented Modeling and Design*, Prentice Hall, Englewood Cliffs, NJ, 1991.
[Schlumberger]	Schlumberger, http://www.cyberflex.com/
[Schmidt, 1997]	D. C. Schmidt, "Applying design patterns and frameworks to develop object-oriented communication software," in P. Salus (ed.), *Handbook of Programming Languages*, Vol. 1, MacMillan Computer, 1997.
[Schwaber & Beedle, 2002]	K. Schwaber & M. Beedle, *Agile Software Development with Scrum*, Prentice Hall, Upper Saddle River, NJ, 2002.
[Schwaber, 2004]	K. Schwaber, *Agile Project Management With Scrum*, Microsoft, Redwood, 2004.
[Shaw & Garlan, 1996]	M. Shaw & D. Garlan, *Software Architecture: Perspectives on an Emerging Discipline*, Prentice Hall, Upper Saddle River, NJ, 1996.

[Shipman & McCall, 1997]   F. M. Shipman III & R. J. McCall, "Integrating different perspectives on design rationale: Supporting the emergence of design rationale from design communication," *Artificial Intelligence in Engineering Design, Analysis, and Manufacturing*, Vol. 11, No. 2, 1997.

[Siewiorek & Swarz, 1992]   D. P. Siewiorek & R. S. Swarz, *Reliable Computer Systems: Design and Evaluation*, 2nd ed., Digital, Burlington, MA, 1992.

[Simon, 1970]   H. A. Simon, *The Sciences of the Artificial*, MIT Press, Cambridge, MA, 1970.

[Sommerville, 2006]   I. Sommerville, *Software Engineering*, 8th ed., Addison-Wesley, 2006.

[Spivey, 1992]   J. M. Spivey, *The Z Notation, A Reference Manual,* 2nd ed., Prentice Hall International, Hertfordshire, U.K., 1992.

[Steelman, 1978]   *Requirements for High Order Computer Programming Languages: Steelman*, U.S. Department of Defense, Washington, DC, 1978.

[Subrahmanian et al., 1997]   E. Subrahmanian, Y. Reich, S. L. Konda, A. Dutoit, D. Cunningham, R. Patrick, M. Thomas, & A. W. Westerberg, "The *n*-dim approach to building design support systems," *Proceedings of ASME Design Theory and Methodology DTM'97*, ASME, New York, 1997.

[Suchman, 2007]   L. A. Suchman, *Human-Machine Reconfiguration: Plans and Situated Actions,* 2nd ed. Cambridge University Press, 2007.

[Sun, 2009]   Sun Microsystems *Code Conventions for the Java Programming Language.* http://www.java.sun.com/docs/codeconv/ 2009.

[Tanenbaum, 1996]   A. S. Tanenbaum, *Computer Networks,* 3rd ed. Prentice Hall, Upper Saddle River, NJ, 1996.

[Taylor, 1911]   F. W. Taylor, *The Principles of Scientific Management*, Harper Bros., New York, 1911.

[Telelogic]   Telelogic, http://www.telelogic.se.

[Tichy, 1985]   W. Tichy, "RCS—A system for version control," *Software Practice and Experience*, Vol. 15, No. 7, 1985.

[TogetherSoft, 2002]   TogetherSoft, *Together Control Center*, Raleigh, NC, 2002, http://www.togethersoft.com.

[Tolkien, 1995]   J.R.R. Tolkien, *The Lord of The Rings*, Harper Collins, 1995.

[Tunde & Harmon Ray, 1994]   A. Ogunnaike Babatunde & W. Harmon Ray, *Process Dynamics, Modeling and Control*, Oxford University Press, 1994.

[Turner & Robson, 1993]   C. D. Turner & D. J. Robson, "The state-based testing of object-oriented programs," *Conference on Software Maintenance*, pp. 302–310, September 1993.

[Twain, 1897]   M. Twain, *Following the Equator: A Journey Around the World*, American Publishing Co., Hartford, 1897, BoondocksNet Edition, 2003.

[Vaughan, 1996]   D. Vaughan, *The Challenger Launch Decision: Risky Technology, Culture, and Deviance at NASA*, The University of Chicago Press, Chicago, 1996.

[Viller & Sommerville, 1999]   S. Viller & I. Sommerville, "Social analysis in the requirements engineering process: from ethnography to method," *International Symposium on Requirements Engineering (ISRE'99)*, Limerick, Ireland, June 1999.

[Warmer & Kleppe, 2003]   J. Warmer & A. Kleppe, *The Object Constraint Language: Getting Your Modes Ready for MDA*, 2nd ed., Addison-Wesley, Reading, MA, 2003.

[Weinand et al., 1988]   A. Weinand, E. Gamma, & R. Marty, "ET++—An object-oriented application framework in C++," in *Object-Oriented Programming Systems, Languages, and Applications Conference Proceedings*, San Diego, CA, September 1988.

[Weinberg, 1971]   G. M. Weinberg, *The Psychology of Computer Programming*, Van Nostrand, New York, 1971.

[Wigand et al., 1997]   R. T. Wigand, A. Picot, & R. Reichwald, *Information, Organization and Management: Expanding Markets and Corporate Boundaries*, John Wiley & Sons, London, 1997.

[Wilson & Ostrem, 1999]   G. Wilson & J. Ostrem, *WebObjects Developer's Guide*, Apple Computers, Cupertino, CA, 1998.

[Wirfs-Brock, 1995]   R. Wirfs-Brock, "Design objects and their interactions: A brief look at responsibility-driven design," in J. M. Carroll (ed.), *Scenario-Based Design: Envisioning Work and Technology in System Development,* Wiley, New York, 1995.

[Wirfs-Brock et al., 1990]   R. Wirfs-Brock, B. Wilkerson, & L. Wiener, *Designing Object-Oriented Software*, Prentice Hall, Englewood Cliffs, NJ, 1990.

[Wood & Silver, 1989]   J. Wood & D. Silver, *Joint Application Design®*, Wiley, New York, 1989.

[Wordsworth, 1992]   J. B. Wordsworth, *Software Development with Z: A Practical Approach to Formal Methods in Software Engineering*, Addison-Wesley, Reading, MA, 1992.

[Yourdon & Constantine, 1979]   E. Yourdon & L. Constantine, *Structured Design*, Prentice Hall, Englewood Cliffs, NJ, 1979.

[Wiki]   Wiki, http://c2.com/cgi/wiki?WikiWikiWeb.

[Yahoo]   Yahoo, http://groups.yahoo.com.

[Zultner, 1993]   R. E. Zultner, "TQM for technical teams," *Communications of the ACM*, Vol. 36, No. 10, pp. 79–91, 1993.

Index

Design patterns

Abstract Factory (328, 341, 710) this pattern shields a system from the concrete classes provided by a specific platform, such as a windowing style or an operating system.

Adapter (319, 711) This pattern encapsulates a piece of legacy code that was not designed to work with the system. It also limits the impact of substituting the piece of legacy code for a different component.

Bridge (321, 712) This pattern decouples the interface of a class from its implementation. Unlike the Adapter pattern, the developer is not constrained by an existing piece of code.

Command (329, 342, 713) This pattern enables the encapsulation of control objects so that user requests can be treated uniformly, independent of the specific request. This pattern protects these objects from changes required by new functionality.

Composite (55, 228, 233, 330, 714) This pattern represents a hierarchy which has dynamic width and depth. The services related to the hierarchy are factored out using inheritance, allowing a system to treat leaves and intermediate composite nodes uniformly.

Facade (254, 715) This pattern reduces dependencies among classes by encapsulating a subsystem with a simple unified interface.

Observer (240, 342, 716) This pattern allows to maintain consistency across the states of one Publisher and many Subscribers.

Proxy (274, 405, 717) This pattern improves the performance or the security of a system by delaying expensive computations, using memory only when needed, or checking access before loading an object into memory.

Strategy (325, 463, 718) This pattern decouples a policy from a set of mechanisms or a context from a set of implementations. Depending on the policy or context, the mechanisms or implementations can be changed at runtime transparently from the client.

Notations

UML use case diagrams (31, 44) Use case diagrams are used to represent the functionality of the system, as seen by an actor.

UML class diagrams (32, 50) Class diagrams are used to represent the structure of the system, in terms of subsystems, classes, attributes, operations, and associations.

UML sequence diagrams (32, 59) Sequence diagrams represent behavior in terms of a series of interactions among a set of objects.

UML statechart diagrams (33, 62) Statechart diagrams represent behavior of a single object as a state machine in terms of events and transitions.

Activity diagrams (33, 65) Activity diagrams are flow diagrams which represent behavior of a set of objects as activities and transitions.

UML deployment diagrams (228) Deployment diagrams represent the mapping of software components to hardware nodes.

Issue models (497) Issue models represent the justification of decisions in terms of issues, proposals, arguments, criteria, and resolutions.

PERT charts (90) PERT charts represent the division of work into tasks and ordering constraints.